Messianism among Jews and Christians

Other Titles in the Cornerstones Series

The Israelite Woman by Athalya Brenner-Idan
In Search of 'Ancient Israel' by Philip R. Davies
Fragmented Women by J. Cheryl Exum
Sanctify Them in the Truth by Stanley Hauerwas
Solidarity and Difference by David G. Horrell
One God, One Lord by Larry Hurtado
Neither Jew nor Greek by Judith Lieu
Jesus: Miriam's Child, Sophia's Prophet by Elisabeth Schüssler-Fiorenza
The Christian Faith by Friedrich Schleiermacher
The Pentateuch: A Social and Critical Commentary by John Van Seters
The Christian Doctrine of God by Thomas F. Torrance
Paul and the Hermeneutics of Faith by Francis Watson
Word and Church by John Webster
Confessing God by John Webster

Messianism among Jews and Christians

Biblical and Historical Studies

Second Edition

William Horbury

Bloomsbury T&T Clark
An imprint of Bloomsbury Publishing Plc

B L O O M S B U R Y
LONDON • OXFORD • NEW YORK • NEW DELHI • SYDNEY

Bloomsbury T&T Clark
An imprint of Bloomsbury Publishing Plc

Imprint previously known as T&T Clark

50 Bedford Square
London
WC1B 3DP
UK

1385 Broadway
New York
NY 10018
USA

www.bloomsbury.com

First edition published 2003. This edition published 2016

British Library Cataloguing-in-Publication Data
A catalogue record for this book is available from the British Library.

ISBN: PB: 978-0-56766-274-3
ePDF: 978-0-56766-275-0
ePub: 978-0-56766-276-7

Library of Congress Cataloging-in-Publication Data
A catalog record for this book is available from the Library of Congress.

Series: Cornerstones

Typeset by Deanta Global Publishing Services, Chennai, India
Printed and bound in India

Contents

Abbreviations

AGJU	Arbeiten zur Geschichte des antiken Judentums und des Urchristentums
ANRW	Aufstieg und Niedergang der römischen Welt
BAR	British Archaeological Reports
BASOR	*Bulletin of the American Schools of Oriental Research*
BETL	Bibliotheca Ephemeridum Theologicarum Lovaniensium
BJP	Brill Josephus Project
BJRL	*Bulletin of the John Rylands Library*
BZNW	Beihefte zur *ZNW*
CBQ	*Catholic Biblical Quarterly*
CCL	Corpus Christianorum, Series Latina
CHJ	*Cambridge History of Judaism*
CIIP	Corpus Inscriptionum Iudaeae/Palaestinae
CIJ	J.-B. Frey, *Corpus Inscriptionum Judaicarum* (i, Rome, 1936; reissued, revised by B. Lifschitz, New York, 1975; ii, Rome, 1952)
CSEL	Corpus Scriptorum Ecclesiasticorum Latinorum
DJD	Discoveries in the Judaean Desert
EB	Encyclopaedia Biblica
EH	Encyclopaedia Hebraica
EJ	*Encyclopaedia Judaica* [to distinguish the two works bearing this title, references include a date]
ERE	*Encyclopaedia of Religion and Ethics*
ET	*Expository Times*
ETL	Ephemerides Theologicae Lovanienses
FAT	Forschungen zum Alten Testament
FJB	Frankfurter Judaistische Beiträge
FRLANT	Forschungen zur Religion und Literatur des Alten und Neuen Testaments
GCS	Die griechischen christlichen Schriftsteller
HDB	*Hastings' Dictionary of the Bible*

HTR	*Harvard Theological Review*
HUCA	*Hebrew Union College Annual*
ICC	International Critical Commentary
IEJ	*Israel Exploration Journal*
JAC	Jahrbuch für Antike und Christentum
JANES	*Journal of the American Near Eastern Society*
JAOS	*Journal of the American Oriental Society*
JBL	*Journal of Biblical Literature*
JE	*Jewish Encyclopaedia*
JEH	*Journal of Ecclesiastical History*
JIGRE	W. Horbury and D. E. Noy, *Jewish Inscriptions of Graeco-Roman Egypt* (Cambridge, 1992)
JJS	*Journal of Jewish Studies*
JNSL	*Journal of Northwest Semitic Languages*
JQR	*Jewish Quarterly Review*
JRS	*Journal of Roman Studies*
JSNT	*Journal for the Study of the New Testament*
JSOT	*Journal for the Study of the Old Testament*
JSP	*Journal for the Study of the Pseudepigrapha*
JSS	*Journal of Semitic Studies*
JTS	*Journal of Theological Studies*
LXX	Septuagint
MGWJ	Monatsschrift für die Geschichte und Wissenschaft des Judentums
MT	Massoretic Text
NT	Novum Testamentum
NTS	*New Testament Studies*
OLZ	Orientalistische Literaturzeitung
OTS	Oudtestamentische Studiën
PAAJR	*Proceedings of the American Academy for Jewish Research*
PEQ	*Palestine Exploration Quarterly*
PG	J. P. Migne, *Patrologia Graeca*
PL	J. P. Migne, *Patrologia Latina*
RAC	Reallexikon für Antike und Christentum
RB	Revue biblique
REB	Revised English Bible

REJ	Revue des études juives
RHPR	Revue d'histoire et de philosophie religieuses
RHR	Revue de l'histoire des religions
RIDA	Revue international des droits de l'Antiquité
RQ	Revue de Qumran
RV	Revised Version
SC	Sources chrétiennes
SJLA	Studies in Judaism in Late Antiquity
SJOT	*Scandinavian Journal of the Old Testament*
SVT	Supplements to *Vetus Testamentum*
TLZ	Theologische Literaturzeitung
TSAJ	Texte und Studien zum Antiken Judentum
TU	Texte und Untersuchungen zur Geschichte der altchristlichen Literatur
TWAT	Theologisches Wörterbuch zum Alten Testament
TWNT	Theologisches Wörterbuch zum Neuen Testament
VC	Vigiliae Christianae
VT	Vetus Testamentum
WUNT	Wissenchaftliche Untersuchungen zum Neuen Testament
ZAW	Zeitschrift für die Alttestamentliche Wissenschaft
ZDPV	Zeitschrift des deutschen Palästina-Vereins
ZKG	Zeitschrift für Kirchengeschichte
ZNW	Zeitschrift für die neutestamentliche Wissenschaft und die Kunde der älteren Kirche
ZPE	Zeitschrift für Papyrologie und Epigraphik
ZTK	Zeitschrift für Theologie und Kirche
ZWT	Zeitschrift für wissenschaftliche Theologie

Introduction to the Second Edition

'Messianism' can stand for all biblically inspired Jewish communal hope, spiritual and political, with or without a messiah figure.[1] Yet the significance of the term can also narrow dramatically. So from the 1960s to the early years of the present century, when this book first appeared, the place of messianism in ancient Judaism was often minimized (see pp. 30–2, below).[2] In ancient as in modern hope the universal reign of God and the exaltation of Israel do indeed come to the fore.[3] For the Second-Temple period it was stressed, however, that the interrelated hope for a coming king—that which can most readily be called 'messianic'—did not always reach expression. How diverse, moreover, was this hope when it *was* expressed!

Yet it remained clear that messianism including hope for a ruler had been central enough in the Second Temple period to influence both Christianity and later Judaism. Exceptions to the minimizing trend emerged in work which kept apocalypses, Targums, rabbinic literature and Jewish risings against Rome in view.[4] The writer's separately published argument for a less minimizing

1 On broad use of 'messianism' from Hermann Cohen to Emmanuel Levinas see D. Biale, *Gershom Scholem: Kabbalah and Counter-History* (Cambridge, MA and London, 1979), 148–55; P. Bouriez, *Témoins du futur: Philosophie et messianisme* (Paris, 2003), translated by M. B. Smith as *Witnesses for the Future: Philosophy and Messianism* (Baltimore, 2010); C. Wiese, *The Life and Thought of Hans Jonas: Jewish Dimensions* (Hanover, NH and London, 2007), 108–110, 154–60. For a 'messianic idea' of this breadth as a frame for both ancient and modern hopes see P. Alexander, 'Towards a Taxonomy of Jewish Messianisms', in J. Ashton (ed.), *Revealed Wisdom: Studies in Apocalyptic in Honour of Christopher Rowland* (Leiden, 2014), 52–72.

2 On this trend and its antecedents see M. Karrer, *Der Gesalbte: Die Grundlagen des Christustitels* (FRLANT 151, Göttingen, 1990), 23–34; W. Horbury, *Jewish Messianism and the Cult of Christ* (London, 1998), 1–2, 5–7, 36–7; id., 'Jewish Messianism and Early Christology', in R. N. Longenecker (ed.), *Contours of Christology in the New Testament* (Grand Rapids, MI and Cambridge, 2005), 3–24; M. V. Novenson, *Christ among the Messiahs: Christ Language in Paul and Messiah Language in Ancient Judaism* (New York, 2012), 39–41.

3 On monarchy exercised by God and by the nation in the Pentateuch see W. Horbury, 'Monarchy and Messianism in the Greek Pentateuch', in M. Knibb (ed.), *The Septuagint and Messianism* (BETL 195, Leuven, 2006), 79–128 (80, 87, 89, 91–3, 97–9).

4 Including G. Scholem, 'Zum Verständnis der messianischen Idee im Judentum', *Eranos Jahrbuch* 28 (1959), 193–239, E. T. 'The Messianic Idea in Judaism', in G. Scholem, *The Messianic Idea in Judaism and other Essays on Jewish Spirituality* (London, 1971), 1–36; R. Le Déaut, *La nuit pascale* (Analecta Biblica 22, Rome, 1963); D. Flusser, 'Jüdische Heilsgestaltungen und das Neue Testament', in id.,

approach, and the related work gathered afterwards in the present book of 2003, formed part of this reaction.[5]

The expectation of a coming ruler, rather than biblically inspired hope in general, is determinative for messianism as studied here.[6] Otherwise, however, the scope remains broad. Messianism as envisaged in this book is attested in early forms in the psalms and prophecies of the Hebrew Bible. It is a theme of Jewish sacred books and their interpretative tradition as they are edited, associated with one another and handed down under the Persians. Messianism is then significant in tradition as well as life among Jews under Greek and Roman rule. The present book brings into view the period from Alexander the Great to the Christian empire of the fifth century, or, in literary history, from Chronicles and the Septuagint to rabbinic literature.

Twelve essays, originally separate but with many internal connections, were revised and amplified to form the chapters of this book. They treat Jewish messianism and the theocentric, national and royal hopes surrounding it as these developed in Greek and Roman settings, including the setting of early Christianity (Chapters 2, 5–8, 11) and the cult of Christ (Chapters 9 and 12).

These chapters and their original introduction are reprinted unchanged apart from small corrections and occasional citation of later work. The present new introduction is intended to complement its predecessor in review of the subject. Each is followed by a list of writings cited. For the revised index to the second edition I am most grateful to Grishma Fredric and her colleagues at Deanta Publishing Services, working on behalf of Bloomsbury T. & T. Clark. In the rest of this introduction to the second edition I seek to place the picture of messianism, which is sketched in this book, in the setting of other current approaches.

Entdeckungen im Neuen Testament, Band 2, *Jesus – Qumran – Urchristentum* (Neukirchen-Vluyn, 1999), 212–52; M. Pérez Fernández, *Tradiciones mesiánicas en el Targum Palestinense* (Valencia and Jerusalem, 1981); M. D. Herr, 'Realistic Political Messianism and Cosmic Eschatological Messianism in the Teaching of the Sages', *Tarbiz* 54 (1985), 331–46; M. Hengel, 'Messianische Hoffnung und politischer "Radikalismus" in der "jüdisch-hellenistischen Diaspora". Zur Frage der Voraussetzungen des jüdischen Aufstandes unter Trajan 115-117 n. Chr.', reprinted from D. Hellholm (ed.), *Apocalypticism in the Mediterranean World and the Near East* (Tübingen, 1983, repr. 1989), 655–86 in M. Hengel, *Judaica et Hellenistica: Kleine Schriften I* (WUNT 90, Tübingen, 1996), 314–43; id., 'Die Bar-Kokhbamünzen als politisch-religiöse Zeugnisse', *Gnomon* lviii (1986), 326–31, reprinted in Hengel, *Judaica et Hellenistica. Kleine Schriften* I, 344–50.

[5] Horbury, *Jewish Messianism and the Cult of Christ*; id., *Messianism among Jews and Christians* (Edinburgh, 2003).

[6] Here my approach differs from that of Philip Alexander (n. 1, above).

Jews and Christians

Judaism and Christianity are viewed together here. It is urged that Jewish messianism, influenced by Greek and then Roman ruler-cult, linked Jewish piety with the cult of Christ and Christian messianism in such a way that in the first and second centuries we can speak of 'one messianism of the Jews and of the Christians' (chapter 9, p. 324, below).[7] In later Judaism, New Testament messianic themes are judged to live on through and beyond the period of the Mishnah, especially in liturgy, Targum and midrash (chapter 10, p. 365, below). Angels and saints were also remembered, it is suggested, in both communities, in a way which could frame reverence for a messianic figure (chapter 12, pp. 388, 412–15, below).

The book thus offers glimpses of Jewish messianism, and also of an associated Christian messianism, before, during and after the age of Christian origins. The place of messianism in the rolling interpretative tradition which accompanied biblical writings in the Jewish community, and was both inherited and further encountered by Christians, is accordingly a concern throughout (on study of scripture and tradition see pp. 33–8, below).[8]

A perspective from scripture and tradition

The perspective adopted is then not quite the same as that of work focused mainly on apocalypses. To quote Norman Cohn on Daniel 7 and its

[7] Compare Scholem, 'The Messianic Idea in Judaism', 15–16: 'The political and chiliastic Messianism of important religious movements within Christianity often appears as a reflection of what is really Jewish Messianism'; but the shared messianism sketched in the present book is judged to comprise both the political element which Scholem saw as Jewish and the mystical element which he saw as Christian. On Scholem's defence of this contrast see P. Schäfer, 'Gershom Scholem und das Christentum', in W. Schmidt-Biggemann (ed.), *Christliche Kabbala* (Pforzheimer Reuchlinschriften 10, 2003), 257–74 (267–70). J. A. Fitzmyer, *The One who is to Come* (Grand Rapids and Cambridge, 2007), 182–3 echoes the similar contrast in J. Klausner, *The Messianic Idea in Israel from its Beginning to the Completion of the Mishnah* (E. T. London, 1956), 517–31. Scholem himself is followed by A. Oppenheimer, 'Messianismus in römischer Zeit. Zur Pluralität eines Begriffes bei Juden und Christen', *Jahrbuch des Historischen Kollegs 1997* (Munich, 1998), 53–74, repr. in id., *Between Rome and Babylon: Studies in Jewish Leadership and Society* (TSAJ 108, Tübingen, 2005), 263–82.

[8] See further E. Grypeou and H. Spurling (eds.), *The Exegetical Encounter between Jews and Christians in Late Antiquity* (Jewish and Christian Perspectives Series, 18; Leiden and Boston, 2009); E. Grypeou and H. Spurling, *The Book of Genesis in Late Antiquity: Encounters between Jewish and Christian Exegesis* (Jewish and Christian Perspectives Series, 24; Leiden and Boston, 2013).

development in II Baruch, II Esdras, the Sibyl, Revelation and second-century Christianity, 'In the apocalypses poetic imagery of great power not infrequently served the imperious needs of what can only be described as a collective megalomania. … This propaganda made great play with the phantasy of an eschatological saviour, the messiah.'[9] Cohn picked out the perilous fascination exerted in the church and in modern society by hope for the overthrow of evil through the world-empire of the saints and their messianic king. He related it to twentieth-century totalitarian régimes as well as to the repeated millennial risings of mediaeval and early modern Europe. At the same time the continuing vitality of the messianism of the apocalypses within post-biblical Judaism was being underlined by Gershom Scholem; for him this messianism of catastrophe leading to utopia was indeed destructive and costly, but also blew 'a kind of anarchic breeze' through the window of what might otherwise be a too firmly well-ordered house. The order of which he spoke arises ultimately from the Pentateuch, heard with its accompanying tradition as a book of divine law and commandments.[10]

The coming kingdom pictured in Daniel and later apocalypses is central below especially in chapter 6, on Jerusalem-centred hope in Paul and his predecessors, chapter 9, on second-century messianism, and chapter 10, on the messianism of Yose ben Yose's synagogue poetry. The book as a whole, however, sets the apocalypses within the Pentateuchally-related interpretative tradition.

By the time of Alexander the Great, the Pentateuch had become the primary sacred text, prophets, psalms and other writings were viewed together with it, and hopes for the future were associated with the books of Moses as well as the prophets (see pp. 157–8, below, for this outlook in Josephus and St John's Gospel). A flexible interpretative tradition accompanied transmission of these books, and is attested in ancient translation and paraphrase. Within this tradition, messianic interpretation could persist irrespective of political circumstances.

This persistence aided the impetus of what may be called a messianic myth. At the same time, however, the orientation of tradition towards the Pentateuch

[9] N. Cohn, *The Pursuit of the Millennium* (London, 1957), 3–5.

[10] Scholem, 'The Messianic Idea in Judaism', 21, set against the background of argument by Albert Schweitzer and others for the importance of apocalypses by Biale, *Gershom Scholem: Kabbalah and Counter-History*, 152–4; on Scholem's debt to Schweitzer see further pp. 39–40, below.

fostered, with emphasis on law as well as prophecy, the 'restorative' as well as 'utopian' tendencies distinguished by Scholem, and moderation of urgent hope.[11] Thus, in a classic instance of restraint, when the daughters of Jerusalem are adjured not to stir up love prematurely (Cant. R. ii, on Song of Sol. 2:7), rabbinic interpreters hear a warning not to rebel or hasten the time appointed for the messiah. The persistence of messianism did not preclude detachment from it.[12]

Approaches to messianism

Messianism among Jews and Christians is understood here, as already noted, in the sense of the expectation of a coming pre-eminent ruler – coming either at the last, as the word eschatology strictly implies, or simply at some time in the future. In any case, the advent may be envisaged as near. Messianism here thus covers treatment of a present ruler in a messianic way.

The term 'messiah' may or may not be used in relevant literary texts, but this broad specification of future rather than simply eschatological expectation acknowledges a measure of continuity between the use of 'messiah' in the Hebrew scriptures for the Lord's 'anointed' (as in royal psalms which have a future as well as a present aspect) and its later use as an often unexplained special term for the coming God-given king.[13]

In this later period messianism is indeed linked with thought of the 'last days' (the term *eschatos* is used in Septuagint renderings of this phrase) which were foreseen according to scripture by Jacob, Balaam and Moses (Gen. 49:1, Num. 24:14, Deut. 31:29; cf. Hos. 3:5). Yet the expectations commonly called eschatological may emphasize hope for the future of Israel, notably the coming glorious kingdom mentioned above, as much as final events for the

[11] M. Fishbane, 'Midrash and Messianism: Some Theologies of Suffering and Salvation', in P. Schäfer and M. R. Cohen (eds.), *Towards the Millennium: Messianic Expectations from the Bible to Waco* (Studies in the History of Religions 77, Leiden, Boston and Köln, 1998), 57–71 (57–8). On restorative emphasis and resistance to it in mediaeval reshaping of messianism see Scholem, 'The Messianic Idea in Judaism', 24–33; on urgency and restraint, pp. 361–2, below.

[12] T. Rajak, 'Momigliano and Judaism', in T. Cornell and O. Murray (eds.), *The Legacy of Arnaldo Momigliano* (Warburg Institute Colloquia 25, London & Turin, 2014), 89–106 (100–102).

[13] On 'messiah' as an unexplained technical term in the Greek and Roman period, and implications of this usage, see Horbury, *Jewish Messianism and the Cult of Christ*, 7–12.

world, so that 'future' is again not inappropriate.[14] For hearers in the Greek and Roman age the context of the 'last days', 'that day' and final events would have been in view in the Pentateuch and prophets; but in themselves many prophecies significant for messianism chiefly foretell future victory and reign (so Gen. 49:10-11, Num. 24:7-9 and 17-19, Isa. 10:33-11:16). Hence, without dismissing 'the clearly eschatological connotations that messianic hope takes on' (A. N. Chester) after the period of the Hebrew Bible, I would add that hope for a future reign may sometimes have outshone other aspects of eschatological hope.[15]

A broad focus on future hope, including strictly eschatological hope, then divides my approach from that of those who tie messianism to eschatology.[16] Among them Chester treats the question with particular care in his monumental studies of messianism.[17] The broader definition has antecedents in the work of H. Gressmann, the more strictly eschatological in that of S. Mowinckel.[18] On the understanding adopted in this book, focused on expectation of a coming ruler, study of messianism embraces royal praise and prophecy in the Hebrew biblical writings. Many current treatments, however, exemplified by that of J. A. Fitzmyer, stick to an eschatological view of messianism and set aside this biblical material.[19] Yet even on this view it is hard to make an absolute distinction between Hebrew biblical texts and later sources. J. J. Collins finds a modest attestation of eschatological messianism in biblical writings from the post-exilic age, and possibly earlier.[20]

In the approach followed here the term 'messiah' is important, as noted above, but some texts which speak of a ruler in other terms are still thought

[14] Each kind of expectation can stand out separately, even though both are presented as final and should therefore be viewed together as eschatological, according to P. Volz, *Die Eschatologie der jüdischen Gemeinde im neutestamentlichen Zeitalter: Nach den Quellen der rabbinischen, apokalyptischen und apokryphen Literatur* (Tübingen, 1934, repr. Darmstadt, 1966), 2.

[15] A. Chester, *Messiah and Exaltation* (WUNT 207, Tübingen, 2007), 202.

[16] Horbury, *Jewish Messianism and the Cult of Christ*, 6–7, discussed by Chester, *Messiah and Exaltation*, 201–3; in his own definition he understands eschatology as importing finality but not necessarily an end of the world.

[17] Chester, *Messiah and Exaltation*, 193–205; id., *Future Hope and Present Reality*, Volume I, *Eschatology and Transformation in the Hebrew Bible* (WUNT 293, Tübingen, 2012), 208–10.

[18] See Horbury, *Jewish Messianism and the Cult of Christ*, 14–23; Chester, *Future Hope and Present Reality*, Volume I, *Eschatology and Transformation in the Hebrew Bible*, 232–5.

[19] Fitzmyer, *The One who is to Come*, 2–5, on this point following Mowinckel.

[20] J. J. Collins in A. Y. Collins and J. J. Collins, *King and Messiah as Son of God: Divine, Human and Angelic Messianic Figures in Biblical and Related Literature* (Grand Rapids, MI and Cambridge, 2008), 43–6.

to attest messianism. Fitzmyer ties his historical reconstruction, however, to attestation of 'messiah', Hebrew *mashiah*, in the sense of a national messiah—first found in his view at Dan. 9:25. The earlier Septuagintal version of the prophecies of Jacob and Balaam in the Pentateuch did indeed make explicit the thought of a coming ruler, but, he stresses, one not yet identified as messiah.[21] Here, however, these Septuagintal references to a ruler are treated as messianic (see this introduction, below). Similarly, Fitzmyer judges pre-Septuagintal attestations of Davidic hope not yet to be messianic, whereas here they are ascribed to a developing messianism.

Yet the broad ruler-focused understanding of messianism followed here, unlike the still broader conceptions represented by P. S. Alexander (see n. 1), itself excludes those attestations of hope which, as noted at the beginning of this introduction, do not mention a messianic figure. In these texts God himself, often pictured as a man of war, the 'double of the messiah' (as Gressmann put it), redeems his people (for examples see chapter 1, pp. 67–71, below). This theocratic emphasis is prominent in some biblical and later Jewish texts which are thought to indicate hostility or indifference to messianism with a messianic figure. It is urged here, however, that their outlook may be compatible with explicitly messianic hope.

Continuity and coherence

A continuity in messianic hope is envisaged here throughout the Second-Temple period and beyond. This view of course does not imply widespread or uniform messianism in all times and places. Yet continuity in varying circumstances was made possible, it is urged, through the transmission of sacred books together with traditional interpretation. Such interpretation is attested in the late Persian and early Greek periods by Chronicles and then by the Septuagint (LXX) Pentateuch, to be discussed later in this introduction (see also pp. 40, 76–7, 90, below). In the second century B.C.E. it has echoes in Ecclesiasticus, the Wisdom of Ben Sira. I would now set the Davidic future hope of Ecclus. 47:11 and 47:22 (pp. 72–5, below) more explicitly beside the

[21] Fitzmyer, *The One who is to Come*, 62–4, 70–72.

future hope for Jerusalem and the sanctuary expressed in Ecclus. 36:12-14 (pp. 231–4, below). Then in the later part of the Hasmonaean age messianic interpretation reappears dramatically in the Qumran texts.

When the present book first appeared A. Laato had been arguing strongly for pre-Hasmonaean messianic hope (p. 32, below). Some found instead, however, a messianic vacuum, especially in the Greek age, or urged that later messianism might be too incoherent to be significant (pp. 64, 67, 159, below). Meanwhile attestation of messianic hope in the Persian period has been reaffirmed by J. Schaper and A. Rofé.[22] The importance of tradition for the continuity of messianism from this time to the Greek age, as Septuagint translations suggest, has also been restated.[23] More limited affirmations of some continuity (see p. 32, below) have likewise been further developed. Thus for Collins his modestly attested early messianism reappears, still in a small way, in the LXX Pentateuch, but later more strikingly in LXX Psalms and Isaiah; messianism has a clear resurgence in the Qumran texts and later writings.[24] Chester not dissimilarly finds 'proto-messianic' passages in the Hebrew psalms and prophets, later calling these, rather, passages with 'latent messianic potential'. He avoids the unqualified 'messianic' in this biblical connection not least because he describes messianic hope as eschatological. From the Greek age to the later Hasmonaean period he acknowledges a 'latent messianism' (stressing, with the present writer, the influence of edited and collected scripture), thereafter recognizing a clear messianic hope.[25] Collins and Chester thus both envisage a relatively restricted pre-Hasmonaean messianism, but they differ strikingly from detections of a messianic vacuum in the Greek age.

[22] J. Schaper, 'The Persian Period', in M. Bockmuehl and J. Carleton Paget (eds.), Redemption and Resistance: the Messianic Hopes of Jews and Christians in Antiquity (London, 2007), 3–14; A. Rofé, 'David their King (whom God will Raise): Hosea 3:5 and the Onset of Messianic Expectation in the Prophetic Books', in D. A. Baer and R. P. Gordon (eds.), Leshon Limmudim: Essays on the Language and Literature of the Hebrew Bible in Honour of A.A. Macintosh (Library of Hebrew Bible/Old Testament Studies 593, London, 2013), 130–35.

[23] J. Schaper, 'Messianism in the Septuagint of Isaiah and Messianic Intertextuality in the Greek Bible', in M. Knibb (ed.), *The Septuagint and Messianism* (BETL 195, Leuven, 2006), 371–80; Horbury, 'Monarchy and Messianism in the Greek Pentateuch', 99–102; to later writers of comparable outlook on tradition listed at 100, n. 39 add L. Prijs, *Jüdische Tradition in der Septuaginta* (Leiden, 1948), criticized by M. A. Knibb, 'The Septuagint and Messianism: Problems and Issues', in Knibb (ed.), *The Septuagint and Messianism*, 3–19 (9).

[24] Collins, *King and Messiah as Son of God*, 42–7.

[25] Chester, *Messiah and Exaltation*, 229–30, 279–84; id., *Future Hope and Present Reality*, Volume I, *Eschatology and Transformation in the Hebrew Bible*, 213–14, 231, 262–3.

Their recognition of continuity from the time of the Qumran texts onwards is in contrast again, as Chester emphasizes, with more minimizing treatments.[26] For this period continuity, at least in use of messianic language, seems also to be implied by M. V. Novenson's argument that (irrespective of any hope or activism) there was consistent use (but diverse development) of scripturally moulded language concerning 'messiahs', and of a group of biblical texts on future rule.[27] This distinctively language-focused approach indicates concern with the subject sufficient to generate language-use, and perhaps retains some kinship with the emphasis on the influence of associated passages of scripture which is represented in this book and often elsewhere (see pp. 33–8, below).

One possible non-literary attestation of continuity in the early Roman period is formed by the risings against Rome mentioned already, and the long-term unrest in which they were high points (pp. 319–24, below, on the second century). Their connection with messianism has remained debatable, but has been affirmed especially for the risings at the time of Trajan's Parthian campaign, and the Bar Kokhba war fifteen years later.[28]

A continuity is also discerned here in specifically Jewish messianic tradition, in the period between the initial rise of Christianity, and the Christian empire of the fourth century and later, when Talmud and midrash were taking shape. Messianic themes of the New Testament are considered here to reflect in many ways the messianism of contemporary Jews in the first and early second centuries. The messianism of Jews in the later Roman empire is envisaged as a continuation within Judaism of this Jewish inheritance, not simply as a fresh development of Jewish messianism under the impact of Christianity (see especially pp. 364–5, below).

This perception of a continuing impetus among Jews for originally Jewish views which had also been taken up in Christianity, as it is presented here in Chapters 9–12, is meant to complement the widely noted recognition of Christian influence. A Christian context has long been envisaged as providing the impulse for Christian-like elements in Talmud and midrash and for

[26] Chester, *Messiah and Exaltation*, 279–80.
[27] Novenson, *Christ among the Messiahs*, 34 and n. 1, 53–63.
[28] See affirmations respectively measured, strong and minimal by Oppenheimer, 'Messianismus in römischer Zeit'; Chester, *Messianism and Exaltation*, 418–20; M. Goodman, 'Messianism and Politics in the Land of Israel, 66-135 C.E.', in Bockmuehl and Paget (eds.), *Redemption and Resistance*, 149–57; further discussion in W. Horbury, *Jewish War under Trajan and Hadrian* (Cambridge, 2014), 275–7, 360–62, 367, 378–88.

Christian-like piety, such as the remembrance of saints discussed in chapter 12, below. Interpretation of rabbinic texts on these lines has developed further.[29] This book, however, seeks also to keep in view the possibility of long-term continuity with the hope and piety of earlier Judaism.

The importance of Byzantium and Syriac-speaking Christianity for those who shaped the Babylonian Talmud has been justly stressed, but the messianic traditions which they presented did not necessarily arise solely in creative redaction. The continuity perceived in this book between messianism at the end of the Second Temple period and in later Judaism is suggested by the Amidah and other old elements of the liturgy, and the tradition of biblical interpretation in the Targums.[30] It is also suggested by the sharing as well as the opposition of second-century and later Jews and Christians in messianic hopes (pp. 241, 321–4, below). Hence, for example, I think there is still a case for attributing the interpretation of the plural 'thrones' in Dan. 7:9 – 'one for Him and one for David' – in the name of R. Akiba, in the Babylonian Talmud, to second-century Jewish opinion (as at pp. 84, 156, 169–71, below) rather than, as Schäfer argues, to anti-Christian polemic by a Talmudic editor.[31]

The question of continuity touches that of coherence. This book suggests a measure of coherence in the messianism of the Greek and Roman periods, despite diversity (see especially Chapters 1 and 4, at pp. 80–90, 159–61, below). Diversity presents itself not only through diverse titles and descriptions in the sources (including David, son of David, prince of the congregation, messiahs of Aaron and Israel, messiah son of Joseph) but also through modern classification of types of messianism (including human versus superhuman, and realistic

[29] Examples include I. J. Yuval, *Two Nations in Your Womb: Perceptions of Jews and Christians in Late Antiquity and the Middle Ages* (translated from Hebrew by B. Harshav and J. Chipman; Berkeley, Los Angeles and London, 2006), 10–91; D. Boyarin, 'Hellenism in Jewish Babylonia', in C. E. Fonrobert and M. S. Jaffee (eds.), *The Cambridge Companion to the Talmud and Rabbinic Literature* (Cambridge, 2007), 336–63; H. M. Zellentin, *Rabbinic Parodies of Jewish and Christian Literature* (TSAJ 139, Tübingen, 2011); P. Schäfer, *The Jewish Jesus: how Judaism and Christianity Shaped Each Other* (Princeton and Oxford, 2012).

[30] For broadly comparable views see Chester, *Messiah and Exaltation*, 413–20 (on the period down to the aftermath of the Bar Kokhba rising); Alexander, 'The Rabbis and Messianism', in Bockmuehl and Paget (eds.), *Redemption and Resistance*, 227–44.

[31] Babylonian Talmud Hag. 14a, Sanh. 38b, discussed by Schäfer, *The Jewish Jesus: how Judaism and Christianity Shaped Each Other*, 68–85. On his view of the Babylonian Talmud see further W. Horbury, 'Rabbinic Perceptions of Christianity and the History of Roman Palestine', in Martin Goodman and Philip Alexander (eds.), *Rabbinic Texts and the History of Late-Roman Palestine* (Oxford, 2010), 353–76 (356–7).

political versus cosmic eschatological), and many distinguishable motifs.[32] Diversity is further underlined when any coherence is found not in messianism with a messiah figure, but in broader concepts, as when a messianic idea is envisaged without the necessity for a messiah, or when messianism is viewed as a series of extensions of the concept of the kingdom of God.[33]

Then, moves away from the notion of one concept, however broad, which might in principle cover diverse types of expectation, have helped, as M. V. Novenson shows, to propagate a sense of the vagueness of messianism.[34] They can also bring instead pictures of competing dynamisms, such as the clash between a theophanic vector, standing for the revelation of the divine, and an apotheotic vector, representing attempts to transcend mortality by transformation into angelic or divine form.[35] Emphasis can then be laid advisedly on the fluid competitions and interactions of diverse ideas.

Classifications showing wide diversity, and new pictures of clash and interaction, can sharpen perception of the individualities of relevant literary texts; but they need not rule out recognition of interrelationships and common features. Messianism as envisaged here is hope with a focus on a coming ruler, but is sensitive externally to contemporary gentile culture, including ruler-cult, and internally to movements in Jewish piety. It finds fluid and diverse expression accordingly. Yet (it is urged) this did not exclude a degree of coherence.

Much of this point is expressed by others. Thus, replacing a unified *Messiasidee* with a picture of dynamic interaction, Schäfer says that the diverse 'ideas' and 'notions' connected with messianic expectations have their own separate dynamic developments, but are in many ways interrelated.[36]Again,

[32] For examples see pp. 80–81, below, on Bousset, Mowinckel and Morton Smith; Herr, 'Realistic Political Messianism and Cosmic Eschatological Messianism in the Teaching of the Sages'; similarly, Oppenheimer, 'Messianismus in römischer Zeit. Zur Pluralität eines Begriffes bei Juden und Christen'; L. T. Stuckenbruck, 'Messianic Ideas in the Apocalyptic and Related Literature of Early Judaism', in S. E. Porter (ed.), *The Messiah in the Old and New Testaments* (Grand Rapids, MI and Cambridge, 2007), 90–113; on motifs, Alexander, 'Towards a Taxonomy of Jewish Messianisms'.

[33] These views are exemplified respectively by Alexander, 'Towards a Taxonomy of Jewish Messianisms'; A. S. van der Woude, *Die messianischen Vorstellungen der Gemeinde von Qumrân* (Assen, 1957), 249.

[34] Novenson, *Christ among the Messiahs*, 34–43 (welcoming in principle the movement away from notions of a messianic idea).

[35] M. Idel, Ben: *Sonship and Jewish Mysticism* (London and New York, 2007), 4–5, in an approach to the history of mysticism which can also be applied to messianism; movement away from a unified messianic idea, particularly as reconfigured by Scholem, was urged in his *Messianic Mystics*, 17–18, 32–5.

[36] P. Schäfer, 'Diversity and Interaction: Messiahs in Early Judaism', in Schäfer and Cohen (eds.), *Towards the Millennium*, 15–35 (17).

Chester stresses diversity, but argues that incongruity and inconsistency should not be overplayed, and that there is a degree of coherence both in Qumran messianism and when, at a later time, a preexistent, transcendent figure and a more earthly messiah can both be envisaged.[37]

This book likewise lays stress on the point that some coherence is recognizable. I argue in this connection for the compatibility of conceptions of Davidic kingship and priestly-royal dyarchy, and of human and superhuman figures (pp. 81–90, below); for an old myth of the birth, wars and reign of the messianic figure (pp. 33, 372–7, below); and for the debt of messianic description to biblical portraits of the king (pp. 81, 90, below).[38]

The Septuagint Pentateuch

For the early continuity sketched above, one literary text has special importance. Attention was drawn in this book once more, following Z. Frankel, to seeming attestation of messianism in the Septuagint Pentateuch, translated for Greek-speaking Jews in Egypt under the Ptolemies in the third century before Christ (see p. 37, below).[39] If this is right, the text forms a bridge in attestation between the Persian period and the time of Ben Sira and the Qumran texts. It confirms too that messianism, here associated with the Torah, already has a recognized place in interpretation of the sacred books.

Relevant Pentateuchal texts include, as noted above, the prophetic Blessing of Jacob, on the tribe of Judah (Gen. 49:8-12), and the prophecies of Balaam,

[37] Chester, *Messiah and Exaltation*, 216–9, 274–5, 293–5.

[38] On dyarchy see further W. Horbury, *Jewish War under Trajan and Hadrian* (Cambridge, 2014), 357–60; on earthly and heavenly figures in a coherent messianism, Chester, *Messiah and Exaltation*, 293–4; on attribution of divine status to royal and messianic figures, J. J. Collins in Collins and Collins, *King and Messiah as Son of God*, 99–100; W. Horbury, 'Josephus and 11Q13 on Melchizedek', in G. Khan and D. Lipton (eds.), *Studies on the Text and Versions of the Hebrew Bible in Honour of Robert Gordon* (SVT 149, Leiden and Boston, 2012), 239–52 (245–50); on messianic narratives as response to Christian stories (by contrast with emphasis, represented in this book, on their probably pre-Christian roots) M. Himmelfarb, 'The Mother of the Messiah in the Talmud Yerushalmi and Sefer Zerubbabel', in P. Schäfer (ed.), *The Talmud Yerushalmi and Greco-Roman Culture*, iii (Tübingen, 2002), 369–89; ead., 'The Messiah Son of Joseph in Ancient Judaism', in R. S. Boustan, K. Herrmann, R. Leicht, A. Yoshiko Reed and G. Veltri (eds.), *Envisioning Judaism: Studies in Honor of Peter Schäfer* (2 vols., Tübingen, 2013), ii, 771–790.

[39] On Z. Frankel, *Vorstudien zu der Septuaginta* (Leipzig, 1841, repr. Farnborough, 1972), 179–91, on interpretative tradition, and id., *Über den Einfluss der palästinischen Exegese auf die alexandrinische Hermeneutik* (Leipzig, 1851, repr. Farnborough, 1972), 48–51, 182–5, 213, on Septuagintal messianism, in their connection with subsequent scholarship, see p. 36, below, and Horbury, 'Monarchy and Messianism in the Greek Pentateuch', 100 n. 39, 103–5.

on the people of Jacob-Israel (Num. 23:7-10, 18-24; Num. 24:3-9, 15-19).[40] The Septuagint (LXX) version of these prophecies and of the Blessing of Moses (at Deut. 33:5) seems to form, as Frankel noted, a testimony to messianic hope.[41] The appearance of messianic Pentateuchal interpretation later on in the Qumran texts, from Judaea under Hasmonaean rule, helped to confirm the place of messianism in exegetical tradition. The richness of the Qumran material suggests, independently of the Septuagint, that the messianic theme will have been part of such tradition before the Hasmonaean age.[42] This inference from Qumran texts is perhaps relatively uncontroversial, but messianism in the Septuagint has formed a focus of debate.[43] The case accepted here needs fresh summary.

The writer's argument presupposes the interpretative tradition mentioned above. During the Persian period, the books of Moses and the prophets and the psalms had begun to be associated, as is seen in Chronicles. It is assumed that the Septuagint translators of the Pentateuch would have been aware of existing interpretation on these associative lines, irrespective of the question whether parts of the sacred books were already known in Greek at the time of the Septuagint translation.[44] Thus the descent of David from Judah (I Chron. 2:15, 5:2, 28:4) has encouraged probable echoes of Isa. 11:1 in the blessing upon Judah as rendered in Gen. 49:9-10 LXX (pp. 161–2, below). It is taken likewise that LXX renderings which suggest a Hebrew original differing slightly from the consonants preserved in the Massoretic text may reflect an existing reading tradition of their Hebrew, as in the famous translations 'there shall come forth a man' and 'higher than Gog' in Num. 24:7 LXX.

The Septuagint translators, then, are not envisaged as offering a freely interpretative translation, but rather as bearing witness, in the course of a predominantly close translation and sometimes no doubt unintentionally,

[40] See chapter 4, at pp. 161, 174–7, below.

[41] Horbury, *Jewish Messianism and the Cult of Christ*, 46–51, with further considerations at pp. 146–7, 263–4, 266, below, and in Horbury, 'Monarchy and Messianism in the Greek Pentateuch', 94–6, 107–9, 121–6.

[42] Horbury, 'Monarchy and Messianism in the Greek Pentateuch', 105–6.

[43] For the debate see especially J. Lust, *Messianism and the Septuagint: Collected Essays*, ed. K. Hauspie (BETL 178, Leuven, 2004) (see p. 37, below; the essays appeared in the years 1978–2003); J. Schaper, *Eschatology in the Greek Psalter* (WUNT 2.76, Tübingen, 1995); Knibb (ed.), *The Septuagint and Messianism*.

[44] On interpretative tradition in relation to the Septuagint see Schaper and Horbury as cited in n. 26, above.

to interpretative traditions of their time.[45] Messianic allusions detected here in the LXX are therefore viewed as part of the impact of the Hebrew Pentateuch as it was understood at the time of the translation; what can be called 'Septuagintal' messianism because of its attestation in the Septuagint is regarded as a reflection or development of interpretative tradition, and is not ascribed simply to creativity on the part of the translators.

To recall the Septuagintal passages in question, all in the Hebrew are prophecies relating to 'the last days' mentioned already (Gen. 49:1, Num. 24:14, Deut. 31:29). Jacob's blessing upon Judah in Gen. 49:9-12 speaks in the Septuagint of a succession of rulers from the lion-like tribe of Judah, the ancestor of David: 'There shall not fail a ruler from Judah, and a governor from his loins, until the things laid up for him come, and he' – probably the ruler rather than Judah – 'is the expectation of the nations.' Then in Numbers 23-4 Balaam views Israel as the people among whom are the glories of rulers (23:21 LXX) and who shall rise up as a lion (23:24). He foretells with the spirit of God in him (24:2 LXX), and in a trance-like state – 'in sleep', or 'in a dream', 'his eyes being opened' (24:4, 24:16, LXX) – that from Israel's seed 'there shall come forth a man' (24:7 LXX) to be lord over many nations with a kingdom higher than Gog, and that a star shall rise from Jacob and a man shall stand up from Israel (24:17 LXX).[46] Lastly, in Deut. 33:5 LXX Moses prophesies that 'there shall be a ruler in the Beloved, when rulers of peoples are gathered together with tribes of Israel'. 'Beloved' interprets the Hebrew title Jeshurun, which signifies the Israelite people (loved by God, Deut. 7:8, etc.; see also p. 301, below).

All three passages in their Septuagintal form forecast the rise of rulers in Israel, within prophecies of the greatness of Israel or the tribes. The unfailing succession of rulers is prominent in Gen. 49:10 and Num. 23:21 LXX. A seemingly increased emphasis in the Septuagint of Genesis 49 and Numbers 24 on a great ruler to come coheres with the imperial emphasis laid in Deuteronomy, in the Hebrew as preserved in the Massoretic text and still more in the Septuagint, on the future monarchy of Israel over other nations.[47] The

[45] For the foregoing see Horbury, 'Monarchy and Messianism in the Greek Pentateuch', 102, 121–2.

[46] The rendering in Num. 24:4, 24:16 LXX, also found in Targum Onkelos, is compared with other explanatory descriptions of trance in LXX by W. Horbury, 'Benjamin the Mystic (Ps. 67:28 LXX)', in Boustan, Herrmann, Leicht, Yoshiko Reed and Veltri (eds.), *Envisioning Judaism: Studies in Honor of Peter Schäfer*, ii, 733–49 (744).

[47] Deut. 15:6, 26:19, 28:1, 28:13, enhanced in the tradition represented in LXX by the repetition at 28:12 LXX of 'you shall rule over many nations, and they shall not rule over you' from Deut. 15:6.

total picture suggested can be compared with the view of a succession of rulers leading eventually to a messianic king-emperor which appears in some later texts, including II Baruch 61-73 (see pp. 81–3, below).

Later work on these Septuagintal texts has included affirmation of a messianic interpretation by M. Rösel, in continuation of his earlier studies, on Genesis and Numbers.[48] Within work which is cautious in recognizing continuity a generally positive view of this suggestion, with a note of pitfalls and a desire for further confirmation, was taken by Andrew Chester.[49] J. J. Collins and A. Salvesen asked, however, whether a predicted individual ruler was indeed seen by the translators as specifically messianic.[50]

Thus Collins finds no messianic overtones in Gen. 49:10. He urges that the rendering 'the things laid up for him', which contrasts with and is probably earlier than the Greek variant (close to messianic rendering found in Targum Onkelos and elsewhere) 'he for whom it is laid up', shows that the translator either did not know or did not accept the widespread later messianic interpretation of the Hebrew, traditionally rendered 'Shiloh' in the English Bible.[51] Yet the wording 'the things laid up for him', in the sense of the messianic kingdom to be revealed in the last days, well fits a messianic interpretation.[52] Secondly, Collins holds that Judah rather than the coming ruler is the expectation of the nations (Gen. 49:10), and he judges that the Septuagint here foretells leadership for Judah, but fails to link that leadership with a messianic king. Within the context of verse 10, however, it seems more natural to take 'ruler' and 'governor' as the antecedent of 'he is the expectation

48 M. Rösel, 'Jakob, Bileam und der Messias: messianische Erwartungen in Gen 49 und Num 22-4', in Knibb (ed.), *The Septuagint and Messianism,* 151–75.

49 Chester, *Messiah and Exaltation*, 280–81; confirmation of the force of the messianism exhibited here might include the development of Numbers 24 LXX in Isa. 19:20 LXX (pp. 179–80, below) and in Philo, quoted in this introduction, below.

50 J. J. Collins, 'Messianism and Exegetical Tradition: the Evidence of the LXX Pentateuch', in Knibb (ed.), *The Septuagint and Messianism,* 129–49, summarized by J. J. Collins in Collins and Collins, *King and Messiah as Son of God*, 54–5; A. Salvesen, 'Messianism in Ancient Biblical Translations in Greek and Latin', in Bockmuehl and Paget (eds.), *Redemption and Resistance*, 245–61 (without knowledge of chapter 4 as presented in 2003).

51 This rendering of the Great Bible (1539–40), following Sebastian Münster (see S. R. Driver, *Genesis* (London, 1904), 386), was taken over by King James's translators and again in RV, and is found in the margin in RSV and NRSV; for 'the things laid up for him' as probably the earlier of the two renderings preserved in the LXX tradition see also Horbury, 'Monarchy and Messianism in the Greek Pentateuch', 109.

52 Frankel, *Über den Einfluss der palästinischen Exegese auf die alexandrinische Hermeneutik*, 50 stresses that the Septuagint here corresponds with Targum Onkelos 'Messiah, *whose is the kingdom*' (my italics), both understanding 'Shiloh' as *she-lo*, 'that which is his'; p. 81, n. 44, below.

of the nations', as Rösel and Salvesen do. More broadly, here Collins says nothing on the association of Judah with his descendant David. This Davidic association of Judah is brought out before the time of the Septuagint Pentateuch in Chronicles, as noted above, and then again afterwards in Ben Sira and the Qumran texts.[53] The unfailing Davidic line, together with the future messianic David noted above, will have been in view in Septuagintal interpretation of the blessing upon Judah.[54]

On Numbers 24 Salvesen seems to accept that the star may be messianic, but she doubts, citing Lust, whether 'man' has messianic overtones, and notes his view that Philo, in his two quotations of Num. 24:7 LXX, speaks of an eschatological Man restoring primaeval Man, not of a king messiah (see in response to Lust here pp. 176–7, below).[55] Philo writes none the less, in the context of these two quotations, that the *anthropos* will have a kingdom which is advancing every day (Philo, *Mos.* i 290, following Num. 24:7 LXX), and that he will lead an army to war which will subdue great nations (Philo, *Praem.* 95, joining Num. 24:7 LXX with Num. 24:17-18 LXX). By contrast with Lust, Knibb and Collins as well as Rösel affirm that messianic implications of the Hebrew are enhanced in Numbers 24 LXX, although Collins stresses that the 'man' is not called 'messiah'.[56]

On Deut. 33:5, 'There shall be a ruler in the Beloved, when rulers of peoples are gathered together with tribes of Israel,' the Septuagint with 'there shall be' reads the Hebrew as referring to the future, whereas the reading tradition represented in the Massoretic pointing indicates a past tense, 'there was'. The LXX future reading of Deut. 33:5 influenced messianically, as M. Gilbert showed, the long Latin text of Ecclus. 24:33-4; here an echo of Deut. 33:4 in verse 33,

[53] I Chron. 5:2, 28:4; Ecclus 45:25, 47:22, discussed in Horbury, 'Monarchy and Messianism in the Greek Pentateuch', 108–9; 4Q252, v 1-4, interpreting Gen. 49:9-10 (p. 73, n. 25, below).

[54] Horbury, 'Monarchy and Messianism in the Greek Pentateuch', 108–9; for the future David see Jer. 30:9; Ezek. 34:23-4, 37:24-5; Hos. 3:5 (on the 'last days'), passages all ascribed to a Persian-period redactor with a messianic state of mind by Rofé, 'David their King (whom God will Raise)'; Talmud Yerushalmi, Ber. ii 4, 5a, in the name of 'our rabbis', following quotation of Hos. 3:5 in discussion of the placing of the benediction 'Jerusalem' in the Amidah: 'whether king messiah is from the living, David is his name, or from those who sleep, David is his name'; p. 170, below.

[55] Salvesen, 'Messianism in Ancient Biblical Translations in Greek and Latin', 247–8; Lust's cited essay on 'The Greek Version of Balaam's Third and Fourth Oracles' is reprinted in Lust, *Messianism and the Septuagint: Collected Essays*, 69–86.

[56] Knibb, 'The Septuagint and Messianism: Problems and Issues', 17–18; Collins, 'Messianism and Exegetical Tradition: the Evidence of the LXX Pentateuch', 142–7; Rösel, 'Jakob, Bileam und der Messias: messianische Erwartungen in Gen 49 und Num 22-4', 168–75 (suggesting that a non-Davidic messiah is in view).

corresponding to Ecclus. 24:23 LXX, is followed by reference to the raising up of a king of David's line. The future reading of Deut. 33:5 recurs, also messianically, in the Palestinian Targum (Neofiti and Fragment-Targum) 'a king from the house of Jacob shall arise'.[57] It reappears, probably again with a messianic allusion, in a New Year piyyut of Yose ben Yose (chapter 10, p. 342, below).[58]

There is then a tradition of understanding the future ruler here messianically. This seemingly messianic prediction of the Septuagintal version of the Blessing of Moses is consistent, as Frankel noted, with the Septuagintal reference to the final 'day of vengeance' (Isa. 61:2) in the immediately preceding Song of Moses (Deut. 32:35 LXX).[59] The second part of Deut. 32:35 in both Hebrew and LXX stresses that such a day is near: 'the day of their destruction is near, and the things ready for them hasten' – in LXX, 'the things ready for *you*' (Israel) '*are present*' (see further p. 237, below).

It has been proposed, however, that the future ruler in Deut. 33:5 LXX is God himself, as in the theocratic hopes noted already.[60] Yet the rendering *archon*, 'ruler' for Hebrew *melekh*, 'king' itself suggests that the translators of Deut. 33:5 understood this phrase of a king other than God. The use of *archon* rather than *basileus* for Hebrew *melekh* in the Septuagint Deuteronomy, represented here and found also for example in the 'law of the king' in Deut. 17:14-15, corresponds to the pious preference in Ezekiel, the Damascus Document and other texts for Hebrew *nasi'*, 'prince' or 'ruler', instead of *melekh*, 'king', a term probably now often reserved for God himself.[61]

[57] For Ecclesiasticus and the Targums see Horbury, 'Monarchy and Messianism in the Greek Pentateuch', 124, citing M. Gilbert, 'Les additions grecques et latines à Siracide 24', in J. M. Auwers and A. Wénin (eds.), *Lectures et relectures de la Bible. Festschrift P.M. Bogaert* (BETL 144, Leuven, 1999), 195–207 (204–5).

[58] Yose ben Yose, *ahallelah elohay*, lines 30–31 in A. Mirsky (ed.), *Yosse ben Yosse: Poems* (Jerusalem, 1977), 92, quoted and discussed at p. 342, below; here in translating the biblical quotation I originally followed the Massoretic pointing and took the tense as past, but in the context of the poem I now think it must be read as future, with these Targums. The unambiguous future of line 31 'to Jeshurun again shall there turn back the kingdom' is then followed by 'as it is written in the law, And there shall be a king in Jeshurun'. A past tense is more awkward in the context. A reference to the messiah later in the poem is recognized by Mirsky (line 55, translated and discussed at pp. 344–5, below).

[59] Frankel, *Über den Einfluss der palästinischen Exegese auf die alexandrinische Hermeneutik*, 213; for the connection of a messiah-like angelic king with this day in interpretation of Isaiah 61:2 'the acceptable year of the Lord, and the day of vengeance of our God' see 11Q13 (11Q Melchizedek) ii 13 'Melchizedek will execute the vengeance of the judgments of God'.

[60] Collins, 'Messianism and Exegetical Tradition: the Evidence of the LXX Pentateuch', 147–8.

[61] A. Rofé, 'Qumranic Paraphrases, the Greek Deuteronomy and the Late History of the Biblical *nasi*', *Textus* 14 (1988), 164–74, followed by C. Dogniez and M. Harl, *La Bible d'Alexandrie: le Deutéronome* (Paris, 1992), 225, on Deut. 17:14, and Horbury, 'Monarchy and Messianism in the Greek Pentateuch', 93–4.

Again, it is objected, against a messianic interpretation of LXX, that the ruler (*archon*) 'in the Beloved' is not differentiated by vocabulary from the others mentioned in the same verse, although two different nouns are used in the Hebrew here.[62] Yet use of the same term need not imply equation, as can be seen from the use of the same Hebrew and Greek words for the Israelite king and the gentile kings who make obeisance to him in Ps. 72 (71):1, 10-11.

Deut. 33:5 LXX then speaks of a future king in Israel.[63] Its 'there shall be a ruler in the Beloved' understands the Hebrew in the messianic way also seen in the Palestinian Targum. Deut. 33:5 LXX seems to represent interpretation of the Hebrew in accord with a future context in Deuteronomy (Deut. 31:29 on the last days; Deut. 32:35 LXX on the day of vengeance) and with earlier prophecies in Genesis 49 and Numbers 24, which in both Hebrew and LXX speak of future Israelite rule. Such interpretation can be envisaged as part of exegetical tradition known to the translators.

Collins incorporates his restriction of messianism to Numbers 24 LXX into an overall view of messianism under Greek rule. Frankel had rooted the messianism which he found more extensively expressed in the LXX Pentateuch in a presumed sense of oppression felt by Egyptian Jews.[64] Collins urges, by contrast, that the smaller place which he gives to messianism in the Septuagintal books of Moses suits the marginality of messianism under the Ptolemies among Greek-speaking Jews; the focus of their hope on benevolent gentile rulers and the general lack of messianic interpretation in their Greek writings other than the Septuagint might suggest that messianism only began to flourish among them in the Flavian period and later, when Jewish-gentile relations had deteriorated.[65] Yet (without wishing to link messianism simply with suffering) one may note that sole emphasis on a communal Jewish sense of security in Ptolemaic Egypt may be over-optimistic.[66] E. Bickerman envisaged like Frankel a sense of exile and subjection in the Greek-speaking diaspora, and Jewish festivals in lower Egypt and Alexandria to commemorate

[62] Salvesen, 'Messianism in Ancient Biblical Translations in Greek and Latin', 249, noting that *archon* here renders both *melekh*, 'king' and *r'osh*, 'head'.

[63] The Septuagint context may suggest a figure combining Mosaic contours with those of the returning imperial David noted above (n. 54).

[64] Frankel, *Über den Einfluss der palästinischen Exegese auf die alexandrinische Hermeneutik*, 49–50, 182–5.

[65] Collins, 'Messianism and Exegetical Tradition: the Evidence of the LXX Pentateuch', 148–9.

[66] M. Idel, *Messianic Mystics* (New Haven and London, 1998), 6–9 suggests many possible life-situations for messianic hope.

deliverance from Ptolemaic persecution are mentioned in III Maccabees and Josephus.[67]

It then seems possible still to argue, after review of alternative proposals, that the LXX Pentateuch translates prophecies ascribed to Jacob, Balaam and Moses in such a way as to suggest that central passages are understood messianically. Messianic interpretation forms part of exegetical tradition as it has come down to the translators, well before the Hasmonaean age, and is continued by them.

Messianism and the Israelite people

Lastly, the messiah as presented in this book is a national figure. The prominence of the people of Israel in hope connected with the messiah was noted at the beginning of this introduction. The future Israel, like the coming kingdom of God, has indeed been viewed sometimes as an object of hope to which messianism is subordinate.[68] The Deuteronomic emphasis on future monarchy of Israel over other nations has been mentioned already (see n. 47, above). Comparably, the rule of the 'people of God' rather than a messiah figure specifically may be envisaged in the second column of the Aramaic 'Son of God fragment' from Qumran Cave 4 (4Q246), in the light of Daniel 7 and other passages (pp. 163–5, below).[69] Reassessments of the applicability of the term 'nationalism' in antiquity have included argument that it is indeed apt for Jewish

[67] E. J. Bickerman, *The Jews in the Greek Age* (Cambridge, MA and London, 1988), 245–6; III Macc. 7:17-20 and Josephus, *Ap.* ii 55, discussed by J. Mélèze-Modrzejewski, *The Jews of Egypt* (E. T. Edinburgh, 1995), 141–53 (he affirms the possibility of repression of the Jews under both Ptolemy IV Philopator and Ptolemy VIII Euergetes). Jewish awareness, even in good times, of possible instability and danger is affirmed in connection with texts including III Maccabees by T. Rajak, 'The Angry Tyrant', in T. Rajak, S. Pearce, J. Aitken and J. Dines (eds.), *Jewish Perspectives on Hellenistic Rulers* (Berkeley, Los Angeles and London, 2007), 110–17.

[68] So N. A. Dahl, *Das Volk Gottes* (Oslo, 1941, repr. Darmstadt, 1963), 89, approving Volz's phrase 'the personification of the future state' to describe the messiah as presented in the Amidah (see Volz, *Die Eschatologie der jüdischen Gemeinde*, 175).

[69] J. J. Collins in Collins and Collins, *King and Messiah as Son of God*, 65–74, restating his view of the Son of God here as messiah, takes him as the figure who 'shall raise up the people of God' (col. ii, line 4); but it seems preferable on balance to translate 'until the people of God shall arise', with G. Vermes and E. Puech, and also, as urged below, to take the personified 'people' as the subject in the following lines (5–9). For the people as judging the earth (lines 5–6), a point for which parallels have been thought lacking (so J. J. Collins, *The Scepter and the Star* (New York, 1995), 159), compare judgment by the saints or the righteous collectively in I Enoch 91:12, Wisd. 3:8, I Cor. 6:2, and one possible understanding of Dan. 7:22. Chester, *Messiah and Exaltation*, 230–33 makes the subject of line 4 the people, but the subject of lines 5–9 the messiah.

as well as other ancient thought.[70] Jews and Christians both viewed themselves as belonging to a body continuous with the congregation of Israel described in the Pentateuch. 'The prince of the congregation, the branch of David', to use Qumran messianic titles (4Q285; p. 374, below), was envisaged within this setting. Apocalypses presenting visions of the messiah can also include visions of Israel or the church (p. 289, below). The 'nationalism' surrounding the messiah is represented in this book especially as manifest in the ancient personifications of 'Israel', the 'people of God', 'synagogue' and 'church'.

In these ways the nation comes to the fore especially in chapter 5, on the apostolic Twelve as a sign of messianic restoration of a primitive God-given constitution, chapter 8, on ecclesial conceptions in the Septuagint and the New Testament, and chapter 10, on Yose ben Yose. God and his people seem to predominate over the relatively rarely mentioned messiah in Yose's hymnody (pp. 330–34, 342–8, 358, 361), although I would now see the messiah as having a slightly stronger profile in Yose than I thought originally (see n. 58, above). This urgent yet also reserved messianism can be compared, however, with the place for a messiah figure in connection with the people – the king in the beloved, Deut. 33:5 – which emerges in chapter 8 from the Pentateuch in its Septuagintal presentation. Here christocentric Christian views of the ecclesia are judged to represent intensification rather than alteration of existing Jewish emphasis. The same is true, it is argued, for the cult of Christ discussed in Chapters 9 and 12 (pp. 314–17, 388–92, 413–15, below).[71]

The connection between king or messiah and sanctuary, holy city, people and land stands out especially in chapter 3, on Herodian kingship and the temple, and chapter 9, on Jerusalem in Pauline and pre-Pauline hope. Here Paul is envisaged as sharing expectation of a future messianic kingdom in a Zion prepared by God.[72] I would now give more notice to links between the

[70] D. Goodblatt, *Elements of Ancient Jewish Nationalism* (Cambridge, 2006); B. McGing, review of A.-E. Veïsse, *Les 'révoltes égyptiennes'* (Leuven, 2004), in *Archiv für Papyrusforschung* 52 (2006), 58–63.

[71] On the cult in connection with Judaism see further W. Horbury, '*Cena Pura* and Lord's Supper', in J. Pastor and M. Mor (eds.), *The Beginnings of Christianity: A Collection of Articles* (Jerusalem, 2005), 219–65, reprinted in Horbury, *Herodian Judaism and New Testament Study*, 104–40; id., 'Beginnings of Christianity in the Holy Land', in G. G. Stroumsa and O. Limor (eds.), *Christianity in the Holy Land: From the Origins to the Latin Kingdoms* (Turnhout, 2006), 7–89 (80–89). On the cult of Christ and Christological development see Horbury, 'Jewish Messianism and Early Christology', 3–24; id., review of L. W. Hurtado, *Lord Jesus Christ*, in *JTS* N.S. lvi (2005), 531–9; A. Chester, 'High Christology – Whence, When and Why?', *Early Christianity* ii (2011), 22–50.

[72] Novenson, *Christ among the Messiahs*, 143–4 follows rather the view that Christ's present reign is envisaged in I Cor. 15:20-28.

concept of the Twelve (chapter 5) and the messianic kingdom (Chapters 6 and 9) in connection with the division of land.[73] Still with a national focus, divine covenants and promises, including ultimately the messiah and the messianic kingdom, are envisaged (chapter 2) as the gifts or grace of God to the congregation; this development of Pentateuchal usage appears in Ezekiel Tragicus, Philo, Paul and beyond.[74]

National and messianic suffering

The suffering of the congregation emerges as the counterpart of the consolation of the messianic age in Yose ben Yose (chapter 10, pp. 330–40, 360).[75] Suffering borne on behalf of the congregation comes to the fore in this book in connection with patriarchs, martyrs and disciples of the Wise (chapter 10, with more general discussion of martyrs and saints in chapter 12); but it is also evinced by the high priest, as Hebrews and various ancient Jewish presentations of the high priest suggest (chapter 7, on priesthood in Hebrews, pp. 279–83). The counterpart of king and messiah in the Pentateuchal dyarchy, he is universally significant but represents above all the congregation in the temple service, with its messianic overtones (chapter 10, on Yose, pp. 353–7, below). Further early traces of suffering appear in connection with an eschatological high-priestly figure, in Qumran fragments (4Q540-541) associated with the traditions found in the Testament of Levi.[76]

The comparable suffering of the messianic king (pp. 341, 360, below) can indeed be suggested by biblical treatments of Moses, the king, and the servant

[73] This point is brought out by S. Freyne, *The Jesus Movement and its Expansion: Meaning and Mission* (Grand Rapids, MI and Cambridge, 2014), 140–43.

[74] See further the commentary by P. Lanfranchi, *L'Exagoge d'Ezéchiel le Tragique* (Studia in Veteris Testamenti Pseudepigrapha 21, Leiden, 2006); J. M. G. Barclay, '"By the grace of God I am what I am": Grace and Agency in Philo and Paul', in J. M. G. Barclay and S. Gathercole (eds.), *Divine and Human Agency in Paul and his Cultural Environment* (London, 2006), 140–57; Horbury, 'Beginnings of Christianity in the Holy Land', 87–8 (on gifts in Jewish and Christian piety); id., 'Psalm 102:14 and Didache 10:6 on Grace to Come', in Baer and Gordon (eds.), *Leshon Limmudim*, 165–72.

[75] The old and central place of mourning for the destruction of the temple in this suffering (pp. 322–3, 338–40, below) is explored by P. S. Alexander, 'Was the Ninth of Av Observed in the Second Temple Period? Reflections on the Concept of Continuing Exile in Early Judaism', in Boustan, Herrmann, Leicht, Yoshiko Reed and Veltri (eds.), *Envisioning Judaism: Studies in Honor of Peter Schäfer*, i, 23–38.

[76] M. Hengel, 'Zur Wirkungsgeschichte von Jes 53 in vorchristlicher Zeit', in B. Janowski and P. Stuhlmacher (eds.), *Der leidende Gottesknecht. Jesaja 53 und seine Wirkungsgeschichte* (FAT 14, Tübingen, 1996), 49–91, repr. in M. Hengel, *Judaica, Hellenistica et Christiana: Kleine Schriften II* (WUNT 109, Tübingen, 1999), 72–114 (92–8); G. J. Brooke, *The Dead Sea Scrolls and the New Testament* (London, 2005), 140–57 (a chapter on 'The *Apocryphon of Levi*^{b} and the Messianic Servant High Priest'); Knibb, 'The Septuagint and Messianism: Problems and Issues', 12–13.

of God, viewed with the Targum and Justin Martyr (*Dial.* lxxxix 1–2) on Isaiah 53.[77] It stands out, however, only in Christianity, and in the rabbinic messiah son of Ephraim or son of Joseph.[78] The debated 'Gabriel stone' seems to offer too little unambiguous text in this regard to show hope fixed on a slain messiah, as I. Knohl urges.[79] Yet the view that messianic suffering was envisaged before Christianity is strengthened by the Qumran 'self-glorification hymn' (4Q491c, cf. 4Q427, 4Q471b). Here claims to have suffered occur in a text shown by Chester to be close to Davidic messianic tradition.[80]

These remarks may suffice to set this book among other approaches, and to indicate the flow of study since the first edition. Ancient messianism is perceived here as a scripturally-rooted element of tradition, integrated with interpretation of the written Torah. It cohered with conceptions of Israel and the church, and also of the kingdom of God (pp. 342–5, 358, below). Under Greek and Roman rule its kinship with ruler-cult was apparent (pp. 118–20, 148–9, 314–17, 380–85, below). Its mingling with mysticism is glimpsed through prayers, hymns and visionary texts (pp. 160, 165–8, 314–16, 411–13, below). The approach taken here views this broad messianism with and within piety focused on the Torah and the temple and synagogue service—somewhat as in the Psalter the second psalm, on the Lord's anointed, continues the first, on meditation in the Torah. Among ancient Jews and Christians these two psalms could be joined or separated; not dissimilarly, messianism evoked both assent and pause for thought.[81]

[77] Hengel, 'Zur Wirkungsgeschichte von Jes 53 in vorchristlicher Zeit'; Horbury, *Jewish Messianism and the Cult of Christ*, 33; I. Knohl, *The Messiah before Jesus: the Suffering Servant of the Dead Sea Scrolls* (Berkeley, Los Angeles and London, 2000); D. Boyarin, *The Jewish Gospels: The Story of the Jewish Christ* (New York, 2012), 129–56.

[78] A. Goldberg (p. 38, below); Fishbane, 'Midrash and Messianism'; P. S. Alexander, 'The Mourners for Zion and the Suffering Messiah: *Pesikta rabati 34*—Structure, Theology and Context', in M. Fishbane and J. Weinberg (eds.), *Midrash Unbound: Transformations and Innovations* (London, 2013), 137–57; Schäfer, *The Jewish Jesus*, 236–71; Himmelfarb, 'The Messiah Son of Joseph in Ancient Judaism'.

[79] I. Knohl, *Messiahs and Resurrection in* The Gabriel Revelation (London and New York, 2009); M. Henze (ed.), Hazon Gabriel: *New Readings of the Gabriel Revelation* (Early Judaism and its Literature, 29, Leiden and Boston, 2011).

[80] Chester, *Messiah and Exaltation*, 242–50.

[81] On Pss. 1–2 as a unity, Talmud Babli, Berakhoth 9b-10a; Talmud Yerushalmi, Taanith ii 2, 65c; Acts 13:33; Justin Martyr, *I Apol.* xl; C. K. Barrett, *A Critical and Exegetical Commentary on the Acts of the Apostles* (ICC, 2 vols., Edinburgh, 1994, 1998), i, 646.

Literature

P. S. Alexander, 'The Rabbis and Messianism', in M. Bockmuehl and J. Carleton Paget (eds.), *Redemption and Resistance: the Messianic Hopes of Jews and Christians* (London, 2007), 227–44.

———, 'The Mourners for Zion and the Suffering Messiah: *Pesikta rabati 34* – Structure, Theology and Context', in M. Fishbane and J. Weinberg (eds.), *Midrash Unbound: Transformations and Innovations* (London, 2013), 137–57.

———, 'Was the Ninth of Av Observed in the Second Temple Period? Reflections on the Concept of Continuing Exile in Early Judaism', in Boustan, Herrmann, Leicht, Yoshiko Reed and Veltri (eds.), *Envisioning Judaism: Studies in Honor of Peter Schäfer*, i, 23–38.

———, 'Towards a Taxonomy of Jewish Messianisms', in Ashton (ed.), *Revealed Wisdom*, 52–72.

J. Ashton (ed.), *Revealed Wisdom: Studies in Apocalyptic in Honour of Christopher Rowland* (Leiden, 2014).

D. A. Baer and R. P. Gordon (eds.), *Leshon Limmudim: Essays on the Language and Literature of the Hebrew Bible in Honour of A.A. Macintosh* (Library of Hebrew Bible/Old Testament Studies 593, London, 2013).

J. M. G. Barclay, '"By the grace of God I am what I am": Grace and Agency in Philo and Paul', in J. M. G. Barclay and S. Gathercole (eds.), *Divine and Human Agency in Paul and his Cultural Environment* (London, 2006), 140–57.

D. Biale, *Gershom Scholem: Kabbalah and Counter-History* (Cambridge, MA, and London, 1979).

E. J. Bickerman, *The Jews in the Greek Age* (Cambridge, MA and London, 1988).

M. Bockmuehl and J. Carleton Paget (eds.), *Redemption and Resistance: The Messianic Hopes of Jews and Christians in Antiquity* (London, 2007).

P. Bouriez, *Témoins du futur: Philosophie et messianisme* (Paris, 2003), translated by M. B. Smith as *Witnesses for the Future: Philosophy and Messianism* (Baltimore, 2010).

R. S. Boustan, K. Herrmann, R. Leicht, A. Yoshiko Reed and G. Veltri (eds.), *Envisioning Judaism: Studies in Honor of Peter Schäfer* (2 vols., Tübingen, 2013).

D. Boyarin, 'Hellenism in Jewish Babylonia', in C. E. Fonrobert and M. S. Jaffee (eds.), *The Cambridge Companion to the Talmud and Rabbinic Literature* (Cambridge, 2007), 336–63.

———, *The Jewish Gospels: The Story of the Jewish Christ* (New York, 2012).

A. Chester, *Messiah and Exaltation* (WUNT 207, Tübingen, 2007).

———, 'High Christology – Whence, When and Why?', *Early Christianity* ii (2011), 22–50.

———, *Future Hope and Present Reality*, Volume I, *Eschatology and Transformation in the Hebrew Bible* (WUNT 293, Tübingen, 2012).

N. Cohn, *The Pursuit of the Millennium* (London, 1957).

J. J. Collins, 'Messianism and Exegetical Tradition: the Evidence of the LXX Pentateuch', in Knibb (ed.), *The Septuagint and Messianism*, 129–49.

N. A. Dahl, *Das Volk Gottes* (Oslo, 1941, repr. Darmstadt, 1963).

C. Dogniez and M. Harl, *La Bible d'Alexandrie: le Deutéronome* (Paris, 1992).

M. Fishbane, 'Midrash and Messianism: Some Theologies of Suffering and Salvation', in Schäfer and Cohen (eds.), *Towards the Millennium*, 57–71.

J. A. Fitzmyer, *The One who is to Come* (Grand Rapids and Cambridge, 2007).

D. Flusser, 'Jüdische Heilsgestaltungen und das Neue Testament', in id., *Entdeckungen im Neuen Testament,* Band 2, *Jesus - Qumran - Urchristentum* (Neukirchen-Vluyn, 1999), 212–52.

Z. Frankel, *Vorstudien zu der Septuaginta* (Leipzig, 1841, repr. Farnborough, 1972).

———, *Über den Einfluss der palästinischen Exegese auf die alexandrinische Hermeneutik* (Leipzig, 1851, repr. Farnborough, 1972).

S. Freyne, *The Jesus Movement and its Expansion: Meaning and Mission* (Grand Rapids, MI and Cambridge, 2014).

M. Gilbert, 'Les additions grecques et latines à Siracide 24', in J. M. Auwers and A. Wénin (eds.), *Lectures et relectures de la Bible. Festschrift P.M. Bogaert* (BETL 144, Leuven, 1999).

D. Goodblatt, *Elements of Ancient Jewish Nationalism* (Cambridge, 2006).

M. Goodman, 'Messianism and Politics in the Land of Israel, 66-135 C.E.', in Paget and Bockmuehl (eds.), *Redemption and Resistance*, 149–57.

E. Grypeou and H. Spurling (eds.), *The Exegetical Encounter between Jews and Christians in Late Antiquity* (Jewish and Christian Perspectives Series, 18; Leiden and Boston, 2009).

E. Grypeou and H. Spurling, *The Book of Genesis in Late Antiquity: Encounters between Jewish and Christian Exegesis* (Jewish and Christian Perspectives Series, 24; Leiden and Boston, 2013).

M. Henze (ed.), Hazon Gabriel: *New Readings of the Gabriel Revelation* (Early Judaism and its Literature, 29, Leiden & Boston, 2011).

M. D. Herr, 'Realistic Political Messianism and Cosmic Eschatological Messianism in the Teaching of the Sages', *Tarbiz* 54 (1985), 331–46.

M. Himmelfarb, 'The Mother of the Messiah in the Talmud Yerushalmi and Sefer Zerubbabel', in P. Schäfer (ed.), *The Talmud Yerushalmi and Greco- Roman Culture*, iii (Tübingen, 2002), 369–89.

———, 'The Messiah Son of Joseph in Ancient Judaism', in Boustan, Herrmann, Leicht, Yoshiko Reed and Veltri (eds.), *Envisioning Judaism: Studies in Honor of Peter Schäfer*, ii, 771–90.

W. Horbury, review of L. W. Hurtado, *Lord Jesus Christ*, in *JTS* N.S. lvi (2005), 531–9.

———, 'Jewish Messianism and Early Christology', in R. N. Longenecker (ed.), *Contours of Christology in the New Testament* (Grand Rapids, MI and Cambridge, 2005), 3–24.

———, '*Cena Pura* and Lord's Supper', in J. Pastor and M. Mor (eds.), *The Beginnings of Christianity: A Collection of Articles* (Jerusalem, 2005), 219–65, reprinted in Horbury, *Herodian Judaism and New Testament Study*, 104–40.

———, 'Beginnings of Christianity in the Holy Land', in G. G. Stroumsa and O. Limor (ed.), *Christianity in the Holy Land: From the Origins to the Latin Kingdoms* (Turnhout, 2006), 7–89.

———, 'Monarchy and Messianism in the Greek Pentateuch', in M. Knibb (ed.), *The Septuagint and Messianism* (BETL 195, Leuven, 2006), 79–128.

———, *Herodian Judaism and New Testament Study* (WUNT 193, Tübingen, 2006).

———, 'Rabbinic Perceptions of Christianity and the History of Roman Palestine', in Martin Goodman and Philip Alexander (eds.), *Rabbinic Txts and the History of Late-Roman Palestine* (Oxford, 2010), 353–76.

———, 'Josephus and 11Q13 on Melchizedek', in G. Khan and D. Lipton (eds.), *Studies on the Text and Versions of the Hebrew Bible in Honour of Robert Gordon* (SVT 149, Leiden and Boston, 2012), 239–52.

———, 'Benjamin the Mystic (Ps. 67:28 LXX)', in Boustan, Herrmann, Leicht, Yoshiko Reed and Veltri (eds.), *Envisioning Judaism: Studies in Honor of Peter Schäfer*, ii, 733–49.

———, 'Psalm 102:14 and Didache 10:6 on Grace to Come', in Baer and Gordon (eds.), *Leshon Limmudim*, 165–72.

———, *Jewish War under Trajan and Hadrian* (Cambridge, 2014).

L. W. Hurtado, *Lord Jesus Christ: Devotion to Jesus in Earliest Christianity* (Grand Rapids, 2003).

M. Idel, *Messianic Mystics* (New Haven and London, 1998).

———, Ben: *Sonship and Jewish Mysticism* (London and New York, 2007).

M. Karrer, *Der Gesalbte: Die Grundlagen des Christustitels* (FRLANT 151, Göttingen, 1990).

J. Klausner, *The Messianic Idea in Israel from its Beginning to the Completion of the Mishnah* (E. T. London, 1956).

M. Knibb (ed.), *The Septuagint and Messianism* (BETL 195, Leuven, 2006).

———, 'The Septuagint and Messianism: Problems and Issues', in Knibb (ed.), *The Septuagint and Messianism*, 3–19.

I. Knohl, *The Messiah before Jesus: the Suffering Servant of the Dead Sea Scrolls* (Berkeley, Los Angeles & London, 2000).

———, *Messiahs and Resurrection in* The Gabriel Revelation (London & New York, 2009).

P. Lanfranchi, *L'Exagoge d'Ezéchiel le Tragique* (Studia in Veteris Testamenti Pseudepigrapha 21, Leiden, 2006).

R. Le Déaut, *La nuit pascale* (Analecta Biblica 22, Rome, 1963).

J. Lust, *Messianism and the Septuagint: Collected Essays*, ed. K. Hauspie (BETL 178, Leuven, 2004).

B. McGing, review of A.-E. Veïsse, *Les 'révoltes égyptiennes'* (Leuven, 2004), in *Archiv für Papyrusforschung* 52 (2006), 58–63.

J. Mélèze-Modrzejewski, *The Jews of Egypt* (E. T. Edinburgh, 1995).

A. Mirsky (ed.), *Yosse ben Yosse: Poems* (Jerusalem, 1977).

M. V. Novenson, *Christ among the Messiahs: Christ Language in Paul and Messiah Language in Ancient Judaism* (New York, 2012).

A. Oppenheimer, 'Messianismus in römischer Zeit. Zur Pluralität eines Begriffes bei Juden und Christen', *Jahrbuch des Historischen Kollegs 1997* (Munich, 1998), 53–74, repr. in id., *Between Rome and Babylon: Studies in Jewish Leadership and Society* (TSAJ 108, Tübingen, 2005), 263–82.

M. Pérez Fernández, *Tradiciones mesiánicas en el Targum Palestinense* (Valencia and Jerusalem, 1981).

T. Rajak, 'The Angry Tyrant', in T. Rajak, S. Pearce, J. Aitken and J. Dines (eds.), *Jewish Perspectives on Hellenistic Rulers* (Berkeley, Los Angeles and London, 2007), 110–17.

———, 'Momigliano and Judaism', in T. Cornell and O. Murray (ed.), *The Legacy of Arnaldo Momigliano* (Warburg Institute Colloquia 25, London & Turin, 2014), 89–106.

A. Rofé, 'Qumranic Paraphrases, the Greek Deuteronomy and the Late History of the Biblical *nasi*', *Textus* 14 (1988), 164–74.

———, 'David their King (whom God will Raise): Hosea 3:5 and the Onset of Messianic Expectation in the Prophetic Books', in Baer and Gordon (eds.), *Leshon Limmudim*, 130–35.

M. Rösel, 'Jakob, Bileam und der Messias: messianische Erwartungen in Gen 49 und Num 22-4', in Knibb, *The Septuagint and Messianism*, 151–75.

A. Salvesen, 'Messianism in Ancient Biblical Translations in Greek and Latin', in Bockmuehl and Paget, *Redemption and Resistance*, 245–61.

P. Schäfer and M. R. Cohen (eds.), *Towards the Millennium: Messianic Expectations from the Bible to Waco* (Leiden and Boston, 1998).

P. Schäfer, 'Diversity and Interaction: Messiahs in Early Judaism', in Schäfer and Cohen (eds.), *Towards the Millennium*, 15–35.

———, 'Gershom Scholem und das Christentum', in W. Schmidt- Biggemann (ed.), *Christliche Kabbala* (Pforzheimer Reuchlinschriften 10, 2003), 257–74.

———, *The Jewish Jesus: How Judaism and Christianity Shaped Each Other* (Princeton and Oxford, 2012).

J. Schaper, *Eschatology in the Greek Psalter* (WUNT 2.76, Tübingen, 1995).

———, 'The Persian Period', in Bockmuehl and Paget (eds.), *Redemption and Resistance*, 3–14.

———, 'Messianism in the Septuagint of Isaiah and Messianic Intertextuality in the Greek Bible', in Knibb (ed.), *The Septuagint and Messianism*, 371–80.

G. Scholem, 'Zum Verständnis der messianischen Idee im Judentum', *Eranos Jahrbuch* 28 (1959), 193–239; E. T. 'The Messianic Idea in Judaism', in G. Scholem, *The Messianic Idea in Judaism and other Essays on Jewish Spirituality* (London, 1971), 1–36.

L. T. Stuckenbruck, 'Messianic Ideas in the Apocalyptic and Related Literature of Early Judaism', in S. E. Porter (ed.), *The Messiah in the Old and New Testaments* (Grand Rapids, MI and Cambridge, 2007), 90–113.

A. S. van der Woude, *Die messianischen Vorstellungen der Gemeinde von Qumrân* (Assen, 1957).

P. Volz, *Die Eschatologie der jüdischen Gemeinde im neutestamentlichen Zeitalter: Nach den Quellen der rabbinischen, apokalyptischen und apokryphen Literatur* (Tübingen, 1934, repr. Darmstadt, 1966).

C. Wiese, *The Life and Thought of Hans Jonas: Jewish Dimensions* (Hanover, New Hampshire and London, 2007).

A. Yarbro Collins and J. J. Collins, *King and Messiah as Son of God: Divine, Human, and Angelic Messianic Figures in Biblical and Related Literature* (Grand Rapids and Cambridge, 2008).

I. J. Yuval, *Two Nations in Your Womb: Perceptions of Jews and Christians in Late Antiquity and the Middle Ages* (translated from Hebrew by B. Harshav and J. Chipman; Berkeley, Los Angeles and London, 2006).

H. M. Zellentin, *Rabbinic Parodies of Jewish and Christian Literature* (TSAJ 139, Tübingen, 2011).

Introduction to the First Edition

These studies review the setting and content of messianic hope in ancient Judaism and early Christianity. The earliest among them appeared in 1981, when their subject was receiving rather less notice in biblical scholarship than is now the case.

To set the collection in context I have picked out some characteristic themes of subsequent study for notice in this introduction. The first is the lively continuance of a time-honoured debate on the importance of messianic hope in ancient Judaism at the time of Christian origins, a debate closely linked in the period under review with a second characteristic theme, the discussion of new sources. Two further notable features of this period are the study of messianism in its connection with the history of ancient biblical interpretation, and the perception of messianism in a social context, as bound up with catastrophe, upheaval and renewal. Finally, the relation of Jewish and Christian conceptions of an exalted messiah with loyalty to one God continues to be a focus of discussion. In comment I urge that although ancient Jewish monotheism is often interpreted with strong emphasis on transcendence, it also had an important place for divine immanence and divine-human mediation and intercommunion.

At the end of the introduction the structure and scope of this book are outlined (see pp. 48–50), and some publications from the period under review are listed (pp. 52–7). Further details of work cited in the introduction by author's name can be found here.

Debate on the importance of messianic hope

When debate on the significance of messianism is considered, the years since 1981 may seem at first sight to have brought nothing new. So world-weary a conclusion would be premature, but it is true that both sides of an old-established argument have continued. The importance of messianism in Judaism before and during the rise of Christianity was repeatedly both doubted and affirmed towards the end of the twentieth century. In modern biblical study this difference of opinion can be traced back continuously (compare the comments at the beginning of chapter 4, below) at least as far as the early nineteenth-century doubts of Bruno Bauer on the very existence of a pre-Christian messianism.[1]

The doubts expressed by Bauer and others gained force among many who were personally more attached than Bauer was to Christian tradition, partly perhaps because a judgment on these lines could readily fit the dissociation of Christ from the Old Testament in the influential Christology of Friedrich Schleiermacher.[2] Bauer himself had stated his doubts fully in 1841 in response to the ascription of vast mythopoeic influence to messianism by D. F Strauss in his life of Jesus; among those who took them up later was one who urged the necessity of a knowledge of Judaism and Jewish scholarship for New Testament study, H. J. Holtzmann, although in the end he came to hold that messianic hope was widespread in the Herodian age.[3] Bauer's doubts were rediffused, however, in the twentieth century, through the fascinating portrait of him in Albert Schweitzer's *Quest of the Historical Jesus*. Bauer had urged, on lines still often followed, that messianism left no clear traces in the Septuagint, the Old Testament Apocrypha, or Philo; apart from Daniel, then, a book which would also later be seen as ambiguous in this regard, it appeared only in post-Christian and possibly interpolated apocalypses like the Parables of Enoch and 2 Esdras, and in the Targums, which again were not so early as to give clear attestation of pre-Christian views. He ironically noted that Strauss' sceptical indication of messianic myth as the staple of the gospel narratives itself depends on the venerable Christian assumption that there

[1] For a brief sketch see Horbury, *Jewish Messianism and the Cult of Christ*, 36–7.

[2] This was the view of A. Hilgenfeld, *Messias Judaeorum* (Leipzig, 1869), vii.

[3] H. J. Holtzmann, 'Die Messiasidee zur Zeit Jesu', *Jahrbücher für deutsche Theologie*. 1867, 389–411; New Testament students are advised to get Jewish learning and to study the works of the representatives of the *Wissenschaft des Judentums* in G. Weber and H. Holtzmann, *Geschichte des Volkes Israel und der Entstehung des Christentums*, i (Leipzig, 1867), xxxvii–xxxviii (Holtzmann was responsible for the treatment of Christian origins). Later on, reckoning now with the work of H. Gunkel, H. Gressmann and W. Bousset on the deep roots and prevalence of messianic myth, he came to hold that Davidic messianic hope had become general ('Gemeingut Aller') at the beginning of the Roman period; see H. J. Holtzmann, *Lehrbuch der neutestamentlichen Theologie* (2 vols., Freiburg i. B. and Leipzig, 1897), i, 68–85 (81); 2nd edn., eds. A. Jülicher and W. Bauer (Tübingen, 1911), i, 85–110 (103) (now specifying Davidic hope).

was indeed a long-standing antecedent messianic expectation to be fulfilled by Christ.[4]

Questions have once again been put to this assumption in the later years now under review, wide-rangingly in J. Becker's Old Testament study (1977, ET 1980), and on particular aspects by many contributors to the collective volumes on messianism edited by J. Neusner, W. S. Green and E. S. Frerichs (1987) and by J. H. Charlesworth (1992); but some scholars have also been consistently re-emphasizing the importance of Jewish messianism as a factor in the rise of Christianity, for example J. C. O'Neill (1980, 1995, 2000) and N. T. Wright (1991, 1992, 1996), on the historical Jesus and New Testament theology, and C. C. Rowland (1982, 1985, 1998) and A. N. Chester (1991, 1992, 1998) on Christian origins. One encouragement to this approach was the long-term influence of Gershom Scholem's collected essays on messianism and his great book on Shabbethai Zebi, which had appeared in English in 1971 and 1973 respectively (see below).

In work specifically on texts associated with ancient messianism, the period began with the issue by G. Vermes, F. Millar and M. Black (1979) of a revised form of E. Schürer's survey and synthesis, which itself had originally comprised a considered rejection of the young H. J. Holtzmann's view (n. 3, above); perhaps the main gap in this section of the revised Schürer is formed by its silence on the Septuagint (see below), but it ranges over the Old Testament Apocrypha and pseudepigrapha, and the Eighteen Benedictions (Amidah), with some reference to the Targums and rabbinic texts, and in the revised version also to Qumran material, surveyed in a new appendix. Particularly helpful, in the present writer's view, is the balanced recognition by Schürer and his revisers of supra-mundane as well as human traits in the portrait of the messiah at the end of the Second Temple period, and their indication of a background for all these in the Old Testament. The revisers rightly allowed, by

[4] B. Bauer, *Kritik der evangelischen Geschichte der Synoptiker*, i (Leipzig, 1841), xvii, 391–3 (Strauss depends here on an 'orthodox' presumption), 393–416 (literary sources on messianism), partly summarized by A. Schweitzer, *Geschichte der Leben-Jesu-Forschung* (2nd edn. of *Von Reimarus zu Wrede*; Tübingen, 1913), 145–7; ET *The Quest of the Historical Jesus, First Complete Edition*, translated by W. Montgomery, J. R. Coates, Susan Cupitt and J. Bowden, ed. John Bowden (London, 2000), 128–30. On Holtzmann's 1867 restatement (n. 3, above) see E. Schürer, *History of the Jewish People in the Age of Jesus Christ*, Division II, ii (ET Edinburgh, 1890), 127, 135–6; this passage was retained in Schürer's revised 1907 edition of the original (*Geschichte des jüdischen Volkes im Zeitalter Jesu Christi*, ii (Leipzig, 1907), 580, 589–90), but not in the corresponding section of the second volume of the revised English translation (1979), cited in the bibliography below.

contrast with Schürer himself, for perpetuation of both aspects of this portrait in later non-Christian Jewish tradition, but they more questionably inclined to a post-Herodian dating for the Parables of Enoch.[5] (Their twofold messianic portrait is perhaps fully illustrated by some texts in which they found only part of it, as is suggested for the Psalms of Solomon in chapter 1, pp. 60–2, below.) In further work on biblical and post-biblical sources both the tendencies indicated above are clear; messianism melts away in the studies of the title 'anointed' by M. Karrer (1990) and of Davidic texts by K. E. Pomykala (1995), but it regains a fair body of attestation in books reviewing Old Testament as well as later material by A. Laato (1997) and the present writer (1998). Cautious affirmation mixed with a good measure of doubt can be tasted in G. S. Oegema (1994, revised ET 1998) and S. Schreiber (2000). A penetrating critical account of recent study of messianism opens J. C. O'Neill's argument for the currency at the time of Christian origins of developed answers to the question 'What would the messiah be like? (O'Neill 2000, 27–72).

New sources in late twentieth-century study

Yet the character of the study of ancient messianism in these years is hardly captured by the simple observation that an old difference of opinion has persisted. Students of the subject, whatever their views, have also been appraising a fund of new or newly-considered source-material. Divergence of opinion has invigorated discussion of the sources, somewhat as the strength of nineteenth-century doubt concerning pre-Christian messianism noted by A. Hilgenfeld (n. 2, above) led him in 1869 to republish the Psalms of Solomon and to issue Greek retroversions of 2 Esd. 3–14 and the then recently recovered Assumption of Moses.

In the later twentieth century, the front rank among recently recovered material was occupied by new texts from Qumran Caves 4 and 11, partly known at the beginning of the 1980s and published in full in the next decade.

5 For a date before the destruction of Jerusalem by Titus see M. Black, in consultation with J. C. VanderKam, *The Book of Enoch or I Enoch* (Leiden, 1985), 183–4, 187–8; G. W. E. Nickelsburg, *1 Enoch 2* (Hermeneia, Minneapolis, 2012), 58–63 (in the later years of Herod the Great, or shortly afterwards). Note further that the lack of attestation for the Parables in the Qumran finds applies also to other late Hasmonaean and Herodian works, including the Psalms of Solomon and the Assumption of Moses; and that chapter lvi, best explained as alluding to the Parthian threat to Jerusalem in 40 B.C., seems to be presupposed in the Revelation of St John the Divine (16:12, cf. 1 En. 56:5–6).

The intensive study which they have evoked can be approached through the re-evaluation of these texts by J. J. Collins (1995) and J. Zimmermann (1998), and through collective works such as that edited by J. H. Charlesworth, H. Lichtenberger and G. S. Oegema (1998). Important yet often ambiguous fragments attest a Hebrew 'messianic apocalypse' (4Q521; not all would assent to this title) in which 'heaven and earth shall listen to his anointed', and two compositions influenced by Daniel: 4Q246, in Aramaic, mentioning one who will be called 'son of God' (see chapter 4, below); and 11Q13, in Hebrew, on Melchizedek (see chapters 1 and 4, below), identifying the bearer of good tidings (Isa. 52:7) as 'anointed of the spirit' (cf. Isa. 61:1). In the present writer's view, 4Q521 and 11Q13 probably reflect conceptions of an exalted messiah, but in 4Q246 the figure who will be called 'son of God' seems more likely to be an adversary. Of clearer significance for the history of messianism are remains of messianic interpretations in Hebrew of texts which were to become classical messianic prophecies for later Jews and Christians, notably Genesis 49 (4Q252, cited in chapter 4, below) and Isaiah 11 (a composition on eschatological war attested in 4Q285 and 11Q14 and discussed in chapter 11, below). These can now be viewed together with messianic passages from Qumran texts published at an earlier date, including the Damascus Document, first edited from Cairo Genizah manuscripts but also attested in fragments from Qumran Cave 4 edited in 1998, and the recension of the Community Rule and its annexes long known from Cave 1 (1QS=1Q28, 1Q28a, 1Q28b).[6] They confirm the pre-Christian currency of messianic hope, suggest developed 'myth' of the kind doubted by Bauer but reaffirmed by Gunkel (chapter 11, below), and anticipate some descriptions of messianic victory in the later apocalypses of Baruch and Ezra, preserved as the Syriac Apocalypse of Baruch and 2 Esd. 3–14.

Messianic hope in ancient biblical interpretation

Late twentieth-century discussion of messianic hope was enlivened not only by new texts, but also by reconsideration of familiar sources. This is true with regard to what is perhaps the major insight of the second half of the twentieth century in

[6] That the two annexes should be viewed as integral to the cave 1 recension of the rule is stressed by P. S. Alexander and G. Vermes, *Qumran Cave 4.xix, Serekh ha-Yahad and two related Texts* (DJD xxvi, Oxford, 1998), 10.

the study of ancient messianism, namely a regained recognition that messianic hope belongs to the stream of interpretative tradition which accompanies the Jewish scriptures throughout antiquity. The texts from the Qumran finds noted above were part of the material which confirmed this perception. Work on these lines from the 1980s onwards directly depends on the efflorescence of the study of ancient exegesis just after the Second World War.

Prominent among the familiar but reconsidered sources have been the ancient versions of the Old Testament, translations which embody much interpretative tradition. Of special note are two groups of translations into ancient Jewish vernaculars, formed by the Greek and the Aramaic versions, respectively. Greek versions, led by the Septuagint (third century B.C. onwards), are mainly known through Christian transmission, apart from manuscript finds in the Judaean wilderness and Egypt. Aramaic translations of Leviticus and Job are fragmentarily attested in texts from Qumran Caves 4 and 11, and Aramaic biblical versions include the Peshitta Old Testament of the Syriac-speaking church, a translation which probably preserves much Mesopotamian Jewish interpretation (see especially the late M. P. Weitzman's introduction to the Peshitta (1999), cited with brief comment in chapter 4, p. 175, below). The most substantial witness to Jewish interpretation among the Aramaic versions is formed, however, by the Targums transmitted in connection with the Hebrew Bible in the continuous literary tradition of the Jewish community. The Targums often follow interpretations also attested in the midrash, but they incorporate material ranging in date from the Second Temple period to the beginning of the Middle Ages. The Septuagint and Targums had an old-established place in the dossier of texts on messianic hope, as can be seen from the summary of Bauer given above; but in the years under review their investigation had received fresh impetus from the post-war revival of concern with the history of biblical interpretation.

This revival coincided with widespread philosophical, literary and theological attention to hermeneutical questions, and in biblical study it converged with fresh appreciation of rabbinic and patristic exegesis and inner-biblical reinterpretation. At the same time exploration of exegetical tradition was being stimulated by the discovery of the Qumran pesharim, beginning with the Habakkuk commentary from Cave 1 (studied in publications by W. H. Brownlee and others from 1948 onwards), by the identification of a complete Pentateuchal Targum text of

Palestinian type in Codex Neofiti 1 in Rome (by A. Díez Macho, 1956), and by the two-stage emergence (1952, 1961) of the Greek Minor Prophets Scroll from Cave 8 in Nahal Hever (Wadi Habra), south of En-Gedi, giving substantial Palestinian attestation of early Jewish revision of the Septuagint.[7]

Books conveying the atmosphere of this early post-war period include I. L. Seeligmann's *The Septuagint Version of Isaiah* (1948), reconsidering the outlook of the translation, H. de Lubac's *Histoire et esprit* (1950), on Origen's exegesis, and K. Stendahl's *School of St Matthew* (1954, revised edition 1968), reviewing the 'formula-quotations' of messianic prophecy in the light of the pesharim; all these illuminate the exegetical roots of messianism and Christology, but the place of messianic hope in interpretative tradition perhaps emerges most clearly from G. Vermes, *Scripture and Tradition in Judaism* (1961, revised impression 1973). Some of the light which this book sheds on messianism in biblical interpretation is indicated in chapter 4, below.

An element in these exegetical studies which has much significance for messianism is formed by interest in figures and symbols, in typological interpretation, and in the earliest Jewish and Christian art. Relevant work includes above all E. R. Goodenough on *Jewish Symbols in the Graeco-Roman Period* (13 vols., 1953–68), and the question of messianic symbols in art was discussed especially in connection with the Dura-Europus synagogue paintings from the early third century A.D., for example by Goodenough and by R. Wischnitzer, *The Messianic Theme in the Paintings of the Dura Synagogue* (1948). This discussion, taken up again in the 1980s and touched on in chapter 12, below, has now extended to more recently discovered representations, including a fifth-century synagogue mosaic from Sepphoris.[8]

[7] W. H. Brownlee, 'The Jerusalem Habakkuk Scroll', *BASOR* cxii (1948), 8–18; A. Díez Macho, 'The Recently Discovered Palestinian Targum', *SVT* vii (1959), 222–45; D. Barthélemy, 'Redécouverte d'un chaînon manquant de l'histoire de la Septante', *RB* lx (1953), 18–29, Y. Aharoni, 'Expedition B—the Cave of Horror' and B. Lifschitz, 'The Greek Documents from the Cave of Horror', *IEJ* xii (1962), 188–99 (197–9) and 201–7, respectively, and D. Barthélemy, *Les devanciers d'Aquila* (SVT x, Leiden, 1963), with outline of the sequence of discovery by E. Tov, *The Greek Minor Prophets Scroll from Nahal Hever (8HevXIIGr)* (DJD viii, Oxford, 1990), 1.

[8] For and against the discernment of a messianic theme at Dura see, respectively, J. Goldstein, 'The Central Composition of the West Wall of the Synagogue of Dura-Europos', *JANES* xvi–xvii (1984–5), 99–142 and P. V. M. Flesher, 'Rereading the Reredos: David, Orpheus, and Messianism in the Dura Europos Synagogue', in D. Urman and P. V. M. Flesher (eds.), *Ancient Synagogues* (2 vols., Leiden, New York and Köln, 1995), ii, 346–66 (the composition is Davidic, but not messianic). Hope for messianic redemption, perhaps with an implied answer to Christian apologetic, was discerned in the Sepphoris composition by Z. Weiss and E. Netzer, *Promise and Redemption: a Synagogue Mosaic from Sepphoris* (Jerusalem, 1996).

Concern with symbols in Jewish and Christian literary exegesis, exemplified especially in books on typology such as J. Daniélou's *Sacramentum Futuri* (1950), encouraged later symbolic studies bearing on messianism, including R. Murray on *Symbols of Church and Kingdom* in Syriac literature (1973), and A. Jaubert (1973) on messianic symbolism in ancient Judaism as a substratum of the earliest Christology.

Renewal in all these areas was in part also, however, a continuation of seminal work on the theological and legal outlook of the ancient versions achieved in the *Wissenschaft des Judentums* of the nineteenth century, notably by Z. Frankel and by A. Geiger (whose *Urschrift und Uebersetzungen der Bibel in ihrer Abhängigkeit von der innern Entwickelung des Judenthums* (1857) had been reissued in 1928, introduced by Paul Kahle).[9] Their studies had vividly demonstrated the interconnection of the Septuagint and the Targums with the development of communal history and thought, and Frankel had underlined the messianic fervour suggested by some Septuagintal renderings in the Pentateuch.[10]

From the 1980s onwards these post-war developments led to the issue of compendia on inner-biblical exegesis and on the interpretation of the Old Testament in the New, such as M. Fishbane's *Biblical Interpretation in Ancient Israel* (1985) or the collection *It is Written: Scripture Citing Scripture* edited in honour of Barnabas Lindars By D. A. Carson and H. G. M. Williamson (1988), and on the history of Old Testament interpretation, with special reference to the ancient versions and the New Testament, as in the collections *Mikra*, edited by M. J. Mulder with H. Sysling (1988), and *Hebrew Bible / Old Testament*, edited by M. Saebo (1996 onwards). Work on interpretation of the Old Testament in the New had always called special attention to messianic exegetical tradition, and in this area the influential contribution of C. H. Dodd and Barnabas Lindars was continued by work such as D. Juel's justified singling-out of *Messianic Exegesis* (1988) or R. B. Hays (1989) on *Echoes of Scripture in the Letters of Paul* (refreshingly sensitive to literary allusion, but perhaps

[9] The remarkable success of Geiger in stimulating work on text and versions is illustrated by S. Heschel, *Abraham Geiger and the Jewish Jesus* (Chicago and London, 1998), but its long term character emerges less than fully because of the book's concentration on New Testament study.

[10] Z. Frankel, *Ueber den Einfluss der palästinischen Exegese auf die alexandrinische Hermeneutik* (Leipzig, 1851, reprinted Farnborough, 1972), 50–1, 182–5, discussed by Horbury, *Jewish Messianism and the Cult of Christ*, 48.

underestimating the extent to which Pauline messianic exegesis follows pre-existing lines; see chapter 6, below).

Within this setting translation of and commentary on the Septuagint and its dependent Greek versions came to the fore, notably in the commentary-series *La Bible d'Alexandrie* initiated by M. Harl (1986 onwards) and in A. Salvesen, *Symmachus in the Pentateuch* (1985), and the messianism of the Septuagint was examined in these commentaries and by writers including J. Koenig (1982), R. Le Déaut (1984), A. van der Kooij (1987, 1998, 1999) and J. Schaper (1995). J. Lust (1985, 1995, 1997; discussed in chapter 4, below) has critically surveyed messianic passages and cautioned against over-interpretation. I have attempted to use Septuagintal attestation of ancient Jewish teaching especially in chapters 4, 5 and 8, below, on the messiah and the Jewish and Christian polity; but it also plays a part in chapters 2, on the thought-world of Ezekiel Tragicus, 6, on Jerusalem-centred hope, and 12, on the saints. Its special bearing on the debated pre-Christian history of messianic hope is discussed in chapter 4, below, and in *Jewish Messianism and the Cult of Christ* (especially 46–52, 90–7, 127–32; see further pp. 13–20, above). The Greek Pentateuch indicates that in the third century B.C. the Torah was interpreted in connection with messianism, and Septuagintal renderings in the Pentateuch and elsewhere illustrate that conjunction of superhuman and human attributes in the messianic figure which was observed by Schürer in other sources.

The Targums have been enriched with newly-edited textual material notably but by no means only through Neofiti 1, mentioned above. Like the Greek versions, they have also received extensive translation and comment, for example from A. Díez Macho and others, *Neophyti 1* (1968–79), from R. Le Déaut on the Palestinian Targums to the Pentateuch (1978–81), and from many authors in the series *The Aramaic Bible*. Re-examination of Targumic material on messianism has come not only in work of this kind but also in more general reviews by S. H. Levey (1974) and, on the Palestinian Targums to the Pentateuch, M. Perez Fernandez (1981); in the course of study of the Targums on particular books or in particular sources (as by W. Smelik on Judges, R. P. Gordon on the Minor Prophets, R. Loewe and P. S. Alexander on the Song of Solomon, and R. Kasher on the Tosephtoth of the Targum to the Prophets); and in many studies of individual passages, for example the last words of David (E. van Staalduine-Sulman, 1999).

The Targumic attestation of messianism belongs together with that offered in Jewish prayer, including the Amidah (discussed in this connection by Schürer and his revisers, by R. Kimelman, and by P. S. Alexander), and with the complex messianic witness of the Talmud and midrash, surveyed and discussed in this period by writers including P. Schäfer, J. Neusner, J. Maier, P. S. Alexander and M. Hadas-Lebel, and considered with special reference to one important source in the Frankfurt studies of Pesikta Rabbathi directed by A. Goldberg.[11] Rabbinic texts attest hostility to as well as interest in messianism, they have sometimes been interpreted—most importantly in the case of the Mishnah, as discussed by Neusner and Alexander—as deliberately neglecting it, and they reflect a long history of Roman, Christian, Parthian and early Islamic rule which includes many possible occasions for the discussion or repression of messianic hope. In the context of biblical interpretation, however, they are impressive as attesting, once again, the persistence of messianic themes in connection with the Pentateuch and Prophets, and the continuation of the twofold messianic portrait reflected in the Septuagint and in other sources of the Second Temple period. Awareness of both Greek and Aramaic biblical interpretation among rabbinic teachers in Galilee will perhaps have encouraged these continuities.[12]

The relative richness of messianic reference in the Targums is compared and contrasted in chapter 10, below, with the more restrained messianism of the liturgical poetry of Yose ben Yose, from about the fifth century. The value of the Targums for the history of messianism lies perhaps not simply in their much-debated points of contact with pre-Mishnaic Jewish and Christian sources, but more especially in their general attestation that the Hebrew Bible in all its parts was interpreted throughout the Roman and Byzantine periods in connection with messianic hope of a kind largely corresponding to that of Second Temple times. P. S. Alexander, underlining anti-messianic tendencies in rabbinic Judaism, puts the Targums next after the liturgy as a factor encouraging the survival of messianism in the Jewish community of late antiquity, despite opposition.[13]

[11] Schäfer, 'Die messianischen Hoffnungen'; Neusner, *Messiah in Context; Judaism and Christianity in the Age of Constantine*; 'Mishnah and Messiah'; Goldberg, *Erlösung durch Leiden;* 'Die Namen des Messias'; Maier, 'Der Messias' (on the earliest period); Alexander, 'The King Messiah in Rabbinic Judaism'.

[12] Horbury, *Jewish Messianism and the Cult of Christ*, 3–4, 99–102.

[13] Alexander, 'The King Messiah in Rabbinic Judaism', 472–3.

Messianism and catastrophe

The continuity of messianism in interpretative tradition from the Greek period onwards, as it is attested by the ancient biblical versions, has therefore received special notice in the second half of the twentieth century and in the years since 1981 now under review. This perception of later twentieth-century study recalls the famous remark of Josephus (*B.J.* vi 312) that the Jews were incited to war against Rome above all by a biblical prediction of a world-ruler from Judaea. Josephus here also points, however, to political and social aspects of messianism which have likewise been much discussed. Thus G. S. Oegema, cited above, brings out the relationship of conceptions of the messiah to current conceptions of great rulers, and in the studies collected here messianism had been similarly linked with Herodian temple-restoration and ruler-cult (chapter 3), the prestige of the high-priest and the priestly aristocracy (chapter 7), and resistance to Rome (chapter 9). Messianism can be associated with the publicity surrounding Jewish rulers of all kinds, whether established in power or at the head of uprisings. Uprisings and 'popular' messianic figures, such as some of the 'sign-prophets' mentioned by Josephus may be judged to be, have of course received much attention, memorably manifest in Morton Smith's dictum 'The most likely way to become a messiah was to begin as a robber', and bringing social questions into the centre of discussion.[14] Messianic elements in the Jewish revolts which broke out under Nero, Trajan and Hadrian have been brought out above all by Martin Hengel (1976, ET 1989; 1983; 1984–5; see also p. 10, n. 31, above).

Of special importance for the understanding of messianism under both socio-political and mystical aspects, however, has been its characterization by Gershom Scholem as 'a theory of catastrophe' (see chapter 10, below; p. 4, above). Scholem appeals in this connection to the series of Jewish apocalypses extending from Hellenistic times into late antiquity and the Middle Ages, and to cataclysmic elements in messianic movements, not least in Sabbatianism.[15]

His diagnosis has been kept in view at the end of the twentieth century not only because the study of Jewish mysticism has flourished, but also because contemporary Jewish religion has continued to include mystical and

[14] Morton Smith, 'Messiahs: Robbers, Jurists, Prophets', 42.
[15] Scholem, *The Messianic Idea*, 7, cf. 1–77; *Sabbatai Sevi*, 8–9, 464–7.

messianic enthusiasm, not to be overrated but sometimes manifest.[16] Scholem regarded his understanding of messianism as applicable to early Christianity, and in New Testament study his insights converged during the later twentieth century with existing interpretation of Jesus and Paul against the background of Jewish apocalypses, set out at the beginning of the century by Johannes Weiss, Albert Schweitzer and F. C. Burkitt, and followed by many later scholars. With Scholem's phrase 'theory of catastrophe', quoted above from a lecture first published in 1959, compare Burkitt's phrase (1909) 'The Christian hope a preparation for catastrophe'; both Burkitt and Scholem were sympathetic readers of Albert Schweitzer.[17]

In the period under review the light shed by Scholem on ascetic, antinomian and ecstatic elements in messianism has been applied to primitive Christianity notably by W. D. Davies (1976, reprinted 1984) and C. C. Rowland (see Rowland (1998), 493–6). The depth of Scholem's insight should not, however, preclude recognition of messianic hope as belonging to a biblically-focused exegetical tradition. The messianic elements in this tradition were current in prosperity as well as adversity; they had the potential for startling empowerment in given political and social circumstances, but they were endowed with a measure of independent continuity by the stream of biblical interpretation to which they belonged (compare the conclusion of chapter 1, below).

Messianism and monotheism

Despite the traditional Christian connection of Christ with Old Testament prophecy, noted above, the New Testament literary deposit of christology and the cult of Christ has often been studied either in separation from Jewish messianism or in contrast with it. The renewed discussion of messianism towards the end of the twentieth century has however to some extent converged

[16] de Lange, *An Introduction to Judaism*, 201–6; modern Jewish movements which link messianism with a conviction that the time of national redemption has come are studied by A. Ravitzky, *Messianism, Zionism, and Jewish Religious Radicalism*, and his work is discussed in connection with Christian origins by J. Marcus, 'Modern and Ancient Jewish Apocalypticism' and 'The Once and Future Messiah', and in connection with Zionism by Y. Amir, 'Messianism and Zionism'.

[17] F. C. Burkitt, 'The Eschatological Idea in the Gospel', in H. B. Swete (ed.), *Essays on Some Biblical Questions of the Day by Members of the University of Cambridge* (London, 1909), 194–213 (194, cf. 207–13); cf. H. B. Swete, *Jewish and Christian Apocalypses* (London, 1914), 44–5. Schweitzer is quoted and followed by Burkitt, 'The Eschatological Idea', 210–11 and Scholem, *Sabbatai Sevi*, 95–7.

with developments in study of the Christian sources, as is exemplified in work by O'Neill, Wright, Chester, Oegema, Laato and Schreiber. At the same time the emergence of the cult of the exalted Christ has formed a central question in New Testament study.

Concern with the religion, not simply the teachings, of Jews and Christians was an abiding element in twentieth-century biblical study, especially in the English-speaking world, despite douches of cold water in times of emphasis on biblical theology.[18] In this instance the relevant Christian customs and conceptions have mainly been derived from Greek and Roman ruler-cult or Jewish angelology, on the one hand, or from a new inner-Christian association of Christ with the God of Israel, on the other. The traces in pre-Christian messianism of influence from ruler-cult and of a superhuman as well as human messianic portrait nevertheless suggest that messianism above all led to the exaltation and worship of Christ (see chapters 9 and 12, below, and my *Jewish Messianism and the Cult of Christ*). This view receives a measure of confirmation from the messianic associations of the principal titles of Christ. Contemporary Jewish treatment of biblical and later figures as saint-like heroes would have helped to form a favourable environment for the posited development (chapter 12, below).

The exalted traits in the messianic portrait mean that, irrespective of the argument just outlined, Jewish messianism as well as the Christian cult of Christ invites consideration of ancient Jewish monotheism. However Jewish loyalty to the one God should be described, for some of its adherents it was not incompatible with the salutation of an exalted messianic king or, in Christian terms, our 'Lord' (Mar(an)a, Kyrios). This point has been explored in some of the varying derivations of the cult of Christ noted above, either with reference to the importance of intermediaries and great angels in Judaism (see for example the work by Fossum, Barker and Gieschen), or with appeal to new Christian experience (as made in different ways by Hurtado and Bauckham). In work represented in this book (especially in chapters 1, 4, 9 and 12) it is taken that the one God was imagined together with lesser divine beings as 'a great king above all gods' (Ps. 95:3), governing a world of spirits. This presupposition

[18] J. Barr, *The Concept of Biblical Theology: an Old Testament Perspective* (London, 1999), 105 (considering New Testament as well as Old Testament study). In a lively appeal for return to the study of Pauline religion J. Ashton, *The Religion of Paul the Apostle* (New Haven and London, 2000) perhaps underrates earlier concern with the subject.

is important for the interpretations of messianism and the cult of the saints offered here, and it can perhaps be clarified through comparison with the different view of ancient Jewish monotheism taken by R. J. Bauckham, in his clear-cut ascription of New Testament christology to association of Christ with the God of Israel.[19]

He urges that theological descriptions of Jewish monotheism, whatever their emphasis, fail to satisfy because they miss the vivid and precise Old Testament perception of the character of God. His own argument can be roughly summarized as follows. In order to appreciate the monotheism characteristic of Jews at the end of the Second Temple period, we should consider the identity of the God of Israel. This deity has a character, outlined especially in the biblical habit of describing him as a world-creator and world-ruler who demands exclusive worship. These characteristics made him unique and distinguished him sharply from all other reality. Yet the same characteristics are there in New Testament descriptions of Christ. That suggests that Christ was seen as part of the unique divine identity. At the same time it also explains how the Christians could genuinely assume that they shared the ancestral Israelite monotheism. A notable clue to their attitude is offered by the influential section of Isaiah now designated chapters 40–55, which will have been read among Christians as a continuous whole, including the passages on God's servant; the expression of 'eschatological monotheism' in this prophecy will accordingly have been received as a declaration of 'christological monotheism'.

Correspondingly, in the Jewish monotheism of this period the uniqueness of the God of Israel was in no way modified (Bauckham urges) by the conception of intermediaries between the deity and humanity. These are either included in the unique identity of God, as can be argued in respect of God's spirit, word, and wisdom; or else, as can be claimed of great angels and exalted patriarchs, they are excluded from the unique divine identity and plainly reckoned as servants of God. Intermediaries of the former but not the latter kind are thought to share in the work of God as creator; in the work of God as ruler, it is exceptional to find just one sole intermediary.

[19] Bauckham, *God Crucified*, 1–56, 77–9; Bauckham, 'The Worship of Jesus in Philippians 2:9–11'; Bauckham, 'The Throne of God and the Worship of Jesus'. The argument builds in part on the treatment of the worship of Christ in Bauckham, *Climax*, briefly noticed in Horbury, *Jewish Messianism and the Cult of Christ*, 116–17.

Similarly, it is argued, the deity no longer shares a 'species identity' as a divinity among divinities. Accordingly, with few exceptions, God's throne is unaccompanied by others; but among the Christians Psalm 110, in which the king is commanded to sit at God's right hand, is widely applied to Christ—without known precedent in Jewish messianic interpretation. Correspondingly again, the Christian exaltation of Christ goes beyond what is attested of the messiah or archangels, for Christ's rule is cosmic and supra-angelic; Christ, like the God of Israel himself, has all authority in heaven and earth (Matt. 28:15), and raises and judges the dead (John. 5:21–3).

An initial comment on the argument from Christian usage summarized in the preceding paragraph may serve to introduce broader considerations. In the particular argument just noted for Christian presentation of Christ in unprecedentedly close association with the one God much seems to be rested, first, on a shortage of non-Christian evidence for messianic application of Ps. 110:1–3; but the Parables of Enoch on messianic enthronement (45:3, etc.), viewed in combination with rabbinic interpretation of both Dan. 7 and this psalm (including the allotment of the Danielic 'thrones' to God and 'David', ascribed to Akiba in a baraitha transmitted at Hag. 14a and Sanh. 38b), and the implications of Mark 12:35–7, have been held to suggest that the beginning of the psalm could indeed be understood messianically at the end of the Second Temple period.[20] Similarly, the exaltation of Christ over heaven and earth and in the general resurrection and judgment is comparable with the messianic exaltation at the last judgment depicted in the Parables of Enoch (46–53, 62–4) and perhaps also in 4Q521 (Messianic Apocalypse) and 11Q13 (Melchizedek), discussed above, and with the supra-angelic exaltation of the messiah later envisaged in rabbinic comment on Isa. 52:13.[21] Again it seems hard to rule out the possibility that exaltation of this kind was current in messianic interpretation at the end of the Second Temple period, and formed the background of the comparable exaltation of Christ. The argument from silence may therefore not be strong in these two instances.

Bauckham's broader argument, which has been briefly summarized, is congruent with two often-noticed aspects of ancient Judaism and nascent

[20] The cautious evaluation by D. M. Hay, *Glory at the Right Hand* (Nashville and New York, 1973), 26–30 shows that this possibility cannot be ruled out.

[21] Targum *ad loc.* and Tanhuma Buber, Genesis, 70a, Toledoth, 20, discussed in Horbury, *Jewish Messianism and the Cult of Christ*, 139.

Christianity. First, in its description of Jewish monotheism, it recalls the militant confession of one God which was often manifest in the Jewish community of the late Second Temple period, in prayer, literary polemic and martyrdom, and in more commonplace custom, for example in the copying of texts. Thus the wish to distinguish the God of Israel seems likely to have been one influence on the practice, attested in some manuscript remains from this period, of writing the tetragram in palaeo-Hebrew characters in texts in the square script, or in Hebrew characters in Greek texts. Secondly, as regards specifically Christian monotheism, this argument highlights the early Christian capacity for creative development, also exhibited in such institutions as 'the Twelve' (chapter 5, below). Moreover, the broader argument—still in development, as the author notes—comprises interesting detailed suggestions, for example on continuous reading of Isa. 40–55 (continuous reading of Isaiah is similarly posited in chapter 6, below).

Yet an argument on these lines perhaps does less than full justice to the Old Testament inheritance of Jews and early Christians. The biblical tradition which they inherited and developed indeed treasures the uniqueness of Israel's God, but it expresses divine immanence as well as transcendence, and assumes not an isolated divine dictator viewed over against all other reality but a divine king in the midst of a council and court of 'gods' or 'sons of God' (Ps. 82:1; Job 1:6, 38:7). Biblical vocabulary and idiom expresses not only assertion of the one God, but also deep-rooted conceptions of a pantheon or divine council, of primordial and personified wisdom, and of superhuman and human spirits: within the circle of these conceptions Israel's deity was not wholly deprived of a 'species identity', for he was 'a great god, and a great king above all gods' (Ps. 95(94):3); and humanity was not wholly shut out from the world of the divinities, for the king could be hailed as a divinely-begotten godlike being (Isa. 9:5(6); Pss. 2:7, 45:7, 110:1–3).[22]

In the Second Temple period the God of Israel was correspondingly viewed as 'king of gods' (4Q200 2, 5, with *ᵉlohim*; Rest of Esther 14:12, Philo, *Conf.* 173, with *theoi*), presiding over yet accompanied by angelic beings recognized as in some sense divine, 'spirits' who could be entitled 'gods' according to the biblical nomenclature illustrated above. The continuing use of this vocabulary will have tended to modify that disappearance of the Creator's 'species identity'

[22] Horbury, *Jewish Messianism and the Cult of Christ*, 88–90, 120–25.

on which stress is laid in the argument under review. Moreover, Israel's God presiding over these lesser divinities as 'God of the spirits and all flesh' (Num. 16:22, 27:16, LXX) was envisaged in comparison as well as contrast with a not wholly dissimilar Greek or Roman pantheon in which many gods were presided over by a 'Father of gods and men' (Homer, *Il.* i 544, etc.). The gods of the heathen might be dismissed as spirits or demons who would be ultimately ineffective (Ps. 96:5), yet they could also be understood as angel-divinities providentially appointed to guide or misguide the nations (Deut. 4:19; Deut. 32:8 (lxx); Ecclus. 17:17; chapter 8, pp. 262–3, below). Similarly, it was possible for Jewish apologists to interpret Greek recognition of a supreme divinity, Zeus, as an attempt to name the true supreme God revealed by Moses (Letter of Aristeas 16; Jos. *Ant.* xii 22; Aristobulus frag. 4, in Eus. *P.E.* xiii 12). Correspondingly again, for many Jews at the end of the Second Temple period, here too continuing biblical, tradition, human beings can be inspired by divine or angelic or demonic spirits, and can be described accordingly as 'sacred spirit' (Moses in Ass. Mos. 11:16) or 'unclean spirits' (the possessed in Mark 3:11).

Against this background of scriptures understood as attesting a world of spirits, the Christian 'Christological monotheism' seems unlikely to have emerged simply as a new association of 'Jesus' with the unique identity of Israel's God (the widespread phrase 'worship of Jesus' may be misleading in this respect). Attention should also be given to the conception of a supreme God accompanied by other great spirits, to the assumed intermingling and contact between the spirits of human beings and divine, angelic and demonic spirits, and to the titles of Jesus, which can have spiritual and angelic as well as royal overtones. Thus 'Christ', which often replaced 'Jesus', suggested the biblical superhuman figure of an inspired king (Isa. 11:2), also called a 'mighty god' or 'angel of great counsel' (Isa. 9:5(6), Hebrew and LXX respectively).

These considerations can be further related to three particular elements of the argument under review. First, by contrast with what is sketched in that argument as the general pattern, the intermediary figures of wisdom and word on the one hand, and great angels and patriarchs on the other, are not always clearly distinguished as, respectively, included within and excluded from the divine identity. An important instance of overlap between the two is the identification of primordial wisdom with the angel of the Lord who appeared to the patriarchs and guided the exodus and conquest. Thus in the Wisdom of

Solomon the wisdom active as mediator from the beginning is identified with the angel of the patriarchs and the exodus (Wisd. 9:9, 10:15–11:1); and this identification seems already to be assumed in Ecclesiasticus, where primordial wisdom is enthroned on the pillar of cloud (Ecclus. 24:4; cf. Exod. 14:19). In Philo the word of God, the Logos, is similarly treated as an angelic figure, 'eldest of the angels, as it were Archangel', and is also identified with the heavenly man of God's first creation (Gen. 1:27) and the Dayspring-man pointed out by Zechariah (6:12) (*Conf.* 41, 60–3, 146), thereby gaining messianic as well as angelic overtones.[23] Christians, similarly again, united the divine wisdom and word with the great angelic spirit of the Hexateuch, and understood all three as the pre-existent Christ (Justin, *Dial.* lxi 1). This influential line of thought thus tended to modify the absoluteness of a distinction between divine word and wisdom, on the one hand, and an angelic servant of God, on the other, and accordingly it made less sharp the distinction between God and all other reality.

Secondly, it has already been noted that, by contrast with what is stressed in the argument under review, Israel's deity seems not to have been wholly deprived of a 'species identity' in the development of Old Testament tradition during the Second Temple period, for the use of 'god' (*ᵉlohim, theos*) to describe demigods or godlike angelic powers continued in force. 'God' is still viewed as accompanied by 'gods'—and godlike spirits can inspire and indwell humankind. Biblical history can indeed be summed up as the commerce of divine wisdom with holy souls on earth; 'in all creations passing into holy souls, she forms friends of God, and prophets' (Wisd. 7:27).

Thirdly, in accord with this conception of divine, angelic and human communion and fellowship, but again in contrast with what is suggested in the argument under review, the sharpness of emphasis on Israel's God as world-creator is modified in the Second Temple period by complementary emphasis on the metaphor of origin as well as that of creation. Thus the biblical vocabulary of 'generation' is complemented by the equally biblical yet also Hellenic vocabulary of 'generation' and 'procession'. Perhaps the most obvious trace of this line of thought is the naming of the first book of the Pentateuch, by a title already attested in Philo, as 'Genesis'—'origin' or

[23] Horbury, *Jewish Messianism and the Cult of Christ*, 94; on messianic associations of Zech. 6:12 and other LXX passages with *anthropos* see chapter 4, p. 175, below.

'generation', in accord with Gen. 2:6 LXX 'the book of the genesis of heaven and earth' and 5:1 LXX 'the book of the genesis of men'—rather than the book, of 'creation' (*ktisis*, cf. Gen. 1:1 LXX *ektisen*).[24] Correspondingly, the new creation of Isa. 65:17, 66:22 (see chapter 6, below) can be spoken of as 'the regeneration' (*palingenesia*, Matt. 19:28). Similarly, human beings or their souls can be thought of as divinely generated; 'we also are his offspring', in words of the Greek poet Aratus which seemed a good summary of divine creation to the Christian author of Luke and Acts (Acts 17:25–6, 28–9), as they already had to the Jewish philosopher Aristobulus (fragment 4, in Eus. *P.E.* xiii 12, cited above). There is some kinship between the human and the divine realms (John 1:13, 13:3; 1 Pet. 1:23; 2 Pet. 1:4; 1 John 3:9).[25] It is against this background, yet in full accord with biblical language, that the divine sonship of Israel (Exod. 4:22) is widely emphasized (for instance in Ecclus. 17:18, in the longer Greek text, and 36:11; 2 Esd. 6:58), and that the Rule of the Congregation from Qumran Cave 1 envisages (1QSa = 1Q28a ii 11–12) that God may 'beget' the messiah (cf. Pss. 2:7, 110:1–3). Wisdom likewise is divinely 'generated' (Prov. 8:25 LXX), but can also be envisaged as 'proceeding' from the mouth of the most High (Ecclus. 24:3), as an 'outflow' of the divine glory or a 'beam' of the invisible light (Wisd. 7:25–6). This vocabulary does not take away the transcendence of the supreme deity, but it complements the overtones of manufacture with those of kinship.

Comparably, Jesus son of Sirach sums up the biblical theme of the works of creation by stressing transcendentally that the Lord is 'above all his works' and 'made them all' (Ecclus. 43:28, 33); but in the same context he has also stretched out a hand to immanence with the complementary expression 'he is all' (Ecclus. 43:27). Yet another complement to the creation vocabulary is provided by exploration of the biblical phrase 'image of God' (Gen. 1:26; 5:1; echoed in Ecclus. 17:3; Wisd. 2:23; and with reference now to wisdom rather than humankind, in Wisd. 7:26).

In these ways the sharp distinction between God and all other reality which is stressed in the argument under review is modified by thoughts of likeness,

[24] Philo, *Abr.* 1 'Of the holy laws written in five books, the first book is called and inscribed Genesis, from the genesis of the cosmos, which it includes at the beginning', discussed with other passages by J. C. Ryle, *Philo and Holy Scripture* (London, 1895), xx–xxi.

[25] Some of the New Testament material on divine generation is set in the context of Hellenic and patristic thought on divine-human kinship by E. des Places, *Syngeneia* (Études et commentaires li, Paris, 1964), 138–41, 183–4, 189.

kinship and communion.[26] The relative prominence of the language of divine generation in the New Testament, illustrated above, underlines the importance of these modifications for the formation of Christology. More broadly, in Judaism towards the end of the Second Temple period the thought of the sheer transcendence of divine kingship was complemented by an understanding of the scriptures as attesting a world of spirits. In this understanding, the one 'God of the spirits and of all flesh' appointed the angel-deities of the nations, and through divine wisdom and godlike angelic powers conversed with human spirits. Exalted conceptions of a messianic king developed, therefore, among both Jews and Christians, against the background of a biblical monotheism in which the supreme deity was imagined together with lesser divine beings, both 'above all gods' (Ps. 95:4) and 'in the midst of gods' (Ps. 82:1). The messianic king embodied an angel-like spirit and touched the society of the 'gods' as well as mortals.

The structure and scope of this book

Biblical and historical studies of messianism which I first published between 1981 and 1998 are revised and collected here to form a series of twelve chapters. They complement, but are not included in, my *Jewish Messianism and the Cult of Christ* (1998).

Some of their contacts with the five characteristic themes of late twentieth-century study picked out above have already been noted. Thus chapters 1 and 4, on the Apocrypha and the Son of man, and the first part of chapter 11, on Antichrist, contribute to discussion of the importance of messianic hope at the time of Christian origins, and the associated discussion of new sources. They can be read as complement to the first part of *Jewish Messianism and the Cult of Christ*, in which it is argued that messianism was widespread before the rise of Christianity. Then the third theme, the study of messianic hope as integrated into the ancient tradition of biblical interpretation, is important throughout the studies collected below. Interpretative texts are central in chapter 1, on the Apocrypha and pseudepigrapha, chapter 2, on Ezekiel the Tragedian, chapters

[26] Compare in general the critique of interpretation of Judaism as a strictly transcendental monotheism offered by Thoma, *A Christian Theology of Judaism*, 124.

5 and 6, on the Phylarchs and Jerusalem, chapter 8, on the Septuagint, and chapter 10, on early synagogue poetry. The fourth theme, the association of messianism with catastrophe, is explored especially in chapters 9–11, on suffering and messianism, on Jews and Christians in the second century, and on conceptions of Antichrist. Finally, the relationship between messianism and monotheism is explored with reference to exalted conceptions of kings, saints and heroes in chapter 3, on Herodian ruler-cult, chapter 9, on the second century, and chapter 12, on the cult of Christ and the cult of the saints. These three chapters can be viewed together with the second part of *Jewish Messianism and the Cult of Christ*, in which homage to an exalted messiah is presented as the great link between Herodian Judaism and the Christian cult of Christ.

The chapters have been arranged below, however, according to a roughly chronological ordering of their subject-matter.

The book is focused on the Herodian period and the New Testament, but looks back to the Apocrypha and pseudepigrapha, and onward to Judaism and Christianity in the Roman empire. It is divided into three sections, headed *The Second Temple Period* (chapters 1–3), *The New Testament* (chapters 4–8), and *Synagogue and Church in the Roman Empire* (chapters 9–12).

Within this framework each section includes some treatment of central themes, such as messianism in the Apocrypha and pseudepigrapha (chapter 1), the Son of man (chapter 4) and Pauline hope for a new Jerusalem (chapter 6), and Jewish and Christian messianism in the second century (chapter 9). There are also, however, studies of some relatively neglected topics, including suffering and messianism in synagogue poetry (chapter 10), and the relation of Christian and Jewish messianism with conceptions of the church (chapter 8) and of Antichrist (chapter 11) and with the cult of Christ and of the saints (chapters 9 and 12).

Throughout, an attempt is made to set messianism in a broad political and religious context. Its links with revolution and social upheaval have received much attention, but these studies seek also to explore its setting in religion and in the conflict of political theories—since the ancient Jewish constitution is both a 'church' and a 'state'. Thus conciliar and priestly constitutional ideals in their bearing on Christian messianism form an important theme here (chapters 5, on the Twelve, and 7, on conceptions of the church; compare also chapter 8, on the Aaronic priesthood), and again one that is relatively little studied.

New Testament subjects which come to the fore include the historical Jesus (chapters 4–5), Paul (chapters 2 and 6), Hebrews (chapter 7), and New Testament theology (chapters 8, 11 and 12, and parts of chapters 2, 9 and 10).

With regard to religion, chapter 2 is a counterpart to chapter 10 in its focus on poetry in honour of Jewish festivals, in this instance pre-Christian Greek Jewish poetry expressing a theology of God's gifts, which may include the messiah; and chapter 3 explores the religious as well as political theme of messianism and ruler-cult through study of Herod's temple restoration and the debated reference in Persius to 'Herod's days', here interpreted as Herodian festivals kept by Jews in Rome. The relation of messianism and Jewish religion with elements in Christian religion becomes central in chapter 9, on chiliasm and the cult of Christ, and chapter 12, on the cult of Christ and the cult of the saints.

Literary tradition, often of considerable freshness and beauty, is important throughout. The poetic texts considered include the festal poetry already mentioned (chapters 2 and 10), hymnody and prayer concerning Jerusalem (chapter 6), and Septuagintal poems from the Pentateuch and Wisdom (chapter 8). One aim has been to allow these writings to speak, despite the need for restraint in quotation.

All the chapters have been revised, and chapters 2–5, 7 and 12 have considerable additions; chapter 6 is mainly new. In revision an attempt has been made to represent at least something of the fresh editing of sources and further study which has taken place since the work first appeared.

Material incorporated below originally appeared in volumes in honour of G. M. Styler (chapter 10), M. D. Hooker (chapter 6), J. P. M. Sweet (chapter 8), and E. Bammel (chapters 3 and 7). The thanks to them included in the first publications are here gratefully expressed again.

Acknowledgement is gratefully made to the following publishers for permission to reproduce material: the Istituto Patristico Augustinianum; Messrs. E. J. Brill; Cambridge University Press; Messrs. T&T Clark; J. C. B. Mohr (Paul Siebeck); Oxford University Press; Sheffield Academic Press.

I am very grateful to Dr. A. N. Chester and Dr. J. N. B. Carleton Paget for commenting on drafts of the introduction, and to Ruth Tuschling for making the indexes. As usual I am deeply indebted to my wife Katharine for encouragement and forbearance.

Particulars of First Publication

The table below gives particulars of the first publication of the essays on which the chapters in this volume are based. The revisions printed here include alteration and addition.

1. Messianism in the Old Testament Apocrypha and Pseudepigrapha: J. Day (ed.), *King and Messiah* (Sheffield, 1998), 402–33
2. The Gifts of God in Ezekiel the Tragedian: 'Ezekiel Tragicus 106: *doremata*', *VT* xxxvi (1986), 37–51
3. Herod's Temple and 'Herod's Days': William Horbury (ed.), *Templum Amicitiae* (Sheffield, 1991), 103–49
4. The Messianic Associations of 'the Son of Man': *JTS* N.S. xxxvi (1985), 34–55
5. The Twelve and the Phylarchs: *NTS* xxxii (1986), 503–27
6. Jerusalem in Pre-Pauline and Pauline Hope: 'Land, Sanctuary and Worship', in J. P. M. Sweet and J. M. G. Barclay (eds.), *Early Christian Thought in its Jewish Setting* (Cambridge, 1996), 207–24 (208–11, 219–24, with alterations and additions)
7. The Aaronic Priesthood in the Epistle to the Hebrews: *JSNT* xix (1983), 43–71
8. Septuagintal and New Testament Conceptions of the Church: M. N. A. Bockmuehl and M. E. Thompson (eds.), *Vision for the Church* (Edinburgh, 1997), 1–17
9. Messianism among Jews and Christians in the Second Century: *Augustinianum* xxviii (1988), 71–88
10. Suffering and Messianism in Yose ben Yose: W. Horbury and B. McNeil (eds.), *Suffering and Martyrdom in the New Testament* (Cambridge, 1981), 143–82
11. Antichrist among Jews and Gentiles: M. Goodman (ed.), *Jews in a Graeco-Roman World* (Oxford, 1998), 113–33
12. The Cult of Christ and the Cult of the Saints: *NTS* xliv (1998), 444–69

Literature

P. S. Alexander, 'The King Messiah in Rabbinic Judaism', in Day (ed.), *King and Messiah*, 456–73

Y. Amir, 'Messianism and Zionism', in Reventlow (ed.), *Eschatology in the Bible and in Jewish and Christian Tradition*, 13–30

R. S. Barbour (ed.), *The Kingdom of God and Human Society* (Edinburgh, 1993)

R. J. Bauckham, *God Crucified: Monotheism and Christology in the New Testament* (London, 1998)

———, 'The Worship of Jesus in Philippians 2:9–11', in R. P. Martin and B. J. Dodd (eds.), *Where Christology Began: Essays on Philippians 2* (Louisville, 1998), 128–39

———, 'The Throne of God and the Worship of Jesus', in Newman, Davila and Lewis (eds.), *The Jewish Roots of Christological Monotheism*, 43–69

J. Becker, *Messianic Expectation in the Old Testament* (1977, ET Edinburgh, 1980)

W. Beuken, S. Freyne and A. Weiler (eds.), *Messianism through History* (Concilium 1993/1, London and Maryknoll, 1993)

J. N. B. Carleton Paget, 'Jewish Christianity', *CHJ* iii (1999), 731–75

J. H. Charlesworth (ed.), *The Messiah: Developments in Earliest Judaism and Christianity* (Minneapolis, 1992)

J. H. Charlesworth, H. Lichtenberger and G. S. Oegema (eds.), *Qumran-Messianism* (Tübingen, 1998)

A. N. Chester, 'Jewish Messianic Expectations and Mediatorial Figures and Pauline Christology' in M. Hengel and U. Heckel (eds.), *Paulus und das antike Judentum* (Tübingen, 1991), 17–89

A. N. Chester, 'The Parting of the Ways: Eschatology and Messianic Hope', in J. D. G. Dunn (ed.), *Jews and Christians: The Parting of the Ways A.D. 70 to 135* (Tübingen, 1992), 239–313

———, 'Messianism, Torah and early Christian Tradition', in G. N. Stanton and G. G. Stroumsa (eds.), *Tolerance and Intolerance in Early Judaism and Christianity* (Cambridge, 1998), 318–41

R. E. Clements, 'The Messianic Hope in the Old Testament', *JSOT* xliii (1989), 3–19

J. J. Collins, *The Scepter and the Star* (New York, 1995)

J. D. Crossan, *The Historical Jesus* (Edinburgh, 1991)

———, *The Birth of Christianity* (Edinburgh, 1999)

W. D. Davies, 'From Schweitzer to Scholem: Reflections on Sabbatai Svi', reprinted from *JBL* xcv (1976), 529–38 in W. D. Davies, *Jewish and Pauline Studies* (London, 1984), 257–77

J. Day (ed.), *King and Messiah in Israel and the Ancient Near East* (Sheffield, 1998)

C. H. T. Fletcher-Louis, 'The Worship of Divine Humanity as God's Image and the Worship of Jesus', in Newman, Davila and Lewis (eds.), *The Jewish Roots of Christological Monotheism*, 112–28

D. Flusser, 'Messiah', *EJ* xi (1971), 407–17

C. A. Gieschen, *Angelomorphic Christology* (AGJU 42, Leiden, 1998)

Arnold Goldberg, *Erlösung durch Leiden. Drei rabbinische Homilien über die Trauernden Zions und den leidenden Messias Ephraim (PesR 34. 36. 37)* (Frankfurter Judaistische Studien, IV, Frankfurt am Main, 1978)

———, 'Die Namen des Messias in der rabbinischen Traditionsliteratur. EinBeitrag zur Messiaslehre des rabbinischen Judentums', *FJB* vii (1979), 1–93

M. D. Goodman, 'The emergence of Christianity', in A. Hastings (ed.), *A World History of Christianity* (London, 1999), 7–24

———, (ed.), *Jews in a Graeco-Roman World* (Oxford, 1998)

M. Hadas-Lebel, 'Hezekiah as King Messiah: Traces of an Early Jewish-Christian Polemic in the Tannaitic Tradition', in J. Targarona Borrás and A. Sáenz-Badillos (eds.), *Jewish Studies at the Turn of the Twentieth Century* (2 vols., Leiden, 1999), i, 275–81

———, ' "Il n'y a pas de messie pour Israël car on l'a déjà consommé au temps d'Ézéchias" (TB Sanhédrin 99a)', *REJ* clix (2000), 357–67

D. Hellholm (ed.), *Apocalypticism in the Mediterranean World and the Near East* (Tübingen, 1983)

M. Hengel, *Die Zeloten* (2nd edn., Leiden and Köln, 1976), ET, with new introduction, *The Zealots* (Edinburgh, 1989)

———, 'Messianische Hoffnung und politischer "Radikalismus" in der "jüdisch-hellenistischen Diaspora": zur Frage der Voraussetzungen des jüdischen Aufstandes unter Trajan, 115–117 n. Chr.', reprinted from Hellholm, *Apocalypticism*, 655–86 in Hengel, *Judaica et Hellenistica, 314–43*

———, 'Hadrians Politik gegenüber Juden und Christen', reprinted from *Journal of the American Near Eastern Society* xvi–xvii (1984–5) [Ancient Studies in Memory of Elias Bickerman], 153–81 in Hengel, *Judaica et Hellenistica*, 358–91

———, *Judaica et Hellenistica: Kleine Schriften i* (Tübingen, 1996)

———, *Essays in Early Christology* (Edinburgh, 1996)

W. Horbury, 'The Beginnings of the Jewish Revolt under Trajan', in H. Cancik, H. Lichtenberger and P. Schäfer (eds.), *Geschichte—Tradition—Reflexion: Festschrift für Martin Hengel zum 70. Geburtstag* (Tübingen, 1996), i, 283–304

———, *Jews and Christians in Contact and Controversy* (Edinburgh, 1998)

———, *Jewish Messianism and the Cult of Christ* (London, 1998)

———, 'Messianism and Early Christology', forthcoming in R. N. Longenecker (ed.), *Contours of Christology in the New Testament* (Grand Rapids, 2002)

———, 'Jewish and Christian Monotheism in the Herodian Age', forthcoming in L. T. Stuckenbruck (ed.), *Perspectives on Monotheism*

L. W. Hurtado, 'The Binitarian Shape of Early Christian Worship', in Newman, Davila and Lewis (eds.), *The Jewish Roots of Christological Monotheism*, 187–213

———, *One God, One Lord: Early Christian Devotion and Ancient Jewish Monotheism* (2nd edn., Edinburgh, 1998)

A. Jaubert, 'Symboles et figures christologiques dans le judaïsme', in J.-E. Menard (ed.), *Exegese biblique et judaïsme* (Strasbourg, 1973), 219–36

D. Juel, *Messianic Exegesis* (Philadelphia, 1988)

M. Karrer, *Der Gesalbte: die Grundlagen des Christustitels* (FRLANT cli, Göttingen, 1990)

R. Kasher, 'Eschatological Ideas in the Toseftot Targum to the Prophets', *Journal for the Aramaic Bible* ii (2000), 22–59

R. Kimelman, 'The Messiah of the Amidah: a Study in Comparative Messianism', *JBL* cxvi (1997), 313–24

J. Koenig, *L'Herméneutique analogique du Judaïsme antique d'après les témoins textuels d'Isaïe* (SVT xxxiii, Leiden, 1982).

A. van der Kooij, 'The Old Greek of Isaiah 19:16–25: Translation and Interpretation', in C. E. Cox (ed.), *Sixth Congress of the International Organization for Septuagint and Cognate Studies, Jerusalem 1986* (Society of Biblical Literature Septuagint and Cognate Studies Series xxiii, Atlanta, 1987), 127–66

———, 'Zur Theologie des Jesajabuches in der Septuaginta', in Reventlow (ed.), *Theologische Probleme der Septuaginta und der hellenistischen Hermeneutik*, 9–25

———, *The Oracle of Tyre: The Septuagint of Isaiah XXIII as Version and Vision* (SVT *lxx*i, Leiden, New York and Köln, 1998)

———, 'The Teacher Messiah and Worldwide Peace. Some Comments on Symmachus' Version of Isaiah 25:7–8', *JNSL* xxiv (1998), 75–82

A. Laato, *A Star is Rising: The Historical Development of the Old Testament Royal Ideology and the Rise of the Jewish Messianic Expectations* (Atlanta, 1997)

N. de Lange, *An Introduction to Judaism* (Cambridge, 2000)

R. Le Déaut, 'La Septante, un Targum?', in R. Kuntzmann and J. Schlosser (eds.), *Études sur le judaïsme hellénistique* (Paris, 1984), 147–95

L. J. Lietaert Peerbolte, *The Antecedents of Antichrist* (Leiden, 1996)

G. Lindbeck, 'Messiahship and Incarnation', in G. Cavadini (ed.), *Whom do you say that I am?* (forthcoming)

S. H. Levey, *The Messiah: an Aramaic Interpretation, the Messianic Exegesis of the Targum* (Cincinnati, 1974)

J. Lust, 'Messianism and Septuagint', in J. A. Emerton (ed.), *Congress Volume: Salamanca, 1983* (Leiden, 1985), 174–91

———, 'The Greek Version of Balaam's Third and Fourth Oracles; the *ἄnqrwpoV* in Num. 24:7 and 17; Messianism and Lexicography', in L. Greenspoon and O. Munnich (eds.), *VIII Congress of the International Organization for Septuagint and Cognate Studies, Paris 1992* (Society of Biblical Literature Septuagint and Cognate Studies Series xli, Atlanta, 1995), 233–57.

———, 'Septuagint and Messianism, with a Special Emphasis on the Pentateuch', in Reventlow (ed.), *Theologische Probleme der Septuaginta und der hellenistischen Hermeneutik*, 26–45

M. Mach, *Entwicklungsstadien des jüdischen Engelglaubens in vorrabbinischer Zeit* (TSAJ xxxiv, Tübingen, 1992)

M. Mach, 'Christus Mutans: Zur Bedeutung der "Verklärung Jesu" im Wechsel von jüdischer Messianität zur neutestamentlichen Christologie', in Gruenwald, Shaked and Stroumsa, *Messiah and Christos*, 177–97

J. Maier, 'Der Messias', in P. Sacchi (ed.), *Il giudaismo palestinese: dal 1 secolo a.C. al 1 secolo d.C.* (Associazione Italiana per lo Studio del Giudaismo, Testi e Studi viii; Bologna, 1993), 157–86

J. Marcus, 'Modern and Ancient Jewish Apocalypticism', *JR* lxxvi (1996), 1–27

———, 'The Once and Future Messiah in Early Christianity and Chabad', *NTS* xlvii (2001), 381–401.

C. R. A. Morray-Jones, 'The Temple Within: the Embodied Divine Image and its Worship in the Dead Sea Scrolls and other Early Jewish and Christian Sources', *Society of Biblical Literature Seminar Papers* xxxvii (1998), 400–31

C. C. Newman, J. R. Davila and G. S. Lewis (eds.), *The Jewish Roots of Christological Monotheism* (Supplements to the *Journal for the Study of Judaism* lxiii; Leiden, Boston and Köln, 1999)

J. Neusner, *Messiah in Context* (Philadelphia, 1984)

———, *Judaism and Christianity in the Age of Constantine: History, Messiah, Israel, and the Initial Confrontation* (Chicago and London, 1987)

———, 'Mishnah and Messiah', in Neusner, Green and Frerichs (eds.), *Judaisms and Their Messiahs*, 265–82

J. Neusner, W. S. Green and E. S. Frerichs (eds.), *Judaisms and Their Messiahs at the Turn of the Christian Era* (Cambridge, 1987)

G. S. Oegema, *Der Gesalbte und sein Volk* (Göttingen, 1994)
———, *The Anointed and his People* (Sheffield, 1999)
J. C. O'Neill, *Messiah* (Cambridge, 1980)
———, *Who Did Jesus Think He Was?* (Leiden, 1995)
———, *The Point of it All: Essays on Jesus Christ* (Leiden, 2000)
A. Oppenheimer, 'Leadership and Messianism in the Time of the Mishnah', in Reventlow (ed.), *Eschatology in the Bible and in Jewish and Christian Tradition*, 152–68
M. Perez Fernandez, *Tradiciones mesiánicas en el Targum Palestinense* (Valencia and Jerusalem, 1981)
K. E. Pomykala, *The Davidic Dynasty Tradition in Early Judaism* (Atlanta, 1995)
E. Puech, *La croyance des esséniens en la vie future: immortalité, résurrection, vie éternelle?* (2 vols., Paris, 1993)
H. Graf Reventlow, *Problems of Biblical Theology in the Twentieth Century* (ET London, 1986)
——— (ed.), *Eschatology in the Bible and in Jewish and Christian Tradition* (*JSOT* Supplement Series ccxliii, Sheffield, 1997)
——— (ed.), *Theologische Probleme der Septuaginta und der hellenistischen Hermeneutik* (Gütersloh, 1997)
A. Rofé, 'The Battle of David and Goliath: Folklore, Theology, Eschatology', in J. Neusner, B. A. Levine and E. S. Frerichs (eds.), *Judaic Perspectives on Ancient Israel* (Philadelphia, 1987), 117–51
———, 'Isaiah 59:19 and Trito-Isaiah's Vision of Redemption', in J. Vermeylen (ed.), *The Book of Isaiah, le Livre d'Isaïe: les oracles et leurs relectures, unité et complexité de l'ouvrage* (*BETL* lxxxi, Leuven, 1989)
C. Rowland, *The Open Heaven* (London, 1982)
———, *Christian Origins: an Account of the Setting and Character of the most Important Messianic Sect of Judaism* (London, 1985)
———, 'Christ in the New Testament', in *Day, King and Messiah*, 474–96
P. E. Satterthwaite, R. S. Hess and G. J. Wenham (eds.), *The Lord's Anointed: Interpretation of Old Testament Messianic Texts* (Carlisle, 1995)
J. Schaper, *Eschatology in the Greek Psalter* (Tübingen, 1995)
P. Schäfer, 'Die messianischen Hoffnungen des rabbinischen Judentums zwischen Naherwartung und religiösem Pragmatismus', reprinted from C. Thoma (ed.), *Zukunft in der Gegenwart* (Bern and Frankfurt am Main, 1976), 95–125 in P. Schäfer, *Studien zur Geschichte und Theologie des rabbinischen Judentums* (Leiden, 1978), 214–43
G. Scholem, *The Messianic Idea in Judaism and Other Essays on Jewish Spirituality* (London, 1971)

———, *Sabbatai Sevi, the Mystical Messiah* (first issued in Hebrew, Tel-Aviv, 1957; revised and augmented ET, London, 1973)

S. Schreiber, *Gesalbter und König: Titel und Konzeptionen der königlichen Gesalbtenerwartung in frühjüdischen und urchristlichen Schriften* (*BZNW* CV, Berlin and New York, 2000)

E. Schürer, G. Vermes, F. Millar and M. Black, *History of the Jewish People in the Age of Jesus Christ*, ii (Edinburgh, 1979), 488–554 (bibliography)

M. Smith, 'What is Implied by the Variety of Messianic Figures?', *JBL* lxxviii (1959), 66–72, reprinted in M. Smith, *Studies in the Cult of Yahweh* (2 vols, Leiden, New York and Köln, 1996), i, 161–7

———, 'Messiahs: Robbers, Jurists, Prophets', *PAAJR* xliv (1977), 185–95, reprinted in M. Smith, *Studies in the Cult of Yahweh* (1996), ii, 39–46

E. van Staalduine-Sulman, 'Reward and Punishment in the Messianic Age (Targ. 2 Sam. 23:1–8)', *Journal for the Aramaic Bible* i (1999), 273–96

L. T. Stuckenbruck, 'Worship and Monotheism in the Ascension of Isaiah', in Newman, Davila and Lewis (eds.), *The Jewish Roots of Christological Monotheism*, 70–89

C. Thoma, *A Christian Theology of Judaism* (*ET* by H. Croner, New York, 1980)

G. Vermes, *The Changing Faces of Jesus* (London, 2000)

N. T. Wright, *The Climax of the Covenant* (Edinburgh, 1991)

———, *The New Testament and the People of God* (London, 1992)

———, *Jesus and the Victory of God* (London, 1996)

A. Yarbro Collins, 'The Worship of Jesus and the Imperial Cult', in Newman, Davila and Lewis (eds.), *The Jewish Roots of Christological Monotheism*, 234–57

J. Zimmermann, *Messianische Texte aus Qumran. Königliche, priesterliche und prophetische Messiasvorstellungen in den Schriftfunden von Qumran* (WUNT ii.104, Tübingen, 1998)

M. P. Weitzman, *The Syriac Version of the Old Testament: An Introduction* (University of Cambridge Oriental Publications lvi, Cambridge, 1999)

R. J. Zwi Werblowsky, 'Mysticism and Messianism: the case of Hasidism', in E. J. Sharpe and J. R. Hinnells (eds.), *Man and his Salvation: Studies in memory of S. G. F. Brandon* (Manchester, 1973), 305–14

The Second Temple Period

1

Messianism in the Old Testament Apocrypha and Pseudepigrapha

Vocabulary and scope

The advantage of the phrase 'Apocrypha and Pseudepigrapha' is that it points to the Old Testament background which is a vital but sometimes neglected aspect of these books. Broadly speaking, the Apocrypha are those writings associated with the Old Testament but outside the Hebrew canon which early Christian tradition approved; these books (Wisdom, Ecclesiasticus and others) were sometimes termed 'outside' or 'ecclesiastical' books, for they were 'outside' the canon, yet read in 'ecclesiastical' usage.[1] Jerome, like a number of his contemporaries and predecessors, especially in the Christian east, endorsed their use yet stressed their non-canonicity, saying that they should be 'set apart among the apocrypha'.[2] With emphasis, rather, on their acceptance in the church, a western view advocated by Augustine and approved by two councils of Carthage (397, 419) and pope Innocent I held them to be in principle (whatever might be the case in practice) fully as authoritative for Christians as the books of the Hebrew canon. The Pseudepigrapha, however, are those writings outside the Hebrew canon, but dubiously ascribed to or linked with biblical authors, which early Christian tradition generally doubted or disapproved; these books (1 Enoch, the Assumption of Moses, 2 Baruch

[1] So Origen, in Eus. *H.E.* 6.25, 2, quoting a Jewish book-list ('outside'); Rufinus, *Symb.* 36 ('there are other books which were called by our forbears not canonical but ecclesiastical').

[2] Jerome, Prologues to the books of Kings and Solomon, in R. Weber (ed.), *Biblia Sacra iuxta Vulgatam Versionem* (2nd edn., 2 vols., Stuttgart, 1975), 365 (original of the quotation here), 957; comparably, a book-list in the Greek *Dialogue of Timothy and Aquila* lists Tobit, Wisdom and Ecclesiasticus under the heading 'Apocrypha' (H. B. Swete, *An Introduction to the Old Testament in Greek* (Cambridge, 1902), 206). On like-thinking predecessors and contemporaries of Jerome see W. Horbury, *Jews and Christians in Contact and Controversy* (Edinburgh, 1998), 208–10.

and many others) included several collectively called 'pseudepigrapha' in ancient book-lists, but they were often simply termed 'apocrypha' in a pejorative sense (so Athanasius, with allusion to pseudepigrapha of Enoch, Isaiah and Moses).[3]

The designation of the approved books not in the Hebrew canon as 'the Apocrypha' which is followed here became familiar in the Middle Ages under the influence of Jerome, and notably his 'helmeted preface' to Kings, *Prologus galeatus*, quoted above.[4] The currency of his terminology will have been enhanced by its entry into the mediaeval tradition of commentary both on scripture and on canon law. Thus, according to the early mediaeval Gloss Ordinary on scripture, 'the canonical books of the Old Testament are twenty-two in number; ... any others ..., as Jerome says, must be placed among the apocrypha'; similarly, in the early-thirteenth-century gloss on Gratian's *Decretum* by Johannes Teutonicus, the range of the word 'apocrypha' is illustrated from its customary application to Wisdom and the other approved Old Testament books not in the Hebrew canon: 'these are called apocryphal; yet they are read [sc. in the church], but perhaps not universally'.[5] Correspondingly, among a number of authors using this vocabulary, the fifteenth-century biblical commentator Alphonsus Tostatus of Avila wrote, with an appeal to Jerome, that Tobit, Judith, Wisdom and Ecclesiasticus 'are received in the church, and read, and copied in Bibles, and yet they are apocryphal'; and in 1540 a non-reformed Franciscan biblical expositor could still recommend to ordinands an answer to the question 'What are the books of the Old Testament?' which

3 Swete, *Introduction*, 281; Coptic text of Athanasius, *Ep. Fest. 39*, discussed and translated in E. Junod, 'La formation et la composition de l'Ancien Testament dans l'Église grecque des quatre premiers siécles', in J.-D. Kaestli and O. Wermelinger (eds.), *Le Canon de l'Ancien Testament. Sa formation et son histoire* (Geneva, 1984), 105–51, 124–5, 141–4.

4 Jerome's mediaeval influence was illustrated especially by J. Cosin, *A Scholastical History of the Canon of the Holy Scripture* (1657; reprinted, ed. J. Sansom, Oxford, 1849). R. Rex, 'St John Fisher's Treatise on the Authority of the Septuagint', *JTS* N.S. xliii (1992), 55–116 (63, n. 23) suggests that Augustine's view was more prevalent in earlier mediaeval writing, Jerome's from about the twelfth century. It may be added that, throughout, the Old Testament was regularly divided between books of the Hebrew canon and other books, as in Isidore of Seville (*Etymol.* 6.1, 9, PL 82.228–9) and the ninth-century Latin version of the Stichometry of Nicephorus by the papal librarian Anastasius (in C. de Boor, *Theophanis Chronographia*, ii (Leipzig, 1885, reprinted Hildesheim, 1963), 57–9).

5 Gloss Ordinary, Preface 'on canonical and non-canonical books' (PL 113.21, from the edition of Douai, 1617); gloss on Gratian, *Decretum*, 1:16, interpreting 'apocrypha' in the passage of the Gelasian Decree which puts the Apostolic Canons 'among the apocrypha' (*Decretum Gratiani ... una cum glossis* (Lyons, 1583), col. 60). Both are quoted by Cosin, ed. Sansom, *Scholastical History*, 218, 224–5 (paras. 135, 140).

ended: 'All the books of the Old Testament are thirty-seven in number, twenty-eight canonical, nine apocryphal.'[6]

By 1540, however, Jerome's terminology had already been taken up in the reform party, notably through the work of Andreas von Karlstadt on the canon (1520). The designation of the relevant Old Testament books as apocryphal which had hitherto been widely current was now soon to be discouraged by the Council of Trent. In 1546 the council reaffirmed the canonicity of most of these books, following Augustine, Innocent I, and subsequent conciliar lists including that of the Council of Florence.[7] In Luther's German Bible of 1534 and Coverdale's English Bible of 1535 these books had been set apart as 'Apocrypha', in accord with their separate registration in ancient and mediaeval lists, and under the name which could in the 1530s still be used irrespective of party; but in 1562 they were perhaps significantly listed in the Sixth of the Thirty-Nine Articles simply as 'other books', not as 'Apocrypha'.[8] The latter term was continued, however, in later English Bibles; in the Authorized Version of 1611 it appeared in the relatively cautious formula 'the books called Apocrypha'. The books of the Hebrew Bible and the Apocrypha therefore correspond, respectively, to the Old Testament books renamed after the Council of Trent by Sixtus Senensis in his *Bibliotheca Sancta* (1566) as 'protocanonical' and 'deuterocanonical'; the Pseudepigrapha correspond to those which he continued to call 'apocryphal'.[9] The frequently reprinted Clementine Vulgate of 1592 followed the practice of separating books separately registered in ancient lists, with regard to those Apocrypha which had not been recommended by Augustine and at Trent, that is 1–2 Esdras

[6] Alphonsus Tostatus, *Opera*, 8 (Cologne, 1613), 12b (preface to Chronicles); Joannes Ferus, *Examen Ordinandorum*, in Ferus, *Opuscula Varia* (Lyons, 1567), 900–26 (910). Compare Cosin, ed. Sansom, *Scholastical History*, 248–9, para. 162 (similar remarks elsewhere in Tostatus' prefaces to Matthew and Chronicles); 261–2, para. 176 (Ferus). The position of Luther's opponent cardinal Cajetan (Thomas de Vio), who also followed Jerome not long before the Council of Trent, seems therefore to have been rather less unusual than is suggested by G. Bedouelle, 'Le canon de l'Ancien Testament dans la perspective du Concile de Trente', in Kaestli and Wermelinger (eds.), *Le canon de l'Ancien Testament*, 253–82 (257–60).

[7] Bedouelle, 'Le canon', 262–9 describes the recurrence at Trent of arguments for expressing a distinction between the two classes of canonical books. Karlstadt's influence is noted without reference to the broad early sixteenth-century currency of the term 'apocrypha' by H.-P. Rüger, 'Le Siracide: un livre à la frontière du canon', in Kaestli and Wermelinger (eds.), *Le Canon de l'Ancien Testament*, 47–69 (58–9).

[8] The Sixth Article here followed the Württemberg Confession, which had been submitted at the Council of Trent in 1552 and avoided some controversial terms.

[9] On the new vocabulary sponsored by Sixtus (who notes the old terms which he is replacing) see Bedouelle, 'Le canon', 268–74, 280–2.

(3–4 Ezra) and the Prayer of Manasses; these were printed by themselves in an appendix.

Yet the beneficial association of the names Apocrypha and Pseudepigrapha with the Hebrew canon has a concomitant disadvantage. It may divert attention from other writings outside the Hebrew Bible which shed light on these books. In particular, the Apocrypha and Pseudepigrapha should be viewed together with the rich tradition of biblical interpretation attested in the Septuagint, Qumran exegesis, Philo, Josephus, the New Testament, the Targums and rabbinic literature. The books of the Apocrypha and Pseudepigrapha, then, are closely related to the Hebrew Bible, an important point which these two names attest; but these books are also to be set within the great stream of early biblical interpretation which was already moving in the Persian period.

In what follows there are some elements of a survey, but an attempt is also made to consider the Apocrypha and Pseudepigrapha as part of the evidence concerning messianism in the Second Temple period as a whole. The present writer has urged elsewhere that throughout this period, roughly from Haggai to Bar Kokhba, messianic hope was more pervasive than is usually allowed.[10] Here it is asked whether the relevant material in the Apocrypha and Pseudepigrapha, scattered chronologically over the years from Alexander the Great to Hadrian, is consistent with such a view. The Apocrypha, in which clear allusions to messianic hope are sparse, are reviewed with regard to the suggestion that between the fifth and the second centuries there was a 'messianological vacuum'. The Pseudepigrapha, in which such allusions are more plentiful, are considered in connection with the view that messianism was predominantly diverse.

The Apocrypha and the question of a messianological vacuum

The Apocrypha of the English Bible have for long been a centrepiece in a regular manifestation of the study of messianism, which may be called the 'no hope list'—the list of books wherein no messianic hope is to be found. The books cited often come from the Hebrew Bible as well as the Apocrypha;

[10] W. Horbury, *Jewish Messianism and the Cult of Christ* (London, 1998), 36–63.

a representative list would include at least Baruch, Tobit, Judith, 1–2 Maccabees, and the Wisdom of Solomon as writings where mention of a messiah might be expected, but is absent.[11] The most obviously messianic book in the Apocrypha, 2 Esdras (4 Ezra in the Vulgate), is also one of those which lacks strong support in ecclesiastical tradition, as is evident from the loss of its Greek text and its fate at the Council of Trent. The Apocrypha, therefore, the group among the books of the Apocrypha and Pseudepigrapha which enjoyed more authority among early Christians and probably also among Jews, seems almost to suggest the unimportance rather than the importance of messianism.

Not all would accept that the distinction drawn by many patristic authors between the groups of books which came to be known as the Apocrypha and the Pseudepigrapha was already current among Jews at the end of the Second Temple period. Some have regarded the two sets of books as virtually indistinguishable in the pre-Christian and primitive Christian periods.[12] Many of the Pseudepigrapha were probably read as widely as many of the Apocrypha, as is suggested for the Judaean Jewish community by the Qumran finds and for early Christian Egypt by quotations and papyri; yet, on the other side, there is a case, accepted by the present writer, for holding that the Christian distinction between the authority to be attached to the two sets of writings probably has pre-Christian antecedents.[13] Hence in what follows it is presupposed that at the end of the Second Temple period, among Jews as well as Christians, most of the Apocrypha are likely to have been more widely acceptable than the Pseudepigrapha, even though they were not necessarily always more influential.

[11] For such lists see W. V. Hague, 'The Eschatology of the Apocryphal Scriptures, I, The Messianic Hope', *JTS* xii (1911), 57–98 (64); A. von Gall, ΒΑΣΙΛΕΙΑ ΤΟΥ ΘΕΟΥ, *eine religionsgeschichtliche Studie zur vorkirchlichen Eschatologie* (Heidelberg, 1926), 376–7; W. Bousset and H. Gressmann, *Die Religion des Judentums im späthellenistischen Zeitalter* (3rd edn., Tübingen, 1926), 222; S. B. Frost, *Old Testament Apocalyptic: Its Origins and Growth* (London, 1952), 66–7; S. Mowinckel, *Han som kommer* (Copenhagen, 1951), 185 (ET *He That Cometh* [trans. G. W. Anderson, Oxford, 1956], 180); Morton Smith, 'What is Implied by the Variety of Messianic Figures?', reprinted from *JBL* lxxvii (1959), 66–72 in M. Smith (ed. S. J. D. Cohen), *Studies in the Cult of Yahweh* (2 vols., Leiden, 1996), i, 161–7 (163) (passing over the Apocrypha); J. Becker, *Messiaserwartung im Alten Testament* (Stuttgart, 1977), 74 (ET *Messianic Expectation in the Old Testament* [trans. D. E. Green; Edinburgh, 1980], 79).

[12] So Swete, *Introduction*, 224–5; J. Barton, *Oracles of God* (London, 1986), 35–81. R. Beckwith, *The Old Testament Canon of the New Testament Church and Its Background in Early Judaism* (London, 1985), 406–8 similarly holds that the first Christians esteemed a number of books from the Apocrypha and Pseudepigrapha alike; but he suggests that Jewish groups valued various sets of books, including the Greek Apocrypha, as adjuncts to the canonical books.

[13] Horbury, 'The Christian Use and the Jewish Origins of the Wisdom of Solomon', in J. Day, R. P. Gordon and H. G. M. Williamson (eds.), *Wisdom in Ancient Israel* (Cambridge, 1995), 182–96 (185–7); J. Day, R. P. Gordon and H. G. M. Williamson, *Jews and Christians in Contact and Controversy*, 25–35, 206–15.

The Apocrypha and Pseudepigrapha overlap in date, but the Apocrypha include a far greater proportion of writings which can be securely assigned to the Greek period.[14] Thus pre-Maccabaean works in the Apocrypha include, together with Ecclesiasticus, probably also 1 Esdras, Tobit, Judith, the Greek adjuncts to Esther, and at least the first part of Baruch (1:1–3:8); coaeval with these books but within the Hebrew canon is the older part of Daniel, pre-Maccabaean work given its present form in the Maccabaean period. To return to the Apocrypha, a second-century date is likely for the Epistle of Jeremy (transmitted in the Vulgate as the sixth chapter of Baruch), the Greek adjuncts to Daniel, and 2 Maccabees, while 1 Maccabees and probably also Wisdom can be assigned to the early years of the first century B.C. The short Prayer of Manasses, handed down in the LXX book of Odes, is probably pre-Christian. 2 Esdras, in which chapters 3–14 include material from the reign of Domitian, is probably the latest of all the books in the Apocrypha; but, as already noted, it teeters on the edge of the class of approved books because of its weak ecclesiastical support. The works from the Apocrypha represented in discoveries from the western shore of the Dead Sea are Tobit in Hebrew and Aramaic, the Epistle of Jeremy in Greek, and Ecclesiasticus in Hebrew. Also attested at Qumran in Hebrew is a Davidic pseudepigraph which through the LXX came near to gaining apocryphal status, Psalm 151. All four texts represented in Dead Sea discoveries are probably from the older material in the Apocrypha.

On these datings the relatively non-messianic Apocrypha are contemporary with other more strongly messianic texts in the LXX and the Pseudepigrapha. These include the LXX Pentateuch in the third century; the Testaments of the Twelve Patriarchs and the LXX Isaiah, Jeremiah, Ezekiel, Twelve Prophets and Psalms in the second; and the Messianic Apocalypse (4Q521), the Psalms of Solomon and relevant parts of the Third Sibylline book in the first century B.C. Messianism is then important, from the time of Herod the Great onwards, in the series of apocalypses beginning with the Parables of Enoch (1 En. 37–71, not attested at Qumran) and including, after the destruction of Jerusalem by

[14] For discussion of date and attestation see especially E. Schürer, *Geschichte des jüdischen Volkes im Zeitalter Jesu Christi* (3rd–4th edn., Leipzig, 1901–9), ET, revised by G. Vermes, F. Millar, M. Black, M. Goodman and P. Vermes, *The History of the Jewish People in the Age of Jesus Christ* (Edinburgh, 1973–87), iii.1–2; on Wisdom, also Horbury, 'The Christian Use and Jewish Origins of the Wisdom of Solomon', 183–5, and 'Wisdom of Solomon', in J. Barton and J. Muddiman (eds.), *The Oxford Bible Commentary* (Oxford, 2001).

Titus, the apocalypses of Ezra (2 Esd. 3–14) and Baruch (2 Baruch, the Syriac Apocalypse of Baruch); two further messianic works, the Fifth Sibylline book and the Christian Revelation of St. John the Divine, should be viewed together with this series.

The widespread silence of the Apocrypha on messianism, together with the ambiguity of Chronicles in this respect, has encouraged the view that a 'messianological vacuum' can be identified in Jewish literature between the fifth and the second centuries.[15] This view is already questioned by the third-century material noted in the preceding paragraph. The LXX Pentateuch, in particular, presents a messianic interpretation of the prophecies of Jacob and Balaam which is so strongly developed that it seems likely to be significant for the fourth century as well as the third, with regard to Chronicles and other possibly messianic material from the later Persian period.[16] Yet part of the strength of the 'vacuum' view lies in its association of silence on messianism, even if the extent of this silence is debatable, with a theocentric emphasis in post-exilic Israelite religion.

This emphasis on 'God who lives for ever, and his kingdom' (Tob. 13:1) has sometimes been understood as involving an opposition to earthly Israelite monarchy which inspired the reapplication of messianic promises to the nation as a whole or to God himself, for instance in Deutero-Isaiah on the 'sure mercies of David' (Isa. 55:3–4) or Zech. 9:9–10 on the lowly king.[17] Despite the close links of kingship with Israel and the kingship of God, the reapplication envisaged by exegetes in instances such as these is not beyond question.[18] A more clearly marked aspect of theocentrism is the readiness to portray the deity himself as a warrior king which is evident throughout the Second Temple period; the two Songs of Moses (Exod. 15; Deut. 32) evince this outlook in a manner which will have been particularly influential, as is illustrated below, given their incorporation into the Pentateuch.

[15] Frost, *Old Testament Apocalyptic*, 66–7; Becker, *Messiaserwartung*, 74–7 (ET *Messianic Expectation*, 79–82); J. J. Collins, *The Scepter and the Star* (New York, 1995), 31–8, 40 (with caution), see pp. 8–9, above.

[16] Horbury, *Jewish Messianism and the Cult of Christ*, 36–51, see pp. 13–20, above.

[17] So Becker, *Messiaserwartung*, 63–4, 67–8 (ET *Messianic Expectation*, 68–70 [Isa. 55], 72–3 [Zech. 9]); R. Albertz, *Religionsgeschichte Israels in Alttestamentlicher Zeit*, ii (Göttingen, 1992), 446 (ET *A History of Israelite Religion in the Old Testament Period*, ii (trans. J. Bowden, London, 1992), 426 [Isa. 55]).

[18] Thus C. R. North, who took Isaiah 55 to speak of transference of the Davidic covenant to the community, specially noted the difficulty of deciding whether this or revival of monarchy is in view (C. R. North, *The Second Isaiah* (Oxford, 1964), 255); and Zech. 9:9 is taken by Albertz, *Religionsgeschichte*, II, 639 (ET *Religion*, ii, 567) to envisage an earthly ruler.

Attention was drawn to the post-exilic importance of this line of thought by H. Gressmann and A. von Gall, with reference to such passages as the enthronement psalms, Zech. 14 and the Isaiah apocalypse (Isa. 24–7). Its vitality throughout the later Second Temple period is confirmed by the hymns to the divine victor in the War Scroll (e.g. 1QM 12.11–12), by the development of the portrait of the divine warrior from Isa. 59:16–18 in Wisd. 5:16–23, and by the bold anthropomorphism with which the Lord is envisaged as a man of war in some rabbinic tradition.[19] Gressmann justly called this hero-deity the double of the messiah.[20] For von Gall the messiah played only a subordinate part in the eschatology of Judaism at the end of the Second Temple period, partly because God himself was so vividly imagined as the coming king, and partly because only extreme nationalists went to the length of envisaging an earthly leader; that is why the messiah is often unmentioned.[21] Thus in von Gall's reconstruction the Apocrypha and Pseudepigrapha, roughly speaking non-messianic and sometimes messianic respectively, would correspond to a dual Old Testament emphasis on the kingdom of God and the kingdom of the messiah, respectively; and in the Greek and Roman periods, just as under the Persians, the theme of the kingdom of God would have been the more important.

As the reference to the book of Wisdom has already suggested, in the Apocrypha a silence on messianism can indeed be accompanied by vivid portrayal of the God of Israel as a hero. Outside the Wisdom of Solomon this combination is especially noticeable in the substantial group of mainly prose and mainly narrative books: 1 Esdras, the Greek adjuncts to Esther and Daniel, Tobit, Judith, 1–2 Maccabees, and (with a smaller proportion of prose) Baruch and the Epistle of Jeremy. Assessment of their silence or near-silence on messianism is indeed affected by their narrative character. We should not expect messianic expectations to be straightforwardly mentioned in prose historical narrative following the biblical model; for in biblical prose directly messianic material is mainly found in prophecies or psalms inserted into the narrative, as is the case with the Song of Hannah or the Pentateuchal

[19] See, for example, Mekhilta de-R. Ishmael, Beshallah, Shirata 4, on Exod. 15:3 (he appeared at the Red Sea like an armed warrior); Pesikta de-Rab Kahana 22.5 (he puts on garments of vengeance and red apparel, as at Isa. 59:17, 63:2).

[20] H. Gressmann, *Der Ursprung der israelitisch-jüdischen Eschatologie* (FRLANT vi, Göttingen, 1905), 294–301.

[21] Von Gall, ΒΑΣΙΛΕΙΑ, 214–57, 291, 374–7.

prophecies of Jacob and Balaam. It turns out, however, that even the poems and prayers in these narratives in the Apocrypha, although they do indeed express hopes for national redemption, regularly lay emphasis on the kingdom of God, not the kingdom of the messiah.

The narrative books give occasion for the expression of redemptive hopes above all because their principal figures have prophetic and martyr-like characteristics. These characteristics are obvious in Daniel and the Three Children, and Eleazar the scribe and the seven brethren and their mother (2 Macc. 6–7); but they are there too in Tobit, who flees from persecution and suffers the loss of all his goods, but returns when times improve (1:19–20, 2:8), and before his death prophesies the glorification of Jerusalem. Baruch speaks prophetically of the consolation of Jerusalem at the ingathering. Mordecai and Esther can to some extent be associated with the martyrs, for in the Greek Esther his perilous refusal to bow to Haman is explained as a Zealot-like refusal to honour man rather than God (13:12–14), and she risks her life and endures a mortal agony of fear (14–15). Martyr-themes also appear in Judith, where the destruction of the temple and the imposition of ruler-cult are feared (3:8, 6:2). To the martyr figures of the prose narratives there should of course be added, from a book which follows the verse tradition of the biblical wisdom literature, the righteous sufferer whose tribulation and vindication are vividly depicted in Wisdom 1–5.

The prophecies in these books are concerned above all with the ingathering and the divine vengeance, considered as a victory over idols and over earthly enemies. Thus in Esther, Judith, Tobit and 1–2 Maccabees stress is laid on the overthrow of Israel's enemies—Persian, Assyrian, or Greek. The prayers and prophecies in the narratives follow suit, often reflecting the influence of the depictions of a warrior-deity in the two Songs of Moses. In the Greek Esther, Mordecai and Esther pray to God as king and victor over idols, in words which echo the enthronement psalms and the greater song of Moses in Deuteronomy 32 (see 13:9, 15 [Lord, thou God, king, God of Abraham, cf. Ps. 47:6–9]; 14:3, 8–12 [king of the gods, cf. Ps. 95:3], 17 [nor have I drunk the wine of the drink offerings, cf. Deut. 32:38]). Similarly, the prayer and thanksgiving of Judith (9:7, 16:3) echo Ps. 76:4 (ET 3), on the Lord who breaks the battle as a warrior king in Zion (cf. also Ps. 46:10 [ET 9]); and in her thanksgiving (16:2–17) this thought leads to a passage echoing Ps. 96

and Exod. 15 which ends with a woe to the nations, for 'the Lord almighty will take vengeance of them in the day of judgment, to put fire and worms in their flesh' (cf. Deut. 32:41–3; Isa. 66:14–16, 24). Judith's thanksgiving is immediately followed by a dedication of the spoils of Holofernes in Jerusalem (Judith 16:18–20), and this scene crowns an important series of allusions to the biblical Zion theme; Judith prays for the defence of the sanctuary (9:8, 13) and stands for 'the exaltation of Jerusalem' (10:8, 13:4, 15:9).

Tobit prophesies the ingathering and the end of idolatry (13–14), again with repeated emphasis on the kingdom of God in his prayer (13:1, 6, 7, 10, 11 and 15), and now with an address to Jerusalem (13:9 onwards). Baruch 4–5 combines echoes of Deuteronomy 32, on Israel's idolatry and the coming punishment of the nations, with an apostrophe to Jerusalem on the ingathering, echoing Isaiah 60. Again, ingathering to the holy place (Exod. 15:17) and vengeance on the oppressor-nations are the main themes of the Jerusalem prayer in 2 Macc. 1:25–9 which reads like an antecedent of the Eighteen Benedictions. Lastly, divine vengeance on oppressors is envisaged in Wisdom 1–5 within the context of a hope of immortality (3:4). At Wisd. 3:1–9 it includes the 'visitation' of righteous souls (cf. Gen. 50:24–25; Isa. 10:3; Ps. 106:4–5 (LXX 'visit us'); Ecclus. 35:17–19; 1QS 3.14, 4.18–19; Ass. Mos. 1:18); and at Wisd. 5:15–23 they are protected at the world-wide judgmental victory of the divine warrior (cf. Isa. 59:16–19, as noted above).

Ingathering to Zion and vengeance on oppressors can of course involve a messianic leader, as in the explicitly messianic ingatherings depicted later on in Pss. Sol. 17:26, 42–4; 2 Esd. 13:39–40, where in each case the event is still emphatically presented as the work of God. Is such a leader ruled out by the sole stress on the kingship of God in these passages from the Apocrypha, with their echoes of the enthronement psalms, Trito-Isaiah on Zion, and the two Songs of Moses?

The answer Yes is not so clear as might perhaps be supposed. First, as already noted, the 'messianological vacuum' itself is by no means airtight. There is no question of centuries kept clear of any breath of messianic hope. The texts just considered from the Apocrypha are contemporary with others in which messianic hope is explicit, including the LXX Pentateuch and Prophets. Secondly, some of the theocentric biblical passages taken up in the Apocryphal texts were themselves interpreted in ways consonant with messianic hope.

Thus the hymns to the divine warrior which were put in the mouth of Moses in Exodus 15 and Deuteronomy 32 had become part of an exodus narrative in which not only the divine king but also Israel's earthly ruler, Moses, was of great importance. Similarly, the Trito-Isaianic prophecies of Zion included during the Persian period the oracle of a redeemer for Zion, immediately following the description of the divine warrior taken up in Wisdom 5 (Isa. 59:20); by the second century they were also read as including another oracle of a saviour (Isa. 62:11 LXX).[22] Comparably, the depiction of the divine avenger in Isa. 63:1–6 was immediately followed by a Zion-oriented prayer (63:7–64:11[12]) in which the thought of redemption by God alone once again came to be intensely expressed (Isa. 63:9 LXX 'not an ambassador, nor an angel, but the Lord himself saved us', anticipating a rabbinic formula well known from the Passover Haggadah); but in this prayer the exodus, the paradigmatic redemption of old, also explicitly involves Moses, the 'shepherd' (Isa. 63:11). Thirdly, the occasions on which it is said that God himself fights Israel's battle do not exclude the figures of Moses and an angel, Joshua, the king, or Judas Maccabaeus and an angel (Exod. 14:14; Jos. 10:14; Ps. 20:7–9; 2 Macc. 11:8–10). This is also true of the War Scroll, in a passage (1QM 11.1–7) which concludes 'Truly the battle is thine and the power from thee. It is not ours. Our strength and the power of our hands accomplish no mighty deeds except by thy power and the might of thy great valour. This thou hast taught us from ancient times, saying, A star shall come out of Jacob …'. Here God's own action is precisely the sending of the messiah, the star from Jacob (Num. 24:17).

In sum, therefore, the prayers and predictions in the Apocrypha which have just been considered show that redemption and judgment could be satisfactorily imagined through concentration on the portrayal of God himself as the hero; but they hardly show that a messianic leader was ruled out. It seems indeed not unlikely that divine redemption could have been taken to involve human leadership of the kind which was archetypally depicted in the Pentateuchal narratives of the exodus.

The silence of the Apocrypha on messianism has claimed attention so far, with the theory of a 'messianological vacuum' in view. In at least three of these

[22] On the 'redeemer' see A. Rofé, 'Isaiah 59:19 and Trito-Isaiah's Vision of Redemption', in J. Vermeylen (ed.), *The Book of Isaiah, le Livre d'Isaïe: les oracles et leurs relectures, unité et complexité de l'ouvrage* (BETL, lxxxi; Leuven, 1989), 407–10.

books, however, the silence is less than total. 2 Esdras will be considered below, with the Pseudepigrapha. The other two books in question are among the most influential of all the Apocrypha, Ecclesiasticus and 1 Maccabees. The relevant passages should be considered in the context of the exaltation of Jewish rulers in these and other books of the Apocrypha. Ben Sira himself of course glorifies Moses, Aaron and Phinehas, without forgetting David, Solomon, the righteous kings, and Zerubbabel (45:1–26, 47:1–22, 48:17–49:4, 11), and Simon the high priest in his own days (50:1–21); but similarly, 1 Esdras honours Ezra 'the high priest' (9:40) as well as the Davidic Josiah and Zerubbabel (1:32, 4:13, 5:5–6); in Judith the high priest Joakim has a central place (4:6–15, 15:8), and in 2 Maccabees Onias the high priest has the attributes of a saint, represented in both legend and vision (3:1–36, 15:12–15). The encomia of the Maccabaean priestly rulers in 1 Maccabees are noted below. In Wisdom, high-priestly praise emerges again in the lines on Aaron, the blameless servant of God who stayed the plague, vested in cosmic glory, for 'in the long robe is the whole world' (18:20–25); and the presentation of King Solomon and a series of Israelite leaders as inspired by celestial wisdom (Wisd. 7–10) is implicitly messianic, in so far as it suggests that Israel may still in the future be similarly blessed.

All these books reflect the glory of the high priest, as that was envisaged in the Second Temple period, but in Ecclesiasticus, 1 Esdras and Wisdom the éclat of the Davidic monarchy is also evident. It is therefore not surprising that David has a place in the Hymn of the Fathers in Ecclesiasticus; but it is striking, in view of the author's strong devotion to the high priest's honour, that David and his covenant are noticed three times.[23] First, Ben Sira proceeds as might be expected from Moses and Aaron to Phinehas; but then (45:25) he fits a reference to the covenant with David in after his reference to the covenant with Levi and Phinehas, and before he goes on to Joshua. The Hebrew text preserved in a Bodleian fragment of the Genizah MS B can be rendered on the following

[23] The political setting has been discussed, since the first publication of this essay, by J. K. Aitken, 'Biblical Interpretation as Political Manifesto: Ben Sira in his Seleucid Setting', *JJS* li (2000), 191–208 (noting that the praise of Simon the high priest could have been taken to imply support for Seleucid as opposed to Ptolemaic rule). On the context of the Davidic lines in the Hymn see J. D. Martin, 'Ben Sira's Hymn to the Fathers: a Messianic Perspective', in A. S. van der Woude (ed.), *Crises and Perspectives* (OTS xxiv; Leiden, 1986), 107–23. The line 'Praise him who makes a horn to flourish for the house of David' in the Hebrew psalm of fifteen verses found in two Cambridge leaves of the Genizah MS B after Ecclus. 51:12 (P. C. Beentjes, *The Book of Ben Sira in Hebrew* (VTSup, lviii; Leiden, 1997), 92–3) is not considered here; the case for the authenticity of these verses (M. Z. (H.) Segal, *Sepher Ben Sira ha-shalem* (2nd edn., Jerusalem, 1958), 352) is outweighed for the present writer by their absence from the grandson's version.

lines, in the light of the grandson's Greek: 'And there is also a covenant with David, son of Jesse, from the tribe of Judah; the inheritance of a Man [the king] is to his son alone, the inheritance of Aaron is also to his seed.'[24] This abruptly expressed passage seems to praise the Levitical covenant of priestly descent though Phinehas by means of a comparison or contrast with the covenant of Davidic succession, as both the Greek and the Syriac versions suggest. Its placing and wording are probably influenced by Jer. 33:17–22, a comparison of the covenants of Levi and David, and one of the passages which promises that there should never be cut off a 'man' to sit on David's throne.[25] In any case, its presence when the context did not demand it suggests the abiding importance of the Davidic tradition and hope even when the high priest is the supreme contemporary figure; there would be no compliment to the priesthood in such a comparison or contrast if the Davidic covenant did not enjoy great prestige and expectation of continuity.

Comparably, the passage devoted to David separately in the praise of the fathers (47:1–11) dwells like Psalm 151 on the God-given strength of his youthful feats, and ends with a reference to his royal throne over Jerusalem; taking up an image with a firm place in Davidic dynastic oracles (1 Sam. 2:10, etc.), Ben Sira concludes that God 'exalted his horn for ever'.[26] In the light of the earlier passage there is no need to minimize this 'for ever', as is sometimes done; Ben Sira's great reverence for Simon the high priest need not imply that he thought the royal line was now subsumed in the high priesthood, never to revive independently.[27] On the contrary, after his ensuing account of Solomon

[24] Pointing *'îš* with R. Smend, and emending to *lbnw lbdw* with I. Lévi, both cited by Segal, *Ben Sira*, 316; for the text see A. E. Cowley and Ad. Neubauer (eds.), *The Original Hebrew of a Portion of Ecclesiasticus (xxxix.15 to xlix.11)*, together with the Early Versions and an English Translation, followed by the Quotations from Ben Sira in Rabbinical Literature (Oxford, 1897), 28–9, with English translation, or Beentjes, *Ben Sira*, 81.

[25] On the royal 'man' in Ecclus. 45:25 and other texts see W. Horbury, 'The Messianic Associations of "the Son of Man"', *JTS* N.S. xxxvi (1985), 34–55 (51, = p. 179, below); for David and his seed as granted the covenant of kingship, see the interpretation of Gen. 49:10 in 4Q252 by means of Jer. 33:17: 'there shall not be cut off one who sits upon the throne for David ... until the coming of the messiah of righteousness, the shoot of David, for to him and to his seed was given the covenant of the kingdom of his people' (my translation; Hebrew text re-edited by G. J. Brooke in Brooke and others, *Qumran Cave 4.xvii* (DJD xxii, Oxford, 1996), 205–6; ET in G. Vermes, *The Complete Dead Sea Scrolls in English* [London, 1997], 463).

[26] On the horn in Davidic oracles and in this passage see D. C. Duling, 'The Promises to David and their Entrance into Christianity—Nailing down a Likely Hypothesis', *NTS* xx (1973), 55–77 (58, 62).

[27] For minimizing interpretation on these lines see J. J. Collins, 'Messianism in the Maccabean Period', in J. Neusner, W. S. Green and E. S. Frerichs (eds.), *Judaisms and Their Messiahs at the Turn of the Christian Era* (Cambridge, 1987), 97–109 (98); J. Neusner, W. S. Green and E. S. Frerichs, *Scepter*, 33–4; K. E. Pomykala, *The Davidic Dynasty Tradition in Early Judaism: its History and Significance*

he expresses at the end of 47:22, in a line of which only a few letters are preserved in Hebrew, the expectation that through God's mercy there will be a 'remnant' for Jacob, and a 'root' for David. M. H. Segal here identified an allusion to a prophecy quoted in Rom. 15:12 as a testimony to a messianic Jewish king of the gentiles, Isa. 11:10 (cf. 1) 'And there shall be on that day a root of Jesse, who shall stand for an ensign of the peoples'.[28] This identification is strengthened by the fact that Isa. 11:1–10 continue the oracles of 10:20–34; these begin with the promise of the return of the 'remnant of Jacob' (10:20–1) which is also echoed in Ecclus. 47:22, and themselves are in the sequel of the oracle of the prince of peace on David's throne (Isa. 9:6–7 [ET 5–6]). The comparable combination of 'the throne of David' (Isa. 9:7 [ET 6]) and 'the house of Jacob' (Isa. 10:20) occurs in the Davidic promise of Luke 1:33. The association of the Davidic oracles of Isaiah 9 and 11 with the 'house' and 'remnant' of Jacob in Isaiah 10 will have been further assisted by the Davidic interpretation of the blessing of Jacob in Gen. 49:9–10. This was current before as well as after Ben Sira's time, as the LXX Pentateuch shows; compare 4Q252 on Gen. 49:10, the Davidic covenant of kingship and 'the messiah of righteousness, the branch of David' (fuller quotation in n. 25, above) with Gen. 49:9 LXX 'from the shoot, my son, you came up', alluding to Isa. 11:1.[29]

In the background of the Davidic passages in Ecclesiasticus there may then be envisaged the combination of the rich narrative material on David (including its development, outside the Hebrew canon, in Psalm 151) with prophetic Davidic oracles, notably those ascribed to Nathan and Isaiah, and probably also with a Davidic interpretation of Jacob's prophecy of kings descended from Judah. Ben Sira's threefold use of this material, within a Levitical atmosphere which might have been expected to muffle Davidic allusion, has a sufficiently

for Messianism (Atlanta, 1995), 131–45; G. S. Oegema, *Der Gesalbte und sein Volk: Untersuchungen zum Konzeptualisierungsprozess der messianischen Erwartungen von den Makkabäern bis Bar Koziba* (Schriften des Institutum Judaicum Delitzschianum 2; Göttingen, 1994), 50–6; revised ET *The Anointed and his People: Messianic Expectations from the Maccabees to Bar Kochba* (JSP Supplement Series xxvii, Sheffield, 1998), 48–54, without special discussion of the texts considered here, likewise judges that kings are solely past authorities for Ben Sira, who lacks messianic hope and tends rather to 'messianize' Simon the high priest. A. Laato, *A Star is Rising: the Historical Development of the Old Testament Royal Ideology and the Rise of the Jewish Messianic Expectations* (University of South Florida International Studies in Formative Christianity and Judaism v; Atlanta, 1997), 242–7 dissents from this view, on arguments overlapping with those presented above.

28 Segal, *Ben Sira*, 329; on this and other allusions to the Davidic promises in Ecclus. 47:22 see also Duling, 'Promises', 61–2. The Isaianic allusion is ignored by Pomykala, *The Davidic Dynasty Tradition*, 145–7 (denying that 47:22 has any messianic aspect).

29 Horbury, *Jewish Messianism and the Cult of Christ*, 50.

strong and consistent emphasis on succession and hope to merit the adjective 'messianic'.

One may compare these passages in Ecclesiasticus with the reference to David's throne for ever made perhaps nearly a century later in 1 Macc. 2:57. Once again the immediate setting of the reference is priestly, in this case the last words of Mattathias the priest, the patriarch of the Hasmonaean line. At the same time, therefore, the surrounding atmosphere is that of the court praise given to the ruling dynasty. In 1 Maccabees the Maccabaean house is 'the seed of those by whose hand salvation (σωτηρία) was given to Israel' (1 Macc. 5:62). Aretalogical poems honour Judas Maccabaeus as a veritable lion of Judah, 'saving Israel' (1 Macc. 3:3–9, 9:21), and Simon Maccabaeus in 'his authority and glory' (14:4–15). The rulers thus have some of the glamour of what could be called in a broad sense a fulfilled messianism; but future hopes probably remain important among Jews in general, as J. A. Goldstein has emphasized, and it seems possible that even in this court praise such hopes find rather more reflection than might be suggested by Goldstein's profile of Maccabaean propaganda.[30] Thus Judas Maccabaeus, 'saving Israel', still prays to God as saviour of Israel (1 Macc. 4:30), and the hymns in praise of Judas and Simon still leave room for divine deliverance to come. Similarly, the prayer of 2 Macc. 2:17–18, which takes it that through the Maccabees God has restored 'the heritage to all, and the kingdom, and the priesthood, and the hallowing', as promised in Exod. 19:6 LXX, still looks for a future ingathering into the holy place, and confirms that the Hasmonaean polity was not regarded as the total fulfilment of the divine promises.

In the last words of Mattathias (1 Macc. 2:49–70) his list of examples for his sons includes not only 'Phinehas our father', as might be expected of a priest, but also David, who 'by his mercy inherited a throne of kingdom for ever' (εἰς αἰῶνας, 2:57). 'Mercy' here seems to be David's own good deeds, as probably in the appeal to his 'mercies' at the end of Solomon's prayer in 2 Chronicles (6:42). The 'throne of kingdom for ever' echoes the promise of 2 Sam. 7:13 'I will establish the throne of his kingdom for ever' (cf. 2 Sam. 7:16; 1 Chron. 17:12, 14; Isa. 9:7 (6)). A similar echo of this promise and of

[30] J. A. Goldstein, 'How the Authors of 1 and 2 Maccabees Treated the "Messianic" Promises', in Neusner, Green and Frerichs, *Judaisms and Their Messiahs*, 69–96, especially 69–81, followed in the main on 1 Macc. 2:57 by Pomykala, *The Davidic Dynasty Tradition*, 152–9; for dissent, see Laato, *Star*, 275–9.

Isa. 9:7(6) can be heard at Luke 1:33 (already noticed in connection with Ecclus. 47:22), 'the Lord God shall give him the throne of his father David, and he shall reign over the house of Jacob for ever'. 'For ever' need not be taken in its fullest sense in Mattathias's speech, as has often been emphasized; but the presence of the phrase suggests that the specifically messianic potential of the Davidic reference has not been nullified by the author or redactor. Similarly, although the stress laid here on David's good deeds fits the presentation in 1 Maccabees of Hasmonaean achievements as Davidic, it also assimilates the past David to the expected future son of David. Thus in the LXX Isaiah, perhaps also from the Maccabaean age, the Davidic messiah's description as a prince of peace is further underlined (Isa. 9:5–6 LXX); and in the Psalms of Solomon, towards the end of the Hasmonaean period, the virtue of the coming son of David is vividly portrayed (Pss. Sol. 17:32–37, noticed further below).[31] In the context of the last words of Mattathias, then, this sentence on David has no special messianic emphasis; but its presence shows that a tradition with a clear messianic aspect was current and could be used despite Maccabaean loyalties.

In Ecclesiasticus and 1 Maccabees alike, therefore, a writer who appears to be a staunch upholder of the current authorities in Judaea finds it natural to allude not just to David, but to the promises concerning his throne and line. These relatively slight references are therefore an impressive testimony to the strength of messianism as part of the biblical tradition. A similar inference can be drawn from the messianism of the LXX Pentateuch, a document used in settings where Jews were profoundly conscious of the importance of loyalty to rulers. In discussion of both Ecclesiasticus and 1 Maccabees by commentators concerned with messianism, stress has naturally been laid, nevertheless, on political circumstances which could have inhibited messianic interpretation of the references to David's throne and line; and Ecclesiasticus and 1 Maccabees have sometimes been assigned accordingly to the 'messianological vacuum'. In the treatment offered above, by contrast, an attempt has been made to show how much in both cases has been taken up from the messianic development of the biblical Davidic promises. Messianism involved an interaction between biblically-rooted tradition and the external political situation; but the roots

[31] The LXX form of Isa. 9:6–7 is associated with Maccabaean Davidic expectation by R. Hanhart, 'Die Septuaginta als Interpretation und Aktualisierung: Jesaja 9:1 (8:23)–7(6)', in A. Rofé and Y. Zakovitch (eds.), *Isaac Leo Seeligmann Volume*, iii (Jerusalem, 1983), 331–46 (345–6).

of the tradition in the biblical books and their accepted interpretation were widespread and deep, as the LXX and later on the Targums show. Messianism therefore had a life in the common mind independently of the special circumstances which might encourage or discourage it. It is notable, finally, that Ecclesiasticus and 1 Maccabees, the books in which a reflection of messianic tradition has been traced, are unlikely to represent marginal opinion; these are the two books of the Apocrypha which have perhaps most clearly been esteemed among Jews as well as Christians in antiquity.[32]

The Pseudepigrapha and the diversity of messianism

The Pseudepigrapha, on the other hand, as noted already, are essentially the books connected with the Old Testament which Christian tradition doubted or disapproved. Disapproval implied interest rather than the lack of it, however, as has already been noted for Christian Egypt; a similar coexistence of disapproval and interest can be conjectured in earlier Jewish opinion, at the time of the copying of the texts of Pseudepigrapha deposited at Qumran. Modern usage has associated with these books some comparable Jewish works under pseudonyms taken from gentile rather than biblical literature, of which only the Sibylline Oracles are mentioned here, and some other books associated with scripture which have been made known through discoveries of MSS, especially at Qumran.[33]

To note the earlier Pseudepigrapha roughly in chronological order, the pre-Maccabaean parts of the Third Sibylline book and of 1 Enoch both include some possibly third-century material. The Testament of Kohath (4Q542) and Visions of Amram (4Q543-9) known fragmentarily in Aramaic from Qumran texts may well also have been composed in the third century.[34]

[32] On Jewish use of Ecclesiasticus in Hebrew see Cowley and Neubauer, *Portion*, ix–xii, xix–xxx (collecting quotations); on 1 Maccabees in Hebrew, Origen in Eus. *H.E.* 6.25, 2, cited above (quoting a Jewish book-list in which 'the Maccabees' is an 'outside' book with a Semitic-language title); Jerome, in the Prologue to Kings cited above, 'I have found the first book of the Maccabees in Hebrew' (Weber, *Biblia Sacra*, i, 365).

[33] On date and attestation of the books mentioned below see especially Schürer, *Geschichte*, ET revised by G. Vermes, Millar, Black, Goodman and P. Vermes, iii. 1–2; Vermes, *Complete Dead Sea Scrolls*.

[34] E. Puech, *Qumrân Grotte 4.xxii, Textes araméens, Première partie, 4Q529-549* (DJD xxxi, Oxford, 2001), 258–64, 285–8.

Other considerations too suggest that much of the expanded Bible attested in Qumran texts and in books like Baruch may come from early in the Greek period. Thus Jubilees, possibly also the Genesis Apocryphon, and the extra-canonical psalms—among which at least Psalm 151 attained near-canonical status—can be assigned to the second century, and this may be the case too with the Temple Scroll and the fragmentary Qumran Second Ezekiel, but still earlier dates are not impossible for all these sources. The Testaments of the Twelve Patriarchs are known in the main through Christian transmission, but their basis is probably of the second century B.C., for much in the work suits Hasmonaean circumstances. Then 3 Maccabees is probably of the second century B.C., although it is often dated much later. The poem known as the Messianic Apocalypse (4Q521) is at latest from the early part of the first century B.C., and the Psalms of Solomon, which also touch the messianic theme, are from the mid-first century B.C. The *Biblical Antiquities* of Pseudo-Philo have a kinship with Josephus' *Antiquities* which is among the features suggesting a late Herodian date, but which might alternatively point to a common source in more ancient biblical paraphrase.

Among writings which enlarge on a particular biblical character or episode, Joseph and Asenath and Jannes and Jambres are probably both from Ptolemaic Egypt, and the Prayer of Joseph and the Testament of Job are usually dated about the time of Christian origins but may be older; 4 Maccabees and the Paralipomena of Jeremiah are perhaps from about the end of the first century A.D. Among works which can broadly be called prophecies, the Parables of Enoch (1 En. 37–71) are of disputed date, but can be ascribed to the Herodian period with fair probability (see chapter 56); the Assumption of Moses is Herodian but from some time after the death of Herod the Great, the fragmentarily attested Eldad and Medad is probably from before the time of Christian origins, and several writings reflect the impact of the destruction of Jerusalem by Titus—the Fourth and Fifth Sibylline books, the Syriac Apocalypse of Baruch (2 Baruch), and perhaps also the Apocalypse of Abraham, although it could be earlier. Outside the Pseudepigrapha category, 2 Esdras and the Revelation of St. John the Divine should be viewed together with this group of apocalypses.

Finally, some more Christianized works like the Life of Adam and Eve, 2 Enoch on Melchizedek, and the Greek Apocalypse of Baruch certainly include Jewish material coaeval with the writings mentioned so far. The Pseudepigraphic writings known through Christian transmission or quotation which are now also attested by Dead Sea discoveries include 1 Enoch, apart from chapters 37–71 (Aramaic), Jubilees (Hebrew), Second Ezekiel (Hebrew), and fragments of the Testaments of Levi (Aramaic) and Naphthali (Hebrew) which are related to the Testaments of the Twelve Patriarchs. As with the Apocrypha, the books attested in these discoveries are all likely to be old, probably pre-Maccabaean.

Hence, the series of Pseudepigrapha begins at latest in the third century B.C., and is substantial in the second century; but it has more material from the Herodian period and from after the Roman destruction of Jerusalem than is the case with the Apocrypha. Nevertheless, the books from the Greek period in the Apocrypha are contemporary with a very considerable literature in the Pseudepigrapha which contributes to a rewritten and expanded Bible; indeed, the Bible assumed in the books of the Apocrypha will probably often have been understood on the lines attested in the Pseudepigrapha. The works classified as Pseudepigrapha because they did not win approval appear to be those which seemed to supplant the books of the Hebrew canon, either by rewriting the text, or by offering new revelations. Hence the Pseudepigrapha include Jubilees and its congeners, the apocryphal Ezekiel, and the whole series of Jewish apocalypses from 1 Enoch onwards, with the half-exception of 2 Esdras; the relatively late date of many apocalypses has also probably worked against them.

The process of rejection seems already to be reflected in 2 Esdras. Here such books as the Pseudepigrapha are defended by what amounts to an attack on the prestige of the twenty-four 'public' books, through a theory of a double revelation to Moses like that later expressed in order to validate oral Torah; in the seventy additional books reserved for the wise is the true spring of understanding and knowledge (2 Esd. 14:45–8; cf. 14:5–6).[35] The serious use which could be made of Pseudepigrapha by Christian readers, despite all disapproval, is illustrated by Origen on the Prayer of Joseph (Origen, *Jo.* ii 186–92 [31], on John 1:6), and by a probably early fourth-century request for

[35] Biblical and extra-biblical passages linked with or reflecting this theory, including Deut. 29:28, 2 Baruch 59:4–11, and Lev. R. 26.7, are compared by M. E. Stone, *Fourth Ezra* (Minneapolis, 1990), 418–19, 441; for specification of the Mishnah and other traditions as revealed to Moses at Sinai, see for example Lev. R. 22.1, quoting Joshua b. Levi on Deut. 9:10.

a loan of 'Esdras' (probably 2 Esdras) in exchange for a loan of Jubilees, now documented in a papyrus letter.[36]

The Pseudepigrapha which attest messianism in particular include, as noted above, the Testaments of the Twelve Patriarchs in the second century B.C., the Psalms of Solomon and relevant parts of the Third Sibylline book in the first century B.C., and a series of apocalypses extending throughout and beyond the Herodian period, notably the Parables of Enoch, the apocalypses of Ezra (2 Esd. 3–14) and Baruch (2 Baruch, the Syriac Apocalypse of Baruch), and the Fifth Sibylline book.[37]

These books have been a focus of the widespread scholarly emphasis on the diversity of messianic hope. Morton Smith drew attention, with reference to Qumran texts and Pseudepigrapha, to the range of positions suggested by silence on messianism, dual messianism (as in the Testaments of the Twelve Patriarchs), and concentration on a single figure; he also noted what he described as an even greater range of eschatological expectation in general, for example in the various sections of 1 Enoch.[38] A. Hultgård, similarly, judges that diversity is so great that the messianic conception of each document should be considered on its own; but he is also able to list some common features.[39] Earlier, W. Bousset had separated and contrasted what he judged to be two very different messianic portraits: that of a human ruler, in the Psalms of Solomon, and that of a superhuman hero, in the apocalypses ascribed to Enoch, Ezra and Baruch.[40] This separation exemplifies a distinction between human and superhuman messianic figures which is often drawn, although it can be added that the characteristics of the two figures merge in many sources.[41] A similar

[36] E. Bammel, 'Die Zitate aus den Apokryphen bei Origenes', reprinted from R. J. Daly (ed.), *Origeniana Quinta* (BETL CV; Leuven, 1991), 131–6 in E. Bammel (ed. P. Pilhofer), *Judaica et Paulina: Kleine Schriften* II (Tübingen, 1997), 161–7; D. A. Hagedorn, 'Die "Kleine Genesis" in P. Oxy. lxiii 4365', *ZPE* cxvi (1997), 147–8 (criticized by R. Otranto, 'Alia Tempora, alii libri. Notizie ed elenchi di libri cristiani su papiro', *Aegyptus* lxxvii (1997), 101–24 (107–8), but defended (convincingly, in the present writer's view) by A. Hilhorst, 'Erwähnt P. Oxy. LXIII 4365 das Jubiläenbuch?', *ZPE* cxxx (2000), 192).

[37] For a survey of their messianism see especially Andrew Chester, 'Jewish Messianic Expectations and Mediatorial Figures and Pauline Christology', in M. Hengel and U. Heckel (eds.), *Paulus und das antike Judentum* (Tübingen, 1991), 17–89 (27–37) and 'The Parting of the Ways: Eschatology and Messianic Hope', in J. D. G. Dunn (ed.), *Jews and Christians: The Parting of the Ways A.D. 70 to 135* (Tübingen, 1992), 239–313 (239–52) (literature); Chester, *Messiah and Exaltation*, 333–52, 471–96.

[38] Smith, 'What is Implied?', 162–6.

[39] A. Hultgård, *L'eschatologie des Testaments des Douze Patriarches* (Acta Universitatis Upsaliensis, Historia Religionum, 6; Uppsala, 2 vols., 1977, 1982), i, 301, 323–35.

[40] Bousset and Gressmann, *Religion*, 228–30, 259–68.

[41] So Mowinckel, *Han som kommer*, 185–9 (ET *He That Cometh*, 280–6).

yet differently ordered separation is accordingly employed by J. J. Collins to describe the Davidic messiah, with special reference to the Psalms of Solomon, on the one hand, and the heavenly saviour king with traits from Daniel 7 on the other; in contrast with Bousset's presentation, the Herodian apocalypses, indebted both to the Davidic tradition and to the Danielic Son of man, are justly considered in both sections.[42]

Can any unity be detected in the messianic portraiture of the Pseudepigrapha? A living tradition of messianic biblical interpretation, such as was discerned above behind Ecclesiasticus and 1 Maccabees, can be expected to proliferate, but it will not lose all coherence. The biblical literary deposit of the circle of ideas surrounding the Davidic monarchy forms a background against which a considerable unity can in fact be perceived, as a number of students of messianism have pointed out.[43] Three points in support of this understanding can be briefly illustrated here.

First, a sharp division between Davidic and non-Davidic expectations is discouraged by the traces in the Pseudepigrapha of a habit of connecting the messiah not just with David, but with the whole series of Jewish kings and rulers, including the judges. A particularly important antecedent is Gen. 49:10, cited already; Jacob, speaking of the latter days, foresees a succession of princes and rulers from Judah, who shall never fail until he comes, to whom the kingdom pertains.[44] Towards the end of the first century A.D. the interpretation of the cloud-vision in 2 Baruch correspondingly makes the messiah sit on the throne of his kingdom (chapters 70–3) at the climax of the series of good rulers—David, Solomon, Hezekiah and Josiah (61, 63, 66). The connection of the messiah not just with David, but with the line of good kings, emerges in a different way in the perhaps roughly contemporary last words

[42] Collins, *Scepter*, 48–73, 173–94.

[43] So, in different ways, H. Riesenfeld and M.A. Chevallier (see Horbury, *Jewish Messianism and the Cult of Christ*, 65), and Laato, *Star*, see also pp. 11–13, above.

[44] For this interpretation see Peshitta ('whose it (fem.) is'), Targum Onkelos ('the messiah, whose is the kingdom'), Targum Neofiti and Fragment Targum (both 'the king messiah, whose is the kingdom'), part of the LXX tradition (ἕως ἐὰν ἔλθῃ ᾧ ἀπόκειται), perhaps followed by Symmachus, and 4Q252, cited in n. 25, above ('the messiah of righteousness, the branch of David, for to him and to his seed was given the covenant of the kingdom of his people'); the emphasis of the main LXX ('until the things laid up for him come') is on the coming of the kingdom to Judah, and the following clause 'and he is the expectation of the nations' then refers back, without full clarity, to the never-failing ruler of the first half-verse in the LXX (M. Harl, *La Bible d'Alexandrie*, 1, *La Genèse* [Paris, 1986], *ad loc.*); the material is surveyed by S. R. Driver, *The Book of Genesis* (London, 1904), 410–15 and M. Perez Fernandez, *Tradiciones mesiánicas en el Targum Palestinense* (Valencia and Jerusalem, 1981), 127–35.

ascribed to Johanan b. Zaccai, 'Set a throne for Hezekiah, king of Judah, who is coming' (*Ber.* 28b); the messiah can be envisaged not only as David, as in Ezek. 37:24–6, but also as one of David's great reforming heirs, the king in whose days Assyria was smitten.[45]

The more straightforward presentation of a royal succession leading up to the messiah, as in Gen. 49:10, reappears in Pseudo-Philo's *Biblical Antiquities*, a work which has a number of points of contact with 2 Baruch.[46] Here Kenaz is presented as one of the kings and rulers mentioned in the prophecy of Jacob; at 21:5 Joshua quotes Gen. 49:10, 'a prince (*princeps*) shall not depart from Judah, nor a leader (*dux*) from between his thighs', and at 25:2 'the people said, Let us set up for ourselves a leader (*dux*) ... and the lot fell upon Kenaz, and they set him up as a prince (*princeps*) in Israel'. This quotation and its development strengthen J. Klausner's messianic interpretation of the paraphrase of the Song of Hannah later in the *Biblical Antiquities* (51.5). Here (cf. 1 Sam. 2:9):

> the wicked [God] shall shut up in the shadows, for he keeps for the righteous his light.
> And when the wicked shall be dead, then shall they perish; and when the righteous shall sleep, then shall they be set free.
> Yet thus every judgment shall abide, until he who has possession (*qui tenet*) shall be revealed.

Klausner suggested that these last words allude to the 'Shiloh' oracle at the conclusion of Gen. 49:10, not quoted at 21:5, understood in the sense 'until he come, to whom it pertains' which was documented above.[47] The messianic king would then be 'revealed' (cf. 2 Esd. 7:28, 2 Baruch 29:3) as judge, as in the Parables of Enoch (61:8–10) and elsewhere. This interpretation in turn fits Jonathan's words to David a little later in the *Biblical Antiquities* (62.9), 'Yours is the kingdom in this age, and from you shall be the beginning of the kingdom that is coming in due time.'[48] The messianic king, on this line of thought, is

[45] A *Sitz im Leben* for this saying in Judaea soon after the destruction of Jerusalem is outlined by M. Hadas-Lebel, 'Hezekiah as King Messiah: Traces of an Early Jewish-Christian Polemic in the Tannaitic Tradition', in J. Targarona Borrás and A. Sáenz-Badillos (eds.), *Jewish Studies at the Turn of the Twentieth Century* (2 vols., Leiden, 1999), i, 275–81.

[46] Stone, *Fourth Ezra*, 39–40; K. Berger, with G. Fassbeck and H. Reinhard, *Synopse des Vierten Buches Esra und der Syrischen Baruch-Apocalypse* (Tübingen, 1992), 4–5.

[47] J. Klausner, *The Messianic Idea in Israel from Its Beginning to the Completion of the Mishnah* (three parts, 1902, 1909, 1921; ET of revised edn., London, 1956), 367.

[48] Messianic interpretation of 51.4 and 62.9 is taken to be possible and probable, respectively, by H. Jacobson, *A Commentary on Pseudo-Philo's* Liber Antiquitatum Biblicarum (AGJU xxxi; Leiden, 1996), i, 250; but he does not regard messianism as a strong concern of the author.

indeed Davidic; but he forms the climax of the whole line of good kings and rulers, including the judges, and can be envisaged not only as David but also as Hezekiah come again.

Secondly, messianic expectation was linked with the royal line, the Jewish constitution, and the relevant biblical figures not as they *were* according to modern historical reconstruction, but as they were *envisaged* from time to time in the Graeco-Roman world. This means that material which now looks multifarious, for it includes messianic treatment of priests, judges and patriarchs, in the Greek and Roman periods would have naturally associated itself with the single succession of legitimate Jewish rulers. Thus the constitutional co-ordination of high-priest and king, as envisaged in the Pentateuchal portrait of Eleazar and Joshua (Num. 27:15–23), is reflected in the dual messianism of the Testaments of the Twelve Patriarchs and the Qumran texts, and, later on, the 'Simeon prince of Israel' and 'Eleazar the priest' coins of the Bar Kokhba revolt. This political theory could evidently cover what was noticed, in an oracular survey of history in a pseudepigraph known from a Qumran copy, as the change of government between the days of the kingdom of Israel and the (post-exilic) time when 'the sons of Aaron shall rule over them' (4Q390 [Apocryphon of Jeremiah C^e] fragment 1, lines 2–5).[49] Furthermore, the succession of rulers is traced back beyond David to the judges (Kenaz in Pseudo-Philo, as just noted) and Moses. So Moses is king, probably in the conception of the book of Deuteronomy (33:5), and certainly in the Pentateuch as understood by Ezekiel Tragicus and Philo and in the midrash;[50] Justus of Tiberias began his history of the Jewish kings with Moses.[51]

Similarly, some biblical redeemer-figures which are often reckoned as angelic rather than messianic in modern study were interpreted messianically in antiquity. This pre-eminently applies to the one like a son of man in Daniel, identified as an angelic figure by many modern interpreters,[52] but regularly

[49] For text and translation see D. Dimant, *Qumran Cave 4, xxi. Parabiblical Texts, Part 4: Pseudo-prophetic Texts* (DJD xxx, Oxford, 2001), 235–44.

[50] Ezekiel Tragicus 36–41, 68–89; Philo, *Mos.* 1.148–62 (ὠνομάσθη γὰρ ὅλου τοῦ ἔθνους θεὸς καὶ βασιλεύς, 158); Targ. Ps.-Jonathan on Deut. 33:5; see further J. R. Porter, Moses and Monarchy (Oxford: Blackwell, 1963); L. Ginzberg, *The Legends of the Jews* VI (Philadelphia, 1956), nn. 170, 918.

[51] Photius, *Bibliotheca*, 33, cited and discussed by Schürer, *Geschichte* (ET *History of the Jewish People*, revised by Vermes and Millar, i, 35–7).

[52] N. Schmidt, J. A. Emerton, C. C. Rowland and J. Day are among many noted by J. J. Collins, *Daniel* (Hermeneia; Minneapolis, 1993), 310, nn. 288–94 as, like himself, representing this interpretative view.

understood as the messianic king at the end of the Second Temple period (in 1 Enoch, 2 Esdras, and probably also Sib. Or. 5:414–33). This royal messianic exegesis seems to be related to the whole scene in Daniel 7 in the saying in the name of Akiba explaining the 'thrones' of verse 9 as two, 'one for him [the Almighty], and one for David' (baraitha in *Hag.* 14a, *Sanh.* 38b).[53] Secondly, Exod. 23:20–1, on the angel or messenger sent before Israel, was understood in rabbinic exegesis as referring to an angel, sometimes identified as Metatron (see *Exod. R.* 32.1–9, on 23.20; 3 En. 12.5); but in probably earlier exegesis by Christians or preserved in Christian sources it was also applied to John the Baptist, perhaps in his capacity as Elijah (Mark 1:2), and to Joshua (Justin, *Dialogue*, 75.1–2), the latter being Moses' successor and a model of the royal deliverer. The indwelling of the spirit is prominent in the Old and New Testament descriptions of both Joshua and John (Num. 27:16, 18; Luke 1:15, 17), and it is likely that they were envisaged as embodied spirits, just as Moses is called 'holy and sacrosanct spirit' in the Assumption of Moses (11:16, quoted below); similarly, in the Prayer of Joseph noted above, Jacob embodies the archangel Israel, and Origen judges accordingly that the Baptist was an angelic spirit. The applications of Exod. 23:20–1 to Joshua and John would then not be so far removed as might appear at first sight from the rabbinic applications of the passage to an angel.

Within the body of Pseudepigrapha, the same kind of ambiguity surrounds a heavenly emissary foretold in the Assumption of Moses (10:1–2):

> And then [God's] kingdom shall appear in all his creation. And then the devil shall have an end, and sadness shall be taken away with him. Then shall be filled the hands of the messenger (*nuntius*) who is appointed in the highest, who will at once avenge them of their enemies.

Here, then, the kingdom of God will appear, and the messenger will be consecrated (his hands will be 'filled', in a biblical phrase used of consecration to the priesthood, as at Exod. 28:41; Lev. 8:33); he is appointed in the highest to avenge the Israelites. This messenger has been interpreted as an angel, notably Michael, but there is a case for understanding him as a messianic

[53] The passages are discussed, together with the treatment of Dan. 7 in Justin, *Dialogue* 32, in Horbury, 'Messianic Associations', 36, 40–8 (= pp. 156–7, 161–3, 170–3, below, see also p. 11, above).

[54] Collins, *Scepter*, 176 (an angel); T. W. Manson, 'Miscellanea Apocalyptica', *JTS* xlvi (1945), 41–5 (43–4) (Elijah); J. Tromp, *The Assumption of Moses: A Critical Edition with Commentary* (Studia in Veteris Testamenti Pseudepigrapha x; Leiden, 1993), 228–31 (a human messenger, Taxo the Levite).

figure.[54] He waits in heaven, as the messiah does (2 Esd. 12:32, cf. 7:28, cited above; 1 En. 46:1–4, 48:6). His hands 'shall be filled'; but although this term for consecration suits priests, and therefore angels, it was more broadly applied in later Hebrew, as appears in 1 Chron. 29:5 and 2 Chron. 29:31. He will avenge the Israelites, like a good king, and as the messianic king was expected to do (1 En. 48:7; cf. Isa. 11:4, 61:2; Ps. 2:9; Ps. Sol. 17:23–7; 2 Esd. 12:32–3, 13:37–8; 2 Baruch 72:2–6). Similarly, 'Melchizedek will execute the vengeance of the judgements of G[od', according to a Qumran text (11Q Melch 2.13). Moses himself in the Assumption is not only 'holy and sacrosanct spirit', *sanctus et sacer spiritus* but also 'great messenger', *magnus nuntius* (11:16–17). In 10:1–2, like a prophet-king, this 'great messenger' foretells another messenger who will vindicate Israel as soon as God's kingdom is revealed—not certainly, yet not improbably, the messianic king envisaged as a great pre-existent spirit.

These considerations underline the ambiguity of another figure sometimes described simply as angelic, Melchizedek in 11Q Melchizedek, quoted above.[55] His initiation of the heavenly judgment and liberation, as it is represented in this fragmentary text, seems close to what is envisaged in the brief description of the messenger appointed in the highest in the Assumption of Moses. Melchizedek is mighty among the rebellious 'gods' (angels) of Psalm 82, but at the same time he is the ancient king of Salem and priestly forbear of David (Ps. 110:3). His messianic associations are borne out by the rabbinic tradition that Melchizedek is one of the four smiths of Zech. 2:3 (Elijah, the Messiah, Melchizedek, and the priest anointed for war, in the version in *Cant. R.* 2.13, 4). In 11Q Melchizedek this departed royal figure is treated as a spirit who answers to what is envisaged in Isa. 61:1–2, when God's day is announced by one who is anointed and upon whom is the spirit of the Lord. He can be compared, however, not only with the angelic powers over whom he has the mastery, but also with great returning kings such as Hezekiah in the last words attributed to Johanan b. Zaccai. Although the fragmentary state of the text makes judgment tentative, it seems on balance likely that he is indeed a messianic figure, a king of old who has gained angelic status and will return as deliverer and judge, as

[55] Vermes, *Complete Dead Sea Scrolls*, 500–2; Collins, *Scepter*, 176; E. Puech, *La croyance des esséniens en la vie future: immortalité, résurrection, vie éternelle?* (Paris, 1993), ii, 516–62; the text has been re-edited by F. García Martínez, E. J. C. Tigchelaar, and A. S. van der Woude, *Qumran Cave 11. ii* (DJD xxiii, Oxford, 1998), 221–41 (not available when this essay was first written), and it receives further discussion in chapter 4, 165–6, below; Horbury, 'Josephus and 11Q13 on Melchizedek'.

could also be expected of Hezekiah or David.[56] In some important instances, therefore, the redeemer-figures classified as angelic could be interpreted as human deliverers linked with the line of Israelite kings and rulers.

Thirdly, the messianic portraiture in the Pseudepigrapha is not wholly suited to the distinctions which have often been drawn between human and superhuman figures. As noted above, a contrast between human and superhuman categories, sometimes identified especially with Davidic and Danielic tradition, respectively, can be accompanied by the observation that the characteristics of each category often merge. Thus, strikingly, one of the few common features noted by A. Hultgård in messianic presentations of the Greek and Roman period is investiture by bestowal of the spirit (passages including Pss. Sol. 17:42[37]; 1 En. 49:1–3; 11Q Melch 18), under the influence of Isa. 11:1 and Isa. 61:1–2;[57] this trait contributes to a conception of the messianic figure as above all the embodiment of an excellent spirit from above. There is in fact a case for seeing the 'superhuman' portrait as more widespread and more continuously attested than is commonly allowed, especially in the light of Septuagintal and rabbinic material.[58] Here attention is restricted to the Pseudepigrapha.

A 'superhuman' portrait has been widely recognized in the Herodian apocalypses. The apocalypses of Ezra and Baruch are roughly contemporary works which have much in common; they perhaps draw on shared traditions of prayer, hymnody and instruction.[59] Comparable portraiture occurs in the Parables of Enoch preserved in Ethiopic (1 En. 37–71), and the Fifth Sibylline book, composed in Greek hexameters (see especially lines 414–33). In 2 Esdras, the Parables of Enoch, and probably also the Fifth Sibylline, traits of the Danielic Son of man combine with those drawn from messianically interpreted passages in the Pentateuch, prophets and psalms.[60] The interpretation of these three texts as referring Danielic and other material to a single messianic figure seems preferable to K. Koch's suggestion that in 2 Esdras and elsewhere a 'two-stage messianology' is envisaged, turning first

[56] So, for example, Hultgård, *L'eschatologie*, i, 306–9; P. A. Rainbow, 'Melchizedek as a Messiah at Qumran', *Bulletin for Biblical Research* (1997), 179–94.

[57] Hultgård, *L'eschatologie*, i, 281, 323–4.

[58] Horbury, *Jewish Messianism and the Cult of Christ*, 86–108.

[59] Stone, *Fourth Ezra*, 39–40; Berger, *Synopse*, 8–9; for II Baruch as earlier see M. Goodman, 'The Date of 2 Baruch', in Ashton (ed.), *Revealed Wisdom*, 116–37.

[60] Pp. 156–61, below; J. VanderKam, 'Righteous One, Messiah, Chosen One, and Son of Man in I Enoch 37–71', in Charlesworth (ed.), *The Messiah* (Minneapolis, 1992), 169–91.

on the messiah and then on the Son of man.[61] Superhuman features in all these sources include pre-existence (2 Esd. 13:26, 1 En. 48:3, 6; probably implied at 2 Baruch 29:3, Sib. Or. 5:414); advent from heaven (2 Esd. 13:3 (from the sea, with the clouds), Sib. Or. 5:414; 1 En. 48:4–7; probably implied at 2 Bar. 29:3); and miraculous annihilation of foes and establishment of kingdom (1 En. 49:2; 2 Esd. 13:9–13; 2 Baruch 29:3–5, 39:7–40:3; Sib. Or. 5:414–28).

Such features can also be perceived, however, in other messianic portraits in the Pseudepigrapha. Thus, advent from heaven is probably implied in Sib. Or. 3:652–6 on the 'king from the sun' sent by God.[62] It seems also, however, that in the seventeenth Psalm of Solomon, widely taken to represent a 'human' messianic figure, traces of a notion of pre-existence emerge in the lines on God's foreknowledge of the messianic king (Ps. Sol. 17:23[21], 47[42]):

> Behold, Lord, and raise up for them their king, the son of David at the time which thou knowest, O God …
> This is the beauty of the king of Israel, of which God has knowledge, to raise him up over Israel, to instruct him.

God knows the time when the king is to be raised up, as in Ps. Sol. 18:6 (5), where the time is the 'day of choice', the day chosen by God; God also knows the king's 'beauty' or 'majesty' (εὐπρέπεια). This noun is one of those used to describe the king's beauty in Greek versions of Ps. 45 (44):4 'in your glory and beauty' (LXX variant recorded by Origen in the Hexapla) and 110(109):3 'in the beauty of the holy one' (Theodotion).[63] These textual witnesses both represent translations which could have come into being later than the Psalms of Solomon, although this is not necessarily so; attempts to revise LXX passages will have been made in the first century B.C., and some forms or antecedents of the version ascribed to Theodotion will certainly have circulated in the Herodian period.[64] In any case, however, the occurrence of εὐπρέπεια in Greek versions of these royal psalms is a pointer to contexts

[61] Within the long-standing and widespread tradition of messianic biblical interpretation vividly sketched by Koch, 'the son of man' would readily have been associated, in the present writer's view, with messianic interpretation of biblical words which can be rendered 'man'; see K. Koch, 'Messias und Menschensohn. Die zweistufige Messianologie der jüngeren Apokalyptik', in E. Dassmann, G. Stemberger et al. (eds.), *Der Messias (Jahrbuch für Biblische Theologie viii)* (Neukirchen-Vluyn: Neukirchener Verlag, 1993), 73–102 (especially 79–80, 85–97); Horbury, 'Messianic Associations', 48–53.

[62] Chester, 'Jewish Messianic Expectations', 35 and n. 50.

[63] F. Field (ed.), *Origenis Hexaplorum quae supersunt* ii (Oxford, 1875), 162, 266.

[64] See E. Schürer, revised by M. D. Goodman, in Schürer, *Geschichte* (ET *History of the Jewish People*, iii.1, 501–4).

likely to be important for interpretation of the psalmodic portrait of a coming king in Psalms of Solomon 17. Both the passages concerned in the Psalms of David are exalted in style. Psalm 45 is a hymn to the king, and its lines on the king's beauty played an important part in second-and third-century Christian concepts of Christ.[65] In Ps. 110(109):3, according to Theodotion 'in the beauty of the holy one' immediately follows 'with you is the rule in the day of your power', and precedes 'from the womb before the daystar I have begotten you'; it is therefore associated both with the king's epiphany on the day of his power, and with his origin 'before the daystar'.

It seems likely, then, that in Ps. Sol. 17:47(42) the king's beauty is considered to be known to God beforehand. It can have been envisaged as in heaven ready to be revealed, on the lines of the expectations about the revelation of the heavenly sanctuary—the 'ready dwelling' in the LXX at Exod. 15:17, 1 Kings 8:39 and elsewhere—which are widely attested from the third century B.C. onwards (for example, at Wisd. 9:8; 2 Esd. 13:36; 2 Baruch 4:1–6).[66] This way of thinking is applied to a messianic figure in passages including the Lucan canticle Nunc Dimittis: 'thy salvation, that which thou hast prepared' (Luke 2:30–1); 2 Esd. 12:42 'the Anointed whom thou hast kept' (cf. 1 Pet. 1:4 'kept in heaven'); and 2 Baruch 29:3, 30:1 ('the messiah shall begin to be revealed ... shall return in glory').

Schürer and his revisers regarded the Psalms of Solomon as contrasting with the Parables of Enoch and 2 Esdras precisely in the presentation of a thoroughly human and non-pre-existent messianic figure.[67] Nevertheless, expectation of the kind just discerned in Ps. Sol. 17 is within the range of ideas independently suggested by Ps. Sol. 18:6(5), cited above, on the day chosen by God for the 'raising up' or 'bringing back' (ἄναξις) of the Anointed.[68] It is consistent with this interpretation that the spiritual endowment of the king is emphasized; in a passage noted above with regard to investiture by bestowal

[65] Irenaeus, *Haer.* iii.19 (20), 2, cited with other passages at p. 314, n. 16, below.

[66] W. Horbury, 'Land, Sanctuary and Worship', in J. Barclay and J. Sweet (eds.), *Early Christian Thought in Its Jewish Context* (Cambridge, 1996), 207–24 (210–11).

[67] Schürer, *Geschichte*, ii, 616 (ET *History of the Jewish People*, revised by Vermes, Millar and Black, II, 519).

[68] H. E. Ryle and M. R. James (eds.), *Psalms of the Pharisees, commonly called the Psalms of Solomon* (Cambridge, 1891), 149–50, on 18:6, found pre-existence to be suggested by ἄναξις, but they rejected this interpretation because they could find no hint of it in Ps. Sol. 17; such hints seem to be given, however, by 17:23 and 42, as interpreted above. In 18:6 T. W. Manson's emendation ἀνάδειξις, 'showing' (Manson, 'Miscellanea Apocalyptica', 41–2; cf. Luke 1:80) would equally suggest a hidden period, on earth or in heaven; but the text, offering a word not familiar from the gospels, seems preferable.

of the spirit, he is pure from sin, and God has made him 'mighty in holy spirit' or 'mighty by a holy spirit' (Ps. Sol. 17:41–2 [36–7]; cf. Isa. 11:2, 61:1). In Pss. Sol. 17–18, then, it seems likely that the glory and beauty of the Davidic king are known to God, waiting in heaven for the appointed time when the son of David is to be raised up.[69]

Against this background it seems likely that Ps.-Philo, discussed above with reference to 2 Esdras and the Parables of Enoch, should also be taken to envisage the revelation of a messiah who will be the heavenly judge. There is likewise a fair probability that the 'messenger' of Ass. Mos. 10:2, consecrated in heaven to avenge Israel, is a preexistent messianic figure. Further, Bousset rightly associated with the 'transcendent messiah' of the Herodian apocalypses the passages in the Testaments of the Twelve Patriarchs on the 'new priest' whose 'star shall rise in heaven, as a king' and on the 'star from Jacob', 'a man like a sun of righteousness', the 'shoot of God' to arise from Judah (T. Levi 18:2–3, T. Jud. 24:1, 4–6).[70] Particularly notable here are links with the star of Balaam (Num. 24:17) and, once more, with the oracle on Judah in the Blessing of Jacob (Gen. 49:10), here linked again with Isa. 11:1 (see n. 29, above). The astral associations suggest that the priestly and royal messianic figures are being envisaged as embodied spirits, on the lines noted above with reference to Ass. Mos. 11:17.

In all the Pseudepigrapha noted at the beginning of this section as attesting the messianic theme, therefore, with the addition of Ps.-Philo and perhaps also the Assumption of Moses, the messianic portraiture includes superhuman characteristics. These are not incompatible with the conception of the messiah as a mortal king (2 Esd. 7:29), perhaps especially because emphasis is laid on his spiritual aspect. These features recall the superhuman glory of the king in such biblical passages as Isa. 9:5 (ET 6); Mic. 5:1 (ET 2); Ps. 45:7, 110:3.

In conclusion, therefore, to summarize this short study, it may be said first of all that the name Apocrypha, inherited from mediaeval usage in its favourable application to approved books outside the Hebrew canon, and the accompanying but less favourable term Pseudepigrapha, recall an early

[69] The interpretation in the text above was formulated before I had seen Laato, *Star*, 283–4, where it is rightly noted that the whole passage is not far from descriptions of 'transcendental divine agents', but the question of pre-existence is left open.

[70] Bousset and Gressmann, *Religion*, 261 (suggesting links with the myth of a king of Paradise); Hultgård, *L'eschatologie*, especially i, 203–13 (on T. Jud. 24), 300–26 (on T. Levi 18 in its Jewish setting).

Christian distinction which is not unlikely to have Jewish origins; some adjuncts to the canonical books were approved, others were disapproved. In the case of the Pseudepigrapha, the coexistence of disapproval with strong interest among early Christians probably replicates an earlier conjunction of contrasting Jewish attitudes to these books, as 2 Esd. 14:44–7 suggest.

The Apocrypha, although in many cases they exemplify silence on messianism and a theocentric concentration on divine deliverance, do not encourage the view that there was a 'messianological vacuum' in the late Persian and early Greek period. This notion is in any case implicitly questioned by the messianism of the LXX Pentateuch; but it is also questioned by the traces of messianic biblical interpretation in Ecclesiasticus and 1 Maccabees. These two influential Apocrypha show that authors who loyally upheld the non-Davidic Judaean authorities of their day were still affected by biblically-inspired messianic tradition, which had a life of its own in communal biblical interpretation independently of circumstances which might specially encourage its development.

The Pseudepigrapha at first glance seem to bear out the widespread view that the messianism of their period was predominantly diverse; but much of their material has an underlying unity arising from its roots in biblical tradition on the king. Modern distinctions between Davidic and non-Davidic expectations, or between angelic and human messianic figures, are overcome in ancient presentations. Thus in the Pseudepigrapha messianic figures can be connected with the whole line of Israelite rulers, from the patriarchs and Moses onwards, and it can be envisaged that past monarchs may attain angelic status as spirits in the hand of God.

Similarly, the widespread distinction between human and super-human messianic portraits seems misplaced; superhuman traits can be detected throughout those Pseudepigrapha which are known for their messianic traditions, and also in material in which messianic expectation is less widely recognized (notably Pseudo-Philo's *Biblical Antiquities*, and perhaps also the Assumption of Moses). It is suggested here that these traits reflect above all the superhuman traits in biblical oracles on the present or future king. The oracular royal portraiture would have been developed in a continuous tradition of messianic biblical interpretation, which was always influenced by political circumstances, but retained its own independent life.

2

The Gifts of God in Ezekiel the Tragedian

ἐγὼ θεὸς σῶν, ὧν λέγεις, γεννητόρων
Ἀβραάμ τε καὶ Ἰσαὰκ καὶ Ἰακώβου τρίτου.
μνησθεὶς δ᾽ ἐκείνων καὶ ἔτ᾽ ἐμῶν δωρημάτων
πάρειμι σῶσαι λαὸν Ἑβραίων ἐμόν.

I am the God of your Forefathers, as you call them,
Abraham, and Isaac, and Jacob, the third.
Remembering those, and remembering also my gifts,
I am here to save my own people of the Hebrews.

(Ezekiel Tragicus 104–7)

What are God's 'gifts' (δωρήματα) in line 106? The interest of the question emerges from the discussion by Jacobson, 109–12.[1] He judges that the interpretation which would most readily be expected, 'gifts from God', is meaningless here. The contextual mention of the patriarchs might indeed encourage the often-suggested paraphrase of 'gifts' as 'promises'; but this, in Jacobson's view, would over-stretch the Greek.

Instead, Jacobson proposes either the interpretation 'gifts made to me' (the meritorious deeds of the patriarchs then being understood as offerings), or the conjectural emendation ἐμῶν δὴ ῥημάτων (the 'words' being God's 'promises'). Although Jacobson does not decide between these alternatives, he concludes that the exegete must adopt one of them.

Perhaps, however, the interpretation 'gifts from me' can be accepted. Some evidence in its favour is reviewed below. The passages concerned support, so it will be argued, this understanding of line 106; but it will be noted, also, that they

[1] Literature cited by author's name is listed at the close of the chapter.

bring more clearly into view a post-biblical Jewish theological idiom, of some significance for the ideas of covenant and grace (see p. 21 and n. 74, above).

I

God's gifts have already been mentioned by the tragedian in line 35, in which Jochebed tells the young Moses of (his) γένος πατρῷον καὶ θεοῦ δωρήματα. Here the word is taken by Jacobson, 110, to bear its ordinary sense, which he thinks is not to be found in line 106. Nevertheless, line 106 closely resembles line 35 in two respects: in both lines, God's gifts are mentioned immediately after a reference to the Hebrew ancestors, and both lines are biblically inspired, but not part of a continuous biblical paraphrase. (Jochebed's speech is non-biblical, and line 106, although its immediate context corresponds to Exod. 3:6a and 8, is itself linked with Exod. 3 only relatively loosely.) This second point may suggest that the phrase was a current expression in the writer's time, with a special meaning which the reader or hearer was expected to grasp. Its connection in both lines with the patriarchs commends the view that in both the gifts of God to Israel in particular are intended, the privileges granted to the patriarchs for 'the people of the Hebrews' (lines 106–7).

II

Before this interpretation of the gifts as national privileges is considered in a broader literary context, the date of Ezekiel Tragicus should be reviewed in the light of discussion, since this essay first appeared, by R. Van De Water. It is usually held that one relatively clear indication of date comes from Eusebius of Caesarea, whose *Praeparatio Evangelica* (written *c.* 313–20) is our main source for the poem; for he notes that his long quotations of Ezekiel Tragicus on Moses are drawn from the first-century B.C. compiler Alexander Polyhistor, and Ezekiel Tragicus must then have written in or before the first century B.C. Van De Water questions this interpretation of Eusebius, and urges that the quotations were taken directly from the poet Ezekiel. Eusebius' quotations would then show that Ezekiel Tragicus was current in the age of Constantine, but would provide no further indication of date.

The argument for quotation of Ezekiel Tragicus through Polyhistor should first be set out more fully. Eusebius is customarily understood to say that he is producing his quotations of the poet Ezekiel (in *P.E.* ix 28–9) from the compilation *Concerning the Jews by Alexander* Polyhistor, who wrote probably between 80 and 40 B.C.; they form part of a long section (*P.E.* ix 17–37) in which Eusebius, naming this work at the beginning, draws on Polyhistor and often names him again in the text as the source (see chapters 17, 19, 20, 21, 23, 25 and 37). On Moses, Eusebius makes an initial reference to Polyhistor in chapter 26, and then successively cites Eupolemus, Artapanus and Ezekiel (chapters 26–9). Clement of Alexandria on Moses (*Strom.* i 23) had likewise quoted successively but more briefly from the same passages of Eupolemus, Artapanus and Ezekiel, in the same order, and had named Alexander Polyhistor not here but a little earlier (*Strom.* i 21); probably he also drew on Alexander for these excerpts (Freudenthal, 12; E. Schürer, revised by M. Goodman, 510–11). The poet Ezekiel himself then could not have written much later than 40 B.C.

Van De Water, arguing against a pre-Christian date such as this, first stresses the silence of Philo and Josephus on Ezekiel Tragicus; secondly, he urges that Eusebius should not be interpreted as citing Alexander here, and was probably quoting the poet Ezekiel directly; thirdly, he notes that the biblical echoes in this poetry occasionally suggest the possibility that the author knew a LXX text revised towards the Hebrew, such as can best be envisaged in the first century A.D.; finally, he proposes a date for Ezekiel Tragicus in the Christian era, suggesting that the exaltation of Moses in the dream described in lines 68–89 is a response to Christian exaltation of Christ.

Van De Water's discussion of Eusebius in particular will be considered in a moment. To comment on his three other points briefly, it may first be said that the silence of Philo and Josephus is not decisive; they are similarly silent on other writing connected with the Pentateuch and current in Greek by the first century B.C., for example the work of Artapanus, who is unambiguously quoted from Alexander Polyhistor by Eusebius (*P.E.* ix 23). Then, to move to Van De Water's third point, revision of the LXX towards the Hebrew is certainly attested by the mid first century A.D., but the process will probably have begun earlier, as the ordinance against changing the LXX imagined in the Letter of Aristeas 310–11 suggests. Lastly, exaltation of Moses is not incompatible with a date before the rise of Christianity, as is suggested by the heightened portrayal of Moses as king in the LXX Pentateuch and in Philo (Horbury, 49; chapter 7, below).

The argument that Eusebius has been wrongly understood as quoting Ezekiel Tragicus through Alexander Polyhistor would be important if valid; but two of the relevant introductory formulae in Eusebius are hard to interpret otherwise than as referring, with two main verbs, first to Alexander and secondly to Ezekiel: *P.E.* ix 29, 12 Τούτοις ἐπάγει, μετά τινα τὰ μεταξὺ αὐτῷ εἰρημένα, λέγων· Ταῦτα δέ φησιν οὕτω καὶ Ἐζεκιῆλος ἐν τῇ Ἐξαγωγῇ λέγων, περὶ μὲν τῶν σημείων τὸν Θεὸν παρεισάγων λέγοντα οὕτως· 'To these things he makes an addition, after some remarks which he has made in the meanwhile, saying: These things Ezekiel too says in this way, speaking in the *Exagoge*, when he brings forward the god speaking about the signs as follows: …'; *P.E.* ix 29, 14 Πάλιν μεθ' ἕτερα ἐπιλέγει· Φησὶ δὲ καὶ Ἐζεκιῆλος ἐν τῷ δράματι τῷ ἐπιγραφομένῳ Ἐξαγωγή, παρεισάγων ἄγγελον 'Again after other things he adds: Ezekiel also says, in the drama entitled *Exagoge*, introducing a messenger …'. Translators who interpret the formulae in this way include Gifford, iii, 471, 473; Holladay, 377, 387, with notes 136, 187; and Nielsen, 100, 102.

The Greek of these two passages, when understood in this way, seems plainly expressed. That is hardly the case, however, on the interpretation proposed by Van De Water, when one subject (Ezekiel) is taken to govern both main verbs on each occasion. Thus in the first passage, it is awkward to render (with Van De Water, 62), 'But saying these things in this manner, after some intervening remarks, Ezekiel, in the *Exagoge*, then adds to these concerning the signs, introducing God speaking as follows'; for Ezekiel, the supposed subject of the first main verb ἐπάγει, is not mentioned until he has also been the supposed subject of the participle λέγων as well as the second main verb φησιν. On this understanding, the Greek is inelegant and verges on obscurity; but it becomes clear if Alexander is the unnamed subject of the first main verb and the participle λέγων, as is assumed in the punctuation reproduced above. In the second passage, it seems impossible to construe μετά exactly as implied in the rendering by Van De Water, 63, 'Again, after he adds other things, Ezekiel, in the drama entitled *Exagoge*, also introduces a messenger'; but the rendering 'after other things, Ezekiel adds and says', which avoids this difficulty but keeps the proposal of a single subject for the two verbs, would still make the Greek appear abrupt and clumsy—for again the subject is not reached until after the reader has encountered both main verbs.

On the other hand, with punctuation as reproduced in the Greek quotations above, implying a separate subject for each verb, the Greek wording in both cases is terse and lucid. The implied subject of the first verb in each case will then be Alexander, last mentioned at the end of chapter 25 and the beginning of chapter 26; some way back, as stressed by Van De Water, but not so far back as to make the implication unclear. These conclusions from the introductory formulae in Eusebius are in turn supported by the indication of Alexander as the source given by the series of quotations from the same passages of the same three authors in Clement of Alexandria, as noted above. Ezekiel Tragicus must then be dated no later than the first century B.C.

III

The view that God's gifts, in lines 35 and 106, are distinctive national privileges receives confirmation, first, from Rom. 11:29 ἀμεταμέλητα γὰρ τὰ χαρίσματα καὶ ἡ κλῆσις τοῦ θεοῦ. Paul can use χάρισμα interchangeably with a number of other words for 'gift', including δώρημα (Rom. 5:15–16). In Rom. 11:29 the patriarchs, once again, have just been mentioned (verse 28), and the gifts are the privileges of the Israelites, whose are (Rom. 9:4) 'the adoption and the glory and the covenants and the lawgiving and the promises, whose are the forefathers (πατέρες), and from whom is the Christ, according to the flesh'.

This list combines gifts especially associated with the exodus (the adoption, the glory and the lawgiving) with the covenants, which recall the patriarchs as well as Moses, and the promises, which are particularly closely linked with the patriarchs; the patriarchs and the messiah are then mentioned separately at the close. The combination of Mosaic and patriarchal themes is of course already present in the book of Exodus, including the passage (3:6–8) which is echoed in Ezekiel Tragicus 104–7. Hence, it would not be unreasonable to hold that the gifts of God in Ezekiel's tragedy, in both Jochebed's speech and the divine speech, are indeed the national covenants granted to the patriarchs. A more precise identification of the promises in mind will be attempted at the close.

A similar conception of God's gifts emerges in 1 Clem. 31–2, a passage which echoes Rom. 9:3. In 1 Clement, as at the end of the list in Rom. 9, the gifts are identified as the personages whose calling signifies covenanted mercy. Abraham, Isaac and Jacob are upheld as examples; and it is then noted that the greatness of the gifts (τῶν … δωρεῶν) given by God appears, when one considers that from Jacob come the priests, the Levites, and the Lord according to the flesh; kings, rulers and governors in the tribe of Judah; and the seed as the stars of heaven in the other tribes (1 Clem. 32.1–2).

Romans and 1 Clement perhaps elucidate a third early Christian allusion to God's gift, John 4:10. The woman's question how it comes about that a Jew should ask drink of a Samaritan woman here receives an answer beginning 'If you knew the gift of God (τὴν δωρεὰν τοῦ θεοῦ), and who it is that says to you …' Once again, the general context is patriarchal, for the well is Jacob's (4:5–6, 12); and the woman's question makes the immediate context national, an emphasis which continues to be prominent (4:20–2). Hence, the gift is likely to signify the privilege granted to the Jews in particular, the patriarchal covenant promising redemption through a messiah (4:26) who, as the immediately following words in verse 10 imply, is now speaking. 'If you knew the gift of God' could then almost be paraphrased 'if you knew that salvation is of the Jews' (cf. 4:22). In this interpretation, the saying is rather more closely integrated with its context than it is when the gift is understood either (as by Barrett) as water, signifying the law, or (as by P. P Sänger in Schneider-Fascher) as a general, comprehensive term. The word then appears as another instance of 'gift' in the distinctive sense of a Jewish national privilege, with probable reference to the messiah rather than the law.

In all three of these early Christian instances, then, the gifts are linked, as in Ezekiel Tragicus, with the patriarchs and the chosen people. In Romans and John a contrast is implied between the specially privileged Jewish nation and the gentiles or the Samaritans, respectively. These features, viewed together with the two occurrences in Ezekiel's tragedy, confirm that a distinctively Jewish usage of words for 'gift' is reflected or continued in the Christian sources. H. Odeberg indeed suggested, without reference to Greek sources, that a Jewish technical term is reproduced at John 4:10. In support he quoted a number of rabbinic texts, the most relevant of which will be considered shortly. Meanwhile Ezekiel Tragicus, taken together with Romans and 1 Clement, shows that his view was essentially correct, and confirms that the usage was pre-rabbinic. It is not only early Christian literature, however, which bears out this judgment. Other inner-Jewish evidence, Greek as well as Hebrew, will now be noted, and the relation of the usage to post-exilic and later developments in the understanding of the Old Testament covenants will be briefly discussed.

IV

The pattern of much Jewish reference to God's giving, in connection with the patriarchs and the exodus, is found in the Pentateuch. Both in Genesis and in the narratives of the exodus, the reports of the promises to the fathers are rich in allusions to giving (see the passages collected by Clines, 31–43). The verb rather than a noun for 'gift' is used, however, and specific benefits are generally listed, without reference to undefined gifts. In one probably late example, Jacob's prayer at Gen. 32:9–12 (the context is J), undefined benefits occur, not as gifts, but as 'mercies' (verse 10). The plural of *ḥesed*, used here in connection with the patriarchs, is connected in like fashion with the Davidic covenant at Isa. 55:3, and in the prayer-passages Ps. 89:50, 2 Chron. 6:42. As would be expected, and as later evidence confirms, prayer was clearly an important setting for the preservation and development of references to God's giving in connection with the covenants.

The preference exhibited in the Pentateuch for the verb, for specificity, and for words other than nouns meaning 'gift' if generalization occurs, doubtless owes something to Hebrew idiom as well as to the weight of revered example. At any rate, the same preference marks many prayers and exhortations of the Second Temple period which recall God's giving in connection with the patriarchs and the exodus. Examples are Neh. 9, Ps. 105, 7–end, 1 Macc. 4:49–61, Abram's prayer in Genesis Apocryphon, col. xxi (expansion of Gen. 13:4), Luke 1:68–75, 2 Esd. 3:4–36, Moses's speech in Josephus, *Ant.* iii 84–8 (expansion of Exod. 19:25), and the benedictions Hoda'ah (M. Yoma vii 2, R.H. iv 5; corresponding to the seventeenth (eighteenth) benediction of the

Amidah) and Geʾullah (B. Ber. 9b; modern text in Singer—Brodie, 44–5; short form in B. Ber. 14b).

Despite the absence of words for 'gift' from these passages on the patriarchs and the exodus, they regularly emphasize God's giving and his benefits. In the Greek and Roman periods it became natural for Jews to view the deity, like an earthly ruler, as 'Euergetes' (as noted, with reference to Greek-speaking Jews, by Knox, 28; knowledge of the benefactor-cult among Jews who used Aramaic is suggested by Mastin, 84). Philo straightforwardly applies the noun to God (so *Op. mundi* 169 'benefactor of mankind'); Josephus avoids this application, possibly with something of the distaste evident at Luke 22:25, but uses the verb, as at *Ant.* iv 213 (God's benefits to Israel). It was then not a long step to introduce nouns for 'gift' into biblically-inspired passages on God's giving. The association of this vocabulary with solid and palpable benefits is illustrated by the application of δωρεά, in literature and papyri of the Hellenistic age, to a grant of land in particular (texts of the third century B.C. are cited by Liddell, Scott, Jones and McKenzie, 464b, s.v.). Somewhat comparably but much later, Jewish inscriptions at Sardis (perhaps fourth-century A.D.) and elsewhere speak of the moneys available to donors as δωρεαί of God (Rajak, 232, 236–9).

Accordingly, Josephus, who was familiar with the Hellenic notion of an exchange of gifts between the gods and men (van Unnik, 365), makes the deity himself, in Amram's dream, draw attention to his own side of the exchange, as 'having granted (δωρησάμενος) their ancestors to become so great a multitude from a few' (*Ant.* ii 212). Here the divine promise appears to be understood as a gift, and the passage was therefore well cited in favour of the interpretation of the 'gifts' in Ezekiel Tragicus 106 as the promises by G. B. Girardi (*Di un Dramma Greco-Giudaico nell' Età Alessandrina* (Venice, 1902), 52; not available to me, but cited by Jacobson, 205, n. 49). Nouns for 'gift' are used by Josephus of the special graces afforded to Israel at the exodus (δωρεαί, *Ant.* iii 14, iv § 212), above all the law (δωρεά, *Ant.* iii 78, 223), the choicest gift (δώρημα, iv 318).

Among these passages, *Ant.* iv 212 is noteworthy, for it recounts the prescriptions for morning and evening prayer ascribed to Moses. These have no explicit biblical warrant, but are clearly linked by Josephus with the Shemaʿ, which he probably knew with the introduction mentioning the exodus found at Deut. 6:4 in the LXX and the Nash Papyrus. 'They are to acknowledge to

God the gifts bestowed upon them, when they were delivered from the land of Egypt' (*Ant.* iv 212). Here the gifts are the benefits to Israel recalled in a prayer perhaps to be identified as an early form of the benediction Ge'ullah, which now follows the Shema'. Thus, a summary of a prescribed prayer, which might be expected to follow the Pentateuchal pattern just noted, instead describes the national privileges as gifts.

Josephus, therefore, uses 'gift' in a sense very close to that which, it is argued, appears in Ezekiel Tragicus. The connection is with the exodus rather than the patriarchs, but patriarchs and exodus are often and closely linked in the Pentateuch. In Josephus, as in the tragedian, the gifts are national privileges. This usage, as is plain in Josephus, fits a characteristically Hellenistic view of the deity as bestower of gifts, and it correspondingly recalls the Roman vocabulary of patronage (Spilsbury, 181–91); but at the same time it remains close to the Pentateuchal emphasis on God as giver.

Philo presents similar phenomena. Two aspects of his usage deserve mention. First, like Josephus, he can employ 'gifts' of God's benefits to the nation (δωρεά, *Praem. et poen.* 79, referring to Lev. 26:7, Deut. 28:1, 7). This can occur, again as in Josephus, in a prayer-passage; the fruits of the promised land, in a paraphrase of the canticle recited by the bringer of first-fruits (Deut. 26:5–11), are 'graces and gifts' (χάριτες καὶ δωρεαί, *Spec. Leg.* ii 219).

Secondly, Philo holds that 'covenants are written for the benefit of those who are worthy of the gift (δωρεά), so that a covenant is a symbol of grace' (*Mut. nom.* 52, in a comment on Gen. 17:2; the same interpretation of a covenant is given at *De sac. Abelis et Caini* 57, on Deut. 9:5).

This view of a covenant as symbolizing God's grace is influential in Philo. Thus the treatise *De migratione Abrahami* begins with a consideration (1–127) of the Abrahamic covenant of Gen. 22:2–3 as comprising five gifts (δωρεαί). Sometimes Philo takes the covenant as God's gift to the wise (so *Mut. nom.* 58), but other passages suggest that this is a development of a simpler view, in which it is, first of all, a gift to those designated as recipients: Noah, and so the God-beloved (Gen. 9:11 in *Somn.* ii 224–5); Abraham (Gen. 22:16 in *De Abr.* 273); or Phinehas (Num. 25:12–13 *Spec. Leg.* i 57). Hence, like Josephus, but now in explicit and frequent connection with the patriarchs, Philo presents the national covenanted privileges as God's gifts. The usage found in Ezekiel Tragicus is therefore attested not only by Christian writers likely to reflect or perpetuate Jewish idiom, but also, directly, by Hellenistic Jewish authors. This conclusion has been affirmed, since the essay was first published, in a fuller examination of Philonic usage by A. M. Schwemer, 83, 92–101.

V

Now, however, the inquiry has touched passages of importance for the understanding of biblical *b^erît* in the Second Temple period. When that question has been examined, some of the evidence just reviewed has been differently interpreted. The post-exilic tendency to give *b^erît* the sense of promise or grant, which in the present inquiry appears as another aspect of the development whereby national privileges came to be described as gifts, has been considered mainly in its relation to the central content (however defined) of Old Testament *b^erît*. Accordingly, it was claimed by Heinemann that Philo had no notion of a covenant (*Bunde*) between God and the patriarchs and Israel; rather, in some of the passages just cited, he understood διαθήκη either as 'divine attribute', an idea which could be equated with the Logos, or as 'last will' (Heinemann, 482–4, 564). Behm, on the other hand, held that Philo was aware of a broader sense of διαθήκη as 'disposition', and that, therefore, he stood closer to the biblical usage of *b^erît*; but that, in his own interpretations, he exploited the current understanding of the Greek word as 'will' (Behm, 131, followed by Jaubert, 314–15, 414–37). It has since been argued, without special reference to Heinemann, that, despite this exploitation, the broader sense 'disposition' was genuinely important for Philo, and that herein he followed the sense which was primary for the LXX translators; and they in turn, it is further suggested, were in this respect true to the central significance of biblical *b^erît*, which should be rendered with terms like 'promise, disposition, allotment' or 'ordinance' (Kutsch, 78–83, 85–7). In response, it has been noted that the LXX rendering may reflect the changing semantics of *b^erît* in the period, rather than the continuation of the understanding thought to be central in biblical times, and that it may well have to be related to specific conditions of Hellenistic Judaism (Barr, 35–6). Since this essay first appeared, the understanding 'will' has again been proposed as important for the LXX translators, but the Ptolemaic currency of provisions for heirs to enjoy the use of property while the testator is still alive has at the same time been picked out as forming one of the associations of διαθήκη (Schenker, 127–8, 129–31); even on this view, then, the LXX rendering is implicitly brought a little nearer to the broader sense 'disposition'.

Philo is pivotal in this discussion; but in the passages cited by Behm, which are all among those already considered above, a play on the meaning 'will' is either slight and subordinate (*Mut. nom.* 51 κλῆρον κατὰ διαθήκας ἀπολείψειν, Colson 'to leave a covenanted portion'), or else not clearly to be identified at all (*De sac.* 57 and *Somn.* ii 223–4, where Deut. 9:5 and Gen. 9:11 are explained, respectively, in the broader terms of granting a gift noted above). Heinemann himself (483, n. 7) had found the meaning 'will' only in the first two of these three passages; he grouped *Somn.* ii 223–4, 237 with two other places claimed as examples of the meaning 'divine attribute', which could be equated with the Logos (*Det. pot.* 68, *Qu. in Gen.* 3.51). In *De somniis* ii, however, the sense 'divine attribute' emerges only in the course of the argument, and does not cancel the meaning 'gift' picked out above; for God's gift (223–4) is said to reflect his nature (237). In the remaining two passages, διαθήκη is paralleled with the divine words (*Det. pot.* 67, taking up the parallelism of Deut. 33:9c), or interpreted as the divine word (*Qu. in Gen.* 3.51, on Gen. 17:13). In each of these three passages διαθήκη has a less strongly doctrinal flavour than Heinemann's summary suggests, but he rightly avoided classifying the first passage as an instance of the meaning 'will'.

The meaning 'will', therefore, plays at most a subordinate part in one of the passages cited to exemplify it, and is certainly neither prominent nor regular in them. These passages, together with others, are better treated as illustrating Philo's view of the national privileges as God's gifts. His connection of διαθήκη with gift then appears within a broader context of his thought than is opened by study of the interpretation of *b*[e]*rît*, and it becomes questionable from the first whether, as Heinemann assumed, Philo makes this connection mainly because he understands διαθήκη as 'will'.

The passages witness, instead, to the Philonic view of the covenants as gifts. This view has been considered, however, in the present connection, precisely because it is not peculiar to Philo. Rather, both Philo and Josephus share a view which already appears in Ezekiel Tragicus. Furthermore, the allusive character of the tragedian's references to it suggests that it was already traditional in his time. Hence, it should be reckoned among possible influences on the LXX rendering. This consideration would favour the view that διαθήκη was taken by the LXX translators to signify 'disposition' in a broader sense than 'will' (Behm, 130; Kutsch, 58–71, 86).

If the LXX rendering was influenced by interpretation of the covenants as gifts it can readily be related, as Barr suggested, both to the changing semantics of *b^erît* and to the circumstances of Hellenistic Jewry. The Pentateuch in its completed form leads naturally, as already noted, to a view of the covenants as gifts; and this completed form may now be judged both to illustrate, and to have encouraged, a shift in the semantic range of *b^erît* towards the sense of 'grant', or the like. This view of the covenants, as has also been noted, fits easily into a Hellenized conception of the deity as a royal benefactor.

The view expressed allusively in Ezekiel Tragicus, and developed in Josephus, Philo and first-century Christian writers, is therefore probably interrelated with the late biblical and Septuagintal interpretation of *b^erît*. In the Greek period, the semantic development already evident in the completed form of the Pentateuch will have encouraged, and have been encouraged by, a view of the covenants as gifts of the divine benefactor. The age of this traditional view of the covenants, its agreement with the emphasis of the completed Pentateuch itself, and its consistency with the conceptions of the deity which became natural under the Hellenistic monarchies, all combine to suggest that it will have been widely influential. That its range embraced Palestine as well as the Diaspora is shown by the rabbinic evidence, which can now be viewed in the perspective of pre-rabbinic usage.

VI

Two of the rabbinic texts quoted by Odeberg resemble prerabbinic passages considered above. First, Simeon b. Yohai used to say (according to B. Ber. 5a, in a passage identified as a baraitha) that three good gifts (*mattānôt*) were given by God to Israel, but all of them only through suffering: the Torah, and the land of Israel, and the world to come. It is here assumed, as in Ezekiel Tragicus, Josephus, Philo and Paul, that the covenanted privileges are gifts; and a fine homiletic turn then presents the common assumption as a consolation.

Secondly, a saying in the name of R. Nathan (late second century A.D.) distinguishes between conditional and unconditional covenants, as exemplified by the covenants with David and the Rechabites. In the Mekhilta this saying is immediately followed by a consideration of things (*d^{e}bārîm*) 'that were given (*nitt^{e}nû*) conditionally—the land of Israel, the temple, and the kingdom of the house of David', as contrasted with 'the book of the law and the covenant of Aaron, which were not given conditionally' (Mekhilta, Yitro, Amalek, ii, on Exod. 18:27; Horovitz—Rabin, 201). The sequence of the two sayings, and the mention of Aaron's covenant in the second, mean that the covenants themselves are viewed as gifts, in the manner exemplified especially fully in Philo. Further, the covenantal privileges listed as given overlap with those noted in Paul (law, [temple-] service, messiah, Rom. 9:4–5) and 1 Clement (the Levitical priesthood, 1 Clem. 32.2).

A further illustration of the currency of the thought of God's special gifts to Israel comes from rabbinic interpretation of the place-name Mattanah (Num. 21:19). Its meaning 'gift' is applied either to the miraculous well of the wilderness journey (so Targum Pseudo-Jonathan *ad loc.*) or to the gift of Torah (so, with reference to the individual rather than the nation, M. Abot vi 2, B. Erub. 54a).

Rabbinic passages therefore exhibit an understanding of national privileges as divine gifts which is continuous with that just studied in pre-rabbinic usage. This theological idiom was not restricted to Greek-speaking Jews. The attribution to Simeon b. Yohai (mid second-century Palestine), viewed together with the examples from Mekhilta and Targum Pseudo-Jonathan, suggests that in this case Josephus probably reflects the usage of his native land as well as the Diaspora. The idiom will then have been common to Jews with different vernaculars, Hebrew, Aramaic and Greek, in both Palestine and the Diaspora, in the latter part of the Second Temple period. Particularly significant of its importance is its occurrence in summaries of prescribed prayers (Josephus, *Ant.* iv 212; Philo, *Spec. Leg.* ii 219).

VII

The description of national privileges as divine gifts is therefore common enough to deserve notice in studies of grace in the writings of the Second

Temple period. Such notice seems not to have been widely accorded, to judge from the silence of the general treatments by Conzelmann and Dittmann. Similarly, even when Philo on grace has been considered in connection with the covenant (Jaubert, 431–7) and with thanksgiving (Laporte, 194–246), this aspect has remained unmentioned.

Here it can only be suggested that the usage surveyed above, in its concentration on God's gifts to the nation, exhibits a connection between Jewish ideas of grace and those of Paul. Paul's characteristic application of 'grace' to redemption through Christ has been held to contrast with Philo's broader usage. Philo constantly finds God's χάρις in his gifts in nature. For 'gift' in this sense he often uses δωρεά, sometimes also δώρημα, χάρις itself (as in *Spec. Leg.* ii 219, quoted above), and, twice only, χάρισμα (*Leg. all.* iii 78, discussed by Moffatt, 114–15). A comparably broad view of God's giving also appears in earlier Jewish literature, without special attachment to χάρις or its Hebrew equivalents (so, for example, Letter of Aristeas 205 [Laporte, 198–9] or Eccles. 3:13, 5:18). Paul, on the other hand, uses χάρις above all for redemption through Christ, and χάρισμα (which he can also apply to redemption, Rom. 5:15–16) for a spiritual rather than a natural gift.

The novelty of Pauline usage has therefore been emphasized (for example, with reference to χάρισμα, by Moffatt, 105, Dörrie, col. 316, and Knoch, col. 353). Nevertheless, in the Jewish usage surveyed above, God's gifts are those imparted to his people whom he wills to redeem (cf. Ezekiel Tragicus 106–7). Accordingly, his gifts in Philo, who shares this usage, are by no means only the gifts of nature. Hence, if consideration of Paul is broadened beyond the etymologically linked χάρις and χάρισμα to include other words for 'gift' it seems that the characteristically Pauline uses of 'grace' and 'gift' for redemption through God's messiah are developments of this Jewish theological idiom.

Thus, when Paul explores the antecedents of 'this grace' (Rom. 5:1), in Rom. 4 and Gal. 3 he gives a re-interpretation of the association of God's gifts to the nation with the patriarchs and the covenantal promises (see especially Ezekiel Tragicus and Philo, sections I and II above). Similarly, the Pauline application of 'gift', and of 'grace' in the sense of 'gift', to redemption through Christ, is a special instance of the habitual Jewish reference to national gifts. These could include covenantal grant (Ezekiel Tragicus, Philo, Rom. 9); the gifts of the exodus deliverance, including the law (Josephus, Rom. 9, Targum

Pseudo-Jonathan, B. Ber. 5a); and the messiah and the world to come (Rom. 9, B. Ber. 5a, Mekhilta). The χάρισμα of Rom. 5:15–16, where the gift is 'this grace' (Rom 5:1) of redemption, received by the called and chosen (Rom. 1:6–7, 9:24–6), therefore specializes χάρισμα as used for the privileges of Israel in Rom. 11:29 (cf. Rom. 9:4–5). (That Rom. 11:29 illuminates the beginning of the Pauline development of χάρισμα is suggested by Conzelmann, 394, n. 10; his view may be strengthened if, as argued here, Rom. 11:29 itself reproduces current Jewish usage.) To move from χάρισμα to δωρεά, the 'unspeakable gift' of 2 Cor. 9:15 includes, as Barrett notes *ad loc.*, a reference to 'the grace of our Lord' mentioned at 2 Cor. 8:9, where χάρις has the sense of 'generosity'; but this moral quality of Christ, mentioned also at Rom. 5:15, is taken by Paul, as the latter verse makes clear, to reflect the prior, redemptive 'grace of God and the gift' (ἡ χάρις τοῦ θεοῦ καὶ ἡ δωρεά, Rom. 5:15). Hence, this characteristically Pauline view of God's grace and gifts, in all its freshness and intensity, appears as a special development of that Jewish view of national privileges as God's gifts which was already traditional for Ezekiel Tragicus.

VIII

In conclusion, it may be possible to specify more closely the particular covenantal gifts in view in Ezekiel Tragicus 106. The whole line echoes a regular item of biblical covenantal terminology, the remembering of the patriarchs and the covenant. This remembering gained liturgical embodiment in an old element of the New Year services, the recitation of 'remembrance-verses'—a catena of biblical texts employing *zkr*—as a prayer for divine remembrance; it forms the second in the triad of similarly-composed prayers inserted into the Amidah, known as *malkuyyôt, zikrônôt, šôfārôt* (M. R. H. iv 5–6). The existence of this prayer at the time of the compilation of the Mishnah implies prior recognition that an appreciable number of Pentateuchal texts can be classified as 'remembrance-verses', and suggests that special attention to these verses will have been customary for some time. Such attention would be a natural response to their prominence in the Pentateuch, where the P passages on remembering the covenant are in some respects strikingly similar to the praises of God in the psalter for his remembrance (Childs, 41–4, citing, among other texts, Exod. 6:5, 8 and Ps. 105:8). It is therefore reasonable to suppose, without implying a particular date of origin for the *zikrônôt*-prayer, that the remembrance-verses were already attracting attention as such towards the end of the second century b.c., at the time of Ezekiel Tragicus. That such attention is conceivable in the Greek-speaking Diaspora as well as Palestine is confirmed by Wis. 18:22, where one such verse, Exod. 32:13, forms the basis of a midrashic insertion into the narrative of Num. 17:6–15 (16:41–50).

Among the remembrance-verses recalled by Ezekiel Tragicus 106 are Exod. 2:24 (just before the biblical passage already invoked by the neighbouring lines of the tragedy), Exod. 6:5, 8 and Lev. 26:42, 45. Unlike the line in the tragedy, however, which speaks of remembering the forefathers and remembering the gifts, in that order, these verses mention the covenant first, and in Leviticus the patriarchs are named in order of juniority rather than of seniority, again by contrast with the play (line 105). A closer parallel is afforded by another verse, already mentioned, Exod. 32:13. Here Moses beseeches the Lord to remember Abraham, Isaac and Israel (line 106, μνησθεὶς δ' ἐκείνων), to whom he swore to multiply their seed and to give their seed the land (line 106, καὶ ἔτ' ἐμῶν δωρημάτων). In these lines of the tragedy, however, the divine speeches from the beginnings of Exod. 3 and 6 are coalesced (as noted by Jacobson, 98). It may then be suggested that the basis of line 106 lies, in the first place, in Exod. 6:3–5. This passage relates, successively, how God appeared to the three patriarchs, established his covenant with them, and now remembers his covenant. Here the order is that of line 106, but the singular covenant, even though a plurality of covenants is perhaps implied by the mention of three patriarchs, contrasts with the plural 'gifts' of the play. Further, again by contrast with the play, the covenant alone is said to be remembered, and the divine appearing, on which the play is silent, receives emphasis. These discrepancies may then suggest that, in the second place, as a summary of the longer passage ending with God's remembrance, the tragedian took the remembrance-verse Exod. 32:13, and made it the immediate pattern of his line. This verse is quoted in the (probably fifth-century) *zikrônôt* of Yose ben Yose (*'epḥad b^e ma'^a śay*, lines 52–5, in Mirsky, 102–3); and in Wisd. 18:22, as already noted, it influenced a narrative based on Numbers. In a somewhat comparable way, it is now suggested, Exod. 32:13 influenced a speech based on Exod. 3 and 6. The 'gifts' in mind in Ezekiel Tragicus 106 could then be identified, from Exod. 32:13, as the sworn promises of seed and land.

Recognition of a Jewish theological idiom in Ezekiel Tragicus 106 has led to various conclusions, which can now be summarized. Some are directly exegetical, others bear on the development of the biblical ideas of covenant and grace.

First, it has appeared that 'gifts' in Ezekiel Tragicus 106 need not be taken as 'gifts to God' and that the line stands in no need of conjectural emendation. By 'gifts' were meant, as in line 35, the national privileges given by God through the patriarchal covenants; and the promises of increase and of the land were probably especially in view (cf. Exod. 32:13).

Ezekiel Tragicus is an early witness to this application of words for 'gift' to the covenantal privileges of Israel. The allusive character of his usage suggests that it was already traditional. This view of its age is consistent with its widespread attestation at the end of the Second Temple period, both among Greek-speaking Jews (see Philo and Josephus) and among those who used Hebrew or Aramaic (see the rabbinic texts). A wide currency is also suggested by its appearance, in Philo and Josephus, in summaries of prescribed prayers.

This Jewish usage was reproduced by St. Paul (Rom. 11:29; cf. Rom. 9:4–5), and extended in 1 Clement. It offers an explanation of the ambiguous 'gift of God' in John 4:10, which should then probably be taken as a reference to the messiah rather than the law.

To turn, secondly, to the idea of the covenant, it has been suggested above that the early development of the usage here surveyed should be viewed together with the post-exilic semantic development of *b*[e]*rît* towards the sense of 'grant' or 'disposition'. Both developments were probably indebted in the same way to biblical thought as well as the *Zeitgeist*; the completed form of the Pentateuch set the covenants in the context of divine giving, and in the Greek period it became natural for Jews to envisage the deity as a kingly benefactor. The thought of the covenants as gifts to the nation may already have influenced the choice of the translation διαθήκη in the LXX. The Philonic passages which have been thought to exploit the meaning of διαθήκη as 'will' seem rather to exemplify the understanding of the covenants as gifts which has been under review.

Lastly, this Jewish understanding of covenanted privileges as God's gifts has appeared as a neglected antecedent of Pauline views of grace. The contrast somtimes drawn between the Philonic and the Pauline treatments of grace should be modified, for both are indebted to the Jewish theological idiom studied here. Paul's characteristic use of 'grace' and 'gift' for the messianic redemption received by God's chosen develops the widespread Jewish use of 'gifts' for the covenantal grants and promises of Israel's redeemer. This Jewish usage, with the special assurance of God's favour to his people which it expresses, had already moulded lines 106–7 in Ezekiel Tragicus.

Literature

J. Barr, 'Some Semantic Notes on the Covenant', in H. Donner, R. Hanhart and R. Smend (eds.), *Beiträge zur Alttestamentlichen Theologie: Festschrift für Walther Zimmerli zum 70. Geburtstag* (Göttingen, 1977), 23–38

C. K. Barrett, *The Gospel according to St. John* (2nd edn., London, 1978)

———, *The Second Epistle to the Corinthians* (London, 1973)

J. Behm, *διαθήκη, TWNT ii* (Stuttgart, 1935), 127–37

B. S. Childs, *Memory and Tradition in Israel* (London, 1962)

D. J. A. Clines, *The Theme of the Pentateuch* (1978, repr. Sheffield, 1982)

F. H. Colson and G. H. Whitaker (trans.), *Philo v* (1934, repr. London and Cambridge, MA, 1968)

H. Conzelmann and W. Zimmerli, *χάρις, χάρισμα, TWNT ix* (Stuttgart, 1973), 363–397

H. Dittmann, H. Dörrie, O. Knoch and A. Schindler, 'Gnade', *RAC* xi (Stuttgart, 1979–80), cols. 313–446

J. Freudenthal, *Hellenistische Studien, Heft 1 & 2, Alexander Polyhistor und die von ihm erhaltenen Reste judäischer und samaritanischer Geschichtswerke* (Breslau, 1875)

E. H. Gifford (ed. and trans., with notes), *Eusebii Pamphili Evangelicae Praeparationis Libri xv* (Oxford, 4 vols. in 5, 1903)

I. Heinemann, *Philons griechische und jüdische Bildung* (Breslau, 1932)

C. R. Holladay, *Fragments from Hellenistic Jewish Authors, ii, Poets* (Atlanta, 1989)

W. Horbury, *Jewish Messianism and the Cult of Christ (London, 1998)*

H. S. Horovitz and I. A. Rabin (eds.), *Mechilta d'Rabbi Ismael* (Frankfurt am Main, 1931, repr. Jerusalem, 1960)

H. Jacobson, *The Exagoge of Ezekiel* (Cambridge, 1983)

A. Jaubert, *La notion d'alliance dans le judaïsme aux abords de l'ère chrétienne* (Paris, 1963)

W. Knox, *St Paul and the Church of the Gentiles* (Cambridge, 1939)

E. Kutsch, *Neues Testament—Neuer Bund? Eine Fehlübersetzung wird korrigiert* (Neukirchen-Vluyn, 1978)

J. Laporte, *La doctrine eucharistique chez Philon d'Alexandrie* (Paris, 1972)

H. G. Liddell and R. Scott, *A Greek-English Lexicon*, new edition by H. S. Jones and R. McKenzie (Oxford, 1925–40)

B. A. Mastin, 'Daniel 2[46] and the Hellenistic World', *ZAW* lxxxv (1973), 80–93

A. Mirsky (ed.), *Yosse ben Yosse: Poems* (Jerusalem, 1977)

J. Moffatt, *Grace in the New Testament* (London, 1931)

F. Nielsen, 'Tragediedigteren Ezekiel. Introduktion og oversaettelse', *Dansk Teologisk Tidsskrift* lxii (1999), 81–105

H. Odeberg, *The Fourth Gospel* (Uppsala, 1929)

T. Rajak, 'The Gifts of God at Sardis', in M. Goodman (ed.), *Jews in a Graeco-Roman World* (Oxford, 1998), 229–39

A. Schenker, '*Διαθήκη* pour b[e]rit. L'option de traduction de la *LXX* à la double lumière du droit successoral de l'Égypte ptolémaïque et du livre de la Genèse', in J.-M. Auwers and A. Wénin (eds.), *Lectures et relectures de la Bible. Festschrift P.-M. Bogaert* (*BETL* cxliv, Leuven, 1999), 125–31

J. Schneider and E. Fascher, *Das Evangelium nach Johannes* (Berlin, 1976)

E. Schürer, revised by M. Goodman, 'Jewish Literature Composed in Greek', in E. Schürer, *Geschichte des jüdischen Volkes im Zeitalter Jesu Christi* (3rd–4th edn., Leipzig, 1901–9); ET *The History of the Jewish People in the Age of Jesus Christ*, revised by G. Vermes, F. Millar, M. Black, M. Goodman and P. Vermes, iii.1 (Edinburgh, 1986), 470–704

A. M. Schwemer, 'Zum Verhältnis von Diatheke und Nomos in den Schriften der jüdischen Diaspora Ägyptens in hellenistischrömischer Zeit', in F. Avemarie and H. Lichtenberger (eds.), *Bund und Tora. Zur theologischen Begriffsgeschichte in alttestamentlicher, frühjüdischer und urchristlicher Tradition* (*WUNT* xcii, Tübingen, 1996), 67–109

S. Singer and I. Brodie (eds.), *The Authorized Daily Prayer Book of the United Hebrew Congregations of the British Commonwealth* (London, 5722–1962)

P. Spilsbury, 'God and Israel in Josephus: a Patron-Client Relationship', in S. Mason (ed.), *Understanding Josephus: Seven Perspectives* (*Journal for the Study of the Pseudepigrapha* Supplement Series xxxii, Sheffield, 1998), 172–91

W C. van Unnik, 'Eine merkwürdige liturgische Aussage bei Josephus (Jos Ant 8, 111–13)', in O. Betz, K. Haacker and M. Hengel (eds.), *Josephus-Studien Otto Michel zum 70. Geburtstag gewidmet* (Göttingen, 1974), 362–9

R. Van De Water, 'Moses' Exaltation: Pre-Christian?', *Journal for the Study of the Pseudepigrapha* xxi (2000), 59–69

3

Herod's Temple and 'Herod's Days'

Ancient accounts of Herod's temple often pass over the name of Herod. He is named as builder neither in Mishnah, Middoth, nor by Philo in his description (*Spec. Leg.* i 71–8; cf. *Leg. ad Gaium* 294–7), nor by Tacitus or Cassius Dio, nor even by Josephus when not following Nicolas of Damascus; the long description in book v of the *War* names Solomon as founder of the temple, but Herod only as builder of Antonia (Josephus, *B.J.* v 185, 238).

These silences can readily be ascribed to the negative views of Herod expressed by Josephus and in rabbinic and Christian sources, and reflected in Strabo's reference to Jewish 'hatred towards Herod' as the justification for Antony's execution of Antigonus (in a passage quoted by Josephus, *Ant.* xv 9–10). Other reasons for silence can be envisaged, however, including in different cases the biblically-influenced and traditional character of the narratives or the writer's sense that the building was a communal achievement. Moreover, as will be seen in a moment, the silence is broken not only when Josephus follows Nicolas, but also when the story of the building of the sanctuary recurs in rabbinic narrative.

E. Bammel has drawn attention to the political value of the temple, and in particular its official oversight, for the house of Herod and Herodian supporters.[1] The accounts of Herod's temple may therefore suitably introduce some reconsideration of Herodian kingship in its Jewish setting. The concentration of historiography on Judaea and its movements of revolt against Rome tends to highlight aspects of the house of Herod which were or were regarded as non-Jewish. Herodian kingship should also be viewed against its broader Jewish background, with fuller reference to the diaspora and to likely

[1] E. Bammel, 'The Trial before Pilate', in E. Bammel and C. F. D. Moule (eds.), *Jesus and the Politics of His Day* (Cambridge, 1984), 423–4, 446; and in a review of M. D. Goodman, *The Ruling Class of Judaea* (Cambridge, 1987) in *JTS* N.S. xl (1989), 213–17 (215); on Josephus on Herod's temple, see J. W. van Henten, *Judean Antiquities 15: Translation and Commentary* (BJP 7B, Leiden & Boston, 2014).

differences of attitude among Jews at home as well as abroad, so that areas of merging as well as contrast gain due prominence.[2]

A small step in this direction is at any rate attempted here. Some of the narratives of the building of Herod's temple in Jerusalem, and Persius' lines on 'Herod's days' in Rome, are considered as foci of positive associations between the house of Herod and the Jews of the Roman empire.

The desiderata just outlined are of course not ignored by historians, and they are prominent in the relatively short pre-war treatments of the house of Herod by H. Willrich and A. Momigliano; more recently, A. Schalit has monumentally presented Herod the Great as a Hellenistic monarch imbued with Augustan ideology, but one sufficiently aware of Jewish feeling to foster a Herodian messianism as the analogue to a ruler-cult, and one whose achievements entitle him to be recognized as a king of Israel; while M. Stern, dissenting from this recognition, has nevertheless indicated many connections as well as conflicts between the Herods and their Judaean Jewish subjects.[3] In Schalit's book, however, although Hellenism is central, the claims of political history accord less prominence to the discussion of Jewish Hellenism, a debate also relevant to assessment of Herodian kingship (and Schalit wrote before M. Hengel's contributions to this debate). Moreover, here and in Stern's writing the emphasis still lies mainly on Judaea, as is naturally also true of the treatment of hostility to the Herods in work on the antecedents of the Judaean revolt of 66–70 by Hengel and Goodman (see nn. 1 and 2, above).

Since the present essay first appeared, D. Mendels has reviewed Herodian monarchy in the context of ancient Jewish nationalism, and the diaspora and Hellenism have received fuller attention from P. Richardson, with a relatively favourable reassessment of Herod the Great and an affirmation of his Jewishness

[2] With regard to Herod the Great, this point has been noted by M. Hengel, *The Zealots* (ET Edinburgh, 1989), 323–4, n. 68 and (since the present essay first appeared) by P. Richardson, *Herod. King of the Jews and Friend of the Romans* (Columbia, SC, 1996; reissued Edinburgh, 1999), xiii, 45, 53, 62, 93–4.

[3] H. Willrich, *Das Haus des Herodes zwischen Jerusalem und Rom* (Heidelberg, 1929); A. Momigliano, 'Herod of Judaea', 'Rebellion within the Empire', sections iv–vii, and 'Josephus as a Source for the History of Judaea', in S. A. Cook, F. E. Adcock and M. P. Charlesworth (eds.), *The Cambridge Ancient History* x (Cambridge, 1934, repr. 1971), 316–39, 849–65, 884–7 (the general standpoint differs from that of Momigliano's post-war work; see n. 37, below); A. Schalit, *König Herodes* (Berlin, 1969; a revised and enlarged version of the text originally issued in modern Hebrew, Jerusalem, 1960); M. Stern, 'A. Schalit's *Herod*', *JJS* xi (1960), 49–58, and (among other writings) 'The Reign of Herod' and 'The Herodian Dynasty and the Province of Judea at the End of the Period of the Second Temple', in M. Avi-Yonah and Z. Baras (eds.), *The Herodian Period* (= *The World History of the Jewish People*, First Series, Volume vii) (London, 1975), 71–178.

(n. 2, above), and from N. Kokkinos, with a contrasting portrayal of the Herods, against the background of F. Millar's exploration of local Syrian cultures, as an alien line of Hellenized Phoenician descent; but in Mendels the inadequacy of a Herodian claim to Jewish kingship is underlined, in Richardson the contrasts between Jewish life in diaspora and homeland emerge more clearly than the similarities, and in Kokkinos the ancient endeavours to dissociate the Herods from the Jewish community are naturally re-emphasized.[4] Hence, although S. J. D. Cohen has reaffirmed Herod's Jewishness, in the sense of his membership of the community revering the God whose temple is in Jerusalem, it is perhaps still useful to recall in outline some of the evidence for more positive Jewish acknowledgement of Herodian kingship, and to note once more the long-recognized overlap of attitudes between the diaspora and Judaea.[5]

Estimates of public opinion must of course reckon with a probable difference between the homeland, where revolts broke out in Idumaea, Judaea, Peraea and Galilee on the death of Herod the Great, and the diaspora, where Herodian monarchs were valued as protectors of the Jews. Among Judaean and Galilaean Jews themselves, however, opinion will also have varied; it is likely that the division between rich and poor emphasized by Josephus, and the overlapping division between town and country, often corresponded to a difference in attitudes to the Herodian government.

Some Jews were supporting the house of Herod in Judaea and Galilee before Herod the Great established his reign. When he was fighting for the crown between 40 and 37 he found Jewish partisans in Galilee, Idumaea and Judaea (especially Jericho); and Jerusalem itself—where leading Pharisees urged submission to Herod—was divided (Josephus, *B.J.* i 291–3, 319, 326, 335, 358, parallel with *Ant.* xiv 395–8, 436, 450, 458, xv 2–3). At the capture of the city the Jewish attacking forces were as hard to restrain as the Romans

[4] D. Mendels, *The Rise and Fall of Jewish Nationalism* (New York, 1992), 213–23; Richardson, *Herod*, 264–6; N. Kokkinos, *The Herodian Dynasty* (Sheffield, 1998), especially 342–62; F. Millar, *The Roman Near East, 31 B.C.-A.D. 337* (Cambridge, MA and London, 1993), especially 235, 345, 351–66.

[5] S. J. D. Cohen, *The Beginnings of Jewishness: Boundaries, Varieties, Uncertainties* (Berkeley, Los Angeles and London, 1999), 23; on overlap of home and diaspora opinion see for example, E. Schürer, *Geschichte des jüdischen Volkes im Zeitalter Jesu Christi*, iii (4th edn., Leipzig, 1909), 188–9 ('Palestinian' Judaism can be found outside as well as inside Palestine, and 'Hellenistic' Judaism inside as well as outside); W. D. Davies, *Paul and Rabbinic Judaism* (1948; 5th edn., Mifflintown, PA, 1998), 1–16 (6–7, reciprocal interchange of thought between Palestine and the diaspora); on a Herodian halakhic instance, E. Bammel, 'Markus 10 11f. und das jüdische Eherecht', *ZNW* lxi (1970), 95–101 (divorce initiated by the wife, as by Herod the Great's sister Salome in her marriage with Costobar, was known in Jewish Palestine as well as the diaspora, despite its condemnation as un-Jewish by Josephus, *Ant.* xv 259).

(*B.J.* i 351 = *Ant.* xiv 479). Since this essay first appeared, I. Shatzman's reassessment of Josephus' reports on the Herodian forces has shown that the majority of Herod's army at the siege of Jerusalem were Jews.[6]

Thereafter, Jerusalem and Jericho will always have had their wealthy Herodian constituency (strengthened by the foundation of Phasaelis and Archelais in the region of Jericho); but it is also notable that the long periods of Herodian rule in the northern tetrarchies found response in the nomenclature of more prosperous Jews. The name Herod is attested in Tiberias in 66 (two leading citizens of that name are mentioned by Josephus, *Vita*, 33), and, much later on, in inscriptions perhaps of the fourth century at Capernaum and Beth She'arim; Philip of Bethsaida (John 1:45, 12:21), like the Herods of Tiberias, can have been named after the tetrarch who was also city-founder.[7] 'Herodians', best understood as supporters of the house of Herod (with H. H. Rowley, n. 31, below), are envisaged both in Galilee and Jerusalem in Mark 3:6, 12:13).

Moreover, Jewish town-dwellers in particular were regularly at close quarters with gentiles, as at Caesarea or Scythopolis, so that a diaspora-like situation, in which a Jewish king could be valued, was reproduced in the homeland. Correspondingly, Herod the Great could be remembered as a Jewish king and benefactor by the wealthy Jewish community of Caesarea, who argued that this largely gentile city was theirs, since its founder was a Jewish king (Josephus, *B.J.* ii 266). In the diaspora itself, Babylonia and Alexandria contributed important groups of Herodian adherents (see Stern, as cited in

[6] The vast majority of Jews supported Antigonus, in the judgment of *M. Stern, 'Social and Political Realignments in Herodian Judaea', The Jerusalem Cathedra ii (1982), 40–62 (40–1)*; this view has also been taken, since the first appearance of the present essay, by M. Goodman, 'Judaea', in A. K. Bowman, E. Champlin and A. Lintott (eds.), *The Cambridge Ancient History, Second Edition, x, The Augustan Empire, 43 B.C.-A.D. 69* (Cambridge, 1996), 740. Herodian numbers may indeed be exaggerated in Josephus, based on Nicolas of Damascus (as in the case of Galilee, according to Schalit, *Herodes*, 90—now questioned by I. Shatzman, as cited below); but the Jewish population was clearly divided, and the significance for this point of the zeal of the Jewish captors of Jerusalem, not mentioned by Stern, is brought out by Schalit, 173, n. 95. For the Jewish majority in Herod's own forces in 37 see I. Shatzman, *The Armies of the Hasmonaeans and Herod* (TSAJ 25, Tübingen, 1991), 153 n. 98, 163–4.

[7] For the inscriptions see B. Lifschitz, *Donateurs et fondateurs dans les synagogues juives* (Paris, 1967), 61, no. 75 (= *CIJ* ii, no. 983) (donor of column at Capernaum), and M. Schwabe and B. Lifschitz, *Beth She'arim*, ii, *The Greek Inscriptions* (Jerusalem, 1967), 17, no. 56; these names suggest some qualification of Goodman, *Ruling Class*, 122, n. 16, where the failure of ordinary Jews to take Herodian names is contrasted with gentile willingness to take the name Agrippa under Agrippa II, but this evidence (indicating a similar Jewish inclination in Herodian territory) is unmentioned. Agrippa II will have been in view when Josephus named a son Agrippa (*V.* 5; 427), as is underlined in two works of importance for the later Herods which were not available when this essay was first written: S. Schwartz, *Josephus and Judaean Politics* (Columbia Studies in the Classical Tradition, xviii, Leiden, 1990), 12; D. R. Schwartz, *Agrippa I* (TSAJ xxiii, Tübingen, 1990), 157, n. 41.

n. 6, above), and Herodian supporters and nomenclature reappear in Rome (see Rom. 16:10–11 and section II (c), below). Many of Herod the Great's descendants gained added prestige from Hasmonaean high-priestly ancestry (which Agrippa I is represented as valuing particularly in Philo, *Leg. ad Gaium* 278); and the acclaim which these Herodian princes could receive from Jews both at home and abroad, in Judaea, Alexandria, the Greek islands and Italy, is loud and clear in the cases of Mariamme's sons Alexander and Aristobulus, and her grandson Agrippa I.

Recognition of the Herods has therefore left widespread traces in the evidence for the unified but varied ancient Jewish community, in which differences of standing and outlook often traversed the difference between homeland and diaspora. The texts considered below against this background come from a dossier which has often been examined. Thus, M. Stern's summary of the claims of Herod the Great to be viewed as a Jewish king largely overlaps with seventeenth-century argument for the Jewishness of Herod, itself a reaction against the treatment of Herod as an alien in patristic interpretation of Gen. 49:10 on the departure of the sceptre from Judah.[8]

Here two items in Stern's summary are reviewed again. The narratives of the temple-building in Josephus and rabbinic literature are compared and studied with regard to Herodian publicity; the possible link between the renewed temple and 'the days of Herod' mentioned by Persius is re-examined; and exegesis of the relevant texts is connected with the broader discussion of Herodian kingship against the Jewish background sketched above. It is urged below that Persius is a further witness to the Jewish observation of Herodian festivals attested by Josephus; and that these passages confirm the importance of the more favourable Jewish attitudes to the house of Herod, bring out the significance of Herod's temple as a royal sanctuary, and illuminate the contacts between Herodian kingship ideology and Jewish messianism.

[8] M. Stern, 'The Reign of Herod', 110–11; cf. F. Spanheim, *Dubia Evangelica* (2 vols., Geneva, 1639), ii, 225–55, summarizing the debate initiated by J. J. Scaliger's assertion of Herod's Jewish descent (cited in n. 31, below). Justin Martyr and Eusebius (cited in n. 18, below) viewed Herod's allegedly Ascalonite origin respectively as an objection to and a support for the claim that Christ came when the sceptre had departed from Judah; this interpretation of Gen. 49:10 is made to rest, rather, on Herod's Idumaean descent in the version of Josephus' account of the deputations to Augustus concerning Herod's will in the fourth-century Christian Latin Hegesippus, *Historiae*, ii 1, 2. Herod is called *alienigena* without further specification in the interpretations of Gen. 49:10 in the same sense by Rufinus, *De Benedictionibus Patriarcharum* i 7 and Augustine, *De Civitate Dei* xviii 45 (translated with further Augustinian material in Ad. Posnanski, *Schiloh I* (Leipzig, 1904), 71–5).

I. Narratives of the building of the temple

(a) Josephus

When Josephus follows Nicolas, and presents Herod as the king of the Jews building the Jerusalem temple (*B.J.* i 400–1, *Ant.* xv 380–425), he echoes court publicity in which three royal associations of the enterprise are heavily underlined. First, in Herod's speech to the people beforehand, it is represented that the Jews' own king is restoring the temple to the height originally planned by Solomon. (Regret for the fall of Solomon's temple, which 'was high', and hope that a future temple will be very high, is reflected at 2 Chron. 7:21; 1 En. 90:29; Sib. v 425.) The forefathers who rebuilt and maintained it after the exile had to be content with the reduced dimensions prescribed by their foreign overlords, Cyrus and Darius and others, in a time of necessity and subjection. Now, however, under Herod, there is peace, prosperity, and friendship with the universally powerful Romans, as opposed to servitude under the Persians and Macedonians, and the king can perform the pious duty of restoration (*Ant.* xv 385–7).

Significantly, the Macedonians are mentioned, but the Maccabees are not. This silence is emphasized by the insertion of a reference to the Maccabees in the tenth-century Jewish paraphrase of this speech in Josippon (50.15–17 in the edition by D. Flusser, i (Jerusalem, 1978), 227). Here it is said that they won freedom and kingship—the points on which Herodian silence is to be expected—but could not rebuild the temple—a point which was indeed made in Herodian publicity (Herod's speech in Jericho in Josephus, *Ant.* xvii 162, quoted below). Those speaking for and under the Herods, however, no doubt thought it better, if possible, not to mention the Hasmonaean house at all.

Secondly, and consistently with the emphasis in the foregoing on Herodian deliverance from national servitude, the rebuilt temple signified Jewish victory under a conquering Jewish king. King Herod dedicated 'barbarian spoils' which were fixed round about the whole new sanctuary, with the addition of those he had taken from the Arabs (*Ant.* xv 402). 'Barbarian' is no doubt a well-worn substitute for 'enemy' in this connection (cf. Virgil, *Aeneid* ii 504), but here it seems to have both a Roman and a Jewish reference. Herod had helped to repulse the Parthians and their allies, the barbarians particularly feared in Rome, and had taken booty from them; they are repeatedly called βάρβαροι in the previous book of the *Antiquities* (e.g xiv 341, 347, 441–5, following Roman usage, in these passages probably mediated by Nicolas, but also adopted by Josephus himself, see *B.J.* i 3). Moreover, the rebuilding of the temple began in 20 B.C., when Augustus visited Syria, added to Herod's territory, and by a display of force in Armenia compelled the Parthian king Phraates IV to restore Roman spoils and standards; this great capitulation was marked by publicity including coins, sculpture, and many references in the poets (e.g. Horace, *Od.* iv 15, 4–8).[9]

It is likely, then, that 'barbarian spoils' are meant to recall the Herodian Jewish contribution to this vaunted achievement of the Augustan peace. At the same time, indeed, Herod was building his temple to Augustus at Paneas (Josephus, *Ant.* xv 363–5). Herod had also, however, fought traditional enemies of the Jews in his ultimately victorious war against the Nabataean Arabs, who had twice defeated Alexander Jannaeus (Josephus, *Ant.* xiii 375, 392, xv 147–60). Here, therefore, Herod had beaten the Hasmonaean record, and 'barbarian' could allude to enemies of the Jews, as in 2 Macc. 2:21, 10:4, and to the Arabs in particular, as in Josephus, *B.J.* i 274. The spoils could therefore legitimately recall, as Herod's speech on the temple restoration is represented as doing, specifically Jewish victory within the context of Roman friendship.

The emphases represented in the speech and the adornment of the temple therefore stamp a Herodian impress on the themes of the deliberately unmentioned Hasmonaean Hanukkah, which recalled how the Maccabees 'put the barbarian hordes to flight, ... recovered the temple ..., and freed the city' (2 Macc. 2:21–2, cf. 10:1–8). Herod, king of the Jews, has given them, again and in fuller measure, victory over barbarian enemies and liberty from alien rule; and—what is more than the recovery of the temple commemorated at Hanukkah—he has restored the house of God to its former Solomonic glory. Conditions in fact answer to the zealotically-tinged ideal sketch of the time of David and Solomon later given in 2 Baruch: 'much blood of the nations that had sinned then was shed, and many offerings were offered at the dedication of the sanctuary. And peace and tranquillity reigned at that time' (Syriac Apocalypse of Baruch 61:2–3).

9 See J. G. C. Anderson in *Cambridge Ancient History*, x (1934), 262–3; passages from Horace, Propertius and Ovid on the return of the standards are listed by E. S. Gruen in *Cambridge Ancient History, Second Edition*, x (1996), 191–2, nn. 235, 238, 240.

Hence, thirdly, the context is not unfitting for the claim in the speech that the temple is the king's act of piety towards God, in return for having obtained the kingdom—which, with the divine will and counsel, he has brought to prosperity (Josephus, *Ant.* xv 383, 387). The themes are at once Graeco-Roman and characteristically Jewish. Herod displays the *eusebeia* which was a prime quality of the Hellenistic monarch (as emphasized by the Jewish sages in the Letter of Aristeas, 255, 261 and elsewhere), and which was eminently shown by Augustus, the great restorer of temples.[10] It was indeed claimed by the house of Herod in the title *eusebes* which was used by Agrippa I and II, and already by Herod the Great himself (as has been shown since the first appearance of this essay by a fresh reading of an inscribed lead weight from Azotus).[11] *eusebeia* is further presented in the War as Herod the Great's own notable quality, when he plans the temple restoration and also (in a speech ascribed to him in his rebuilt temple) when, eight years later, he names his successors (Josephus, *B.J.* i 400, 462, cf. *Ant.* xvi 132–3). The restoration of the Jerusalem temple is understood in the earlier speech as part of a divine–human exchange of benefits, a Graeco-Roman concept (as exemplified in n. 10, above) which had entered Jewish piety in convergence with the later biblical references to divine gifts, studied in chapter 2, above; thus, in David's prayer in 1 Chron. 29:14, his offerings for Solomon's temple are a return of God's gifts, and the opening of Solomon's prayer at the dedication of the temple (1 Kings 8:23 = 2 Chron. 6:14) includes in Josephus a contrasting recognition that it is impossible to recompense God in the exchange (*Ant.* viii 111, see n. 10, above).

[10] Hailed, for example, as a benefactor who has put the gods themselves under an obligation, in Ovid, *Fasti* ii 59–64 (especially 63–4 templorum positor, templorum sancte repostor | sit superis, opto, mutua cura tui); closer to Jewish emphasis on the priority of the divine side of the exchange (in agreement with the Stoic view that God needs nothing, Letter of Aristeas 211, Acts 17:25) is the recommendation of Augustus' restoration policy in Horace, *Od.* iii 6, 1–5 delicta maiorum immeritus lues | Romane, donec templa refeceris.| … dis te minorem quod geris, imperas. For the Greek background of the concept of exchange of benefits see W. C. van Unnik, 'Eine merkwürdige liturgische Aussage bei Josephus (Jos Ant 8, 111–113)', in O. Betz, K. Haacker and M. Hengel (eds.), *Josephus-Studien* (Göttingen, 1974), 362–9 (364–6).

[11] Inscriptions of Agrippa I and II (notably OGIS 419, from Sia in the Hauran, giving both father and son the title *eusebes*) are quoted by Schürer, *Geschichte*, ET, i, revised by M. Black, G. Vermes and F. Millar (Edinburgh, 1973), 452 n. 42, 475 n. 15 (on Herodian Sia see Millar, *The Roman Near East*, 38, 394–6); for *eusebes* in the titulature of Herod the Great see A. Kushnir-Stein, 'An Inscribed Lead Weight from Ashdod: a Reconsideration', *ZPE* cv (1995), 81–4. Temple-oriented Herodian *eusebeia* is further considered by the present writer, 'Der Tempel bei Vergil und im herodianischen Judentum', in B. Ego, A. Lange and P. Pilhofer (eds.), *Gemeinde ohne Tempel* (Tübingen, 1999), 149–68, repr. in Horbury, *Herodian Judaism and New Testament Study*, 59–79.

In accord with the Jewish overtones of the passage Schalit, followed by A. Hultgård and Th. A. Busink, finds a Davidic messianism behind the references to God's favour to the king; and although, as Stern shows, it is unlikely that Herod claimed Davidic descent, he is presented here as a divinely appointed and guided king who is a second and perhaps still greater Solomon (in his building, comparably, as Busink notes, his retention of the old 'Solomon's Porch' will have designedly set off the greater size and splendour of his own new work).[12] The comparison with Solomon is reinforced in the *Antiquities*, where the account of Herod's temple is preceded by the story of the Essene prophecy that he would be king of the Jews and enjoy exceptional good fortune until the end of his life, when his neglect of piety and justice would bring down the divine wrath (xv 373–9); Solomon, likewise, prospered by divine providence until idolatry brought wrath upon him (1 Kings 11 as interpreted in Josephus, *Ant.* viii 190–211). Further, Herod erected a marble monument at the tomb of David and Solomon (*Ant.* xvi 182–3). Herod is therefore presented as a divinely blessed king of the Jews, a king whose work approximates to that of the divinely promised royal deliverer of the people—a king, that is, over whom the aureole of messianism must hover.

Messianism in the Herodian period cannot be dissociated from contemporary ruler-cult (see Hultgård (n. 12, above), i, 326–76), and could fasten simply on Jewish rather than specifically Davidic origins, a viewpoint following naturally from the importance of Pentateuchal messianic texts such as Num. 24:7 and 17 (and the absence of any Davidic reference in the 'law of the king', Deut. 17:14–20), and corresponding to the expectation of someone 'from the country' of the Jews (Josephus, *B.J.* vi 312). In this presentation, then, a messianic atmosphere is being fostered around a non-Davidic reigning king, somewhat as appears to have occurred earlier with Hyrcanus I, or later on among the following of Bar Cocheba; it is likely that temple-building was already associated with the messianic king.[13] Early

[12] Schalit, 475–6; A. Hultgård, *L'eschatologie des Testaments des Douze Patriarches* (2 vols., Uppsala, 1977 and 1982), i, 376; Th. A. Busink, *Der Tempel von Jerusalem von Salomo bis Herodes*, ii (Leiden, 1980), 1061–2; Stern, 'A. Schalit's Herod', 55–8.

[13] On Hyrcanus, see Josephus, *Ant.* xiii 299–300, interpreted by *E. Bammel 'ΑΡΧΙΕΡΕΥΣ ΠΡΟΦΗΤΕΥΩΝ', TLZ lxxix (1954), cols. 351–6*, now reprinted with an addition in E. Bammel, mit einem Nachwort von Peter Pilhofer, *Judaica et Paulina: Kleine Schriften II* (WUNT xci, Tübingen, 1997), 133–9; on Bar Cocheha, Schürer, Black, Vermes and Millar, i, 543–5. On the temple, note that the thought of a messianic temple-builder was clearly widespread after 70 (e.g. Sib. v 423–5, Targ. Isa. 53:5, Zech. 6:12–13), but that the hope for a better, God-given temple at the last had then long been

Christian understanding of the Herodians as those who held Herod to be the messiah (n. 31, below) was doubtless influenced by the interchangeable use of 'king of the Jews' and 'Christ' in Matt. 2:2 and 4, but this use itself reflects the messianism of Jewish kingship. Later Herodian invocations of a messianic atmosphere include Archelaus' appearance enthroned in the temple, discussed below (an unsuccessful attempt), and Agrippa I's enthusiastic reception by the Jews of Alexandria (Philo, *Flaccus*, 25–39; section II (d), below).

The restoration was therefore made to point, in an Augustan but also Jewish messianic manner, to Herodian Jewish victory, peace and piety, and to the divine appointment of Herod as king. This presentation fits his studied favour towards Pharisees and Essenes, mentioned with emphasis just before the account of the restoration (Josephus, *Ant.* xv 370–1).

These royal aspects of the enterprise are underlined by the completion of the sanctuary on Herod's accession day, which was observed with special distinction on this occasion. (Josephus, *Ant.* xv 423). It has been noted that Herod's building projects usually served not only his ardour for personal fame, but also broader purposes of state (particularly, in this case, the needs of the national economy and religion); when the king took his place as founder of the new temple on his accession day, the solemnity suggests not only awareness of these needs, but also an intention to present the house of Herod as a great Jewish monarchy.[14] Thenceforth his accession day will also

current; see Tobit 14:5, and Exod. 15:17 LXX ἕτοιμον κατοικητήριον 'ready dwelling', discussed since the first appearance of this essay by Horbury, 'Land, Sanctuary and Worship', in J. Barclay and J.P.M. Sweet (eds.), *Early Christian Thought in its Jewish Context* (Cambridge, 1996), 207–24 (208–11). Zech. 6:12 LXX and 1 En. 53:6 probably indicate that the messiah could be expected to build or adorn it. See W. Bousset and H. Gressmann, *Die Religion des Judentums im späthellenistischen Zeitalter* (3rd edn., Tübingen, 1926), 239; J. Nolland, 'Sib. Or. iii. 265–94, an Early Maccabaean Messianic Oracle', *JTS* N. S. xxx (1979), 158–66 (the restoration of the temple by Cyrus and Zerubbabel is presented in Sib. iii as a pattern for the last times), with J. J. Collins, 'Messianism in the Maccabean Period', in J. Neusner, W. S. Green and E. Frerichs (eds.), *Judaisms and Their Messiahs at the Turn of he Christian Era* (Cambridge, 1987), 97–109 (99, restricting any significance for the Sibyl's eschatology to the possibility that final Jewish restoration will come through a gentile king like Cyrus; but, if an eschatological reference is allowed, the allusion to judgment more naturally suggests a messianic figure, as stressed by H. N. Bate, *The Sibylline Oracles, Books III–V* (London, 1918), 30–1).

14 E. Netzer, 'Herod's Building Projects: State Necessity or Personal Need?', *The Jerusalem Cathedra i* (1981), 48–61; M. Broshi, 'The Role of the Temple in the Herodian Economy', *JJS* xxxviii (1987), 31–7; K. Galling, 'Königliche und nichtkönigliche Stifter beim Tempel von Jerusalem', *ZDPV* lxviii (1950), 138–42 (141, accession-day dedication shows Herod as a royal patron of the temple on the pattern of the prince in Ezekiel, and, still more, of Hellenistic monarchs).

have been a Herodian dedication festival comparable with Hanukkah, the themes of which had been given a Herodian impress in the publicity just surveyed.

The temple was a traditional place of national assembly;[15] but the specifically dynastic themes of the new building were invoked when Herod named his successors in Herod's temple, and the white-robed Archelaus greeted his new subjects there from a golden throne on a dais before he offered sacrifice (Josephus, *Ant.* xvi 132–5, xvii 200–12, paralleled in *B.J.* i 457–66, ii 1–9). Archelaus' throne on a dais may be compared with the dais provided for Solomon at the dedication of the temple, according to 2 Chron. 6:13; Josephus assumes that Solomon will have been seated there (*Ant.* viii 107). A similar dais is to be put up in the temple court for the king to read the law, seated, at the feast of Tabernacles in the sabbatical year, according to the Mishnah (Soṭah vii 8). The Jewish and Roman traditions of Herodian piety were renewed by Agrippa I with a more sensitive *captatio benevolentiae* when he offered sacrifices of thanksgiving in due form, and dedicated in the temple the golden chain given him by Caligula (Josephus, *Ant.* xix 295); his reputation for modest hesitancy in claiming royal rights in the temple is also illustrated by the Mishnaic tradition that in the sabbatical year he read the law standing, not sitting, and that his eyes filled with tears when he read from Deut. 17:15 the command that the king should be an Israelite (Soṭah, *ibid.*). The royal associations of the temple were clearly considered likely to encourage support for the monarch, but the question how far these associations were accepted is underlined by the silence on Herod in the accounts of his temple noted at the beginning. Satire which may have earlier antecedents appears in R. Kahana's description of 'Herodian doves' in rows in their cote cooing 'Kyrie, kyrie'—apart from one dissenter who comes to a bad end for saying 'Kyrie *cheirie* [slave]' (Babylonian Talmud, Hullin, 139b; see Schürer, Vermes, Millar and Black, i, 310, n. 77).

[15] Evidence from Josephus and elsewhere is gathered by Ad. Büchler, *Types of Jewish-Palestinian Piety from 70 B.C.E. to 70 C.E.* (London, 1922), 205–8; for the idea compare 1 En. 89:50, 69, 90:29, 33, 36; Test. Benj. 9:2, and probably already 2 Sam. 7:10. An important Pentateuchal antecedent is Exod. 15:17 (cited in n. 13, above), where assembly in the sanctuary immediately follows entry into the land; see Horbury, 'Land, Sanctuary and Worship', 208–11.

(b) The Babylonian Talmud

It is therefore notable that the strongly Herodian account in which Josephus follows Nicolas[16] finds clear echoes in Talmudic tradition. The legend that rain fell only at night during construction (Josephus, *Ant.* xv 425) recurs in rabbinic exegesis of Lev. 26:4 'Then I will give you rain in due season' (Sifra, Behuqqotay, Pereq 1.1; Lev. R. 35.10; Babylonian Talmud, Ta'anith 23a). Moreover, an alternative version of the building of the sanctuary appears in the haggadah of the Babylonian Talmud (Baba Bathra 3b–4a). The final sequence of this rabbinic narrative is strikingly close to that of Nicolas' account.

Nicolas' narrative, as presented by Josephus, *Ant.* xv 365–425, runs as follows. (i) The king represses dissent, employs many spies, and even disguises himself to hear what his subjects are saying. (ii) He demands an oath of loyalty, gets rid of objectors, but excuses Pollion the Pharisee and Samaias and their disciples, and the Essenes. (iii) Manaem the Essene had prophesied that Herod would be king. (iv) Herod plans to rebuild the temple, and explains his purpose in a speech beforehand. (v) The temple is described at length. (vi) The new sanctuary is swiftly completed within eighteen months, on Herod's accession day; the work was expedited, because rain fell only at night.

The haggadah transmitted in the Babylonian Talmud begins with Herod's rise to power as a slave of the Hasmonaean house who kills the royal family, save for one princess; but she prefers suicide to marriage with him. Then, however (Baba Bathra 3b, end) it approximates to the sequence in Josephus just outlined, (i) The sages expound Deut. 17:15, teaching that the king must be an Israelite, and Herod kills them all except for Baba ben Buta, whom he blinds. (ii) He tries to trick Baba into treasonable talk, but is pleased by his prudent answers, and expresses regret (now in his own person) at having killed the sages; Baba advises him to rebuild the temple. (The story is told here in the Gemara of the tractate Baba Bathra with regard to the question, brought into connection with the Mishnah on building jointly-owned walls [Baba Bathra 1.1], whether

[16] G. Hölscher, 'Josephus 2', *PW* ix.2 (1916), cols. 1934–2000 (1973–82) ascribes some material in this section, including some legends with rabbinic parallels, to a Jewish author who revised Nicolas; but Nicolas represents himself as entirely at home when he speaks in defence of the Jews (*Ant.* xvi 31–57; cf. xii 126), his native Damascus had a very large Jewish community with numerous non-Jewish sympathizers, especially among the women (*B.J.* ii 559–61; did this apply to Nicolas' own family?), and the material with rabbinic parallels considered here can therefore be ascribed either to him (so, probably, 421–3, on the swift completion of the sanctuary) or to Josephus himself (so, probably, 425, on the regulated rain, a story appended from 'our fathers').

a synagogue may be pulled down before a replacement is available; just this question concerning the temple is said to have dismayed the people when they heard Herod's plan, according to Josephus, *Ant.* xv 388–9.) (iii) Baba advises that Roman objections can be avoided if a messenger to Rome takes three years on his mission; meanwhile the temple can be pulled down and rebuilt. (iv) Herod does so, and Roman prohibition and reproof arrive too late. (v) He who has never seen the building of Herod has never seen a beautiful building; Herod wanted to plate it with gold, but the sages said that its variegated marble was more beautiful, for it was like the waves of the sea.

Josephus and the rabbinic narrative both include, in differing order, spying by Herod in person; dissent punished by execution, with some exception; friendly converse between Herod and a sage; rapid completion of the temple by Herod; and independently expressed praise for its beauty. The Talmudic Herod is a plebeian and alien usurper, a tyrant and a man of blood—a powerful caricature placarding the condemnations which are mixed with praise in Josephus—but both narratives make Herod's personal spying and repression the back-ground of the temple rebuilding. The stress then falls in the rabbinic narrative, as in Josephus, on the prompt execution of Herod's grand design. Further, when the brilliant marble structure is praised, it is specifically called—in striking contrast with the silences noted above—'the building of Herod'; 'he who has never seen the building of Herod has never seen a beautiful building in his life' (Babylonian Talmud, Baba Bathra, 4a; cf. Sukkah, 51b).

The historical writing of Nicolas or Josephus probably played a part in the origins of this haggadah, through Jewish readers who reacted positively at least to this aspect of the presentation of Herod.[17] That the tradition concerning him cannot have been fixed wholly negatively in tannaitic material known in Babylonia is shown not only by the transmission of this amoraic story in Baba

[17] The swift completion of the building in Baba Bathra 4a need not be a sign of the lateness of the narrative (as held, because of its contrast with the many years occupied by the building of the temple as a whole, by J. Neusner, *The Rabbinic Traditions about the Pharisees before 70*, i (Leiden, 1971), 391); the sanctuary alone is probably in view, as in Josephus. With the proposal made in the text above, compare the argument for the indirect derivation of Hasmonaean narratives in the Babylonian Talmud (notably in Qiddushin 66a and Sanhedrin 19a–b) from Nicolas through Josephus presented by J. Efron, *Studies on the Hasmonaean Period* (ET, SJLA xxxix, Leiden, New York, Copenhagen and Cologne, 1987), 161–97, 215–18 (first read by the present writer after completion of this essay); Efron, 185 notes the similarity in style between Qiddushin 66a and Baba Bathra 3b. A more favourable view of Nicolas' historical value than Efron adopts is taken here, but the relationship between Josephus and the haggadah of the Babylonian Talmud is assessed similarly. The general importance of literary sources in the rabbinic transmission of folk-tales is shown by E. Yassif, 'Traces of Folk Traditions of the Second Temple Period in Rabbinic Literature', *JJS* xxxix (1988), 212–33.

Bathra 3b–4a, but also by the partly parallel Sukkah 51b, where 'the building of Herod' is positively treated in discussion attributed to Babylonian rabbis of a baraitha not mentioning Herod but concluding 'he who has not seen the temple when it was standing [literally, 'in its building'] has never seen a beautiful building'. (M. Eduyoth 8.6, on the method of rebuilding the temple with due reverence, is noteworthy as another tannaitic tradition not mentioning Herod but probably implying a favourable view of Herod's temple.)

In any case, however, it is notable that Baba Bathra 3b–4a includes, together with condemnation of Herod as a tyrannical usurper, warm and specific acknowledgement of his achievement as temple-builder. Approbation is underlined by the claim that the king did this good work on rabbinic advice, and the warmth with which his benefaction is acknowledged contrasts with the critical tone of the application of the story in Num. R. xiv 8, to interpret Num. 7:64 'a sin offering'—because Herod's temple was built by a sinful king. The closeness of the narrative of the building of the sanctuary in Baba Bathra 3b–4a to Josephus, and its divergence at this point from the negative view of Herod found in the context and widely reflected in rabbinic sources, suggests that Nicolas' publicistic account of the warm reception of the work was not without foundation (as could be inferred also from the rabbinic accounts of the regulated rain, the reverent reconstruction, and the beauty of the building), and that the temple continued to be admired specifically as Herod's building.

(c) The temple restoration and attitudes to the house of Herod

Three of the criticisms placarded in Baba Bathra 3b and also found in Josephus would have been blunted in so far as Nicolas' presentation was accepted. First, if the house of Herod had usurped the place of the Hasmonaeans, the new Herodian building made it possible to claim that 'in the hundred and twenty-five years of their reign' the Hasmonaeans 'had been unable to accomplish anything like this for the honour of God' (Herod's speech at Jericho shortly before his death, in Josephus, *Ant.* xvii 162). The themes of the Hasmonaean Hanukkah, as already noted, were subsumed in and (in respect of the new building) surpassed by the Herodian dedication.

Secondly, the dynasty of the Herods might be plebeian, but its lofty ambition, expressed in the temple building, enjoyed the divine favour (Josephus, *B.J.* i 400, cited above). The strength of the objection that the house of Herod was not a royal family is most clear in Josephus' *Antiquities*, where it is more prominent than the charge of Idumaean birth (see *Ant.* xiv 78, 300 (contrast *B.J.* i 241), 403 (king Antigonus), 430=*B.J.* i 313 (the old bandit of Arbela), and 491). Hölscher (n. 16, above) suspected in these passages the hand of the anti-Herodian Jewish reviser of Nicolas, but this description well fits Josephus himself, proud of his Hasmonaean descent (see his criticism of Nicolas, *Ant.* xvi 184–7). That Josephus' view was more widely shared is suggested, however, by its attribution to Antigonus and his bandit partisan, and its appearance in the gibe of 'slave' in Baba Bathra 3b–4a [*'abda*]—where, again, it is more prominent than the charge of alien descent—and in Hullin 139b (cited in I (a), above) [*cheirios*].

Thirdly, however, Hasmonaean propaganda made the house of Herod not only plebeian, but also alien; Herod was a commoner *and* an Idumaean, in Antigonus' answer to Herod's proclamation before the wall of Jerusalem (*Ant.* xiv 403). Idumaean origin, explained here by Josephus as making one a half-Jew, was by no means inconsistent with zealous Jewish patriotism, as observed with regard to the house of Herod by A. Kasher (as cited in n. 18, below); but it was clearly open to suspicion (see Goodman (n. 1, above), 117, 222–3). This relatively mild charge was no doubt strengthened because Herod's mother was Arabian (Josephus, *B.J.* i 181), and was still further heightened when it was combined with the charge of plebeian origin, in a story that Herod's grandfather was a slave of the temple of Apollo in Ascalon.[18]

[18] See Justin Martyr, *Dial.* 52.3; and Africanus to Aristides, in Eusebius, *H.E.* i 6, 2–3 and 7, 11 (cf. *Chronicle*, Olympiad 186; *Dem.* viii 1). Ephrem Syrus, commenting on the Diatessaron, takes the Roman census of Luke 2:1–3 rather than Herodian government as his witness to the fulfilment of Gen. 49:10 (see n. 8, above). This is perhaps because, since the story of Herod and the wise men comes later in the Diatessaron, the census forms the first convenient context for noting that the sceptre had departed from Judah, in accordance with the Pentateuchal testimony. In any case, Ephrem too calls Herod an Ascalonite. See the Syriac comments on Diatessaron 2.17 and 3.7, in L. Leloir, 'Le commentaire d'Éphrem sur le Diatessaron. Quarante et un folios retrouvés', *RB* xciv (1987), 481–518 (490–3, 500–1). At the time of Herod's Arabian campaign the priests said that he was 'an Arabian, uncircumcised', according to the Slavonic Josephus, passage corresponding to Greek *B.J.* i 364–70 (ET in H. St.J. Thackeray, *Josephus* iii (Loeb Classical Library, London and Cambridge, Mass., 1957), 636–8: discussion by R. Eisler, ΙΗΣΟΥΣ ΒΑΣΙΛΕΥΣ ΟΥ ΒΑΣΙΛΕΥΣΑΣ (2 vols., Heidelberg, 1929 and 1930), i, 340–8). Justin and Africanus are discussed by J. Jeremias, *Jerusalem in the Time of Jesus* (ET London, 1969), 331–2 (Africanus' stress on the currency of the story in Greek histories favours derivation from Ptolemy of Ascalon), Schalit, *Herodes*, 677–8 (favouring Jewish anti-Herodian origin), E. M. Smallwood, *The Jews under Roman Rule* (Leiden, 1976, corrected reprint 1981), 19–20, n. 50 (allowing either Jewish or Christian origin), M. Hengel, *Rabbinische Legende und frühpharisäische Geschichte: Schimeon b. Schetach und die achtzig Hexen von Askalon* (Abhandlungen der Heidelberger Akademie der Wissenschaften, Ph.-hist. Klasse, 1984, 2), 43 (following Schalit); and A. Kasher, *Jews, Idumaeans, and Ancient Arabs* (Tübingen, 1988), 62–5, 126–30 (a Christian, not a Jewish story). Since the first appearance of this essay, Ascalonite origin has been used as a key to interpretation of the Herodian dynasty by N. Kokkinos (n. 4, above); an Ascalonite element in Herod the Great's ancestry is credible, and his mixed origin clearly aroused suspicion, but it is less clear that it will in itself have led Herod unsurprisingly to a merely official

In practice, then, these charges might make Herodian rule seem to breach the law of the king in Deut. 17:15, excluding 'a foreigner that is not thy brother' (cf. Isa. 1:26, 'I will restore thy judges as at the first', echoed in the eleventh benediction of the Amidah, and Jer. 30:21); rabbinic sources envisage Deut. 17:15 as troubling both Agrippa I and Herod the Great (Mishnah, Soṭah 7.8, and Babylonian Talmud, Baba Bathra, 3b, both cited above). The Christian connection of this charge with Gen. 49:10 corresponds to Jewish preoccupation with this verse also as a guarantee of indigenous government, as the LXX, Qumran paraphrase and the Targums suggest.[19] (The fourth-century Hegesippus, probably a baptized Jew, takes Idumaean descent to be a reason for regarding Herod as alien (n. 8, above).) Charges on this score were therefore damaging; Herod met them with a claim to descent from the foremost Jews who came out of Babylon to Judaea (Josephus, *Ant.* xiv 9), but the rebuilding was clearly also intended to present the house of Herod as an illustrious Jewish dynasty.

According to a fourth criticism, not reflected in Baba Bathra 3b–4a, Herod favoured non-Jews above Jews in his benefactions. Diaspora Jews probably in fact gained some toleration on account of these benefactions, as argued by A. H. M. Jones (n. 51, below). The adverse view of them reflected in Josephus seems likely to represent Josephus' own opinion; but, once again, his opinion was probably more widely shared. In the speech of the Jewish deputies in Rome after Herod's death he is said to have adorned gentile cities at the expense of cities in his own realm (Josephus, *B.J.* ii 85, parallel with *Ant.* xvii 306). Similarly, in the narrative of his life Herod is said to have treated gentile cities so well that he seemed to be forming a defensive ring to contain his own subjects (*Ant.* xv 326–30), and characteristically to have been the benefactor of gentiles rather than Jews (xvi 158–9, in reflection on his benefactions to the Greek cities), never bestowing any gift worth mentioning on a Jewish city—by

Judaism, as suggested by Kokkinos, *The Herodian Dynasty*, 343–51 (contrast Kasher, as just cited, on Idumaean Jewish patriotism). Justin ascribes the allegation of Ascalonite connections to Jews, but Africanus (with a detailed narrative) to gentile historians; it may perhaps be conjectured that an Ascalonite story, which claimed the great king for the city with a touch of the anti-Jewish 'poison of Ascalon' (Philo's phrase, *Leg. ad Gaium* 205), was known both to Ptolemy the writer on Herod (probably to be identified with Ptolemy of Ascalon) and to anti-Herodian Jews.

19 Posnanski (n. 8, above), 20–31; M. Perez Fernandez, *Tradiciones mesiánicas en el Targum Palestinense* (Valencia and Jerusalem, 1981), 123–7, adds reference to Neofiti and to a Qumran comment on Gen. 49 (4Q252, frg. 6) published by J. M. Allegro, 'Further Messianic References in Qumran Literature', *JBL* lxxv (1956), 174–87 (174–6), and now re-edited by G. J. Brooke in Brooke and others, *Qumran Cave 4.xvii* (DJD xxii, Oxford, 1996), 205–6.

contrast with Agrippa I, who was beneficent towards his own people as well (xix 328–31).

Here his benefactions in Jerusalem are unmentioned; the theatre and amphitheatre (*Ant.* xv 268) could no doubt be classed as unacceptable gifts, but his monument at the tomb of David and Solomon and, above all, the temple are striking omissions. They are mainly explained, perhaps, by the likelihood that the complaint in question stems not from Jerusalem but from Jewish communities near the gentile cities which he adorned (most fully listed by Josephus, *B.J.* i 422–8); his benefactions to Ascalon, for example, were perhaps resented by the mainly Jewish Jamnia, or those to Ptolemais by the neighbouring Galilaeans. It is also true, however, that even his pious Jerusalem benefactions were received coolly by some of the inhabitants. Significantly, the monument to David and Solomon was popularly explained by a story that the king was trying to plunder their tomb, and Herod is represented as complaining that his expenditure on the temple has been ungratefully received (by those involved in the attempt to remove his eagle, *Ant.* xvii 162–3). The efforts to present the temple as a Jewish benefaction will have been correspondingly great.

The differing attitudes to the house of Herod noted above in the Judaean and Galilaean as well as the diaspora Jewish population suggest that such efforts will not have been entirely vain. This view is borne out by Josephus' own transmission of Nicolas' publicity (with annotations), and by its clear echoes in rabbinic literature. There is evidence, also, for a more detached view of the house of Herod, at some distance from the Hasmonaean propaganda of the three criticisms noted first above. Thus, in the Assumption of Moses 6, the Hasmonaean priest kings are criticized equally with Herod the Great, who is condemned for his cruelty but not for plebeian or Idumaean origin or for usurpation; indeed, it is held that 'he will judge them as they deserve', *iudicabit illis quomodo digni erunt* (6:6). This opinion corresponds, as has often been noted, to the advice of the Pharisee Samaias during the siege of Jerusalem that Herod, who was destined to punish them, should be admitted (Josephus, *Ant.* xiv 176). In its stress on divine providence the prophecy in the Assumption of Moses has points of contact not only with the advice attributed to Samaias, but also, despite its more negative expression, with the emphasis on Herod's royal destiny in Nicolas' treatment of the temple. The relatively detached spirit of these judgments seems to reappear later on in the laconic chronicle-tradition transmitted in the name of R. Jose b. Halafta (mid second century); without mentioning Roman rule, or endorsing Hasmonaean propaganda, it covers the period from, the kingdom of Greece to the destruction of the temple simply by noting two Jewish monarchies of equal duration: 'kingdom of the Hasmonaean house, 103 years; kingdom of the house of Herod, 103 years' (Babylonian Talmud, Abodah Zarah, 8b–9a, parallel with B. Ratner (ed.), *Seder Olam Rabba* (Wilna, 1897), 142).

To summarize section I as a whole, Nicolas' history, advancing this presentation of Herod, was taken over by Josephus despite his criticisms (*Ant.* xvi 184–7), and is likely to have been known to other Jews at the end of the first century A.D. The story of the building of the sanctuary, like some other episodes from Nicolas' Hasmonaean and Herodian history, made its way either independently or through Josephus into the rabbinic haggadah. Despite the sensitivity of the issue of the sanctity of the temple, the rabbinic forms of the story have nothing but praise for what is called 'the building of Herod'.

In Nicolas' account the rebuilding shows Herod as a Jewish king piously restoring the temple to its Solomonic glory, and as a victor who has conquered the Jews' traditional enemies and (by aiding the repulse of the Parthians) has contributed to the Augustan peace after civil war, a blessing as important to Judaea as to Italy. He appears, therefore, as a Jewish king touched by the aura of messianism. This aura will have been regularly rediffused by the celebration of his accession day, which was now also a feast of dedication. The temple restoration thereby reinforced the Herodian form of ruler-cult.

The main points of Hasmonaean propaganda were directly opposed to this presentation, and the persistence of favourable comment on Herod's temple in rabbinic tradition, and on Herod as temple-builder in Baba Bathra 4a, suggests that the court publicity reflected by Nicolas was not wholly unheeded. The attestation of views which seem to show some detachment from the Hasmonaean case, together with the evidence that Jews at close quarters with gentiles valued Herodian kings as patrons, helps to indicate a climate of opinion in which the Herodian presentation, supported dramatically by 'the building of Herod', could have found some hearing.

During the period from Nicolas to Josephus Herod's descendants, Agrippa I above all, had followed his footsteps in presenting themselves as Jewish kings and patrons. In Josephus' time Justus of Tiberias composed his Herodian history of the Jewish kings, from Moses to Agrippa II (Photius, *Bibliotheca*, 33). Josephus, by his comparison of Herod the Great with Agrippa I, makes the obvious but important point that the criticisms levelled at Herod the Great were not all thought to apply to his successors. As has now appeared, the temple was a focus in this period for more positive views of the house of Herod as a Jewish monarchy, including what may be called a Herodian messianism.

The significance of the temple in the diaspora, where the collection of the temple tax was a prized and threatened privilege defended by Herod (Josephus, *Ant.* xvi 28), means that the Herodian presentation of the rebuilding will have had an impact throughout the Jewish world. Some evidence for diaspora response to the Herodian rebuilding and the house of Herod will now be reviewed in connection with Persius' lines on 'Herod's days'. It will be suggested that Persius is a further witness to the Herodian festivals with which, as has emerged from Josephus on the temple, a remembrance of the dedication of the sanctuary was now associated.

II. Persius on 'Herod's Days'

(a) Alternative explanations

If 'Herod's days' were indeed days kept in honour of a Herod, the relevant lines from Persius' fifth satire (Persius v 179–84) allow a valuable glimpse of the prestige of Herodian princes among the Jews of Rome towards A.D. 60. On the other hand, Herod may simply be named by Persius as a well-known king who was taken to represent the Jewish people. The passage would then still attest a Herodian reputation for Jewish loyalty; but the 'days' would be days characteristically observed by Jews, perhaps the sabbaths shortly to be mentioned by Persius, rather than specifically Herodian commemorations. These alternatives have long been debated. Three full recent commentaries on the passage opt, after discussion, for identification of the 'days' as sabbaths.[20]

[20] M. Stern, *Greek and Latin Authors on Jews and Judaism*, i (Jerusalem, 1974), 435–7; R. A. Harvey, *A Commentary on Persius* (Leiden, 1981), 177–82; W. Kissel, *Aules Persius Flaccus, Satiren* (Heidelberg, 1990), 744–5.

Independently of this question, the lines are an important and vivid portrayal of a Jewish quarter and a Jewish festal dinner in Rome under Nero, and one of the attestations of the attraction of Jewish rites for Romans. The Herodian problem posed by the passage is reconsidered here in the light of some evidence and discussion which is not to the fore in the commentaries just mentioned, including Herod's dedication of the sanctuary on his accession-day.

Persius v, lines 179–84, run as follows in the editions by W. V. Clausen (Oxford, 1956, 28; 1959 (and revised reissue, 1992), 24):

> … at cum
> Herodis uenere dies unctaque fenestra
> dispositae pinguem nebulam uomuere lucernae
> portantes uiolas rubrumque amplexa catinum
> cauda natat thynni, tumet alba fidelia uino,
> labra moues tacitus recutitaque sabbata palles.

They may be rendered, following A. Pretor with slight adaptations:

> Then again when Herod's days come round, and lamps wreathed with violets and ranged along the greasy window-sills have vomited their murky cloud, when the tail of the tunny overlapping the red dish floats in its sauce and the white jar brims with wine, you move your lips in silence and grow pale over the sabbaths of the circumcised.[21]

These lines of the satire are part of an imaginative Stoic exhortation addressed to the man enslaved by his passions, here pictured in the grip of superstition. Jewish observances form the first example of the strange rites by which he is too readily overawed; further examples follow from the cults of Isis and Cybele. The train of thought is displayed in Dryden's vigorous version:

> Thy Superstition too may claim a share:
> When Flow'rs are strew'd, and Lamps in order plac'd,
> And Windows with Illuminations grac'd
> On *Herod*'s Day; when sparkling Bowls go round,
> And *Tunny*'s Tails in savoury Sauce are drown'd
> Thou mutter'st Pray'rs obscene; nor do'st refuse
> The Fasts and Sabbaths of the curtail'd *Jews*.[22]

[21] A. Pretor, *A. Persii Flacci Satirarum Liber* (new edition, Cambridge, 1907), 86.

[22] *The Satires of Decimus Junius Juvenalis*. Translated into English Verse by Mr Dryden, And several Other Eminent Hands. Together with the *Satires of Aulus Persius Flaccus*. Made English by Mr Dryden (London, 1697), 484–5.

(b) The scholia

The alternative interpretations of *Herodis ... dies* either as Herodian commemorations or as other days known to be observed by Jews first appear in outline in the scholia on Persius. The comments preserved under the name of Cornutus include varying forms of the note:

> hic Herodes apud Iudaeos regnavit temporibus Augusti in partibus Syriae. Herodis ergo diem natalem Herodiani observant. Aut etiam sabbata, quo die lucernas accensas et violis coronatas in fenestris ponunt.[23]

> This Herod reigned among the Jews in the times of Augustus in the region of Syria. The Herodians therefore observe Herod's birthday. Or also the sabbaths, on which day they put in the windows lamps lit and wreathed with violets.

The excerpts from the scholia published by Buecheler and Leo and quoted above do not give a full view of the textual tradition, in part of which, for instance, another comment on Herod's days appears before that just quoted.[24] Five main forms of the text have been distinguished.[25] For this essay I have compared O. Jahn's edition of 1843; the editions of 1520 (representing a different form of text) and 1590 (including the scholia, from a text allied to that followed by Jahn, selected by J. J. Scaliger for publication by P. Pithou in 1585); and editions of scholia from MSS in Prague and Berne.[26] 'Cornutus' preserves much from antiquity, perhaps from commentaries on Persius such as Jerome mentions (*Adversus Rufinum* i 16); but it also includes mediaeval additions, notably from the school of Auxerre in the ninth century.[27]

[23] O. Jahn, F. Buecheler and F. Leo, *A. Persii Flacci D. Iunii Iuvenalis Sulpiciae Saturae* (Berlin, 1910), 54–5.

[24] It explains them, probably by assimilation to the Floralia mentioned in line 178, as 'dies cupidinei'; see Kvicala, as cited in n. 26 below, 37.

[25] Clausen (1956), xiv; P. K. Marshall, 'Persius', in L. D. Reynolds (ed.), *Texts and Transmission: A Survey of the Latin Classics* (Oxford, 1983), 293–5; on the forms of the text of Cornutus, D. M. Robathan, F. E. Cranz, P. O. Kristeller and B. Bischoff, 'A. Persius Flaccus', in F. E. Cranz and P. O. Kristeller (eds.), *Catalogus Translationum et Commentariorum: Mediaeval and Renaissance Latin Translations and Commentaries*, iii (Washington, 1976), 201–312.

[26] O. Jahn, *Auli Persii Flacci Saturarum Liber, cum scholiis antiquis* (Leipzig, 1843) (see the comments by Clausen (1956), xiv); *Auli Flacci Persii Satyrographi Clarissimi opus emendatum* ... (Venice, 1520); *A. Persii Satyrarum Liber i. D. Iunii Iuvenalis Satyrarum Lib. v. Sulpiciae Satyra i. Cum veteribus commentariis nunc primum editis. Ex bibliotheca P. Pithoei IC. cuius etiam Notae quaedam adiectae sunt* (Paris, 1590) (see Robathan and Cranz, 236–7); J. Kvicala, *Scholiorum Pragensium in Persii satiras delectus* (Abhandlungen der königlichen böhmischen Gesellschaft der Wissenschaften, Sechste Folge, vi, 1873–4; Prague, 1873); E. Kurz, *Die Persius-Scholien nach der Bernerhandschriften. III. Die Scholien zu Sat. IV–VI* (Burgdorf, 1889).

[27] Clausen (1956), xxiii–xxiv; J. E. G. Zetzel, 'On the History of Latin Scholia, II: The Commentum Cornuti in the Ninth Century', *Medievalia et Humanistica*, x (1981), 19–31.

In these circumstances any attempt to distinguish ancient from mediaeval material must be tentative, but content and textual variation appear to support the following suggestions.

First, in the extract from the scholia quoted above, the opening comment on Herod wholly lacks New Testament allusion, and places Herod's Jewish kingdom simply in Syria (contrast Luke 1:5 'rex Iudaeae', and the references to Judaea, Jerusalem and the land of Israel in Matt. 2:1–3, 21–2); the wording therefore seems better suited to an ancient *grammaticus* than to a mediaeval commentator.

Secondly, the same is largely but not entirely true of the following comment. Its initial reference to Herod's birthday could derive from the New Testament on 'Herod' (Antipas: Matt. 14:6, Mark 6:21), but it is just as likely to reflect general ancient custom. By contrast, the ensuing mention of 'Herodiani' almost certainly depends on the New Testament or Christian sources. The comment was accordingly ascribed to Carolingian revision by Jahn (1843), cxxxv.

It seems possible, however, that mediaeval accretion may be limited to the word 'Herodiani'. The sequence 'Herodis … Herodiani' is confused in the textual tradition; the order of the proper nouns can be reversed, or a second 'Herodis' can appear instead of 'Herodiani', and the Prague scholia as edited by Kvicala present a text without 'Herodiani', as follows: 'Herodis igitur diem natalem observant, ut etiam sabbata …'.[28] It may be suggested that this text represents an earlier form of the tradition, and that 'Herodiani' is a gloss by a reader familiar with the New Testament; its insertion into the text caused the contusion now evident. Formerly, the subject of the sentence had been 'Iudaei', understood; 'they therefore keep Herod's birthday, as also the sabbaths …'. It is also worth noting, without resting too much weight on a place (the beginning of a clause) perhaps particularly liable to alteration, that the text with 'ut' makes better sense before 'etiam', and may be more original.

To summarize, there is a case for supposing the word 'Herodiani' to be a gloss on a comment which otherwise comes from non-Christian antiquity, and which originally explained 'the days of Herod' as royal birthdays observed by the Jews. It possibly also described their observation as being like that of the sabbaths. The scholiast's reference to the sabbaths, however, was widely understood as an alternative explanation, as the reading with 'aut' attests.

[28] Persius 1520, f.xc, verso 'Herodiani … Herodis'; Kurz, 38; Kvicala, 38.

In this second understanding one may suspect the operation of the tendency often found in commentary to harmonize, and to explain unknowns by identification with knowns. In the scholia on this passage the puzzling 'Herodis … dies' were explained by identification with the known Floralia, mentioned just before (line 178; n. 24, above), as well as with the known sabbaths, mentioned just afterwards.

The scholia therefore already present the two alternative explanations noted under (a), above, although one possibly early form of the comment in question unifies the elements otherwise taken as alternatives. In any case, the reference to the Herodians is more likely to be a gloss on an old comment than a sign that the comment which includes it is Christian. In non-Christian antiquity, therefore, 'the days of Herod' were already explained as royal birthdays, and the identification with the sabbaths was probably also already current, perhaps as a harmonizing explanation.

(c) Later exegesis

How were the alternative explanations presented by later exegetes? By contrast with the scholia, the limited number of renaissance commentators on Persius consulted for this essay incline markedly towards explanation of 'Herod's days' as sabbaths (B. Fontius, A. A. Nebrissensis)[29] or as Jewish festivals in general (Ascensius, Johannes Britannicus, J. B. Plautius, J. Murmellius).[30]

J. J. Scaliger therefore made a fresh beginning when, in his notes on Eusebius' *Chronicle* (1606), he integrated the scholion on Herod's birthday (part of the material he had selected for Pithou) with the patristic and later view that the Herodians honoured Herod as messiah—a view which had perhaps already contributed to the appearance of 'Herodiani' in the scholia.[31] Scaliger urged that, as Persius read in the light of the scholion could be taken to attest, Herodians in the time of Nero still sacrificed in honour of Herod

[29] Persius 1520, f.xc, verso; Persius 1551, 609A; on these commentators see Robathan and Cranz, 265–7, 278.

[30] Persius 1551, 602B, 603D, 606C, 609D; see Robathan and Cranz, 273–8, 283–4.

[31] J. J. Scaliger, *Thesaurus Temporum …, Animadversiones in Chronologica Eusebii* (Leiden, 1606), 150 (on Eusebius' annal for the year 1983 from Abraham); Jerome spoke both for this view of the Herodians (*Adversus Luciferianos*, 23) and against it (in his commentary on Matt. 22:15), and it was favoured by Ps. Tertullian, Epiphanius and others, followed by H. Grotius and other scholars, cited by H. H. Rowley, 'The Herodians in the Gospels', *JTS* xli (1940), 14–27 (15–16). It was also adopted by Cornelius a Lapide (1639) in his comments on Matt. 2:1, 2:15 and 22:16.

the Great and celebrated his birthday. Furthermore, Herod was of Jewish descent, and Christian apologists from Eusebius and Augustine onwards were therefore unjustified in maintaining that Gen. 49:10 was fulfilled when rulers and governors ceased from Judah at the accession of Herod the foreigner (nn. 8 and 18, above).

These arguments evoked lively contradiction, and Scaliger's interpretation of 'Herod's days' won only qualified acceptance in contemporary commentary on Persius in England;[32] but it was adopted by two influential editors of Persius, Isaac Casaubon and Otto Jahn, although each broadened and modified it.

Casaubon, to whom Scaliger inscribed a copy of his work on Eusebius (Cambridge University Library, Adv. a. 3.4), preferred Scaliger's association of the passage with Herod the Great, and compared the Herodian group with the Roman sodalities founded to honour emperors after their deaths by sacrifices and other commemorations (for such associations in Asia Minor see Price (n. 54, below), 118). Casaubon allowed, however, that Agrippa I might have been intended, and that royal accession days could have been observed not just by Herodians, but by Jews in general.[33] This is of course a reasonable inference from the narrative of the dedication of the temple in Josephus.

Jahn, accepting that celebrations of Herod's birthday by Herodians seem to be intended, added that Persius could hardly be expected to show accurate knowledge, and that Herod's name was particularly familiar to Roman readers (Jahn (1843), 208). These additional considerations are important among those which have commended the alternative interpretation of 'Herod's days' as a reference to characteristically Jewish observances.

More recent exponents of the 'days' as birthdays or accession days include J. Conington and A. Pretor (echoing Jahn's caution), among commentators on Persius;[34] W. Schmidt, writing on birthdays in antiquity (with reference, again,

[32] T. Farnaby, *Iunii Iuvenalis et Auli Persii Flacci Satyrae Cum Annotationibus* (4th edn., London, 1633), 184, *ad loc.* (the days are either those observed by the nation obedient to Herod, the Jews, or else Herod's birthday, celebrated like an accession day; the comment is reproduced unchanged from the first edition, London, 1612); J. Bond, *Auli Persii Flacci Satyrae Sex. Cum posthumis Commentariis ...* (London, 1614), 119, *ad loc.* (paraphrasing line 179 as referring to the sabbaths of the Jews and Herod's birthday). Bond therefore combined Scaliger's proposal with the alternative interpretation, but Farnaby left the question open.

[33] I. Casaubon, *De rebus sacris et ecclesiasticis exercitationes xvi* (London, 1614), 48; I. Casaubon, *Auli Persi Flacci Satirarum Liber* (3rd edn., London, 1647), 458–9, *ad loc.*

[34] J. Conington, *The Satires of A. Persius Flaccus* (2nd edn., Oxford, 1874), 113; Pretor, 86–7.

to associations for their observance);[35] F.-J. Dölger, in the fifth volume of his work on the symbolism of the fish (but in the second volume he had thought differently);[36] and among writers on Jewish history and the New Testament, H. Willrich (in a relatively full treatment), A. Momigliano (in his pre-war work), A. Schalit, H. W. Hoehner and E. Bammel.[37]

These interpretations have throughout been flanked, however, by explanations of the days not as Herodian festivals, but as other days characteristically observed by Jews. Thus M. de Roa, writing just before Scaliger's Eusebian study appeared, was followed and echoed later in the seventeenth century by John Spencer when he preferred to take the phrase as an allusion to Jewish holidays and sabbaths; for Herod's fame as a representative of Judaism de Roa cited the statement that Pompey conferred the high-priesthood on Herod, in Strabo, *Geog.* xvi 2, 46.[38] Then Scaliger was vigorously opposed by his Jesuit adversary N. Serarius, who gave his main attention to the questions raised concerning Christian tradition that Herod was non-Jewish, but also emphasized that the days mentioned by Persius could be understood as sabbaths and festivals, especially Tabernacles and Purim; for the name of Herod as standing for Jewish piety in Roman satire he compared Juvenal vi 159 on the barefoot celebration of sabbaths by kings in Judaea, in the context of a reference to Agrippa II.[39]

35 W. Schmidt, *Geburtstag im Altertum* (Religionsgeschichtliche Versuche und Vorarbeiten vii.1, Giessen, 1908), 70 (Roman Jews formed a kind of *collegium*), 130.

36 F.-J. Dölger, ΙΧΘΥΣ (5 vols., i Rome, 1910, ii–iii Münster i. W., 1922, iv Münster, 1927, v Münster, 1943), ii, 94 and nn. 8–9, 95, 543 (Persius describes a sabbath fish-dinner, which gives a good idea of the Diaspora Jewish *cena pura*); v, 384–5 (Persius says that the Jewish community ate fish at their festal meal on Herod's birthday in Rome).

37 Willrich, *Das Haus des Herodes*, 96–7, 180 (not cited in the commentaries by Stern and Harvey (n. 20, above)); Momigliano, 'Herod of Judaea', 332 and n. 1 (a feast called after Herod the Great, perhaps a birthday or accession day); Schalit, *Herodes*, 480, n. 1128 (following Schmidt, as cited in n. 35, above, and asking additionally if the Roman Jewish *collegium* may have Herod Antipas in view); H. W. Hoehner, *Herod Antipas* (Cambridge, 1972), 160–1, n. 5 (the proverbially magnificent birthdays of the Herods); E. Bammel, 'Romans 13', in Bammel and Moule (cited in n. 1, above), 365–83 (368, n. 22 (the celebration of Herod's birthday by the Jews of Rome)). A difference between Momigliano's two groups of writings on Jewish history, between 1930–35 (when he affirmed the importance of Hellenism within the Jewish community) and after 1970 (when he minimized that importance) is brought out and discussed by F. Parente, reviewing A. Momigliano, *Pagine ebraiche a cura di Silvia Berti*, in *Quaderni di Storia*, Year xv, no. 29 (1989), 171–8; the decision on *Herodis … dies* reflects the standpoint discerned by Parente in the earlier work; see further Rajak, 'Momigliano and Judaism', 103–6.

38 M. de Roa, *Singularium locorum ac rerum libri v … de die natali sacra at profana* (Lyons, 1604), 187–8; J. Spencer, *De Legibus Hebraeorum Ritualibus et earum Rationibus* (2 vols., Cambridge, 1727), ii, 1123 (book iv, chapter 6, first published in this edition; Spencer died in 1693).

39 N. Serarius, *Rabbini et Herodes … Adversus Ios. Scaligeri Eusebianas Annotationes, et Io. Drusii Responsionem* (Mainz, 1607), 290–1.

Many interpretations of this kind, however, identify the days more precisely either as sabbaths or as the days of Hanukkah. The lights and the fish menu described in lines 180–3 suit both. Sabbath lights specified as such were gently mocked by Persius' contemporary, Seneca (*Ep.* xcv 47), and Hanukkah lights are attested in Josephus (*Ant.* xii 325) and the Mishnah (Baba Kamma vi 6). Fish was a festal delicacy, especially but not only eaten on the sabbath (Mishnah, Bezah ii 1; Tosefta, Bezah ii 1 (colias for the festival)).

The sabbath identification is commended by the specific mention of sabbaths in line 184. C. Vitringa, amassing evidence on sabbath lights, accordingly held that the scholiast was deceived in his reference to birthdays; Herod (Agrippa I) was clearly mentioned as a type of the Jewish people, and Persius alluded to the sabbath lights and meal.[40] Vitringa was cited and followed by E. Schürer; in the revised English translation of Schürer's work the specific identification of 'Herodis … dies' as sabbaths has been dropped, but the passage is still treated as a description of the sabbath, and more recent historians who follow suit without discussion include M. D. Goodman and N. Kokkinos.[41] This identification of the days is widespread. It was adopted in Latin lexicography by Lewis and Short (but not by P. G. W. Glare);[42] among commentators on Persius, by G. Nemethy, T. F. Brunner, R. A. Harvey and W. Kissel;[43] in study of the Jews of Rome, by A. Berliner, H. J. Leon and R. Penna;[44] in study of the sabbath, by L. Doering;[45] in study of Jewish symbolism, by F.-J. Dölger in his earlier discussion (n. 36, above), and by E. R. Goodenough (who favours connection with the sabbath *cena pura*, but leaves open the possibility that Herod's birthday is intended);[46] and in collections of texts on the Jews

[40] C. Vitringa, *De Synagoga Vetere libri tres* (2 vols., Franeker, 1696), i, 194–5 (book i, part 1, chapter 9).

[41] Schürer, *Geschichte*, iii (3rd edn., Leipzig, 1909), 166, n. 49; ET, revised by M. Black, G. Vermes, F. Millar, M. D. Goodman and P. Vermes, iii. 1 (Edinburgh, 1986), 161, n. 60; Goodman. 'Judaea', in *Cambridge Ancient History, Second Edition*, x (1996), 739, n. 3; Kokkinos, *The Herodian Dynasty*, 349.

[42] C. T. Lewis and C. Short (eds.), *A Latin Dictionary* (Oxford, 1879), 850, and P. G. W. Glare (ed.). *Oxford Latin Dictionary* (Oxford, 1982), 792, s.v. Herodes.

[43] G. Nemethy, *A. Persii Flacci Satirae* (Budapest, 1903), 302, and *Symbolae Exegeticae ad Persii Satiras* (Budapest, 1924), 12, no. xxi (supporting the interpretation from Juvenal vi 159, as Serarius did; see n. 39, above); T. F. Brunner, 'A Note on Persius 5.179ff.', *California Studies in Classical Antiquity*, i (1968), 63–4; Harvey and Kissel, as cited in n. 20, above.

[44] A. Berliner, *Geschichte der Juden in Rom von der ältesten Zeit bis zur Gegenwart* (2 vols. in 1, Frankfurt am Main, 1893), i, 101–2 (noting that others identify the days as Hanukkah or a Herodian festival); H. J. Leon, *The Jews of Ancient Rome* (Philadelphia, 1960), 38; R. Penna, 'Les juifs à Rome au temps de l'apôtre Paul', *NTS* xxviii (1982), 321–47 (324).

[45] L. Doering, *Schabbat* (TSAJ 78, Tübingen, 1999), 285, 288 n. 24.

[46] E. R. Goodenough, *Jewish Symbols in the Greco-Roman Period* (13 vols., New York, 1953–68), i (1953), 36; ii (1953), 106; v (1956), 42–3.

from Greek and Roman sources, by T. Reinach, M. Stern, M. Whittaker and M. H. Williams.[47]

The identification of the days as the eight days of Hanukkah, commemorating the Maccabaean dedication of the temple, can be made without qualification (as by H. Vogelstein, n. 48, below). It has also been suggested, however, that the 'days of Herod' marked a feast of dedication with Herodian aspects. Thus J. de Voisin held that either Hanukkah, or the feast of dedication of Herod's temple, might be in view; J. Derenbourg supposed that the festival was Hanukkah, but that Herod, well known at Rome, was named by Persius instead of the Hasmonaeans; and S. Krauss, criticizing the sabbath explanation as forced, ingeniously argued that under Herod the Hasmonaean Hanukkah was renamed the feast of Herod—the title echoed in Persius—and that in response the lights of Hanukkah were introduced, to preserve the officially discouraged recollection of the Hasmonaeans.[48] O. S. Rankin, examining Krauss' theory, could not agree that the sabbath explanation was forced, especially in view of the difficulty of Persius; he also noted that a Herodian origin for Hanukkah lights seems incompatible with 2 Maccabees, but he allowed that the construction of Herod's temple could have affected the understanding of Hanukkah significantly.[49] Section I, above, has offered some confirmation for the view shared by Krauss and Rankin, that Herod's temple stood for a dynastic outlook at odds with the Hasmonaean emphasis of Hanukkah; it has seemed likely that Herod's accession day also became a new feast of dedication.

This review of interpretation has underlined reasons which incline many to find ordinary rather than unfamiliar Jewish observances reflected in Persius here. He specifically mentions the sabbaths; and the lights and the fish dinner, so vividly described, fit well-known sabbath and festival customs. These points are emphasized by Stern, Harvey and Kissel (n. 20, above). It is held, in interpretation of the passage on these lines, that Persius' Jewish knowledge

[47] T. Reinach, *Textes d'auteurs grecs et romains relatifs au Judaïsme* (Paris, 1895), 264–5; Stern, as cited in n. 20, above; M. Whittaker, *Jews and Christians: Graeco-Roman Views* (Cambridge, 1984), 71; M. H. Williams, *The Jews among the Greeks and Romans: a Diasporan Sourcebook* (London, 1998), 55–6, no. II.115.

[48] H. Vogelstein and P. Rieger, *Geschichte der Juden in Rom* (2 vols., Berlin, 1895–6), i, 81; J. de Voisin, *Theologia Iudaeorum* (Paris, 1647), 94 (book i, chapter 5); J. Derenbourg, *Essai sur l'histoire et la géographie de la Palestine, d'après les Thalmuds et les autres sources rabbiniques* (Paris, 1867), 165, n. 1; S. Krauss, 'La fête de Hanoucca', *REJ* xxx (1895), 24–43, 204–19 (36).

[49] O. S. Rankin, *The Origins of the Festival of Hanukkah* (Edinburgh, 1930), 80–6; this full discussion was not mentioned in the subsequent treatments of 'Herod's days' cited in the present essay.

was probably limited; but that Greek and Roman perception of the Herods, as attested in Strabo on Herod's high-priesthood and in Juvenal on royal sabbaths (cited by de Roa, Serarius and Nemethy, see nn. 38, 39 and 43, above), would have allowed Persius to take Herod as representing the Jews and Jewish custom.

On the other hand, this perception is not very different from that probably held by diaspora Jews who valued royal patronage. Those who explain the days as Herodian birthdays or accession days accordingly view them against the background of Jewish support for the house of Herod, especially in the Diaspora. The history of study has shown how readily the observance of Herodian days would fit the conditions of Jewish life in the Herodian age. Thus the probable importance of contemporary ruler cults for an understanding of the Jews' response to their monarchy was indicated by Scaliger and Casaubon. The Roman Jews who kept the days might be Herodians (Scaliger) or the community in general (Casaubon), as in the probably later and earlier forms, respectively, of the scholion discussed in section II (b), above. The possible significance of Herod's newly-dedicated temple in connection with the days emerges from the explanations of de Voisin and Krauss. Discussion of the scholion also showed that the sabbath explanation may in early instances have owed much to the practice of explaining the unknown by identification with a nearby known.

The understanding of 'Herod's days' as Herodian commemorations which is suggested below draws on the presentation of Herod's accession day, in section I, above, as a dedication festival and a focus of Herodian court theology. The interpretation offered here is a modified form of that expounded most fully by H. Willrich. His arguments will now be reviewed with some additions. Four aspects of the background are thereby considered in turn, as follows: Jewish—gentile relations, the bearing of gentile dynastic celebrations on Herodian observances, the Jews in Rome, and the setting in Roman satire.

(d) 'Herod's Days' as royal birthdays or accession days

Willrich (as cited in n. 37, above) set the lines in Persius, first, against the general background of Jewish-gentile tension. Roman Jewish observance of Herodian birthdays or accession-days (probably monthly, in the usual Hellenistic and Roman manner) would be natural, he urged, as part of a bid for official protection; we know that Herod the Great celebrated his accession-day, and that Roman Jews organized themselves in synagogues of 'Augustesians' and 'Agrippesians'; they are likely to have paid their respects to their patrons, including the house of Herod, just as in 13 B.C. the Jews of Berenice in the Libyan Pentapolis made a decree to honour M. Tittius at each new moon.[50]

The Roman synagogues mentioned are perhaps more likely to be associations of slaves and freedmen from the households of Augustus and M. Agrippa, but the general importance of the motive suggested by Willrich has been shown more recently from Josephus' procedure in recording Jewish privileges; Herod's defence of the Ionian Jews (Josephus *Ant.* xvi 28) was noted at the end of section I, above, and it has been plausibly suggested that his benefactions to Greek cities (continued by his successors) played an important part in gaining toleration for diaspora Jews.[51] Graeco-Roman observance of royal birthdays and accession days in the manner to which Willrich alluded is documented by Schürer and his revisers with evidence including the Rosetta Stone (196 B.C., on the monthly birthday and accession-day of Ptolemy V) and 2 Macc. 6:7 (the monthly birthday of Antiochus IV), and, for the Herods, Mark 6:21, on Antipas, and Josephus, *Ant.* xix 321, on Agrippa I (birthdays), and Josephus, *Ant.* xv 423, on Herod the Great, cited above (accession-day).[52] How naturally *Herodis ... dies* can be taken in this sense appears from a law of Valentinian II, Theodosius I and Arcadius (7 August 389) in which, after a note of special days (from the Kalends to the Easter season and Sundays), they require like reverence 'for our days too' (*nostris etiam diebus*)—then explained as the days on which they were born or began to reign (Theodosian Code ii 8, 19).[53]

[50] καθ' ἑκάστην σύνοδον καὶ νουμηνίαν, 'at each [?sabbath] assembly and new moon'; see lines 16–17 of the text republished with commentary by J. M. Reynolds in J. A. Lloyd (ed.), *Excavations at Sidi Khrebish, Benghazi (Berenice)*, i (Supplements to Libya Antiqua, 5, 1977), 244–5, no. 17, and in G. Lüderitz, *Corpus jüdischer Zeugnisse aus der Cyrenaica* (Wiesbaden, 1983), 151–5, no. 71; the date 13 B.C. is supported, and the situation is connected with the hostility (including threats to the temple tax) indicated in Josephus, *Ant.* xvi 160–1, 169, by M. W. Baldwin Bowsky, 'M. Tittius Sex.f. Aem. and the Jews of Berenice (Cyrenaica)', *American Journal of Philology* cviii (1987), 495–510. (I am grateful to Dr J. N. B. Carleton Paget, of Peterhouse, Cambridge, for drawing my attention to this article.) The importance of new moon festivals in the diaspora at the beginning of the Christian era is shown by T. C. G. Thornton, 'Jewish New Moon Festivals, Galatians 4:3–11 and Colossians 2:16', *JTS* N.S. xl (1989), 97–100.

[51] Schürer, *Geschichte*, revised ET, iii.1, 96; T. Rajak, 'Was There a Roman Charter for the Jews?', *JRS* lxxiv (1984), 107–23 (122–3); A. H. M. Jones, *The Herods of Judaea* (Oxford, 1938, corrected reprint 1967), 104–5.

[52] Schürer, Vermes, Millar and Black, i (Edinburgh, 1973), 347–8 (part of n. 26).

[53] P. Krueger, *Codex Theodosianus* (2 vols., Berlin, 1923 and 1926), i, 65–6.

Secondly, Willrich asked if there were Jewish parallels for a relatively short-lived celebration of the kind proposed, and how it might have related to various kings of the house of Herod. He pointed out that the observance of Herod's birthday or accession-day by Jews in Rome could be compared with the localized or relatively short-lived celebration of other Jewish festivals, like the feast of the Septuagint in Alexandria. 'Herod's days' in the time of Persius, who will hardly have written this passage long before 60, would have been a special continuance by Roman Jews of festal days of Herod the Great.

This identification of the Herod in question was not certain, in Willrich's view, but he preferred it. He noted that Agrippa I and II, who were significant for the Jews in Rome, seem to be excluded because they did not use the dynastic name (although others applied it at least to Agrippa I; see Acts 12:1); and that Herod of Chalcis, likewise prominent in Rome (Josephus, *Ant.* xx 13–16, 103–4; *B.J.* ii 217, 221–3), was less important than Herod the Great. The latter's unpopularity might seem to speak against the observance of his days after his death, but this consideration was outweighed, in Willrich's judgment, by the likelihood that the days had the capacity for survival often found in festivals, and that their discontinuance might have seemed an affront to the house of Herod; moreover, Herod's friendship with Augustus would have benefited the Roman Jews particularly.

Here Willrich seems justified in stressing both the likelihood that Roman Jews honoured the house of Herod, and the uncertain identification of the particular Herod of *Herodis ... dies*. Nevertheless, the argument that days in honour of Herod the Great were observed after his death and are mentioned here could be rested not only (with Willrich) on his friendship with Augustus, but also (following the lead of de Voisin and Krauss) on his building of the temple. The completion of the sanctuary on his accession-day will have made the day thereafter also a feast of dedication, an addition which might be expected to strengthen the impetus of the day. Further, the continuation of honour to a monarch after his death is known (as already noted by Scaliger and Casaubon, nn. 31 and 33, above) in the royal cults of the Graeco-Roman world, notably where they are connected with dynasties rather than individuals.[54]

[54] F. W. Walbank, 'Monarchies and monarchic ideas', in F. W. Walbank, A. E. Astin, M. W. Frederiksen and R. M. Ogilvie (eds.), *The Cambridge Ancient History, Second Edition*, vii.1, *The Hellenistic World* (Cambridge, 1984), 97–8, on Ptolemaic and Seleucid dynastic cults; S. R. F. Price, *Rituals and Power: The Roman imperial cult in Asia Minor* (Cambridge, 1984), 61–2, 118, on second-century celebration of the birthdays of Augustus and Livia.

The theory of such cultus as acknowledgement of exceptional benefactions is sympathetically outlined by Nicolas of Damascus (Fragment 125) and by Philo (*Leg. ad Gaium* 149–51), and Jews will have expected to render to their own royal benefactors, as Alexandrian Jews did to the emperor, 'all the honours which the laws permitted' (Philo, *Flacc.* 97).[55] In this context, it would not be surprising if Jews continued to keep the festal days of the founder of the Herodian dynasty and the rebuilder of the temple after his death.

Such honours commonly ceased, however, when the monarch died;[56] moreover, hostility to Herod the Great after his death was expressed by the throngs of Roman Jews who supported the Judaean embassy of opposition to Archelaus' succession (Josephus, *B.J.* ii 80–3). Further, accession days are replaced without affront by the equivalent days of an accredited successor. It is therefore perhaps rather more likely that *Herodis ... dies* should be days of later Herodian kings. The festal days of Herod the Great had the lustre of the founder of the dynasty and the re-founder of the temple; his successors took over this aureole with the dynastic name 'Herod', which was used by Archelaus, Antipas and Herod of Chalcis, and was applied to Agrippa I. Their festal days, too, will have been 'Herod's days'. About the year 50 Agrippa II succeeded Herod of Chalcis as protector of the temple, and it may be suggested that his birthdays or accession-days, inheriting associations with the house of Herod and with Herod's temple, were still known when Persius wrote, perhaps ten years later, by the traditional name of Herod's days.

Thus far, then, Willrich's indication of Jewish—gentile tension as a strong motive for Jewish honour to Jewish kings has been endorsed, and it has been suggested that, although there is much to be said for the proposal that the 'days' belong to Herod the Great, it is perhaps somewhat more likely that, at the time of Persius, they should have been days of the reigning Agrippa II.

A third element of Willrich's case was his argument that the circumstances of the Jews in Rome in particular favoured his interpretation. To those already noted—their organization under the names of powerful patrons (or of the households to which they belonged), and their benefit from the friendship

[55] That the panegyric on Augustus in Philo, *Leg. ad Gaium* 143–7 derives from a composition used in the Alexandrian synagogues is envisaged, following W. Weber, by E. Bammel, *Jesu Nachfolger: Nachfolgeüberlieferungen in der Zeit des frühen Christentums* (Heidelberg, 1988), 19.

[56] Price, *Rituals*, 61–2, with regard to Roman emperors.

of Augustus and Herod—he added the presence of Herodian supporters in Rome, as in Puteoli.

This consideration opens the larger question of the importance of the gentile element among Herod's supporters. Willrich himself emphasized that, although Greeks were undoubtedly prominent in Herod's court and following, Greek or Roman names might cover Jewish personages, and he evidently held that the Roman supporters were mainly Jews.[57]

Here Willrich perhaps thought especially of references in Josephus to Herod's 'friends', in the sense of close political adherents, in connection with Herodian princes in Rome.[58] The passages include Josephus, *Ant.* xvi 87 (Herod's correspondence with all his friends made his son Antipater well known in Rome); *B.J.* i 602–6, paralleled in *Ant.* xvii 80 (Herod's friends in Rome induced by Antipater and his friends to accuse Archelaus and Philip); and *B.J.* ii 104–5, paralleled in *Ant.* xvii 328–31 (Herod's friends support the welcome of the youth who posed as Mariamme's son Alexander in Puteoli and Rome). Willrich will also have had in mind, however, two further passages related to these, on the Roman lodgings of the princes: *Ant.* xv 343, on the true Alexander and his brother in Rome at the house of Pollio, 'one of those most zealous for Herod's friendship'; and *Ant.* xvii 20–1, on the Roman nurture of Archelaus, Antipas and Philip—in the case of the two former (Philip's host is not mentioned) 'by a certain Jew', according to B. Niese's conjecture Ἰουδαίῳ in xvii 20, where MSS give ἰδίῳ, 'by a member of [the royal] household'.

In the case of Alexander and Aristobulus (*Ant.* xv 343), Willrich held that, especially since Herod would hardly have offended his Jewish subjects by lodging them with a gentile, their host Pollio was more likely to be a Jewish Herodian supporter than (as W. Otto had argued) Virgil's patron C. Asinius Pollio, who was consul when Herod received the title of king.[59] Willrich's position on Pollio corresponds to his view that the Roman friends in general were wealthy Jews, as might be suggested by their part in the welcome of the

[57] Willrich, 101–2, 181; for Greek-speaking Jews connected with the Herodian family, see T. Rajak, *Josephus* (London, 1983), 53–5; courtiers of Herod the Great usually taken to be non-Jews, but open to reassessment in the light of Willrich's remark, include the tutors Andromachus and Gemellus (Josephus, *Ant.* xvi 241–3; Schürer, *Geschichte*, ET revised by Black, Vermes and Millar, i, 311).

[58] Ptolemaic, Seleucid and Roman imperial usage of the title 'Friend' is documented by E. Bammel, ΦΙΛΟΣ ΤΟΥ ΚΑΙΣΑΡΟΣ, *TLZ* lxxvii (1952), cols. 205–10.

[59] Willrich, 184–5, against W. Otto, 'Herodes', *PW* viii, Supp. 2 (1913), cols. 69 and 103.

false Alexander. Apart from general considerations, however, an identification with Asinius Pollio is discouraged, as Willrich noted, by the fact that Josephus himself makes no explicit connection between the princes' host and Asinius Pollio, whom he has mentioned twice in the previous book of the *Antiquities* (xiv 138 (through Strabo, as 'Asinius') and 389), whereas he might have been expected to underline the distinction of Herod's friend.[60] Further, it can be asked whether Asinius Pollio, who was not a close adherent of Augustus and withdrew from politics under the principate, would have been chosen by Herod or Augustus as the princes' host or described by Josephus as zealous for friendship with Herod; for Herod had indeed formerly, like Asinius Pollio, been loyal to Caesar and Antony, but had now, unlike Pollio, transferred his allegiance to Augustus.[61]

These particular objections probably do not exclude Asinius Pollio altogether. Josephus can distinguish between individuals of the same name who might otherwise be confused (n. 60, above), but there is no such distinction here. The objection derived from Asinius Pollio's personal detachment from Augustus retains some force, but it must be balanced against the possibility that he was, as L. H. Feldman urged, sympathetic with Judaism; this might be suggested by the subject-matter of the Fourth Eclogue, which Virgil addressed to him, by Herod's advancement during his consulate, and by his patronage of the Alexandrian historian Timagenes, who gave a friendly description of the Hasmonaean Aristobulus I.[62] Otto's identification of Asinius Pollio as Herod's friend was independently defended, however, by Schalit. He questioned whether a Jewish host would have been viewed as of sufficient eminence to be named in this context, which emphasizes the distinction of the princes' reception (their

[60] Josephus habitually, however, points out possible confusions arising from recurrences of the same name, as is noted in connection with Volumnius (with the example of *Ant.* xvii 343, on Archelaus and his steward Archelaus) by E. Bammel, 'Die Rechtsstellung des Herodes', reprinted from *ZDPV* lxxxiv (1968), 73–9, in E. Bammel, *Judaica: Kleine Schriften* I (Tübingen, 1986), 3–9 (3, n. 2).

[61] The career and outlook of Asinius Pollio are described by R. Syme, *The Roman Revolution* (Oxford, 1939, reprinted 1985), 5–6, 291, 482–6, 512, and are likewise taken to be inconsistent with this identification by M. Grant, *Herod the Great* (London, 1971), 145. The force of Willrich's argument is perhaps recognized in the doubts concerning the identification expressed by E. Groag and A. Stein, *Prosopographia Imperii Romani* (2nd edn., Berlin and Leipzig, 1933), A 1241, 253; Asinius Pollio had been regarded as the host in the first edition.

[62] L. H. Feldman, 'Asinius Pollio and His Jewish Interests', *Transactions of the American Philological Association* lxxxiv (1953), 73–80, followed by Stern, *Authors*, i, 213; G. Zecchini, 'Asinio Pollione', *ANRW* ii 30, 2 (1982), 1265–96 (1279–81); and D. R. Schwartz, *Agrippa I*, 43–4 (further literature). Timagenes is Strabo's authority in a description of Aristobulus quoted by Josephus, *Ant.* xiii 319 and taken by Stern, *Authors*, i, 223 to show that (by contrast with other Alexandrian writers) Timagenes was not hostile to the Jews.

admission, also, to the house of Augustus himself is heavily stressed).[63] Once again, doubt might be prompted by Asinius Pollio's detachment, but Schalit's observation would also suit R. Syme's tentative suggestion that the friend was Augustus' unspeakable intimate Vedius Pollio.[64] Asinius Pollio, the Pollio last mentioned by Josephus, cannot be ruled out, however, given the consideration from Augustus which his eminence enjoyed, despite his political detachment. He remains on the whole perhaps the strongest candidate for identification with this otherwise unspecified Pollio.[65] In any case, Schalit's discernment of the aims of the passage makes it likely on the whole that the host belonged to the gentile rather than the Jewish element of the Roman friends.

In the case of Malthace's sons Archelaus and Antipas, Niese's conjecture Ἰουδαίῳ at Josephus, *Ant.* xvii 20, noted above, would make their host unambiguously Jewish; but ἰδίω_ι, the reading of the MSS, makes good sense if rendered 'a member of the household', is supported by the Latin, and should probably be followed. It is then an open question whether this high-ranking Herodian domestic, who was perhaps also the host of Philip, was Jewish, gentile, or partly Jewish; but in any case, he was a member of the household rather than one of the group of friends.

Thus far, then, the friends of Herod in Rome appear as a mixed Jewish–gentile group. To move beyond the considerations noted by Willrich, Roman Jews of less wealth and standing connected with the house of Herod can be discerned with fair likelihood in Rom. 16:10–11, where 'those of Aristobulus' perhaps belong to the household of a Herodian prince, the brother or the son of Herod of Chalcis; the uncle and the nephew Aristobulus are both mentioned in Josephus, *B.J.* ii 221, and an Aristobulus who is probably the nephew is mentioned with Herod of Chalcis in Claudius' letter of 45 to Jerusalem, as reproduced in *Ant.* xx 13. Paul's kinsman Herodion, who is mentioned in Romans immediately afterwards (16:11), is probably a former Herodian slave, perhaps from this same household.[66]

[63] Schalit, *Herodes*, 413–4, n. 936; for the court-like overtones of admission to Augustus, see Syme, *Roman Revolution*, 385.

[64] R. Syme, 'Who was Vedius Pollio?', reprinted from *JRS* li (1961), 23–30 in R. Syme, *Roman Papers* (ed.) E. Badian, ii (Oxford, 1979), 518–29 (529).

[65] Goodman, 'Judaea', 742, n. 6 regards Asinius Pollio as probable, but Vedius Pollio as also possible.

[66] J. B. Lightfoot, *Saint Paul's Epistle to the Philippians* (4th edn., reprinted London, 1908), 174–5, followed by C. E. B. Cranfield, *A Critical and Exegetical Commentary on the Epistle to the Romans*, ii (Edinburgh, 1979), 791–2 (regarding the uncle as the likeliest of three candidates for the identification), and P. Lampe, *Die stadtrömischen Christen in den ersten beiden Jahrhunderten* (Tübingen, 1987), 135–6, 148 (leaving the precise identification open).

Since the first appearance of this essay a further instance of Herodion as a Jewish name in Rome has been identified by D. Noy (acknowledging a suggestion by M. H. Williams). The name is found, spelt as Ἡροδίων, in a probably third- or fourth-century inscription on marble from the Jewish catacomb of the Vigna Randanini (CIJ 173); the text, which was formerly discussed as possible evidence for a synagogue 'of the Herodians', is republished by Noy on the basis of his own reading (1993) and new interpretation as JIWE ii 292. This identification is rejected by N. Kokkinos because of unexpected spelling (Omicron for Omega), late date, and wholly Jewish context;[67] but these arguments do not seem strong. For the spelling, compare Omicron for Omega in the dative of the name Theodora (Θεοδόρῃ) in a contemporary and comparably carefully lettered marble plaque from the same catacomb (CIJ 83 = JIWE ii 206). For the date, compare the continuation of the Jewish use of the name Herod into the fourth century, attested in inscriptions at Capernaum and Beth She'arim, as noted above (n. 7). On the context, note that these inscriptions also come from Jewish contexts (synagogue and catacomb, respectively). It seems likely, therefore, that just as the name Herod could recur in Jewish contexts in post-Herodian Galilee, so Herodion could recur in a Jewish context in Rome.

Herodian connections are also possible in the synagogue of the Volumnesians (attested in Roman inscriptions including CIJ 402 = JIWE ii 100), if it takes its name from Herod's friend Volumnius, procurator of Syria in 8 b.c.[68] Of the individual Roman Jews named in literary sources outside the New Testament (eight from the Herodian period are listed by H. Solin), only Livia's slave Acme and Josephus himself have known connections with the house of Herod;[69] but Solin's list does not include the members of the Herodian family who lived or stayed for long periods in Rome. These data give at least some indication of sections of the Jewish population, notably slaves or freedmen of households with a Herodian connection, where the friends of Herod might find support.

[67] Kokkinos, *The Herodian Dynasty*, 313, n. 169.

[68] The Volumnesian identification is accepted by Penna (as cited in n. 44, above), 327, but judged dubious by Smallwood, *Roman Rule*, 138, because Volumnius is not known to have been a benefactor of the Jews; but this consideration is not so strong if the synagogue members are thought to have belonged to his household. He was a supporter of Herod, as shown (with emphasis on Josephus, *Ant.* xvi 269), by Bammel, 'Rechtsstellung' (as cited in n. 58, above), n. 2; and as a procurator of Syria he could have returned to Rome with Jewish slaves in his household. For further literature and discussion see now Noy's commentary on JIWE ii 100.

[69] H. Solin, 'Juden und Syrer im westlichen Teil der römischen Welt', *ANRW* ii. 29.2 (1983), 587–789, 1222–49 (658–9); Acme was executed by Augustus for intriguing with Antipater to bring about the death of Herod's sister Salome (Josephus, *B.J.* i 661).

The Roman Jews in general were known in the city for their public demonstrations.[70] Two of these have a recorded connection with the house of Herod. At the second hearing before Augustus to determine Herod's will more than eight thousand Jews thronged to the temple of Apollo on the Palatine to stand by the Judaean embassy opposing Archelaus (Josephus, *B.J.* ii 80–3, parallel with *Ant.* xvii 300–3). The friends of Herod and his sons failed to muster popular support on this occasion, no doubt because they were divided, as the Herodian family was (*B.J.* ii 81). It was quite otherwise on the occasion soon afterwards when the friends, as already noted, supported the enthusiastic reception of the false Alexander. The young prince, as he was thought to be, was borne in a litter with a royal retinue through the narrow streets, perhaps in the quarter (probably in Trastevere) described by Persius, amid the acclamations of vast crowds of Jews (Josephus, *B.J.* ii 101–10, parallel with *Ant.* xvii 324–38). Here, as when Agrippa I was later welcomed by the Jews of Alexandria, there is the atmosphere of what may be called a Herodian messianism (section I, above).

In the *Antiquities* Josephus characteristically notes that the impostor was popular because he was thought to be the son of the Hasmonaean Mariamme. With a satire written half a century after this scene in view, it should be added that popularity derived by Herodian princes from this source went towards the strengthening of the Herodian house, for Agrippa I, his brother Herod of Chalcis, and his son and daughter Agrippa II and Berenice, all important in Rome, all shared this descent.

In sum, therefore, the evidence seems to be against the view that there was little or no connection between the Herodian princes in Rome and the Roman Jewish community.[71] The Herodian friends probably included Jews as well as gentiles, some of the slaves and freedmen who were an important element in the community (Philo, *Leg. ad Gaium*, 155) are likely to have been associated with house-holds of the Herodian family or its sympathizers, and the community as a whole could be united in acclamation of a (supposed) Herodian prince.

[70] The pressure exerted by a crowd is regarded as typically Jewish by Horace, interpreted by *J. Nolland, 'Proselytism or Politics in Horace, Satires I, 4, 138–43', VC xxxiii (1979), 347–55.*

[71] This is the opinion of Penna, 'Les juifs à Rome', 336 and n. 145, and (with reference to Agrippa I) D. R. Schwartz, *Agrippa I*, 43; to the contrary, good relations between Herodian princes and the Jewish aristocracy in Rome, on the analogy of the Herodian cultivation of wealthy Alexandrian Jews, are envisaged by S. Schwartz, *Josephus and Judaean Politics*, 140, n. 101.

The Roman Jewish community was therefore a setting in which the celebration of Herodian festivals can appropriately be envisaged. Two further aspects of the acclamation scene bear this out. First, the corresponding scene at Alexandria called forth a famous Greek counter-demonstration, including satirical cries of *Marin*, 'our lord', and Philo gives a reason for it which suggests the great political advantage accruing to the Jewish population from the possession of a king: each Alexandrian Greek was as vexed because a Jew had been made a king as if he himself had been deprived of an ancestral kingdom (Philo, *Flacc.* 29). This underlines the point already noted that, against the general background of Jewish—gentile tension, the Roman Jews would be likely to pay attention to the Herodian royal family, so often represented in Rome. Secondly, the crowds recall that honour to a king was not, as has perhaps sometimes been assumed in argument on 'Herod's days', a mere official form arousing no general interest. In the case of the imperial cult it has been emphasized that the official prescriptions were not an empty formality (Price (n. 54, above), 117–21), and similar considerations would apply to Jewish honours.

Lastly, Willrich questioned the sabbath interpretation against the background of references to Judaism in Roman poetry. 'Herod's days', he urged, would be a strange designation for the sabbaths, which were well known to Romans (cf. Krauss, as cited in n. 48, above); one might perhaps expect 'Saturn's day', as in Tibullus (i 3, 18; Stern, *Authors*, i, no. 126, 318–20). He did not consider, however, the counter-argument from Juvenal vi 159 (noted in II (c), above): *dedit hunc Agrippa sorori | observant ubi festa mero pede sabbata reges*, 'Agrippa gave this [gem] to his sister, where kings keep festal sabbaths barefoot' (Serarius and Nemethy, nn. 39 and 43, above). Juvenal, referring here to Agrippa II and Berenice, treats Judaea as the place where kings keep the sabbath with exotic piety, and Persius might likewise coin a phrase in which the sabbaths are *the* days of a Jewish king.

This counter-argument would be reinforced, and Willrich's doubt concerning the sabbath interpretation would lose much of its justification, if 'Herod' were indeed a metonymy for 'Jews' elsewhere in Latin verse. This has more recently been urged by Harvey (n. 20, above), with reference to Horace, *Ep.* ii 2, 184 *Herodis palmetis pinguibus*; here, in a passage on differences of taste and character, one brother is said to prefer an idle life to 'Herod's rich palm-groves', while the other, wealthy and untiring, works from dawn to dusk. Harvey takes Persius to be following Horace, and understands the phrase as equivalent to 'the rich palm-groves of the Jews'; but this seems questionable, because the palm-groves of Herod in particular, near Jericho, were famous. Antony had given them to Cleopatra, and Octavian restored them to Herod after Actium (Josephus, *B.J.* i 361, 396). Further, as C. Macleod pointed out, the passage deals with ambition, and an allusion to the notable ambition of Herod in particular adds to its force.[72]

Hence, if Juvenal's line suggests that the interpretation of the phrase as an abrupt equivalent for 'sabbaths' cannot be ruled out, Horace's phrase starts the counter-consideration that the knowledge of the Jews and Judaism available to Roman satirists should not be minimized. Just as Horace's reference to Herod's palm-groves seems to be precise and accurate, so his at first surprising allusion to 'tricesima sabbata' (*Sat.* i 9, 69) probably reflects Jewish usage. Here too it has been argued that this is simply a reference to weekly sabbaths, under a fanciful name devised by the poet; but it is much more likely to refer to new-moon festivals observed by the Jews of Rome (see Stern, *Authors*, i, 129, 324–6, and Thornton, 'Jewish New Moon Festivals', cited in n. 50, above). Persius' *Herodis dies* are similarly unparalleled, but appear in a context in which otherwise, like Horace, the poet shows considerable knowledge of the Jews in Rome, offering our best description of a diaspora festal meal. Even if there were not the background of Herodian influence studied here, it would be reasonable to suppose that Persius was using an uncommon but genuine Jewish name for a festival.

The Herodian associations of the Roman Jewish community, and the far from negligible knowledge of the Jews exhibited by satirists who lived in Rome, therefore support the specifically Herodian interpretation of 'Herod's days' outlined above. These days were probably royal festivals, as is suggested by independent references in Josephus and the New Testament to the celebration of Herodian birthdays and accession days. The phrase *Herodis … dies* in Persius is perhaps best explained by the suggestion that the birthdays or accession-days of Agrippa II had inherited an existing designation, 'Herod's days'.

72 C. Macleod, *Horace, The Epistles Translated into English Verse with Brief Comment* (Rome, 1986), 82.

III. Conclusions

Conclusions reached above can now be summarized as follows.

Herodian publicity, as echoed in the strikingly similar accounts of Herod's temple-restoration in Josephus' *Antiquities* and the Talmud, found a great focus in the dedication of the sanctuary on Herod's accession-day (section I, above). The restored temple, with all its 'goodly stones and votive offerings' (Luke 21:5), was thereby incorporated into the Herodian form of ruler-cult (sections I (a) and II (d), above).

Jewish observance of the Herodian festivals corresponded to the importance of the Herodian kings as Jewish patrons and representatives. Herod the Great was presented in the temple restoration as a great king of the Jews, like the kings of old. Examination of Nicolas' narrative, as transmitted by Josephus (section I (a), above), confirmed the interpretation of Herod's policy as thoroughly Augustan, yet thoroughly Jewish: an appeal to the pre-Maccabaean biblical heritage (I (c), above).[73] The Talmudic echo of this presentation (I (b), above) suggests that it was not entirely rejected. It gave an answer to some current criticism of Herod the Great, and its virtue as a shield of his house will have been continually renewed by the impressive temple restoration itself (Mark 13:1; Luke 21:5), which proceeded continuously until about the year 64 (Josephus, *Ant.* xx 219).

It can therefore be suggested once again that *Herodis ... dies* in Persius v 180 are Herodian birthdays or accession days—most probably those of Agrippa II (section II (c)–(d), above). The Jews of Rome under Nero about the year 60 would then have kept a Herodian festival, as was already thought to be the case in comment on Persius from the later Roman empire (section II (a)–(b) above). The suggestion in the form advanced above is a variant of an interpretation of Persius put forward by J. J. Scaliger, which has been perhaps most fully expounded and defended in recent times by H. Willrich. It associates the passage in Persius with the unambiguous evidence in Josephus and the New Testament for Jewish celebration of Herodian festal days.

[73] E. Bammel, 'Sadduzäer und Sadokiden', reprinted from ETL lv (1979), 107–15 in Bammel, *Judaica* (as cited in n. 60, above), 117–26 (118–20); he follows Wellhausen's view of Herodian policy, but points also to the Augustan background, and shows how policy was put into effect.

This argument brings into view a number of links between the Herodian monarchy and the Jewish community, in the diaspora and in the homeland. Herodian kings or princes have appeared at the centre of a Jewish community, in Rome, Alexandria or Jerusalem. These scenes were noticed together with some of the less dramatic traces of Jewish Herodian support at the beginning of the essay, and comparable evidence for Herodian links with the Jews of Rome was somewhat more fully considered in II (d). Hence, without discounting the influence of the Zealot movement or the complexities of reaction to each individual monarch, one may acknowledge, with rather more readiness than is sometimes allowed, a measure of Jewish recognition of the Herods.[74]

The house of Herod protected a temple which was the focus of Jewish communal life throughout the world. Herod the Great as temple builder was invested in Nicolas' presentation with an atmosphere of what can be called, with due reserve, Herodian messianism (I (a) and (c), above). Later Herodian monarchs evoked and shared this atmosphere, in a Jewish counterpart to the contemporary ruler-cults (I (c) and II (c)–(d), above). The connections and contrasts between the two appear especially in the career of Agrippa I, hailed as lord among the Jews of Alexandria and as godlike in the theatre at Caesarea. The Herodian form of ruler-cult, sometimes viewed merely as a concession to Graeco-Roman manners, was also a medium for the expression of Jewish national feeling. It corresponded to real needs of the Jewish community for protection and for self-assertion, both at home and abroad. This aspect of Herodian kingship was Jewish as well as Greek and Roman, and it deserves further consideration among the antecedents of the cult of Christ.[75]

[74] So H. Vogelstein, *Rome* (Philadelphia, 1940), 28–9. From this standpoint the allowance made by Goodman, *Ruling Class*, 122–3 for favourable attitudes to Agrippa I and II among Jews would be endorsed, and the Jerusalem and Judaean negative views of the Herods which he emphasizes would be complemented by some notice of likely variations.

[75] See now the present writer's *Jewish Messianism and the Cult of Christ* (London, 1998), especially 68–77, 134–6, 144–5, pp. 118–20, above; pp. 314–17, 380–5, below.

The New Testament

4

The Messianic Associations of 'The Son of Man'[1]

I

Was 'the son of man', for Jews at the beginning of the Christian era, a messianic title? During an earlier cycle of intensive study, reviewed by Schmidt, that more than well-worn question received influential negative answers from Lietzmann, Wellhausen, Dalman (differing in other respects from Wellhausen), and S. R. Driver—although Fiebig returned an affirmative of striking clarity.

The affirmative later came to be more widely received; but, whereas Fiebig had regarded the phrase as open to a messianic understanding by Jews in general (Fiebig, 95), Billerbeck, finding this interpretation solely in 1 Enoch, restricted the currency of the usage to 'apocalyptic circles' (Strack-Billerbeck, 485, 958). Such a restriction was not whole-heartedly endorsed by Bousset, who enrolled the gospels as further witness to titular understanding of the phrase by Jews (Bousset (1), 268; (2), 13); but it was probably encouraged by his own association of the phrase with a pre-existent heavenly messiah, differentiated from the human messiah of the Psalms of Solomon, and held to be attested distinctively (but, in view of some Septuagintal evidence, not quite exclusively) in the apocalypses (Bousset (1), 259–68).

Mowinckel combined elements of Fiebig's view with Bousset's theory. 'Son of man', he held, was widely regarded as one with the messiah, but in apocalyptic circles the phrase meant, not the messiah (unless by a secondary process of identification), but a distinct, heavenly, eschatological deliverer (Mowinckel, 360–5).

[1] This paper was written, in its first form, for a symposium of the Cambridge New Testament Seminar in honour of the seventh-fifth birthday of Professor C. F. D. Moule.

Doubts had meanwhile once again been expressed, especially in England, concerning the prevalence of 'the son of man' as a messianic title. It was now assumed that a distinctive 'apocalyptic messiah', as envisaged by Bousset, was in question. It was noted, however, that the fullest source for the expectation of such a figure, the Parables of Enoch, was of uncertain date, by no means clearly pre-Christian, and part of a work with some claim to be rated among the 'hundred worst books' (H. L. Goudge, endorsed by Campbell, 148). The expectation of a heavenly messiah, even if pre-Christian, was probably current only among the public for books like Enoch, a body not necessarily representative of Jews in general. The phrase 'son of man' was much more likely to have been associated with Dan. 7, a passage certainly generally known among pre-Christian Jews. As used by Jesus, it was not a title, but a reference to the Danielic figure, understood as a symbol for the saints, in the sense of the loyal Israelites (so, for example, Manson, 72–4 (citing his earlier studies); Dodd, 116f. (with reference also to Psalms 8 and 80; Moule (2), 11–14; Hooker (1), 183–90, and (2), 155f., 158f., 165–8).

T. W. Manson's exposition was criticized by Bowman, 285a, for minimizing the importance of the interpretation of Daniel in the first century A.D. Nevertheless, the powerful development of Manson's view, as noted at the end of the foregoing paragraph, has meant that the question whether 'the son of man' was a messianic title is widely regarded as expecting the answer 'No'. It is negated, for example, by Kim, 19, even though he thinks that, in the pre-Christian period, the Danielic figure could already have been viewed as a heavenly messiah.

This negative opinion has recently been strengthened (as noted by Hooker (2), 158f.) by a return to Lietzmann and Wellhausen, in which the theories of Bousset and of T. W. Manson are both alike ruled out. G. Vermes rejects the view that 'the son of man' was messianically titular at the time of Jesus (see Vermes (2), 327f.; (3), 168–77, 188f.; (4), 95–7); but he joins this rejection with a second, positive argument, for interpretation of the gospel sayings as circumlocutional. Vermes is endorsed in both respects (with modification of the second argument) by P. M. Casey, in a detailed study of the history of the exegesis of Dan. 7; and these authors are followed by Barnabas Lindars, who applies the results of the two arguments (revising Casey's revision of the second) to the whole reconstruction of the historical Jesus (Casey (1), 137–9, 224–8 and (2), 46–54, 150; Lindars, vii–ix, 1–16, 158–61).

For clarity's sake, however, it should be noticed that, as Vermes has emphasized, the argument against the titular character of 'the son of man' is distinct from the argument for a circumlocutional use of the phrase by Jesus (Vermes (3), 188). The two arguments do not stand or fall together. Thus J. C. O'Neill, in appendix 2 of his book *Messiah*, argues for a circumlocutional use by Jesus, but leaves open the question of titular usage; and M. D. Hooker, on the other hand, accepts that such titular usage is unlikely, but modifies Vermes' other argument by urging that, in the mouth of Jesus, the phrase was not only circumlocutional, but also, and more importantly, Danielic—an identification with the mission of the people of God (O'Neill (1), 103–15; Hooker (2), 165–8). Prof. O'Neill's discussion forms part of his broader contention that Jesus believed himself to be messiah but refrained from saying so, in reverent accord with a binding custom that one who so believed should not proclaim himself (hinted at in John 19:7 'by our law he ought to die, because he made himself the son of God'); D. Flusser had also urged, without reference to such a custom, that Jesus, like the Teacher of Righteousness in the Damascus Document, was a messiah awaiting the time when he would be revealed as such (Flusser, 108–9; O'Neill (3), 89–91). In further work since this essay first appeared, O'Neill has affirmed, with acknowledgement to the argument on titular usage set out below, that titular as well as circumlocutional usages of 'the son of man' were current in the time of Jesus, and that both figure in sayings material attributed to him with a good claim to authenticity; the titular usages (e.g. Matt. 24:37–9, Luke 17: 26–30) referred to the messiah in general but not to Jesus' own status, and the circumlocutional ones (e.g. Matt. 8:20, Luke 9:58) to humanity in general or Jesus in particular but not to the messiah, so that in neither case did these genuine son-of-man sayings constitute a messianic claim (O'Neill (2), 45–54, 122–32; (3), 80–4). A somewhat comparable combination of usages by Jesus is suggested by B. D. Chilton; but he underlines the importance of generic rather than simply circumlocutional senses of the phrase, in a modification of Vermes like that urged by Casey, as cited above (compare also O'Neill on applications to humanity in general) (Chilton, 259–68). Chilton takes the usage described here as titular to be, as urged by Moule, a reference to the Danielic figure in particular; Jesus would have meant by it an angel with whom he saw himself as paired, in accord with the angelic as well as messianic associations of the phrase to be found both in Dan. 7 and in the Parables of Enoch and Revelation (Chilton, 273–87). These further discussions thus continue, for all their differences, to bring out the distinct character of the arguments concerning titular and circumlocutional usage, respectively.

The present study, concentrated on messianism rather than Aramaic idiom, will therefore treat only one of the two arguments advanced by Vermes. In his view, which, as just noted, found formidable advocates in the past, and has won wide acceptance in the present, the phrase 'the son of man' was not employed as a title, and did not evoke any messianic concept at the time of Jesus. In what follows it will be urged that, on the contrary, the messianic interpretation of Dan. 7 is likely to be early enough to have given 'the son of man' a messianic association at the beginning of the Christian era; and that a distinct, but comparable, early messianic interpretation of words for 'man', which appears to be rooted in non-Danielic biblical passages, strengthens the probability that messianic significance could have been perceived in 'the son of man' on its own. The phrase necessarily had a wide semantic range; but it is likely that it included, within that range, established messianic associations, such that it could have been taken by Jewish hearers or readers as a reference to the messiah. In this sense, it will be suggested, the phrase was indeed a messianic title.

II

Writers who differ widely on Dan. 7 converge when considering 1 Enoch, 2 Esdras, and sometimes also the interpretation of Dan. 7:9 ascribed to Akiba (Hag. 14a, Sanh. 38b). In these texts they recognize an approximation between the understanding of Dan. 7 and the messianic hope. Thus Mowinckel finds an identification of the heavenly son of man as the messiah; Gese, a more explicit continuation of the development of Davidic messianism to which he ascribes Dan. 7 itself; and Vermes, denying that 'the son of man' was a title, still allows that 'the biblical Aramaic idiom, "one like a *son of man*", in Dan. 7:13, though not individual and Messianic in its origin, acquired in the course of time a definite Messianic association' (Mowinckel, 360–2; Gese, 143–5; Vermes (3), 176; (5), 38–40, 175–7). An argument against this conclusion from the Parables of Enoch and 2 Esdras was presented, with instructive appeal to the history of scholarship, by M. Müller, 66–88 (not available to me when this essay was first published); a brief response, bringing out implications of section IV, below, was offered in Horbury (1), 482–3. Also since the present essay first appeared, it has been re-emphasized that (as was argued by Emerton, 236–8) the man from the sea in 2 Esd. 13 can be seen against the background of Ugaritic texts to have the traits of Baal in conflict with Yam and Mot and of the Lord in comparable Old Testament passages, even though it is allowed that the explanation of the vision in verses 21–58 moves in the direction of a messianic interpretation (Hayman, especially 7–8, 13). On the other hand, the messianic associations of 'one like a son of man' in the Parables of Enoch and 2 Esdras, and the value of these texts as independent witnesses attesting common assumptions which were probably more widespread, have been reaffirmed by Collins, 451–66.

This widely recognized messianic understanding of Dan. 7 corresponds, as is emphasized below, to the establishment of links between Dan. 7 and other biblical passages which were thought to refer to the messiah. Daniel was highly esteemed as prophecy, as Josephus shows (*Ant.* x 267f., cited by Moule (2), 14 and 16). Josephus' silence on chapter 7 should be ascribed not to the insignificance of the passage in his eyes (as suggested by Kim, 35), but to his view of it as a prophecy of the downfall of Rome (Fraidl, 20 n. 3; Casey, 121). His concern with Daniel, as Eduard Meyer showed, is only one instance of the early and widespread impact made by the book (Meyer, 332f.). Nevertheless, Josephus' comments on Daniel suggest that he characteristically viewed it together with the whole corpus of the law and the prophets. He emphasizes that Daniel's words will be fulfilled, in the same way that he speaks of the impending fulfilment of Balaam's oracles (*Ant.* iv 125, also implying the downfall of Rome, as noted by Fraidl, *loc. cit.*), and of Moses' predictions to the tribes (*Ant.* iv 303, 320; cf. 2 Baruch 84:2–4), and of the prophecy of Isaiah and the twelve prophets (*Ant.* x. 35). In his synoptic view of messianic prophecy, beginning from the fundamental law, but embracing the prophets, with special attention to Daniel, together with it, Josephus exemplifies the outlook envisaged behind the interconnection of messianic passages considered below.

Two Johannine passages have a claim to reflect, like Josephus, the broad biblical basis found for the messianic hope by first-century Jews; one of them suggests, further, the association of 'the son of man' with this hope. In John

1:45 'we have found him of whom Moses in the law, and the prophets, wrote'. Further, in John 12:34, 'we have heard out of the law that the Christ abides for ever, and how do you say that the Son of man must be lifted up?' Here, at least for the simple, the son of man seems to be identified with the messiah, and the messiah is thought, as in 1:45, to be prophesied in the law. (Bruce, 51, is representative when he comments that there is no need to suppose that 'the son of man' was current as a synonym for the messiah, and thinks that the passage may reflect a Christian equation of the two.) On the supposition that Jewish views are authentically reflected, the ensuing question 'Who is this son of man?' would most naturally be thought to arise not from the obscurity of the title (as suggested by Kim, 35), but from perplexity that the son of man, the messiah, should suffer (so Meyer, ii, 337 n. 1, and Vermes (3), 162; cf. Trypho in Justin, *Dial.* xxxii). According to these Johannine passages, then, 'the son of man' was titular enough to evoke the thought of the messiah in first-century Jewish hearers, and their messianic beliefs primarily attached not to newly revealed apocalypses, but to the law and the prophets.

John therefore, taken at face value, suggests that 'the son of man' had been incorporated into the messianic hope. Josephus confirms that, as would be expected, Daniel was viewed together with the law and the prophets, the sources from which, as the two Johannine passages show, the messianic hope was held to spring. The background against which 'the son of man' should be considered would accordingly be not Dan. 7 alone, but (as Bowman's criticism suggests) the messianic interpretation of the law and the prophets, into which Dan. 7 also had been drawn. Such interpretation, as will be argued in the following section, had already given the messianic hope a relatively stable core by the beginning of the first century A.D. The influence of this interpretation, with its characteristic interconnection of messianic texts, is in mind when it is suggested, below, that 'the son of man' would have gained messianic significance not only from messianic exegesis of Dan. 7, but also from the messianic understanding of words for 'man' found elsewhere in the Bible. This significance would have been sufficiently marked to warrant, in the sense outlined at the end of the previous section, the description 'messianic title'.

The history of the subject, as has become plain, offers strictly limited comfort to such a view; but the proposal can appeal to two otherwise sharply divergent studies of ancient Judaism as a whole. First, Bousset, in *Die Religion des Judentums im späthellenistischen Zeitalter*, argued that the use of a general expression like 'man' for a messianic title is comparable with the titular use of a word like ἀνατολή (the same argument was advanced, with reference to 'man' rather than 'the son of man', by Vermes (I), 63). Bousset continued by noting that, if 'man' is applied so frequently to a messianic figure as seems to be the case in the Parables of Enoch, it has gone very far along the road towards recognition as a messianic title (Bousset (1), 266 n. 1; compare the recent statement of this view of Enochic usage by Black (2), 201–3). Secondly, however, G. F. Moore, who strongly dissented from Bousset's view of the apocalypses as good witnesses to Judaism, nevertheless himself independently held, in his book *Judaism*, that the discovery of the messiah in Daniel's 'son of man' was not likely to be original with the followers of Jesus or with himself—this, on the basis, not of 1 Enoch, but of Akiba's interpretation of the plural 'thrones' in Dan. 7:9 as one for the Almighty, and one 'for David' (Moore, ii, 336f.).

III

So much for the rags of academic respectability at which this argument may clutch; but the reader will ask if it has any clothes at all, for it suspiciously resembles what Lindars, following Paul Winter, now describes as a modern myth (Lindars, 3–8). It asserts (1) that there was a relatively fixed core of messianic belief at the time of Christ; and (2) that 'the son of man' was already associated with this belief. Now, therefore, it must be asked what primary evidence there may be for these assertions.

(1) Was messianism, at the beginning of the Christian era, in any degree a stable and generally accepted set of beliefs? In the early 1950s, opposite views on this point were advanced by Dodd and T. W. Manson. Dodd, in *According to the Scriptures* (1952), wrote that 'χριστός was a vague though extremely honorific title.... It was not until after the fall of the Temple, perhaps not until the second century, that there was any clearly formulated, and generally accepted, messianic dogma' (Dodd, 114). Manson, by contrast, in the *Servant-Messiah* (1953), pointed to the remarkable concord in the expectation of the Davidic king-messiah evinced between different sources, probably pre-

Christian or contemporary with the gospels: Psalms of Solomon 17 and 18, Philo, *de praemiis et poenis*; and the Fourteenth Benediction of the Amidah. Their concord was borne out, so Manson suggested, by the messianic uprisings of contemporary Jewish history (Manson, 23–35). Casey is among those who incline towards Dodd's view (Casey, 136–9), but here he differs from Vermes, who quotes the same texts as Manson, in an argument leading to the same conclusion, but with two important additions: first, he shows that Qumran evidence also attests the significance of the Davidic messiah, and, secondly, he notes that two of the sources quoted—the Psalms of Solomon and the Fourteenth Benediction—are prayer-texts, and therefore likely to enshrine widely held views (Vermes (3), 130–4).

To go beyond the evidence cited by Manson and Vermes, one may note that the importance of the Davidic hope, and the likelihood that it was relatively fixed by the beginning of the Christian era, are already suggested by its prominence in the Old Testament. Especially noteworthy, together with Isa. 11:2–5 is the mention of David as ἄρχων εἰς τὸν αἰῶνα (Ezek. 37:25) in the influential concluding chapters of Ezekiel, after the resurrection of the dead and the ingathering, and before the war with Gog of the land of Magog: that is to say, in the middle of what was read as an outline of the eschatological events.

Further, by the first century the Davidic hope of the prophets had been linked with the law, especially with the blessings of Judah in Gen. 49 and Deut. 33 (cf. 1 Chron. 5:2, 28:4), and with the oracles of Balaam in Num. 24; and it is in the law as well as the prophets, as suggested already, that a Jew of the time would instinctively look for messianic texts. The link between law and prophets emerges, for instance, from Gen. 49:9f. LXX, where, after 'Judah is a lion's whelp', verse 9b runs 'from the shoot, my son, you came up'. Βλάστος 'shoot', is strikingly put in the place of Hebrew *ṭerep*, 'prey'; and it is the word used for the 'blossom' of the vine in the chief butler's dream, Gen. 40:10. This vine was itself interpreted messianically and sacerdotally, in an exegesis attributed to Bar Cocheba's uncle, Eleazar of Modin (Hullin 92a). When 'from the shoot' is followed by ἀνέβης, 'you came up', however, the rendering also constitutes a reminiscence of Isa. 11:1 LXX, 'a bloom shall come up' (ἀναβήσεται) 'from the root'. A comparable connection between these two verses is presupposed (as noted by Vermes (1), 43) in Rev. 5:5 'the lion of the tribe of Judah, the root of David', and, probably, in 2 Esd. 12:31f., where the seer's lion is identified as the Anointed, who (in the Syriac text) 'shall spring up out of the seed of David'. Similarly, in the next verse of the Septuagint Genesis, as is well known, ἄρχων 'ruler' renders Hebrew *sēbeṭ*, 'sceptre'; and Vermes draws attention to a comparable connection between this verse and Isa. 11:1 in Qumran commentaries on both passages (Vermes (3), 133). These exegetical interconnections, of a type recently studied by Koenig and Heater, tend to unify and strengthen the complex of messianic texts; and it is noteworthy that they are developed so far, in specifically messianic interpretation, by the period of the Septuagint and the Qumran texts.

Hence, there are good grounds for holding that the messianic hope of the first century A.D. was thought to be rooted in law as well as prophets, as the Johannine passages and Josephus would suggest; and that, in the expectation of the Davidic messiah, it already had a stable core of widely shared and relatively fixed belief. (For further study of the 'core' question since this essay first appeared, see pp. 11–13, above; Horbury (2), 36–108; O'Neill (3), 27–72.)

IV

It can now be asked, (2) To what extent was 'the son of man' associated with this messianic hope? Two classes of evidence will be considered. The first is drawn from the messianic exegesis of Dan. 7; the second, reviewed in the following section, is from a distinct, but comparable, messianic interpretation of words for 'man'.

At the beginning of section II it was noticed that a messianic understanding of Dan. 7:13 is widely recognized by students in 1 Enoch, 2 Esdras, and the interpretation of the 'thrones' attributed to Akiba (one early item in more extensive rabbinic evidence). Frequent application of a biblical text to the messiah means that key words in that text are likely to gain messianic associations. Thus in Gen. 49:9, just considered, 'Judah, a lion's whelp' leads to Rev. 5:5, where 'the lion' is titular, and is identified with 'the root', another title, arising from Isa. 11:1; and 'a lion's whelp' leads also, in 2 Esd. 11:37. to what may be called a fully paid-up lion, beheld ramping and roaring by the seer, and interpreted to him as 'the anointed one' (12:32). The comparison with a lion in Gen. 49:9 was thus developed, by virtue of the messianic application of the verse, into a title signifying the messiah. The description of a man-like figure in Dan. 7:13 could have initiated a similar development, as was suggested in the comments by Bousset and (with reference to 'man' in other biblical contexts) by Vermes, noted at the end of section II, above.

The force of this consideration obviously depends upon the age and frequency of the messianic exegesis of Dan. 7:13. That it was common, and that it probably goes back at least to the last quarter of the first century A.D., can be seen especially clearly from the discussion by Vermes (3), 170–7. Lindars, going one step further, accepts that the gospel source Q, and Jewish interpretation in 1 Enoch and 2 Esdras, drew independently upon a messianic exegesis of Dan. 7 which was already current (Lindars, 159). It may be inferred that he would regard it as well established by the middle of the first century A.D.

Casey, however, is not confident that the messianic interpretation of Dan. 7 is earlier than 2 Esdras; and, unlike Vermes and Lindars, he does not believe that the saying attributed to Akiba is a testimony to the messianic interpretation, or evidence for its date (Casey, 85–9, 136f.). The early evidence for the interpretation should accordingly be reviewed.

It should be noticed, first, that the saying attributed to Akiba is one of a number of attestations, in sources of different character, from the end of the first century A.D. and the beginning of the second. It stands together with 1 Enoch, 2 Esdras, and Sib. v. 414–33 (dated before Bar Cocheba, and perhaps in the last years of the first century A.D., by J. J. Collins in Charlesworth, i, 390). From later in the second century come the remarks on Dan. 7 assigned to Trypho by Justin, *Dial.* xxxii (between 155 and 160, according to Harnack, i, 281).

In all these sources, except the last, the messianic interpretation is assumed without argument. Consistently with this phenomenon, Trypho is envisaged by Justin as accepting that Dan. 7 is a prophecy of the messiah, and as objecting solely to the identification of the glorious Danielic figure with the crucified Christ. Trypho's speech permits the interpretation that he expects a great and glorious human messiah, and its authenticity as a report of Jewish messianism need not, therefore, be impugned (as by Higgins, 301).

The messianic interpretation is therefore assumed in sources of disparate provenance: two Jewish apocalypses, a rabbinic tradition, a Sibylline oracle from Egyptian Jewry, and a Christian report of Jewish messianic belief. The first four of these sources, representing both Palestine and the Diaspora, come from not long before and after A.D. 100. This exegesis is likely, then, to have been widespread at a considerably earlier date.

Are there indications of its pre-Christian currency? Kim's suggestion that it is attested in an Aramaic Qumran fragment needs further substantiation; for the figure called 'son of the Highest' in 4Q246 (partly published by Fitzmyer (1) 91–4) could be viewed negatively in the text, particularly if the passage on his titles echoes Ps. 82:6 (a possibility not considered in the discussion by Kim, 20–2). Since this essay first appeared, the text (one partly-preserved and one complete column, each of nine lines) has been edited in full by E. Puech (2), who brings out its wealth of Danielic allusion and classifies it as a fragment of an apocryphon of Daniel. It probably does not constitute further evidence for the messianic interpretation under review, but it is of note for the present argument in at least two ways.

First, the view that the lines (i 9–ii 1) on a figure who will be called 'son of God' and 'son of the Highest' attest a messianic interpretation of the 'one like a son of man' in Daniel has much to be said for it, as is shown by Collins (2), 154–72; but the conclusion that this figure hailed with lofty titles is that of an evil king seems preferable (Puech (2), 178–84), and it fits the thematic importance of a coming evil king in Daniel and elsewhere (ch. 11, below), and of ruler-cult in Daniel and its early interpretation (Dan. 6:8–10 (7–9)); LXX Dan. 3:12, 18 'your image'; Mastin, as cited p. 71, above; Horbury (2), 72, 74).

Secondly, however, the text goes on to present (ii 4–9) what seems to be a vivid personification of 'the people of the saints of the most High' (Dan. 7:18–27); war and oppression will last 'until the people of God arise' (4Q246 ii 4), when 'all the provinces will do him [the people] homage; the great God is his strength, he will wage war for him' (2:7–8). For this personification of 'the people of God', in expression of similar sentiments, compare the influential oracle of Nathan in 2 Sam. 7:10 'and I will appoint a place for my people Israel, and will plant him, and he shall dwell in his own place, and shall be disturbed no more; and the children of iniquity shall not again oppress him, as at the first' (the singular pronouns referring to 'my people Israel' in the Hebrew here are rendered by English plurals in AV, RV, REB, NRSV). The view of Israel which is implied in these lines of 4Q246 would then be broadly comparable with the presentation of Israel as God's first-born (Exod. 4:22) in the prayer of the Words of the Luminaries (4Q504 1–2 cols. iii–iv (xiv–xv), moving from Israel as son to the honouring of 'your people' by the gentiles).

This interpretation of 4Q246 2:5–9 seems on balance more satisfying, as Puech urges, than renderings (such as that expounded by Fitzmyer (2), 43–51) which depend on the assumption that after line 4 an unnamed king, probably the figure to be hailed as divine son in line 1, comes into view in place of the 'people' just mentioned in line 4; and the reference of lines 5–9 to God's people, in direct continuation of line 4, can appeal (see Puech (2), 174–8, 183) to biblical and post-biblical passages on the nation as divinely favoured. Thus 4Q246 2:7–8, just quoted, echo the divine promises to Zion that kings and nations shall bow down before her (Isa. 49:23, 60:14), taken up again in Enoch's vision of the beasts and birds worshipping the sheep (1 En. 90:30), and then the assurances of Moses, of the priest marching with the army, and Joshua that the Lord will make war for Israel (Exod. 14:14; Deut. 1:30, 3:22; Deut. 20:4; Jos. 23:10) (these biblical passages, which seem particularly close, can be added to those cited in Puech's commentary).

These lines so understood are still of note in the present context, however, because they suggest that early interpretation of Dan. 7 included meditation on 'the people of the saints' as well as the correlated 'one like a son of man'. This line of thought would have been in agreement with the prominence of the flock of 'sheep' and the 'righteous' in the second Dream-vision of Enoch and the Apocalypse of Weeks; see 1 En. 90:19–38 (from the second Dream-vision), cited above, and 91:12–13 (from the Apocalypse of Weeks), following the Aramaic text 'a sword shall be given to the righteous, to execute righteous judgment upon all the wicked, and they shall be delivered into their hands …' (4Q212, col. iv, lines 15–18). The use of the Aramaic language for the transmission of the text in 4Q246, as for the Enochic prophecies just cited, will have allowed in principle a relatively widespread reception. Argument that 'the son of man' as used by Jesus indicated the Danielic figure understood as a symbol of 'the people of the saints' (see especially Moule and Hooker, cited in section I) can therefore be strengthened by reference to the importance of the personified 'people' in this strand of early Danielic interpretation. Note, however, that the Enochic dream-vision focused on the sheep finds its culmination in a white bull symbolizing an Adam-like messianic king; comparably with the sheep, he is feared and entreated (cf. Ps. 72:5) by the beasts and birds (1 En. 90:37, as interpreted by Black (3), 20–1, 279–80; Nickelsburg, 406–7). Given the correlation of people and messianic king exemplified here (and noted in general terms by Puech (2), 182), the people-oriented strand in meditation on Dan. 7 was also compatible with the messianic interpretation of the Danielic 'one like a son of man' which became common and is studied in this chapter.

Another Qumran find, the Hebrew text 11Q13 (11Q Melchizedek), has already received a short discussion in chapter 1 (pp. 85–6, above). This text suggests that the book of Daniel was drawn into messianic interpretation before the rise of Christianity, but it probably cites the ninth rather than the seventh chapter of Daniel. The fragments are assigned to three columns of the manuscript in the fresh edition by García, Tigchelaar and van der Woude (221–41), published since this essay first appeared. Continuous text is available only in col. ii, the greater part of which has been recovered; it includes description of the end of days as the tenth jubilee and (with a series of allusions to Isa. 61:1–2) as the proclamation of liberty to the captives by Melchizedek (2.4–6) in his 'year of grace' (2.9), when he will also execute the divine vengeance (2.13). He is the 'god' who 'will judge in the midst of the gods' and rebuke their wickedness (Ps. 82:1–2, applied in 2:10–12 to Melchizedek condemning Belial and his spirits).

The prediction is further confirmed (11Q13, col. ii 15 onwards) by interpretation of Isa. 52:7, a passage which like Isa. 61:1 presents a figure with 'good tidings'. The bearer of good tidings in Isa. 52:7 is identified (2:18) as 'the anointed of the spirit' (cf., again, Isa. 61:1) 'as Dan[iel] said [...'. The subsequent lacuna is filled by the editors from Dan. 9:25, 'until an anointed, a prince, seven weeks'. A quotation from this passage would suit the earlier reference in 11Q13 (2:7–8) to 'the first week of the jubilee' and to 'making atonement' (*l^e^kapper*, cf. Dan. 9:24 *u-l^e^kapper*). The 'anointed of the spirit' is often interpreted as a (possibly prophetic) figure distinct from Melchizedek (so Puech (1), pp. 553–4; García, Tigchelaar and van der Woude, 232); but the allusion to Isa. 61:1 in this phrase suggests that it refers rather to Melchizedek himself, a king whose activity has just been presented in the terms of Isa. 61:1–2 in 11Q13 2:4–6; 9; 13, as noted above (so Hultgård, i, 307–8; Rainbow, 193). The presentation of Melchizedek in this text, as a formerly earthly king who comes again as a great spirit or demi-god (*^e^lohim*) with deliverance from heaven, has been compared to that of the son of man in the gospels (so, for example, Puech (1), 556–8). This overall resemblance is noteworthy, and the possibility of a debt to Dan. 7 in 11Q13 is underlined by the phrase 'peo]ple of the saints of God' (*ʿa]m qᵉdoshey ʿel*) in 11Q13 2.9; but the contribution of 11Q13 to the present argument lies also in the Danielic citation of ii 18. It emerges here that the book of Daniel was drawn, before the rise of Christianity, into the complex of messianic biblical interpretation. The ninth rather than the seventh chapter was probably in view, given the special suitability of Dan. 9:25 to the context; but the general likelihood that the seventh chapter too received a messianic exegesis before the rise of Christianity is enhanced by 11Q Melchizedek through this appeal to Daniel as well as the seeming echoes of Dan. 7 in portrayal of the deliverer and the delivered 'saints'.

Pre-Christian currency for this exegesis is rather more strongly supported by Ezekiel the Tragedian (first-century B.C. or earlier, as argued in chapter 2, pp. 92–5). In Ezekiel's play Moses dreams of a great throne, and a noble man, crowned and sceptred, sitting upon it; but this figure beckons to Moses, hands over the sceptre to him, tells him to sit on a (or the) great throne, and gives him a royal crown. He then departs from the thrones, and Moses sees all earth and heaven, and counts the stars, which fall before his knees. Raguel tells Moses that the dream presages his future rule and prophetic knowledge.

The resemblances between this passage (lines 68–89) and both Ps. 110:1–4 and Dan. 7:9ff. are noted by Jacobson, 90f., and influence from Dan. 7 is definitely identified by van der Horst, 24: Moses, comparably with the man-like figure in Dan. 7:13f., approaches the throne and receives sovereignty. At many other points the description is probably indebted to other biblical sources. Two further considerations, however, are consistent with the suggestion of influence from Dan. 7 in particular. First, the sovereignty exercised by the man-like figure in Daniel is underlined in the probably interpretative rendering of the Old Greek (LXX), where (in contrast with Theodotion) the one 'as a son of man', having come, 'was present as ancient of days' (Stuckenbruck, especially 271–6). The presentation of the enthronement of Moses in the dream is therefore in line with a strand in early understanding of the seventh chapter of Daniel. Secondly, the plural 'thrones' in Ezekiel Tragicus 76 ἐκ θρόνων χωρίζεται has been explained as simply an elegant variation on the singular (commentators cited by Holladay, 444); but it seems likely also to reflect biblically-rooted Jewish conceptions of the deity enthroned with great powers or favoured spirits beside him, and to accord significantly with the Danielic scene. So in the Wisdom of Solomon, without clear knowledge of Daniel yet probably in line with existing convention, the divine 'thrones' are shared by wisdom (9:4), but, in a variation comparable with that of Ezekiel Tragicus here, the deity is asked to send her from the singular 'throne' of his glory (9:10); and, later on in another section of the book, the divine word leaps from 'royal thrones' in heaven (18:15). Comparably, the earthly king David has 'thrones' (Wisd. 9:12; cf. Ps. 122:5). Similarly, in Dan. 7:9 plural 'thrones' are set. In Revelation, here with clear knowledge of the book of Daniel, there is a throne with the surrounding thrones of the elders (4:3–4), and in a later passage 'thrones' (20:4), and then 'a great white throne' (20:11). In Ezekiel Tragicus, comparably, a singular 'great throne' (lines 68–9, 74) is occupied by the 'noble man' until he seats Moses upon it and 'departs from the thrones' (line 76). The variation in these lines is therefore probably more than simply stylistic, and it recalls not just current convention in depiction of the divine thrones, but also the Danielically-influenced literary visions of Revelation. These two considerations, derived respectively from the Greek Daniel and from Ezekiel's diction, do not amount to additional attestations of Danielic influence on Ezekiel Tragicus here. They show, however, that the proposal that this narrative is influenced by Dan. 7 is consistent both with the early history of Danielic interpretation, and with an element in Ezekiel's diction which has evoked comment. Danielic influence is probably rightly detected in the central action of the narrative.

For the present purpose this is significant. As other Danielic passages are treated as familiar in 1 Macc. 1:54; 2:59f., a work roughly contemporary with Ezekiel's play, so here the narrative of 7:13f. in particular has left its mark. The part played by the man-like figure in Daniel is taken by the man Moses, who is to be endowed with sovereignty and the gift of prophecy (lines 85–9), and who was viewed in the first century A.D. and later as a prototype of the messiah. (See Acts 7:35 with Vermes (3), 97f., citing, among other passages, Josephus, *Ant.* xx 97, on Theudas, and Targ. S. of S. 4:5 'your two redeemers who will redeem you, Messiah son of David and Messiah son of Ephraim, are like Moses and Aaron …'.) Ezekiel's presentation is itself likely to have been formed not only by Dan. 7, but also by messianically interpreted psalms, such as 45 and 110 (both compared by Jacobson, 90f.). Moses' dream in Ezekiel's tragedy (not discussed by Vermes, Casey and Lindars) can therefore be said to presuppose an exegesis of Dan. 7:13f. which is very close to the messianic exegesis under review; and the probability that this messianic exegesis is pre-Christian is considerably strengthened thereby.

Thus far, the variety of the sources in which the messianic exegesis is attested at the end of the first century A.D. has suggested that it was widespread considerably earlier; 11Q Melchizedek has shown, if the reading is true, that Daniel was quoted as a specifically messianic prophet at Qumran; and Ezekiel the Tragedian, whose understanding of Dan. 7:13f. is close to the messianic exegesis has been seen to strengthen the likelihood that it was current in the pre-Christian period. Note is now taken of a feature of the attestations from the first and second centuries A.D. which points in the same direction, their dependence on a combination between Daniel and other messianic biblical texts.

The combination of texts manifest in each passage arises from the process of interpretative interconnection, which was exemplified from Gen. 49:9f. (section III, above). Thus, 1 Enoch and 2 Esdras draw in different ways on a link between Dan. 7 and Isa. 11. In the second parable of Enoch, which begins with a vision based on Dan. 7, the Elect One has the spirit of wisdom and understanding (1 En. 49:3 Isa. 11:2), and has been identified as the messiah (1 En. 48:10) and the son of man to whom belongs righteousness (1 En. 46:3; cf. Isa. 11:4f. and 'messiah of righteousness' in a Qumran comment on Gen. 49:10 (4Q252; Allegro, 175; G. J. Brooke in Brooke *et al.*, 205–6; ch. 1, n. 25, above) and in Targ. Jer. 33:15 (Vermes (1) 53 n. 2)). Similarly, in the third parable, the enthroned son of man (1 En. 62:2f. will exercise the attributes described in Isa. 11:2–4 (parallels tabulated and discussed by Theisohn, 57–63; cf. 100–13). In both parables, the combination of the enthronement of the son of man by the Lord of Spirits with the doom of the kings (1 Enoch 45:3, 46:3–6, 62:1–3) depends on a link between Dan. 7 and Ps. 110 (Theisohn, 98), and probably also Ps. 2, where the kings rebel against the Lord and his Anointed (Nickelsburg & VanderKam, 262), and Ps. 48:4–6. Similarly, again, in 2 Esdras, the man flying with the clouds of heaven burns up his foes by his words and breath (2 Esd. 13:3 f., 10; cf. Dan. 7:13; Isa. 11:4).

The possibility of allusions to Isa. 11:4 in 1 Enoch and 2 Esdras is allowed by Emerton, 237, with reference also to a comparable allusion in Ps. Sol. 17:27;

but he prefers to derive the description of fire from the mouth in 2 Esd. 13:10 from the abundantly attested storm imagery of Old Testament theophanies, for example, Ps. 18:8. In both 1 Enoch and 2 Esdras, however, the man-like figure is identified as the messiah; and, in view of the pre-Christian messianic application of Isa. 11 already noted in both Hebrew and Greek sources in section III, above, as well as in Ps. Sol. 17, this chapter seems the more likely source for the description in 2 Esdras. Isa. 11:4, in a less inflammatory interpretation, was also influential within the Septuagint of Isaiah, at 32:2 (as noted by Koenig, 143, with acknowledgement to R. R. Ottley); it seems likely to the present writer (section V, below) that the latter verse was also understood messianically by the translator (another interpretation in Koenig, 146 n. 14).

Comparably with the combination of texts in 1 Enoch and 2 Esdras, Akiba's saying (Casey's view of which is discussed below) presupposes a link between Dan. 7 and a text on messianic session, probably Ps. 110:1. Again, the Fifth Sibylline, within the Danielic frame of the blessed man who comes from heaven in the last time of the saints (lines 414, 432; cf. Dan. 7:13, 22, and Num. 24:17 LXX), sets a picture coloured by other messianic texts; it includes his God-given sceptre (Pss. 2:9, 45:7f., 110:2; cf. 1Q Recueil des Bénédictions (1QSb), col. v, line 24 (adaptation of Isa. 11:4 follows immediately), and Ezekiel the Tragedian, 1.74); his burning-up of the cities and nations of the wicked (line 419; cf. Num. 24:18f., Isa. 11:4); and his rebuilding of Jerusalem and the temple (lines 420–7; cf. 2 Sam. 7:10–14; Ezek. 37:24–8; Hag. 2:7; Zech. 7:12). The dependence of this Sibylline passage on Dan. 7:13 is unjustifiably discounted by Casey, 120; he does not mention the references to the heavens and the time of the saints.

Lastly, Trypho, having heard out Justin's declamation of the whole of Dan. 7:9–28, replies 'O man, these and other like scriptures compel us to await one great and glorious, who receives the everlasting kingdom as son of man from the ancient of days' (Justin, *Dial.* xxxii). It is therefore expected by Justin that, as will indeed have occurred before the passages just examined could take shape, Dan. 7:13f. would have been set by Jewish interpreters together with 'other like scriptures' thought to refer to the messiah.

In these passages, therefore, Dan. 7:13f. have been combined (to note only the shared allusions) with Isa. 11:2–4 (1 Enoch, 2 Esdras, and the Fifth Sibylline), Ps. 110 (1 Enoch, 2 Esdras, the Fifth Sibylline, and probably Akiba's saying; so, already, Ezekiel the Tragedian), and Ps. 2 (1 Enoch; 2 Esdras (God's king on Mount Zion; Ps. 2:6; cf. 2 Esd. 13:6f., 35f.), and the Fifth Sibylline). The wide range of origin of the passages, embracing both Palestine and the Diaspora, means that their shared links between texts are likely to be old. In the case of Ps. 110 this likelihood is confirmed by Ezekiel the Tragedian. The specifically messianic interpretation of Dan. 7 is indicated especially by the shared link with Isa. 11, as well as with messianically interpreted psalms. From consideration of the common use of this combination of texts, it would be natural to ascribe the origin of the messianic interpretation to a period very considerably earlier than that of the attestations themselves.

Before this consideration is drawn together with those already advanced, it is necessary to recur to the saying in Akiba's name; for Casey, as noted already, discounts it as evidence for the messianic interpretation of Dan. 7:13 (Casey, 86–8). Akiba's assertion that one of the 'thrones' mentioned in Dan. 7:9 is 'for David' is referred by Casey, 87, to the historical David rather than the messiah; but this is implausible, especially when the messianism of the early second century is remembered, because of the messianic understanding of 'David' already prominent in the Old Testament (as noted in section III, above, with reference to Ezek. 37:25; cf. Jer. 30:9; Ezek. 34:23f.; Hos. 3:5 (with jBer. 5a, quoted by Moore, 2, 326). It is objected, further, that Akiba's reference to Dan. 7:9 does not necessarily imply any particular interpretation of Dan. 7:13 (Casey, 87; so also Dalman, 391, withdrawing his earlier view). If 'David' refers to the messiah, however, the likelihood of such an atomistic exegesis in this instance is not strong; for verse 13, as already noted, was widely associated with the messiah. (Add, to the four other passages discussed above, Sanh. 98a (in the name of Joshua b. Levi, third century) and Num. R. 13.14, on Num. 7:13 (anonymous); in both these places, as in the other passages already noted, the messianic application of Dan. 7:13 is a matter of course.) Moses' dream in Ezekiel the Tragedian also probably implies a connection, as suggested above, between the thrones and the transmission of sovereignty in verses 13f. Lastly, Casey suggests that the ascription of one of the thrones to 'David' was intended as a contribution to the widely discussed problem of reconciling a plurality of thrones with the unity of God; this solution, he thinks, could have been offered without any associated messianic interpretation of verse 13. It has already been noticed, however, that an association with 'David' in verse 9 is likely to imply acceptance of the messianic exegesis of verse 13; and A. F. Segal, accordingly, in his review of rabbinic discussion of 'two powers', finds in this saying a messianic interpretation of the one like a son of man, and thinks it likely to be early. The later rabbinic tendency (represented in the disagreement which Akiba's saying is reported to have met) was to unify such conflicting representations of the deity as seemed to be suggested by the ancient of days and the man-like figure (A. F. Segal, 47–9). This saying can therefore continue to be viewed as an important indication that, in the Palestinian rabbinic movement of the early second century, as well as in the Parables of Enoch, II Esdras, the Fifth Sibylline, and Justin's picture of Trypho, Dan. 7:13 was regarded as a messianic text; see p. 11, above.

The considerations evoked by these attestations can now be viewed together. The range and variety of the sources for the messianic exegesis, at the end of the first century A.D. and the beginning of the second, immediately suggest that it was widespread at an earlier date. Secondly, the likelihood that it arose in the pre-Christian period receives general support from the quotation of Daniel as a messianic prophet at Qumran, if 11Q Melchizedek is correctly read; and ascription to this period is more particularly suggested by the witness of Ezekiel the Tragedian, whose understanding of Dan. 7:13f. in view of the rôle of Moses as prototype of the messiah, is very close to the messianic exegesis. Thirdly, the common dependence of the attestations from *c.* A.D. 100 upon a combination of Dan. 7:1 with other messianically interpreted texts indicates a prior exegetical development, such that the messianic exegesis probably arose very considerably earlier than these attestations of it. The three considerations all point in the same direction. In particular, the indications of prior exegetical development, viewed together with the interpretation in Ezekiel the Tragedian, speak for an origin no later than the early first century A.D., and possibly much earlier.

New Testament evidence for a messianic interpretation of Dan. 7:13, however its attribution is more precisely to be determined, could then be regarded (as by Lindars, 159, in the case of Q) as a further attestation and development of the widespread Jewish interpretation. Thus, it would be possible to consider the combination of Dan. 7:13 with Ps. 110:1 in Mark 14:62 not simply as Christian exegetical development (it is so explained by Casey, 182, and Lindars, 110–12), but as a further employment, whether by Jesus (to whom the saying is ascribed by Moule (1) 86; (2) 27) or an early Christian, of a combination of texts which also influenced both Ezekiel the Tragedian, and the attestations of the messianic exegesis which have just been examined.

In the nature of the evidence, the dating of the messianic exegesis which has now been attempted can be no more than an assessment of probabilities. The argument offered here, as will have been noticed, is often close to that presented by Vermes (for example, in the evaluation of Akiba's saying). It differs, however, so far as primary evidence is concerned, in including discussion of the Fifth Sibylline together with the other contemporary attestations considered by Vermes, and in its attention to possibly relevant pre-Christian sources, notably 11Q Melchizedek and Ezekiel the Tragedian. In respect of interpretation, it differs in the synoptic view taken of the attestations, and in the emphasis laid on their variety, and on the common exegetical development which nevertheless seems to be presupposed in them all. The probability has then appeared to lie, as Moore thought, on the side of a significantly earlier origin than Vermes and Casey would suggest.

The question then posed is whether one can, with Vermes, exclude the possibility that the phrase 'the son of man' was capable of being understood as a messianic title, at the time of Jesus. Vermes holds that rabbinic derivation of the messianic names Anani and Bar Niphle from *ʿanānē*, 'clouds' in Dan. 7:13 proves that 'the son of man' in that verse was never understood as a title (Vermes (3) 172, with reference to Tanhuma Buber, Genesis, Toledoth, 20 (cited above) and Targ. 1 Chr. 3:24, on Anani; cf. Sanh. 96a, on Bar Niphli); but these names, more immediately derived from the Davidic passages 1 Chron. 3:24 and Amos 9:11 respectively, rather witness to the messianic understanding of Dan. 7:13 as a whole than to the non-titular character of other words in it. Thus the importance of 'son of man' as well as 'clouds' in Dan. 7:13 for the Targumist at 1 Chron. 3:24 is noted by Willi, 120. The other consideration advanced by Vermes is the lack of a clear titular usage of 'the son of man' in the various messianic interpretations of Dan. 7:13 (Vermes (3) 172f., 175). This observation does not mean, however, that the phrase was insignificant. The parables of Enoch do not use it without further qualification; but their repetition of it in various forms, in contexts clearly indebted to Dan. 7:13, strongly suggests an impression left by those particular words in the verse. As Bousset noted (end of section II, above), they have gone far along the road to becoming a title. Similarly, when 2 Esdras speaks of 'one in the likeness of a man', and 'that man' who 'flew with the clouds of heaven' (2 Esd. 13), the phrase 'one like a son of man' in Dan. 7 has made its mark. Likewise, although the Sibyl, with ἀνήρ, makes the slightly more veiled allusion which befits her, it is probable that she echoes this phrase in Daniel when she sings of the 'blessed man' from the heavens in the time of the saints (Sib. 5:414, 432).

Hence, the lack of a clear titular usage of 'the son of man', emphasized by Vermes, does not mean that the phrase was passed over. On the contrary, it was echoed and repeated, in contexts in which, through the interpretation of Dan. 7:13, it was associated with the messiah. There is therefore reason to suppose that, from the messianic exegesis of Dan. 7:13, 'the son of man' would have been likely to develop into an expression which could be taken as a reference to the messiah, comparably with the development of 'lion' noticed at the beginning of this section. These messianic associations of 'the son of man', it will now be suggested, would have been further strengthened by interpretative usage, not primarily connected with Dan. 7 in which biblical words for 'man' took on a specialized messianic reference.

V

In the second class of evidence mentioned at the beginning of the previous section, and now to be considered, messianic significance attaches to words and expressions for 'man', in interpretation of passages other than Dan. 7.

Thus, first, 'king messiah' and *bar nāš* are associated in the Targum of Ps. 80, where the phrases render MT *bēn* (verse 16) and *ben ʾādām* (verse 18) respectively. The same personage, 'the man of thy right hand' (verse 18), is naturally envisaged in both verses, once *bēn* is taken as 'son'; and Septuagint and Peshitta, accordingly, give the equivalent of 'son of man' at each occurrence. The Hebrew text of the psalm, when verse 16 is thus understood, places solemn emphasis on 'son', 'man', and 'son of man', in prayer for national deliverance with recollection of the exodus; that is to say, as the Targum of verse 16 makes plain, in a context which could readily evoke the thought of the messiah. 'Son of man' is not a synonym for *bēn* in the Hebrew text, or (as stressed by Casey, 91) for 'king messiah' in the Targum; but its close link with these words, in text and Targum of a national prayer, gives the phrase a messianic association independent of Dan. 7. The Targumist (as pointed out by McNeil, 420) will have understood 'messiah' and 'son of man' as parallel designations. In the Septuagint psalm the phrase 'son of man', given added solemnity by repetition, would gain comparable significance from its context. Here, then, in the Hebrew psalm, as it was understood from the time of the Septuagint, and in the Aramaic and Greek versions, the phrase 'son of man' is solemnly used, and can be said to have acquired messianic associations.

Other words for 'man' are interpreted messianically in the examples which follow. Particularly noteworthy are two instances of ἄνθρωπος, 'man', as a messianic title, in the Septuagint of Balaam's oracles: a fundamental passage, as the name of Bar Cocheba shows, for messianism in the first and second centuries A.D. Thus, in Num. 24:7, 'water shall pour from his buckets' becomes in the Septuagint 'there shall come forth a man … who shall rule many nations.' (ἐξελεύσεται appears to be an interpretative echo of Isa. 11:1 ἐξελεύσεται ῥάβδος; compare the use of (ἐξ)έλευσις for a messianic advent, pointed out by Kilpatrick, 136–43.) The messianic interpretation continues with the transformation of Agag into Gog, in the following verse. Verse 7, in Targum Pseudo-Jonathan, has the words 'king' and 'redeemer', and in Onkelos 'king'; and in the Greek, with ἄνθρωπος, it is twice quoted as a messianic oracle by Philo (*Mos.* i. 290; *pr. et p.* 95), is followed closely in the wording of the messianic prediction in Test. Judah 24:1, and is probably also echoed in Test. Naphtali 4:5. The origin of the almost universal messianic interpretation of this verse is discussed by Vermes (1) 159f., with a reference to Isa. 45:8 and the messianic associations of *ṣedeq*; but the significant point in the present connection is that, given this interpretation of Num. 24:7, the Septuagint rendering could hardly have arisen unless ἄνθρωπος were already recognized as a messianic title. This point is reinforced by the star-oracle of Num. 24:17, where *šēbet*, 'sceptre', identified as the prince of the congregation in CD 7.21, and as the messiah in Targums Onkelos and Pseudo-Jonathan (the versions are reviewed by Vermes (1) 59), is rendered 'man', ἄνθρωπος, in the Septuagint. The Peshitta, in verse 7, in accordance with the Septuagint, has *gabrā* 'man'; a point of interest, again, in the present connection, in view of the probably Jewish origin of the Peshitta Pentateuch. In verse 17, on the other hand, Peshitta *reša* 'head' spells out the implications of LXX ἄνθρωπος but is itself closer to *šalit* 'governor' in Targum Neofiti (combined there with *paroq* 'redeemer') or to ἡγούμενος in the quotation in Justin Martyr, *Dial.* cvi.4. The Neofiti rendering, viewed together with Onkelos and Ps.-Jonathan as noted above, underlines the likelihood that the text quoted by Justin represents a Jewish revision of the LXX. Such a revised Greek text was perhaps known to the Peshitta translator here.

In a full discussion of Peshitta origins published since this essay first appeared, the late M. P. Weitzman argued that the earlier books of the Hebrew Bible were translated into Syriac *c.* A.D. 150 in a non-rabbinic Jewish community, probably in Edessa (Weitzman, especially 244–62). However the translators' Jewish community is to be characterized, Weitzman's study shows that the Peshitta Pentateuch is likely to have drawn on the LXX in a Jewish rather than a Christian context. The agreement of both LXX and Peshitta at Num. 24:7 with wider Jewish exegetical tradition is noted by Weitzman, 70.

A word for 'man' has messianic significance in a number of other passages discussed by Vermes, who makes acknowledgement also to Brownlee (Vermes (1) 56–66). Noteworthy among these are Isa. 66:7 (*zākār*, Targum 'her king'), 2 Sam. 23:1 (*geber*), and Zech. 6:12 (*'īs*), where 'man' receives strong emphasis in statements taken to identify a messiah; the usage is not clearly symbolic, but it is such as to favour the messianic application seen in the Septuagint Numbers. Connecting these and other passages, including Num. 24:7, 17, with the messianic use of *geber* and *zākār* in 1QH[a] xi (iii). 7–10 (and with *geber* and *'īs* in the less clearly messianic 1QS iv. 20–2), Vermes concluded that these commonplace nouns acquired the characteristics of a proper name (Vermes (1) 63).

In a book unknown to me when this essay was first published, M. Perez Fernandez put forward much the same argument as is presented in this section. He urged, mainly on the basis of the evidence cited in the preceding paragraph together with a special study of the Targums of Num. 24:7 and 17, that ἄνθρωπος and *geber* could be used with a messianic connotation, and that this usage consequently contributed to the messianic understanding of 'son of man'; such understanding of the phrase will not have been derived solely from Dan. 7 (Perez, especially 260–9).

Two studies of Jewish interpretation of Num. 24:7 and 17 in Greek which have appeared since this essay was first printed should be considered at this point. First, by contrast with the argument offered above, J. Lust has urged that ἄνθρωπος in Numbers 24 LXX does not have clear messianic overtones; in verse 7 it is ambiguous, despite other elements in the Greek rendering which could point to kingship, and in verse 17 it seems even to do away with the royal character of the expected figure, which might have been suggested by the 'star' of the first half of the verse (Lust, 236–41). Moreover, in the external witness to the Greek text of these verses, apart from Philo, ἄνθρωπος is attested only in relatively late Christian writers, from about the time of Origen onwards (Lust classes the quotation of verse 17 in Test. Judah 24:1 and the allusion to the 'man' of both verses in Test. Naphtali 4:5 as Christian insertions); the earliest clear Christian attestation, in Justin Martyr (*Dial.* cvi.4, quoted above), reflects not ἄνθρωπος but ἡγούμενος in verse 17, and the Latin text of Irenaeus similarly has *dux*—and it is likely too, as Lust well notes, that this form of verse 17 is reflected when Micah 5:1 is quoted with ἡγούμενος at Matt. 2:6 (compare Horbury (2), 200, n. 87). Philo, then, is for Lust the sole early external witness to ἄνθρωπος, and he is held to have understood it not messianically, but as a reference to humanity in general (a sense akin to the understanding of the verse in the later patristic tradition as a prophecy of Christ's humanity). It is not impossible, Lust thinks, that Philo himself introduced 'the man' into the Greek of verse 7 for the first time, although it could certainly have stood in the text which he knew, and could have been understood by the earlier translator on the lines which Philo later followed. In verse 17, which Philo does not quote, ἄνθρωπος is in any case in itself without messianic connotations, in Lust's view. It will have established itself in the Greek of both verses, he suggests, perhaps partly through the influence of the anthological association of Num. 24 with Isa. 11 (compare Horbury (2), 93), which is attested in Qumran texts and in early patristic writings (note the assonance of ἄνθρωπος and Isa. 11:1 ἄνθος), and partly through the attraction of a reference to humanity in verse 7 and the influence of Philo on Christian users of the LXX (Lust, 241–52).

In response it can be said, first, that in both verse 7 and verse 17 the word appears prominently in a Greek context which, as Lust agrees, suits and even enhances the expectation of a coming ruler. It will have been thought by the translator to suit that context, a context which aligns verse 7 with the clearly ruler-oriented verse 17. This verse in Hebrew foretells the 'star' and 'sceptre', in LXX 'star' and 'man'. Secondly, this immediate context in the Greek of Num. 24

would soon have encouraged a messianic understanding of the term, even if, contrary to what seems probable, this understanding was not already a factor when the rendering was chosen. Thirdly, such an understanding would have been strengthened by the long-standing association of Num. 24 with Isa. 11, attested in both Hebrew and Greek sources before the rise of Christianity (add to Lust's citations the allusion to both texts, together with Ps. 2, in Ps. Sol. 17:21–2, 24). Fourthly, as regards the history of the text, the Peshitta as cited with Weitzman's comment above increases the general likelihood that ἄνθρωπος in verse 7 antedates Philo. Fifthly, it is by no means so clear as Lust suggests that Philo understood the passage non-messianically; Philo here appears to expect the Israelites in their time of future blessing to be following a great leader (cf. Horbury (2), 85 and n. 77). Lastly, the understanding of the term by Greek-speaking Jews who knew the LXX cannot be divorced from the messianic understanding of the two verses attested in the Targum. (See also p. 17, above.)

Further instances of ἄνθρωπος with messianic overtones in the LXX will be considered in a moment. Before that, however, it should be noted that the points just made concerning Philo and the Targums receive support from a second study of Num. 24 in Greek, in this case focused on Philo. C. T. R. Hayward compares Philo's interpretation of Balaam's prophecies in verses 3–9, 15–19 with the Targums; he finds that both Philo and the Targums connected these oracles with Jacob's prophetic blessing in Gen. 49:8–12, concerning the lion-like Judah and the ruler to arise from him, a passage discussed above for its exegetical interconnections with Isa. 11 (section III) and its contribution to the vision of the messiah as a lion in 2 Esdras (section IV). Its connection also with Balaam's prophecy in the LXX is noted by Horbury (2), 48–51. This link will have been encouraged by the comparison with a lion in Num. 24:9. Hayward shows that both Philo and the Targumists on Num. 24 expect a lion-like deliverer to spring from the leonine tribe (Hayward, 32–6). Probably, therefore, ἄνθρωπος, like *geber* and other Hebrew vocabulary discussed by Vermes and Perez, could be used with a messianic connotation.

There is further evidence to support this conclusion. First, in Mishnaic Hebrew *ʾīš* 'man' could evidently sometimes be honorific, as appears from the polite form of address to the high priest, *ʾīšī kōhēn gādōl* (Mishnah, Yoma i.3, 5): literally 'my man', but better rendered freely 'my lord'. In this instance it is not impossible that the Mishnah preserves usage of the Second Temple period.

Secondly, the specifically royal and messianic associations of 'man' would be strengthened not only by the texts noted above, but also by the repeated promise that there should never be cut off a man (*'îš*) to sit on David's throne (1 Kings 2:4; 8:25; 9:5; 2 Chron. 6:16; 7:18; Jer. 33:17).

Thirdly, the messianic understanding of *'îš* has further testimony in ancient Jewish interpretation. First, in LXX Isa. 32:2, after the messianic overtones of verse 1a in the Hebrew, 'a king shall reign in righteousness', have been somewhat stressed by the rendering 'a righteous king shall reign', the Hebrew text beginning 'and a man (*'îš*) shall be as a hiding-place from the wind …' becomes 'and the man (ὁ ἄνθρωπος) shall be hiding his words, and shall be hidden as from rushing water; and he shall be manifest in Zion as a rushing river, glorious in a thirsty land'. According to Koenig, 146 n. 14, 'the man' in LXX means, by contrast with the Hebrew, every man; the generality of the king's subjects are alarmed at his strict righteousness, and lie low. This view debits the translation at worst with bathos, and at best with decidedly paradoxical praise of the messianic reign. It seems better to follow up R. R. Ottley's observation (endorsed by Koenig, 143 n. 5, as noted in section IV above), that the rendering of *ruaḥ* in this verse by 'words' echoes Isa. 11:4 LXX. The latter verse, as often noted already, was messianically interpreted; and the Septuagint translation of Isa. 32:2 makes consistent sense if 'the man' means the messianic king. He is first hidden, then revealed (cf. 2 (Syriac) Baruch 24:3, and the comparable texts discussed by Vermes (3), 137f.); he will then be glorious as a rushing river (compare the fountain, breaking into great waves, which symbolizes the dominion of the messiah in the vision of 2 (Syriac) Baruch 36:4f., 39:9, and the messianic interpretation of the 'water' of Num. 24:7, noted above). Hence 'man' here, in the Hebrew text, is likely to have been taken by the Septuagint translators as a signal meaning 'messiah'.

Again, Ps. 87:5 *'îš wᵉ'îš*, 'a man and a man', perhaps to be rendered 'man after man', is divided in LXX '… a man shall say, both "A man (ἄνθρωπος) was born in her", and "Himself, the Highest, founded her" '. It would be natural to take the second 'man' in LXX messianically. That the whole Hebrew phrase could indeed be understood in this way is indicated by Targum 'king David and Solomon his son', and Midrash Tehillim lxxxvii. 6, in the name of Judah b. Simon (late fourth-century Palestine) 'the nations of the world will bring gifts to king Messiah, as it is said, A man and a man is born in her (Ps. 87:5);

these are the messiahs of the Lord, Messiah son of David and Messiah son of Ephraim'.

Again, in the second line of Ecclus. 45:25, immediately after a line on David 'son of Jesse, of the tribe of Judah', the Hebrew consonantal text begins *nḥlt'š*. M. H. Segal points *'ēš*, interpreting 'an inheritance of fire-offerings', in agreement with the reference to Aaron in the second half of this second line; but Smend and Peters (cited by M. H. Segal, *ad loc.*) point *'īš*, interpreting 'the inheritance of a man', and applying the phrase to David, in accordance with the repeated Davidic promise noted above. The second line can then be read as a comparison, in the manner of Jer. 33:17–22, between the covenants of David and Aaron, and it binds the Davidic reference of the previous line more neatly and forcefully into its larger Aaronic context than a totally Aaronic second line can do (against the argument of M. H. Segal, *ad loc.*). In the present connection it is notable that, whether or not *'īš* is the true punctuation, it seems to have been that understood by Ben Sira's grandson, who rendered the Hebrew by 'the inheritance of a king'; that is to say, in 'man' he heard royal and messianic overtones.

Fourthly, further to the passages discussed in the first publication of this essay, it may be added that the influence of the messianic ἄνθρωπος of the LXX Pentateuch (Num. 24:7, 17, discussed above) can be detected in Isa. 19:20 LXX. Here the 'saviour' (*moshia'*) of the Egyptian Jews in the Hebrew text receives the long rendering 'a man (ἄνθρωπος) who shall save us'. 'Such a rendering of a participle is quite unusual in LXX Isaiah (and in the rest of the LXX as well)' (van der Kooij, p. 141). Contrast the more straightforward short rendering σωτήρ, 'saviour' to which the LXX here was revised in Aquila, Symmachus and Theodotion (Horbury (2), 50, 147). Within the context of the LXX Isaiah van der Kooij (142) finds the closest parallel in 8.8 (ἄνθρωπον ὃς δυνήσεται κεφαλὴν ἆραι), and he notes that ἄνθρωπος indicates an important person here and elsewhere in Isaiah LXX (including 32:2, discussed above). Still within the Isaianic context, he adds that the immediately following words in Isa. 19:20 LXX, 'judging (χρίνων) he shall save us', link the 'man' of 19:20 with the ruler from Jesse who shall judge (Isa. 11:3–4 LXX κρινεῖ), and with him who shall be 'judging' (κρίνων) enthroned 'in the tabernacle of David' (Isa. 16:5 LXX). Moreover, the sequel 'And the Lord shall be known to the Egyptians' (Isa. 19:21) implies that the saviour-judge of verse 20 is Jewish (van der Kooij, 143). Within the LXX Isaiah, therefore, the Greek rendering of 19:20 suggests expectation of a Jewish judge and deliverer who strongly resembles the coming Davidic king prophesied in chapters 11 and 16. To van der Kooij's illumination of this Isaianic context it may be added that the use specifically of ἄνθρωπος in this connection in Isa. 19:20 LXX is likely to reflect the prominent and influential usage of this word in the LXX Pentateuch at Num. 24:7 and 17, discussed above with reference also to the interpretative association of Num. 24 with Isa. 11.

Lastly, in Sib. 5:414 'a blessed man', already discussed, it is likely that this messianic interpretation of 'man' has converged with the allusion to Dan. 7:13, and the imagery of Pss. 45, and 110, and Isa. 11. Similarly, in Test. Judah 24, the influence of Num. 24 LXX comes together with that of Pss. 45, 110; Isa. 11. One may suspect a similar background of exegesis, combining messianic 'man' with Isa. 11:4, behind Acts 17:31 'to judge the world in righteousness by a man whom he ordained'.

When this additional evidence for messianic interpretation of 'man' is combined with the passages already noted, it emerges, first, that there is a substantial biblical basis for such a development. A number of Davidic and messianic texts lay solemn emphasis upon a word for 'man': 2 Sam. 23:1 (*geber*); 1 Kings 2:4, 8:25, 9:5; 2 Chron. 6:16, 7:18; Jer 33:17; Zech. 6:2 (in all these, *ʾîš*); Ps. 80:18 (*ben ʿādām*). The messianic development from these texts was also favoured by the honorific employment of *ʾîš* in other connections (M. Yoma).

Further, the messianic interpretation of 'man' was known not only in the Diaspora (Septuagint Numbers and Isaiah, Peshitta Numbers, Greek Ecclesiasticus, Greek Testaments of Judah and Naphtali, Philo, Fifth Sibylline) but also in Palestine (Hebrew Ecclesiasticus, Qumran Hodayot, Judah b. Simon in Midrash Tehillim); and there is pre-Christian evidence in both categories. Num. 24:7 LXX is a particularly impressive witness to the strong influence of the interpretation, its early date, and its combination with other messianic exegesis; but each of these features can be found elsewhere in the evidence.

This second class of evidence, considered on its own, would therefore lead one to conclude that, by the beginning of the Christian era, words for 'man' could be understood in biblical interpretation as references to the messiah. This conclusion, as *ben ʿādām* in Ps. 80 underlines, is of significance for 'the son of man' as well as 'man'.

VI

To sum up the two classes of evidence which have now been considered in sections IV and V, it may be said that messianic exegesis of Dan. 7:13 probably arose not later than the early first century A.D., and possibly much earlier. Key words in such messianically interpreted passages were subject to a tendency towards titularity, and 'son of man' was significant enough to have been affected in this way. The messianic associations of the phrase would have been strengthened by a distinct, but comparable, pre-Christian messianic interpretation of words for 'man', to be found in connection with biblical passages other than Dan. 7:13.

Evidence exemplified in section III, above, suggests that, at the beginning of the Christian era, the Davidic hope already constituted a relatively fixed core of messianic expectation, both in Palestine and in the Diaspora. Exegetical interconnections attest that the son of man' is likely to have acquired, within its wide range of meaning, definite associations with this hope. There is no need to envisage a separate 'son of man concept', of the type criticized by Vermes (4), 95–7 and Lindars, 8. More probably, as has been argued here, 'the son of man' had become one of the words and phrases which could readily be understood as a reference to the messiah. In that sense, it can be called a messianic title.

A conclusion may perhaps be allowed to sketch, in the briefest catechetical form, a response to three obvious objections. First, how would such an interpretation comport with Jesus' reserve concerning messiahship? Answer, the range of meaning of the phrase allowed it to be both self-referential and messianic; in its aspect of opacity, which the hearer was invited to pierce, it resembled the parables. Secondly, why, then, was it not commonly used in the church as a title for Christ? Answer, partly, perhaps, because of its special link with the Second Coming, and partly also because the meaning which was most obvious to the gentile, 'human being', ran directly against the honorific tendency of Christology; its rarity as a title is therefore comparable with the relative rarity of χριστός in its Jewish sense of 'messiah', rather than as a proper name. It is consistent with this view that later Christian traces of the phrase as a title occur where Jewish influence is likely (Acts 7:56; Gospel of the Hebrews, in Jerome, *de viris illustribus*, 2; Hegesippus in Eusebius, *H.E.* ii. 23, 13; Latin text of Asc. Isa. 11:1; cf. Bousset (2), 13–15, 20). Lastly, does not this argument recklessly obscure the light cast on the ministry of Jesus, as Moule especially has shown (e.g. Moule (1), 86–90), by the Danielic imagery of vindication? Answer, not necessarily so, a disavowal which the treatment above of 'the people of God' in 4Q246 may already have signalled; for if 'the son of man' is rightly understood as messianic, it does not thereby cease to be Danielic.

Literature

J. M. Allegro, 'Further Messianic References in Qumran Literature', *JBL* LXXV (1956), 174–87

M. Black (1), *An Aramaic Approach to the Gospels and Acts* (3rd edn., Oxford, 1967)

——— (2), 'Aramaic Barnasha and the "Son of Man"', *ET* xcv (1984), 200–6

——— in consultation with J. C. VanderKam (3), *The Book of Enoch or I Enoch* (Leiden, 1985)

W. Bousset (1), *Die Religion des Judentums im späthellenistischen Zeitalter* (3rd edn., revised by H. Gressmann, Tübingen, 1926)

——— (2), *Kyrios Christos* (2nd edn. (1921), reprinted Göttingen, 1966)

J. Bowman, 'The Background of the Term "Son of Man"', *ET* lix (1948), 283–8

G. J. Brooke et al., *Qumran Cave 4.xvii* (DJD xxii, Oxford, 1996)

F. F. Bruce, 'The Background to the Son of Man Sayings', in H. H. Rowdon (ed.), *Christ the Lord* (Leicester, 1982), 50–70

J. Y. Campbell, 'The Origin and Meaning of the Term "Son of Man"', *JTS* xlviii (1947), 145–55

M. Casey (1), *Son of Man* (London, 1979)

——— (2), *From Jewish Prophet to Gentile God* (Cambridge, 1991)

J. H. Charlesworth (ed.), *The Old Testament Pseudepigrapha* (2 vols., London, 1983, 1985)

B. D. Chilton, '(The) Son of (the) Man, and Jesus', in B. Chilton and C. A. Evans (eds.), *Authenticating the Words of Jesus* (Leiden, 1999), 259–87

J. J. Collins (1), 'The Son of Man in First-Century Judaism', *NTS* xxxviii (1992), 448–66.

——— (2), *The Scepter and the Star* (New York, 1995)

G. Dalman, *Die Worte Jesu*, i (2nd edn., Leipzig, 1930)

C. H. Dodd, *According to the Scriptures* (London, 1952)

S. R. Driver, 'Son of Man', *HDB* iv (1902), cols. 579–89

J. A. Emerton, 'The Origin of the Son of Man Imagery', *JTS* N.S. ix (1958), 225–42

P. Fiebig, *Der Menschensohn* (Tübingen and Leipzig, 1901)

J. A. Fitzmyer (1), *A Wandering Aramaean* (Society of Biblical Literature Monograph Series xxv, Missoula, 1979)

——— (2), *The Dead Sea Scrolls and Christian Origins* (Grand Rapids and Cambridge, 2000)

D. Flusser, 'Two Notes on the Midrash on 2 Sam. vii', *IEJ* ix (1959), 99–109

F. Fraidl, *Der Exegese der siebzig Wochen Daniels in der alten und mittleren Zeit* (Graz, 1883)

H. Gese, *Zur biblischen Theologie* (Munich, 1977)

A. Harnack, *Die Chronologie der altchristlichen Literatur bis Eusebius*, i (Leipzig, 1897)

A. P. Hayman, 'The "Man from the Sea" in 4 Ezra 13', *JJS* xlix (1998), 1–16

C. T. R. Hayward, 'Balaam's Prophecies as Interpreted by Philo and the Aramaic Targums of the Pentateuch', in P. J. Harland and C. T. R. Hayward (eds.), *New Heaven and New Earth, Prophecy and the Millennium: Essays in Honour of Anthony Gelston* (Leiden, Boston and Köln, 1999), 19–36

H. Heater, Jr., *A Septuagint Translation Technique in the Book of Job* (CBQ Monograph Series xi; Washington DC, 1982)

A. J. B. Higgins, 'Jewish Messianic Belief in Justin Martyr's Dialogue with Trypho', *NT* ix (1967), 298–305

C. R. Holladay, *Fragments from Hellenistic Jewish Authors, ii, Poets* (Atlanta, 1989)

M. D. Hooker (1), *The Son of Man in Mark* (London, 1967)

——— (2), 'Is the Son of Man Problem really insoluble?', in E. Best and R. McL. Wilson (eds.), *Text and Interpretation* (Cambridge, 1979), 155–68

W. Horbury (1), review of M. Müller, *Der Ausdruck 'Menschensohn' in den Evangelien*, *JTS* N.S. xxxviii (1987), 480–83

——— (2), *Jewish Messianism and the Cult of Christ* (London, 1998)

P. W. van der Horst, 'Moses' Throne Vision in Ezekiel the Dramatist', *JJS* xxxi (1983), 21–9

A. Hultgård, *L'eschatologie des Testaments des Douze Patriarches* (2 vols., Uppsala, 1977 and 1982)

H. Jacobson, *The Exagoge of Ezekiel* (Cambridge, 1983)

G. D. Kilpatrick, 'Acts vii.52 ΕΛΕΥΣΙΣ', *JTS* xlvi (1945), 136–45

S. Kim, *The Son of Man as the Son of God* (*WUNT* xxx, Tübingen, 1983)

J. Koenig, *L'Herméneutique analogique du Judaïsme antique d'après les témoins textuels d'Isaïe* (*SVT* xxxiii, Leiden, 1982)

A. van der Kooij, 'The Old Greek of Isaiah 19:16–25: Translation and Interpretation' in C. E. Cox (ed.), *Sixth Congress of the International Organization for Septuagint and Cognate Studies, Jerusalem 1986* (Society of Biblical Literature Septuagint and Cognate Studies Series xxiii, Atlanta, 1987), 127–66

B. Lindars, *Jesus Son of Man* (London, 1983)

J. Lust, 'The Greek Version of Balaam's Third and Fourth Oracles; the *ἄnqrwpoV* in Num. 24:7 and 17; Messianism and Lexicography', in L. Greenspoon and O. Munnich (eds.), *VIII Congress of the International Organization for Septuagint and Cognate Studies, Paris 1992* (Society of Biblical Literature Septuagint and Cognate Studies Series xli, Atlanta, 1995), 233–57

B. McNeil, 'The Son of Man and the Messiah: A Footnote', *NTS* xxvi (1980), 419–21

T. W. Manson, *The Servant-Messiah* (Cambridge, 1953)

E. Meyer, *Ursprung and Anfänge des Christentums* (3 vols., Berlin, 1921–3)

J. Milik, 'Milkî-ṣedeq et Milkî-resa' dans les anciens écrits juifs et chrétiens (1)', *JJS* xxiii (1972), 95–144

G. F. Moore, *Judaism* (3 vols., Cambridge, MA, 1927–30)

C. F. D. Moule (1), 'Neglected Features in the Problem of "the Son of Man" ', reprinted from J. Gnilka (ed.), *Neues Testament und Kirche [Festschrift for R. Schnackenburg]* (Freiburg i.B., 1974), 413–28 in C. F. D. Moule, *Essays in New Testament Interpretation* (Cambridge, 1982), 79–90

——— (2), *The Origins of Christology* (Cambridge, 1977)

——— (3), ' "The Son of Man": Some of the Facts', *NTS* xli (1995), 277–9, reprinted in C. F. D. Moule, *Forgiveness and Reconciliation, and other New Testament Themes* (London, 1998), 205–7

S. Mowinckel, *He That Cometh* (ET Oxford, 1959)

M. Müller, *Der Ausdruck 'Menschensohn' in den Evangelien: Voraussetzungen and Bedeutung* (Leiden, 1984)

J. C. O'Neill (1), *Messiah* (Cambridge, 1980)

J. C. O'Neill (2), *Who Did Jesus Think He Was?* (Biblical Interpretation Series xi, Leiden, 1995)

——— (3), *The Point of it All: Essays on Jesus Christ* (Leiden, 2000).

G. W. E. Nickelsburg, *1 Enoch 1* (Hermeneia, Minneapolis, 2001).

——— and J. C. VanderKam, *I Enoch 2* (Hermeneia, Minneapolis, 2012).

M. Perez Fernandez, *Tradiciones mesiánicas en el Targum Palestinense* (Valencia and Jerusalem, 1981)

E. Puech (1), *La croyance des esséniens en la vie future: immortalité, résurrection, vie éternelle?* (2 vols., Paris, 1993)

——— (2), '246. 4QApocryphe de Daniel ar', in Brooke et al., *Qumran Cave 4.xviii*, 165–84

N. Schmidt, 'Son of Man', *EB* iv (1907), cols. 4705–40

A. F. Segal, *Two Powers in Heaven* (Leiden, 1977)

M. Z. (H.) Segal, *Sepher Ben Sira ha-shalem* (2nd edn., Jerusalem, 1958)

H. L. Strack and P. Billerbeck, *Kommentar zum Neuen Testament aus Talmud and Midrasch*, i (Munich, 1922)

L. T. Stuckenbruck, ' "One like a Son of Man as the Ancient of Days" in the Old Greek Recension of Daniel 7, 13: Scribal Error or Theological Translation?', *ZNW* lxxxvi (1995), 268–76

J. Theisohn, *Der auserwählte Richter* (Göttingen, 1973)

G. Vermes (1), *Scripture and Tradition in Judaism* (Leiden, 1961; 2nd impression, Leiden, 1973)

——— (2) 'The Use of bar nash / bar nasha in Jewish Aramaic', *Appendix E in Black (1)*, 310–28

——— (3), *Jesus the Jew* (London, 1973)

——— (4), *Jesus and the World of Judaism* (London, 1983)

——— (5), *The Changing Faces of Jesus* (London, 2000)

M. P. Weitzman, *The Syriac Version of the Old Testament: An Introduction* (University of Cambridge Oriental Publications lvi, Cambridge, 1999).

T. Willi, *Chronik* (*Biblischer Kommentar, Altes Testament*, xxiv, fascicle 2; Neukirchen-Vluyn, 1999)

5

The Twelve and the Phylarchs

I

In modern study of Christian origins, especially among those writers concerned with Jewish history who have been said to form a 'third quest' of the historical Jesus (Wright, 83–4), some New Testament traces of an emergent constitution have received attention. How can the constitutional implications of the ministry of Jesus and his disciples be related to the contemporary Jewish polity, and to the subsequent growth of the Christian ecclesia?

Answers to this question may include comment on the twelve, a body which appears through references in the gospels, the Acts and Paul to have been at the heart of the continuity between the ministry of Jesus and the later Christian communities. Such comment is exemplified in B. F. Meyer, 134, 154; cf. 242, with an emphasis which can roughly be labelled ecclesial, and in Sanders (1), 326; (3), 184–7; Wright, 299–300, 532; Allison, 101–2; Frederiksen, 89–98; Freyne, 140–3, with an emphasis which can roughly be labelled national or Israelite. All six authors affirm, despite varying emphases, that Jesus did indeed appoint twelve, who stood for the twelve tribes and the restoration of Israel. Crossan, 337, by contrast, puts such numbers down to the evangelists and does not discuss the possible rôle of a group of twelve in Christian origins, despite his interest in Pauline evidence for the Jerusalem church (Crossan, 423–4); but he indicates a range of Old Testament associations of a body of twelve (or seventy). Can one go further towards determining the constitutional significance of a body of twelve for a Jew of the first century A.D.?

One possible model for the twelve, the group of tribal princes, seems to be relatively neglected. In what follows attention will be drawn to it, and an attempt will be made to characterize its interpretation in ancient Judaism.

Finally, against this background, brief comment will be offered on the place of the twelve in early church order and in the ministry of Jesus.

II

A prominent group of twelve, in the Pentateuch and elsewhere in the Hebrew Bible, is formed by the twelve princes of the tribes. Moses and Aaron chose them, by divine direction, to be their associates in the great census (Num. 1:4 and 7). In the Septuagint these *n^e^sîʾîm* or *n^e^sîʾey ha-ʿedah* usually appear as ἄρχοντες (τῆς συναγωγῆς) but by the first century A.D. Josephus and some other Jewish writers of Greek refer to them as 'phylarchs'. Thus, for example, the 'princes of Israel' (Num. 7:2), who are identified in the same verse of the Hebrew text as 'the princes of the tribes' who took the census, are additionally specified in the Septuagint as 'twelve', and appear in the corresponding passage of Josephus as 'phylarchs' (Josephus, *Ant.* iii 220). Philo, speaking of the patriarchs as 'the rulers of the nation, twelve in number', interestingly adds that 'it is the custom to call them phylarchs' (*fug. et inv.* 73), and the usage is also known to Josephus (*Ant.* iii 169). (Compare the complementary Septuagintal usage of 'patriarch' for the princes of the tribes, 1 Chron. 27:22 (section IV, below).) Josephus and others therefore called the princes of the tribes by an honourable name which could also be applied to the twelve patriarchs themselves.

These developments in Josephus and elsewhere already suggest that the twelve princes were alive in the first-century mind as a group of rulers comparable with the patriarchs and, perhaps, inheriting their authority. In a volume of essays which emphasized the importance of institutions in primitive Christianity Austin Farrer suggested that the group of twelve disciples was indeed modelled upon the twelve princes and, thereby, the twelve patriarchs (Farrer (1), 120–4; cf. (2), 21–2); but his suggestion, so far as the present writer is aware, has remained isolated in recent study.

Once, however, as Bengel's note on Matt. 19:28 shows, the thought that the twelve were modelled upon the phylarchs was more commonplace. In the seventeenth century it figured in political theory as well as biblical comment. Hugo Grotius (1641) interpreted Matt. 19:28 as a promise made on the analogy of the ancient state of the Hebrew kingdom, wherein the phylarchs had a dignity closely approaching the majesty of the king (Grotius, ii.1, 188, *ad loc.*). Spinoza (1670) viewed the Mosaic polity as a theocracy, from which the Hebrew monarchy was a disastrous decline, but he agreed with Grotius that the phylarchs had an important constitutional position. Rejecting the rabbinic view that Moses instituted the sanhedrin, Spinoza held that he chose the phylarchs to form the army, to divide the promised land, and, after the division, to handle all the affairs of war and peace in their own tribes; under these princes the tribes formed a federation comparable with the Estates of the Netherlands (*Tractatus Theologico-Politicus*, xvii, and note 38, in Wernham, 162–71, 186f., 252–5).

In England Grotius' view was given precision and development by Henry Hammond (1653). In his annotation on Matt. 19:28 he observed that the sons of Zebedee cherished the expectation 'of some earthly greatness, particularly of that (so familiar among them) of the φύλαρχαι; and he paraphrased the promise with 'You ... shall in the new age or state (taking its beginning from the resurrection and ascension of Christ) have a power in the church instated on you, as my successors, somewhat proportionable to that of the several Rulers of the tribes among the Jews.' Here the apostles' ecclesiastical jurisdiction, in succession to their master, is carefully described as in some ways comparable to that of the phylarchs. The same comparison was incorporated by Hobbes into his unified description of civil and ecclesiastical polity: 'For as Moses chose twelve princes of the tribes, to govern under him; so did our Saviour choose twelve apostles, who shall sit on twelve thrones, and judge the twelve tribes of Israel' (*Leviathan*, xli, in Oakeshott, 320).

Any advocate of a cause might welcome the hard-headed Hobbes as support for the more imaginatively speculative Farrer; but there is a less frivolous reason for recalling these seventeenth-century scholars. Their studies show that, at a time when the Mosaic and apostolic constitutions were fiercely scrutinized for their bearing on government in church and state, the importance of the phylarchs in the Old Testament stood out clearly—as emerges most strikingly from their key position in Spinoza's reconstruction of the theocracy—and that the likelihood that they formed a model for the twelve apostles seemed strong. It is not surprising that patristic homily on relevant Old Testament passages already made the same connection between the princes and Matt. 19:28 (Origen, *in Exod. hom.* xi.6, on 18:21; *in Iesu Nave hom.* xviii.1).

The biblical passages on the phylarchs (reviewed in the following section) come mainly from P, Ezekiel and Chronicles. In modern study, therefore, their constitutional significance for pre-exilic Israel has been less prominently discussed. The phylarch has been variously interpreted as sacral prince (Noth) or elected representative (Speiser) (see Halpern, 207–10). Source-criticism shows, nevertheless, that Spinoza's distinction between the princes and the sanhedrin is rooted in the texts. Phylarchs and elders appear for the most part in different sources (Halpern, 212–13). In the Pentateuch, the elders characterize JE rather than P (apart from Lev. 4:15; 9:1), and the *nāśîʾ* is regular in P, but unknown elsewhere (apart from Exod. 22:27 (28)). Thus Exod. 24:1, 9–11, perhaps a separate tradition in E (Childs, 500–1), a scene with Moses, Aaron, priests and elders, stands over against Exod. 34:30–2 (P), a scene with Moses, Aaron and the phylarchs. As between these passages, later harmonized by LXX and Rashi (sections IV and VI, below), constitutional views already differ.

Hence, however much the importance of the phylarchs in the Old Testament, and, consequently, their possible relevance to the apostles, has been underlined by later study of the Bible, it remains to be asked whether that importance was indeed (in Hammond's words) 'so familiar among them' in first-century Palestine. Some indications in Josephus have already suggested that this could have been the case; but the rabbinic tradition from which Spinoza departed held the sanhedrin rather than the twelve princes to be centrally important, and a modern account of 'rule in Jewish tradition', intended to reflect the influence of Maimonides and rabbinic thought, can ignore the phylarchs entirely, in its biblically-based exposition of Jewish political theory (E. Marmorstein, 13–28). Similarly, they receive only occasional reference in the study of Jewish political theory in the Second Temple period published since this essay first appeared by Goodblatt, 6–130. Would they have occurred more readily to a first-century Jew?

III

The twelve princes of the tribes do indeed appear to have cut a bolder figure in Jewish biblical exposition of the early Roman period. Increasing attention to the rabbinic chain of tradition, with its emphasis on the sanhedrin, would increasingly tend to dim their éclat, even though the biblical narratives concerning them continued to be read. Their importance in earlier interpretation of the narratives will be considered in a moment. First, however, it may be convenient to note the main biblical passages from which expository speculation could begin.

The *nāśî'* is not to be cursed (Exod. 22:27), and a special sin-offering is appointed for him (Lev. 4:22–6). 'The princes of the congregation' are mentioned in the narratives of the manna (Exod. 16:22) and of the delivery of the law to the people, when the face of Moses shone (Exod. 34:31). Princes play a more active part when they present the jewels of ephod and breastplate (Exod. 35:27), supervise the census (Num. 1–2), bring special offerings at the dedication of the altar (Num. 7:1–88), stand ready to assemble at the trumpet-blast (Num. 10:4), command the tribal hosts with their standards (Num. 10:4–28), and hand over their rods for the choice of the priestly tribe (Num. 17:16–28(1–13)). 'The well which the princes (*śārîm*) dug' can recall them (Num. 21:18), and they are named after Moses and Eleazar the priest, in the fashion of a council, in the stories of Zelophehad's daughters (Num. 27:2, 36:1; cf. Jos. 17:4), the spoiling of Midian (Num. 31:13), and the petition of the Reubenites and Gadites for an inheritance (Num. 32:2); correspondingly, it is they who are appointed, with Eleazar and Joshua, to divide the land (Num. 34:16–29). 'My princes', comparably, are to give land for a new allotment (Ezek. 45–8).

Beyond the Pentateuch, the princes continue to be prominent in the stories of the settlement. Still appearing as a council, they are taken in by the wily Gibeonites (Jos. 9:15–21), they supervise the division of the land (Jos. 14:1; 21:1), and ten of them are deputed with Phinehas to investigate the altar built in Gilead (Jos. 22:9–34). Under the monarchy, the princes are among those assembled for the dedication of the temple (1 Kings 8:1, see below).

In Chronicles *nāśî'* is more often a notable within the tribe (as 1 Chron. 7:40) than a tribal head (as 1 Chron. 2:10); but the heads of the tribes, usually *śārîm*, take a constitutional part resembling that of the princes of the congregation in P. Thus the Chronicler gives their names, and recounts their presence at David's charge to Solomon and their offerings to the temple (1 Chron. 23:2; 27:16–22; 28:1; 29:6). They are conjoined with the king in giving orders at Hezekiah's reformation (2 Chron. 29:30; 30:2, 12; cf. 31:8), and their association with the king in providing offerings is centrally important in the Chronicler's passovers under Hezekiah and Josiah (2 Chron. 30:24; 35:8; cf. 1 Chron. 29:6); the *śārîm* (LXX ἄρχοντες) in these passages compare in wealth and piety with the *n*^{e}*sî'îm* of Num. 7 (LXX again ἄρχοντες).

The approximation between princes of the congregation in P and princes (heads) of tribes in Chronicles indicates the relevance of a group of post-exilic passages in which 'princes' (*śārîm*, ἄρχοντες) are mentioned with high precedence in a recital of the elements in Israel's constitution: kings, princes, priests, (prophets,) fathers (Neh. 9:32, 34; Dan. 9:6, 8; Baruch 1:16; 2:1). Comparably, the 'heads' of tribes are mentioned first at Num. 30:2 (P), Deut 5:20; 29:9. The influence of such passages perhaps appears at one important place, 1 Kings 8:1 (2 Chron. 5:2), where the assembly comprises elders, heads of tribes and princes of fathers, but in LXX Kings (not Chronicles) simply elders. If LXX represents an earlier text of Kings (so Burney, 104–5, with analysis of terminology), Chronicles and the Hebrew text of Kings arise from an attempt to reconcile elders and princes within a single constitution.

The bulk of this biblical material, particularly that which depicts the princes as a kind of council, obviously lends itself to the constitutional speculation which is already discernible as one motive behind the narratives themselves. The princes are also associated with the two important commandments mentioned first. These constitutional and regulative passages invite halakhic interpretation. On the other hand, the material includes a number of memorable stories. Some of these are indeed elaborated in the haggadah, and, although the halakhic material just noted may be presumed to have engaged the most serious attention of a first-century Jew, the princes would have been stirred to life in his imagination by whatever haggadic developments of the stories were known to him. Hence, it may be excusable to take the two divisions of material in this paragraph in reverse order, and to begin a brief and selective survey of early interpretation with the princes in the haggadah.

One complex of interpretation gives a noteworthy example. The biblical accounts of the tabernacle, its service and its ministry are strikingly elaborated in Josephus, Philo and the midrash. Within this set of narratives, the princes stand out especially clearly when they present their offerings (Num. 7:1–88). This long chapter, beginning 'on the day that Moses had fully set up the tabernacle', was of halakhic interest in connection with the *ma'*^{a}*mād* or standing body of priests, Levites and laymen which, serving with the courses, represented the nation at the daily sacrifices (Yadin 204, n. 3); but this interest is bound up with the conviction, abundantly expressed in the haggadah, that the princes' offerings stand for Israel's response to the Almighty, who, in the newly-consecrated tabernacle, has drawn near to his beloved people like the bridegroom in Solomon's Song (see, for instance, Pesikta de-Rab Kahana (hereafter PRK) i.l, on Cant. 5:1 'I am come into my garden, my sister, my spouse'). Hence the phylarchs' offertory procession evokes lyrical comment, of appropriate fulness, especially from Palestinian homilists of the third and fourth centuries (see Num. R xii.16, on 7.2, to xiv.18, on 7.88). In a characteristic interpretation, later words from Cant. 5:1, 'Eat, O friends; drink, drink deep, O beloved', are taken as the Almighty's invitation to his guests, the twelve princes (Num. R xiii.2, on 7.12; Cant. R v. 1, 1 (R. Simeon b. Yosanyah and R. Berekiah)).

The understanding of the princes' offerings so dazzlingly developed by these homilists was a time-honoured one. Even apart from any allusion to Solomon's Song, Josephus similarly emphasized that the princes, in Num. 7 represented the people in their new and closer walk with God (*Ant.* iii 219–22). 'The multitude judged that God was tabernacling together (ὁμόσκηνον) with them ... and they offered gifts to God according to their tribes. For the phylarchs came together, two by two ... Each of them brought, moreover, other sacrifices, called "saving" ' (σωτηρίους, following the Septuagintal rendering of *sh*^{e}*lamim* in the Pentateuch). It is reasonable to suppose that an elaborated account of the princes' offerings in Num. 7, probably drawing out their significance as representing Israel's devotion, circulated in Palestine before A.D. 100 as part of the larger repertory of narrative and homily concerning priesthood, sanctuary and sacrifice; especially since Num. 7 was read at Hanukkah (M. Meg. 3.6).

Secondly, under the heading of haggadic interpretation of the princes, note should be taken of additions to the biblical passages on the phylarchs, and the establishment of connections between them (a process already noted in the biblical text of Num. 7:2, section II, above). These developments are sometimes minor in themselves, but collectively they indicate a creative concern with the twelve princes as biblical characters, for they come from a wide range of sources. This selection follows the biblical order.

By the goatskins with which Jacob obtained his blessing (Gen. 27:16) he atoned for the princes of his tribes, for the prince's sin-offering is a kid of the goats (Pithron Torah, on Lev. 4:22 (Urbach 10f.)). 'The officers of the children of Israel' in Egypt (Exod. 5:14f., 19) were the princes (Sifre Num. 45, on 7.2; these officers were the members of the sanhedrin, according to Sifre Num 91 and Targum Pseudo-Jonathan, both on Num. 11:16). The prince Nahshon and his house 'gathered much' manna (Exod. 16:18, in Mekhilta, Beshallah, Wayyassa, iv, on Exod. 16:16 (Horovitz-Rabin, 167)). Moses summoned the princes before the battle with Amalek (addition to Exod. 17:9, in Josephus, *Ant.* iii 47). The twelve spies (Num. 13:23f., LXX ἀρχηγοί) are described as phylarchs (Philo *Mos.* i.22). Contrary to what is most naturally suggested by Num. 7:17 (2), the princes and the people together inscribed the rods (Josephus, *Ant.* iv 63–6); indeed, Moses sealed them with the phylarchs' signet-rings (1 Clem. 43). The princes who dug the well (Num. 21:18) were the phylarchs (Tos. Sukkah iii.11; Tanhuma Numbers Bemidbar 2, on 1:1 (481), Huqqath 21, on 21.17–18 (573); Dura Europos mural (probably; Gutmann, 141f.)), although competitors for the identification include the sanhedrin (Neofiti margin on Num. 21:18) and others (CD vi. 6, Philo, *Mos.* i. 256). The apostate Zimri, 'prince of a father's house' in the tribe of Simeon (Num. 25:14), becomes ἡγούμενος of the tribe (Josephus, *Ant.* iv 141; the word is used of the princes, 1 Chron 27:16 LXX), 'head' or 'prince' of the whole tribe (Sifre Num. 131, on 25.5; Tanhuma Buber, Numbers, Phinehas, 3, on 25.10 (Buber, 151); Sanh. 82a, followed by Rashi on Num. 25:6). At the allotment of land Eleazar, clothed with Urim and Thummim, presided, and the princes drew the lots (addition to Num. 26:52–6, 34:17f., in B.B. 122a). The 'phylarchs' are the first category of those summoned to hear the last song and blessings of Moses (Deut. 31:28 LXX); and it is they who take up the stones from the bed of Jordan for a memorial of the crossing (addition to Jos. 4:4 in Josephus *Ant.* v 20).

It is not, of course, contended here that all these interpretations were current during the New Testament period. A first-century circulation seems highly probable for the first example considered at length (Num. 7); among the eleven developments in detail just listed, the first probably arose after the cessation of sacrifice, but the Septuagint, Philo, Josephus and 1 Clement account for six. What is suggested, rather, is that this combination of later and earlier material exhibits the continuity of creative interpretative interest in the twelve princes. This concern is evident in the rabbinic midrash, but it simply continues an interest which had already prompted alterations and additions in the biblical paraphrase of the first century and earlier, from which a significant proportion of the examples has been taken. This imaginative interest in the interpretation of the phylarchs can therefore properly be assumed as an influence in first-century Palestine.

IV

That the phylarchs should be included among the possible models of the company of 'the twelve' was suggested in section II, above, with reference to their prominent place in seventeenth-century reconstructions of the Mosaic and apostolic polities, which could be considered as a reflection of their importance in the Old Testament text itself. It was then asked whether this importance, which rabbinic concentration on the sanhedrin tended to obscure, would indeed have been recognized by a first-century Jew. An affirmative answer to this question has now been given (section III, above), on the basis of a selective review of the phylarchs in the haggadah. Yet, granted the important point that the phylarchs 'lived' as biblical characters in the first-century Jewish imagination, it remains to consider the first division of material distinguished at the beginning of section III, the constitutional and regulative passages in their halakhic interpretation.

This type of interpretation bears closely upon an inquiry into the place of the New Testament twelve in contemporary Jewish thought, for it was of primary importance for ancient Jewish interpreters, and is invited, as already noted, by the nature of many of the Old Testament passages themselves. Here it is approached, first, by way of traces of the idea of a constitution including a body of twelve tribal princes; and secondly, in the following sections, through Josephus and other sources wherein this idea seems to stand in conflict or connection with the idea of government by sanhedrin. The object will be to ascertain what constitutional or regulative associations a first-century Jew might have associated with the twelve phylarchs.

First, traces of the thought of a constitutionally important body of twelve tribal chiefs are not infrequent. The prominence of the princes in 1 Chronicles, as compared with 1 Kings (section III, above), already suggests this thought; and the place of Zerubbabel and his eleven companions, at the head of the list of returning exiles (Ezra 2:2 = Neh. 7:7) is often viewed as a trace of it (Schürer-Vermes-Millar, ii, 201).

However this may be, the phylarchs clearly gain further political importance in the LXX, despite the translation ἄρχοντες which can equate them with elders (sections II, above, and VI, below). Moses spoke concerning vows 'unto the heads of tribes, to the children of Israel', but in the LXX simply 'unto the rulers of the tribes of the children of Israel' (Num. 30:2). At the giving of the Ten Commandments there drew near 'all the heads of your tribes, and your elders', but in the LXX 'all the leaders (ἡγούμενοι) of your tribes, and your *gerousia*' (Deut 5:20 (lxx 23)); here the elders are identified as the council, but it is envisaged that the tribal leaders, probably the phylarchs (cf. 1 Chron. 27:16 LXX ἡγούμενος), will take precedence over them. This view of what is intended in the LXX is supported by a later passage in which, in the Hebrew text, Moses exhorts 'your heads, your tribes, your elders and your officers, all the men of Israel' (Deut. 29:9); but the Septuagintal version of this list begins 'your rulers of tribes (ἀρχίφυλοι) and your gerousia'. Here the phylarchs are plainly mentioned first of all, even before the council. Comparably, they are added, as already noted, as the first category of those who hear the last words of Moses (Deut. 31:28, LXX).

With these passages one should view Exod. 34:30 LXX πρεσβύτεροι ('elders of Israel' for MT = 'children of Israel',). The alteration reconciles the following verse, 34:31, on Moses, Aaron and the princes, with the comparable earlier account of Moses, Aaron and the elders (Exod. 24:1, 9–11, see section II above). After the alteration in 34:30 the princes can be understood, in the light of the LXX passages just mentioned, as the leading members of the council.

In 2 Chronicles LXX, similarly, 'the princes of hundreds'—who take precedence immediately after the high priest in the important constitutional context of Joash's coronation—become 'the patriarchs' (2 Chron. 23:20 LXX); the same word is chosen, in a counterpart of Philo's application of 'phylarch', to render an unambiguous Hebrew reference to the rulers of the tribes (1 Chron. 27:11 LXX), and they rather than the inner-tribal heads are probably meant by the translator to take the highest place the court affords in 2 Chron. 23. The phylarchs are also inserted, in a cultic context but again probably not without political connotations, when the twelve he-goats, a sin-offering for all Israel at the dedication of the second temple (Ezra 6:17, 8:35), are specified in 1 Esd.

7:8 as corresponding to the number of the twelve φύλαρχαι (cf. Lev. 4:22; Num. 7:87, speaking for RV 'princes' rather than REB 'patriarchs' at 1 Esd. 7:8). The addition of 'twelve' at Num. 7:2, LXX (section II, above) likewise picks the princes out as a body.

The political precedence awarded in these Septuagintal passages also appears in the Jewish historian Eupolemus (second century B.C., quoted from Alexander Polyhistor by Eusebius, *praep. ev.* ix. 30, 8): David 'handed over the government to his son Solomon, in the presence of Eli the high priest and the twelve princes of the tribes' (Wacholder, 151). From the biblical list of princes, priests and Levites (1 Chron. 23:22) Eupolemus retains only the twelve and the high priest (on whose name 'Eli' see Wacholder, 151 and Spiro, 104, n. 29). He perhaps considers that, with the high priest, the phylarchs form the council (so Wacholder, 154). As will be seen shortly, Josephus seems to attack this view.

In these Greek Jewish sources a significant place in the Jewish polity is clearly accorded to the twelve princes. Qumran texts have provided other evidence for this particular point, together with more general indications of the constitutional importance of the number twelve. They also attest, without reference to twelve, the continuing influence of the Pentateuchal image of the phylarchs at the head of the tribal formations. Thus, in an edition not available to me when this essay was writen, C. A. Newsom (26–7, 32–5) shows that the angelic *n*[e]*śî'îm* mentioned several times in the Songs of the Sabbath Sacrifice (so 4Q 403 1 i, lines 1, 10, 21, 26 'chief princes'; 4Q 400 3 ii 2 'deputy princes') are probably the chief priests and deputy chief priests of the seven heavenly sanctuaries, envisaged on the model of the tribal princes in such passages as Num. 1:16, 7:2, 10:14, and enjoying a precedence among the angels such as the princes have on earth. On the number twelve, however, the present argument converges with the studies of Qumran and the twelve by Flusser and Baumgarten.

In the Isaiah pesher, as Flusser notes, the pinnacles of the new Jerusalem (Isa. 54:12) are the twelve chief priests, and its gates of carbuncle the twelve heads of tribes (4QpIsa[d], cf. Rev. 21:14; corrected text and translation in Baumgarten, 146–50). This interpretation can be related to the provision in the War Scroll for *ma'*[a]*mādôt* consisting of twelve priests, twelve levites and twelve tribal princes (1QM ii. 1–3). Of clearest constitutional importance is the similar ordinance in the Temple Scroll, compared by Baumgarten: the king shall have a council of 'twelve *nᵉśîʾîm* of his people', twelve priests, and twelve levites, above whom his heart shall not be lifted up, and whom he shall always consult (Deut. 17:20 as interpreted in 11Q Temple lvii.11–15). These three passages, in which the twelve princes themselves clearly figure, can be viewed together with two others, discussed by both Flusser and Baumgarten, in which the *number* twelve is important; the Manual of Discipline evisages a council of twelve men and three priests (1QS viii.1), and the Ordinances provide for a court of twelve, including two priests (4Q Ordinances ii. 4, iii. 4).

Baumgarten, enlarging on Flusser's suggestion of a Qumran background for the New Testament twelve, argues that the New Testament views of the apostles as tribal judges (Matt. 19:28) and of the heavenly elders as a body of twenty-four (Rev. 4:4, etc.; see Charles on 4:10, and Geyser, 392–7) depend not only on Qumran notions of the composition of courts, but also on various ancient traditions about the membership of the sanhedrin. Views that the court should be duodecimally based are reflected, he finds, in these (notably in Sanh. 17a, where seventy-two is explained as six from each tribe). His conjecture rests, however, in large part, on the clearer importance of the number twelve in the composition of the Qumran courts.

The non-sectarian Jewish evidence from the Septuagint and Eupolemus, not discussed by Flusser and Baumgarten, may now be thought to confirm the likelihood of duodecimal Jewish antecedents for both the New Testament and the rabbinic texts. Here a further, less direct trace of the constitutional significance of the phylarchs may be added. In pre-Christian passages of the Testaments of the Twelve Patriarchs the expectation of the resurrection includes the hope that the twelve patriarchs will be raised as governors of their tribes (Test. Judah 25:1–2, Benj. 10:7; cf. Zeb. 10:2 (individual patriarch); date and theme discussed by O'Neill, 95 and Hultgård, i, 260–1, 235–6, 246–7, 254). This hope for patriarchal government of the tribes recalls the connections between patriarchs and phylarchs already noted in LXX, Philo and Josephus. The midrash on Num 21:17–18 already discussed correspondingly says that the patriarchs are called princes (*sarim*) (Tanhuma Numbers, Huqqath, 21, as cited in section III, above; parallels include Num. R. 19.26, on 21.18).

To sum up the present section, it may be said that the constitutional importance of the twelve princes in particular is clear in the Septuagint (Numbers, Deuteronomy, Chronicles and 1 Esdras), Eupolemus, and, as Flusser and Baumgarten have noted, in three Qumran texts (4QpIsa, 1QM, 11Q Temple). It is also implied by the hope that the twelve patriarchs will arise to govern their tribes (Testaments of Judah, Zebulun and Benjamin). More generally, the idea of a governing body of twelve is accepted in 1QS and 4Q Ordinances, and is conjectured by Baumgarten, with probability, to have influenced early rabbinic tradition. The Qumran texts, viewed against the earlier background of P, Chronicles, Ezra and the LXX as well as the second-century Eupolemus and the Testaments of the Twelve Patriarchs, appear to be conservative rather than idiosyncratic in the prominence they give to the princes. In this particular the Greek sources bear out Vermes' general conclusion that the tribally-based Qumran order represents an earlier view of the Jewish polity (Schürer-Vermes-Millar, ii, 201). For the present inquiry, however, it is specially notable that, from the LXX to Qumran, constitutional prominence continued to be given not only to the tribes, but also to the phylarchs themselves.

Thus far, it seems that the Gospel company of twelve, in the first century A.D., could well have awakened in their contemporaries associations with the ancestral Jewish polity, τὸ δωδεκάφυλον ἡμῶν (Acts 26:7), and with the constitutional significance of the twelve tribal princes in particular. The previous section has shown that an interest in the phylarchs can be assumed in the biblical interpretation of this period. Yet, as is plain from Josephus, direct institutional embodiment of the tribal view of the Jewish polity had become archaic in the first century. The view itself remained influential, because of its biblical roots, but it had to compete, as already noted, with the practical and ideological importance of two political institutions, the high-priesthood and the council, which were also rooted in the Bible. Before a judgment on the significance of the twelve apostles can be more fully formed, it must be asked how far the constitutional importance of the princes could survive, in Josephus and other sources, side by side with the idea of government by high priest and sanhedrin.

V

Josephus, who regards the council of elders under high-priestly presidency as the backbone of the constitution, treats the twelve princes with striking ambiguity. In his sketch of the Mosaic polity he allows, if necessary, for a king (with Deut. 17:14), who shall do nothing without the high priest and the elders (here Josephus is in noteworthy accord with the Temple Scroll, as cited in the previous section); but this Deuteronomic provision is only made in case the nation cannot be content with a (kingless) 'aristocracy', the authentic Israelite constitution (*Ant.* iv 223f.). This preference for aristocracy may owe something to Dionysius of Halicarnassus, as noted by Downing, 60. At any rate, the aristocratic polity is clearly identical, for Josephus, with the 'theocracy' (*Ap.* ii.165) under which the Jews, by ancestral custom, obey the priests (as Pompey is told, according to *Ant.* xiv 41). The national decline from sacerdotal aristocracy occurred in the time of the judges; the biblical description of the lapse following the settlement is amplified in Josephus by 'the aristocratic form of government was already becoming corrupted, and they did not appoint councils of elders (γερουσίαι) or any other magistracy (ἀρχή) formerly ordained by law' (addition to Judg. 2:11–23 in Josephus, *Ant.* v 135).

The phylarchs evidently fail to fit neatly into Josephus' narrative of the 'aristocratic' period before this decline. On the one hand, as noted earlier, Josephus can introduce the phylarchs into the biblical narrative, or heighten their rôle (*Ant.* iii 47, iv. 64, v. 20, cited in section III, above). He not only leaves the phylarchs their place in charge of the census (*Ant.* iii 287), but also specially notes, on the basis of the list in Num. 1:5–16, that Moses 'enrolled' Manasseh and Ephraim 'among the phylarchs' (κατέλεξεν εἰς τοὺς φυλάρχους, *Ant.* iii 288); this fulfils Jacob's charge to his sons (*Ant.* ii 195), and here Josephus seems to regard the phylarchs' authority as patriarchal.

On the other hand, all the biblical passages wherein the princes seem to form a council (as noted in section III, above) are consistently altered by Josephus. In almost every instance the phylarchs disappear, and a reader of Josephus only would be unaware that they are mentioned and given importance at the corresponding places in the Bible. A brief review of these paraphrases by Josephus may bring out their character more clearly.

First, shortly after describing the census, Josephus mentions the silver trumpet which summons the princes. Here he calls them ἀρχαί (adaptation of Num. 10:4 in Josephus, *Ant.* iii 292). This broad designation, 'the authorities', can also be used to cover magistracies inferior to the council (as in *Ant.* v 135, just quoted). It compares with the generalizing LXX of Num. 10:4 'the rulers, leaders of Israel', but contrasts with the exact trumpet inscription 'princes of God' in the War Scroll (*n^esî'ey el* 1QM iii.3; Yadin 48, 268). Josephus gives a still more general rendering than LXX, perhaps because the trumpet summons the princes to meet in council, and he wants an expression that will cover the council envisaged in his own political theory, the *gerousia*.

Such a suspicion seems to be borne out by his treatment of other passages in which the princes appear as a council. Moses alone is mentioned at the points where the princes figure in the stories of the spoiling of Midian and the plight of Zelophehad's daughters (Josephus, *Ant.* iv 162, 174f.). Again, 'the princes' or 'the heads of the fathers of the tribes', who with Moses and Eleazar receive the petition of Reuben and Gad, become simply those ἐν τέλει, 'in authority' (adaptation of Num. 32:2, 28 in Josephus, *Ant.* iv 171).

In the three other relevant passages care has evidently been given to a representation of the ideal sacerdotal 'aristocracy', into which a model king has been introduced in the person of Joshua. Two of Josephus' paraphrases accordingly dismiss the princes entirely, in favour of a *gerousia* presided over by the high priest. Thus, in the Bible the princes alone are responsible for the misguided promise to the Gibeonites, but in Josephus it is made by 'Eleazar the high priest with the *gerousia*' (addition to Jos. 9:15–21 in Josephus, *Ant.* v 55, 57). Similarly, the ten princes deputed to investigate the altar of witness become simply ten men held in honour by the Hebrews (adaptation of Jos. 22:14 in Josephus, *Ant.* v 104); but they are now despatched not just by 'the children of Israel', but, in good constitutional form, by Joshua and the high priest Eleazar and the *gerousia* (addition to Jos. 22:13 in *Ant.* v 103).

In Josephus' version of the story of the Gibeonites it might seem that the phylarchs straightforwardly constitute the council of elders, as was probably the case in Eupolemus (section IV, above). Any complete identification of the princes with the council seems questionable, however, in view of the passages where vaguer terms for 'authorities' are substituted by Josephus. This doubt is underlined by the third and last of the paraphrases in which the phylarchs have become part of an ideal Mosaic polity.

Here the phylarchs are clearly named together with the council, in connection with the division of the promised land. This passage is the only one of the seven under review in which a biblical mention of the princes survives in Josephus. Difference of opinion on the authority for the allotment of the land is already apparent in the Bible itself. Joshua alone divides the land, according to Jos. 18:10; but Eleazar (named before Joshua) and the princes or heads of the fathers of the tribes are associated with him, according to Num. 34:17f., Jos. 14:1; 19:51; 21:1. Josephus, in his paraphrase of Jos. 18:10, naturally follows the last-mentioned texts, which represent P and its influence, the chief biblical source of Josephus' own theory of sacerdotal aristocracy; but he says that Joshua took with him Eleazar and the *gerousia* 'with the phylarchs' (*Ant.* v 80).

In the six paraphrases considered hitherto either the phylarchs were excised, so that Moses appeared to act alone, or the potentially more comprehensive 'authorities' or high priest and council were substituted for them. The survival of the phylarchs in this seventh instance perhaps owes something to the context, for they are prominently associated with the division of the land not only in the biblical passages just quoted (cf. Ezek. 45:8), but also in the midrash (B.B. 122a (section III, above), and PRK v. 9). They survive here in Josephus, however, only to be named after the *gerousia*. It is unclear whether they belong to the council, or are thought of as a separate and perhaps subordinate group.

That Josephus could envisage the phylarchs as part of a larger council, as in the Temple Scroll (section IV, above), is suggested by his substitution of more comprehensive terms, including *gerousia* (twice), in four of the other passages just considered. The present paraphrase can be understood in the same way, but its order of words underlines the authority of the council. Herein it contrasts with Deut. 29:9 LXX quoted in section IV, above, where the phylarchs are mentioned before the council; but it significantly accords with Targum Pseudo-Jonathan on the same verse, beginning 'your heads of sanhedrin and the rulers of your tribes' ('*^{a}mark^{e}ley shibteykhon*) in that order. In *Ant.* v 80, then, the isolated survival of the phylarchs with but after the council tends to exalt the council as a whole, and to reduce the phylarchs to a section within the council rather than at its head.

In six of the seven paraphrases under review, therefore, the phylarchs are eliminated; in two of these six, more comprehensive 'authorities' appear instead; in another two, high priest and council are substituted. In the seventh, which has just been considered, the council is again inserted, and added to Joshua and the high priest; but in this instance it appears 'with the phylarchs', who, although they have this once been allowed to remain, are probably envisaged as no more than a group within it. Thus Josephus, despite his heightening of the phylarchs' rôle elsewhere, regularly dismisses them, or at least minimizes them, sometimes clearly in favour of high priest and council, whenever he paraphrases passages wherein the phylarchs themselves appear as a council of constitutional significance.

Josephus' noticeable measure of consistency in the paraphrase of these constitutionally relevant passages recalls the fact that one of his two purposes in the *Antiquities* was to describe the constitution (*Ant.* i 5). In the book he puts forward his own view of the Jewish polity, outlined at the beginning of this section; and it is in the light of this purpose that his apparently self-contradictory treatment of the phylarchs may be thought to make sense. He dismisses or minimizes them not because he suddenly scorns those whom once he delighted to honour, but because he is an advocate of government by high priest and council, and must show this to be the 'order of a polity' (*Ant.* iii 84) which, as he strongly stresses, was revealed on the mount and in the tabernacle (on his view of the revelation of a constitution, Horbury (2), 56–7; = 239–40, below).

Josephus' working out of this purpose is further evinced by his insertion of the *gerousia* in passages unconnected with the phylarchs. The levitical priests and the judge foreordained by Moses as a court of appeal are high priest, 'prophet' and *gerousia* (adaption of Deut. 17:9 in Josephus, *Ant.* iv 218); Moses is escorted to his passing by high priest, *gerousia* and general, all unmentioned in the biblical narrative (addition to Deut. 34:1 in Josephus, *Ant.* iv 324); Joshua is made to behave as a constitutional monarch, for he reports the oath taken by the two spies in Jericho 'to the high priest Eleazar and the gerousia' (addition to Jos. 2:23f.) in Josephus, *Ant.* v 15); and, as in Josephus' narrative of the altar of witness (*Ant.* v 103, mentioned earlier in this section), so also in the case of the Benjamites the *gerousia* advises parley before war is declared (addition to Judg. 20:8–11 in Josephus, *Ant.* v 151). Josephus' advocacy of the high priest and the council of elders is unmistakable.

Since this essay first appeared, and independently of it and of one another, Goodblatt (94–7) and Pearce (35–9) have considered the presentation of a *gerousia* by Josephus in the *Antiquities*; from differing standpoints each notes, comparably with the foregoing paragraphs, the treatment of the princes as members of a body of elders, and Goodblatt suggests (comparably with the following paragraph, but without reference to Ps.-Philo) that Josephus was indebted to existing paraphrase.

Josephus was perhaps not without precedent in his suppression and transformation of the phylarchs. Another pre-rabbinic paraphrast, Pseudo-Philo, in his Biblical Antiquities, likewise deletes them where they are prominent in the Bible (Num. 1 in Ps.-Philo 14; Num. 17:21 (6) in Ps.-Philo 17.2; Jos. 14:1 in Ps.-Philo 20.9), or turns them into elders (Jos. 22:13–15 in Ps.-Philo 22.2), despite strong emphasis on the twelve tribes (e.g. Ps.-Philo 10.3, 14.1, 19.5, 20.9, 25.2–26.15, 49.2). To judge by the long Kenaz narrative, where the author had little biblical material, his preferred constitution was headed by captain, high-priest and elders (25:6, 28:3). Here again he is like Josephus, with somewhat less emphasis on priestly rule. It seems likely that these probably roughly contemporary authors drew on a common narrative tradition, wherein the phylarchs were dropped in the interest of ruler, high-priest and elders.

The ambiguity of Josephus' treatment of the phylarchs therefore arises from a form of the conflict observed by Spinoza between their biblical importance and the theory of the sanhedrin. Josephus gives the princes a more definite share in patriarchal glory than the Bible does, and recognizes them as representatives of Israel (paraphrase of Num. 7; section III above); but he systematically deprives them of the conciliar status which they clearly receive in the biblical text. Both aspects of this treatment were probably already familiar. Re-statement of its negative side, as seen in Josephus and Ps.-Philo, will nevertheless have been evoked in the first century A.D. by the prestige of high priest and council, and by the heightened presentation of the phylarchs found in many older but still current sources (LXX, Eupolemus, Qumran texts, and Testaments of the Twelve Patriarchs, reviewed in the previous section). That others shared the outlook of Josephus is suggested not only by Pseudo-Philo, but also by signs of the same conflict of political theories in rabbinic texts now to be considered.

VI

The targums continue the generalizing side of LXX interpretation. The common Greek rendering ἄρχοντες included, however, within its wide range, the possibility pursued by Josephus that the phylarchs are councillors. Ἄρχοντες join with elders in sources for a Jerusalem council (Ezra 10:8 LXX (for Hebrew *sarim*; elders only at 1 Esd. 9:4); 1 Macc. 14:28; Acts 4:5, 8), and the Alexandrian Jewry has a *gerousia* with ἄρχοντες in Philo, but seventy 'elders' in the Talmud (Philo, Flacc. 80; j Sukkah v 1, 55a); ἄρχοντες could sometimes be used interchangeably with πρεσβύτεροι (Harvey, 321; evidence most fully in Lietzmann (162–9), who warns that the terms need not always overlap).

The same link with the council is probably though less plainly allowed by the comparable targumic renderings *rabrᵉbin, rabrᵉbane,* or *ᵃmarkᵉlin*, 'great men' or 'rulers'. Both are probably old; the former also occurs in the Peshitta Pentateuch (*rawrᵉbānēʾ*), and the meaning of the latter was debated (Horayoth 13a, Lev. R. v.3). Possible conciliar overtones emerge in view of the correspondence of *rabrᵉbin* with the plural of Hebrew *gadhôl* and Greek μέγας (eg. Gen. 12:17 LXX, Onkelos and Pseudo-Jonathan, of 'great' afflictions); the Greek and Hebrew words can stand independently for councillors. Thus Mattathias in 1 Maccabees is ἄρχων καὶ ἔνδοξος καὶ μέγας (2:17), and in a midrash *gᵉdhôley yisraʾel* 'the great men of Israel' describe Isa. 3:14 'the elders of his people and his princes' (שריו, LXX here ἄρχοντες, targum variant *rabrᵉbohi* (Stenning, 13)), who are enthroned as assessors in the heavenly court (Dan. 7:9 interpreted in Tanhuma Buber, Leviticus, Qedoshim 1; p. 72, on Lev. 19:1). The targums therefore probably allow a conciliar link, and certainly exclude any potential conflict of jurisdiction between the princes and the elders of the sanhedrin, when these renderings occur in verses where the princes could be regarded as a council (e.g. Num. 7:2, 10:4, 17:17, 21:(2, 6), 27:2, 31:13, 32:2; in all these LXX ἄρχοντες, Onkelos *rabrᵉbin*, Neofiti *rabrᵉbane*, Peshitta *rawrᵉbānēʾ*, Pseudo-Jonathan *ᵃmarkᵉlin* (combined with *rabrᵉbin* in 7:2)).

Definite advocacy of the sanhedrin also appears, however, as already noted (section III, above), in a tendency to ascribe ancient worthies to its membership (the officers of the Israelites in Egypt, who were also identified with the princes, Pseudo-Jonathan on Num. 11:16; the princes who dug the well, Neofiti margin on Num. 21:18). As the former of these examples shows, this tendency could run directly counter to exaltation of the phylarchs; at Deut. 29:9, as noted in the previous section, the Septuagintal precedence of phylarchs over council is reversed by Pseudo-Jonathan, and at Deut. 31:28 'the elders of your tribes' becomes in LXX 'your phylarchs' (section IV, above), but in Pseudo-Jonathan 'the wise men of your tribes'.

Despite the strength of this tendency the targums preserve, like Josephus, some traces of the phylarchs' importance. Thus, in the account of the tribal formations under the standards (Num. 10:14–28), Pseudo-Jonathan adds to the biblical naming of each prince the introduction 'the great man who was appointed'. In a particularly striking reversal of the commendation of the sanhedrin, 'the elders of the congregation' appear in the targum as 'the twelve elders of the congregation who are appointed rulers over the twelve tribes' (Pseudo-Jonathan on Lev. 4:15, discussed by Mantel, 43, n. 240). This rendering is in opposition to Sanh. 13b, where the 'congregation' is the sanhedrin (see below); but it accords with the biblical context, where the elders might be expected to represent the congregation, and the sin-offering of 'the prince' is soon mentioned (Lev. 4:22). Advocacy of the sanhedrin, continuing Josephus' propaganda for the *gerousia*, has here not excluded a reference, perhaps of earlier origin, to the phylarchs as a ruling council.

A biblical basis for the composition and procedure of the sanhedrin is sought with special concentration in the Mishnah and early halakhic midrash. In this context the 'prince' and the 'congregation' could acquire new, technical senses; but the recognition of the *nāśî'* as a tribal prince could persist here as well as in the targum. Thus Lev. 4:13–23, on the sin-offerings of the 'whole congregation' and the prince, the passage from which a verse in targumic rendering has just been considered, formed the basis of Mishnaic discussion of errors of judgment by the sanhedrin. 'Congregation' was understood as 'court', and 'prince' (verse 22) not as tribal prince, but as king (Mishnah, Horayoth ii.5–iii.3; cf. Tosefta Horayoth i.9, ii.2). Despite the fundamental halakhic importance of this interpretation, it was still rightly asked 'Who is a "prince" (*nāśî'*)?' (Mishnah Horayoth iii.3, Tosefta Horayoth ii.2); the answer given is 'king', but the comment in the Babylonian Talmud (Horayoth 11 a) is indeed that a tribal prince like Nahshon might reasonably though wrongly be envisaged. The understanding of *nāśî'* in verse 22 as tribal prince survived in Pithron Torah *ad loc.* (cited in section III, above), and probably influenced Pseudo-Jonathan on verse 15, just quoted.

The honour of the phylarchs is also strikingly upheld in the opinion that, whenever the congregation was addressed, the princes were spoken to first

(Sifre Num. 73, on 10.34). By contrast, according to Babylonian Talmud, Erubin 54b, the laws were expounded in order to Aaron, his sons, the elders, and finally all the people; the precedence here given to priesthood and council would have pleased Josephus, and, just as he often did, it excludes the princes as a special group. Indeed, Exod. 34:31, wherein Aaron and the princes meet Moses before the people do, is interpreted by Rashi in the light of this Talmudic passage, the princes being understood (comparably, up to a point, with Exod. 34:30 LXX) as the elders, or as among the elders, of Exod. 24:14 (sections II and IV above). Sifre, however, keeps the primacy given to the princes at Exod. 34:31, and also to the 'heads' of tribes at Num. 30:2, where they are the first to hear Moses on vows, Deut. 5:20, where they are the first to approach Moses, and Deut. 29:9, where they are again his first addressees. In the three last-mentioned passages, as noted already (section IV, above), LXX gives added emphasis to the precedence of the phylarchs.

Sifre on the princes' primacy as recipients of the laws may be compared with the tradition, found in later compilations, that the princes ranked immediately below Eleazar; they and he would wait each morning on Aaron, who with the rest would then wait on Moses (Tanhuma Buber, Numbers, on 20:25 (addition to Huqqath, 131–2); Pithron, on Num. 20:25, in Urbach, 187–8). Rashi on Num. 30:2, in contrast with his comment on Exod. 34:31, speaks simply of Moses' custom of honouring the princes by communicating the divine message first of all to them, and does not mention the elders. Here he may well have drawn directly on Sifre; but in any case his comment, together with the tradition preserved in Tanhuma Buber and Pithron Torah, shows that the primacy of the princes' council could still be mentioned in rabbinically-influenced Jewish exposition, even on a subject so closely bound up with the theory of the sanhedrin as the reception of the Torah.

Hence, despite pervasive concern with the sanhedrin, the princes could still be envisaged in halakhic interpretation as the phylarchs (Horayoth 11a; Sifre Num. on 7:2). The targums tend to dissolve the princes' corporate identity by generalizing translation, which can merge them in the sanhedrin in the tradition of LXX, Pseudo-Philo and Josephus; they also displace the princes from their precedence over the sanhedrin, in the tradition of Josephus but against one marked tendency of LXX. Nevertheless, the princes can be mentioned as a ruling council (Pseudo-Jonathan on Lev. 4:15), qualified to receive the divine commandments first of all (Sifre Num. 73, on 10.31–4). Septuagintal tendency to emphasize the princes' precedence finds at least a measure of continuation.

Some survival of the princes' earlier éclat was probably encouraged by their natural place in tribally-based views of the Jewish polity. Such views impinge on the theory of the sanhedrin when it is considered as a body representing the twelve tribes. Thus, 'when the heads of the people are gathered together with the tribes of Israel' (Deut. 33:5) is taken to refer to the seventy elders gathered in sanhedrin, representing the corporate union of the tribes (Sifre Deut. on 33:5; Pithron, in Urbach, 334); but, according to Sanh. 17a, Moses is puzzled whether to choose six or five members of the sanhedrin from each tribe, as in either case he reaches a total different from the seventy requested in Num. 11:16. In these passages consideration of the sanhedrin itself is affected by that tribal conception of Israel which would also encourage attention to the more conveniently numbered tribal princes.

VII

The significance of the biblical passages on the phylarchs was recognized in ancient Jewry, as has now been seen, both by development and by selective suppression. From the making of the LXX to the rabbinic homily of the amoraic period, the princes lived in haggadic exposition (section III above). Their first-century Greek Jewish designation 'phylarch' (section II above) suggests a share in patriarchal glory, confirmed in Josephus' two-sided presentation; and in rabbinic exposition the princes figured uninterruptedly as national representatives in such important traditional narratives as that of the phylarchs' offerings (section III). In halakhic interpretation, however, continuity was broken by the conflict of constitutional ideals, already evident in the biblical texts as between the phylarchs in P and the council of elders in JE. In one group of sources, comprising the Septuagint, Eupolemus, three Qumran texts and the Testaments of the Twelve Patriarchs (section IV, above), clear constitutional importance is ascribed to the twelve biblical princes and their successors. In Josephus and Pseudo-Philo, on the other hand (section V, above), the princes are deprived of their biblical precedence, the biblical references to them as a council are almost all suppressed, and, instead, the high priest and the council of elders are given a much heightened rôle. The same tendencies emerge in rabbinic exegesis (section VI, above), with its concentration on the sanhedrin; but the special status of the phylarchs was sometimes remembered, perhaps in connection with the tribal view of Israel. In first-century Palestine both the haggadic interpretation of the princes, and the conflict between the constitutional models offered by the phylarchs on the one hand and the high priest and elders on the other, can be assumed to have been familiar.

Three stages in this conflict can be roughly distinguished in the sources considered above. In the first stage, represented by the LXX passages noted in section IV, the twelve princes form a body taking precedence immediately after high priest and monarch, and before the *gerousia*. Eupolemus, who chooses simply to mention king, high priest and phylarchs at Solomon's accession, may well share this view, but is too fragmentarily preserved for certainty. In the second stage, represented by the Temple Scroll, and probably also reflected in the Isaiah pesher and the War Scroll (section IV, above), the twelve princes, or rather their successors, form part of a larger council. A third stage appears in Josephus, Pseudo-Philo and the targums. They still allow a link between the princes and the council, but their generalizing translations obscure the specific reference to twelve princes which is clear in the three Qumran texts. Now the princes are largely dissolved as a corporation, by generalizing renderings or the suppression of biblical references, and emphasis falls on the high priest and council; if the princes are still mentioned as a body, the council as a whole takes precedence over them (so Josephus, probably, and Pseudo-Jonathan).

These roughly distinguished stages in the conflict between two constitutional models have some correspondence to periods of time. It is not improbable, as noted above, that the positive constitutional development of the twelve reflects an early form of post-exilic Jewish polity, which was antiquated by the increasing importance of a larger council. By the first century, the practical significance of the theory of high priest and council is confirmed by the predominance of this constitution in the first period of Jewish self-determination in the revolt of A.D. 66. Clearly, however, these stages, though broadly successive in time, could overlap and conflict in the thought of contemporaries; and they did so in first-century Palestine, as comparison of the Qumran texts and Josephus indicates.

The haggadic development of the princes, and their place in the conflict of constitutional models, are therefore significant for the understanding of the twelve and the apostles. Two interpretations of early Christian evidence against this background may be summarily suggested.

First, in the realm of church order, the variations and connections in Luke-Acts between the twelve and the apostles on one side, and the elders of the Jerusalem church on the other, can be ascribed in part to an inner Christian manifestation of the broader Jewish constitutional conflict. Wellhausen stressed that references to the twelve (eleven) in the gospels and Acts cluster in the resurrection narratives and their sequels (Wellhausen, 141). Here the eleven or the apostles receive knowledge for teaching (Luke 24:45; cf. Acts 2:42), commission (Luke 24:48; Acts 1:8; Matt. 28:19; John 20:21), and the Spirit (Luke 24:49; Acts 1:5, 8; 2:1–14, 37 (2:1 continues 1:26; 2:2 καθήμενοι suggests dignitaries); John 20:22). Authority to remit sins is given in this setting in John 20:23 (cf. Matt. 18:18; 16:19). The emphasis on authority to govern is marked in Matt. 19:28, parallel with Luke 22:30 (Bammel, 45–7), but mission predominates in the resurrection narratives, in Mark 3:13–19; 6:7–13 and parallels (especially 3:14–15; 6:7). The weight placed on authorization, particularly evident in the visionary contexts indicated by Wellhausen, is best ascribed to the claims and prestige of a governing body of apostles (compare the exaltation of constitutional models in the Jewish interpretation just considered). Such a body appears in Acts 4:35; 9:27 and especially (as Wellhausen (144) again stressed) in the constitutional language of Acts 6:2. (οἱ δώδεκα convene τὸ πλῆθος τῶν μαθητῶν). On the other hand 'elders' form a council together with apostles at Acts 15:2, 4, 6, 22, 23, 16:4, and elders—but not a group of apostles—are mentioned at Acts 11:30, 21:18. The 'seventy' or 'seventy-two' of Luke 10:1, 17–20 reflect, it may be suggested, a pre-Lucan attempt to include the elders in the apostolic commission. (E. Meyer, i, 276, 279–80 takes another view, but inclines to pre-Lucan origin; the proposal that Jerusalem elders stand behind the passage was once made by W. L. Knox, but he later thought it temerarious (Knox, ii, 49, n. 2).) Preoccupation, death or absence of apostles (Acts 6:2, 12:2, 19) may of course have tended to exalt the elders; but Jewish interpretation of the princes suggests another factor also, the strength of the contemporary tendency towards merging an authoritative body of twelve into a council of elders.

Since this essay first appeared, attention has been drawn again (with emphasis on Jewish as well as Christian influence in respect of the number twelve) to literary traces of the notion of a body of twelve elders in the church, notably when bishops appoint twelve elders in the Pseudo-Clementine *Recognitions* (iii 68, vi 15) and *Homilies* (xi 36) and in the regulations of *Testamentum Domini* i 34; 40; also to comparisons between the council of presbyters and the apostles, for example in Ignatius, *Magn.* vi 1 or *Const. Ap.* ii 28, 4 (here the presbyters are συνέδριον καὶ βουλὴ τῆς ἐκκλησίας); and also to Jerome (*Ep.* 146) and other sources on the election of bishops by *presbyteroi* at Alexandria in the second and third centuries (van den Broek (1) 64–5, (2) 108–10). It has been correspondingly suggested both that in Jewish-Christian tradition James the Lord's brother as bishop of Jerusalem was envisaged with twelve elders, as names in the Jerusalem episcopal list in Eusebius might indicate (van den Broek (1) 63–5); and that the second-century Alexandrian church eldership was modelled on that of the Alexandrian Jews (mentioned at the beginning of section VI, above), but was a body of twelve (van den Broek (2) 110–11). Further, with acknowledgement to van den Broek (1) and to the argument for the influence of the number twelve offered above, it has been conjectured that in Jerusalem under James the Lord's brother the relatively few remaining members of the original apostolic Twelve were indeed incorporated into a body of twelve elders (Bauckham, 74–5). On different lines, however, it has been urged that the mention of elders without apostles in Acts 11:30, 21:18 reflects the church order familiar to Luke and his reviser rather than conditions in Christian Jerusalem in the 40s and 50s (Taylor, 90–1, on Acts 11:30). The texts and customs which form the basis for all these suggestions again indicate the converging influence of theories of a body of twelve and a council of elders in the early church, and the importance both of Pentateuchal precedent and contemporary Jewish interpretation of it. On Jerusalem as reflected in Luke-Acts, Bauckham's suggestion attractively combines the Acts references to Jerusalem church elders with and without apostles in a way which suits slightly later church custom, but does not include comment on Luke 10; Taylor's judgment fits well with the passages from Acts and the Pastoral Epistles cited at the beginning of the last paragraph, but makes less allowance than the view adopted here for the influence of the constitutional ideal of a council of elders at the earliest stage of Jerusalem Christianity. The view that the Jerusalem church had long included a body of elders distinct from the Twelve is favoured, irrespective of Luke 10, by the passages cited above from Acts 15–16 as well as 11:30, considered together with the preference for a council of elders evinced in Jewish treatments of the constitution discussed above.

The same constitutional preference can also be recognized, it may be urged, in notices of elders in diaspora Christianity (Acts 14:23, 20:17; 1 Tim. 5:17; Titus 1:5; 1 Pet. 5:1; 2 John 1; 3 John 1), sometimes in writings which also envisage a twelve-tribe polity (James 5:14 (1:1); Rev. 4:4, etc. (7:4, etc.); 1 Clem. 47.6, 54.2, etc. (31:4, 43:2, 55:6)). The conventional view that these attest a Christian eldership modelled on the Jewish is doubted by Harvey, partly (he states) because Jerusalem sanhedrists differed considerably from Christian presbyters, partly because the duties of diaspora elders are unclear, and the name πρεσβύτερος is rare in the epigraphic evidence, whereas ἄρχοντες are common (Harvey, 319–26). Yet (section VI above, Harvey, 321) these names could be interchangeable; and the relevant model was not simply or primarily the contemporary Jewish council, but also the Mosaic συναγωγή or ἐκκλησία wherein, thanks to the LXX translators, οἱ πρεσβύτεροι Ἰσραήλ and πάντες οἱ ἄρχοντες τῆς συναγωγῆς dwelt together in unity (the phrases are quoted from Exod. 34:30–1 LXX, discussed in sections II and VI above).

In a full discussion of elders published since this essay first appeared R. A. Campbell again urges that among both Jews and Christians at the time of the rise of Christianity the terms translated 'elder' were honorific but imprecise. By contrast with titles such as ἄρχων, they referred to a status rather than a definite office; and they did not necessarily evoke the thought of Pentateuchal models (Campbell, especially 28–66, 159–63; an overlap rather than a contrast with ἄρχων is suggested by some Jewish texts, as noted at the beginning of section VI, above). In the light of sections V and VI above it seems that although, as Campbell shows, the sources do not permit detailed definition of the office of elder (the same is true of a number of ancient Jewish and Christian communal titles), they do attest the power of the constitutional ideal of a council of elders, and the association of this ideal with the constitutional pattern sketched in the Pentateuch.

Secondly, with regard to the ministry of Jesus, the twelve appear against the background of Jewish interpretation as a body which, like the phylarchs, must needs attract constitutional speculation. With Jewish models in view the calling of the twelve seems likely, nevertheless, to have conferred authority from the first; but it also stands out as distinctive in important respects.

Constitutional speculation has left the deposit indicated by Wellhausen, but the present writer follows those who, like Roloff (430–9) and Sanders (98–101), ascribe the twelve to the period of the ministry. The inclusion of the traitor's name in the lists of the twelve can perhaps be singled out from the evidence pointing in this direction.

The passages most susceptible to constitutional modification are those concerning the titles and authority of the twelve. When examined with a view to the period of the ministry, they show contrast as well as agreement with Jewish treatment of the phylarchs.

First, the names 'twelve' (Mark 3:14; 1 Cor. 15:5, etc.) and the potentially broader 'apostles' (Luke 6:13; Mark 6:30, etc.) contrast with the continuance of Pentateuchal titles in the War Scroll, where 'the prince of the whole congregation' heads twelve 'princes of God' who command the tribes (1QM iii.3, v. 1–2). This contrast is striking, in view of the importance in early Christianity of the Pentateuchal terms 'ecclesia' and 'elder'. The word 'twelve', however, also evokes the repertory of Jewish speculation on the tribes and their rulers.

Secondly, in the passages on authorization, the emphasis lies on the *sending* of the twelve, and their authority to preach and cast out devils (Mark 3:14–15, 6:7, and parallels). This distinctive emphasis is continued in the passages set after the resurrection, noticed above, where the commission to witness and teach is central. The theme of government, on the other hand, which is central in the treatment of the phylarchs, is restricted to Matt. 19:28 and parallel, with which the passages on binding and loosing, Matt. 18:8 and parallels, can perhaps be associated. Contrary to expectation this theme is not explicit, apart from John 20:22–3, in the post-resurrection narratives, although it is perhaps implied in the gift of the Spirit (Acts 2:3–4; cf. Num. 11:25). It accords with the distinctive emphasis on sending that, if the suggestion offered above on Luke 10:1 has any force, the narrative was intended to include the elders among those sent (rather than otherwise authorized). It seems, then, that the name 'apostle' corresponds to the aspect of the authorization of the twelve which was pre-eminent for early Christians (cf. Gal. 2:8, discussed with other evidence for Paul's claims by Moule (1), 158–9). This phenomenon suggests that, with all allowance for development, the sending of the twelve was, as Mark indicates, the principal feature of their original authorization.

The surprising lack of emphasis on government in the post-resurrection material also suggests, however, that Matt. 19:28; Luke 22:30 deserve serious consideration as evidence for the period of the ministry. The saying coheres with the title 'twelve', already noted, and both cohere with three contemporary associations of a body of twelve, as suggested by development of the narratives of the phylarchs. First, the twelve princes were doubly linked with the monarchy, both by biblical connection with Moses, Joshua, David and Solomon (note Eupolemus, section IV above), and by their title *nāśîʾ*, ἄρχων, applicable also to the past and future king (David, Solomon, the Prince of the Congregation, Moses, Bar Cocheba; Ezek. 34:24; 1 Kings 11:34; 1QSb v.21–9; Acts 7:35, Second Revolt coins (Schürer-Vermes-Millar-Black, i, 606)). Secondly, the twelve princes each have their own command. Thirdly, restoration of their rule over the tribes can form part of the hope of redemption, as seen above from Qumran texts and the Testaments of the twelve Patriarchs (cf. PRK v.9). The second and third associations are explicit in Matt. 19:28, and the first coheres with the view of members of the twelve that their master was messiah (Mark 8:30, 10:38).

These considerations do not apply equally to both forms of Matt. 19:28; Luke 22:30 (discussed by Bacon, 116–18, 432–3; Bammel, 45–7; Davies, 363–5; Catchpole, 373–8; Sanders, 98–106). The generalized Lucan form, however, recalls Jewish generalizing of the phylarchs as well as patristic generalization of the apostles (Origen, *in Matt. comm.* xv. 24, on 19:28); it is probably secondary (so Harnack, 67–8; Schulz, 332 n. 68; the opposite view in Catchpole, 377 n. 2).

There is ground, therefore, in the likely development of the saying and in its broader associations, for Sanders to conclude that Matt. 19:28 is a prediction, 'on the whole authentic', that the twelve will judge the tribes at the end. In conjunction with the phenomenon of the twelve it is a sign, for both Sanders and B. F. Meyer (134–6, 153–4), that Israel's restoration was central in Jesus' hope. For Farrer this was also true, if restoration be viewed as renewal; the twelve signified renewal of the patriarchate (the Mosaic appointment of the princes being so interpreted) in connection with a new covenant and a renewed Israel (Farrer (1), 121). In Sanders (3), published after this essay first appeared, the saying reflected in Matt. 19:28 is made the starting-point for an outline of Jesus' understanding of his rôle: he envisaged himself as God's viceroy, at the head of the judges of Israel (the Twelve), and subordinate only to God himself. This outline would fit the connotations of the term 'messiah', in the present writer's view, but Sanders holds that at this period they were far from clear (compare Sanders (2), 295–8; (4), 113–15, discussed in Horbury (3), 41, 78, 112–13); he suggests that Jesus probably did not think of himself as bearer of this title, but that his disciples bestowed it on him after his crucifixion in the setting of belief in his resurrection. The title then in fact roughly corresponded to Jesus' own historical claim, probably an even loftier one, that (as implied by his authority over the Twelve) he would be viceroy over the coming kingdom of God (Sanders (3), 238–43).

Two prominent aspects of the teaching of Jesus tend, however, to qualify this shared view; and they can perhaps be linked with the contrasts already noted between the twelve and the phylarchs. First, explicit reference to Israel is strikingly rare in the kingdom teaching (Dahl, 147–8). The absence of Pentateuchal titles for the twelve can be matched by the contrast between the Lord's Prayer and the more explicitly national Eighteen Benedictions, even in the shortened form Habinenu (jBer. 8a, Ber. 29a, both printed by Staerk 20), or between the parables of the kingdom and the equally theocentric, but also vehemently patriotic treatment of the kingdom in Yose ben Yose's synagogue poetry (Horbury (1), 159–66, = 305–11 below). Secondly, messianism was disputed between disciples and master (Mark 8:32–3, 10:35–8); the restraint imposed on the disciples' fervour accords with the contrast between the emphasis on government in the traditions of the phylarchs, and the emphasis on mission in the authorization of the twelve.

These considerations do not impair recognition of Jesus as a Jew appealing to Israel, which—he takes for granted—is the elect people of God (Mark 7:27); but they direct attention to the apparent discrepancy between Matt. 19:28 and the corrective answer to the disciples' request for places in the kingdom (Mark 10:37–40). Sanders stresses the accord between this request and Matt. 19:28, but also holds that Jesus probably turned the request aside (Sanders, 147, 233). The present writer fully accepts these judgments, but would conclude from them, with the broader considerations in view, that there is a strong possibility that Matt. 19:28 arose during the ministry, yet is inauthentic. It would then represent the messianic fervour of the disciples and their associates, fanned perhaps by the princely model and the circumstances of the Galilaean mission (Mark 6:6–13; Taylor 622, treating the Lucan form of the saying as genuine, thinks this setting the most probable).

On this view, when Jesus 'made twelve' (Mark 3:14), the government of Israel or new Israel was not primarily in question. Jewish speculation on the phylarchs nevertheless supports the argument of Sanders 232 that the action can hardly have been 'mere' symbol; the predecessors and models of the twelve were thought to be significant for practical disputes of constitutional authority. Yet, the contrast between the evidence for the twelve and the phylarchs also suggests that there is truth in allusions to 'renewal' (Farrer (1), 121, 124; Sanders, 229–30). Jesus' distinctive purposes in choosing the twelve, so far as they can be approached, are perhaps best sought through the evidence for an emphasis on sending in the authorization of the twelve, for a reserve on national restoration and messianism, and for a strongly theocentric kingdom teaching. These data suit a work which can be called new (cf. Moule (2), 54), the urgent preparation of contemporary Israel for the kingdom of God. For this the twelve would have received immediate authority. Their authorization thus suits expectation of the kingdom, when messengers are being sent, rather than a kingdom already established, in which provision is being made for government. This is still true, as noted above, of the passages set in the context of appearances of the risen Christ. In this respect there seems to be continuity between the emphases of the period of the ministry, in which the messianic zeal of the body of disciples was to some extent both shared and shaped by their master, and the period of the early church, in which lively expectation of a kingdom of Christ in Jerusalem long continued (see chapters 6 and 9, below). In both periods he was hailed as messianic king, and it seems probable that during the period of the ministry he came to hold that he was called to this office; the authority implied when he 'made twelve' can readily be understood as royal, on the lines suggested by the links with Moses, Joshua, David and Solomon noted above.

Jewish treatment of the phylarchs, finally, is not without significance for the course of events reported in the gospels. Against this background, news of the twelve would confirm, for observers, that Jesus had messianic pretensions. (Moses and Joshua, with whom the princes were closely linked, formed models for Theudas and the Egyptian (Vermes, 97–8; Knox, ii, 143) as well as the Prince 'of the Congregation' (Num. 27:16–17; cf. Mark 6:34).) Further, the choice of the twelve suggests a distinctive mentality. Jesus thereby attached himself to an archaic, non-synedrial and eschatologically charged constitutional model. The sophisticated interpreter, like Josephus or Pseudo-Philo, combined the twelve-tribe union with synedrial government; a body of twelve has a primitive air beside the constitutionally more flexible prayer 'Restore our judges' (Isa. 1:26) in the Eleventh Benediction. Jesus changed the associations of the constitutional model, but contemporary interpretation of the phylarchs suggests that a mind which could summon up 'the twelve' worked on lines uncongenial to 'the rulers and elders and scribes in Jerusalem' (Acts 4:5).

Literature

D. C. Allison, *Jesus of Nazareth: Millenarian Prophet* (Minneapolis, 1998)

B. W. Bacon, *Studies in Matthew* (London, 1930)

E. Bammel, 'Das Ende von Q', in O. Böcher and K. Haacker (eds.), *Verborum Veritas* (Festschrift für G. Stählin, Wuppertal, 1970), 39–50

R. Bauckham, *Jude and the Relatives of Jesus in the Early Church* (Edinburgh, 1990)

J. M. Baumgarten, 'The Duodecimal Courts of Qumran, the Apocalypse, and the Sanhedrin', reprinted from *JBL* xcv (1976) in J. M. Baumgarten, *Studies in Qumran Law* (Leiden, 1977), 145–71

J. A. Bengel, *Gnomon Novi Testamenti* (4th edn., London, 1855)

R. van den Broek (1), 'Der Brief des Jakobus an Quadratus und das Problem der judenchristlichen Bischöfe von Jerusalem (Eusebius, H.E. IV, 5, 1–3)' in T. Baarda, A. Hilhorst, G. P. Luttikhuizen and A. S. van der Woude (eds.), *Text and Testimony: Essays on New Testament and Apocryphal Literature in Honour of A. F. J. Klijn* (Kampen, 1988), 56–65

——— (2), 'Juden und Christen in Alexandrien im 2. und 3. Jahrhundert' in J. van Amersfoort and J. van Oort (eds.), *Juden und Christen in der Antike* (Kampen, 1990), 101–15

S. Buber (ed.), *Midrasch Tanchuma* (3 vols., Wilna, 1885)

C. F. Burney, *Notes on the Hebrew Text of the Books of Kings* (Oxford, 1903)

G. B. Caird, *Jesus and the Jewish Nation* (London, 1965)

R. Alastair Campbell, *The Elders: Seniority within Earliest Christianity* (Edinburgh, 1994)

D. R. Catchpole, 'The Poor on Earth and the Son of Man in Heaven'. *BJRL* lxi (1979), 335–97

R. H. Charles, *A Critical and Exegetical Commentary on the Revelation of St John* (ICC, 2 vols., Edinburgh, 1920)

B. S. Childs, *Exodus* (London, 1974)

J. D. Crossan, *The Birth of Christianity: Discovering what happened in the Years immediately after the Execution of Jesus* (New York, 1998; Edinburgh, 1999)

N. A. Dahl, *Das Volk Gottes* (Oslo, 1941, reprinted Darmstadt, 1963)

W. D. Davies, *The Gospel and the Land* (Berkeley, Los Angeles and London, 1974)

F. G. Downing, 'Redaction Criticism: Josephus' Antiquities and the Synoptic Gospels (I)', *JSNT* viii (1980), 46–65

A. M. Farrer (1), 'The Ministry in the New Testament', in K. E. Kirk (ed.), *The Apostolic Ministry* (London, 1946), 118–32

——— (2), *St Matthew and St Mark* (Westminster, 1954)

D. Flusser, 'Qumran und die Zwölf', in C. J. Bleeker (ed.), *Initiation* (Supplements to Numen, xii, Leiden, 1965), 134–46

P. Frederiksen, *Jesus of Nazareth, King of the Jews* (London, 2000)

S. Freyne, *The Jesus Movement and its Expansion: Meaning and Mission* (Grand Rapids, Michigan & Cambridge, 2014)

A. S. Geyser, 'The Twelve Tribes in Revelation: Judean and Judeo-Christian Apocalypticism', *NTS* xxviii (1982), 388–99

D. Goodblatt, *The Monarchic Principle: Studies in Jewish Self-Government in Antiquity (TSAJ* xxxviii, Tübingen, 1994)

H. Grotius, *Annotationes in Libros Evangeliorum (1641),* in H. Grotius, *Opera Theologica* (3 vols., London, 1679), ii.1

J. Gutmann (ed.), *The Dura-Europos Synagogue: a Re-evaluation (1932–1972)* (Missoula, 1973)

B. Halpern, *The Constitution of the Monarchy in Israel* (Harvard Semitic Monographs xxv, Chico, 1981)

H. Hammond, *A Paraphrase and Annotation upon all the Books of the New Testament* (1653; 2nd edn., London, 1659)

A. Harnack, *Sprüche und Reden Jesu* (Leipzig, 1907)

A. E. Harvey, 'Elders', *JTS* N.S. xxv (1974), 318–32

W. Horbury (1), 'Suffering and Messianism in Yose ben Yose', in W Horbury and B. McNeil (eds.), *Suffering and Martyrdom in the New Testament* (Cambridge, 1981), 143–82 [= ch. 10, below]

——— (2), 'The Aaronic Priesthood in the Epistle to the Hebrews', *JSNT* xix (1983), 43–71 [= ch. 7, below]

——— (3), *Jewish Messianism and the Cult of Christ* (London, 1998)
A. Hultgård, *L'eschatologie des Testaments des Douze Patriarches* (2 vols., Uppsala, 1977 and 1982).
W. L. Knox, *The Sources of the Synoptic Gospels* (ed. H. Chadwick, 2 vols., Cambridge, 1953 and 1957)
H. Lietzmann, 'Zur altchristlichen Verfassungsgeschichte', *ZWT* lv (1914), 97–153, cited above from H. Lietzmann, *Kleine Schriften* (TU lxvii, Berlin, 1958), 141–85
H. Mantel, *Studies in the History of the Sanhedrin* (Harvard Semitic Studies xvii, Cambridge, MA, 1961)
E. Marmorstein, *Heaven at Bay* (Middle Eastern Monographs x, London, 1969)
B. F. Meyer, *The Aims of Jesus* (London, 1979)
E. Meyer, *Ursprung und Anfänge des Christentums* (3 vols., Berlin, 1921–4)
Midrash Tanhuma (New York and Berlin, 1927)
C. F. D. Moule (1), *The Epistles of Paul the Apostle to the Colossians and to Philemon* (Cambridge, 1957)
——— (2), *The Birth of the New Testament* (3rd edn., London, 1981)
C. Newsom, *Songs of the Sabbath Sacrifice: a Critical Edition* (Harvard Semitic Studies xxvii, Atlanta, 1985)
M. Oakeshott (ed.), *Leviathan, by Thomas Hobbes* (Oxford, 1960)
J. C. O'Neill, *Messiah* (Cambridge, 1980)
S. Pearce, 'Josephus as Interpreter of Biblical Law: the Representation of the High Court of Deut. 17:8–12 according to Jewish Antiquities 4.218', *JJS* xlvi (1995), 30–42
J. Roloff, 'Apostel / Apostolat / Apostolizität i. Neues Testament', *TRE* iii (1978), 430–45
E. P. Sanders (1), *Jesus and Judaism* (London, 1985)
——— (2), *Judaism: Practice and Belief 63 BCE–66 CE* (London, 1992)
——— (3), *The Historical Figure of Jesus* (London, 1993)
——— (4), 'Paul', in J. Barclay and J. Sweet (eds.), *Early Christian Thought in its Jewish Context* (Cambridge, 1996), 112–29
E. Schürer, *Geschichte des jüdischen Volkes im Zeitalter Jesu Christi* (3rd–4th edn., Leipzig, 1901–9); *ET* of 2nd edn. (1886–90), *The History of the Jewish People in the Age of Jesus Christ* (Edinburgh, 1890–1); *ET* of 3rd–4th edn., revised by G. Vermes, F. Millar, M. Black, M. Goodman and P. Vermes (Edinburgh, i (1973), ii (1981), iii.1 (1986), iii.2 (1987))
S. Schulz, *Q: Die Spruchquelle der Evangelisten* (Zurich, 1972)
A. Spiro, 'The Ascension of Phinehas', *PAAJR* xxii (1953), 91–114
W. Staerk, *Altjüdische liturgische Gebete* (Kleine Texte lviii, Bonn, 1910)
J. F. Stenning (ed.), *The Targum of Isaiah* (Oxford, 1949)

Justin Taylor, SM, with an excursus by M.-É. Boismard, *Les Actes des deux apôtres, v, Commentaire historique (Act. 9:1–18:22)* (Paris, 1994)

V. Taylor, *The Gospel according to St. Mark* (London, 1952)

E. E. Urbach (ed.), *Sefer Pitron Torah* (Jerusalem, 5738–1978)

G. Vermes, *Jesus the Jew* (London, 1973)

B. Z. Wacholder, *Eupolemus* (Cincinnati, 1974)

J. Wellhausen, *Einleitung in die drei ersten Evangelien* (2nd edn., Berlin, 1911)

A. G. Wernham (ed. and trans.), *Benedict de Spinoza: The Political Works* (Oxford, 1965)

N. T. Wright, *Jesus and the Victory of God* (London, 1996)

Y. Yadin (ed.), *The Scroll of the War of the Sons of Light against the Sons of Darkness* (Oxford, 1962)

6

Jerusalem in Pre-Pauline and Pauline Hope

At the beginning and the end of the Herodian age poets and visionaries could link hope for a coming Davidic king very closely with hope for Jerusalem and the temple. Not long before the reign of Herod the Great, the association was vividly expressed in lines from a prayer in the Psalms of Solomon asking God to raise up the king, the son of David:

> He shall glorify the Lord at the centre of all the earth,
> And he shall purify Jerusalem, making it holy as of old;
> So that nations shall come from the ends of the earth to see his glory,
> bringing as gifts her sons who had fainted,
> And to see the glory of the Lord, with which God glorified her
> (Ps. Sol. 17:32–5).

Similarly close links between the king on the one hand, and the holy city and the holy hill on the other, reappear towards the end of the Herodian age in 2 Esd. 13, where he reigns from the top of Zion, and in the Fifth Sibylline book, where the blessed man from the sky with a God-given sceptre adorns the city beloved by God and builds up a vast sanctuary with a great tower, that the righteous may behold the longed-for divine glory (lines 414–27). The association between king, city and sanctuary evident in all three texts is of course itself founded on biblical presentations of Davidic kingship in connection with Jerusalem and the sanctuary, for instance in the narratives of David and Solomon or in such Psalms as 2, 122 and 132.

Paul was active in a messianic movement in the period of the Herodian kings Agrippa I and II, but he can seem on the face of it to retain mere vestiges of this association. The Christ of Paul is still recognizably the Lord's Anointed, as many Pauline interpreters have shown (C. E. B. Cranfield, M. Hengel and others are cited in discussion of the title *Christos* in Horbury (3), 142–4);

but the holy city and the holy place, where Paul mentions them, can often be understood symbolically. Thus, the transference of the language of sanctuary and sacrifice to Christian life is prominent in Paul, but this is only one of several considerations which together suggest to W. D. Davies that although Paul maintained his reverence for Jerusalem and the sanctuary, these became marginal for him by contrast with his inheritance 'in Christ'. Herein Paul exemplified the revolutionary character of Christian messianism as a whole (Davies, 164–220, 370–3).

This weighty judgment well fits the emphasis laid by other writers on the importance of the heavenly rather than the earthly Jerusalem for early Christianity in general (so—all with some qualification—L. Perrone, G. Stroumsa and C. Markschies), and on the importance of spiritual and eschatological interpretations of land and city for rabbinic as well as Greek Jewish writings (so Weinfeld, 213–21; cf. Alexander, 471, n. 30). Moreover, these trends in Christian and Jewish interpretation are sometimes held to have been particularly well-marked in traditions of the Second Temple period which would have influenced nascent Christianity. Thus the Jerusalem temple in particular might then have received less esteem from Diaspora Jews, as urged by D. R. Schwartz (2), although Diaspora remittance of the temple tax and Diaspora literary praise of the temple (as in the Letter of Aristeas and the Sibylline Oracles) suggest that this was not the ruling attitude; and sanctuary and sacrifice, including the cult of the Jerusalem temple, might have been criticized in principle by Jews such as those whose voice is heard in the Fourth Sibylline book, as suggested by M. Simon and others (although this seems to me a misunderstanding of the Fourth Sibylline; see Horbury (4), 162–5).

Yet, does this judgment concerning Paul in any case do full justice to the place of city and sanctuary in Paul's own future hope? The question is prompted not only by Paul's reverence for Jerusalem, fully recognized by Davies, but also and especially by Paul's debt in both Romans and Galatians to the prophecies of a restored land or city in the later chapters of Isaiah. Thus Gal. 4:26–30 quote Isa. 54:1 'Rejoice, O barren', and Rom. 11:26–7 quote Isa. 59:20–1 in the form 'a redeemer shall come from Sion'.

For Irenaeus and Tertullian, by contrast with many later Christian exegetes, Pauline perceptions of the heavenly city fitted well into chiliastic hope for a kingdom of the saints ruled by Christ in the new Jerusalem (cf. chapter 9, below). In this hope the link between the king and the holy city and the holy hill once again reappears with clarity. Now this Christian chiliasm itself depended especially on the later chapters of the book of Isaiah, as has been brought out by S. Heid (16–30, 231–2). It will be urged below that St. Paul, who is likewise indebted to these chapters, stands within the stream of biblical interpretation which issued in the passages on a paradisal kingdom of Christ and the saints in Zion in the Revelation of St. John and in Papias, Justin Martyr, Irenaeus and Tertullian. These passages include, especially in Tertullian, as strong an emphasis on the spiritual and heavenly character of the new Jerusalem as has been detected in Paul. They also suggest, however, when viewed in conjunction with pre-Pauline texts, that Paul too associated hope for the parousia of Christ with hope for a recreated Jerusalem.

The first part of this study indicates some relevant strands in pre-Pauline biblical interpretation which seem to reappear in Paul. It is suggested that the Isaianic texts had been linked in exegetical tradition with other passages on the sanctuary, notably the Song of Moses at the sea, the prophecy of Nathan to David, and Solomon's prayer at the dedication; and that 1 Enoch both exemplified and influenced this trend.

There was then (it is urged below) a developed body of interpretation on Jerusalem and the sanctuary in the time of Paul. It includes that contrast between Jerusalem above and to come, on the one hand, and the present city and sanctuary, on the other, which is drawn so strongly in Galatians. The contrast belongs, however, to a broader interpretative context in which the function of the present holy place is also regularly acknowledged, and the association of the sanctuary above and that below is emphasized, within a setting of lively hope and longing for the creation of new Jerusalem. In the second part of the present study it is urged that Paul takes up elements of this unified body of interpretation in various contexts, and that he expresses hope for a kingdom of Christ in a recreated, not just a heavenly, Jerusalem.

I

Three characteristics of the interpretative tradition into which Paul entered seem of particular importance for assessment of his appeal to Isaianic prophecy on Zion. They are the habit of considering oracles on Jerusalem collectively; the prominence among them of affirmations of divine preparation and building, in the past or yet to come; and the union of these affirmations with prophecy of newly-created heavens, earth and Zion to form a picture of paradisal bliss in a new Jerusalem.

An influential set of exegetical associations then emerges. There are links between Isaianic and other Jerusalem prophecies, between Isaiah and the Pentateuch, and between the Pentaeuch and Isaiah on the one hand and apocryphal prophecy on the other, especially the book of Enoch. (Rich material on Jerusalem above, sometimes overlapping with that considered here, is discussed by Schwemer (2), 197–228.) Pre-Pauline treatment of this exegetical complex shows the divinely-founded sanctuary above in close association as well as in contrast with the holy place on earth, and the latter too as divinely ordained; and it suggests also that Pauline references to Zion, eternal building and new creation, topics which are sometimes treated separately in study, may reflect a single set of expectations.

Renewed Jerusalem in prayer and expectation

The actuality of Jerusalem prophecies when Paul wrote is displayed especially by their currency in contemporary life and thought. They were remembered in prayer and sacred song, and thought of collectively, for example in Tobit, Ecclesiasticus and the Hebrew Apostrophe to Zion from Qumran Cave 11. The mingling of prophecy and hymnody in much of this material is epitomized in a phrase of the Jewish Sibyl on Jerusalem: καλὴ πόλις ἔνθεος ὕμνων, 'fair city of inspired song' (Sib. 5:263).

The tradition of prayer for people, land, city and sanctuary goes back to the Hebrew Bible (Isa. 63:17–64:12; Ps. 122; Lam. 5, etc.). The form which it received in Ecclesiasticus (36:10–17) and (2 Maccabees 1:27–9, 2:17–18) was developed in the Amidah (Eighteen Benedictions), the daily prayer which was taking shape in the time of Paul, to an extent which allowed E. J. Bickerman to view the Amidah as originally a civic prayer for Jerusalem; the ingathering, the city, the sanctuary and the Davidic kingship are the subjects especially of benedictions 10, 14 and 17 (16) (translated in Schürer revised, ii, 457–61).

Request for the fulfilment of prophecy is prominent in prayer of this kind. 'Raise up the vision spoken in thy name' (Ecclus. 36:17b); 'may the Lord perform what he has spoken concerning Israel and Jerusalem' (Ps. Sol. 11:8); compare the hymn 11Q Apostrophe to Zion 17 (close to Ecclus. 36:17b), and the prayer 2 Macc. 1:29, both quoted below.

These passages recall such promises as Exod. 15:17 (planting in divinely-prepared sanctuary); Lev. 26:3–13 (peace in the land, my tabernacle among you); Isa. 2:2–4 = Micah 4:1–4 (Zion and the temple mount exalted); Isa. 49:14–26 (Zion graven on the palms of God's hands); Isa. 54, 59:16–60:22, 62, 65:17–25, 66:5–24 (building of city as adornment of bride, redemption and new creation of Jerusalem with joy); Jer. 31 (rebuilding of Jerusalem as 'virgin of Israel', joy and plenty, new covenant); Ezek. 17:22–4 (planting and flourishing in the mountain of the height of Israel) and 37:21–8 (after the revival of the dry bones: ingathering, one nation, David their prince for ever, covenant of peace, sanctuary in their midst for evermore); Haggai 2:6–9, Zech. 14 (sanctuary and worship).

Within this group of prophecies an important position was eventually held by the oracle or 'vision' (*ḥazon*, LXX ὅρασις) of Nathan, communicated to David after he had brought the ark into Zion (2 Sam. 7:4–17; 1 Chron. 17:1–15; cf. Ps. 89:19–37). Its promise of a perpetual Davidic dynasty (2 Sam. 7:12–16) is so strong that it has been called 'the matrix of biblical messianism' (Gordon, 236). Correspondingly, its earlier prediction of a divinely-given 'place' and planting for Israel (2 Sam. 7:10) was taken, by analogy with the similar prediction of planting in Exod. 15:17, as the promise of a future divinely-given holy place (see the following section).

Much of this body of prophecy is ultimately indebted to the ancient circle of ideas on the divine foundation of the hill of Zion, but the vision of Nathan, Leviticus and Ezekiel also reflect emphasis laid on the (in principle mobile) local manifestation of the deity.

Oracles like these are already mentally grouped in Ps. 87:3 as understood in the LXX—'glorious things of thee *were* spoken (ἐλαλήθη)'. The prophet Jeremiah was himself believed to make intercession for Jerusalem (2 Macc. 15:14), so that prayer on these lines was the earthly counterpart of a petition offered in heaven. Thus Tobit in Nineveh was pictured as praying for Jerusalem, and then prophesying that 'the house of God shall be built in it for ever with a glorious building, as the prophets have foretold' (14:5). The reverential passive 'shall be built' implies the God-given temple of Exod. 15:17, and perhaps also 2 Sam. 7:10, and the reference to the prophets recalls the end of Tobit's hymn-like prayer, 'For Jerusalem shall be builded with sapphires …' (Tobit 13:16–17), which is a paraphrase of Isa. 54:11–12; 'builded' recalls Isa. 54:14 as interpreted in the LXX, discussed further below. These passages in the book of Tobit are fragmentarily attested in Aramaic and Hebrew texts from Qumran Cave 4 (13:16–17: 4Q196 (Aramaic), 4Q200 (Hebrew); 14:5: 4Q198 (Aramaic)). A broadly comparable combination of Jerusalem-centred prophecy and prayer was perhaps made in the (? second-century B.C.) Hebrew text partly preserved in 4Q522, fragment 9 ii (predicting David, 'the rock of Zion', and the building of 'the house for the Lord') and fragments 22–5 (Ps. 122, praying for the peace of Jerusalem); E. Puech notes that the inclusion of the psalm sets a question-mark against the otherwise plausible attribution of these fragments to an apocryphal prophecy of Joshua (Puech (2), 71). A hymn like Tobit's in its praise of 'the everlasting king' (Tobit 13:7, 11), but with reference now to prophecies such as Isa. 65:17–19 on the sanctuary as the centre of the future joy of the righteous, seems to be implied by 1 En. 25:7 (discussed further below) 'Then I blessed the God of glory, the everlasting king, who prepared for righteous mortals such things …'.

In St. Luke's Gospel it is envisaged, plausibly enough in the light of the texts just reviewed, that there were those 'who were looking for the redemption of Jerusalem' (Luke 2:38)—a phrase recalling two coin legends of the First Revolt, 'liberty of Zion' and 'of the redemption of Zion' (Schürer revised, i, 605). The evident power of these phrases as slogans indicates the intensity of the hope which prayer and hymnody on Jerusalem represent, and to which they contribute.

Throughout the Second Temple period, therefore, the tradition of prayer for land and holy place formed an important *Sitz im Leben* for the 'glorious things' spoken of Zion in prophecy. 'Receive the vision that was spoken of thee', says the poet to Zion with urgent hope, in allusion to Ps. 87:3 on Zion as well as to the 'vision' of Nathan (see especially 2 Sam. 7:10, 13, 17; 1 Chron. 17:9, 12, 14–15; Ps. 89:20) on the house of God and the throne of David (11Q Apostrophe to Zion 17, in 11Q5, col. xxii, lines 13–14; García and Tigchelaar, ii, 1176).

Echoes of such prayer in Paul are heard above all in his prayer for Israel. In Rom. 10:1 his 'supplication' draws not directly on a group of oracles, but on a list of the great Israelite privileges, including the service of the sanctuary (λατρεία), and the Israelite ancestry of the messiah (Rom. 9:4–5); this list (cf. chapter 2, pp. 95–7, above) follows a contemporary pattern of enumerating gifts, but hereby recalls some of 'what he [God] has spoken concerning Israel and Jerusalem' (Ps. Sol. 11:8, quoted above). The list therefore perhaps helps to bring in later on in Romans the Isaianic quotation (combined with an allusion to Jer. 31:33), 'the redeemer shall come from Sion' (Rom. 11:26). Another brief echo of prayer for Israel can be heard, despite difference in tone, near the end of Galatians, when the Jerusalem-linked Isaianic theme of 'new creation' (καινὴ κτίσις) leads immediately to 'Peace be on them, and mercy, and on the Israel of God' (Gal. 6:15–16). The intensity of the corresponding hope can perhaps be traced when he notes the servitude of 'Jerusalem that now is' (Gal. 4:25), and when he sees the 'earthly house of the tabernacle' (cf. 1 Chron. 9:23) as a place where we long for the dwelling from heaven (2 Cor. 5:1–2).

The kinship sometimes evident between Paul and the tradition of prayer for 'Israel and Jerusalem' encourages the further observation that, just as Paul is likely in general to have known the prophetic oracles in topical clusters, so one such cluster will have been formed by Zion-oracles. The general point has often been made in connection with Paul's probable debt to testimony-collections, for example in Rom. 9–11; but the habit of grouping oracles is illustrated particularly clearly, and with special reference to Zion, by the prayer-tradition which has just been considered. Paul's Isaianic Zion-testimonies in Gal. 4:27 and Rom. 11:26–7 are unlikely to have been quoted without awareness of other similar oracles; each will have evoked for him not just a single passage, but a group of Zion-oracles, especially those in the later chapters of Isaiah, and the whole biblical topic of Zion.

Zion prepared and built

The phrase 'prepared and built' from the visions of Sion in 2 Esdras (13:36 *Sion … parata et aedificata*) brings together two threads of biblical Zion-tradition which also emerge in Paul. Divine preparation can be discerned in 1 Cor. 2:8 ἃ ἡτοίμασεν 'the things that God prepared', divine building in the symbolically employed temple language of 2 Cor. 5:1, οἰκοδομὴν ἐκ θεοῦ ἔχομεν 'we have a building from God'.

These conceptions emerge clearly in the Apocrypha and pseudepigrapha, but their biblical roots are deep. The divinely prepared sanctuary is ready in heaven in the Wisdom of Solomon, on the tabernacle 'which thou didst prepare beforehand from the beginning' (ἀπ' ἀρχῆς; Wisd. 9:8; cf. Exod. 15:17; Prov. 8:23); and this is probably also implied in Wisd. 10:10, on the revelation to Jacob of God's kingdom and the knowledge of holy things. Correspondingly, the Syriac Apocalypse of Baruch, after the capture of Jerusalem by Titus, envisages the forthcoming revelation of the city already prepared 'here' (in heaven) beforehand, at the time when God determined to make paradise, then shown to Moses on Sinai when he saw the pattern of the tabernacle and its vessels, and now kept like paradise with God (2 Baruch 4:1–6). The further traces of this expectation of a future divinely-prepared Jerusalem in Old Testament apocrypha and pseudepigrapha, in the Targums and rabbinic literature are widely recognized (for instance in Charles, 6–7; McKelvey, 25–41; Bogaert, i, 421; Attridge, 222–4; Ego, 56–61). The old-established and familiar character of this hope emerges especially clearly, however, from the witness to it which is mainly explored below. This is found in the LXX Pentateuch, Prophets and Psalms, with correspondence in Hebrew as well as Greek sources from the Second Temple period. These interpretative texts build on a broad basis in the Hebrew bible itself.

Thus, in the Hebrew text of the biblical books, a divinely prepared holy place is mentioned at Exod. 15:17. This central prophecy has been noted already; it was read in the Hasmonaean age as a prophecy yet to be fulfilled, as appears from 2 Macc. 1:29, quoted below. It has a narrative analogue in Ps. 78:54, 69. This psalm, together with Ps. 87, about to be mentioned, helped to ensure that the divine foundation of the holy hill here below was kept in view (see part (*c*) of this section, below). The tabernacle, the candlestick and Solomon's temple all follow a divinely-given pattern (Exod. 25:9, 40; Num. 8:4; 1 Chron. 28:19). God's throne is correspondingly 'prepared from of old' (Ps. 93:2). Zion is 'his foundation' (Ps. 87:1) and he himself founds or will found it (Ps. 87:5). The engraving of Jerusalem on the palms of his hands (Isa. 49:16) can be seen against this background as both a souvenir and a plan. Similarly, Jacob's declaration on waking that 'this is none other than the house of God ... this stone shall be God's house' (Gen. 28:17, 22) can suggest, in the light of the biblical references to earthly construction on a heavenly pattern, that his dream must have included a vision of the divinely-prepared temple.

The two lines of interpretation concerning 'preparation' and 'building' which are combined in 2 Esdras lead back into this biblical setting. From the Hebrew biblical books and the Septuagint, 'prepared' in 2 Esdras takes up the Mosaic prophecy of a place for God's dwelling which his own hands have 'prepared' (Exod. 15:17 and related passages on the heavenly dwelling from 1 Kings 8:12, etc., and 2 Chron. 6:1, etc., noted below). 'Built' takes up a theme perhaps rooted primarily in Solomon's claim to 'build' the house (1 Kings 5:17–19 (3–5), paralleled in 2 Chron. 2:3–5 (4–6); and 1 Kings 8:13, 17–20, 27, paralleled in 2 Chron. 6:2, 7–10, 18). He was divinely commanded to do so (Nathan's oracle in 2 Sam. 7:13 and 1 Chron. 17:12, recalled by David in 1 Chron. 22:10, 28:6, and by Solomon in 1 Kings 5:19 (5)), but his claim to build a house for God is strikingly modified by his concomitant and contrasting recognition of God's dwelling in heaven (2 Chron. 2:5 (6); 1 Kings 8:12, 30, 39, 43, 49, paralleled in 2 Chron. 6:1, 21, 30, 33, 39). This extended treatment of the theme of building in connection with David and Solomon is clearly influential, but 'Jerusalem' with the passive participle 'built' most immediately echoes the phrase 'Jerusalem the built' (Ps. 122:3 *ha-b*[e]*nuyah*, οἰκοδομουμένη), and it recalls the ancient claim that Zion was divinely built, and prophecies of its future divine building, both exemplifed in biblical texts discussed below. The lines of interpretation concerned with 'preparation' and 'building' intertwine with a third, treated in the following section, which takes up the language of 'creation'.

(a) Zion prepared

Zion 'prepared' will be considered first. Some of the relevant passages suggest that, although Gal. 4:27 is perhaps the earliest clear witness to the notion of a heavenly Jerusalem (Ego, 14, citing other sponsors of this judgment), the expectation of a divinely-prepared holy place above was already well established in Paul's time. Other texts in this group also indicate that a contrast between the earthly and the heavenly divine dwelling, such as is found in Paul, could in pre-Pauline interpretation be consonant with hope for an ultimate full divine glorification of Jerusalem on earth.

1. The Song of Moses at the Sea (Exod. 15:17)

The tradition of Zion 'prepared' gains strength from its roots in Exod. 15:17, at the climax of a prophetic hymn attributed to Moses himself and placed at a turning-point of the exodus narrative (this hymn is further discussed in chapter 8, below).

> Mayest thou [or, Thou shalt] bring them in and plant them in the
> mountain of thine inheritance,
> In the place for thy dwelling (*makhon le-shibt*[e]*ka*; LXX ἕτοιμον
> κακτοικητήριόν σου 'thy ready dwelling') which thou madest, O Lord,
> The sanctuary, Lord, which thy hands made ready (*kon*[e]*nu*, LXX ἡτοίμασαν)
> (Exod. 15:17)

A clue to the early interpretation of this passage is given in 2 Maccabees:

> Plant thy people in thy holy place, as Moses said
> (2 Macc. 1:29 (cf. 2:18), citing Exod. 15:17)

Here the Mosaic hymn, which in its biblical context could be taken to speak of the forthcoming entry into the land, is treated as a prophecy still not completely fulfilled.

Its phrase 'the place for thy dwelling' (15:17, *makhon le-shibt*[e]*ka*) links the 'preparation' with the 'building' tradition, for it recurs exactly in MT in Solomon's claim to have built a 'place for thy dwelling (*makhon le-shibt*[e]*ka*) for ever' (1 Kings 8:13, paralleled in 2 Chron. 6:3). In the Septuagint, *makhon* in 1 Kings 8:12–13 (placed in LXX after 8:53) finds no clear correspondence, but in 2 Chron. 6:3 *makhon* is rendered by ἕτοιμον, 'ready', recalling Exod. 15:17 LXX and probably indicating a pre-existent divinely-prepared dwelling. This influential Pentateuchal translation, 'ready dwelling', discussed further below, interprets *makhon* 'place' paronomastically by *nakhon* 'ready', a term applied in Isa. 2:2 to the 'mountain of the Lord's house' at the last and in Ps. 93:2 to the divine throne.

The phrase in Exodus is also very close to *m*[e]*khon shibteka*, used of the heavenly divine dwelling at 1 Kings 8:39, paralleled in 2 Chron. 6:30, and Ps. 33:14; in all three verses the LXX translators used the same phrase 'ready dwelling' which is found in Exod. 15:17, as quoted above. Further notable applications of *makhon* to a present or future sanctuary occur in Isa. 4:5 'all the place of mount Zion and her assemblies', and 18:4 (the deity speaks) 'in my place'; Ezra 2:68 to set up God's house 'on its place' (LXX 2 Esdras here ἑτοιμασία 'preparation' is a further reflection of the Pentateuchal rendering 'ready'); Dan. 8:11 'the place of his sanctuary was cast down'.

The song of Moses (Exod. 15:17 in particular) on the divinely-prepared sanctuary into which the people will be led was correspondingly read as a Mosaic prophecy of a new temple—the coming divinely-prepared temple—in texts found at Qumran and in rabbinic interpretation (Schwemer (1), 347–9, 356–7). The texts discussed below are chosen to bring out the old-established character of this reading, to illustrate the exegetical connections made between Exod. 15:17 and the prophetic books, including Isaiah, and to show that the biblical association and contrast between the coming divinely-made sanctuary and the earthly temple was continued without negation of either side.

First, then, a famous Qumran exegetical text (4Q174) is reconsidered, to show that strong hope for the new temple is accompanied by a biblically-grounded contrast with the present sanctuary, which is at the same time an acknowledgement of its function; then, conversely, the prayer for Jerusalem in Ecclesiasticus, which echoes Exod. 15:17 but is sometimes judged to be concerned exclusively with the present temple, is interpreted as hinting also at hope for renewal; and finally the connection of Exod. 15:17 on 'preparation' with the prophecy of Nathan in 2 Samuel is recalled from 4Q174, a further connection with Isa. 65–6 on new creation is shown from the Temple Scroll, and the age and pervasiveness of the influence on future hope exercised by Exod. 15:17 is illustrated from the LXX Pentateuch and Prophets, including Isa. 54, and the New Testament.

2. *4Q Florilegium: The present and the promised sanctuary in future hope*

First, future hope in the terms of Exod. 15:17 is seen in a composition which contrasts the future sanctuary with the present temple, but also acknowledges the function of the present temple. Exod. 15:17 is important in the Hebrew text from Qumran Cave 4 designated Florilegium (see 4Q174, col. i, lines 1–7, attested in fragments 1–2 and 21; freshly collated text and translation with comments in Puech (1), ii, 574–8). The verses Exod. 15:17–18, promising a divinely-built sanctuary, are quoted and interpreted in lines 2–5, as part of an exegesis of Nathan's oracle in 2 Sam. 7:10, quoted in line 1. This promised divinely-built sanctuary is then contrasted with Israel's sanctuary, once laid waste by strangers (lines 5–6); 'but he said to build him a sanctuary of man (*miqdash adam*), that they might be making incense smoke (*maqtirim*) for him in it [or, 'making sacrifices smoke for him in it'], the works of praise before him' (lines 6–7). The connection of 'praise' (*todah*) with making sacrifices smoke (*qatter*) occurs at Amos 4:5.

The divine command mentioned here ('he said') seems best taken as that in Nathan's oracle 'he [Solomon] shall build a house for my Name' (2 Sam. 7:13a); for the introductory 'he said' in 4Q174, compare David's speech in 1 Chron. 28:6 'And he said to me: Solomon thy son, he shall build my house and my courts'. The phrase *miqdash adam* can accordingly be rendered 'a sanctuary made by human beings', and understood (with D. R. Schwartz (1), 88) as a reference to the temple of Solomon, who built the house 'only to make [incense or offerings] smoke' (*l^{e}haqtir*) before him' (2 Chron. 2:5 [6])—words in which Solomon summarizes the fuller statement of purpose which he has just given: 'to make to smoke (*l^{e}haqtir*) before him sweet incense, and for the continual shewbread, and for the burnt offerings morning and evening' (2 Chron. 2:4 [5]).

After this point lines 7–11 then continue with an exegesis of 2 Sam. 7:11–14, but verse 13a 'he shall build a house for my Name' will have been treated in connection with verse 10 and in advance of the rest of the oracle because the sanctuary was taken to be the subject of verse 10 (see the previous section). The relative clarity of these links with Solomon—in the echo of 2 Chron. 2:5 (6)—and with the context—shaped by exegesis of the vision of Nathan, with its reference to Solomon as temple-builder—commend an understanding of *miqdash adam* as Solomon's temple rather than as the 'sanctuary of Adam' constituted by paradise (as in Jub. 8:19, quoted in the following section), or (as argued by Puech (1), ii, 584–91) an eschatological 'sanctuary *consisting* of human beings', or (as suggested in a rich discussion by Brooke, 286–91), a sanctuary both 'of men' and 'of Adam', that is the community of the elect in which the re-establishment of the Edenic sanctuary is inaugurated. The echo of 2 Chron. 2:5 (6) makes it difficult to hold (with Brooke, 287) that an interpretation of 2 Sam. 7:13a 'he shall build a house for my name' has been designedly omitted in the exegesis of Nathan's oracle in 4Q174.

It may be added that, on the interpretation of *miqdash adam* as Solomon's temple followed here, the treatment in 4Q174 of the command in Nathan's oracle that Solomon should build the temple (2 Sam. 7:13a) as suggesting a contrast with the divinely-made sanctuary is comparable with the treatment of the same passage in Nathan's oracle in the Wisdom of Solomon (9:8). Here Solomon's prayer includes the words 'thou didst say (εἶπας) to build a temple in thy holy mount, and an altar in the city of thy tabernacling, a copy of the holy tabernacle, which thou didst prepare beforehand from the beginning'. The beginning of the paraphrase of Nathan's oracle in Wisdom, 'Thou didst say to build', is strikingly close to that in 4Q174, 'he said to build'; then in Wisdom, as in 4Q174, a word which can be rendered 'sanctuary' or 'temple' (ναός) is substituted for the biblical 'house'. Wisdom now further amplifies by mentioning an altar, but this addition again recalls 4Q174, which continues with the reference to making incense or sacrifices smoke discussed above. Finally, however, Wisdom goes on to recall (from 1 Chron. 28:11–12, 19) that Solomon's temple is to be 'a copy' (μίμημα) of the tabernacle divinely prepared beforehand, a recollection which brings out not only likeness, but also contrast. This contrast corresponds with that discerned above in 4Q174, and in both cases it reflects the contrast which is repeatedly drawn in the biblical narratives of David and Solomon between God's earthly house and heavenly dwelling, as was noted at the beginning of this section. The similarity of the treatment of 2 Sam. 7:13a in 4Q174 and the Wisdom of Solomon is not considered in the discussions of 4Q174 cited here, but it offers some confirmation that the understanding of *miqdash adam* as Solomon's temple is on the right lines. In 4Q174, then, as in the Wisdom of Solomon, the biblical contrast is continued; but in both cases the earthly as well as the heavenly temple is divinely ordained.

3. *Ecclesiasticus: Future hope in the praises of the present Jerusalem*

Secondly, then, it is unsurprising that the application of Exod. 15:17 to a coming divinely-prepared temple which is exemplified in 4Q174 did not preclude its application to the existing hill and sanctuary of Zion, as in Ass. Mos. 1:17–18, discussed below with texts on the 'creation' of Jerusalem. This application to the earthly Zion could indeed be made in a fashion which, correspondingly, allows for the other side of the biblical contrast, that is, the hope of Zion's eternal divine glorification and the implication of a divine renewal.

Thus in the early second century B.C. the Jerusalemite poet Jesus son of Sirach alludes to Exod. 15:17 in such a way that the temple here below seems divinely 'prepared'. This suits his whole-hearted assertion of its present indwelling by the pre-existent divine glory, which in his poem is identified with wisdom. The glory of wisdom, and her identification with the sanctuary, are brought out in J. C. Lebram's suggestion that her place in Ecclesiasticus corresponds to that of a Greek city-goddess. Wisdom's self-praise in Ecclesiasticus includes the saying 'he created me from the beginning, before the world; in the holy tabernacle I served before him, and thus was I established in Sion' (Ecclus. 24:9–10, not extant in Hebrew); and this claim seems to be echoed in the Zion prayer, quoted above in the previous section, in the first part of a line which can be rendered as follows from the Cairo Genizah Hebrew (MS B, here represented by the Cambridge fragment T.-S. 16.313, ed. S. Schechter in Schechter and Taylor, 16):

> Give testimony to that which was from the beginning of thy works,
> and raise up the vision spoken in thy name.
> (Ecclus. 36:14 (15))

Kister (308–9 and n. 17) illuminatingly interprets 36:14a by 24:9, but the reference in 36:14a is perhaps not primarily to wisdom as pre-existent Torah, as he suggests in the light of the identification of wisdom with Torah at 24:23: In 24:10 wisdom 'serves' liturgically, and although this can be understood (as by Smend, 218) as a reference to the Torah as regulating the cult, it seems less strained to understand it of wisdom as the divine presence or spirit in the sanctuary (one of two possibilities suggested by Segal, 148). This interpretation of wisdom commends itself in 36:14 especially in view of the importance of the temple and the divine glory in the immediate context of this verse.

The two preceding verses (36:12–13) may be rendered from the Cairo Genizah Hebrew:

> Have mercy on the city of thy holiness, Jerusalem, the place of thy dwelling.
> Fill Zion with thine honour, and thy temple with thy glory.

In Ecclus. 36:12a 'have mercy' echoes Ps. 102:14 'thou shalt arise and have mercy upon Zion'. Then in 12b 'the place of thy dwelling' recalls Exod. 15:17 and 1 Kings 8:13, 2 Chron. 6:2 *makhon le-shibtᵉka*, where the existing holy place of Zion seems primary, and also *mᵉkhon shibteka*, used of the heavenly divine dwelling at 1 Kings 8:39 and other places noted above. In Ecclus. 36:13 'fill … thy temple (*heykhal*) from thy glory' recalls the glory which filled the tabernacle and the temple and was hoped for in even greater brightness (Exod. 40:34–5; 1 Kings 8:11, paralleled in 2 Chron. 5:14; 2 Chron. 7:1; Haggai 2:7); from the 'building' line of tradition, compare Ps. 102(101):17 LXX 'for the Lord shall build Sion, and be seen in his glory', and the Apocalypse of Weeks, at 1 En. 91:13 'there shall be built the *heykhal* of the kingdom of the Great One in the greatness of his glory for all generations of ages' (Aramaic text in 4Q212, col. iv, line 18; García and Tigchelaar, i, 444). The continuing importance of this expectation appears in the lines on the future divine glory appearing in the holy place cited at the beginning of this study from the Psalms of Solomon and the Fifth Sibylline book, and it can also be seen in the Targums and rabbinic literature; 'thine eyes shall see thy teachers (or, thy Teacher)' (Isa. 30:20) becomes in the Targum 'thine eyes shall be seeing his Shekhinah in the house of the sanctuary' (Churgin 101, quoting comparable rabbinic sayings from Soṭah 49a).

The concern with the sanctuary and divine glory which emerges in these ways just before the half-line on 'that which was from the beginning of thy works' seems still to be part of the context in the half-line which follows, 'raise up the vision spoken in thy name'. The 'vision' is likely, as in the Apostrophe to Zion discussed in the previous section above, to be the 'vision' of Nathan, with special reference, as in the Florilegium, to the promise 'I will appoint a place for my people Israel, and plant him' (2 Sam. 7:10). Nathan is one of the prophets commemorated by name in the Hymn of the Fathers, later in Ecclesiasticus (47:1).

The prayer of Ecclesiasticus 36:12–14 in the Hebrew, therefore, expresses hope for full manifestation of the glory of the divine wisdom now present but veiled in the sanctuary, and for the fulfilment of the Zion prophecies with their references to new building, above all the 'vision' of Nathan (as in 11Q Apostrophe to Zion, discussed in the previous section). Hayward 135, having taken 36:14 differently, and having stressed ben Sira's respect for the existing temple, urges that he hoped essentially for the ingathering. This hope was indeed continually bound up with glorification (as at Hag. 2:7–9) and will certainly have been important for ben Sira (cf. again Exod. 15:17, as echoed in 2 Macc. 1:29, quoted above); but the allusions in 36:14 to wisdom in the temple and to Zion prophecies suggest that the poet hoped also for divine manifestation in a renewed sanctuary.

This interpretation of 36:14 seems consistent with Ecclus. 49:12, on the temple restoration of Zerubbabel and Joshua son of Josedech. The second line of this verse, in the Cairo Genizah Hebrew text from MS B (here represented by the Cambridge fragment T.-S. 16.314, edited by S. Schechter in Schechter and Taylor, 19), may be rendered:

> they raised high the holy temple (*heykhal qodesh*),
> that which was prepared for everlasting glory
>
> (Ecclus. 49:12b)

This Hebrew text here is identical with or very close to that which lies behind the grandson's Greek translation. Against the background of Hebrew and Septuagintal interpretation of Exod. 15:17 and related passages outlined above, 'prepared' here (Hebrew *ha-m*[e]*khonan*, Greek ἡτοιμασμένον) appears as one more paronomastic interpretation of *makhon*, in the *piyyuṭ*-like style of this poet (Schechter in Schechter and Taylor, 27–9), to allude to the temple as divinely prepared. The verb *konen* chosen in the Hebrew, and the verb ἑτοιμάζω chosen to render it in the Greek, are those encountered in Exod. 15:17 'the sanctuary, Lord, which thy hands made ready' (MT *kon*[e]*nu*, LXX ἡτοίμασαν). They are separately applied to future rebuilding in Isa. 54:11 (LXX ἑτοιμάζω, cited above), and 54:14 (MT *tikkonani*, 'thou shalt be made ready'). The 'everlasting glory' could then be understood not only of the perpetual divine indwelling expected for the divinely-prepared *makhon* by King Solomon (1 Kings 8:13; 2 Chron. 6:2) but also of an even more glorious divine manifestation still to come, when witness is borne to the glory of the wisdom now veiled, 'that which was from the beginning of thy works' (36:14). The vision of the unveiled divine glory in the sanctuary is the climax of hope, as noted above, in texts ranging from the Apocalypse of Weeks to the Fifth Sibylline book and the Targum of Isaiah (see also Yose ben Yose, at pp. 342–3 below).

4. Association of Exod. 15:17 with Nathan's vision and Isa. 65–6 on new Jerusalem

Each of the two texts now considered draws attention to the exegetical interconnection established between Exod. 15:17 and other prophetic texts. The remembering of Zion prophecies collectively which was surveyed above will of course have contributed to this process. Thus in the earlier part of the passage in 4Q174 Exod. 15:17 is clearly understood as promising a future temple, but lines 1–2 also interpret 2 Sam. 7:10 as a reference to 'the house' to be established 'in the latter days, as it is written … Lord, which thy hands have made ready' (Exod. 15:17); that is to say, the lines on the planting of Israel and the preparation of the sanctuary in Exod. 15:17 had by this time become associated with the similar line from the vision of Nathan, 'I will appoint a place [*maqom*, not *makhon*] for my people Israel, and plant him' (2 Sam. 7:10). The relevant words from 2 Sam. 7:10 are attested in fragment 4 of 4Q174, and Puech follows A. Steudel in placing them immediately before the later words from the same verse which begin line i of col. 1 as printed from fragments 1–2 and 21; but through these later words the association of Exod. 15:17 with 2 Sam. 7:10, from the vision of Nathan, was already evident from 4Q174 as first published. This prophecy of Moses and the vision of Nathan both probably receive allusion within a short space in the prayer for Jerusalem in Ecclesiasticus discussed above. Here 36:12 alludes, with *m*^{e}*khon shibteka*, to Exod. 15:17, and no doubt at the same time to Solomon's prayer at the dedication (1 Kings 8:12, etc., and 2 Chron. 6:1, etc.); 36:14, with *hazon*, probably alludes to the 'vision' of Nathan.

Exod. 15:17, understood as promising a future temple, was connected also with the 'new creation' of Isa. 65:17–18 (cf. 66:22) 'I create new heavens and a new earth … I create Jerusalem'. These Jerusalem-oriented passages from the end of Isaiah lie behind references to new creation or making new in the Hymns and the Community Rule from Qumran Cave 1 (1QS (1Q28) iv 24 'new making' or 'making new' recalls Isa. 66:22 as well as 43:19), and a connection of them with Exod. 15:17 emerges from the Temple Scroll: 'I shall dwell with them for ever and ever, and I shall hallow my sanctuary with my glory, for I shall make my glory abide upon it until the day of creation, when I shall create my temple to establish it (*lehakhino*) for all days, according to the covenant which I made for Jacob at Beth-el' (11Q19 (11QTa) xxix 9–10; García and Tigchelaar, ii, 1250). The connection of 'creation' with the sanctuary here is given by Isa. 65:18, but in view of the importance of 'my glory' in this passage it was perhaps also strengthened by Isa. 4:5, quoted in part above, where 'the Lord shall create' a cloud of glory 'over all the place of mount Zion and its assembly'. With the view of the covenant at Beth-el (Gen. 28:10–22, 35:1–15) taken in the Temple Scroll here compare Test. Levi 9:3–4 'When we came to Beth-el, Jacob my father saw a vision concerning me, that I should be a priest for them'; Wisd. 10:10, cited above, 'wisdom ... showed him [Jacob] God's kingdom, and gave him knowledge of holy things'; and in rabbinic midrash, Ber. R. lxix 7, recording an interpretation of Jacob's words 'This is none other than the house of God' (Gen. 28:17) as his response to a vision of the future temple built, destroyed, and again rebuilt.

The link made in the Temple Scroll between the last two chapters of Isaiah and Exod. 15:17—understood as promising a divinely-built temple—recurs in the prophecies of paradisal bliss at Jerusalem discussed below. Moreover, it seems likely that in the Temple Scroll the divinely-built temple is thought to have been shown to Jacob beforehand, somewhat as it provided for Moses the pattern of the tabernacle and the candlestick, and for David and Solomon the pattern of the temple (Exod. 25:9, 40; Num. 8:4; 1 Chron. 28:19).

These passages from 4Q Florilegium and the Temple Scroll also bring out the prevalence of this understanding of Exod. 15:17, and strengthen the view that the 'new house' brought by the lord of the sheep in the second dream-vision of Enoch is the divinely-built temple, envisaged as pre-existent (1 En. 90:29; McKelvey 29–30, writing before the first edition of the Temple Scroll, and not discussing 4Q174 in this connection, judged this interpretation to be probable but not certain).

5. *Exod. 15:17 in the setting of the Septuagint*

The early date of the interpretation of Exod. 15:17 as an unfulfilled prophecy of 'Sion prepared', and the extent of its interconnection with other texts, both perhaps emerge most clearly of all from the Septuagint. First, the LXX translation 'ready dwelling' in Exod. 15:17 suggests that this verse was already taken to promise a pre-existent God-given temple in the third century b.c.; for 'ready' (ἕτοιμος) signifies divinely prepared (see the following line of the verse), as in the imminent eschatology of Deut. 32:35 LXX 'for the day of *their* destruction is near, and the things which are ready for *you* are present'. These verses come respectively from the lesser and greater Songs of Moses, which were considered together in the time of Philo (*Plant.* 54–9, probably moralizing a current eschatological interpretation), and no doubt earlier too. The phrase 'the things which are ready for you' in the greater Song (Deut. 32:35) seems to be echoed with reference to the paradisal Jerusalem in 1 En. 25:7, already quoted and to be discussed further below.

Secondly, Exod. 15:17 LXX affected the Greek scriptures elsewhere. Thus the rendering 'I make ready (ἑτοιμάζω) for you carbuncle as stone' in Isa. 54:11 LXX, on the new Jerusalem, cited above, probably echoes Exod. 15:17 'made ready', on the divinely-prepared sanctuary, and fits well with Isa. 49:16 LXX and Peshitta 'I have represented you on the palms of my hands' (like a designer). Again, in the Greek scriptures the rendering 'ready dwelling' for the Hebrew phrase 'the place of thy dwelling' from Exod. 15:17 became standard, as noted above, in Solomon's dedication prayer in Kings and Chronicles and in other passages. That this phrase was current in Aramaic as well as Greek is suggested by the appearance of its near equivalent *ʿ^{a}tar m^{e}zumman* 'the place prepared' in the Fragment Targum and Targum Neofiti (and vestigially in Targum Pseudo-Jonathan) on Exod. 15:17.

The body of Zion-oracles remembered in prayer for Jerusalem and the temple therefore had a central Pentateuchal element of Mosaic prophecy. Exod. 15:17, in conjunction with Deut. 32:35 on 'the things which are ready for you', was near the root of an expectation of a divinely-prepared city and sanctuary which has been best-known from the Wisdom of Solomon, the Syriac Apocalypse of Baruch and rabbinic texts, but is already attested at an earlier date in the LXX Pentateuch, Prophets and Psalms, in 1 Enoch, the Temple Scroll and 4Q Florilegium. It exerted broad influence through a web of exegetical interconnections, notably with the vision of Nathan, Solomon's prayer at the dedication and the later chapters of Isaiah. Its links with Nathan's vision and Solomon's prayer worked to preserve in interpretation the biblical pattern both of contrast and association between heavenly dwelling and earthly temple. This pattern could be traced in 4Q Florilegium, despite a 'heavenly' emphasis, and in Ecclesiasticus 36, despite an 'earthly' emphasis.

This old-established biblical interpretation also influenced Christian literature, for example at 1 Pet. 1:5 'ready to be revealed in the last time'; against the Septuagintal background just noted it seems likely that 'ready' here echoes Exod. 15:17, and primarily qualifies the 'inheritance' 'kept in heaven for you' (verse 4; cf. Exod. 15:17; Deut. 32:35), and not just 'salvation', the noun which 'ready' follows in verse 5. In Paul himself this influence can be detected at 1 Cor. 2:9 'the things which God has made ready', discussed further below.

(b) Sion Built

The separate importance of the closely-associated 'building' line of tradition in the Second Temple period emerges especially from the prominence in the apocalypse of Ezra (2 Esd. 3–14) of 'the built city' as a description of Sion seen in visions (2 Esd. 10:27, 42, 44, 13:36, quoted above; discussion by Stone 129–30). As noted above, this phrase sounds like an echo of 'Jerusalem the built' (Ps. 122:3 *hab*ᵉ*nuyah*, οἰκοδομουμένη), a phrase clearly applied to the heavenly city when it is rendered in the Targum 'Jerusalem that is built in the firmament' and in the midrash 'Jerusalem that Jah built' (Tanhuma, Pequde, 1, on Exod. 38:21, also quoting the Targum; ed. Berlin and New York, 1927, 171b). The phrase also recalls, however, other verses on the holy place as divinely built (Ps. 78:69 'he built his sanctuary', 102:17 'the Lord built Zion') or as built by divine command (1 Kings 8:13 'I have surely built', cf. 8:20, 27), and prophecies of future divine building (Jer. 31:4 (LXX 38:4) 'Again will I build thee and thou shalt be built'; Ps. 147:2 'The Lord is the one who builds Jerusalem'; Ps. 102 (101):16 LXX 'for the Lord shall build Sion').

These expectations of divine re-building are echoed in Tobit 13–14, as quoted above, especially 'the house of God shall be built in it for ever with a glorious building, as the prophets have foretold' (14:5), and again when Jubilees, probably in the second century B.C., awaits the time when 'my sanctuary shall be built among them for all eternity … and Zion and Jerusalem shall be established' (1:27); compare the Apocalypse of Weeks, as quoted above, 'there shall be built the *heykhal* of the kingdom of the Great One in the greatness of his glory for all generations of ages' (1 En. 91:13, following the Aramaic text in 4Q212, col. iv, line 18; García and Tigchelaar, i, 444). This will be the new creation when 'the sanctuary of the Lord is created in Jerusalem on mount Zion' (Jub. 1:29), 'mount Zion, which in the new creation will be hallowed for the hallowing of the earth' (4:26). In all these passages the reverential passives indicate divine, not simply human, work.

1. Descriptions of the new building

Akin to the visions of Sion in 2 Esdras are a series of imagined descriptions of the newly-built city, including such biblical prophecies as Zech. 2:5–10 (1–5), but beginning with the appearance in Ezekiel's vision of 'the building (lxx οἰκοδομή) of a city opposite' (Ezek. 40:2 LXX). Here the LXX rendering ἀπέναντι 'opposite' (corresponding to *mi-neged*, rather than MT *mi-negeb*) perhaps already attests the Targumic and rabbinic view that the heavenly city is just above or opposite the earthly (see below; this would supply a contributory cause for the text-form attested in the LXX, shown probably to be secondary by Gese 10–11). Another detailed description of the future city and sanctuary is attested in fragmentary Aramaic texts from Qumran Caves 1, 2, 4, 5 and 11, and has been given the title 'New Jerusalem'; it includes prescriptions for the cult, and its elaboration recalls the detailed description of the future temple in the Temple Scroll. Chyutin 112, noting that the Syriac Apocalypse of Baruch (59:4) takes a record of the pattern of Zion to have been shown to Moses, suggests that the writer of the apocalypse may here allude to this 'New Jerusalem' text.

The influence of these full descriptions of the 'building', from Ezekiel onwards, emerges in the late Herodian age in a cluster of visionary texts. These include Rev. 21:1–22:5 (without 'building' terms other than 21:18 ἐνδώμησ ις, on the material of the wall, but with considerable detail); and Sib. 5:420–7, summarized at the beginning of this study, on the glorifying of the beloved city and the great tower which the blessed man 'formed' (ἔπλασσεν). In two further prophecies from this time, however, the term 'building' comes again to the fore. These are 2 Esdras, cited already for its references to the 'built city', and the Syriac Apocalypse of Baruch (2 Baruch), on 'the Building of Zion' (cf. Ezek. 40:2 LXX 'building') which will be shaken, built again, desolated, but afterwards renewed in glory (2 Baruch 32:2–4); 'the pattern of Zion and its measures', were shown to Moses (59:4, cited above), for the 'building' of the city was already prepared 'here' (in heaven) beforehand, at the time when God determined to make paradise, and was then shown to Moses on Sinai when he saw the pattern of the tabernacle and its vessels—and is now kept like paradise with God (4:1–6). The strength of this theme of the primaeval and future 'building' is illustrated in a fashion of interest for Paul on both 'building' and 'new creation' by the Septuagintal rendering of Isa. 54:11–17. Here—renderings at variance with MT are italicized—the city set with jewels is told 'in righteousness shalt thou be *built*', and again 'behold, I am founding [or, creating] *thee* … I have founded [or, created] *thee*' (οἰκοδομηθήσῃ … κτίζω σε … ἔκτισά σε, at Isa. 54:14, 16–17, LXX). It is notable that this passage was drawn into the sphere of influence of both 'preparation' (verse 11, noted earlier) and 'building' (verse 14, just quoted).

2. Jerusalem below aligned with Jerusalem above

One further interpretation of the 'place' (*makhon*) in Exod. 15:17 affects both 'preparation' and 'building' texts, and can suitably be noted now that both lines of interpretation have been illustrated. Just as *makhon* can be paronomastically identified with *nakhon* in the LXX, and *maqom* in 4Q Florilegium, so in Targumic and rabbinic texts it can be repointed as *m[e]kuwwan* 'set correspondingly'—to the heavenly sanctuary; and the phrase *makhon le-shibt[e]ka* can be understood accordingly both in the Song of Moses on 'preparation' and in Solomon's prayer on 'building'. So the Mekhilta of R. Ishmael includes among interpretations of Exod. 15:17 the passage:

> 'A place (*makhon*) for thee to dwell in'—set correspondingly (*m[e]kuwwan*) to thy dwelling-place. This is one of the statements to the effect that the throne below corresponds to the throne above; and so it also says, The Lord is in his holy temple, the Lord's throne is in heaven [Ps. 11:4]; and it also says, I have surely built thee a house of habitation, set correspondingly to thy dwelling-place for ever [1 Kings 8:13].
>
> (Mekhilta of R. Ishmael, Beshallah, Shirata, x; Lauterbach, ii, 78)

This interpretation occurs in the Targums, including Targum Pseudo-Jonathan on Exod. 15:17 and on Gen. 28:17. Its midrashic employment is sometimes associated with Simeon b. Yohai (mid second century A.D.), for example at Ber. R. 55.7, when it seems to form the pattern of his interpretation of 'Moriah' (Gen. 22:2) as 'seen correspondingly to the sanctuary above', and at Ber. R. 69.7, where Jacob's words at Bethel 'and this (*w[e]-zeh*) the gate of heaven' (Gen. 28:17) are taken to show that the distance from the holy place below to the heavenly sanctuary above is eighteen miles, for *w[e]-zeh* taken numerically adds up to eighteen. It seems to be assumed again in Targ. Ps. 122:3, quoted in part above: 'Jerusalem that is built in the firmament, as a city to be joined for itself together on earth.' These exegeses presuppose an established view that the heavenly city and sanctuary is positioned above the earthly. The late second-century currency of this view is independently attested in Tertullian's report (*Marc.* iii 24, 4) of the appearance of the city in the skies over Judaea, further discussed in chapter 9, below. Ego 96 suggests early tannaitic origins for the corresponding interpretation of 'a place for thy dwelling' in Exod. 15:17 and Solomon's prayer.

A case can be made accordingly for its currency towards the end of the Second Temple period. Josephus in his paraphrase of Solomon's prayer at the dedication (1 Kings 8:13) comes close, with the addition of Stoic colouring, to the rendering given in the Mekhilta: 'We know that thou, O Master, hast an eternal dwelling in those things which thou didst create for thyself, heaven and air and earth and sea … But I have constructed this temple to thy Name so that from it we may, when sacrificing and ministering, send up our prayers into the air to thee' (Josephus, *Ant.* viii 107–8). Here, interpreting 1 Kings 8:13 'a place for thy dwelling', he brings Stoic views of the divine as permeating the universe, especially the aerial regions (so Cleanthes in Cicero, *N.D.* i 37), together with the notion that the deity is in particular to be found up in the air above Jerusalem.

In the roughly contemporary Syriac Apocalypse of Baruch, just cited for its lines on the 'Building of Zion' on earth and with God, Baruch calls out bitterly in his lament: 'Ye priests, take the keys of the sanctuary, and cast them into the height of heaven, and give them to the Lord' (2 Baruch 10:18, discussed with parallels by Charles, 17–18). In this passage the temple above is not specifically mentioned, but there is a similar presumption that the deity is just over Jerusalem—which will be delivered up for a time, until its perpetual restoration (6:9). In passages cited already, however, the 'building of Zion' below answers to a heavenly original kept with God and to be revealed in the end (4:1–6), when the 'building' below is to be renewed in glory (32:4). In the composition taken as a whole, it seems that both the deity and his heavenly Building are close to the earthly building. In 2 Esdras, similarly, although 'the built city' can only be seen in vision from the field where there has been no building (10:53–4), it is in the end precisely when the man from the sea stands upon the top of mount Sion that 'Sion shall come, and shall be showed to all, prepared and built' (13:35–6).

Paul's 'Jerusalem above' which is also to come (Gal. 4:25–6) therefore combines the old expectation of a future Jerusalem, illustrated above from a series of Hebrew, Aramaic and Greek witnesses in connection with 'Sion prepared', with the conception of a heavenly Jerusalem, illustrated above in connection with 'building' as well as 'preparation'. The LXX phrase 'ready dwelling' suits both lines of interpretation. The association of the heavenly with the earthly city and sanctuary which has just been illustrated suggests that, if Rom. 11:26 may tentatively be viewed together with 1 Thess. 4:17, the two epistles present a consistent picture of Christ descending from Zion above to be met by the ingathered saints 'in the air' above Jerusalem.

Recreated paradisal Jerusalem

These expectations were in turn associated with hopes for the joy of the righteous in paradisal bliss in what would later be termed a millennial reign, centred on the divinely prepared Jerusalem sanctuary. These hopes built not only on Exod. 15:17 but also on the description of new creation and joy in Jerusalem in Isa. 65–6. Compare the association of Exod. 15:17 and Isa. 65:17–18 presupposed in the passage quoted above from the Temple Scroll, 11Q19 xxix 9–10.

1. Primordial and future creation of Zion

The emphasis on Jerusalem's re-creation in Isa. 65:18 'that which I am creating: behold, I am creating Jerusalem a joy and her people a rejoicing' helps to give other creation texts concerning Jerusalem a future as well as a primaeval dimension. Such texts include Isa. 4:5, quoted above, on the 'creation' of glory over the *makhon*, and Exod. 15:17 and other passages on the divine 'making' and 'founding' of the holy place and the holy hill. Thus the primordial divine creation of the hill of Zion here below, in line with Exod. 15:17 as interpreted by Ps. 78:54 and Ps. 87:5, all three texts reflecting very old mythology, is still presupposed in the later Herodian age in the Assumption of Moses. Here Joshua is to deposit the books of Moses *in loco quem fecit ab initio orbis terrarum, ut invocetur nomen illius*, 'in the place which [God] made from the beginning of the world, that his Name might be invoked' (Ass. Mos. 1:17–18, as interpreted in Horbury (1), 401–2); cf. Exod. 15:17 'the place for thy dwelling which thou didst make, O Lord'. This ancient tenet of the primordial creation of the holy place has continuing vitality still later in rabbinic speculation on antemundane creations or planned creations (a baraitha in Pes. 54a and Ned. 39b lists seven items including the house of the sanctuary; Ber. R. i 4 and Midrash Tehillim xciii 3 list six items including the house of the sanctuary). The importance of the primordial creation of Zion encourages hope for new creation precisely at 'my holy mountain Jerusalem', as envisaged in Isa. 65–6.

2. Ingathering to a paradisal new Jerusalem

The hopes for a paradisal new creation of Jerusalem are vividly expressed in 1 En. 25, perhaps roughly contemporary with Ecclesiasticus, where wisdom in the Jerusalem temple is compared with a paradisal tree and rivers (Ecclus. 24:13–17, 25–6; Barker, 88), and with Jubilees, where the Garden of Eden is 'the holy of holies and the Lord's dwelling-place' (8:19, discussed by van Ruiten, 218–24). In 1 Enoch the tree of life will be transplanted into 'the holy place, by the house of God, the everlasting king'. The righteous 'will come into the holy place' with joy, and the fruits and scents of the tree will give them lives of antediluvian length (1 En. 25:5–6). 'Then', says the seer, in words quoted above, 'I blessed the God of glory, the everlasting king, who prepared (Greek ἡτοίμασεν) for righteous mortals such things, and created them, and commanded that they should be given them' (1 En. 25:7).

Here once again the future hope is modelled on the ingathering and planting in the holy place foretold in Exod. 15:17; the righteous will come into it for the rejoicing at the chosen place which is prescribed in Deut. 12:12, 18, and prophesied for Jerusalem and 'my holy mountain' at Jer. 31:12–14 (joy and abundance in the height of Zion); Ezek. 17:22–4 (planting of a tree, as in Enoch, and flourishing, in the mountain of the height of Israel), 20:40–2 (ingathering, oblation and manifestation of divine holiness in the mountain of the height of Israel; cf. 34:13–14); and Isa. 65:17–25, 66:10–14, 20–4, with emphasis on long life (Isa. 65:20–2, 66:14), delight in Jerusalem's abundance (Isa. 66:10–11), and ingathering to 'my holy mountain Jerusalem' (66:20). So in 1 En. 25 God has now consoled the desolate Jerusalem by making her wilderness 'as Eden … as the garden of the Lord' (Isa. 51:3), and Israel by making her tents 'like gardens by the river side' (Num. 24:5–6). With a return to the influential language of the two songs of Moses reviewed above, the seer then (1 En. 25:7) blesses God for what he 'prepared' (Exod. 15:17; Deut. 32:35). He is at once (1 En. 26:1) transported to the mid-point of the earth, and (1 En. 26:2–27:4) sees the holy mountain (of Zion) and the accursed valley (of Hinnom) in which, respectively, the pious will bless the Lord at the judgment, and the sinners will be made a spectacle for them (cf. Isa. 66:13–14, 23–4).

The importance of Isa. 65–6 as well as Exod. 15 for Jerusalem-centred hope on these lines is suggested by touches in the LXX of Isa. 65–6 which emphasize the interrelationship of these chapters with 1 En. 25–7. Examples (LXX phrases which lack full correspondence in our Hebrew are italicized in the translations below) occur at Isa. 65:22, LXX 'as the days of the tree *of life* shall be the days of my people' (so also the Targum on this verse), cf. 1 En. 25:5–6 on the length of days conferred by the fruits and fragrance of the tree in the holy place; Isa. 66:23, LXX 'all flesh shall come up before me to worship *in Jerusalem*', cf. 1 En. 27:3 'here shall the pious bless the Lord of glory'; and Isa. 66:24, LXX 'they shall be *for a spectacle* (ὅρασις) to all flesh', cf. 1 En. 27:3 'the spectacle of righteous judgment'.

The 'delight' of Isa. 66:11 and the 'holy mountain' of Isa. 66:20 are combined with 'the mountain of the height of Israel' from Ezek. 17:24 in a prophecy of bliss from the Pesher on Psalm 37 attested in fragments from Qumran Cave 4 (4Q171, fragments 1 and 3–4, col. iii, lines 9–11). Here 'they that are blessed of him shall inherit the land' (Ps. 37:22) refers to 'the congregation of the poor', and the promise 'shall inherit the land' is amplified as 'they shall inherit the mountain of the height of Israel, and in his holy mountain shall they delight'. A little earlier, on Ps. 37:19 'they shall not be ashamed in the evil time', it has been said that 'the converts of the wilderness', probably the same group, 'will live for a thousand generations in salvation, and theirs is all the inheritance of Adam' (4Q171, fragment 1, col. iii, lines 1–2). Here they have paradisal length of days, as in Isa. 65:22 LXX, but with allusion probably to Deut. 7:9 'a thousand generations', as in CD vii 4–6. Earlier still in the psalm, the promise of 'delight' has already been made to the meek in verse 11, in wording like that of verse 22 ('they shall inherit the land, and shall delight …'); the Pesher on verse 11 (4Q171, fragment 1, col. ii, lines 9–12) identifies them as 'the congregation of the poor' (discerned again, as noted above, in verse 22), and it gives a paraphrase of verse 11 which would comfort the poor and hungry, but sounds strikingly carnal to the well-fed: 'those who inherit the land shall delight, and shall grow fat in all the delight of flesh'. In the Pesher, then, 'shall delight' in Ps. 37 has been associated with 'shall delight' in Isa. 66:11 on Jerusalem (both texts employ the relatively rare verb *hith'anneg*), and the result is a prophecy of bliss and long life in Zion. It joins hands with the vividly carnal messianic prophecies in 2 Baruch (29:3–6) and Papias of the time when 'those who have hungered will rejoice' (2 Baruch 29:6; cf. Luke 6:21), but it remains an interpretation of Isa. 66.

In later development of this tradition the bridal imagery of Isa. 52:1, 54:1–13, 61:10–11, 62:4–5 joins the recollection of Isa. 65–6 and Exod. 15; before the rejoicing of the righteous 'the bride shall appear, even the city coming forth' (2 Esd. 7:26), and this is indeed, as a later chapter says, 'Sion … prepared and builded' (2 Esd. 13:36). It is bound together in thought with paradise, the tree of life, the 'preparation' of the world to come and its plenty, and the 'building' of the city: 'since for you is paradise opened, the tree of life is planted, the time to come is prepared, plenteousness is made ready, a city is builded', *vobis enim apertus est paradisus, plantata est arbor vitae, praeparatum est futurum tempus, praeparata est abundantia, aedificata est civitas* … (2 Esd. 8:52). In a similar Christian apocalypse the new Jerusalem (Rev. 21:2) is the bride 'made ready' (Isa. 54:11 LXX, itself echoing Exod. 15:17), comparably associated with the tree of life (Rev. 22:14, 19) and paradise (Rev. 2:7, 3:12).

This approach to the exegetical tradition of paradisal bliss in Zion has then confirmed for the Second Temple period S. Heid's indication of the great importance of the later chapters of Isaiah in early Christian treatment of this topic, but it has also pointed to the influence of other texts, notably the Mosaic prophecy of Exod. 15:17 and the disputed but popular prophecy of Enoch. The combination of Pentateuchal and Enochic oracles with Isaiah is likely to have been especially powerful.

In Paul himself the association of Exod. 15:17 with the prayer and prophecy concerning Zion in Isaiah seems to appear in the adaptation of Isa. 64:3 (4) towards Exod. 15:17 at 1 Cor. 2:9 '… the things which God has made ready for those who love him'; compare MT, which may be rendered '… a God beside thee, that shall work [or, make] for the one who waits for him', and LXX '… beside thee and thy works, which thou shalt do [or, make] for those who await mercy'. The version in Paul appears to paraphrase the last clause on the lines of LXX, with explicit reference to the divine works, but now with their 'preparation' beforehand and pre-existence especially in view, in the line of interpretation connected with Exod. 15:17 LXX 'thy ready dwelling … the sanctuary which thy hands made ready', Deut. 32:35 LXX 'the things that are ready', and 1 En. 25:7 'who prepared for righteous mortals such things'. The list in 2 Esd. 8:52, quoted above, probably enumerates the main 'things which God has made ready' envisaged in 1 Cor. 2:9, 'things' which all belong to paradisal Zion.

A second and more general Pauline comment arises from the strong Isaianic association of new creation with Jerusalem. In exegetical tradition this association, clearly made in the Hebrew text of Isa. 65–6, was underlined not only by the paradisal picture of Zion in 1 En., Isa. 65–6 LXX, and the Pesher on Ps. 37, but also by the Septuagintal rendering of Isa. 54:14–17 with parts of κτίζω (see the previous section), which allows the prophecy to be heard as an earlier divine declaration on the creation of Zion. 'New creation' in Paul should probably therefore be reckoned as another reflection of the set of interpretations and expectations concerning Zion.

Summary of Part I

Three characteristic features of the interpretative tradition on Zion which was current in Paul's time have now been viewed. In each case some considerations emerged which might assist understanding of the place of Jerusalem in Pauline hope. The summary below may then also serve to introduce the second part of this study, in which the Pauline writings themselves come to the fore.

The review of exegetical tradition began from Zion as ἔνθεος ὕμνων, the subject of inspired hymnody. It was urged that recollection of Zion prophecies collectively was encouraged by the custom of prayer and hymnody for Israel and Jerusalem, and this custom was illustrated by texts surviving in Hebrew, Aramaic and Greek. Such prayer appears to be echoed in Paul. It both reflects and contributes to the intensity of hope for the renewed holy place and the divine glory. This Zion-centred intensity is perceptible in Paul, for example at Gal. 4:25–6 and 2 Cor. 5:1–2.

Some important elements in the group of biblical traditions remembered collectively were then identified. At the heart of the Zion-oracles was the Mosaic prophecy of a divinely-prepared holy place (Exod. 15:17 'place of thy dwelling', LXX 'ready dwelling'). It was associated with the greater Song of Moses on 'the things which are ready for you' (Deut. 32:35), with Nathan's 'vision' communicated to David, with Solomon's prayer at the dedication, and with later prophecies including Isa. 54 and 65–6. These interconnections are well seen from the LXX, but they also appear in Hebrew texts such as 4Q Florilegium and the Temple Scroll.

2 Esd. 13:36 on 'Sion prepared and built' was taken to indicate two important threads in interpretation. A notable thread concerned with divine 'preparation' depends on Exod. 15:17, but another thread concerned with 'building' further displays the influence of Nathan's 'vision', Solomon's prayer, Ezekiel's vision of a 'building', and Ps. 122 on Jerusalem 'the built'.

From these lines of interpretation it emerged that a divinely-prepared holy place above and to come had been widely envisaged before Paul's time. Exod. 15:17 LXX 'ready dwelling', a rendering which influenced many other texts, suggests that this expectation was known when the LXX translation of the Pentateuch was made in the third century B.C.

It was urged that the biblical contrast and association between the earthly and the divinely-prepared holy place are not lost even in 4Q Florilegium and Ecclesiasticus, which have the reputation of emphasizing either future hope or present achievement, respectively. Association as well as contrast was underlined by rabbinic interpretation of Exod. 15:17, 1 Kings 8:13 and Ps. 122:3 as locating the heavenly sanctuary in close correspondence with the earthly, and this interpretation was probably already known at the end of the Second Temple period. It was suggested that Gal. 4:26–30 and 2 Cor. 5:1–2 stand within the tradition of contrast and association, and that Rom. 11:26 somewhat comparably presupposes parousia from the city above, associated with that below.

The recreated paradisal Zion formed the final aspect of exegetical tradition to be considered. It emerged that hopes for paradisal bliss in a newly-created Zion, on lines that would later be termed millennial, were expressed especially through association of Exod. 15:17 with Isa. 65–6. They are displayed in 1 En. 25, to which Isa. 65–6 LXX come strikingly close, and in the Pesher on Psalm 37 preserved in 4Q171, which in this respect forms an interpretation of Isa. 66. Interpretation exemplified in Revelation and 2 Esdras brings together the divine preparation of Exod. 15:17, the bridal preparation of Zion envisaged in earlier chapters of Isaiah, including Isa. 54, and the paradisal Zion hopes of Isa. 65–6—two chapters which themselves in the book as we have it respond to the lament and prayer for Zion in 63–4. It was suggested that the development of Isa. 64:3 (4) in 1 Cor. 2:9 can be situated within the exegetical association of Exod. 15:17 with these later chapters of Isaiah.

The importance for the origins of chiliasm of sequential reading of the later chapters of Isaiah (and not simply of the Johannine Apocalypse) has been rightly emphasized by S. Heid; but it emerged, as just noted, that in the Second Temple period these chapters were linked too with prophecy on the holy place in the Pentateuch, especially Exod. 15:17, and with apocryphal prophecy of a paradisal Jerusalem, especially 1 En. 25–7. The importance of the Pentateuchal links emerges from 1 Enoch itself, and of the Enochic links from the Septuagint of Isaiah.

Paul himself, then, is likely to have envisaged Zion-oracles as a group. His contacts with the exegetical strands considered here are not restricted to Gal. 4:26–30 and Rom. 11:26–7, the passages primarily under consideration, although in both these cases the Pauline texts appear to situate themselves within an attested tradition. Other passages found to suggest contact with the exegetical tradition on Zion have included 1 Cor. 2:9 on the things prepared, 2 Cor. 5:1–2 on the eternal and the present dwelling, and Gal. 6:15–16 on new creation and prayer for Israel. More generally, the Pauline themes of Zion, building from God and new creation, which are associated with differing aspects of his teaching, can be seen to arise from a single group of Zion-centred interpretations and expectations.

II

Non-Pauline Christian continuation of this interpretative tradition during and after Paul's lifetime includes the gospels and Acts on 'not made with hands', and Hebrews on mount Sion and the city prepared, as well as Rev. 20–22. It was the Old Testament and apocryphal tradition surveyed above, however, which chiefly contributed to the development of Christian chiliasm (reviewed together with non-chiliastic interpretations of the heavenly Jerusalem by Hill (2) and Markschies (2), 311–29). In chapter 9, below, this Christian phenomenon is understood as in part a manifestation of contemporary anti-Roman messianism in the majority Jewish community, as that is reflected in the apocalypses of Baruch and Ezra and the fourth and fifth books of the Sibylline Oracles (completed after the destruction of Jerusalem by Titus and used by Christians as well as Jews) and in the Jewish disturbances of the second century. This argument is further illustrated from the Epistle of Barnabas and the writings of Justin Martyr in Horbury (2), 146–53.

1. Paul as interpreted in Christian chiliasm

Noteworthy figures in the church in this connection, from the first century to the third, include John the Divine, Papias, Justin Martyr, Irenaeus and Tertullian. Hopes for an earthly kingdom of Christ in a recreated Jerusalem were not shared by all Christians, as Justin Martyr admitted with regret (*Dial.* 80.2), but they were clearly influential in the church. An early witness to them is the Preaching of Peter, quoted by Clement of Alexandria (*Strom.* vi 15) to the effect that the apostles found in the books of the prophets Christ's death and sufferings, 'and the rising and the taking up into the heavens before the foundation [or creation] of Jerusalem (πρὸ τοῦ Ἱεροσόλυμα κτισθῆναι)'. This final phrase has sometimes been regarded as corrupt, but it was surely rightly referred to the new Jerusalem by J. E. Grabe (quoted in Potter, ii, 804–5). It suits the Hebrew text of Isa. 65:18 'I create Jerusalem', but in the LXX its use of κτίζω recalls rather Isa. 54:16–17 'behold I found [or, create] thee', discussed above. For the use of this short phrase without explanation compare the unexplained 'making new' in the Community Rule (1QS iv 24, quoted above). For the Preaching of Peter, then, after the assumption of Christ into the heavens, there is to follow the creation of new Jerusalem as the kingdom of Christ and the saints.

The chain of witness cited to confirm these hopes came to include Paul. Thus Justin picked out especially (*Dial.* 81.1–2) Isa. 65:17–25 on new heaven, new earth, Jerusalem as a joy, and 'the days of my people'; but Irenaeus (*Haer.* v 33–5) added to this and other passages from Isaiah, notably 54:11–14, some further Old Testament witness, especially from Jeremiah (Jer. 31:10–14, on joy in Zion; Baruch 4:36–5:9, on the brightness of Jerusalem displayed everywhere 'under heaven'), and Christian testimony from 'John the Lord's disciple' (v. 35), in the Revelation of John, and 'Elders, disciples of the Apostles' (v. 36), including Papias the 'hearer of John' (v. 33). Into these quotations, however, Irenaeus incorporated also 'the Apostle writing to the Galatians' on the Jerusalem above, the mother of us all (Gal. 4:26); he was not thinking of 'some wandering Aeon', says Irenaeus scornfully, but of 'the Jerusalem which is delineated by hands' (Isa. 49:16). His final outline of stages in creation and recreation (v. 36) culminates in Isaianic and Pauline words: one God 'promised the inheritance of the land to the fathers, brought it forth in the resurrection of the just, fulfils the promises in the kingdom of his Son, and afterwards paternally bestows those things which neither eye saw, nor ear heard, nor have entered into the heart of man' (1 Cor. 2:9, Isa. 64:4).

Tertullian similarly makes Paul the mainstay of his argument for a kingdom on earth which is none the less from heaven, 'in the city of God's making, Jerusalem, let down from heaven, which the apostle also points out as our mother above [Gal. 4:26]; and saying that our *politeuma*, that is our citizenship, is in the heavens [Phil. 3:20], he assigns it to some heavenly city. This is the city which Ezekiel knows, and John the apostle saw' (*Marc.* iii 24, 3–4). Like Irenaeus, Tertullian takes Gal. 4:26 as a reference to the city above which will come down to earth, but he adds that it must also be in view in Philippians on heavenly citizenship (on Phil. 3:20 in its Pauline context see Schwemer (2), 228–38, favouring the 'citizenship' interpretation exemplified in Tertullian here). From the Old Testament Tertullian adds Ezekiel's vision of the 'building' to set beside the vision of John. That he was also indebted both to Enoch (whose book he defends in *Cult. Fem.* 3) and to Isa. 65–6 is indicated by the last chapter of *De Spectaculis*, on the future spectacle of judgment: 'what a kingdom of the righteous! what a city of new Jerusalem! But there are other spectacles too still to come, that last and unending day of judgment … what kind of things are those, which neither eye has seen nor ear heard, nor have come up into the heart of man? [1 Cor. 2:9]' (*Spec.* 30). The judgment which forms this great spectacle is the 'spectacle (ὅρασις) to all flesh' of Isa. 66:24 LXX, further described in 1 En. 27:3 on 'the spectacle of righteous judgment' in the 'accursed valley' of Hinnom, discussed above. The final allusion to 1 Cor. 2:9 once again links Paul with depiction of 'the kingdom of the righteous'; this text, also connected with the kingdom on earth by Irenaeus, closely recalls Isa. 64:4, and was discussed above for its links with the traditions of divine preparation and paradisal Jerusalem.

2. Paul on Zion and messianic reign

Paul could then be understood in the second and third centuries, without special awkwardness, as a witness to hope for a kingdom of the righteous in the heavenly Zion on earth. Against this background, it may be suggested that in Gal. 4:26–30 (quoting Isa. 54:1 'Rejoice, O barren') and Rom. 11:26–7 (quoting Isa. 59:20–1 in the form 'a redeemer shall come from Sion') Paul envisaged a coming messianic reign in the divinely prepared Jerusalem, bringing together the king with the city and the sanctuary on the Old Testament pattern noted at the beginning. Hints at a Jerusalem-centred messianic reign in both passages would be consonant with the eschatological importance of Zion or the land in Rom. 9:25–6 (Davies, 195–6).

To present this suggestion briefly, in the larger Pauline context the most important passage for the question is 1 Cor. 15:20–8. The present writer follows those who hold that in 1 Cor. 15 Paul envisages a Zion-centred messianic reign, beginning with a second coming of Christ. As is shown in verses 25–8 by the exposition of Pss. 110:1, 8:6 on the subjection of enemies, this reign involves the crushing victory over hostile forces granted to the king, God's son, in Zion, on the lines sketched in Psalms 2:6–9, 110:1–6. Comparable developments of this theme of messianic victory (studied further in chapter 11, below), often also with reference to one great foe and with allusion to Isa. 11:4, are found in 2 Esdras (4 Ezra) 13:6–13, 32–50 (God's son on mount Sion destroys gentile foes); Syriac Apocalypse of Baruch 40 (the messiah executes the enemy leader outside Jerusalem), 72–3; 1QSb 'with the breath of your lips may you slay the wicked' (1Q28b, col. v, lines 24–5; Puech (1), 442); and probably 4Q285 (the prince of the congregation, the seed of David, puts a foe to death). In Christian sources this execution of foes in the messianic victory is pictured at 2 Thess. 2:8 and Luke 19:27.

Two informative studies represent the opinion that, rather, the heavenly reign of the ascended Christ is in view in 1 Cor. 15. C. E. Hill (1) urges, among other arguments, that Pss. 110:1, 8:6 regularly elsewhere refer to a heavenly reign; but this is not clear in all cases cited, as at Phil 3:20–1, which also well fits an earthly reign (Bockmuehl, 235; Schwemer (2), 238). For de Boer, 134–5, Paul differs from Revelation precisely in failing to specify an *interim* reign, and probably views the whole time since the resurrection as war somewhat like that described in the War Scroll; but messianic reign traditions better account for the Pauline conjunction of destruction of enemies with a strong emphasis on reigning.

To return now to Galatians, Isa. 54:1 has associations which strongly favour this interpretation. Some of those which it gained in interpretation were noted in comments above on the LXX rendering, which presents building as bridal preparation in verses 11–14 (cited by Irenaeus) and introduces the divine foundation or creation of the city in verses 14–17. The oracle as it stands in the

Hebrew Bible, however, is spoken to an unnamed female addressee; but by the end of the Second Temple period it was linked with the land and with Zion in particular.

First, 'Rejoice, O barren' is among the very few prophetic texts quoted by Philo (*Praem.* 158), and this in connection with the Pentateuchal promises of national redemption; he takes it of the land, revived through its sabbath of desolation (Lev. 26:42–5), bringing forth a new generation of saints (Deut. 30:5), and this sense is given before he adds an allegory. It seems likely that Isa. 54:1 was already traditionally associated with the fundamental Pentateuchal hopes of a renewed land.

Secondly, connection of Isa. 54:1 with Zion in particular will have been encouragedby the similarity between verse 2 'Enlarge the place of thy tent … lengthen thy cords, and strengthen thy stakes' and an earlier passage in the book of Isaiah, 33:20, where Jerusalem is mentioned by name and then described as 'a tent that shall not be removed', with its cords and stakes. The Hebrew and Greek rendered by 'tent' and 'stakes' are the same in both passages, in MT and in LXX, respectively.

Thirdly, pre-Pauline association of Isa. 54 with the coming glorious Zion is indicated by allusion in the LXX and in literary works made known by the Qumran finds. Thus in the LXX Isa. 54:11, on the city prepared with precious stones, seems to be linked with the divinely-built temple of Exod. 15:17 by the rendering in LXX Isaiah 'I make ready (ἑτοιμάζω) for you'. Compare Exod. 15:17 LXX 'thy ready dwelling (ἕτοιμον κατοικητήριόν σου), which thou, Lord, didst make, the sanctuary which thy hands made ready (ἡτοίμασαν)'; Micah 4:1 LXX 'and in the last days the mountain of the Lord shall be manifest (ἐμφανές), ready (ἕτοιμον) upon the peaks of the mountains'; and Wisd. 9:8 'the holy tabernacle which thou didst make ready beforehand (προητοίμασας) from the beginning'. In Hebrew compositions, correspondingly, a pre-Pauline connection of verse 1 with the city is suggested by the echo of verse 2 'spread wide the place of thy tent' in 11Q Apostrophe to Zion 18 'Be exalted and spread wide, O Zion' (11Q5, col. xxii, line 14); and by the allusions to verse 6, and also to verses 1 and 2, which are intertwined with language from Lam. i–ii on Zion in 4Q179.2 (Lamentations), lines 3, 6–7: 'in thy tent' (cf. verse 2) … 'like a woman grieved, like a woman forsaken' (cf. verse 6) … 'like a barren woman' (cf. verse 1).

Before the time of Paul, therefore, the prophecy of Isa. 54 was associated with the coming divine renewal of the land and the coming divinely-prepared Zion. The influence of Isa. 54:1–2 understood as a prediction of future glory addressed to Jerusalem is vividly shown shortly after the time of Paul by the vision of the mourning woman transformed into a large city in 2 Esdras 10:26–7. 'She suddenly uttered a loud and fearful cry'; compare Isa. 54:1 'cry aloud', in the LXX 'break forth and cry'. Then '... the woman appeared to me no more, but there was a city builded, and a place showed itself of great foundations'; compare Isa. 54:2 'spread wide the place of thy tent', Isa. 54:11 1QIsa[a] and LXX 'thy foundations', and Ps. 87 (86):2 'his foundation (LXX 'foundations') on the holy hills', and note that Ps. 87:3 and Isa. 54:2 were successively echoed in the Apostrophe to Zion, verses 17 and 18, quoted individually above. These echoes in 2 Esdras seem not to be widely recognized (the points of similarity in 2 Esdras 10:25–7 and Isa. 54:1–2, 11 are not discussed in the comments on the Ezra-apocalypse by Box, Violet, Stone and Lichtenberger); but they are clear enough to merit notice in the present context. Just as the seer's later vision of the messiah as a lion (2 Esd. 11:36–12:39) grows out of the interpretative tradition concerning Gen. 49:9 'Judah, a lion's whelp' (compare chapter 4, above, p. 133), so here his vision draws on existing application of Isa. 54:1–2 to Zion.

The two texts quoted by Paul, Isa. 54:1 (Gal. 4:26) and 59:20–1 (Rom. 11:26), both recur later on in rabbinic exposition of the new Jerusalem; thus in Pesikta de-Rab Kahana 20:3 the third-century Palestinian homilist Levi connects Isa. 54:1 with Sarah, as in Galatians, and ultimately also with 59:20, quoted in Romans. The rabbinic association of these texts with the new Jerusalem is probably traditional.

Further, Isa. 54 will have been studied continuously with Isa. 52–3. Thus the Targum, understanding 53 messianically, links 53 and 54 by taking 53:5 of the messiah rebuilding the temple, and 54:1 of Jerusalem—now named explicitly as the addressee. In second-century Christianity, similarly, Justin Martyr quotes the whole of Isa. 52:10–54:6 as a baptismal proof-text (*Dial.* 13, discussed with other evidence by Heid, 24–8). The two chapters are likely to have been read in sequence by Paul, who would then naturally understand 54 of a messianic city restoration, as did Christians and Jews rebuked by Origen (*comm. in Joh.* x 25) and Jerome (commentary on Isaiah, book 15, on 54:1).

In Gal. 4:25–6 'the Jerusalem above' is contrasted with 'the Jerusalem that now is', and appears accordingly as the Jerusalem to come; a future reference is also implied in the language of promise and inheritance (Barrett, 164–5; Wilken 281, n. 42). When 'Rejoice, O barren one' (Isa. 54:1) is quoted in this context, against the background just outlined it is likely that the coming divinely-built Jerusalem is in view. 'Cast out the bondwoman and her son, for [he] shall not inherit . . .' (Gal. 4:30, quoting Gen. 21:10) then refers to exclusion from the new Jerusalem. This will requite the present persecution described in Gal. 4:29, just as the joy of the new Jerusalem will console those now persecuted. The ties which Christians already have with Jerusalem above need not rule out an expectation of its coming (*contra* W. D. Davies, 197–8). This future interpretation would suit the advice of Ps.-Demetrius on elocution, quoted by H. D. Betz to explain this passage, to the effect that a series of considerations should conclude with a darkly-hinting and therefore terror-striking argument (Betz, 240).

The interpretation offered by Paul here (4:24 'which things are an allegory') is regarded by Markschies (2), 306–7, as weakening the connection of 'Jerusalem above' with the concrete reality of 'Jerusalem that now is', for the latter is made to represent servitude under the law, while 'Jerusalem above' stands for conformity to Christ. Martyn, 440–3, 462–6, and Sanders, 95–7 similarly concentrate on the symbolism and scope of Paul's interpretation, taking it to be directed against Jerusalem Christians sponsoring a non-Pauline mission; they, not the inhabitants of Jerusalem as a whole, are represented by 'Jerusalem that now is'. Attempts such as these to define the symbolism of 'Jerusalem that now is' are inevitably debatable, but they do justice to the clearly polemical intention of Paul's argument. Yet, do they sufficiently allow for what Schwemer calls the 'apocalyptic realism' of Paul (Schwemer (2), 227–8)? Paul starts with a polemical allegory, but when he reaches the contrast between Jerusalem 'now' and to come he is thinking of a known city, its vividly imagined heavenly counterpart, and speedy divine vindication and retribution. Hence the 'servitude' of present Jerusalem may include what Paul would regard as servitude to law, but is first of all her servitude to gentile power. The bitterness of the language would then import, as suggested already in comparison of this passage with 2 Cor. 5:1–2 in part I, fierce longing for the 'liberty of Zion' and 'redemption of Zion' through the coming of the heavenly Jerusalem and the kingdom of Christ.

Finally, in Rom. 11:26 the quotation of Isa. 59:20 as 'a redeemer shall come from Sion' is also readily explained by traditions of a messianic reign. It is indeed sometimes, though not always, understood as reflecting expectation of the return of Christ precisely from Jerusalem above (an interpretation denied by Wright, 250–1, allowed as possible by Dunn, 306–7, and affirmed by Markschies (1), 3; (2), 305; Schwemer (2), 226, 237–8). '*From* Sion', by contrast with MT 'to' or LXX 'for the sake of', probably reflects Ps. 110:2 'The Lord shall send the sceptre of your power from Sion: rule in the midst of your enemies'. (Note that 'sceptre' in other passages could be taken as a term for the messianic ruler, as in Gen. 49:10 and Num. 24:17 LXX, CD vii 19.) The application of this verse from Ps. 110 is illustrated in 2 Esdras (4 Ezra), where the messiah rules and destroys the wicked from the top of the renewed Zion (13:6–13, 35–8)—the scene probably imagined in 1 Cor. 15:25, and discussed above at the end of the consideration of 'Sion built'. As noted already, in the light of Josephus on Solomon's prayer of dedication, the descent of the messiah from the heavenly Zion would be consistent with 1 Thess. 4:17 'in the air'.

The two Isaiah quotations in Galatians and Romans therefore seem likely to cohere with one another in sketching a messianic reign in the new Jerusalem. Their mutual consistency is underlined by their links with the interpretative tradition on Zion reviewed in the first part of this study, and by their setting in Paul among a number of contacts with this tradition. Thus the contrast in Galatians continues the biblical contrast marked especially in Solomon's prayer, has the intensity of future hope which is repeatedly felt in interpretation of Exod. 15:17, and stands together with the plangent contrast in 2 Cor. 5:1–2. The depiction of the whole scene in Galatians, from the city above to the coming reward within and retribution outside, recalls the recreated paradisal Jerusalem with the accursed valley outside in Isa. 65–6 and 1 En. 25–7, and the series of 'things prepared' in 1 Cor. 2:9, quoted by Tertullian to crown a more lurid depiction. Similarly, the redeemer from Zion in Romans comes like the man of 2 Esdras 13 from and with the heavenly city, and resembles the saviour expected from the heavens where we are citizens in Phil. 3:21 and Christ coming down from heaven in 1 Thess. 4:16–17. Paul's expectation as reflected in Galatians and Romans would then retain the time-honoured association between king, city and sanctuary found in the Psalms of Solomon before him, and in the Fifth Sibylline book later on.

Literature

P. S. Alexander, 'The King Messiah in Rabbinic Judaism', in Day (ed.), *King and Messiah*, 456–73

H. W. Attridge, *Hebrews* (Hermeneia; Philadelphia, 1989)

M. Barker, *The Gate of Heaven: The History and Symbolism of the Temple in Jerusalem* (London, 1991)

C. K. Barrett, 1982 (1976). 'The Allegory of Abraham, Sarah and Hagar in the Argument of Galatians', reprinted from *Rechtfertigung, Festschrift für Ernst Käsemann zum 70. Geburtstag* (Tübingen and Göttingen, 1976), 1–16 in C. K. Barrett, *Essays on Paul* (London, 1982)

H. D. Betz, *Galatians* (Philadelphia, 1979)

E. Bickerman, 'The Civic Prayer for Jerusalem', reprinted from *HTR* lv (1962) in E. Bickerman, *Studies in Jewish History*, ii (Leiden, 1980), 290–312

M. Bockmuehl, *The Epistle to the Philippians* (London, 1997)

M. C. de Boer, *The Defeat of Death: Apocalyptic Eschatology in 1 Corinthians 15 and Romans 5* (JSNT Supplement Series xxii, Sheffield, 1988)

P. M. Bogaert, *L'apocalypse syriaque de Baruch* (2 vols., Paris, 1969)

G. H. Box, *The Ezra-Apocalypse* (London, 1912)

G. J. Brooke, 'Miqdash Adam, Eden and the Qumran Community', in Ego, Lange and Pilhofer, with Ehlers (eds.), *Gemeinde ohne Tempel*, 285–301

R. H. Charles, *The Apocalypse of Baruch translated from the Syriac* (London, 1896)

P. Churgin, *Targum Jonathan to the Prophets* (New Haven, 1927)

M. Chyutin, *The New Jerusalem Scroll from Qumran: a Comprehensive Reconstruction* (JSP Supplement Series xxv, Sheffield, 1997)

W. D. Davies, *The Gospel and the Land* (Berkeley, Los Angeles and London, 1974)

J. D. G. Dunn, *The Theology of Paul the Apostle* (Edinburgh, 1998)

B. Ego, *Im Himmel wie auf Erden: Studien zum Verhältnis von himmlischer und irdischer Welt im rabbinischen Judentum* (WUNT ii.34, Tübingen, 1989)

B. Ego, A. Lange and P. Pilhofer, with K. Ehlers (eds.), *Gemeinde ohne Tempel, Community without Temple: Zur Substituierung und Transformation des Jerusalemer Tempels und seines Kults im Alten Testament, antiken Judentum und frühen Christentum* (Tübingen, 1999)

I. M. Gafni, ' "Pre-Histories" of Jerusalem in Hellenistic, Jewish and Christian Literature', *JSP* i (1987), 5–22

F. García Martinez and E. J. C. Tigchelaar, *The Dead Sea Scrolls Study Edition* (2nd edn., 2 vols., Leiden and Grand Rapids, 2000)

H. Gese, *Der Verfassungsentwurf des Ezechiel (Kap. 40–48) traditionsgeschichtlich untersucht* (Tübingen, 1957)

R. P. Gordon, *1 & 2 Samuel: a Commentary* (Exeter, 1986)

R. Hayward, 'The New Jerusalem in the Wisdom of Jesus Ben Sira', *SJOT* vi (1992), 123–38

S. Heid, *Chiliasmus und Antichrist-Mythos: Eine frühchristliche Kontroverse um das Heilige Land* (Hereditas vi; Bonn, 1993)

M. Hengel and A. M. Schwemer (eds.), *Königsherrschaft Gottes und himmlischer Kult im Judentum, Urchristentum und in der hellenistischen Welt* (Tübingen, 1991)

M. Hengel, S. Mittmann and A. M. Schwemer (eds.), *La Cité de Dieu, Die Stadt Gottes* (Tübingen, 2000)

C. E. Hill (1), 'Paul's Understanding of Christ's Kingdom in 1 Corinthians 15:20–28', *NT* xxx (1988), 297–320

——— (2), *Regnum Caelorum: Patterns of Future Hope in Early Christianity* (Oxford, 1992)

W. Horbury (1), review of J. Tromp, *The Assumption of Moses: a Critical Edition with Commentary* (Leiden, 1993), in *VT* xlv (1995), 398–403

W. Horbury (2), *Jews and Christians in Contact and Controversy* (Edinburgh, 1998)

——— (3), *Jewish Messianism and the Cult of Christ* (London, 1998)

——— (4), 'Der Tempel bei Vergil und im herodianischen Judentum', in Ego, Lange and Pilhofer, with Ehlers (eds.), *Gemeinde ohne Tempel*, 149–68

M. Kister, 'A Contribution to the Interpretation of Ben Sira', *Tarbiz* lix (1990), 303–78

J. Z. Lauterbach, *Mekilta de-Rabbi Ishmael* (3 vols., Philadelphia, 1933)

J. C. H. Lebram, 'Jerusalem, Wohnsitz der Weisheit', in M. J. Vermaseren (ed.), *Studies in Hellenistic Religions* (Leiden, 1979), 103–28

L. I. Levine (ed.), *Jerusalem: Its Sanctity and Centrality to Judaism, Christianity and Islam* (New York, 1999)

H. Lichtenberger, 'Zion and the Destruction of the Temple in 4 Ezra 9–10', in Ego, Lange and Pilhofer, with Ehlers (eds.), *Gemeinde ohne Tempel*, 239–49

C. Markschies (1), *Between Two Worlds: Structures of Earliest Christianity* (1997; ET London, 1999)

——— (2), 'Himmlisches und irdisches Jerusalem im antiken Christentum', in Hengel, Mittmann and Schwemer (eds.), *La Cité de Dieu, Die Stadt Gottes*, 303–50

J. L. Martyn, *Galatians* (Anchor Bible xxxiiiA, New York, 1997)

R. J. McKelvey, *The New Temple* (Oxford, 1969)

L. Perrone, ' "The Mystery of Judaea" (Jerome, Ep. 46): the Holy City of Jerusalem between History and Symbol in Early Christian Thought', in Levine (ed.), *Jerusalem*, 221–39

M. Poorthuis and Ch. Safrai (eds.), *The Centrality of Jerusalem: Historical Perspectives* (Kampen, 1996)

J. Potter (ed.), *Clementis Alexandrini Opera* (2 vols., Oxford, 1705)

E. Puech (1), *La croyance des Esséniens en la vie future: immortalité, résurrection, vie éternelle?* (2 vols., Paris, 1993)

——— (2), *Qumrân Grotte 4.xviii, Textes hébreux (4Q521–4Q528, 4Q576–4Q579* (DJD xxv, Oxford, 1998)

J. T. A. G. M. van Ruiten, 'Visions of the Temple in the Book of Jubilees', in Ego, Lange and Pilhofer, with Ehlers (eds.), *Gemeinde ohne Tempel*, 215–27

E. P. Sanders, 'Jerusalem and its Temple in Early Christian Thought and Practice', in Levine (ed.), *Jerusalem*, 90–103

S. Schechter and C. Taylor, *The Wisdom of Ben Sira: Portions of the Book Ecclesiasticus from Hebrew Manuscripts in the Cairo Genizah Collection presented to the University of Cambridge by the Editors* (Cambridge, 1899)

E. Schürer, *The History of the Jewish People in the Age of Jesus Christ* (new ET, revised and edited by G. Vermes, F. Millar, M. Goodman, M. Black and P. Vermes), i, ii, iii.1, iii. 2 (Edinburgh, 1973, 1979, 1986, 1987)

D. R. Schwartz (1), 'The Three Temples of 4Q Florilegium', *Revue de Qumran* x (1979), 83–91

——— (2), 'Temple or City: What did Hellenistic Jews See in Jerusalem?', in Poorthuis and Safrai (eds.), *The Centrality of Jerusalem*, 114–27

A. M. Schwemer (1), 'Irdischer und himmlischer König. Beobachtungen zur sogenannten David-Apokalypse in Hekhalot Rabbati 122–126', in Hengel and Schwemer (eds.), *Königsherrschaft Gottes und himmlischer Kult*, 309–59

——— (2), 'Himmlische Stadt und himmlischer Bürgerrecht bei Paulus (Gal 4:26 und Phil 3:20)', in Hengel, Mittmann and Schwemer (eds.), *La Cité de Dieu, Die Stadt Gottes*, 195–243

M. Z. (H.) Segal, *Sepher Ben Sira ha-shalem* (2nd edn., Jerusalem, 1958)

P. W. Skehan and A. A. Di Lella, *The Wisdom of Ben Sira* (New York, 1987)

R. Smend, *Die Weisheit des Jesus Sirach erklärt* (Berlin, 1906)

M. E. Stone, *Fourth Ezra* (Hermeneia; Minneapolis, 1990)

G. G. Stroumsa, 'Mystical Jerusalems', in G. G. Stroumsa, *Barbarian Philosophy: the Religious Revolution of Early Christianity* (Tübingen, 1999), 294–314

B. Violet, *Die Apokalypsen des Esra und des Baruch in deutscher Gestalt* (GCS xxxii, Leipzig, 1924)

M. Weinfeld, *The Promise of the Land: the Inheritance of the Land of Canaan by the Israelites* (Berkeley, Los Angeles and Oxford, 1993)

R. L. Wilken, *The Land Called Holy: Palestine in Christian History and Thought* (New Haven and London, 1992)

N. T. Wright, *The Climax of the Covenant* (Edinburgh, 1991)

7

The Aaronic Priesthood in the Epistle to the Hebrews

Hebrews 7:5 treats tithe with an actuality which is noted by historians, but is on the whole undeveloped in study of the background of the epistle. Tithing, the commandments upon which formed the very essence of the law according to one rabbinic dictum (Shabb. 32a, in the name of Simeon b. Gamaliel), receives more discussion in Hebrews 7 than anywhere else in the New Testament—'and that is not much' (Morton Smith, 353, n. 8); but even this little sets a query against estimates of the author, offered in different ways by Moffatt and by Käsemann and his followers, as one who knew the levitical priesthood through his Bible rather than contemporary Judaism.

The view is here advanced for consideration that Jewish development of the biblical teachings on the priesthood had a formative influence on the epistle, both in its treatment of Jewish practice and in its fundamental and distinctive arguments concerning the priesthood of Christ. Some Jewish texts on the priesthood are accordingly compared with Hebrews on two points of tithe and ritual (section II, below), on the interrelation of law and priesthood in Heb. 7–8 (III), and on the figure of the high priest in Heb. 2:17–3:1, 4:14–5:10 (IV). It will aid their evaluation if a general characterization of the Jewish outlook ascribed to the writer of the epistle is first outlined (section I, below), even though this must depend for support to a considerable degree on the particular instances which follow.[1]

[1] The writer is much indebted to Professor C. F. D. Moule for his comments on an earlier draft. Writings cited by author's name are listed at the end.

I

The view here envisaged as formative for the author of Hebrews can be described either as a first-century constitutional theory (Roth (2), 297–301), or as one type of Jewish 'doctrine of the church' (Baumbach, 33–6); it comprises both, for it is, more loosely defined, a Judaism within which the body of ideas biblically associated with the sons of Aaron is primary. As political theory it was given the name 'theocracy' by Josephus (*Ap.* 2.165); he imagined it being put to Pompey in the words 'the ancestral custom is to obey the priests of the God whom we worship' (*Ant.* xiv 41), although with Deut. 17 he himself allowed a place, if the nation should not be content with God alone as their ruler, for a king who should do nothing without the high priest and the advice of the elders (*Ant.* iv 223f.). Still in the theoretical sphere, the influence of the view is evident when Philo treats the high priest as the 'principal part' in the body politic (*Spec. Leg.* 3.131; cf. *Somn.* 2.187); its aspect as an ecclesiastical polity begins to appear when the high priest prays for the whole *systema* of the Jews (2 Macc. 15:12). In practice it initially moulded the independent Jewish government of the First Revolt (Roth (2)), and it left its impress in the legend 'Eleazar the priest' on the coins of the Second; it was formative both for Josephus and his militant adversaries (Lebram, 253). Passages supporting priestly hegemony, especially in Jubilees and the Testament of Levi, have often been linked (as by Charles on Jub. 31:15) with the special claims of John Hyrcanus; but they are equally applicable to the whole Hasmonaean succession (Bammel, col. 353). In fact, as the pre-eminence of Aaron and Phinehas in Ecclus. 45 shows—and also the account of Jewish hierocracy given by Diodorus Siculus from Hecataeus of Abdera (Bar-Kochva, 18–43), although it is dated to the reign of John Hyrcanus by Lebram (246–8)—these ideas have pre-Maccabaean roots. Josephus' term 'theocracy' has long been rightly applied to the polity of P, wherein Joshua shall stand before Eleazar the priest, at whose word Israel shall go out and come in, and the high priest's death marks an epoch (Num. 27:21, 35:28; discussed by Wellhausen, 149–51).

In this theocratic understanding 'the polity of Israel' (Eph. 2:12) is of course at the same time an ecclesiastical polity whereby God's word is declared and Israel is cleansed from sin. The priest is 'the messenger of the Lord of hosts' (Mal. 2:7, perhaps echoed in Diodorus' Hecataeus, 5 [see Stern, i, 31]);

and the high priest 'shall make an atonement for the priests, and for all the people of the congregation' (Lev. 16:33). The more than national scope of the reconciliation ascribed to his ministry well emerges in the cosmic interpretation of his garments; 'in the long robe is the whole world' (Wisd. 18:24), and, correspondingly, 'the high priest of the Jews offers prayers and thanksgivings not only on behalf of the whole race of men, but also on behalf of the elements of nature, earth, water, air and fire' (Philo, *Spec. Leg.* 1.97). This fundamental point is made in various ways in Philo, Josephus and Wisdom (Goodenough, 99, 120); its centrality in ancient Judaism is confirmed by the early synagogal poetry of the Day of Atonement. Here, in Yose ben Yose (probably fifth century), the robe of blue is 'like the brightness of the firmament' (Yose, *'azkhir geburoth*, 165, in Mirsky, 155; so also Josephus, *Ant.* iii 184); and the thought that the temple-service stabilizes creation, well-known from rabbinic sources, is reflected in the customary subject-matter of the poems (Pesikta de-Rav Kahana 1.4f., on Num. 7:1, discussed with parallels in Horbury, 167; = 349, below). The theocracy of the sons of Aaron was thus conceived as mediating divine rule in no attenuated sense.

The writer to the Hebrews would thus be seen as profoundly influenced, like Josephus and Philo, by the theologico-political ideas of the Pentateuchal 'theocracy'. For the sake of clarity this view should be related to other assessments of his outlook (surveyed by H. Anderson since the first publication of this essay, with similar affirmation of the widespread ancient Jewish witness to relevant views, but special emphasis on the apocalypses and 4 Maccabees). First, the assessment of the outlook of Hebrews offered here is compatible with the data taken especially seriously by Moffatt, that the author of the epistle was an able writer of Greek and a student of the Septuagint; for the Pentateuchal sacerdotalism was developed in the Septuagint and in Jewish writings current in Greek from Aristeas to Josephus. By contrast with Moffatt, however, and with Käsemann's attribution of the high-priestly theme to Christian liturgy indebted, like Philo, to a gnostically-recoined Jewish messianism (Käsemann, 107f., 124–40), the writer to the Hebrews is envisaged here not as a scholarly Hellenist *tout court*, who had nothing to do with contemporary Judaism, but as one who was in touch, like Philo and Josephus, with a living Jewish faith.

This view would not, however, be incompatible with the supposition that he was indebted to Christian tradition in the manner suggested by C. J. A. Hickling, in a consideration of striking resemblances between Heb. 2 and Johannine thought and style; for on this suggestion, by contrast with those of Moffatt and Käsemann, it is envisaged that the theology of both John and Hebrews could derive from an element in the first-century Christian population which was 'closely in touch with educated Greek-speaking Judaism' (Hickling, 115). The present writer would simply underline the closeness and directness of the contact with Jewry to be presumed in the case of the author of Hebrews.

In the light of G. F. Moore's work A. C. Purdy long ago argued, against Moffatt on the one side and the appeal to some unusual, distinctive type of Judaism on the other, that Hebrews on priesthood and sacrifice was 'dealing with a problem which was *yet alive* in *normative* Judaism' (Purdy, 264; italicization added). The label 'normative' is perhaps better avoided, for in the context of a reference to Moore it may seem to imply that first-century Judaism is to be judged anachronistically from the standpoint of tannaitic literature alone. The present writer, holding like Purdy that the common traditions of Jewry are the most relevant in this case, would rather associate the Pentateuchal faith reflected in the Greek of Hebrews with a phrase of Solomon Schechter, as adapted by J. H. A. Hart to evoke the substantial community of thought between Philo and Palestinian Jewry: 'the catholic Judaism of the first century'.

Secondly, therefore, such a view as is here advanced differs from two more recent placings of the author against a Jewish background, those which set him either among the Qumran sectaries or among the early merkhabah mystics. In each case, as it seems to the present writer, ideas which Hebrews derives from the common stock of Jewry are mistakenly thought to indicate a link with restricted Jewish groups. Thus the sacerdotalism of Qumran, well brought out in connection with Hebrews by Kosmala (11–13, 76–96), is simply one striking instance of the Pentateuchally-rooted thought already noted; G. R. Driver, 543, judges that the comparable set of parallels adduced by Y. Yadin reflects the common debt of Hebrews and Qumran to more widespread Jewish tradition. Similarly, the strength of a comparison with merkhabah mysticism lies not in kinship between Hebrews and esotericism, but in the likelihood, clearly shown with regard to Hebrews by Hofius, that the Hekhaloth texts and 3 Enoch preserve earlier and more widely-attested features of Jewish cosmography. Such significant themes for Hebrews as the heavenly ascent and the angelic liturgy are treated in the Hekhaloth, as is emphasized by Schäfer (202, 205f., 215–18, 223–5), in much the same way as in the midrash and the pseudepigrapha. The descriptions of heaven in the later mystical texts are probably indebted, by way of a lengthy transmission, to biblical exegesis connected with the temple-service (Hofius, 12); the heavenly sanctuary (Exod. 25:40, 26:30) and its service appear in pre-rabbinic as well as rabbinic texts (Test. Levi 3; Meg. 12b; further texts in Wenschkewitz, 45–9, and Hofius, 13–15, 18f.); and the association of such exegesis with the sons of Aaron is suggested both by the cosmic interpretation of their vesture, noted above, and by the mention of levitical ancestry, in accounts of heavenly ascents, as a qualification for admission to the vision (Moses, in Pesikta Rabbathi 20.11 [Grözinger, 145–7]; R. Ishmael, in 3 En. 1.3, 2.3).

On the other hand, although some continuous tradition probably links pre-rabbinic apocalyptic visionaries with the early tannaitic mystics and the later *yoredhe merkhabah* of the Hekhaloth texts, Hebrews should perhaps be read as representing a more broadly corporate outlook on visionary tradition. The distinction between elementary and advanced teaching, in Heb. 5:12–6:2, need not be associated specially with 'ancient Jewish merkhabah-esotericism', as by Hofius, 74. The relatively reticent allusions in Hebrews to the heavenly sanctuary and its service, and the general admission of the brotherhood to the city of God (12:22), contrast with the more explicit Hekhaloth descriptions of the several heavens, and their inaccessibility to all but the privileged mystic; there are no accounts of visions in Hebrews, whether apocalyptic or Philonic (Michel, 557; Moffatt, lv). Yet the writer links liturgy and mystical piety, and seems near to Philo's view that approach to the divine is open to the righteous (Horbury, 'Benjamin', 748–9). The hints of an approved method of study and prayer in the later texts, which correspond to their association with esoteric teaching in select groups (Alexander, 167–72), contrast with the intensely moral and more broadly corporate character of the brotherly exhortation to draw near in Hebrews. As a homiletic composition for members of a worshipping body Hebrews probably has less in common with the Hekhaloth texts than with the Dura-Europos synagogue mural, *c*. A.D. 245, of Aaron beside a temple with the striking detail of an open sanctuary (Schubert, 45–7).

Akin to these suggestions of a sectarian or esoteric setting is the identification of the addressees as 'Christians from a "dissenting Hebrew" background'—perhaps from 'a dissenting synagogue in Rome'—for whom the Jerusalem temple is not an experienced reality' (Murray, 205). On this proposal, part of a stimulating attempt to clarify discussion of ancient Judaism, 'Jews' would be differentiated from 'dissenting Hebrews' by the touchstone of loyalty to the Jerusalem temple. 'Hebrews' would define themselves by their 'dissent' from this loyalty. Their antecedents, it is suggested, are in the circles represented by Enoch; in the first century A.D. they included Samaritans and Qumran sectarians; and some New Testament books, the Epistle to the Hebrews among them, accordingly reflect a 'dissenting Hebrew' background.

Welcome as is the proposal to discriminate on the basis of so clearly fundamental an institution as the temple, it must be asked whether these suggestions do not conjure up far more 'dissent' than the evidence warrants. 1 Enoch on the temple need not have been inconsistent with loyalty to Jerusalem (compare pp. 223, 244–5, above). Further, the two groups definitely assigned to the dissenting class, the Samaritans and the Qumran sectaries, are united by this suggestion in a manner which they themselves might not have welcomed. Samaritans held that Gerizim rather than Zion was the holy hill, but the Qumran texts seem to attest full conviction of the election of Zion, and to accept temple and priesthood as divinely appointed, simply criticizing the priests who in fact officiate; the authors of these texts have more in common with the 'Jews' of the hypothesis than with the 'Hebrews'. The Judaism of the period therefore offers a considerably less commodious foothold for ascription of the Epistle to sectarians than these proposals would suggest.

The catholicity in Judaism of the theocratic view here suggested as formative for the thought of the epistle is confirmed not only by its Pentateuchal basis, but also by its abiding influence after A.D. 70 both in Palestine and the Diaspora. In the Jamnian period the priesthood of Palestine was still judicially and politically important, with a place in messianic hopes which seemed close to realization (Alon, 318–23; Gereboff, 248f., 449f.; for the priesthood as a body in messianic hope, 2 Baruch 68:5; Hullin 92a, quoted at the close of section III, below); the Eighteen Benedictions significantly end with the Aaronic blessing, long reserved for pronunciation by the priests alone (Hoffmann, 54f.). In the same epoch Josephus made the fate of the sacerdotal polity one of the two great themes of his *Antiquities* (1.5), and defended it in *contra Apionem* as a true theocracy. The vitality of levitical ideas in the early church appears, probably independently of Hebrews, in 1 Clement (Jaubert, 198–200, 202f.); the phenomenon may not be unconnected with contemporary Judaism, for it has often been noticed that Jewish inscriptions, both from Palestine and the Greek-speaking Diaspora, attest the kudos of priestly descent (Wenschkewitz, 39, n. 3 [the Jewish catacomb of Monteverde]; J. Z. Smith, 16f. [Rome and Beth She'arim]; Kraabel, 84 [Sardis and Dura]). Examples from the Second Temple period, mainly but not solely giving names of women of priestly descent, include Semitic-language and Greek ossuary inscriptions from the Jerusalem region (Milik no. 22 = CIIP 183 [Menahem of the sons of Jachim, cf. 1 Chron. 24:17]; Rahmani no. 871 = CIIP 534 [Jehohannah, grand-daughter of Theophilus the high priest]; Ilan no. 8 = CIIP 297 [Megiste *hierisa;* Greek, from Aceldama]), and an Egyptian epitaph of 27 B.C. in Greek (Marin *hierisa*) from Tell el-Yehoudieh, ancient Leontopolis (CIJ 1514 = JIGRE 84).

In the Mishnah, however, the triple concern of Leviticus with sanctuary, sacrifice and priesthood is strikingly modified in Seder Qodashim, as Jacob Neusner notes, by a silence on the priesthood; this Order of the Mishnah continues with the two other subjects of Leviticus, and Hebrews heightens the contrast between Bible and Mishnah by its own continuance with all three (Neusner (1), 21f., 37, 43f.). Yet this silence is likely to betoken, not the insignificance of the priesthood, but reserve towards its claims, which retained, as noted in the foregoing paragraph, a political as well as an ecclesiastical aspect. The abiding importance of the priesthood is suggested by the attention paid to priestly genealogy in another Order of the Mishnah, Nashim. Strong interest in the subject evidently persisted both in the Jamnian period and, after Bar Cocheba, at Usha, this despite the hostility to priestly exclusiveness in contracting marriages evinced in traditions attributed to Johanan ben Zaccai and his pupil Joshua ben Hananiah (Eduyoth 8:3; Yebamoth 15b; Büchler, 20, 22). The reason, Neusner suggests, is concern that the coming restoration of the cult should not be impeded by inadequate genealogical care of the priesthood (Neusner (2), v, 197). The later Palestinian inscriptions of the priestly courses, comparably, show the importance of the priesthood for synagogue worshippers, as is independently indicated by the Targums, the early homiletic midrashim, and early liturgical poetry (Horbury, 167, 179; = 312, 324, below). The Aaronic mural is by no means isolated as regards the thought which it suggests. It is this body of theocratic thought and practice, biblical in its roots, catholic in its attestation throughout ancient Jewry, which is here suggested as the background of the argument of Hebrews.

II

The possibility that the writer to the Hebrews knew priestly tradition seems especially strong when he diverges from the Pentateuch on practical points of administration and ritual, yet in his divergence approaches post-biblical Jewish sources. One such divergence is the seemingly difficult statement of the law of tithe in 7:5, already mentioned. 'They of the sons of Levi that receive the priest's office have commandment to take tithes of the people'; but the commandment in question, Num. 18:21, assigns tithe to all the levitical tribe, not just to its priestly members. The priests are not commanded to tithe 'the people' directly; they are entitled to a further tithe out of the levitical tithe (Num. 18:26–28) as well as to first fruits (Rom. 11:16) and sacrificial portions (1 Cor. 9:13; Heb. 13:10); but the tithe itself goes to all 'the sons of Levi'.

The unexpected wording may arise because the author is thinking first and foremost of priests (6:20; 7:1, 3), and only now does descent from Levi become significant. Even so, there remains an awkwardness which led one commentator conversant with rabbinic texts to conjecture *lewin* for *laon*, so as to obtain a straightforward reference to the priestly 'tithe of the tithe' (Biesenthal, 184–7). The difficulty seems best explained from the practice, with which the passage was associated by Jeremias (106) and Stern (41f.), whereby tithe had long been paid directly to the priest. By contrast with the Pentateuch, Neh. 10:38 significantly adds that the Aaronic priest is to accompany the Levite when he takes tithe. Josephus once says simply that tithe is due to the Levites (*Ant.* iv 240), but he also summarizes Num. 18:21 with the expansion (not in the Targum) that tithe is due from 'the people' (*laos*, as Heb. 7:5) 'to the Levites themselves and to the priests' (*Ant.* iv 68; cf. 4:205 'to the priests and Levites'). Josephus also reports the 'edicts of Caesar' which assign tithe to Hyrcanus and the priests (*Ant.* xiv 203); his Hecataeus speaks of 'priests of the Jews who receive a tithe of the revenue and administer public affairs' (*Ap.* 1:188, perhaps reflecting Hasmonaean usage [Bar-Kochva, 159–60]); and he himself, Nehemiah-like, contrasts the profit made from tithes in Galilee by his priestly colleagues with his own refusal to accept tithes he could have claimed (*Vita*, 63, 80). Tithe is due to the priest, and the Levite is not mentioned at all, in Jud. 11:13–15, Tobit 1:6–8, and Jub. 13:25–27, 32:15. Philo, however (see Leonhardt, 201–7), once clearly describes tithe as the due of the Levite in particular (*Spec. Leg.* 1:156f.), and knows the 'tithe of the tithe' (*Det.* 2), although he once mentions tithe more ambiguously among the first fruits due *tois hieromenois* (*Virt.* 95)—a word which he uses for priestly and non-priestly Levites together (*Mos.* 2.174). According to rabbinic texts the matter was debated in the Jamnian period; against those, including Akiba, who maintain the letter of Num. 18:21, Eleazar b. Azariah upholds its interpretation as a grant of tithe to the priest; Ezra punished the Levites by taking it from them (Ket. 26a, discussed by Zahavy, 30–4). The difficulty is plaintively evoked in a comment on Hyrcanus' abolition of the confession at the presentation of tithes (Soṭah 9:10): 'The Merciful One said that they should give them to the Levites, whereas in fact we give them to the priests' (Soṭah 47b–48a).

In his comment on Heb. 7:5 P. E. Hughes rejects the explanation from contemporary practice, for the allusion to the priests among the Levites fits the author's context, as noted above, and he normally draws simply on the Old Testament; but the latter point is debatable, and the contextual solution does not do full justice to the awkwardness of verse 5 as a simple summary of the specifically mentioned 'commandment', or its resemblance to the equally awkward summaries of Josephus and Eleazar b. Azariah.

A second instance comes from the series of unexpected summaries of the Pentateuch in Heb. 9. In verse 13 'the blood of goats and bulls' from the Day of Atonement (Lev. 16:5f.) is linked with 'the ashes' of the Red Heifer (Num. 19:17–22), which in the Bible has 'no connexion whatever with atonement-day' (Moffatt, 122). A post-biblical connection, however, is rightly envisaged by Michel, 313, on the basis of Maimonides' account of the Day, quoted by Delitzsch, and first-century reports that the high priest slays the Heifer (Josephus, *Ant.* iv 79) and sprinkles its blood (Philo, *Spec. Leg.* 1:268); he had already referred to the link made between the Heifer and the Day in Yoma 1a

(Michel, 168). The connection can also be confirmed from the Mishnah, which records that the priest set apart for the Day of Atonement was sprinkled from the ashes of the Heifer (Parah 3.1, in the name of the first-century Hanina, Prefect of the Priests). This rite is celebrated in the poetry of the Day:

> They sanctified him and cleansed him from sin with the waters of separation,
> answering to the sin-cleansing with blood and the oil of anointing

(Yose, *ʾattah konanta ʿolam be -rob ḥesed*, 76; Mirsky, 183, compares jYoma 1.1, 48c). The sprinkling with the waters mingled from the ashes is here regarded as equivalent to Aaron's purification with blood and oil (Exod. 29:21, the order of which is followed; the parallel Lev. 8:30 mentions the oil first); the seven days' consecration of Aaron and his sons is treated as the pattern of the high priest's preparation for the Day. Seven days' preparation was also required before the burning of the Heifer (Parah 3.1). The procedure, like that of the Day of Atonement, was hotly disputed between Pharisees and Sadducces (Bowker, 57–62, with translations of the rabbinic texts). The association of the two rites in Heb. 9:13 thus probably reflects not unconcern over details of the cult (so Daly, 272f.), and not (only) the exigencies of argument (so N. H. Young, 205), but first-century understanding of the Day of Atonement.

Other passages, of which we cannot now speak particularly, might well reward study on these lines. Here there is only room to note, more generally, that the Pentateuchal interpretations just compared with Hebrews discourage a rigid antithesis between biblical and contemporary knowledge in the author. Josephus' treatments of Num. 18:21, one according to the letter, two others adapted to the practice which he knew from his own experience as a priest, show especially clearly that a Jewish writer could expound the Septuagint without any allusion to contemporary Jewish usage which he undoubtedly knew. Similarly, an interest in the vanished tabernacle, as displayed in the halakhic literature of the Day of Atonement, by no means necessarily implies neglect of the present. Hence it cannot be assumed so unquestioningly as by Moffatt, 114–16, or Schenke, 426 (on the basis of 9.1–5), that the writer to the Hebrews was poorly acquainted with the temple. As examination of 7.5 and 9.13 has suggested, his Septuagintal exposition is not incompatible with knowledge of sacerdotal practice.

III

The priestly ideology bound up with practice emerges, it may be suggested, in two broad aspects of the argument of Heb. 7–8. The first is the significance of 'Levi' (7:5, 9), introduced when the author's real interest is in 'the levitical *priesthood*' (7:11). The awkwardness of this potential inclusion of Levites in an argument about priests, already noted from 7:5 on tithe, can be appreciated further in the light of the Levites' request in A.D. 62 for greater recognition over against the priests; the concession of their demands was characteristically viewed by Josephus as a national transgression which could not be expected to go unpunished (*Ant.* xx 216–18, discussed by Meyer, col. 727). The writer to the Hebrews is carried over this awkwardness by his biblical view of 'the covenant of Levi' as the covenant of the *priests* (Mal. 2:1–10).

It is a familiar fact that in the Pentateuch as now preserved the Levites, 'given to Aaron and his sons' (Num. 8:19; cf. 3:9, 18:6), take second place to the priests, whose appointment and dues are mentioned first (Exod. 28–30, 40:12–16, and Lev. 8; Num. 3:1–4 [priests] before Num. 3:5–13 and Num. 8 [Levites]; Num. 18:1 and 6 [priests] enclosing Num. 18:2–5 [Levites]; Deut. 10:6 [Eleazar succeeds Aaron] before Deut. 10:8f. [separation of Levites]; Num. 18:8–20 and Deut. 18:3–5 [priestly dues] before Num. 18:21–4 and Deut. 18:6–8 [Levites' portion]). The notable descendants of Levi (Exod. 6:16–27) are Aaron and Moses (in that order, verses 20 and 26), Eleazar, and Phinehas—who received 'the covenant of an everlasting priesthood' (Num. 25:12f., quoted in Ecclus 45:24; 1 Macc. 2:54). This Aaronic view of Levi is encouraged by his blessing (Deut. 33:8–11), for it mentions the distinctively priestly prerogatives of Urim and Thummim, legal interpretation, incense-offering and whole-offering. The Pentateuchal presentation could be epitomized by Num. 17:3 (18) 'Thou shalt write *Aaron's* name upon the rod of *Levi*'.

That Aaron's adoption of Levi's tithe simply continues this Pentateuchal tendency was recognized by Wellhausen (165–7). Two further consequences of its continuation are manifest in later sources and relevant to Hebrews. First, Levi becomes above all the patriarch of the priests (Ecclus. 45:6, 17; Jub. 31:16f., 32:1–15; Test. Levi 2–5, 8–12, 14–18; Joseph and Asenath 28:15 [blessing by Levi]); the Exodus 6 genealogy influences both the Aramaic Testament of Levi (as shown by Becker, 96–9) and the late third century B.C.

Jewish chronographer Demetrius, who traces Levi's progeny down to 'Aaron and Moses' (Demetrius, quoted from Alexander Polyhistor by Eusebius, *Pr. Ev.* 9.21; fragment 2 in Freudenthal, 222). The climax of this development is the Day of Atonement poetry already quoted, in which the narrative of the high priest's duties is introduced by praise of Levi and his descendants, once again patterned after the genealogy of Exod. 6:16–27. In Hebrews 'Moses said nothing about priests' to the tribe of Judah (7:14); but he did (it is implied) to the tribe of Levi, repeatedly mentioned since 7:5. This is probably an implied allusion to Moses' blessing of Levi (Deut. 33:8–11), viewed with Ecclus. 45:17 (echo), 4Q Testimonia, and Targum Pseudo-Jonathan (see this section, below) as part of the credentials of the Aaronic priesthood.

A second consequence is the mention of priests in addition to or in place of Levites. Where the Bible speaks of Levites only, a later source may add the priests (Num. 1:53 with Josephus, *Ant.* iii 190; Ezra 8:15, 17 with 1 Esd. 8:42, 46). On the other hand, the nation may be divided into priests and people only, with no separate mention of Levites, although the high priest may be singled out additionally (Lev. 16:33, quoted above; Ecclus. 50:13 ('the sons of Aaron' and 'all the congregation of Israel'); Bar. 1:17 (high priest, priests and people); 1 Macc. 14:41, 47 ('the Jews and priests'); 1 Macc. 14:44 ('the people' and 'priests'); 'Aaron' and 'Israel' (1QS viii, and often in Qumran texts); Yoma 7.1 and Soṭah 7.7f. (separate benedictions for 'the priests' and 'Israel'). Lastly, the high priest alone may be distinguished (Num. 27:19, 22, from the congregation, when Moses lays hands on Joshua; Ecclus. 50:20, from the congregation, in blessing; 2 Macc. 15:12, from the *systema* [see section I, above]; Philo, *Spec. Leg.* 3.131, from the *ethnos*). In these same ways, in Hebrews, priests are added to Levites, or rather substituted for them (7:5); the priesthood alone is differentiated from the people (7:11); and the high priest alone is distinguished (7:27; cf. 2:17, 5:3, 9:7).

Hebrews therefore shares in biblical exegesis and constitutional language which shows the influence of developments of the Aaronic view of Levi found in the Pentateuch. The references to Levi rather than Aaron in chapter 7 are not a sign of polemical alignment with Test. Levi 18 (as suggested by Spicq, II, 124f.). Equally, Philo's association of the patriarch with the Levites (e.g. *Det.* 63–7) is not reflected in the epistle. Levi was probably simply introduced into the argument of priests without hesitation, because the writer had inherited the priestly view.

The larger argument within which Levi appears (6:20–8:13) has other presuppositions comparable with those of the theocracy. Christ being high priest (6:20), both the levitical ministry, and the law of Moses which presupposes it (7:11f.), are antiquated; he who has obtained a more excellent ministry is also the mediator of a better covenant (8:6). In this train of thought Moses' law and Aaron's priesthood are viewed as interdependent, and a high priest whose ministry supersedes that of Aaron is also considered able to mediate a covenant superseding that obtained by Moses.

The law, however, according to G. Hughes (15–19), has logical precedence over the priesthood in this argument; for tithe is 'according to the law' (7:5), 'Moses spoke' concerning those who are priests 'according to the law of a carnal commandment' (7:14, 16; cf. 7:28), and this primacy of law corresponds to the author's fundamental concern with God's 'address' to men (1:1f.).

This interpretation seizes a vital strand of the author's thought, his conviction that God 'has spoken', but seems not fully to reckon with his treatment of Christ's priesthood (6:20) as axiomatic, the supersession of both law and covenant being made to follow from it; Moffatt could take 7:12 as indicating that, in the author's whole outlook, 'the covenant or law is subordinated to the priesthood' (xl; cf. 96, 103). Further, God's address in time past is probably not to be identified solely with the law; it was also heard in the call of God to Aaron (5:4–6, 9:4), comparable for the author with the divine appointment of Christ (5:5f.; cf. 1:2), and giving rise to a single 'levitical institution' (Nairne, lxvii) wherein law and priesthood are co-ordinate. Thus it may be said either that 'the law *makes* men high priests' (7:28) or, from the other side, that the levitical priests '*have* a commandment', one of their privileges (7:5); again, the law should make perfect (7:19), yet this should come about through the priestly ministration (7:11, 10:1). Indeed, the law is subordinate in the sense that it does depend upon the levitical ministry (7:11f.); that 'Moses said nothing about priests' with regard to Judah (7:14) is mentioned not because of the primacy of the law, but in order to clarify the statement that a change of law follows from a change of priesthood (7:12), the point which becomes 'yet more abundantly evident' from Christ's eternal priesthood (7:15f.).

It is therefore legitimate to recognize, in the thought of Hebrews, the interdependence of priesthood and law, and the decisive importance of the high priest in the whole levitical institution. These convictions have obvious

Pentateuchal roots. Only after calling Aaron (Exod. 28:1) does God reveal the priestly laws directing 'Aaron' (Exod. 28:14, etc.) in the closing chapters of Exodus, in Leviticus, 'the law of the priests' in rabbinic as well as Septuagintal parlance, and in Numbers. In Josephus' paraphrase the choice of Aaron by divine revelation (*Ant.* iii 188) is the prelude to consecration of tabernacle and priests, and an account of the sacrifices, offerings and laws of purity. By a partly comparable conception, Levi is designated priest in Jacob's vision (Test. Levi 9:3); Isaac then teaches him 'the law of the priesthood' on sacrifices and offerings (Test. Levi 9:7) or 'the judgment of the priesthood' concerning purity laws (Aramaic and Greek fragments in Charles (2), 247 [the Greek is translated from a Semitic language, the Aramaic itself possibly descends from a Hebrew original, according to Becker, 72f.]; context favours the interpretation of 'judgment' [*din, krisis*] as 'law' rather than [as suggested by Charles (2), lv, with reference to Deut. 18:3 *mišpāṭ*] 'priestly due'). In this passage, judged by Becker to derive ultimately from a pre-Christian oral source later than Jubilees (Becker, 91–3, 103f.), the laws already exist (Test. Levi 9:6), and are probably thought to be those communicated to Isaac in Jub. 21; but they find their application when God calls his priest, and Jacob's dream, confirming the two visions granted to Levi himself, underlines the independent importance of God's call. Its significance in the case of Aaron, already clear in the Pentateuch, is further brought out by Josephus; in Amram's dream it is revealed that Aaron and his descendants will hold God's priesthood for ever, and the stories of Korah, Dathan and Abiram and the blossoming rod show that Aaron was 'thrice elected by God' (*Ant.* ii 216, iv 66). God's choice of Aaron is similarly emphasized in 1 Clem. 43. In the Pentateuch and Josephus the priestly laws, envisaged as given for the first time, appear as a consequence of Aaron's call

These accounts of the institution of the priestly line confirm that Aaron's call is likely to carry significant weight in Hebrews. They also illuminate the interdependence of law and priesthood, and the viewpoint from which the law could seem subordinate. Such a view of the law is further encouraged by its association with the tabernacle (Exod. 25:22; Num. 7:89). Josephus emphasizes this, abridging Exod. 19–32 so as to draw the gift of the law into close connection with the promise of God's *parousia* in the tabernacle (*Ant.* iii 202). Moses is given two summary statements, neither of which is fully paralleled in the Bible. On return from the mount when the decalogue is given, he says that God has declared to the Hebrews a blessed manner of life and the order (*kosmos*) of a polity, and has announced his imminent arrival in the camp (iii 84; warnings against the overthrow of this 'order', *Ant.* iv 193, 292, 312). Secondly, on return from the forty days in the cloud, the episode of the Golden Calf being omitted, Moses says to the people that God has shown him their polity, and has desired that a tabernacle should be made for him, indicating its measurements and fashion; Moses then displays the tables of the commandments (*Ant.* iii 99–101). After the consecration of the tabernacle and its ministers, Moses writes out the book containing the polity and the laws from instruction received during visits to the tabernacle, as Exod. 25:22 suggests (*Ant.* iii 212, 232); finally, as noted in Deut. 31:9, he hands over the book to the priests (*Ant.* iv 304). Thus Josephus associates the 'polity', one of his two great themes (*Ant.* i 5), with the divine presence in the tabernacle; for the revelation of the political *kosmos* begun on Sinai is continued 'from above the mercy seat' (Exod. 25:22). Hence, whereas Aaron, Nadab and Abihu only 'see God' on the mount by an exceptional grace (Exod. 24:1f., 9–11), in the tabernacle Moses receives the continuation of the Sinaitic oracles by an access which is their normal priestly privilege. Aaron's successors continue to approach the mercy seat whence the laws were given (Lev. 16:2), and have custody of the book containing them. Josephus' association of law and tabernacle is therefore also, in this respect, an association of law and priesthood, with the implication that the priest is the law's uniquely empowered interpreter (cf. *B.J.* iii.352).

Levi's blessing makes this implication explicit, for he is given Urim and Thummim and the commission to teach the law (Deut. 33:8, 10). The priest with Urim and Thummim is 'enlightening' (Neh. 7:65, LXX; Bammel, col. 356); and this interpretation of Urim is linked with the teaching office of verse 10 in the quotation of Levi's blessing in 4Q175 (Testimonia), line 17 (*w^{e}yāʾîrû* 'and they shall enlighten' for MT *yôrû* 'they shall teach'). Qumran again reproduces a more widespread exegesis, for the Septuagint has *dēloi* for Urim (verse 8), echoed by *dēlōsousin* (verse 10). The long tradition on the Urim is described by Bammel, cols. 351–5; the corresponding tradition of the teaching priest is equally fundamental to the theocracy. Its prominent Pentateuchal and prophetic basis (e.g. Lev. 10:10f.; Deut. 17:8–12, 21:5, 33:8–11; Jer. 18:18; Ezek. 44:23f.; Mal. 2:6f.) supports the descriptions of the high priest as the 'messenger of the commandments of God' (cf. Mal. 2:7), in the Hecataeus of Diodorus Siculus (section I, above), and of the priests as charged with the administration of public affairs, in the Hecatacus of Josephus (*Ap.* i.188, quoted in section II, above). Josephus himself regards it as the glory of the Jewish polity that the priests exercise an 'exact supervision of the law' as judges and exactors of penalties; the high priest in particular, with his fellow-priests, 'will sacrifice to God, guard the laws, adjudicate in matters of dispute, punish those convicted of crime' (*Ap.* ii.187, 194).

'The people received the law', according to Heb. 7:11f. 'under' the levitical priesthood; a change of priesthood means a change of law. The theocracy of the Pentateuch, and its interpretation by Josephus and others, have provided three examples of ways in which the law could seem to rest upon the priesthood: in the priority of Aaron's call over 'the law of the priests', the association of the revealed polity with the mercy seat approached only by Aaron's successors, and the descriptions of the priests as guardians of the law. A later example, in the style of folk-lore rather than political philosophy, sets the giving of the law within the annals of the priesthood. The following extract from Yose's alphabetical *ʾattah konanta ʿolam be-rob ḥesed*, lines 66–73 (Mirsky, 181f.) is typical of a number of Day of Atonement poems (Horbury, 171–3; = 353–5, below). Its two four-line stanzas represent the letters *Pe* and *Tsade* respectively. Each begins with a word from the priestly vocabulary: *peraḥ*, 'sprig' (cf. 'sprigs of the priesthood' Yoma 1.6 and often), and *ṣiṣ*, the 'plate' (*petalon*) of the mitre (Exod. 28:36; etc.; Bammel, cols. 354–6); the two words are used in the Bible for the 'buds' and 'blossoms' of Aaron's rod (Num. 17:23 [8]). The poet, having spoken of Jacob, continues:

A sprig from his tribes to serve thee thou didst tithe
for his tithing to thee his wealth at the pillar (Gen. 28:22):
Thou didst make the fruit of the righteous flourish from the stem of Levi,
Amram and his descendants as a vine and its tendrils.
Thou didst visit thy flock by the hand of a faithful man (Num. 12:7)
to deliver her from Zoan and to bring her over the waters of the 'handful' (Isa. 40:12).
Thou didst crown him with sanctification of day and covering of cloud,
until he should lead captivity captive and take her of the household for spoil (Ps. 68:19, 13)
With the plate of the priestly crown thou didst endue thy holy one (Ps. 106:16),
and he shall leave it as an inheritance to his sons after him,

Treasured, preserved for everlasting generations;
and contemners of their glory shall be swallowed up and stricken.
O Rock, thou didst adorn them with a multitude of gifts,
and from the king's table didst ordain their food.
Thou didst command them to abide at the gate of thy tabernacle
to consecrate them during seven days.

Here Levi is himself Jacob's tithe, as in Jub. 32:3 (parallels in Charles, *ad loc.*); his stem flourishes like the vine of the chief butler's dream (Gen. 40:9f.). Its tendrils represent Amram's children, as in Ber. R. 88.5 (cited by Mirsky, *ad loc.*); in an alternative tradition, attributed to Bar Cocheba's uncle Eleazar of Modin, they are the temple, the king and the high priest, the buds and blossoms are the 'sprigs of the priesthood', and the grapes are the libations (Ḥullin 92a). The giving of the law appears as its acquisition by Moses, son of Amram, of the tribe of Levi; it follows from the fruitfulness of Levi's stem, the story of which goes on, as in Ecclus. 45:18–22, to the punishment of Korah (the later poem has Uzziah also) and the gifts of heave-offering and sacrificial portions. Aaron's consecration is mentioned in conclusion as the pattern of the high priest's preparation for the Day of Atonement. The narrative here and in comparable poems deepens the emphasis of the genealogy of Exod. 6:16–27, which provides their outline; the law is embraced within the levitical history issuing in the service of tabernacle and temple.

This later synagogal development of Exod. 6 and Ecclus. 45 confirms that the passages wherein Josephus and others make the law seem to rest upon the priesthood, in continuation of the Pentateuchal tendency, represent a widespread manner of thinking. The interdependence of law and priesthood in Heb. 7–8, the treatment of law as subordinate to priesthood, and the decisive importance there attributed to the high priest can justifiably be set within this mode of ancient Jewish thought, and viewed as further signs of the influence of the Pentateuchal theocracy.

IV

A similar conclusion as to influence can be drawn from the markedly ethical passages on the high priest in Heb. 2:17–3:1, and 4:14–5:10. These passages are interwoven with traditions concerning Christ; only 5:1–4 expressly apply to the Aaronic high priest. There is, nevertheless, a continuous emphasis on priestly compassion, and the entire sequence deserves comparison with the ethical presentations of the high priest inspired by Jewish theocratic views.

R. A. Stewart's inquiry into the idea of a sinless high priest in ancient Judaism also showed affinity between Hebrews and Jewish sources on the virtues to be expected from the priesthood. This affinity seems still not fully recognized in subsequent studies of the priesthood in Hebrews; in his comments on these passages Attridge notes some points of contact, but Vanhoye elaborates the contrast between Hebrews and Jewish literature on this subject drawn, with a reference to Dean Farrar's similar opinion, by Spicq on Heb. 2:17. In what follows some attempt is made to continue Stewart's inquiry, with a view less to the special question of sinlessness than to the more general ethical presentation of the high priest in Hebrews.

In the Pentateuch, a formidable combination of fierce zeal and loving-kindness characterizes both Levi and Phinehas (cf. Gen. 49:5–7 'their anger' [note also the approval of zealous slaughter by the sons of Levi, Exod. 32:26–9] with Deut. 33:8 'thy pious one'; Num. 25:11f., zeal rewarded by the covenant of peace). Aaron, more infirm of purpose, is distinguished, rather, by his staying of the plague, which can be understood as a deed of mercy (Num. 17:11–15 [16:46–50]), and he and his sons give the blessing of peace (Num. 6:26).

Ancient Jewish interpretation by no means neglects the zeal of Levi (Judith 9:4; Jub. 30:18; Test. Levi 5:3) or of Phinehas (Ecclus. 45:23, etc.; further texts and discussion in Hengel, 154–81 [Phinehas], 182–4, 192f. [Levi]). Nevertheless, the 'peace' of the Aaronic blessing involves not only Phinehas 'the peaceful man and evident priest of God' (Philo, *Mut.* 108) but also the sons of Levi (Mal. 2:5) and the disciples of Aaron, who love and pursue peace (Hillel, according to Aboth 1.12). This second and perhaps less-studied line of interpretation is especially relevant to Hebrews.

Ethicizing interpretation of this kind is common to Semitic and Greek sources, as is suggested by the closely similar Qumran and Septuagintal versions of Levi's blessing, and by the conjunction of Philo and the Mishnah in the foregoing paragraph. Comparably, the Wisdom of Solomon and Hebrew synagogal poetry alike replace the patriarchal names, in hagiographical fashion, with ethical nicknames like 'the peaceful man'. Aaron, the unnamed 'blameless man' of Wisdom (18:21), is in a *piyyuṭ* likewise simply 'thy holy one' (Yose, cited above, following Ps. 106:16; Ecclus. 45:6).

The epithet 'merciful' (Heb. 2:17), whence the theme of compassion is later developed (Heb. 4:14–5:10), recalls the biblical association of kindness and peace with the priesthood, noted above with regard to the patriarchs of the tribe. The priests inherit the covenant of life and peace from Levi, God's 'pious' or 'kind' one (*hasîd*, LXX *hosios*, Deut. 33:8), who was 'governing in peace' (Mal. 2:6, LXX). Hence, although it was indeed held, in Judith and other sources noted above, that Simeon and Levi took a wholly-justified vengeance on Shechem with the weapons of violence (Gen. 49:5) which guard the heroine in Joseph and Asenath, in the latter work it is Levi who twice enforces the duty of mercy to the enemy (23:8–10, 29:3–5; cf. 28:15), and whose hand Asenath grasps in affection and veneration (23:8). In this acknowledgement of the feminine appreciation of priestly compassion Joseph and Asenath resembles the midrashic portrait of Aaron; whereas only men mourned for Moses, Aaron was lamented by the women as well (Targum Pseudo-Jonathan on Num. 20:29; Tanḥuma on Numbers, addition to Parashath *Ḥuqqath*, paragraph 2, in Buber, *Numbers*, 132).

The topic of priestly mercy is much developed. 'Merciful and faithful' (Heb. 2:17) is close to the description of Aaron, in a targumic version of Levi's blessing, as *ḥasîd*—'pious' or 'merciful'—'entire' and 'faithful'; these qualities emerged when he was tempted (cf. Heb. 4:15) at Massah and Meribah (Targum Pseudo-Jonathan on Deut. 33:8). In the midrash, the verse 'mercy and truth are met together: righteousness and peace have kissed each other' (Ps. 85:11) interprets the meeting and kiss of Aaron and Moses (Exod. 4:27); Moses is righteousness, Aaron is peace (Mal. 2:6), and Aaron is mercy (*ḥesed*)—because of Deut. 33:8, *ḥasîd*—Moses is truth (Tanḥuma on Exodus 25, on 4:27; Buber, ii, Exodus, 15f.). The Aaronic attributes of mercy and peace gathered round the high priest in the halo of the Day of Atonement; in an alphabetical version of the poem for the Day, 'How glorious was the high priest', based on Ecclus. 50:5–21, he came forth in 'piety' or 'kindness' (*ḥasîdût*), 'for it was added to him', with 'peace' upon his lips and 'forgiveness' in his countenance (Geniza text in Edelmann, 16 [Hebrew] and 40; on this category of poems Roth (1), 172f.).

In Hebrews the compassion of the high priest who is 'able to feel with us in our weaknesses' and 'able to bear reasonably with the ignorant' (Heb. 4:15,

5:2), is expressed in words from the Hellenistic ethical vocabulary, but should not be dissociated (as by Käsemann, 151f.) from the Hebraic style of such biblically-moulded descriptions as those just mentioned. Within Hebrews the passage is an expansion of the earlier epithet 'merciful', and in Jewish sources unaffected by the Hellenistic idiom the thought of priestly compassion is developed in a comparable way. Thus, in a striking anticipation of Hebrews noted by Stewart, 128, Levi grieves over the race of men (Test. Levi 2:4); and in the saying ascribed to Hillel already quoted, the disciple of Aaron is 'loving the (fellow-)creatures, and drawing them near to the law' (Aboth 1.12). Moreover, Levi, Aaron and the high priests were described with Greek ethical terms in other Jewish sources wherein, as in Hebrews, the biblical influence is also evident.

Four such Hellenized descriptions of high priests may be mentioned, because, much though they differ from one another, they all come close to the passage on compassion in Heb. 4–5. First, Eleazar the high priest is said to have sent the Septuagint translators to Alexandria with an Aristotelian 'magnanimity' which Josephus delights to imitate in putting forth his own biblical paraphrase (*Ant.* i 12); and, according to an earlier writer, the high priest's emissaries were worthy of his own virtue, cultivating the mean in their unostentatious readiness to listen (Aristeas, 122). This passage is closer in thought to Heb. 5:2 than is the verbally closer commendation by Philo of Aaron's *metriopatheia*, in a philosophical version of the midrashic contrast between Aaron and Moses, as nothing more than a second best to the *apatheia* of the stricter Moses (Leg. *All.* 3.132–5).

Secondly, two accounts of sacerdotal supplication may be compared with Heb. 2:18, 4:15 and 5:7f. In a well-known narrative Josephus relates how Jaddua the high priest faithfully kept his oath to Darius. When Alexander consequently marched in anger 'against the high priest of the Jews', Jaddua, 'in *agōnia* and fear', commanded the people to pray, and himself made petition with a sacrifice (*Ant.* xi 318f., 326). Similarly, in 2 Maccabees, the godly high priest Onias appears in Judas Maccabaeus' dream as *kalos kai agathos*, reverend yet meek in manner (2 Macc. 15:12). During his life, when he led the supplications against Heliodorus' presumption, there was *agōnia* throughout the city; and the corresponding *agōnia* of his own soul (compare that of Jaddua) was so plainly manifest in his shuddering that it was pitiable to see the high priest praying in such distress (2 Macc. 3:14, 16f., 20f.). His meekness recalls 5:2 (for *metriopathein* 'is allied to *praotēs*' [Moffatt, 62]), his sharing of the general *agōnia* the 'sympathy' of 4:14, and its setting of earnest supplication, like Jaddua's sacrifice, the 'strong crying' of 5:7.

Lastly, a near-burlesque companion-piece on priestly meekness is the scene in Joseph and Asenath (33:7–16), worthy of a silent film, in which Simeon draws his sword against Pharaoh's wicked son. Levi, at once perceiving his brother's hostile intent by prophetic intuition, promptly stamps on his right foot and signs to him to restrain his anger. Levi then addresses the blackguardly prince 'with a meek heart and a cheerful countenance'; pointing out that he and his brother are God-fearing men, but that, if the prince persists in his villainy, they will indeed fight. Both brothers then draw their swords, and remind Pharaoh's son of what happened at Shechem. The prince falls down, shaking with fear, but Levi raises him up with a gracious 'Fear not, but beware', and the two go out leaving the villain trembling. The characteristic combination of meekness and strength appears also in the story of Jaddua, before whom Alexander in the end prostrates himself (Josephus, *Ant.* xi 331–3); in the present context the story of Levi is of special interest as a laboured example of *metriopathein* (Heb. 5:2).

These ethical descriptions of Eleazar, Jaddua, Onias and Levi correspond to the view that Aaron was himself chosen priest for his virtue (by God, Josephus, *Ant.* iii 188; by Moses, *Ap.* ii.186f., and Philo, *Mos.* ii.142); the priests themselves can be called 'blameless' (*Ant.* iii 279), the nickname for Aaron in Wisd. 18:21 (see above).

Nevertheless, an aspect of the high priest's sympathy in Hebrews is his 'infirmity', which necessitates the sacrifice for his own sins (Lev. 16:6; Heb. 5:2f., 7:27f., 9:7, 13:11); it is linked with his manhood (2:17f.; 5:1). Similarly, in contemporary Jewish authors, 'the priest is primarily a man'—and so Moses legislates for his marriage (Philo, *Spec. Leg.* i. 101); and the death of Nadab and Abihu 'was a disaster for Aaron considered as a man and a father', although he bore it valiantly and, being already invested with the holy robe, refrained from mourning (Josephus, *Ant.* iii 208–11).

The repeated mention in Hebrews of Aaron's sacrifice for himself recalls its prominence in the narrative of the first sacrifices (Lev. 9; see vv. 7–14); his infirmity is further evident when accidental impurity debars him from eating the sin-offering (Lev. 10:19). This biblical concern is continued, as Stewart notes, in the ethical and ritual law of the priesthood in the Aramaic Testament of Levi (quoted above), and in midrashic comments on the potential sinfulness of the high priest (Stewart, 128, 130f.). In provisions for the Day of Atonement there is a corresponding emphasis on the high priest's sacrifice for himself (Lev. 16:6), the words of his confessions of sin for himself and his house and for the sons of Aaron (Mishnah, Yoma 3.8, 4.2), and the precautions lest he fall asleep and contract impurity during the night before the Day (Mishnah, Yoma 1:4–6); in the last years of Herod the Great the high priest Matthias son of Theophilus had done so (Josephus, *Ant.* xvii 166).

Another aspect of 'infirmity' is the high priest's need of instruction in his duties; Aaron follows orders from Moses when he offers the first sacrifices, and they enter the tabernacle of the congregation together (Lev. 9:2, 5–8, 10, 21, 23). Aaron learned like an apt pupil (Philo, *Mos.* ii. 133); and, as Stewart notes, it was held, in fourth-century rabbinic homily, that the Shekhinah did not dwell with Moses when he performed this ministry, but only with Aaron after his consecration (Lev. R. 11.6, discussed by Stewart, 130). Nevertheless, the charge of ignorance was often deployed against Aaron's successors, sometimes not without justification (as by Josephus in the case of Phanni, the stone-mason made high priest by the Zealots [*B.J.* iv.156, endorsed by Roth (2), 316]), sometimes as an element in ritual controversy. According to the Mishnah, the elders of the priesthood used to adjure the high priest not to change the order of service for the Day of Atonement that had been committed to him; and then 'he turned aside and wept, and they turned aside and wept' (Yoma 1.5)—'he, because he was thought a simpleton, and they ... because they were put to this necessity' (Yose, *ʾattah konanta ʿolam be-rob ḥesed*, line 82 [with Palestinian Talmud, Yoma 1.5, 39a, quoted by Mirsky, 184]). Here, where the high priest is thought to share the corporate shame of the sons of Aaron, his 'often infirmities' verge, as in Hebrews but in a distinctive fashion, upon the theme of priestly sympathy.

The theme of sympathy is linked in Hebrews not only with the high priest's infirmity, but also with his representative character. '*We* have a high priest' who is 'the apostle and high priest of *our* confession' and who, it can even be said, 'became *us*' (Heb. 8:1, 3:1, 7:25); the Aaronic priest, correspondingly, is 'appointed for men' (Heb. 5:1). The obvious link between priestly sympathy and representation also appears in Jewish sources, as in 2 Maccabees 3, discussed above, and the emphasis on the high priest's representativeness (Lev. 16:33, see above) is as strong as it is in Hebrews. Aaron was given 'the priesthood of the people' (Ecclus. 45:7), for 'we need one to discharge the priestly office and to minister for the sacrifices and for the prayers on our behalf' (Josephus, *Ant.* iii. 189); the high priest prays, as common kinsman of all, on behalf of the whole body of Jewry, all mankind, and the entire universe (2 Macc. 15:12; Philo, *Spec. Leg.* i. 97, iii. 131, quoted above). More restrictively, the high priest is called an 'apostle' of the elders and priests—*sheluḥenu*, 'our emissary'—in Yoma 1.5, just quoted, where the emphasis on limitation probably reflects Pharisaic polemic; but the thought broadens again into the honorific biblical representation when synagogal poetry depicts his emergence from the holiest as 'the faithful messenger', 'sending to those that sent him righteousness and healing' (Yose, *'asapper gedoloth*, line 59, and *'azkhir geburoth*, lines 268f., in Mirsky, 206, 171).

The compassion of the high priest, and his solidarity with mankind, which come to expression with particular force in Hebrews, are therefore Pentateuchal themes which received comparable development in other post-biblical sources. In these, as in the traditions concerning Christ taken up in Hebrews, there is a potentially moving contrast between divine appointment and human frailty. Even when the writer to the Hebrews probably draws on sources related to the Gospels, he remains within the bounds of what is appropriate to his priestly expressions. If the manhood of God's Son melts the heart (2:17f.), so in its degree does the manhood of God's high priest in his bereavement (Josephus, *Ant.* iii 208–11); the endurance of temptation (Heb. 2:18, 4:15) and the sorrowful supplication (Heb. 5:7) both well befit a high priest (Deut. 33:8; Pseudo-Jonathan; 2 Macc. 3:16f., 21).

The presentation of the high priest in Hebrews cannot therefore readily be contrasted with Old Testament and Jewish views. Such a contrast emerges in the late twentieth-century commentary tradition even in the context of much sensitivity to ancient Jewish literature (Braun, 70, on Heb. 2:17; Weiss, 304, on 5:2; Gordon, 67, on 2:17). Yet sacerdotal 'mercy' cannot be regarded as new and distinctive (with Michel, 165, on Heb. 2:17, and Vanhoye (1), 461–3); still less is the solidarity of the high priest with men opposed to the viewpoint of the Old Testament and 'the traditional ideas of the most religious Jews' (as maintained by Vanhoye (1), 457f, and in an otherwise scrupulous study of Heb. 5:1–4 by Vanhoye (2), 446f., 455f.)., On the contrary, the leading characteristics of the priesthood, according to Heb. 2:17–3:1 and 4:14–5:10—mercy, faithfulness, compassion, sympathy, forbearance, earnestness in prayer, humanity, infirmity, representativeness—have all been amply attested in Jewish sources, both Hebrew and Greek, especially in the line of interpretation which developed the Aaronic blessing of peace. As was especially obvious from Malachi 2:6 LXX, Aristeas, 2 Maccabees, Philo and Josephus, the principal virtues in this list could be woven into a hagiographical commendation of the high priest as a fitting governor of the theocracy, and Yose's poems confirm that both the self-sacrificing virtue of Aaron and the royalty of the priesthood continued to be remembered in synagogue prayer (Horbury, 173f.; = 356, below). The special contribution of Hebrews should probably be sought not in new ideas about the priesthood, but in the interconnections established by a profound and sensitive homilist between well-known existing ideas and Christian traditions concerning Christ.

V

Käsemann wrote that 'the religio-historical derivation of the idea of the high priest in Hebrews is the single most difficult problem of the epistle. Any exegesis which sees itself forced at this point to have recourse to purely Old Testament and Jewish roots, whereas elsewhere it cannot deny Hellenistic influence on Hebrews, will be divided and unclear' (Käsemann, 116).

The difficulty indicated by Käsemann arises partly from the presentation of the idea in the epistle itself, and it cannot be wholly resolved, even though his antithesis between Hebraic and Hellenic influence is untenable in practice, simply by a reference to the change, since he wrote, in the general understanding of the Hellenization of Judaism. His solution by a derivation, through Christian liturgy, from gnostically-remoulded Jewish messianism, has the merits of holding together Philo and the rabbis, and of linking the central priestly passages of Hebrews with the rest of the Epistle. Its own difficulty lies perhaps especially in the fact that it is in effect, as noted above. one more appeal to an otherwise unknown, distinctive type of Judaism.

The question thus singled out by Käsemann has evoked, more than any other feature of the epistle, the various derivations mentioned in section I—from Christianity, from some unknown form of Judaism, or from Judaism of a sectarian or otherwise unusual description. The more pedestrian approach adopted here is only an approach, for such important aspects of priesthood in Hebrews as the nature of Christ's heavenly ministry remain undiscussed. Nevertheless, it can invoke the pedestrian Muse without apology, for it is an attempt to see whether walking in well-worn old paths of Jewish literature, and in the common traditions of ancient Jewry through which they pass, may not be a reliable means of progress towards the distinctive ideas of Hebrews. The unity of basis which Käsemann desiderated can perhaps be claimed, thus far, but it is an Old Testament and Jewish basis which, like the epistle itself, has assimilated the idiom of Greek.

It has appeared, from three limited inquiries, that some peculiarities of Hebrews in its treatment of Jewish practice (section II), and the presuppositions of some central and distinctive arguments of the epistle—on the priesthood and the law in Heb. 7–8 (section III) and the ethical attributes of the high priest in Heb. 2–5 (section IV)—are all found together in the thought and practice shaped by the Pentateuchal theocracy. Within this context of thought Hebrew and Greek Jewish sources have been seen to converge, both in particularities such as a common debt to Exodus 6 or a common interpretation of Deut. 33:10, and in such larger topics touched by Hebrews as the practice concerning tithe, the co-ordination of law and priesthood, and the ethical presentation of the priest as a man of peace. If Hebrews can justifiably be read within this context, as the inquiries suggest, is any light shed on the historical setting of the epistle?

Michel's comment on the close links between Hebrews on priesthood and contemporary Jewish tradition and politics, may now perhaps be allowed to modify his own earlier historical conclusions. Hebrews on priesthood is not wholly detached (as maintained by Michel, 55f.) from the real historical debates of the period of the First Revolt. It is true that the writer does not enter into these debates, but he shares some of the disputed views. Tithe belongs to the priest (7:5), a much-discussed interpretation supporting practice which was notoriously abused, according to Josephus, by the high-priestly families under Felix and Albinus (*Ant.* xx 181, 206f.); the Red

Heifer and the Day of Atonement are considered together with reference to purification (9:5), and they are both said to have been disputed in this respect between Sadducces and Pharisees; Levi is the priests' patriarch, and the Levites' claims go unnoticed (an attitude which helps to explain the Levites' complaints in 62); and the presuppositions of 7–8 and the earlier passages on the high priest reflect his political as well as ecclesiastical significance (against Michel, 215), and belong to the sacerdotal polity restored for a time during the First Revolt.

Clear pointers towards authorship and geographical location can perhaps hardly be expected, when the ideas concerned were so widely influential. It is worth noting, however, on the basis of the foregoing paragraph, that the thought of the epistle concerning priests would well accord with the Palestinian origin shortly before the First Revolt proposed by Nairne and by Moule (59f., 97f., 160f.). Sections II and III above also suggest one objection to the ancient attribution to Barnabas (the merits of which are shown by Robinson, 217–19), for a Levite would perhaps hardly have treated Levi and the tithe in so priestly a fashion as the writer to the Hebrews has appeared to do. His closeness to Josephus rather than to Philo on these same points might constitute a marginal consideration in favour of Palestinian rather than Alexandrian authorship, if Philo could be taken as representative; but the Alexandrian and Egyptian Jewish communities had many contacts with Judaea, and the variety of outlook manifest in Judaea was probably also found in Jewish Egypt. Lastly, within the New Testament Hebrews attests a priestly outlook which can be considered together with the knowledge of the priesthood and priestly families reflected in varying ways in Matthew, Luke-Acts, and John (Horbury, 'Caiaphas', 44–5).

The line followed here thus leads to reassessment of some characteristics of Hebrews which have been too quickly judged inconsistent with Judaea before the First Revolt, although of itself it does not rule out other places and times of origin. Its indications are clearer, however, with regard to the thought-world of the Epistle. These observations may serve at least to float the suggestion that the antecedents of the priestly thought characteristic of Hebrews should be sought neither in Christianity, nor in sectarian or esoteric Judaism, but in the pervasive influence of the Pentateuchal theocracy.

Literature

P. S. Alexander, 'The Historical Setting of the Hebrew Book of Enoch', *JJS* xxviii (1977), 156–80

G. Alon, *Jews, Judaism and the Classical World* (ET, Jerusalem, 1977)

H. Anderson, 'The Jewish Antecedents of the Christology in Hebrews', in J. H. Charlesworth (ed.), *The Messiah* (Minneapolis, 1992), 512–35

H. W. Attridge, *Hebrews* (Hermeneia: Philadelphia, 1989)

E. Bammel, *ΑΡΧΙΕΡΕΥΣΠΡΟΦΗΤΕΥΩΝ, TLZ* lxxix (1954), cols. 352–6, reprinted in E. Bammel, *Judaica et Paulina: Kleine Schriften II, mit einem Nachwort von Peter Pilhofer* (WUNT xci; Tübingen, 1997), 133–9

B. Bar-Kochva, *Pseudo-Hecataeus On the Jews: Legitimizing the Jewish Diaspora* (Hellenistic Culture and Society xxi; Berkeley, Los Angeles and London, 1996)

G. Baumbach, ' "Volk Gottes" im Frühjudentum', *Kairos* N.F. xxi (1979), 30–47

J. Becker, *Untersuchungen zur Entstehungsgeschichte der Testamente der zwölf Patriarchen* (Leiden, 1970)

J. H. R. Biesenthal, *Das Trostschreiben des Apostels Paulus an die Hebräer, kritisch wiederhergestellt* (Leipzig, 1878)

J. Bowker, *Jesus and the Pharisees* (Cambridge, 1973)

H. Braun, *An die Hebräer* (Tübingen, 1984)

S. Buber (ed.), *Midrasch Tanchuma* (3 vols in 1; Wilna, 1885)

G. W Buchanan, *To the Hebrews* (Garden City, NY, 1972)

Ad. Büchler, *Die Priester und der Cultus im letzten Jahrzehnt des Jerusalemischen Tempels* (Vienna, 1895)

R. H. Charles (1), *The Book of Jubilees* (London, 1902)

——— (2), *The Greek Versions of the Testaments of the Twelve Patriarchs* (Oxford, 1908)

R. J. Daly, *Christian Sacrifice* (Washington, 1978)

G. R. Driver, *The Judaean Scrolls* (Oxford, 1965)

R. Edelmann, *Zur Frühgeschichte des Mahzor* (Stuttgart, 1934)

J. Freudenthal, *Hellenistische Studien* (Breslau, 1875)

J. Gereboff, *Rabbi Tarfon* (Missoula, 1975)

E. R. Goodenough, *By Light, Light* (New Haven, 1935)

R. P. Gordon, *Hebrews* (Sheffield, 2000)

K.-E. Grözinger, *Ich bin der Herr, dein Gott! Eine rabbinische Homilie zum Ersten Gebot (PesR 20)* (Bern and Frankfurt am Main, 1976)

J. H. A. Hart, 'Philo and the Catholic Judaism of the First Century', *JTS* xi (1909), 25–42

M. Hengel, *Die Zeloten* (Leiden, 1961)

C. J. A. Hickling, 'John and Hebrews: The Background of Hebrews 2:10–18', *NTS* xxix (1983), 112–16

L. A. Hoffmann, *The Canonization of the Synagogue Service* (Notre Dame, 1979)

O. Hofius, *Der Vorhang vor dem Thron Gottes* (Tübingen, 1972)

W. Horbury, 'Suffering and Messianism in Yose ben Yose', in W. Horbury and B. McNeil (eds.), *Suffering and Martyrdom in the New Testament* (Cambridge, 1981), 143–82

———, 'The "Caiaphas" Ossuaries and Joseph Caiaphas', *PEQ* cxxvi (1994), 32–48

G. Hughes, *Hebrews and Hermeneutics* (Cambridge, 1979)

P. E. Hughes, *A Commentary on the Epistle to the Hebrews* (Grand Rapids, 1977)

T. Ilan, 'The Ossuary and Sarcophagus Inscriptions', in G. Avni and Z. Greenhut (eds.), *The Akeldama Tombs* (IAA Reports, No. 1; Jerusalem, 1996)

A. Jaubert, 'Thèmes lévitiques dans la Prima Clementis', *Vigiliae Christianae* xviii (1964), 193–203

J. Jeremias, *Jerusalem in the Time of Jesus* (ET, London, 1969)

E. Käsemann, *Das wandernde Gottesvolk* (*FRLANT*, N.F. xxxvii, Göttingen, 1939)

H. Kosmala, *Hebräer—Essener—Christen* (Leiden, 1959)

A. T. Kraabel, 'Social Systems of Six Diaspora Synagogues', in J. Gutmann (ed.), *Ancient Synagogues* (Chico, 1981), 79–91

J. C. H. Lebram, 'Der Idealstaat der Juden', in O. Betz, K. Haacker and M. Hengel (eds.), *Josephus-Studien* (Göttingen, 1974), 233–53

J. Leonhardt, *Jewish Worship in Philo of Alexandria (TSAJ* LXXXIV, Tübingen, 2001)

R. Meyer, 'Levitische Emanzipationsbestrebungen in nachexilischer Zeit', *OLZ* xl (1938), cols 721–8

O. Michel, *Der Brief an die Hebräer* (6th edn., Göttingen, 1966)

J. T. Milik, 'Le iscrizioni degli ossuari', in B. Bagatti and J. T. Milik, *Gli scavi del 'Dominus Flevit', i, La necropoli del periodo romano* (Jerusalem, 1958, reprinted 1981), 70–109

A. Mirsky, *Yosse ben Yosse: Poems* ([Hebrew]; Jerusalem, 1977)

J. Moffatt, *A Critical and Exegetical Commentary on the Epistle to the Hebrews* (Edinburgh, 1924)

C. F. D. Moule, *The Birth of the New Testament* (3rd edn., London, 1981)

R. Murray, 'Jews, Hebrews and Christians: Some Needed Distinctions', *NT* xxiv (1982), 194–208

A. Nairne, *The Epistle to the Hebrews* (Cambridge, 1921)

J. Neusner (1), *A History of the Mishnaic Law of Holy Things, Part Six* (Leiden, 1980)

——— (2), *A History of the Mishnaic Law of Women* (5 vols.; Leiden, 1980)

M. Philonenko, *Joseph et Aséneth* (Leiden, 1968)

A. C. Purdy, 'The Purpose of the Epistle to the Hebrews in the Light of Recent Studies in Judaism', in H. G. Wood (ed.), *Amicitiae Corolla: A volume of Essays presented to James Rendel Harris* (London, 1933), 253–64

L. Y. Rahmani, *A Catalogue of Jewish Ossuaries in the Collections of the State of Israel* (Jerusalem, 1994)

J. A. T. Robinson, *Redating the New Testament* (London, 1976)

C. Roth (1), 'Ecclesiasticus in the Synagogue Service', *JBL* LXXI (1952), 171–8

——— (2), 'The Constitution of the Jewish Republic of 66–70', *JSS* ix (1964), 295–319

P. Schäfer, 'Engel und Menschen in der Hekhalot-Literatur', *Kairos N.F.* xxii (1980), 201–25

H.-M. Schenke, 'Erwägungen zum Rätsel des Hebräerbriefes', in H. D. Betz and L. Schottroff (eds.), *Neues Testament und christliche Existenz* (Tübingen, 1973), 421–37

U. Schubert, *Spätantikes Judentum und frühchristliche Kunst* (Vienna, 1974)

Morton Smith, 'The Dead Sea Scrolls in Relation to Ancient Judaism', *NTS* vii (1960–1), 347–60

J. Z. Smith, 'Fences and Neighbours: Some Contours of Early Judaism', in W. S. Green (ed.), *Approaches to Ancient Judaism ii* (Chico, 1980), 1–25

C. Spicq, *L'Epître aux Hébreux* (2 vols.; Paris, 1952–3)

M. Stern, *Greek and Latin Authors on Jews and Judaism i* (Jerusalem, 1974)

R. A. Stewart, 'The Sinless High-Priest', *NTS* xiv (1967–8), 126–35

A. Vanhoye (1), 'Le Christ, grand-prêtre selon Héb. 2, 17–18', *Nouvelle revue théologique* xci (1969), 449–74

——— (2), 'Situation et signification de Hébreux v. 1–10', *NTS* xxii (1977), 445–56

H.-F. Weiss, *Der Brief an die Hebräer* (Göttingen, 1991)

J. Wellhausen, *Prolegomena to the History of Israel* (ET, Edinburgh, 1885)

H. Wenschkewitz, *Die Spiritualisierung der Kultusbegriffe Tempel, Priester und Opfer im Neuen Testament* (Leipzig, 1932)

R. Williamson, 'The Background of the Epistle to the Hebrews', *ET* LXXXVII (1976), 232–7

N. H. Young, 'The Gospel according to Hebrews 9', *NTS* xxvii (1981), 198–210

T. Zahavy, *The Traditions of Eleazar ben Azariah* (Missoula, 1978)

8

Septuagintal and New Testament Conceptions of the Church

Visions *of* as well as for the church were known at the time of Christian origins. The dreamers of dreams in Israel saw the people as a threatened flock, and Jerusalem as a mourning and rejoicing mother and bride (1 En. 89–91; 2 Esd. 9–10); and the Christians followed them with visions of the church and the holy city as a mother and bride, an aged yet joyful woman and a tower (Rev. 12:1–6, 19:7–8, 21:2; Hermas, *Vis.* i–iii). These visions of sorrow and hope in turn contributed to patristic and later distinctions between a visible and an invisible church, presenting a contrast which could be used to console or reform the empirical congregation.

The four apocalypses just cited were of disputed value in ancient times, and remained on the verges of the LXX and New Testament book-collections. Their visions of the church were shaped, however, by the more generally accepted scriptures. 'No doubt a genuine vision lies behind, but the details evoke scriptural passages' (Sweet 1979, 195). The visions concretize some of the similitudes applied to Israel and Jerusalem in the Old Testament.

Against the background formed by these apocalypses it seems likely that, when the scriptures were read at the time of Jesus and Paul, even non-visionary hearers shared conceptions of the congregation which arose from association and development of the manifold biblical descriptions and images. The Christians were keenly aware of their separate loyalty (1 Cor. 16:22), but this was owed to the messiah of Israel; they spoke and thought of themselves as essential Israel, and applied to themselves most of the relevant biblical vocabulary. So in the biblical manner, without special introduction, Paul could speak of betrothing the Corinthian church as a pure virgin to Christ (2 Cor. 11:2). To a great extent, therefore, New Testament conceptions of the church were ready-made before the apostles preached; and this is true not only of the imagery most readily applicable to the pre-existent or ideal church, but also of descriptions of the empirical assembly.

To *what* extent, exactly, were such conceptions ready-made? One important contribution towards an answer is offered by the Greek translations constituting the LXX, individually and as a collection of books (briefly surveyed by Schürer and Goodman 1986, 474–504). The LXX translations are mainly pre-Christian, and formatively influenced the Greek-speaking Christianity reflected in the Greek New Testament; and the collection as a whole shared something of the enormous prestige accorded to the Greek Pentateuch in particular (the 'Septuagint', or work of the seventy translators, in the strict sense), and was abidingly revered by Christians, from the New Testament period onwards.

Here attention is concentrated on the two Songs and the Blessing of Moses (Exod. 15 and Deut. 32; Deut. 33), and the Wisdom of Solomon. These texts form no more than a particle of the LXX material for conceptions of the congregation, but their significance is considerable. The Pentateuch is the oldest and most widely familiar part of the LXX; the two Songs and the Blessing took a high place, even within this sacrosanct corpus, as prophecies of Moses. This is plain from Philo and Josephus, and can be glimpsed from the New Testament (Rev. 15:3–4).[1] The two Songs were also transmitted as the first two canticles in the LXX book of Odes. This book is a Christian collection in its present form, and it attests the importance of the two Songs in Christian thought and worship; at the same time it probably reflects Jewish usage in its treatment of the Songs of Moses and other Old Testament canticles independently of their biblical context. The Song of Exod. 15 enjoyed widespread veneration among Jews (Hengel, 1995, n. 6) and had a specifically communal character, discussed below. Deut. 32 is regularly called 'the Great Ode' in Philo (*Leg.* iii 105 and elsewhere), perhaps partly as 'the Greater' Song of Moses as opposed to the lesser Song in Exod. 15 (*Plant.* 59, cited in n. 1, above); and in the context of

[1] See Philo, *Plant.* 54–9, where the two Songs of Moses are considered together; *Virt.* 72–7, on the Deuteronomic Song and Blessing; and *Mos.* ii 288–9, on the Blessing; also Josephus, *Ant.* ii 346, iv 303, on the two Songs as composed by Moses in hexameters and preserved in the temple, and iv 320, on the prophetic Blessing. The joint influence on the New Testament of a pair of eschatological verses from the two Songs (Exod. 15:17 and Deut. 32:35) is considered against this background in Horbury 1996, 210–11. In Rev. 15:3–4 'the song of Moses, the servant of God' is that of Exod. 15, but the song sung by the victorious martyrs echoes and parallels that of Deut. 32.

Maccabaean martyrdom it was quoted as 'the Ode of Open Protest' (2 Macc. 7:6, recalling Deut. 31:21 LXX) (see Harl in Dogniez and Harl 1992, 319–20). In the New Testament, similarly, the two Songs were both influential, and the greater Song with its martyr-links was one of 'the early church's favourite texts' (Sweet, 1979, 240).

The book of Wisdom, by contrast, is relatively late, perhaps of the early first century B.C.; but in thought it shows kinship with the Pauline writings, it is another document of martyr-theology, and it was probably known to first-century Christians (Horbury, 1995). The LXX collection of books, in which Wisdom and other approved but non-canonical works are associated with the generally accepted scriptures, probably represents a widespread Jewish reading practice which was continued by early Christians.[2]

All these texts are poetic compositions, presented in Greek in lines which echo the stressed metre of Hebrew verse. They differ markedly from Greek verse written in the quantitative classical metres, and probably reflect by their very form a pride in the ancestral biblical tradition.

The general context of this small-scale inquiry is that explored especially by Dahl 1941, the relation of early Christian conceptions of the church to conceptions of the nation and congregation current in ancient Judaism. Within the study of Septuagintal theology (briefly surveyed with examples by Le Déaut 1984, 175–85, and Schaper 1995, 1–2 and n. 449), this political or ecclesiological topic has gained sporadic attention (notably from Seeligmann 1948, 110–21, on Isaiah). Examination of the Songs and Blessing of Moses in this connection is facilitated by the valuable Septuagintal commentaries of Le Boulluec and Sandevoir 1989 and Dogniez and Harl 1992. The use made of Deut. 32 in ancient Jewish and early Christian literature is surveyed by Bell 1994, 200–85.

Here the LXX is read with an eye not simply to the importance of the Greek bible for Greek-speakers, but also to the likelihood that it often reflects interpretations current in the homeland as well as the diaspora, even among Jews whose main language was not Greek. The contacts between Septuagintal and rabbinic exegesis noted from time to time below point in this direction.

[2] M. Hengel, by contrast, holds that the collection was essentially Christian, albeit influenced initially by Jewish practice in Rome (Hengel, 'Schriftensammlung', discussed by Horbury 1997b); but the consistent Christian wish to accord with Jewish biblical usage suggests that the collection was more representatively Jewish than he allows.

LXX material, used with due caution, may then at times suggest something of conceptions current among Aramaic-speaking Christians, as well as the Greek-speakers whose outlook is more directly mirrored in many New Testament writings.

The passages particularly considered deal with Israel during the exodus, the miraculous time of union between the people and their God (Exod. 4:22, 19:4–6; Deut. 32:10–14; Isa. 63:11–14; Jer. 2:2; Ezek. 16:8) and the pattern of future redemption (Deut. 30:3–5; Isa. 11:11; Ezek. 16:60; Mic. 7:15). Conceptions of the congregation are studied first through five attributes which stand out in the two Songs and Wisdom, and are also prominent in the New Testament, and then through some community titles common to the Jewish and Christian material.

Attributes of the Church

To begin with the lesser Song of Moses, it is through and through congregational as well as prophetic. As presented in Exod. 15 it is communal rather than individual, and forms a congregational hymn. This is clear in the Hebrew as well as the LXX. The hymn was sung not only by Moses, but also by the children of Israel. The singers are articulated into a men's section and a women's section, as befits a comprehensive assembly. In the LXX they still more clearly form a double choir of men and women; Miriam the prophetess was precentor of (ἐξῆρχεν) the women (Exod. 15:20–1).[3] This method of performance recalls Greek and Roman employment of antiphonal male and female choirs, for instance in Horace's ode for Augustus' Secular Games of 17 B.C.; it probably had reflections in Jewish practice at the time of Christian origins, as Philo suggests when, echoing Exod. 15:21 LXX, he says that the choir of the Therapeutae models itself on that formed at the Red Sea 'when the prophet Moses was precentor of (ἐξάρχοντος) the men, and the prophetess Miriam precentor

[3] *Exarchos*, the noun corresponding to the verb used in LXX here, could denote the song-leader in Greek cults (E. R. Dodds (ed.), *Euripides: Bacchae* (2nd edn., Oxford: Clarendon Press, 1960), 87, on line 141, where the chorus say that Bacchus himself is the *exarchos*); the noun is applied by Philo to the male and female precentors of the Therapeutae, in a passage ending with a paraphrase of Exod. 15 using the verb, quoted in the text below (Philo, *V. Contempl.* 83, 87). Since this essay first appeared, Septuagintal and other ancient usage of the verb has been surveyed, and used to interpret a title found in epitaphs from the Roman Jewish catacomb of Monteverde, by Williams 2000.

of the women' (Philo, *V. Contempl.* 85–9). Practice is similarly suggested by probably second-century rabbinic debate on the performance of the song, handed down in the names of R. Akiba, R. Nehemiah and others (Mishnah, Soṭah 5.4; Tosefta, Soṭah 6.2–3).

The Song of Exod. 15 thus has a congregational atmosphere which is enhanced in the LXX. Its LXX presentation has a number of features which reappear in New Testament conceptions of the church. Five at least anticipate attributes of the church as encountered and envisaged by Paul in particular.

The first of these is a constitutional point: the congregation comprises both men and women. The assignation of parts to men and women in a single assembly which has just been noted is an arrangement in principle taken for granted in 1 Cor. 11–14. Thus, as is often pointed out, it seems uncontroversial that women may pray or prophesy in the assembly (1 Cor. 11:5); these activities are close to the prophetically-led women's hymnody of Exod. 15 LXX. The details left room for debate, as 1 Corinthians amply shows, but the principle of an articulated assembly with parts for men and women is a Pentateuchal and prophetic one, made still plainer in the LXX interpretation at this point. This principle contrasts with and to some extent modifies the more frequently noticed teaching on the subordination of women in the Pentateuch and its ancient interpretation. The principle of women's participation is further reflected in ancient Jewish practice (discussed in Horbury 1999), for example in the provision of a women's court in Herod's Jerusalem temple; and elsewhere in Paul, as when (perhaps using an existing testimony-collection) he quotes prophecy concerning sons (2 Sam 7:8) in the adapted form 'you shall be to me for sons and daughters' (2 Cor. 6:18). The church following this principle reflected the Pentateuchal ethos of a comprehensive national community, despite its relatively small local 'churches'.

Secondly, the hymn of the assembly in the LXX is a confession of faith. 'They believed (ἐπίστευσαν) in God, and in his servant Moses. Then Moses and the children of Israel sang this ode to God' (Exod. 14:31–15:1 LXX). The assembly here is a congregation of those who believe in God and his appointed ruler. This point becomes central in New Testament conceptions of the church, as when οἱ πιστεύοντες or πιστεύσαντες denote church members in famous phrases from Acts 2:44, 4:32 on 'believers'; compare the ecclesiastical aspect of 'all who believe' and 'those who believe' in Rom. 3:22, Gal 3:22. These phrases, no doubt in conjunction with the continuing importance of the LXX for early Christians, worked on patristic tradition and helped to shape later definitions of the church as 'a congregation of the faithful'.[4] This point is illustrated in the earliest patristic antecedents of such definitions. Thus, in Cyprian's influential treatise on church unity, the church is 'the new people of those who believe' (*novus credentium populus*), and the phrase is followed by a quotation of Acts 4:32 (Cyprian, *De Unitate*, v 19 (25)). Compare also, nearly a century earlier, Justin Martyr, *Dial.* lxiii 5: 'the word of God addresses as daughter [in Ps. 45(44):10 LXX] those who believe in him [Christ], as being of one soul and one gathering together (συναγωγή) and one ecclesia, the ecclesia which came into being from his name and shares his name—for we are all called Christians'. Here a reminiscence of Acts 4:32 on the believers as of one soul is not unlikely, for possible contacts with Acts 4:13, 25–7 occur in Justin's *First Apology* (xxxix 3, xl 6, 11). However this may be, his *Dialogue* here exemplifies early continuation of the conception of the church as an ecclesia of believers, illustrated above from Acts and Paul, and strikingly presented in the introduction of the lesser song of Moses (Exod. 14:31–15:1 LXX).

Moreover, two small correspondences between these verses in Exodus and expressions later used by Paul deserve notice. In 14:31, the people have faith not just in God, but in God and his servant Moses. This binary pattern (found also at Num. 21:5, here of *dis*belief) is comparable with the Pauline expression of communal faith in one God, and one lord—who as messianic leader takes Moses' place (1 Cor. 8:6). Secondly, these two consecutive verses in Exodus. 14:31 and 15:1, when read together present praise as the fruit of faith. The two verses were indeed thus read together in rabbinic exegesis (so the Mekhilta, quoted below, with homiletic emphasis on the importance of faith); but this already occurred in the Persian period, as appears from the exodus narrative in Ps. 106 (LXX105):12 'And they believed in [God's] words, and sang his praise'. The progression from faith to praise which the consecutive reading embodies

4 For 'congregation of the faithful' see Bishop John Hooper's fourth article of 1552, close to 'congregation of faithful men' in the 1552 text which became the Nineteenth of the Thirty-Nine Articles (both are quoted, with a further comment by Hooper using the word 'multitude', as in Acts 4:32, by C. Hardwick, *A History of the Articles of Religion* (Cambridge: Deighton, 1851), 290); the similar 'blessed company of all faithful people' had been used in the thanksgiving after communion composed for the English Prayer-book of 1549. All are probably influenced by Luther, whose view of the church as a 'communion of saints' in the sense of a congregation of pious believers builds on patristic tradition shaped by Acts as well as Paul (see the text, below).

later reappears in Paul: 'with the heart it is believed …, with the mouth it is confessed' (Rom. 10:10). Here Paul for a moment reverses the sequence 'mouth … heart' derived from his earlier quotation of Deut. 30:14 (Rom. 10:8). As 'confession' (*exomologesis*) in the Greek biblical tradition regularly has the sense of hymnic 'praise', in the Psalter and elsewhere (for example, Tobit 14:1; Ecclus. 39:13–15 LXX), it is not unlikely that Paul has in mind the classical instance of congregational faith and praise at the Red Sea. Ps. 106 was quoted in Rom. 1; and the mouth, important in Paul here, is picked out in Wisdom precisely in connection with the Song at the sea: 'Wisdom opened the mouth of the dumb' (Wisd. 10:21).

It is very possible, therefore, that the sequence Exod. 14:31–15:1 lies behind Rom. 10:10. In any case, however, the pattern of communal faith leading to communal confession which is given here in Exodus will have facilitated Christian views of the church as the community of faith and confession. The believing assembly of men and women in the lesser Song of Moses can be contrasted with God's 'sons and daughters' who provoked him, according to the greater Song, as 'children in whom is no faith (*pistis*)' (Deut. 32:19–20 LXX). The two Songs together, in their LXX form, therefore enforce the conception of the church as a community of faith and confession. They belong to the biblical material which qualified the view that the congregation is perpetuated chiefly by physical descent.

A third and related conception of the church, as the assembly whose confession is divinely inspired, appears in the interpretation of the lesser Song as attested in the Wisdom of Solomon. The prophetically-led congregational hymn of praise was taken to have been inspired, perhaps even ecstatic. In this hymn God opened the mouth of the dumb, and made the tongues of babes to speak clearly (Wisd. 10:20–21; cf. Isa. 35:6); and they roamed like horses and skipped like lambs as they praised the Lord who delivered them (Wisd. 19:9; cf. Isa. 63:13 and Ps. 114:6). In Philo, similarly, they are 'in ecstasy', ἐνθουσιῶντες, men and women alike (Philo, *V. Contempl.* 87).

The interpretation shared by Wisdom and Philo appears also in rabbinic tradition, for example in the Mekhilta: 'As a reward for the faith with which Israel believed in the Lord, the holy spirit rested upon them and they uttered the Song, as it is written, And they believed in the Lord … Then Moses and the children of Israel sang … (Exod. 14:31–15:1)' (Mekhilta, Beshallah, 6 (7), on

Exod. 14:31). The formula 'the holy spirit rested upon Israel and they uttered the Song' is also found in versions of the rabbinic debate on the performance of the Song which has already been mentioned (Mekhilta, Shirata, 1, on Exod. 15:1; Tosefta, Soṭah 6.2, cited above).

The ecstatic aspect of this inspired utterance also reappears in rabbinic tradition, in general agreement with Wisdom and Philo. Thus, sucklings and unborn babes in the womb joined in the Song, together with the ministering angels—as 'God is my strength and my song' (Exod. 15:2) suggests when set beside 'Out of the mouths of babes and sucklings hast thou established strength' (Ps. 8:2–3). This probably second-century exegesis is found among other places at Mekhilta, Shirata, 1, on Exod. 15:1. Comparably, the beginning of the Song of Songs, 'Let him kiss me with the kisses of his mouth', was uttered by Israel at the Red Sea, in an exegesis ascribed to the late third-century Caesarean teacher Hanina bar Papa; the verse so interpreted is paraphrased in the midrash with a variation on the formula of inspiration noted above, 'let him make the holy spirit rest upon us, and we will utter before him many songs' (Cant. R. i 2, 1)—probably taken to include the Song of Songs, with its exalted hints of mystical union, as well as the Song of Moses.

The LXX as understood in Wisdom and Philo therefore represents widespread interpretative tradition. Paul's assumption that the congregational cry of Abba is uttered by the Spirit (Rom. 8:15; Gal 4:6) is closer in expression to the rabbinic version of this tradition, where 'holy spirit' regularly occurs; but it seems none the less to be continuous with the Septuagintal view of the redeemed congregation as uttering a hymn by divine inspiration.

A fourth attribute of the community of the exodus is a relation between the congregation and the angels, both bad and good. This emerges with special reference to the hostile angels in the greater Song.

> When the Highest divided the nations, when he dispersed the children of Adam, he set the bounds of the nations according to the number of the angels of God; and the Lord's portion was his people, Jacob, the lot of his inheritance, Israel.
>
> (Deut. 32:8–9 LXX)

As is often noted, the translation 'the angels of God' here in verse 8 presupposes a Hebrew text such as is known from Qumran Cave 4, to be rendered with

'El' rather than, as in most English versions, 'Israel'; and the 'sons of El' are understood as angels, as happened with the 'sons of God' in Job. Some Greek copies have the rendering 'sons' (followed with discussion by Harl in Dogniez and Harl 1992, 325–6); but it was no doubt considered to refer to angels, as in the majority Greek text. For the present purpose the translation process reconstructed here is less important than the understanding which governs it, also attested at Ecclus. 17:17 and Jub. 15:30–2, in line with Deut. 4:19–20: each nation is allotted to an angel (from among the sun, moon and stars, all the heavenly host, the gods whom the heathen worship, according to Deut. 4:19); but the Lord himself takes his own people. The people of God is therefore eyed jealously by the angel-deities of the nations, but protected by God (and his angels).

This understanding in turn leaves well-known traces in New Testament teaching. Sometimes its ecclesiological aspect remains largely implicit, for example when Paul states that we are redeemed by Christ from the power of the 'elements of the world' and 'not-gods' (Gal. 4:3–5, 8–10), most plausibly understood as the cosmic host of the angel-deities of the nations; here it is membership of the redeemed people belonging to the true God which brings protection from the hostile powers to whom the nations are allotted, but the church is unmentioned. The importance of the church in this connection emerges more clearly in Eph. 3:8–12, where the manifold wisdom of God will be made known to the principalities and powers in the heavens through the church (Eph. 3:10, διὰ τῆς ἐκκλησίας)—God's own people, now consisting, as it is presumed that the heavenly powers who eye his portion can see, both of Jews and gentiles. The church is viewed here, like God's own people in Deut. 32:8, as an object of interest to the angels of the nations—all the more because their own subjects, the gentiles, are falling away to become fellow-citizens with the saints, belonging to God (Eph. 2:19).

Lastly, the congregation of Israel is united around a ruler, Moses in the exodus and another to come. This has already emerged through the binary faith of the congregation in God and in Moses, noticed above in connection with the introduction of the lesser Song (Exod. 14:31–15:1 LXX). The importance of congregational faith in Moses is enhanced elsewhere in the LXX Exodus, in its version of the narrative of the signs given to Moses (Exod. 4:1–9 LXX, where by comparison with MT 'in you' is added after 'believe' in verses 5, 8 and 9).

The significance of Moses as a ruler and the pattern of a messiah is evident in Philonic and rabbinic passages on Moses as king; see for example Philo, *V. Mos.* i 148, 158 (he was named god and king of the whole nation); Midrash Tehillim i 2, on Ps. 1:1 (like David, he was king of Israel and Judah, as shown by Deut. 33:5—a passage from the Blessing of Moses discussed below). This point gains New Testament confirmation not only from Acts 7:35–8, on the legation of Moses as ruler and redeemer, but also from Paul's striking statement that all the fathers 'were baptized into Moses' (1 Cor. 10:2), as the Christians were 'baptized into Christ' (Rom. 6:3).

To return to the Pentateuch, in his final Blessing Moses foretells, according to the LXX, that 'there shall be a ruler in the Beloved, when the rulers of the nations are gathered together at one time with the tribes of Israel' (Deut. 33:5 LXX). The future 'there shall be', contrasting with the past tense represented in the Massoretic pointing and in the rabbinic interpretation quoted above, makes this verse in the LXX a messianic oracle comparable with those of Jacob and Balaam (Gen 49:9–12; Num. 24:7, 17 LXX); but Deut. 33:5 LXX differs from these passages in envisaging the coming ruler as a monarch 'in the Beloved'—the elect people of God—reigning in an imperial council and forming the focus of the unity of Israel and, beyond, of the tributary nations of the world. Here the Blessing in its LXX form is not far from the Stoically-influenced Philonic and Pauline conception of the nation as one body, headed by the high priest or Christ, respectively (Philo, *Spec. Leg.* iii 319; Rom. 12:5) (Dahl 1941, 226–7; Moule 1977, 83–5). Hence, although the messianic links of the congregation in these LXX texts are less prominent than New Testament links between the church and Christ, the LXX presents in the lesser Song and the Blessing of Moses the picture of a church led by Moses as ruler, or by the greater messianic ruler still to come.

Thus far, then, the material studied from the LXX has disclosed five attributes of the congregation which are also prominent marks of the New Testament church. Constitutionally and liturgically, it is a body in which men and women each take part, and it is governed by a divinely-appointed ruler. To turn to theological attributes, it can be described as a community of faith, the congregation of the redeemed who believe and confess. Correspondingly, in this corporate confession it is a community of the divinely inspired, and its confession is led by prophecy. As God's own peculiar people and portion, it is watched by the angel-deities to whom the heathen nations are allotted. Its faith is faith not only in God, but also in the appointed ruler, and a great ruler to come will be the focus of its unity. The shape and ethos of the Pauline churches is anticipated here; and although the theological attributes are not made normative in these texts, the fact that they are exhibited by the congregation of the exodus as described in the Pentateuch accords them authority and influence.

These attributes give some substance to the view of the church outlined in the LXX passages considered here. The sketch which begins to emerge constitutes a far-reaching anticipation of New Testament conceptions. Now this outline can receive further definition from the overlap between some LXX titles used for the congregation, and New Testament titles for the church.

Titles of the Church

Within the two Songs, the Blessing and Wisdom the principal title of the exodus congregation is 'people' (*laos*). The Pentateuchal texts also have the correlative 'Jacob', 'Israel', and (for the national name Jeshurun) 'Beloved'. There is also occasional reference to *ekklesia* and 'saints'. Here the evidently national title 'people' will be treated first, followed by the still national but less plainly ethnocentric 'Beloved', 'ecclesia', and 'saints'. All these terms reappear in the New Testament vocabulary referring to the church, but their fresh application is not always straightforward.

The self-definition of the assembly as the people (*laos*) of God just encountered in the 'Great Ode' is central in the LXX material considered here. In the lesser Song of Exod. 15 the congregation, articulated into men and women, identify themselves emphatically as the elect people of God, 'this people whom you redeemed', 'this people whom you possessed' (Exod. 15:13, 16). The greater Song, correspondingly, remembering the allotment of God's own people to himself in the presence of the angels of the nations (Deut. 32:8 LXX, discussed above), expects the day when 'the Lord will judge his people', when the angels shall worship him and the nations shall rejoice 'with his people', and 'he shall purify his people's land' (Deut. 32:36, 43 LXX). In the Blessing, similarly, he has had pity on his people, and there is none like Israel, 'a people saved by the

Lord' (Deut. 33:3, 29). Finally, in the later chapters of Wisdom the term *laos* is even more clearly a focus of expressions of divine election; thus, in passages on the exodus, Wisdom delivered a holy people, God did good to his people and fed them with angels' food (10:15, 16:2, 20); the Egyptians, on the destruction of their first-born, confessed 'the people' to be God's son (18:13); his people journeyed miraculously on when the Egyptians found a strange death, and in all things God magnified his people (19:5, 22). The theory of divinely-ordered yet rational miracle elaborated in Wisdom itself serves especially, as these verses show, to exalt God's 'people' (Sweet 1965, 123–4).

The word *laos* used here in the LXX, and emerging in Wisdom as *tout court* a current name for Israel, is rarely applied directly to the Christians in Paul. Like the name Israel, it occurs with primary reference to the Jewish people rather than as a straightforward title of the church (Dahl 1941, 210). This is probably the case when Deut. 32:43 LXX 'rejoice, you nations, with his people' is quoted at Rom. 15:10. Earlier in Romans, however, those gentiles whom God has called are held now to share, correspondingly, in the title of his people and his children, as prophesied in Hosea: 'I will call the not-people (as) my people; and her that was not beloved (as) beloved' (Hos. 2:25, freely quoted and followed by Hos. 2:1 LXX, at Rom. 9:24–5). Here Paul probably uses an existing testimony-chain, the compilation of which attests his own conviction that the gentile Christians share the election of the Israelite *laos*. Thus for Christians it was their 'fathers', with spiritual privileges like their own (1 Cor. 10:1–4), who sinned when 'the people sat down to eat and drink' (1 Cor. 10:7, quoting Exod. 32:6). Correspondingly, another Pentateuchal verse on the 'people' is used in exhortation to Christians at 2 Cor. 6:16, in a passage perhaps drawn from a source, as mentioned above. Here the series of texts on the congregation as the temple of God begins with Lev. 26:11–12, quoted in a form near to Ezek 37:27, 'I will dwell among them … and they shall be my people'. The use of this text as the first of the series supports the view that a Pentateuchal understanding of the assembly as made up of men and women contributed to the specification of 'daughters' at the end of the series, as noted above.

The Christians thus belong to the *laos*, but the title is not restricted to the church. This is implied also in Acts, where *laos* can be applied to the Jewish people, as noted below, but 'God made a visitation to take from the gentiles a people for his name' (Acts 15:14; cf. Deut. 32:8; Rom. 9:24). The same interpretation seems likely also to apply to famous texts on Christians as (belonging to) the people of God in Hebrews (4:9, 10:30, from Deut. 32:40); 1 Peter (2:9–10, from Exod. 19:5–6, 23:22; Hos. 2:25); and Revelation (18:4 'come out of her, my people', from Jer. 51:45). These books offer no anti-Jewish definition of *laos*, by contrast with the frequent employment, from the Epistle of Barnabas onwards, of phrases such as 'the new people' (Epistle of Barnabas 5.7; see also Cyprian, *De Unitate* v 19 (25), quoted above). The other side of this coin is New Testament continuation and awareness of the Jewish use of *laos* as a Jewish national title. This was illustrated above from Rom. 15:10 on 'his people'; but is also reflected in Acts (as at 7:17; 26:17, 23; 28:17, all in speeches by Christian Jews to non-Christian Jews) and Jude (verse 5). Phrases like 'the new people' imply a doctrine of supersession, but they also recognize and continue the centrality in biblical and contemporary Judaism of self-definition as 'people of God'—the point brought home by the prominence of *laos* in the LXX texts considered here. *laos* can therefore be reckoned only with qualification among New Testament titles for the church, but the LXX references to an elect *laos* are central in New Testament *conceptions* of the church.

The election of the Jewish nation was also strikingly asserted in the LXX rendering of Jeshurun, the name for Israel occurring in the greater Song and the Blessing of Moses, by ὁ ἠγαπημένος, 'the beloved' (Deut. 32:15, 33:5, 26, followed in the LXX translations of Isaiah (44:3) and the Psalms (29 (28):6); see below). This interpretation fits the immediate context of Deut. 32:15, a description of God's particular care for Israel from the time of his original choice (Deut. 32:8–14), as well as the larger biblical context of the divine love shown in the exodus (compare 'your sons whom you loved', Wisd. 16:26). 'Beloved' appears as a messianic title in the New Testament (Eph. 1:6) and in continuing Christian usage (for example, Epistle of Barnabas 3.6); in both these instances ἠγαπημένος is used, but the similar ἀγαπητός also occurs in this sense, as in the Greek text of the Ascension of Isaiah (3:17).

'Beloved', which could in principle be represented by either Greek word, was probably already applied by pre-Christian Jews not only to Israel, but also to the messiah; thus in the Psalms the former sense seems to appear at Ps. 29 (28):6 LXX (ὁ ἠγαπημένος), the latter in the inscription of Ps. 45 (44) LXX 'for the beloved' (ὑπὲρ τοῦ ἀγαπητοῦ) (Schaper 1995, 78–9, taking Ps. 29 (28):6 LXX also as messianic, by contrast with the above).

The thematically related term 'son' has a similar dual application to Israel and the messiah (Exod. 4:22; Ps. 2:7). The stress on election in LXX application of the title 'beloved' to the congregation may be compared with the stress on Israel's sonship in Hebrew prayer known from Qumran: 'thou hast made us sons to thee before the eyes of all nations, for thou didst call Israel My son, my first-born' (4Q504 iii 1–2, lines 3–5, quoting Exod. 4:22).

In the New Testament the singular 'beloved' as a title is restricted to the messiah (Eph. 1:6, already cited, but not in the epistles generally acknowledged as Pauline; for the title compare Mark 1:11, 9:7, and parallels, for the sense Col. 1:13 'son of his love'). The plural 'beloved of God', however, is a title of the Christians collectively, as at Rom. 1:7 (ἀγαπητοί), 1 Thess. 1:4, 2 Thess. 2:13, Col. 3:12 (ἠγαπημένοι); cf. Rom. 11:28 (ἀγαπητοί), of Israel. The link between the applications to Christ and to the church appears in the immediate context of Eph. 1:6, a blessing on God who 'picked us out through him [Christ] … to be holy and blameless before him in love having foreordained us …' (Eph. 1:4–5). Against the LXX and New Testament background just noted, 'in love' here (ἐν ἀγάπῃ) probably refers to God's love for his people in election (so Origen), not theirs for one another. This passage could then rank with Eph. 5:1 '[God's] beloved children' (τέκνα ἀγαπητά) (cf. Wisd. 16:26) as attesting the sense of the church title 'beloved' in slightly different language.

This usage directly continues, and applies to the church in each place, the assertion of communal election made by the rendering 'beloved' in the greater Song and Blessing of Moses. Its continuity with the LXX is emphasized by the importance of 'beloved of God' (Rom. 1:7, 1 Thess 1:4; cf. Eph. 1:4–5, 5:1), despite the concurrence of the integrally related concept that the church was loved by Christ; the two are fused at Rom. 8:39.

The most famous and influential of all church titles, *ekklesia*, occurs in the introduction of the 'Great Ode': 'Moses spoke to the end the words of this ode in the ears of all the ecclesia of Israel' (Deut. 32:1 LXX). This title was quickly adopted by Christians (1 Thess. 1:1, etc.), by contrast with their qualified use of *laos*. Paul often uses it in the form 'ecclesia of God' (1 Cor. 1:2, etc.), thereby underlining the Christian share in the special relationship to God bestowed on the *laos*. Although *ekklesia* recalled the Israelite 'ecclesia in the wilderness' (Acts 7:38), for which it was regularly used in LXX Deuteronomy, it was not restricted to this sense. Factors which freed it from the strongly national associations of *laos* will have included its absence from LXX Genesis to Numbers, where *synagoge* is used for the Israelite congregation. Another such factor will have been the broad usage of both *ekklesia* and *synagoge*, and the Hebrew *qahal* and *ʿedah* and Aramaic *qehala* and *kenisha*, to which they often respectively correspond, for other assemblies as well as that of all Israel. Thus an application of Aramaic *qehala* to a pious group is found at Babylonian Talmud, Ber. 9b, on the prayer practice of 'the holy congregation' in Jerusalem. (The use of this Aramaic phrase here and elsewhere is discussed in connection with New Testament vocabulary by Jeremias 1969, 247–9.) Hence *ekklesia* could be used for the separate Christian 'churches of the saints' (1 Cor. 14:33; cf. Ps. 89 (88):6 LXX 'the ecclesia of the saints'); but it also presented the churches as continuous with the congregation of Israel described in the LXX Pentateuch.

Finally, 'the saints' appear as Israel corporately in the lesser Song and the Blessing of Moses. God is 'glorified among the saints (ἁγίοι)' (Exod. 15:11 LXX), and 'all the sanctified (ἡγιασμένοι) are under his hands' (Deut. 33:3 LXX). The first of these passages could have been taken as a reference to angels, but was perhaps more readily applicable to the congregation, the saints who are glorifying God by the hymn of Exod. 15 which they are singing. The second passage is applied to the martyrs in 4 Macc. 17:19. In the book of Wisdom, comparably, the martyr 'was numbered among the sons of God, and his lot is among the saints' (5:5); the theme of Israel's sonship (Exod. 4:22) with which 'the saints' of Israel are here connected was noted above in Qumran prayer and elsewhere in Wisdom (16:26; cf. 18:13). Again in Wisdom, at the first Passover the Israelites covenanted 'that the saints (ἁγίοι) should share alike in good things and in dangers' (Wisd. 18:9).

This Jewish designation of Israel as 'saints' is reflected in Acts when gentile Christians receive 'a lot among the sanctified' (Acts 26:18; cf. 20:32, and the use of *laos* for the Jewish people noted above in Acts). Phrases speaking of the 'inheritance' or 'lot' of the saints recur, with the same emphasis on sharing the privileges of Israel, at Eph. 1:18; Col. 1:12 (compare the stress on the church as beloved noted above in Eph. 1:4–5, 5:1; Col. 3:12). The privileges are still implied by 'the saints' without 'lot' in Eph. 2:19, cited above. This group of phrases on the 'saints' inheritance from Acts, Ephesians and Colossians correspondingly recalls the 'Great Ode' not only on 'the sanctified', but also on the election of Israel as falling to God's own 'inheritance' (Deut. 32:8 LXX, discussed above).

The Christians, sharing this inheritance, are in the same way collectively entitled 'sanctified' (1 Cor. 1:2) or, more usually, 'saints' (for example in 1 Cor. 14:33, quoted above, and in epistolary addresses such as Rom. 1:7; Phil. 1:1). This title can readily accompany the title 'beloved', as at Rom. 1:7, Col. 3:12, both cited above. In the case of 'saints' a Pentateuchally-rooted title has been taken up, once again, in the Jewish community, as the LXX Pentateuch and Wisdom attest; and the Christians continue its application to Israel, but also apply it specially to their own churches.

The four titles now considered present the congregation of the exodus as the redeemed people of God, God's beloved, and as the ecclesia of Israel made up of the 'sanctified' or 'saints'. When these titles are viewed together with the attributes noted above, the congregation as presented in this LXX material is more fully characterized. Constitutionally, it is both national and ecclesiastical, a national assembly for divine service, in which men and women take an appointed part. Theologically, it is not only a people descended from the Hebrew ancestors, but also a congregation of the saints who have faith in God and his servant Moses, and confess their divine Lord. Their corporate hymn of faith is divinely inspired, and collectively they are God's own Beloved, led and unified by God's appointed ruler, a people on whom the hostile gaze of the angel-deities is bent in vain.

To return to the opening question, just how far does this picture anticipate Christian conceptions of the church? The view of the congregation of the exodus offered in this LXX material would not be wholly inadequate as a sketch of the church in the New Testament. Thus the Corinthian emphasis on spiritual gifts, and Paul's call in reply for decency and order, could both invoke the example of the Pentateuchal congregation as presented here in the LXX. The constitutive nature of faith for the church, as met in Acts and Paul, is as much a feature of the Septuagintal portrait as is the importance of Jewish descent. The congregation appears in the LXX under designations characteristically used by Christians, 'the church' and 'the saints', and the Pauline phrase 'ecclesia of God' (as at 1 Cor. 1:2) recalls the Septuagintal view of the people as the Lord's own portion.

On the other hand, it has become clear that the transition from this portrayal to Christian conceptions and doctrines of the church was not wholly straightforward. The conviction that Israel corporately were God's chosen and beloved, as LXX interpretation so strongly emphasizes, did not disappear. In this point the Paul of Romans was at one with the Paul of Acts (Rom. 11:28, 15:10; Acts 26:23, 28:17, cited above). Hence, despite expectation that Israel in the end would be saved through Christ (Rom. 11:25–7), and despite thorough Christian participation in the concept of the people of God, 'people' was not readily adopted as a church title until Christian claims to be the new elect people took root.

A second point in which the Christian development seems distinctive without being discontinuous is the link regularly made in New Testament sources between the congregation and the messiah. So in Paul the church is 'the ecclesia of God', but it belongs primarily to God's messiah, and then, thereby, to God: 'you are Christ's, and Christ is God's' (1 Cor. 3:23). This is a messianic expansion of the affirmation that the congregation belongs to God noted above at Deut. 32:8. Similarly, Paul betroths the Corinthian church like a virgin to Christ (2 Cor. 11:2), not directly to God; the church is beloved by Christ as well as God, as noted already; and the Christians form one body in (here probably in the sense 'because of') Christ (Rom. 12:5), or the body of (belonging to) Christ (1 Cor. 12:27) (for these interpretations of the phrases see Moule 1977, 71–2). The communal faith is 'the faith of Jesus Christ' (Rom. 3:22; Gal 3:22); although for many exegetes this faith is the faith exhibited by Christ, in the present writer's view the phrase more probably implies both faith that Jesus is the Christ of God, the bringer of God's redemption, and also faith in Christ like Israel's faith in Moses (the ecclesiastical aspect of 'believing' in these two Pauline passages was noted above).

Here, however, as this comparison recalls, the LXX has presented an antecedent noticed above, the binary faith of Israel in God and Moses (Exod. 14:31; cf. Num. 21:5). Similarly, the conception of the church as the congregation belonging to and unified by the messiah (Rom. 12:5; 1 Cor. 12:27) is anticipated in the lesser Song and the Blessing of Moses (Deut. 33:5). Here the New Testament development can be called not an adaptation, as in the case of *laos*, but an intensification, occasioned by the ardent realized messianism of the Christians.

It can then be said, in conclusion, that the messianic element in Christian faith, and the concurrent Christian modification of the concept of the people of God, are foci of what can be called new in New Testament conceptions of the church. Far more, however, is inherited from Judaism as represented by the LXX tradition, including what might be thought characteristically Christian associations of the church with faith, confession, inspiration and the messiah.[5]

Literature

R. H. Bell, 1994. *Provoked to Jealousy: the Origin and Purpose of the Jealousy Motif in Romans 9–11* (WUNT ii.63, Tübingen: Mohr/Siebeck)

N. A. Dahl, 1941. *Das Volk Gottes* (Oslo: Dybwad)

C. Dogniez and M. Harl, 1992. *La Bible d'Alexandrie, 5, Le Deutéronome* (Paris: Les Éditions du Cerf)

M. Hengel, with R. Defines, 1994. 'Die Septuaginta als "christliche Schriftensammlung", ihre Vorgeschichte und das Problem ihres Kanons', in M. Hengel and A. Schwemer (eds.), *Die Septuaginta zwischen Judentum und Christentum* (Tübingen: Mohr/Siebeck), 182–284

———, 1995. 'The Song about Christ in Earliest Worship' (revised English translation), in M. Hengel, *Studies in Early Christology* (Edinburgh: T&T Clark), 227–91

W. Horbury, 1995. 'The Christian Use and the Jewish Origins of the Wisdom of Solomon', in J. Day, R. P. Gordon and H. G. M. Williamson (eds.), *Wisdom in Ancient Israel* (Cambridge: University Press), 182–96

———, 1996. 'Land, Sanctuary and Worship', in J. P. M. Sweet and J. M. G. Barclay (eds.), *Early Christian Thought in its Jewish Setting* (Cambridge: Cambridge University Press), 207–24

———, 1998. *Jews and Christians in Contact and Controversy* (Edinburgh: T&T Clark)

———, 1999. 'Women in the Synagogue', in W. Horbury, W. D. Davies and J. V. M. Sturdy (eds.), *The Cambridge History of Judaism*, iii (Cambridge: Cambridge University Press), 358–401

J. Jeremias, 1969. *Jerusalem in the Time of Jesus, translated by F. H. and C. H. Cave, with the author's revisions* (London: SCM Press)

A. Le Boulluec and P. Sandevoir, 1989. *La Bible d'Alexandrie, ii, L'Exode* (Paris: Les Éditions du Cerf)

[5] I am most grateful to M. N. A. Bockmuehl for comments and suggestions.

R. Le Déaut, 1984. 'La Septante, un Targum?', in R. Kuntzmann and J. Schlosser (eds.), *Études sur le judaïsme hellénistique* (Paris: Les Éditions du Cerf), 147–95

C. F. D. Moule, 1977. *The Origin of Christology* (Cambridge: Cambridge University Press)

J. L. W. Schaper, 1995. *Eschatology in the Greek Psalter* (WUNT ii.76, Tübingen: Mohr/Siebeck)

E. Schürer and M. Goodman, 1986. *E. Schürer, Geschichte des jüdischen volkes im Zeitalter Jesu Christi* (3rd–4th edn., Leipzig, 1901–9); ET *The History of the Jewish People in the Age of Jesus Christ*, revised by G. Vermes, F. Millar, M. Black, M. Goodman and P. Vermes (i, ii, iii.1, iii.2; Edinburgh: T&T Clark), iii.1, 470–704

L. Seeligmann, 1948. *The Septuagint Version of Isaiah* (Leiden: Brill)

J. P. M. Sweet, 1965. 'The Theory of Miracles in the Wisdom of Solomon', in C. F. D. Moule (ed.), *Miracles* (London: Mowbray), 115–26

———, 1979. *Revelation* (London: SCM Press)

M. H. Williams, 'Exarchon: an Unsuspected Jewish Liturgical Title from Ancient Rome', *JJS* li (2000), 77–87, repr. in M. H. Williams, *Jews in a Graeco-Roman Environment* (WUNT 312, Tübingen, 2013), 141–53

Synagogue and Church in the Roman Empire

9

Messianism among Jews and Christians in the Second Century

I. Introduction

The only difference between Jews and Christians, according to Peter in the *Clementine Recognitions*, concerns the advent of the messiah: 'inter nos atque ipsos de hoc est solo discidium'.[1] Comparable opinions appear in authors who are more central in the apologetic tradition. In Justin's *Dialogue* the Jew Trypho ascribes the neglect of the law by Christians to their error concerning the messiah, an error 'which Justin has propounded zealously (*Dial.* 8). Tertullian similarly concludes that no question is more disputed between Jews and Christians than the coming of the Christ, 'nec alia magis inter nos et illos conpulsatio est quam quod iam venisse non credunt' (*Apol.* 21, 15).[2] Hence, 'credere *in Christum*' became shorthand for the transition from Judaism to Christianity.[3]

This view of the difference between Jews and Christians as essentially or mainly relating to the messiah is already common in the New Testament,[4] but it has long seemed that it may rest on an illusion. For the Jews, in reality, was not the law the principal thing? Thus, the Mishnah compiled in Galilee at the end of the second century has little to say concerning the messiah, and in the diaspora the synagogues, focal points of Jewish life, were associated especially

[1] *Rec. Clem.* i, 50, 5; cf. 43, 2: 'de hoc enim solo nobis qui credimus in Iesum, adversum non credentes Iudaeos videtur esse differentia'.

[2] Further comparable statements are gathered in the commentary by J. E. B. Mayor, *Q. S. F. Tertulliani Apologeticus* (Cambridge, 1917), *ad loc.*

[3] For example, Justin, *Dial.* 47, 1 (πιστεύειν); Pseudo-Cyprian, *ad Vigilium* (the Jew Papiscus 'et in Jesum Christum filium Dei credidit'); *Epistula Severi* 12 (826) 'in Christum crede' (advice to unbaptized Jew; fifth-century Minorca); so already sometimes, perhaps, the Fourth Gospel, e.g. 12:42).

[4] For example, at Acts 9:22, 18:5 (cf. 2:35, 4:18, 5:40 and 42); John 7:40–52.

with the reading of the law.[5] Correspondingly, both the New Testament and the later Christian anti-Jewish writings envisage important disagreements on the subject of the law, for example at John 5:16; Justin, *Dial.* 8, 4. Further, the Christian minority was not necessarily important in Jewish eyes. Many therefore conclude that the picture of a lively *conpulsatio* between Jews and Christians concerning the messiah is Christianized and distorted; warnings on these lines are given, for example, by E. P. Sanders in the New Testament field and by Johann Maier on Jewish—Christian relations in the patristic age.[6]

Nevertheless, if the patristic testimony magnifies the preoccupations of the minority in the imagined debate—the Christian side, it also reflects genuine interests of the majority—the Jewish side. Thus, the LXX Pentateuch already included striking expressions of messianic hope (notably at Gen. 49; Num. 24:7, 17), and such expressions are abundant in the Pentateuchal Targums.[7] Further, Jewish concern with the early Christians, and with Christian messianic hopes in particular, is attested by the traces of Jewish anti-Christian polemic, with special reference to the Christ of the Christians, found in Celsus as quoted by Origen and in rabbinic sources.[8] Here, indeed, J. Maier is prominent among those who interpret the passages otherwise, but the present writer would submit that his reconstruction of their prehistory does something less than justice to the striking accord on this subject between Jewish and pagan sources, and between these sources and the allegations of Jewish criticisms in Justin and Tertullian.[9] In the convergence of these indications of Jewish messianic hopes and anti-Christian polemic with the patristic notices of Jewish-Christian *conpulsatio* on the messiah there appears a basis for the investigation of messianism as a phenomenon common to both Jews and Christians in the second century.

[5] See Acts 15:21; Tertullian, *Apol.* 18, 8 ('palam lectitant').

[6] E. P. Sanders, *Jesus and Judaism* (London, 1985), 281–6 and n. 57 (circumcision was the focus of disagreement, although Christians may also have suffered for the sake of their loyalty to a discredited leader); J. Maier, *Jesus von Nazareth in der talmudischen Überlieferung* (Darmstadt, 1978), 6f. and *Jüdische Auseinandersetzung mit dem Christentum in der Antike* (Darmstadt, 1982), 200–2.

[7] J. Lust, 'Messianism and Septuagint', in J. A. Emerton (ed.), *Congress volume: Salamanca, 1983* (SVT xxxvi; Leiden, 1985), 174–91, accepts as messianic the passages cited here, but holds that the messianic character of Septuagintal interpretation is often over-estimated; on the other hand, some further passages could probably be added to his dossier of messianic texts. On the Targums see M. Pérez Fernández, *Tradiciones mesiánicas en el Targum Palestinense* (Valencia and Jerusalem, 1981).

[8] Celsus in passages such as those quoted by Origen, *c. Celsum* i, 28, 32 (on the Jewish source see E. Bammel, *Judaica* (Tübingen, 1986), 265–83); Tosefta, *Hullin* ii, 22, 24; b. *Sanh.* 43a.

[9] Maier, *Jesus*, 219–37, 264f., discussed by W. Horbury, *Jews and Christians in Contact and Controversy* (Edinburgh, 1998), 105–8.

Here the attempt is made to trace a persistent dependence of the Christian minority on the Jewish majority in messianic hope. Such a dependence may be defined as cultural, in so far as the Christians, despite the distinctive features of their teachings and institutions, formed a kind of subculture of the Jews (as is especially evident in early Christian Old Testament interpretation).[10] It can also be called a doctrinal and institutional dependence, however, in that teachings and customs were often formed by an instinct, to be illustrated below, either to follow or to differ from what was perceived as the Jewish norm.

The persistence of this dependence on the side of the Christians during the second century may also, however, be significant for the understanding of contemporary Jewish opinion. In Justin's *Dialogue* his debate with Trypho on Christianity is preceded by a conversation between Trypho and his friends about 'the war in Judaea'—Bar Cocheba's revolt (Justin, *Dial.* 9, 3). This touch in a literary work once again suggests that Christian second-century sources may reflect not simply the Judaism of the pre-Christian period, but also something of the outlook of contemporary Jews. The persistence of Christian dependence in messianic questions would then indicate the continuing importance of messianic interpretations of the law among Jews under the Antonine and Severan emperors, and might illuminate the historical background of the Mishnah of R. Judah ha-Nasi.

It will now be asked first, therefore, if one can properly speak of a 'messianism', sensitive to contemporary Jewish opinion, among Christians of the second century; and secondly, if the hypothesis of a dependence of Christians upon Jews in messianic hope finds confirmation in, and thereby sheds light upon, contemporary Jewish history.

II. Messianism among the Christians

The concepts of Christ current among second-century Christians have often been discussed with reference to the history of doctrine;[11] but perhaps it is also

[10] For example in Christian use of revised Jewish Greek versions ('Theodotion' and Aquila), or Christian inquiry into the biblical canon 'according to the Hebrews' (e.g. Origen, preface to *com.* Ps. i–xxv, quoted by Eusebius, *H.E.* vi, 25, 1–2).

[11] For example by P. Beskow, *Rex Gloriae* (Stockholm, 1962), 187–211, and *passim*; J. N. D. Kelly, *Early Christian Doctrines* (London, [5]1977), 138–54; J. Daniélou, *A History of Early Christian Doctrine before the Council of Nicaea*, 3 vols. (ET, London and Philadelphia, 1964, 1973, 1977), *passim*.

proper to speak of them as evidences of a messianism. They begin to appear in this light when a connection is made between two well-known manifestations of second-century piety which are not always viewed together, the cult of Christ, and chiliasm.[12]

The cult of Christ can be sensed especially in the phenomenon of hymns sung 'Christo, quasi deo' (Pliny, *ep.* 96, 7).[13] Seen from without, this element in Christian worship perhaps recalled particularly the cults of heroes and of sovereigns.[14] Thus, in the hymn of Clement of Alexandria, which is redolent of παιδεία both in the sense of education and in the sense of a corps of παῖδες, the Christ is hailed as king βασιλεῦ ἁγίων … βασιλεῦ παίδων ἀνεπάφων (lines 11, 31–2 of the hymn in Clement of Alexandria, *Paed.* iii, 12).[15] Through the testimony tradition it was emphasized not only that the Christ came 'as a little boy … who had neither form nor beauty' (Isa. 53:2, LXX), a point advanced by Clement against esteem for merely outward grace, but also that he would come again as 'the king' called 'fair in beauty beyond the sons of men' (Ps. 44 [45]:2–3, LXX).[16] Although these differing aspects could cause him to be imagined as a seemingly insignificant boy[17] or a Protean figure,[18] his beauty was pre-eminent in art and hymnody, and in many visions.

[12] The accord between Christian chiliasm and Jewish messianic hopes is underlined with reference to the land by R. L. Wilken, 'Early Christian Chiliasm, Jewish Messianism, and the Idea of the Holy Land', *HTR* lxxix (1986), 298–307.

[13] Beskow, *Rex Gloriae*, 162–5.

[14] Justin, *I Apol.* 21–2 (Hermes, Asclepius, Dionysus, the emperors), with commentary by A. W. F. Blunt, *The Apologies of Justin Martyr* (Cambridge, 1911), 34–8; Celsus in Origen, *c. Celsum*, iii. 36 (Antinous; meant as an insult, but having enough truth in it to sting; see below on Christ as παῖς).

[15] Note the addition of βασιλεύς in Christian adaptation of the Fourth Eclogue (Oration of Constantine, 19). On Clement's hymn the present writer would venture to diverge in one point of emphasis from the commentary by H.-I. Marrou, in C. Mondésert, C. Matray and H.-I. Marrou, *Clément d'Alexandrie: Le Pédagogue* iii (Paris, 1970), 192–207; παῖς and παῖδες in the hymn seem to refer not just to early childhood, the sense stressed by Marrou (e.g. in the summary, p. 192, n. 2), but also to later boyhood (cf. n. 21, below). Thus in lines 31–2, just quoted, the sense of παῖδες ἀνέπαφοι is perhaps not wholly represented in his rendering 'enfants innocents', for the Greek phrase also bears some correspondence to 'pueri casti', a phrase used to describe the male section of a double choir singing a hymn by Horace, *carmen saeculare*, line 6.

[16] Irenaeus, *Haer.* iii, 19 (20), 2 (alluding to both verses) and Tertullian, *adv. Marc.* iii, 7, paralleled in *adv. Iud.* 14 (quoting both verses); see Cyprian, *test.* ii, 13 (Isa. 53:2, and other texts quoted by Tertullian, *loc. cit.*), 29 (Ps. 44:3); on Isa. 53:2, cf. Justin Martyr, *Dial.* 14, 8 (the two advents) and Clement of Alexandria, *Paed.* iii, 1, 3 (with the note by Marrou, *ad loc.*), *Strom.* iii, 17; vi, 17 (beauty). Second- and third-century texts on Christ's outward appearance are gathered by W. Bauer, *Das Leben Jesu im Zeitalter der neutestamentlichen Apokryphen* (1909, reprinted Darmstadt, 1967), 311–14.

[17] Acts of John 88 (boy on the sea-shore); Pseudo-Cyprian, *de montibus Sina et Sion*, 13–14 (servant-boy guarding vineyard in hide).

[18] *Acta Io.* 88–91; Origen, *c. Celsum* vi, 77.

Thus, Christ appears in catacomb paintings as a young shepherd in the likeness of Orpheus or Hermes;[19] a literary analogue is the description of the Orpheus-like minstrelsy of Christ the Word in Clement of Alexandria, *Protr.* i.[20] Similarly, Christ receives the title παῖς in the hymn of Clement (παῖς κρατερός, line 61), not without the biblical overtones of 'servant' and 'son', but mainly in the sense of a divine 'youth'.[21] It is as a shepherd and 'a most fair young man' (νεανίας) that he appears in Perpetua's vision,[22] as in others recounted in the acts of the martyrs and the apocryphal acts of the apostles.[23] The same concept is perhaps reflected in Justin Martyr, i *Apol.* 35, where *bēn* in Isa. 9:6 (lxx υἱός) is rendered νεανίσκος.

In the cult of Christ, therefore, as attested in hymnody, art, and the associated visions of 'the king ... fair in beauty', he was conceived on the model of the divine *iuvenis*, the model to which Virgil and Horace had assimilated the young Augustus,[24] sometimes against the same pastoral background.[25]

One more aspect of the cult of Christ deserves special note in the present connection. The conceptions of Christ just mentioned bear many resemblances not only to gentile conceptions of heroes and rulers, but also to Jewish descriptions of the messiah current in the Graeco-Roman world. Thus, the Orpheus-Christ in art and literature has long been thought to develop a Jewish Orpheus-David (n. 20, above). Comparably, A. Hultgård has suggested that the messianic teachings of the Testaments of the Twelve Patriarchs were

[19] J. Stevenson, *The Catacombs* (London, 1978), 100f.; R. L. P. Milburn in G. W. H. Lampe (ed.), *The Cambridge History of the Bible* ii (Cambridge, 1969), 283.

[20] The view that this Orphic Christ is adapted from a Jewish Orphic David as represented at Dura (third century) and Gaza (sixth century) (so, for instance, W. K. C. Guthrie, *Orpheus and Greek Religion* (London, [2]1952, 264), is challenged by C. Murray, 'The Christian Orpheus', in *Cahiers archéologiques* xxvi (1977), 19–27 and re-asserted by H. Stern, 'De l'Orphée juif et chrétien', *ibid.*, 28; it is consistent with Ps. 151 as attested in Hebrew in 11Qpsa, although this form of the text is probably not original (M. Smith, 'Psalm 151, David, Jesus, and Orpheus', *ZAW* xciii [1981], 247–53 [250 and n. 8]).

[21] Solomon is somewhat comparably called παῖς Ἑβραῖος by Clement, *Protr.* viii, with prime reference to the young king as 'a youth of good parts' (παῖς εὐφυής, Wisd. 8:19) who prayed for wisdom (1 Kgs. 3:7–9; Wisd. 7:7–14); that παῖς in Wisd. 8:19 can indicate present adolescence as well as past childhood is shown by C. Larcher, *Le Livre de la Sagesse*, ii (Paris, 1984), *ad loc.*

[22] Greek Martyrdom of Perpetua, 20 (ed. J. A. Robinson, Cambridge 1891, 77).

[23] Several instances are gathered by G. W. H. Lampe, *A Patristic Greek Lexicon* (Oxford, 1961), s. vv. νεανίας, νεανίσκος. Among these the Acts of Xanthippe 15 (ed. M. R. James, *Apocrypha Anecdota*, Cambridge 1893, 68), in which Christ in the form of a young man takes the guise of Paul, recalls the story that Philumene, the prophetess of Apelles, saw visions of a boy who was sometimes Christ, sometimes Paul (F. J. A. Hort, 'Apelles', in *Dictionary of Christian Biography*, i (London, 1877), 127f.).

[24] So Virgil, *ecl.* i, 42; *geo.* i, 500; Horace, *carm.* i, 2, 42; cf. Cicero, *Phil.* v, 42 'divinus adulescentulus'; see E. Fraenkel, *Horace* (Oxford, 1957), 214–19.

[25] Stevenson, *Catacombs*, 100.

influenced by ruler-cults.[26] Further, there are kingly epiphanies of the messiah in two writings probably composed about the beginning of the second century, Fourth Ezra (the man from the sea) and the Fifth Book of the Sibylline Oracles (the man from the heavens).[27] The Jewish literature of testaments, prophecies and oracles was continued by Christians, as happened with each of the three books just mentioned. Herein it appears how the cult of Christ was in substantial continuity with Jewish messianism, despite resemblances to pagan cults and the Christian assertion *adversus Iudaeos* that the Christ had come. Thus, in the Latin Fourth Ezra, the second chapter belongs to the second-century Christian composition sometimes called Fifth Ezra; and here is found, prefaced to the book which ends with the Jewish vision of the man from the sea, a Christian vision of the expected 'shepherd', the young son of God who stands on Mount Sion crowning the saints, 'iuvenis statura celsus' (4 Ezra 2:42).[28]

The position taken here may be clarified by reference to a well-known divergence of opinion on the origin of christology. In the influential view of W. Bousset, the cult of Christ as Kyrios arose among diaspora Christians in Antioch and elsewhere by derivation from the gentile cults of 'lords many' (1 Cor. 8:5).[29] M. Hengel and C. F. D. Moule are important among those who have shown that, by contrast with this view, the thought-world and speech of the Jewish communities are more likely to have been seed-beds of the cult of Christ.[30] Here, in general accord with their indications of Jewish origin, it is suggested that the second-century cult of Christ, with all its points of resemblance to the cults of heroes or sovereigns, is in the main a development of Jewish presentations of the messiah;[31] but it is also held that these Jewish

[26] A. Hultgård, *L'eschatologie des Testaments des Douze Patriarches*, 2 vols. (Uppsala, 1977 and 1982), i, 326–76.

[27] Royal elements in these passages are noted by W. Horbury, 'The Messianic Associations of "the Son of Man" ', in *JTS* N.S. xxxvi (1985), 33–55 (44f. = pp. 168–9, above).

[28] The possibility that this passage may reflect pre- or non-Christian conceptions of the 'son of God' is envisaged by R. A. Kraft, 'Towards Assessing the Latin Text of "5 Ezra": the "Christian" Connection', *HTR* lxxix (1986), 158–69 (166). If the passage is Jewish and not Christianized, it will be a further attestation of gentile influence on Jewish messianism, but its adoption by Christians will still exemplify the continuity between that messianism and the cult of Christ.

[29] W. Bousset, *Kyrios Christos* (Göttingen, ²1921), especially 99f. followed by R. Bultmann, *Theologie des Neuen Testaments*, § 7 (Tübingen, 1948), 52.

[30] M. Hengel, *The Son of God* (ET London, 1975), especially 17–56; C. F. D. Moule, *The Origin of Christology* (Cambridge, 1977), especially 36–43, 148–50.

[31] Jewish antecedents to the cult in particular are considered by Beskow, *Rex Gloriae*, especially 45–7, 157–60.

presentations, like their Christian developments, had themselves inevitably taken forms influenced by the gentile cults. The gentile influence which Bousset stressed is therefore here thought to have affected the Jewish as well as the Christian phases of messianism.

Continuity between Jewish and Christian hopes has been more generally recognized in the second phenomenon under review, the chiliasm of Christian second-century writers. Thus Jerome states it as a dilemma that, if he takes the millennium of the Apocalypse according to the letter, he will be Judaizing; but that, if he expounds it spiritually, he will seem to contradict many of the older authorities, 'multorum veterum videbimur opinionibus contraire' (Jerome, *com. Is.*, introduction to book xviii). His list of these authorities runs from the second to the third century, comprising Tertullian, Victorinus, Lactantius, and 'among the Greek writers, Irenaeus (to pass over others)'; of these 'others', the most important second-century writers are the author of the Epistle of Barnabas, Papias and Justin Martyr.[32] Justin viewed the millennium in Jerusalem as an important part of a right faith (*Dial.* 80–1), and although he knew of good Christians who denied it, and the question was later warmly disputed, there is no doubt of the widespread second-century influence of chiliastic hopes. Their roots were in Old Testament promises as interpreted by the Jews, and conjoined (as in Justin) with prophecies in the gospels and the Apocalypse.[33]

Much else in the Christian literary inheritance gave general encouragement to concrete expectations. Thus the work comprising Luke and Acts anticipates an apologist like Justin not only in outlining a gospel to the gentiles, but also in presenting messianic hopes with emphasis on Jerusalem.[34] Correspondingly, second-century writers who are not millennarian may still retain a lively and concrete hope, and these communal expectations have left their trace even in Clement of Alexandria.[35] Nevertheless, Christian chiliasm, and other concrete

[32] The views of the second-century chiliasts and their successors are discussed by Kelly, *Doctrine*, 474–5, 479–80, and K. Berger, *Die griechische Daniel-Diegese* (Leiden, 1976), 80–7.

[33] C. Mazzucco and E. Pietrella, 'Il rapporto tra la concezione del millennio dei primi autori cristiani e l'Apocalisse di Giovanni', *Augustinianum* xviii (1978), 29–45, conclude that second-century authors depend mainly on Old Testament sources, a point which underlines the resemblance of Christian and Jewish hopes.

[34] L. Gaston, *No Stone on Another* (Leiden, 1970), 244–369, with reference to such passages as Luke 2:38, 21:8, 24:21; Acts 1:6.

[35] M. Mees, 'Jetzt und Dann in der Eschatologie Klemens von Alexandrien', *Augustinianum* xviii (1978), 127–37 (136f.).

expressions of Christian hope, are unlikely to be indebted to the Jews only through the literary tradition. The importance of the contemporary Jewish community in Christian expectation is evident, for instance, in Marcion, who seems to have understood the prophets as genuinely foretelling the advent of the messiah of the demiurge, 'in restitutionem iudaici status' (Tertullian, *adv. Marc.* iv, 6, 3).[36]

Anti-gnostic controversy is notable among other factors making for literal interpretation of 'the promises',[37] but the importance of the Jewish position in this regard is underlined by Christian sensitivity to Jewish criticism of Christian hopes. The Jew of Celsus claimed, for example, that the Christians' Christ was not like a good general, because he could not keep his followers' loyalty (Origen, *c. Celsum* ii, 12; cf. 29). The comparison implies that he lacked the generalship which was a standard attribute of the ideal Hellenistic monarch, and was ascribed to Moses, Joshua, and the king messiah.[38] Origen answers partly by noting that even great philosophers have been deserted, and partly and more comprehensively by referring to Christian hopes for a second coming, when their Christ will manifest all the attributes of power and glory desiderated by Jewish critics. Another comprehensive Christian defence was the claim that the promise of the kingdom to the Jews had been transferred to the church; in Fifth Ezra, for example, the Lord commands 'Adnuntia populo meo, quoniam dabo eis regnum Hierusalem, quod daturus eram Israhel' (4 Ezra 2:10). More particular answers were given with regard to the individual prophecies. Thus Mic. 4:1–7, on the future reign of the Lord in Mount Sion, is known by Justin Martyr to be understood messianically by Jewish teachers; but he claims that the afflicted and cast out who will be gathered in (verse 4) are the Christians, not the Jews who have been justly punished and cast out in war (Justin, *Dial.* 109–10).[39]

The lively hopes focused in the widespread second-century chiliasm can now, therefore, be viewed together with the equally widespread cult of Christ. In both cases the Christian evidence has seemed to be moulded in large part

[36] E. Evans (ed. and tr.), *Tertullian adversus Marcionem*, 2 vols. (Oxford, 1972), I, xiii; II, 274.

[37] M. Simonetti, *Profilo storico dell'esegesi patristica* (Rome, 1981) p. 29.

[38] Beskow, *Rex Gloriae*, 209–10 (generalship as royal attribute applied to Christ); see Clement of Alexandria, *Ecl. proph.* 6, 2–3 (Moses and Joshua); cf. *Ps. Sol.* 17:33–7.

[39] If Justin correctly reports Jewish opinion here, and if Jews took dispersion after war to include exile and captivity under Hadrian after the Second Revolt (as Jewish prophetic interpretation transmitted by Jerome [e.g. on Obad. 20] suggests), their understanding of this oracle implies lively hopes for an ingathering, and should be noted in evaluation of reports of Jewish unrest at the end of the century (nn. 54 and 58, below).

by past and present Jewish piety. The cult of Christ is not always closely linked to the hope of his second coming, as Clement of Alexandria shows; but such a link will have been made where this hope was lively, as in the acts of Perpetua. In that conjunction it seems possible to see a Christian messianism properly so called, that is, the robust expectation of a king messiah, who receives ardent communal loyalty. The point is underlined by J. Lawson's observation, that for Irenaeus the hope of a kingdom of Christ and the saints in Jerusalem belonged to the emotional centre of his faith.[40]

Equally, however, this Christian messianism seems to have been a neuralgic point. Here, particularly, the Christians were sensitive to the corresponding beliefs of the Jewish communities, and here the Jews attempted to quell the unauthorized Christian variations of Judaism. The apologetic picture of Jewish—Christian debate concentrated on the messiah was in large measure historically justified. The Christians were doubtless the more profoundly affected by the exchange, for they felt themselves a minority beside the 'populus amplus' of the Jews and their proselytes.[41] Now, therefore, it can be asked whether the hypothesis of the dependence of Christians on Jews in messianism, which has seemed defensible thus far, finds confirmation in the history of the Jews themselves.

III. Jewish history in the second century

The part played by messianic hopes in Jewish history during the second century is debated. It is clear, however, that the century was marked by disturbances among many of the Jews of the Roman Empire, and among inhabitants of the province of Judaea, whether Jewish, Greek or Roman. Four Parthian wars were waged by Rome (under Trajan and Marcus Aurelius, and twice under Septimius Severus); in the second half of the century there were two revolts of Romans in Syria, under Avidius Cassius and Pescennius Niger; and near the beginning of the century there were two great Jewish revolts, under Trajan principally in the Diaspora and under Hadrian in Judaea.

[40] J. Lawson, *The Biblical Theology of St. Irenaeus* (London, 1948), 288–90.

[41] Tertullian, *adv. Marc.* iii, 21, 3: 'et revincet populum amplum [Isa. 2:3], ipsorum imprimis Iudaeorum et proselytorum'.

In these two Jewish revolts, messianism was probably important under Trajan, and almost certainly so under Hadrian, because the Jewish leaders will have been viewed in the light of the general atmosphere of communal hope.[42] Up to a point this observation is also true of R. Judah 'the Prince'—*ha-naśî*—at the end of the century, when he was recognized by the Romans as head or 'patriarch' of the Jewish community; the age of the Severi in which this took place appears largely if not wholly as an oasis of peace for the Jews of the holy land,[43] and the development of the Jewish patriarchate, accompanied by the editing of the Mishnah, marked the beginning of the ascendancy of the rabbinic movement.[44]

The dependence of Christians on Jews in messianism can be discerned (it is here suggested) in the literary deposit of three disturbances in second-century Judaean history. First, the argument in *Barn.* 16 is probably to be understood as presupposing that Jews are rebuilding the Jerusalem temple with Roman sanction, as 'the servants of the enemy' (οἱ τῶν ἔχθρων ὑπηρέται, 16.4).[45] Christians, including the writer, believe that this is happening (a corresponding Jewish belief is probably reflected in rabbinic midrash);[46] and the writer evidently fears, in this chapter as in earlier passages of the epistle, that the addressees may go over to the Jews (cf. *Barn.* 3.6, 4.6). For these Christians the Romans are 'the enemy', as in the Apocalypse; that is to say, those addressed in Barnabas share the Jewish view of Rome which appears in 4 Ezra and the Fifth Sibylline book.[47] An oracle, perhaps adapted from Dan. 9:24–7, is now quoted (*Barn.* 16.6) as a promise of reconstruction: 'for it is written, that when the week is ended a temple of God shall be built gloriously in the name of the Lord' (cf. *Sib.* v, 415–33, also with Danielic allusions).[48] The writer gives a spiritual interpretation (16:7–10), probably because his addressees understood

[42] See W. Horbury, *The Jewish Revolts under Trajan and Hadrian*, forthcoming.

[43] See M. Avi-Yonah, *The Jews of Palestine* (ET Oxford, 1976), 39–42; Severus and Antoninus favoured the Jews, according to Jerome on Dan. 11:34 ('Judaeos plurimum dilexerunt').

[44] Avi-Yonah, *Jews of Palestine*, 54–64.

[45] P. Richardson and M. B. Shukster, 'Barnabas, Nerva and the Yavnean Rabbis', *JTS* N.S. xxxiv (1983), 31–55; on further debate see Horbury, *Jewish War under Trajan and Hadrian* (Cambridge, 2014), 298–300. Hadrian's temple of Zeus is preferred by R. Hvalvik, *The Struggle for Scripture and Covenant* (WUNT ii.82, Tübingen, 1996), 18–23; but on this view Barn. 16 becomes harshly paradoxical.

[46] *Ber. R.* 64, 10, discussed by Richardson and Shukster, *Barnabas*, 47–50. Here Rome orders rebuilding, a point not noted by Hvalvik, 20–1.

[47] On the two Jewish sources see G. Stemberger, *Die römische Herrschaft im Urteil der Juden* (Darmstadt, 1983), 25–30, 53–8.

[48] Allusions to Dan. 7:13, 22 are made in *Sib.* v, 414, 432.

the promise *ad litteram*; thus Cerinthus, according to his critics, expected the restoration of the sacrifices.[49] The rebuilding of the temple could be expected of the messiah, as appears, among other places, in the Sibylline passage just noted; and it seems that the Christians to whom *Barn.* 16 was addressed were sensitive to the messianic hopes of the Jewish community, and were drawn to it when those hopes appeared to be in course of realization.

Secondly, Bar Cocheba is said by Justin Martyr to have commanded Christians to be punished severely, 'if they would not deny Jesus as the messiah, and blaspheme' (Justin, I, *Apol.* 31; quoted by Eusebius, *H.E.* IV, 8, 4). In the light of the susceptibility to Jewish hopes and the hostility to Rome just noted in Barnabas, it would not have been unreasonable for Bar Cocheba to expect that many Christians would come over to the Jewish community at the time of his success. Justin, in his *Dialogue*, reserves a particularly strong condemnation for those who have once acknowledged the Christ of the Christians, but then 'go over for whatever cause to the polity of the law, having denied that he is the Christ' (*Dial.* 47, 4–5). To make this denial, to 'blaspheme' (Acts 26:11; cf. 1 Cor. 12:3), sealed the transition, just as the confession of Jesus as Christ (see n. 3, above) marked the transition to the Christian body. In view of the importance of Bar Cocheba's revolt in the background of the *Dialogue*, noted in section I, above, it is possible that those who Judaized in the revolt are included in Justin's condemnation. However this may be, the likelihood that some Christians did so is underlined by the great praise of the martyrs who would not confess a false Christ of the Jews, in the Ethiopic text of the Apocalypse of Peter.[50] In this second instance from Judaean history the attractive force of messianic hopes in realization was strengthened by the pressure of persecution, but it is probable that, as appeared from *Barn.* 16, many Christians found it natural to Judaize in the atmosphere of messianism.

In the third instance, from the reign of Septimius Severus, historical reconstructions differ radically; but much of the sparse evidence becomes consistent if there was Jewish messianism in Judaea, and Christian sympathy with it. Tertullian, arguing that the millennium will be enjoyed on earth

[49] Gaius and Denys of Alexandria, as reported by Eusebius, *H.E.* iii, 28, 2 and 5.

[50] *Apocalypse of Peter*, 2, considered and translated by C. Maurer and H. Duensing in E. Hennecke, W. Schneemelcher and R. McL. Wilson (eds.), *New Testament Apocrypha* (ET, 2 vols., London, 1963 and 1965), ii, 664, 669; an allusion to Bar Cocheba can be detected with fair probability, but as usual in such prophecies the expressions are veiled and traditional, and the oracle could also be understood of an Antichrist not identified more particularly.

not in existing conditions but in a new Jerusalem which will come down from heaven, appeals to the sight of a heavenly city seen in Judaea 'during the eastern expedition'—that is, Severus' second Parthian campaign of 197; 'constat enim ethnicis quoque testibus in Iudaea per dies quadraginta matutinis momentis civitatem de caelo pependisse' (Tertullian, *adv. Marc.* iii, 24, 4).[51] The setting of the 'eastern expedition' recalls the constant Jewish hope and Roman fear of Parthian conquest, a conception which formed a lively element in both Jewish and Christian messianic expectation, particularly in connection with the return of the ten tribes from beyond the Euphrates.[52] Eusebius' Chronicle has an ambiguous notice (for the year 197) 'Iudaicum et Samariticum bellum'; and in the *Historia Augusta* the life of Severus, thought to rest on sources of some value, has well-known notices of a 'Jewish triumph' for the young Caracalla 'because Severus had been successful in Syria too', of rights conferred upon the Palestinians, and of a prohibition against the adoption of Judaism or of Christianity (HA, *Severus*, 16; 7; 17, 1).[53] These pieces of information cohere if Eusebius' phrase is taken to indicate Jewish and Samaritan unrest;[54] gentile Palestinians were encouraged, but Jews and Christians were punished. The interpretation reported by Tertullian of the appearance in the Judaean morning skies would then reflect the hopes of Jews in revolt at a time of Parthian war, and the corresponding expectations of Christians, probably including some in the army.[55] The Jewish and Christian views would have combined to impress the 'gentile witnesses', probably fellow-soldiers, whom Tertullian mentions. His own use of the story shows how readily it fitted Christian hopes, which at this time and in the following years were stirred by persecution in Syria and Egypt, among other places.[56] Serapion, bishop of Antioch 199–211, wrote a lost work addressed to Domnus, who had Judaized during persecution

[51] Evans, *Tertullian adversus Marcionem* i, xviii, 246–9.

[52] See, for example, Josephus, *B.J.* i, 5, *Ant.* xi, 133; Simeon b. Yohai (mid second century) on Mic. 5:4, in *Lam. R.* i, 13; 4 Ezra 13:45f.; *Sib.* iv, 138f.; Rev. 16:12; Avi-Yonah, *Jews of Palestine*, 66, 83; M. Sordi, *Commodianus*, Carmen apol. 892 *ss.*: rex ab oriente, *Augustinianum* xxii (1982), 203–10.

[53] Various interpretations are discussed in the commentary by M. Stern, *Greek and Latin Authors on Jews and Judaism* ii (Jerusalem, 1980), nos. 513–15.

[54] Sulpicius Severus and Orosius so interpreted it; Denys of Tell Mahre and Bar Hebraeus understood it as 'war between Jews and Samaritans', the sense preferred in a review of these interpretations by Avi-Yonah, *Jews of Palestine*, 77.

[55] On Christian legionaries in the time of Tertullian, see A. Harnack, *Militia Christi* (1905, ET Philadelphia, 1981), 74–84 (not considering this passage).

[56] R. B. Tollinton, *Clement of Alexandria*, 2 vols. (London, 1914), ii, 314–24 (Appendix I).

(Eusebius, *H.E.* vi, 12, 1). On the other hand, the evidence in Jerome and rabbinic sources for favour shown to the Jews (and especially their patriarchs) by the Severi, and the lack of clear rabbinic reference to rebellion, lead perhaps the majority of historians to conclude that there was no Jewish revolt in Judaea at this time, and to interpret Eusebius' Chronicle in some other ways.[57] The approach to messianism followed here might suggest that there is weight in the opinion of the minority, notably W. H. C. Frend, who affirm (with special reference to contemporary Christian history) the likelihood of Jewish disturbances.[58] Rabbinic sources show that neither the reign of Septimius Severus nor the patriarchal co-operation with Rome was universally popular among Jews.[59] The dynasty of R. Judah the Prince would then represent a Jewish élite who, as on other occasions in Jewish history (and as happened with comparable friends of Rome in other provinces) were not always successful in controlling anti-Roman feeling.[60] In this case, then, the hypothesis of Christian dependence on Judaism in messianism would receive some confirmation from its utility as a key to otherwise ambiguous evidence for Jewish second-century history.

In Judaea, therefore, it seems that Jewish messianism made a strong impression upon Christians, who had closely similar hopes and who also sometimes shared Jewish attitudes to Rome. Influence from the Jewish side emerged clearly from *Barn.* 16, and in the revolt under Hadrian it probably prompted agreement as well as reaction among Christians. With these instances in view, it seems likely that the same influence helps to explain the disputed evidence for Jewish disturbances under Septimius Severus, and that

[57] See n. 54, above, and Stern, *Authors*, II, 623–5, 627; E. M. Smallwood, *The Jews under Roman Rule* (1976, corrected reprint Leiden, 1981), 488–9, allows the possibility of a temporary increase in national unrest, but no more.

[58] Tollinton, *Clement*, 318f., and Juster, cited by Stern, *Authors*, ii, 624 (the Jews had sided with Niger); W. H. C. Frend, *Martyrdom and Persecution in the Early Church* (Oxford, 1965), 319–21 and 'Open Questions Concerning the Christians and the Roman Empire in the Age of the Severi', *JTS* N.S. xxxv (1974), 338–51 (343).

[59] *Midrash Zuta* on Ct. I, 6 (ed. S. Buber, 14), in S. Krauss, *Griechen und Römer* [Monumenta Talmudica I] (1914), reprinted Darmstadt, 1972), 63, no. 117 (text, translation and notes), gives the reign of Severus as the third of three long reigns which the Jews were destined to endure as a punishment; Babylonian Talmud, *B.M.* 83b (objections to collaboration), discussed with other comparable material by Avi-Yonah, *Jews of Palestine*, 71.

[60] Smallwood, *Jews under Roman Rule*, 486, emphasizes the strength of the anti-Roman feeling opposed and sometimes shared by the patriarchs; on the rôle of upper-class provincials in quelling unrest, see P. A. Brunt, 'The Romanization of the Local Ruling Classes in the Roman Empire', in D. M. Pippidi (ed.), *Assimilation et résistance à la culture gréco-romaine dans le monde ancien* (Bucharest and Paris, 1976), 161–73; reprinted in P. A. Brunt, *Roman Imperial Themes* (Oxford, 1990), 267–81, where see also 517–31, on the rôle of the élite in the First Revolt.

Christians then also responded sensitively to the expectant atmosphere of the Jewish communities.[61]

IV. Conclusion

In sum, therefore, it seems that the apologetic depiction of Jewish-Christian debate on the messiah, noted above in Pseudo-Clement, Justin and Tertullian, reflects not only the characteristic claims of the Christians but also something of the authentic messianism of Jews in the second century. This reflection indicates the continuing dependence of Christians upon Jews in messianism. Among the Christians, the cult of Christ and chiliasm are both developments of current Jewish messianic thought and expectation, and the two Christian phenomena together form a totality which can properly be called messianism. Christian dependence on the Jews in this sphere finds confirmation in second-century Jewish history, and in turn suggests the continuing importance of messianic hopes in Judaea at the end of the century.

This particular Jewish influence was an important element in the broader cultural influence exerted by the Jewish community on the Christian body. Its effect among the Christians derived especially from their sense of themselves as a minority and as newcomers by comparison with the established 'populus amplus' of the Jews and their proselytes. Accordingly, divergence as well as agreement from Jewish positions can indicate that it was the Jewish positions, first of all, with which Christians thought they should reckon. Hence, despite fierce *conpulsatio* over the advent of the Christ, it remains possible, at least to the time of the compilation of the Mishnah, to speak of *one* messianism of the Jews and of the Christians.

[61] I would envisage a mixture of realism and utopianism throughout the second century in Jewish messianism, rather than the shift away from realism after 135 suggested by A. Oppenheimer, 'Leadership and Messianism in the Time of the Mishnah', in H. Graf Reventlow, *Eschatology in the Bible and in Jewish and Christian Tradition* (Sheffield, 1997), 152–68.

10

Suffering and Messianism in Yose ben Yose

'If the Sage ranked higher than a Prophet, the Precentor [*Vorbeter*] was at the least a Psalmist', wrote Zunz of the post-biblical development in Judaism;[1] but the Sage has had the lion's share of attention from students of rabbinic religion. This is partly, of course, a consequence of Zunz's own conclusion that the surviving relics of early synagogal poetry are post-Talmudic. Since he wrote, however, the Cairo Geniza has multiplied these relics,[2] and it has come to be generally recognized that the early *piyyuṭim* considerably antedate the Arab conquest.[3] Of the earliest poets known by name, Yose ben Yose, Yannai and Kalir, the first two are set at various times in the Amoraic period, up to and including the sixth century.[4] Talmud and liturgy are held to disclose still earlier poems, reciprocally related to midrashic literature in the process of formations.[5] Johann Maier nevertheless still constitutes an admirable exception when he gives space to the early *piyyuṭim* in an account of religion in the Talmudic period.[6]

A story current from the fifth century onwards relates it as remarkable that Eleazar, son of R. Simeon b. Yohai, should have been both a teacher of Scripture and Mishnah and a precentor.[7] The discontinuity as well as the link

1 L. Zunz, *Die Ritus des synagogalen Gottesdienstes geschichtlich entwickelt* (Berlin, 1859), 6.

2 P. E. Kahle, *The Cairo Geniza*, 2nd edn. (Oxford, 1959), 34–48.

3 On the *piyyuṭ* and its origins I. Elbogen, *Der jüdische Gottesdienst in seiner geschichtlichen Entwicklung*, 3rd edn. (Frankfurt am Main, 1931, reprinted Hildesheim, 1962), 280–305 is supplemented in the Hebrew translation, ed. J. Heinemann (Tel Aviv, 1972), 210–28, and translated with the supplements into English by R. P. Scheindlin as I. Elbogen, *Jewish Liturgy: A Comprehensive History* (New York, 1993), 219–37; cf. S. W Baron, *A Social and Religious History of the Jews*, 2nd edn., vol. vii (New York, 1958), 89–105; G. Stemberger, *Geschichte der jüdischen Literatur* (Munich, 1977), 96–100; L. J. Weinberger, *Jewish Hymnography: A Literary History* (London, 1998), 1–28; E. Ben-Eliyahu, Y. Cohn and F. Millar, *Handbook of Jewish Literature from Late Antiquity* (Oxford, 2012), 126–39.

4 J. Heinemann and J. J. Petuchowski, *Literature of the Synagogue* (New York, 1975), 208.

5 Elbogen-Heinemann, 211; Heinemann-Petuchowski, *Literature of the Synagogue*, 209.

6 J. Maier, *Geschichte der jüdischen Religion* (Berlin, 1972), 153–8.

7 Pesikta de-Rav Kahana (PRK) 27.1 (ed. B. Mandelbaum (2 vols., New York, 1962), ii, 403f.); Lev. R. 30.1 (ed. M. Margulies (5 vols., Jerusalem, 1953–60), iv, 790, with citation of parallels including Cant. R. on 3, 6). The texts of Mandelbaum and Margulies, each continuously paginated throughout, are cited below by editor's name.

between house of study and synagogue is here underlined. *Piyyuṭim*, belonging to worship rather than to debate or homily, may therefore complement more strictly rabbinic sources.

There follows accordingly a modest venture in adding to the passages commonly discussed with reference to views of suffering and messianism in the rabbinic period. Surveys of both subjects used for this study restrict themselves to rabbinic texts in the narrower sense, although the relevance of the *piyyuṭim* is noted.[8] Here attention is confined to Yose hen Yose, the earliest of the named poets.[9]

Yose's significance for our purpose derives especially from the *Sitz im Leben* of his poems, but is enhanced by their likely date. A. Mirsky, whose work in producing the first critical edition of Yose with commentary makes this attempt possible, dates him about the fifth century.[10] This means that he is an independent source from the period of the early haggadic midrashim. Genesis Rabbah and Lamentations Rabbah are ascribed to the beginning of the fifth century, and the earliest homiletic midrashim, Leviticus Rabbah and Pesikta de-Rav Kahana, are held to have been compiled during it. A number of parallels between Yose and the midrashim are consistent with such datings, but noteworthy differences in emphasis also emerge.

For Mirsky's dating, not the earliest that has been proposed, stylistic considerations are important. Whereas Yannai and Kalir are rich in characteristically rabbinic material, Yose uses it only occasionally, while hymn-like compositions that are probably earlier than Yose (such as the *Alenu* prayer)[11] have no trace of it at all.[12] In respect of rabbinic matter Yose's contacts appear to be with Palestinian rather than Babylonian tradition.[13]

8 Rachel Rosenzweig, *Solidarität mit den Leidenden im Judentum*, Studia Judaica x (Berlin, 1978); P. Schäfer, 'Die messianischen Hoffnungen des rabbinischen Judentums zwischen Naherwartung und religiösem Pragmatismus', in C. Thoma (ed.), *Zukunft in der Gegenwart* (Bern, 1976), 96–125 (on the *piyyuṭim*, 96) (not available to me as reprinted in Schäfer, *Studien zur Geschichte und Theologie des rabbinischen Judentums*, AGJU xv (Leiden, 1978)); on a single important saying and its parallels, E. Bammel, 'Israels Dienstbarkeit', in E. Bammel, C. K. Barrett and W D. Davies (eds.), *Donum Gentilicium* (for D. Daube; Oxford, 1978), 295–305.

9 Besides Mirsky, cited in the following footnote, see on Yose J. H. Schirmann and A. Sáenz Badillos in *Encyclopedia Judaica* 2nd edn (2007), xxi, 398; Elbogen, *Der jüdische Gottesdienst*, 306–8, with additional note in Elbogen-Heinemann, 231 (ET, 238–9); Maier, *Gesch. der jüdischen Religion*, 155–7; Ben-Eliyahu, Cohn and Millar, *Handbook*, 131–2.

10 A. Mirsky, *Yosse ben Yosse: Poems* (Hebrew: Jerusalem, 1977), 13.

11 Elbogen, *Der jüdische Gottesdienst*, 80f. (ET, 71–2).

12 Mirsky, *Yosse ben Yosse*, 12f.

13 Ibid., 29–31, acknowledging and enlarging upon an observation of S. D. Luzzatto. At 32–6 Mirsky lists parallels with *Pirqe Rabbi Eliezer*, the date of which, he suggests, should be reconsidered in their light.

His name forms an independent ground for the view that he is of Palestinian origin.[14]

His surviving poems are mostly handed down in connection with the liturgy of the 'Days of Awe', New Year and Atonement. Saadia in his early tenth-century Order of Prayer gives a Tekiata for New Year and an Avodah for the Day of Atonement, both by Yose.[15] The Tekiata, thought to have been written originally as a version of this part of the New Year liturgy itself,[16] is used by Saadia rather as his choice among many current hymns. Its three poems *I will praise my God, I fear amid my doings* and *I will flee for help* (*ʾahallelah ʾelohay, ʾefḥad be-maʿasay, ʾanusah le-ʿezrah*) incorporate respectively the *catenae* of texts inserted in the Tefillah at New Year, known as *Kingdoms, Remembrances and Trumpets* (Mishnah, Rosh ha-Shanah 4.6). The Avodah of Yose chosen by Saadia is *I will recount the mighty works, ʾazkhir gevuroth*, Yose's longest composition in this genre, in which (below, pp. 348–9) it was customary to recite the works of God from Creation to the institution of the Aaronic ministry of the Tabernacle, thereafter describing, with Mishnaic quotations, the Temple-service (*ʿavodah*) of the Day of Atonement; a debt to Ecclesiasticus, especially chapter 50, is apparent.[17] Shorter examples of the Avodah by Yose are *I will tell the great works, ʾasapper gedoloth*, recovered from Geniza fragments, and *Thou hast established the world in the multitude of mercy, ʾattah konanta ʿolam be-rov ḥesed*, preserved in the French rite and its North Italian offshoot of Asti-Fossano-Moncalvi (*Apam*).[18] 'Still to-day the visitor who … hears … the Avodah of Kippur in isolated communities like that of Asti is struck by certain resemblances to the modes and phrasing of the Gregorian chant.'[19] Also for the Day of Atonement are *Truly our sins, ʾomnam ʾashamenu*, a Selihah of the type known as Hataʾnu from its refrain 'we have sinned'; another lament, *We have no High Priest, ʾeyn lanu kohen gadol*; and possibly *Once thou didst make us the head, ʾaz le-roʾsh tattanu*, a second Hataʾnu.

14 Mirsky, *Yosse ben Yosse*, 13.

15 I. Davidson, S. Assaf and B. I. Joel, *Siddur R. Saadja Gaon* (Jerusalem, 1941), 225–33, 264–75.

16 [E.] D. Goldschmidt (ed.), *Maḥzor la-yamin ha-norʾaim* (2 vols., Jerusalem, 1970), i, 45 of the Introduction. He prints and annotates the Tekiata in the text, 238–42, 251–6, 265–70. The ancient *Tekiata de-vey Rav*, used in present-day New Year rites, is translated and discussed in Heinemann-Petuchowski, *Literature of the Synagogue*, 57–69.

17 C. Roth, 'Ecclesiasticus in the Synagogue Service', *JBL* LXXI (1952), 171–8.

18 Goldschmidt, *Maḥzor la-yamim ha-norʾaim*, ii, 23 of the Introduction. He prints and annotates Yose's *ʾomnam ʾashamenu* and *ʾattah konanta ʾolam be-rov ḥesed* in the text, 20–4, 465–79.

19 Leo Levi, 'Sul rapporto tra il canto sinagogale in Italia e le origini del canto liturgico cristiano', in *Scritti in Memoria di Sally Mayer* (Jerusalem, 1956), 141.

The simple style of these generally acknowledged poems, on which the remarks below are based, depends for effect on devices such as paronomasia, alphabetic arrangement, or the repetition of a final word or refrain. Rhyme is not used—a writer of the Geonic period indeed classed Yose as a poet without rhyme[20]—although it occurs in one of the four poems of less sure attribution printed by Mirsky in an appendix. Yose's characteristic beauty was singled out by Graetz as the terse phrase whereby, for example, the Hasmonaeans, in words recalling Rom. 15:16, are 'offering kingship as priestly service', *mekhahane melukhah*.[21]

So biblical a poet as Yose would perhaps have viewed the concerns designated in the title of this study by 'suffering' and 'messianism' under such headings as 'tribulation' and 'consolation'. However that may be, transposition into scriptural words underlines that biblical interconnection of the two topics which was memorably traced by E. C. Hoskyns.[22] Such an interconnection emerges also from the principal occasions for which Yose writes. The messianic hopes of New Year spring from present tribulation, and on the Day of Atonement that tribulation, token though it be of Israel's sin, is also the deep whence arises the cry for pardon and redemption.

The christological interpretation of suffering in the New Testament encourages attention to this constant association of suffering with messianic hope. The link appears with special clarity in Gershom Scholem's understanding of messianism as 'not so cheerful' as belief in progress, indeed as 'a theory of catastrophe'.[23] To unite the expressions of suffering and messianism is a characteristic of the *piyyuṭ* throughout its history.[24] Yose's material on the two topics will be treated separately, but his words are often relevant to both at once.

Suffering

(a) The interpretation of suffering

Yose's poems bear out Rachel Rosenzweig's observation that the ancient Jewish sensitivity to communal suffering overshadows awareness of universal

[20] W. Bacher, 'Aus einer alten Poetik (Schule Saadja's)', *JQR* xiv (1902), 742–4 (742)

[21] H. Graetz, 'Die Anfänge der neuhebräischen Poesie', *MGWJ* ix (1860), 20. The phrase is from *'ahallelah 'elohay*, line 28.

[22] 'Tribulation—Comfort', in E. C. Hoskyns, *Cambridge Sermons* (London, 1938), 121–9.

[23] G. Scholem, *The Messianic Idea in Judaism* (London, 1971), 37f., 7f., and index s.v. 'Catastrophe'.

[24] L. Zunz, *Die synagogale Poesie des Mittelalters* (Berlin, 1855), esp. 5f., 129; similarly Elbogen, *Der jüdische Gottesdienst*, 289.

and individual pain.[25] The present sufferings most prominent in Yose are the twin corporate afflictions of servitude and the loss of the Temple service. It is often hard to judge how far the descriptions of calamity are symbolic; but the bitterness of outward, historical experience certainly informs Yose's poems.

The Service has failed from the House of Service;
and how shall we serve the Pure One (*zakh*) when a stranger (*zar*)
makes us serve?...
The joy (*gil*) of the Lots [Lev. 16:8] has ceased from us;
and how shall we go up with joy (*gilah*) when we are in exile (*golah*)?
(*ʾeyn lanu kohen gadol*, lines 3 and 5)

For this predominantly corporate outlook suffering is naturally comforted by messianic hope. Yose's regular consolations are derived especially from the Danielic scheme of the four kingdoms, fore-shadowing the end of servitude, and the bridal imagery of the Song of Songs, to assure the return of the Beloved to his desolate dwelling. His biblical interpretations involve the biblical understandings of suffering as punitive, probative and meritorious. As in rabbinic texts, these views appear together without entire consisteney.[26]

The punitive view of suffering makes intense awareness of corporate affliction the counterpart of an equally intense consciousness of sin. So, in a lament the closeness of which to historical experience is emphasized by Mirsky, *Yosse ben Yosse*, 56, 'we have eaten up the righteousness of our Fathers', the merits of the patriarchs are exhausted (*ʾomnam ʾashamenu*, 13, cf. *ʿefḥad be-maʿasay*, 4; the question how long the merits of the patriarchs endured is discussed in Lev. R. 36.6).[27] The congregation are thrown back on sheer grace, and still have not kept the commandments.

Thou didst strengthen us when our hand failed [Lev. 25:35];
thou didst make known to us 'This do, and live'—
yet hands were not stayed upon us, as her that was overthrown in a
moment [Lam. 4:6].
(*ʾomnam ʾashamenu*, 42–4)

[25] Rosenzweig, *Solidarität*, xiv, 56, 83f.

[26] Rabbinic views of suffering are discussed by Rosenzweig, *ibid.* esp. 56–8, 83f., 188, 224; S. Schechter, *Studies in Judaism*, first series (London, 1896), 259–82; and J. W. Bowker, *Problems of Suffering in Religions of the World* (Cambridge, 1970), 32–7.

[27] Margulies, 851–3.

Zunz paraphrases this last line: 'Yet we stretched out no helping hand, behaving like Sodom that was overthrown in a moment',[28] refusal to 'strengthen the hand of the poor' being 'the iniquity of thy sister Sodom' (Ezek. 16:49); and the reference is accordingly to failure in the very commandment, the pattern of which is the divine grace mentioned two lines earlier. It is not surprising to find strong emphasis (below, p. 356) on the effect of the Day of Atonement as making Israel 'perfect and upright' (*ʾazkhir gevuroth*, 275; *ʾasapper gedoloth*, 60). The messianic significance of this consciousness of sin lies in the view that sin delays the kingdom, an assumption manifest in prayers that Israel may be purified and glorified for the return of the divine presence (below, p. 343). Repentance, the precondition of redemption according to one prominent but debated rabbinic view (below, pp. 339–40) may be implied but is left unmentioned.

The view that suffering may be a test is particularly clear in the lines on Abraham (below, p. 335). It verges on the further view, vital to the link between suffering and hope, that suffering will be compensated or rewarded by God. Once again assumed rather than enunciated, it can for example, be combined with the punitive view in an explanation of Roman dominion.

> The *hairy man* flattered his father with his venison,
> and inherited with the voice of weeping the sword and the KINGDOM.
>
> (*ʾahallelah ʾelohay*, 29)

Here Yose follows the midrash that Esau (Edom-Rome), because he *wept* (Gen. 27:38), was granted the *sword* and the *dominion* (Gen. 27:40) (Mid. Teh. 80.4).[29] This is at once the reward of his suffering, the punishment of Jacob-Israel, and an implied promise that Israel's present tears will likewise be rewarded with the kingdom.

(b) The figure of the Synagogue

Yose's images for *kenesseth yisraʾel*, the Synagogue of Israel are at the heart of his poetry. The passages cited already exemplify a concentration on the fate of his people, which, natural though it be in liturgical settings, contrasts with

[28] Zunz, *Die synagogale Poesie*, 163.

[29] References to this and other midrashim in Goldschmidt, *Maḥzor la-yamim ha-norʾaim*, i, 241, and Mirsky, *Yosse ben Yosse*, ad loc. On Esau see G. D. Cohen, 'Esau as Symbol in Early Medieval Thought', in A. Altmann (ed.), *Jewish Medieval and Renaissance Studies* (Cambridge, MA, 1967), 19–48.

the universalist language found together with the nationalist in the hymn-like prayers of the *Tekiata de-vey Rav*.[30] The Synagogue in Yose is a figure of past and future glory but present suffering. Central among his images is that of the bride, for which he combines the Song of Songs with Jer. 2 and Ezek. 16 in a manner perhaps already apparent in 2 Esd. 5:23–7, and familiar in rabbinic sources from tannaitic passages attributed to R. Akiba onwards.[31]

The three poems of Yose's Tekiata are especially rich in this imagery. The first, *I will praise my God, ʾahallelah ʾelohay*, is mainly triumphant in tone. It begins confidently with the conquest of Canaan. Israel (lines 13–15) is the master, king Arad the Canaanite his slave; Israel are the seed of the blessed, Canaan the accursed; Israel 'the hosts of the KINGDOM' (*melukhah*, repeated at the end of each line from the *malkhuyyoth*-text Ob. 21), whereas Canaan are (lines 17f.)

> strangers
> in the land of the children of Shem, the seed of the KINGDOM

and victory is harshly evoked with 'the son of Nun slaughtered them'. Then, however, with an abrupt change of tone like that of Ps. 44:10, Israel themselves are sheep for the slaughter (line 25, of Haman's plot) and doves (*yonim*) sold to Greeks (*yewanim*) (line 28, of Antiochus iv; cf. Joel 3:6), until finally Esau, last of the 'four kingdoms' rules them. Yet his younger brother will surely inherit (line 30); and in a concluding passage of triumph incorporating the *malkhuyyoth* the Synagogue is the bride 'clear as the sun' of Song of Songs 6:10, awaiting the divine glory in Zion (line 36, introducing Isa. 24:23), and, once again—now with a definitely present reference—God's hosts (line 52, introducing Num. 23:21). This messianic conclusion is discussed below (pp. 342–6); here it is only necessary to note the successive images for Israel: master, seed of the blessed ones, army, seed royal, sheep, doves, bride, and again army. Those of triumph precede and follow those of suffering.

A forcible expression of suffering is the simple negation of the imagery of triumph. So, outside the Tekiata, the language of filiation and the metaphor of the bride recur in lamentation.

[30] Mirsky, *Yosse ben Yosse*, 15f.; I. Elbogen, 'Die messianische Idee in den altjüdischen Gebeten', in *Judaica: Festschrift zu Hermann Cohens siebzigstem Geburtstage* (Berlin, 1912), 669–79 (672f.).

[31] R. Loewe, 'Apologetic Motifs in the Targum to the Song of Songs', in A. Altmann (ed.), *Biblical Motifs* (Cambridge, MA, 1966), 159–96 (161); Bammel, *Israels Dienstbarkeit*, 302; Rosenzweig, *Solidarität*, 53–6.

We were reckoned *the holy seed, sons of the living God*:
we are polluted, and called a people who bring defilement on
the Name.
(*ʾomnam ʾashamenu*, 35f; cf. Isa. 6:13; Hos. 2:1 (1:10); Ezek. 22:5)

We have offered no frankincense (*levonah*) on the mount of *Lebanon*
[the Temple, 1 Kings 7:2]
and how shall the sin be whitened (*yelubban*) of her that is *fair as the*
moon (*levanah* [Song of Songs 6:10])?
The pure myrrh has ceased from her that is *perfumed with myrrh*
[Song of Songs 3:6]
and how, on the mount of myrrh [Moriah, the Temple-mount,
2 Chron. 3:1] shall there rest the *bundle of myrrh* [Song of Songs 1:13]?
(*ʾeyn lanu kohen gadol*, 23, 25)

These negations of course serve to intensify the hope that Synagogue may again be affirmatively described as a holy people, the children of God, a fair bride awaiting the divine bridegroom on his holy hill.[32]

Bridal imagery could be linked triumphantly in midrash with the four-kingdom scheme. Israel 'looked forth as the morning' under Babylon with Daniel, was 'fair as the moon' under Media with Esther, 'clear as the sun' against the Greeks with Mattathias and his sons, and will be 'terrible as an army with banners' to Edom (Song of Songs 6:10 interpreted in Exod. R. 15.6).[33] Yose uses the same link more subtly in a sustained evocation of alternating fear and hope as Israel moves from tribulation to comfort. In *I will flee for help* (Isa. 10:3), the third poem of the Tekiata, he frames the bridal imagery with the symbolism of timorous creatures such as sheep and dove, met already in the mournful central section of the first poem of the Tekiata (p. 331 above). Synagogue, convinced of the divine presence in her worship, takes heart (line 2–3) to 'chirp' (Isa. 10:14) for help for the 'scattered sheep' (Jer. 50:17), dumb before the (Gentile) 'shearers' who oppress her (Isa. 53:7). Yet though the bridegroom said 'Let me hear thy VOICE' (Song of

[32] For Song of Songs 1:13 applied to the resting of the Shekhinah in the rebuilt Temple see Pesikta Rabbati 20.8, edited, with commentary discussing parallels, by K.-E. Grözinger, *Ich bin der Herr, dein Gott!: Eine rabbinische Homilie zum Ersten Gebot* (*PesR 20*), Frankfurter Judaistische Studien ii (Bern and Frankfurt am Main, 1976), 36, 124–6, 6*.

[33] Text with translation and notes in S. Krauss, *Griechen und Römer*, Monumenta Talmudica V.i (reprinted Darmstadt, 1972), 34.

Songs 2:14; each line of the poem ends with *qol*), he fled when he found no Law in her (line 6). Encouraged by recollection of patriarchs and prophets (lines 7–12), Synagogue goes in search of him like the bride of the Song of Songs (lines 13f.). The bridegroom is no longer to be found, as of old, at the Sea or in the Wilderness; he once spoke from the Temple, but 'I have defiled his beloved dwelling' (lines 15–18). This 'I', where 'they' might have been expected, strikingly marks the acute consciousness of sin already noted, especially apparent at this stage in the poem. The first person singular, for which no scriptural source is suggested by Mirsky and Goldschmidt *ad loc.*, may perhaps arise from Ezek. 8, interpreted as 'the lodger turning out the master of the house' in Lev. R. 17.7 (Margulies, 387).

Synagogue remembers, however, that she was precious in the bridegroom's sight (Isa. 43:4); for her he cast down the kingdoms in their order until this present (Roman) dominion of the 'Beast of the reeds' (Ps. 68:31), and, although the time of deliverance is hidden from her in her misery, she knows (here Yose prepares for the *Shofaroth*-texts) that she will rejoice to hear (Song of Songs 5:2) the Beloved knocking at the doors (lines 19–29). 'For ever will he make me the seal upon his heart, as once under the apple tree he raised me up with a VOICE.' This line 30, with its allusions to Song of Songs 8:6 and 5, is at once given its (standard)[34] interpretation by 'the voice of the trumpet exceeding loud' in Exod. 19:16, now cited as the first of the *Shofaroth*. Emboldened as she recalls the giving of the Law, Synagogue prays earnestly for the gathering of the dispersion, reverting to the imagery of desolate biblical birds (Hos. 11:11; Ps. 84:4, 56:1 (title); Isa. 27:13; Zech. 10:8).

> The sparrow from Egypt has cried from the wilderness,
> and the dove from Assyria has sent forth her VOICE.
> Visit the house-sparrow, seek out the silent dove:
> blow for them on the trumpet and hiss for them with a VOICE.
>
> (lines 36f.)

There follows immediately the third of the *Shofaroth* (Isa. 27:13), and the poem ends with twenty further lines of messianic hope, considered below (pp. 346–8). Its treatment of the Song of Songs is comparable with that of

[34] For the Song of Songs interpreted of divine love in the giving of the Law, see Loewe, 'Apologetic Motifs', 161 and (on 8.6) 172.

PRK 5.6–9, but the midrash is more consolatory in tone. Thus, whereas PRK 5.8 (Mandelbaum, 90) notes positively from Song of Songs 2:8 that Israel saw the 'leaping' Holy One in Egypt, at the Sea and at Sinai, Yose's lines 15–18, alluding to the same verse, depend on the thought that this was once the case, but is so no longer.

(c) The fathers, the slain, and the disciples of the wise

The suffering of Israel is also expressed in the sufferings of representative figures. Patriarchs and martyrs (the 'fathers' and the 'slain', *'efḥad be-ma'asay*, 4, 47) are prominent here, and it is probable that the rabbis and their pupils also have a place.

The patriarchs are frequently described in terms of glory. They are the 'ancient mountains' of Deut. 33:15, through whose worth Israel was redeemed from bondage (*'efḥad be-ma'asay*, 41, with Targum Ps.-Jon. *ad loc.*; Lev. R. 36.6 (above, n. 27)). In the *sidre 'avodah*, as in contemporary midrash, Adam has the *wisdom* and *beauty* of Ezek. 28:12–15, and God spreads his jewelled couch within the wedding-canopy of Eden (*'azhhir gevuroth*, 39f.; *'attah konanta 'olam be-rov ḥesed*, 27f; cf. PRK 44; Lev. R. 20.2).[35] Jacob's wrestling is viewed not as affliction but as victory; 'blazing fire flees when it wrestles with him' (*'azkhir gevuroth*, 102; cf. *'attah konanta 'olam be-rov ḥesed*, 64). Like the division of the sea by Moses, the halting of the sun by Joshua, and the raising of the dead by Elijah and Elisha, it can be cited to demonstrate man's God-given lordship over creation (*'attah konanta 'olam be-rov ḥesed*, 24; cf. PRK 1.3).[36]

Equally strong, however, is the emphasis on patriarchal suffering. Adam received divine comfort after Abel's murder.

> This One bound up the wound of the primaeval creature
> when he began to drink the cup mixed for the generations.
>
> (*'azkhir gevuroth*, 65)

The consolation, as in Gen. 4:25, was Seth; and with an allusion to Ps. 147:3 the verse expresses the straightforward view stated in messianic form in 2 Cor.

[35] Mandelbaum, 66f; Margulies, 446.
[36] Mandelbaum, 5.

1:3–5. Tribulation is interpreted as testing especially in the case of Abraham. God 'tested him ten times' (*'asapper gedoloth*, 16), as in Mishnah, Aboth 5.3. The most important of these tests in Yose is the sacrifice of Mount Moriah, to which *'asapper gedoloth* immediately proceeds. The Akedah is considered separately below at pp. 352–3; here we need only note the benefits of this testing for Israel. Abraham can be appealed to as advocate: 'Perhaps he will accept of you, because you obeyed the VOICE'; and Isaac's silent self-oblation gives a ground for petition: 'Look upon the lamb of Moriah; may the dumbness of his mouth be righteousness for her that did not obey the VOICE' (*'anusah le-'ezrah*, 8f.; for the patriarchs as advocates cf. PRK 23.7 (Mandelbaum, 339f.)). Readiness to die is also seen in Moses and Aaron. Moses prayed: 'Blot me out, I pray thee', for the sake of the people; and Aaron braved the plague: 'he bounded with the censer until the plague was stayed' (*'efḥad be-ma'asay*, 5, 8; Exod. 32:32; Num. 17:11–13 (16:46–8)).

The 'martyrological' character of the Akedah has often been noted, and the epithet is applied specifically to Yose's version in *'azkhir gevuroth*, 91–4 (below, pp. 352–3) by Maier, *Gesch. der jüdischen Religion*, 119. It is worth gathering a few other passages in Yose that for convenience may be called martyrological, even though they speak neither of witness, with the New Testament, nor of sanctification of the Name, with the rabbis (but note the phrase 'defilement of the Name', above, p. 332). In all of these passages the sufferers are once again closely linked, or even identified, with the people as a whole. Earlier quotations have described Israel as 'sheep for the slaughter' and 'doves' (above, p. 331), or as a 'scattered' and 'dumb' sheep 'driven away' in exile (above, p. 332; cf. Jer. 50:17, immediately followed by a promise of punishment on the Gentile nations). A line on the Synagogue as bride, however, departs from an otherwise closely followed scriptural model, the *zikhronoth*-text Jer. 2:2, in order to mention the slain as especially remembered by God:

> The High One has greatly longed for the bride of youth:
> her slain and her afflicted have come to REMEMBRANCE.
>
> (*'efḥad be-ma'asay*, 47)

'Her slain', *harugeyha*, recalls the rabbinic phrase *haruge malekhuth*, 'those slain by the Empire', applied especially to the so-called 'Ten Martyrs' under Hadrian. The 'fourth kingdom' was regarded in rabbinic thought as worse than its predecessors precisely in this respect, that it made many martyrs.[37] Suffering under the empire is also probably described in *ʾomnam ʾashamenu*, 40: 'we have been slaughtered, great and small, as fish swallowed up in the net'; and it is clearly lamented in *ʾeyn lanu kohen gadol*:

> How can we toss the blood [Mishnah, Yoma 1.2] when our blood is shed?
> … How can we be purified by wood [Ezek. 41:22) when we have stumbled under the wood [Lam. 5:13]?
>
> (lines 8 and 32, second halves)

Mirsky notes that Targ. Lam. 5:13 interprets 'have been crucified'. It is possible that the last line also constitutes a bitter hint at the Christian Empire in particular; 'wood' comes to be used in anti-Christian polemic.[38] In any case, in accord with the constant use of the first person throughout the poem, the slain are again identified with the whole people. The refrain 'we have sinned', after every second line, immediately follows both references. Martyrdom is thus contextually interpreted as punishment for the nation's sin; the positive values attached to suffering elsewhere in Yose may be in the mind of poet and congregation, but remain unexpressed.

Lastly, the Wise and their disciples are by no means so prominent in Yose as in contemporary rabbinic homily, but the poet is aware of them and appears to think of them in connection with representative suffering. His awareness emerges in a significant adaptation of Ps. 123:2; Isa. 30:20, where he says of the High Priest in divination that 'his eyes are to his teacher [the Shekhinah] as those of disciple to master', *ke-thalmid la-rav* (*ʾazkhir gevuroth*, 154). The disciples of the Wise seem to be regarded as suffering figures in the concluding prayer of *ʾefḥad be-maʿasay*, which incorporates the *zikhronoth*. The poet has just mentioned the good works of the generation redeemed from Egypt (lines 33f., introducing Ps. 111:4), and is about to speak of the merits of the patriarchs (line 41, introducing Exod. 2:24). At this point he prays (lines 36f.):

> Look, O God, upon the dwellers in the gardens [Song of Songs 8:13]
> hearkening to those who converse on the law for REMEMBRANCE;
> Their work is before thee, and their reward is with thee—

[37] Krauss, *Griechen und Römer*, 20n., 24.

[38] For the cross as 'wood' see M. Sokoloff and J. Yahalom, *Jewish Palestinian Aramaic Poetry from Late Antiquity* (Jerusalem, 1999), 216–17 (*qis*); Jerome, *In Ep. ad Gal.* 2.3, on 3.13 (14) (Deut. 21:23).

> theirs who *eat the bread of carefulness* [Ps. 127:2]—in the *book of* REMEMBRANCE,
> as it is written by the hand of thy prophet, Then they that feared the LORD spake one with another; and the LORD hearkened, and heard, and a book of remembrance was written before him, for them that feared the Lord, and that thought upon his name [Mal. 3:16].

Israel as a whole is the garden-dweller, according to Canticle Rabbah *ad loc.*; but here the feminine singular participle of Massoretic Text becomes masculine plural, and the verses closely follow Mal. 3:16, which is applied to converse on Torah in Aboth 3.3. It is likely, therefore, as Mirsky shows, that the 'gardens' (*gannim*) here are houses of study (compare the metaphorical use of *tarbiṣ* for 'academy'), and their 'dwellers' the disciples of the Wise who 'eat the bread of carefulness'. The context in Yose means that the rabbinic students' costly devotion must be regarded as meritorious and representative. His thought will then be close to that vividly expressed in the homily of PRK 11.24, where Simeon b. Yohai's son Eleazar says, when he has laboured in Torah as much as he can, 'Let all the sufferings of Israel come upon me.'[39]

Yose's allusions to patriarchs and martyrs have a hagiographical ring. Abraham is an intercessor, Isaac's death is atoning, and the martyrs are especially remembered by God. Miracles, as is natural in writing of this tendency (cf. Heb. 11:33f.), are regarded for the moment as man's work rather than God's. Jewish veneration of the tombs of the patriarchs and the Maccabaean martyrs is attested well before Yose's time, and it is in the century after him that a pilgrim describes Jews as well as Christians offering incense at the patriarchal shrine in Hebron.[40] Yose's relatively slight reference to the disciples of the Wise is in so similar a vein as to recall that the tombs of rabbis, too, had begun to be venerated (see chapter 12, below). The *pièce justificative* of the Meronites, who in response to dream-apparitions of R. Simeon b. Yohai stole his son Eleazar's body and translated it to the father's tomb in Meron, is found among other places in a composition of Yose's time, PRK 11.23. In such contexts suffering is seen as meritorious and beneficial; 'the sufferer … becomes an object of

[39] Mandelbaum, p. 200; the parallel Ecc. R. 11.2 edited with notes by G. Dalman, *Aramäische Dialektproben*, 2nd edn. (reprinted Darmstadt, 1960), 35 and discussed in connection with Matt. 26:28 by Dalman, *Jesus—Jeschua* (Leipzig, 1922), 158f.; these traditions and related account of Rabbi discussed by Rosenzweig, *Solidarität*, 176–88.

[40] E. Bammel, 'Zum jüdischen Märtyrerkult' as cited p. 376, below.

veneration';[41] Israel benefits, and the sufferings of the Synagogue as a whole tend to be seen as a precious sign of favour rather than, or at least as well as, retribution.

> What then is there left to you to say, since the prophets speak of fixed periods concerning the other [three] captivities, whereas for this [present] one they fix no period, but on the contrary add that the desolation will last to the end?
>
> Your affairs have gone beyond all tragedy ... Where now are the things that you hold sacred? Where is the high priest? Where are the garments, the breastplate and the Urim?
>
> (Chrysostom, C. *Iud.* 5.10 (resumed in 6.2 and 6.5)[42]

So Chrysostom rhetorically addresses the Jews in 387, when Church members were inclined to frequent the Synagogue for festivals including those 'Days of Awe' for which Yose wrote. There is a striking identity between the twin afflictions—servitude and loss of the Temple service—singled out in the patristic commonplaces vigorously echoed by Chrysostom, and those that have figured most prominently in Jewish communal expression as represented by Yose. Chrysostom goes on to treat Lev. 8, which is remembered at the heart of the Day of Atonement Avodah. In both the external and the inner-Jewish source, moreover, the connection is made between these sufferings and the sin that they imply. To note the extent of these shared presuppositions is also, however, to be made more keenly aware of the wholly different general tendency of Yose's poems. Deeply though they lament present suffering, they offer assurance even in the negations of former glory of *We have no high priest* (above, p. 332).

Here the link between Yose and contemporary midrash emerges clearly. Instances in which both draw on a common stock of ideas have already been noted. Rachel Rosenzweig is able to present the midrash as a mode of overcoming suffering,[43] and the compilations ascribed to the fifth century are indeed rich in words of comfort. Joseph Heinemann finds a leading theme of Leviticus Rabbah to be that the sufferings of Israel are in reality 'nothing but loving-kindness and atonement'.[44] He refers especially to chapters 16, 17 and

[41] Schechter, *Studies in Judaism*, 275.
[42] *PG* xlviii, 899, 905, 911.
[43] Rosenzweig, *Solidarität*, 7, 52.
[44] J. Heinemann, 'The Art of Composition in Leviticus Rabba' (Hebrew), *Hasifrut* II (1971), 808–34 (822a); cf. Heinemann, 'Profile of a Midrash', *Journal of the American Academy of Religion* xxxix (1971), 141–50 (148).

26, the last-named (on the Day of Atonement) belonging in his view originally to Pesikta de-Rav Kahana (where chapter 26 is parallel). Similarly, quite apart from this chapter, a large section of Pesikta de-Rav Kahana (chapters 16–22) is devoted to consolation.[45] These and other works likely to stand near in time to Yose's poems contain sayings that give the corporate afflictions themselves a strong positive interpretation. So a homily in the name of the third-century Palestinian Samuel bar Nahmani, current in several versions, says that the destruction of Jerusalem (Jer. 38:28) is in fact a cause of rejoicing, since it brought Israel the ἀποχή, quittance (Gen. R. 41(42).3)[46] or ἀπόφασις, annulment (Lev. R. 11.7)[47] of her iniquities. According to Lam. R. 1.51,[48] on that day Menahem ('Comforter', the Messiah) was born, giving hope for the Temple's rebuilding.[49] Again, the saying ascribed to Akiba; 'Poverty is as becoming to the daughter of Jacob as a red band on the neck of a white horse', occurs at Pesikta de-Rav Kahana 14.3 and Lev. R. 13.4; 35.6.[50] E. Bammel shows that it is implicitly messianic: servitude is a part of redemption itself.[51]

Contrasts, however, also appear between Yose and such otherwise comparable midrashic material. They arise in part at least from the fact that Yose speaks in the name of the congregation, while the midrash is closer to words spoken in homily *to* the congregation. Yose expresses, in the manner appropriate to the day of the Jewish year, the sufferings that the preacher addresses as consoler and apologist. Hence Yose allows himself, as with the figure of the Synagogue in *I will flee for help* or in the lines on patriarchal suffering and martyrdom (above, pp. 334–5), to enter with less explicit allusion to comfort than is typical of these midrashic passages into the corporate affliction and longing for redemption. Hence also, perhaps, the strong midrashic tie between suffering and repentance[52] is absent from Yose. He takes no side on the question whether redemption depends on Israel's prior repentance.[53] His concern is not (unless implicitly) to urge repentance, but

45 W. G. Braude and I. J. Kapstein, *Pesikta de-Rab Kahana* (London, 1975), xxi.

46 J. Theodor and Ch. Albeck (eds.), *Bereschit Rabba* (reprinted Jerusalem, 1965), 1, 407.

47 Margulies, 337, apparatus to line 5.

48 Dalman, *Dialektproben*, 14f.

49 The traditions cited here are discussed by Rosenzweig, *Solidarität*, 32f.

50 Mandelbaum, 241f.; Margulies, 281, 824.

51 Bammel in Bammel-Barrett-Davies, *Donum Gentilicium*, 303.

52 Rosenzweig, *Solidarität*, 153f, 223f., brings out the strength of the belief that suffering implies sin.

53 The rabbinic material is surveyed by A. Marmorstein, 'The Doctrine of Redemption in Saadya's Theological System', in E. I. J. Rosenthal (ed.), *Saadya Studies* (Manchester, 1943), 103–18 (106–12); cf. Schäfer, 'Hoffnungen', esp. 98–100, 110–12, 118 and Bammel in Bammel-Barrett-Davies, *Donum Gentilicium*, 302–4.

to express the communal confession of sin and prayer that *God* will purify and redeem his people. His poems thus recall the significant closing words of Mishnah, Yoma: 'The Holy One, blessed be he, cleanses Israel'; and, though they are hardly intended as argument, suggest something of the weight behind the view that redemption is in God's hand alone. Inevitably thereby they lack something of that strongly ethical emphasis on man's co-operation with divine redemption that Schäfer identifies as an important rabbinic contribution to messianic hope.[54]

Despite these points of contrast in treatment, Yose's interpretations of suffering are close to those of the rabbinic midrash. Just as, in Solomon Schechter's exposition of rabbinic thought, 'by a series of conscious and unconscious modifications' the sufferer 'passed from the state of a sinner into the zenith of the saint',[55] so the suffering Synagogue in Yose receives at one and the same time chastenings for sin and the tokens of divine favour. Here Yose may be comparable with the New Testament as well as the rabbis. As M. D. Hooker has shown, the Apostle appears to include all his sufferings, without discrimination of cause, in the fellowship of Christ's sufferings.[56] For Yose, however, the present sufferings of the community are messianic in a sense less bound up with the messianic figure. Servitude and the loss of the Temple service contain within themselves the hope of their reversal in redemption.

Messianism

'King Messiah will arise and restore the KINGDOM of David to its former dominion. He will *build up* the sanctuary *and gather together the outcasts of Israel* [Ps. 147:2]. All the laws will be restored in his days as they were of old, and sacrifices will be offered' (Maimonides, *Mishneh Torah* xiv. 11.1).[57]

[54] Schäfer, 'Hoffnungen', 118.
[55] Schechter, *Studies in Judaism*, 281.
[56] M. D. Hooker, 'Interchange and Suffering', in W. Horbury and B. McNeil (eds.), *Suffering and Martyrdom in the New Testament: Studies presented to G. M. Styler by the Cambridge New Testament Seminar* (Cambridge, 1981), 80–1.
[57] (Amsterdam, Joseph and Emmanuel Athias, 1702), iv, f. 306*b*; translation and discussion of this passage in Scholem, *Messianic Idea*, 28–32.

The twin afflictions lamented by Yose become in reverse the twin hopes of messianism. The summary of Maimonides shows these hopes for the kingdom and the Temple-service to be at the heart of messianic tradition, even though he goes on to restrict them by his own this-worldly interpretation. A miraculous redemption, in keeping with earlier tradition, is however expected by his predecessor Saadia, in whose *Beliefs and Opinions* (a.d. 933) the same hopes inform a synthesis of rabbinic messianism in which thirteen stages have been discerned.[58] They include the death of Messiah son of Joseph at the advent of the antichrist Armilus, the battle of Gog and Magog, and the advent of Messiah son of David, before the three fundamental events of the gathering of the exiles, the resurrection of the dead, and the rebuilding of the Temple. Saadia admitted Yose's poems into his Order of Prayer no doubt largely because they were widely current; but his deliberate choice of them from among a great many others also suggests that their messianism, less elaborate than his own though it may well be, did not strike him as inconsistent with the views that he was to synthesize.[59] His scheme of redemption is in fact close to apocalyptic works such as the early seventh-century *Zerubbabel.*

The works mentioned so far present messianism in a unified manner. In rabbinic writings, not least the midrashim likely to be near Yose's time, it is of course reflected fragmentarily. Yose's poems have the interest of appearing to presuppose a connected scheme of redemptive events. One cannot, however, expect such a scheme to be precisely described in poetry. Kalir's poem *In those days and at that time* is very close to *Zerubbabel*, but fails to mention Armilus by name; and a messianic *piyyuṭ* in Saadia's name is far from giving the detail of his prose account.[60] With this caution in view Yose's messianic passages are now considered. The headings of the kingdom and the Temple service roughly correspond, with certain overlaps, to the principal themes of the Tekiata and the Avodah poems respectively.

[58] Marmorstein in Rosenthal, *Saadya Studies*, 113.

[59] Saadia is likely to have compiled the *Siddur* after his travels ending in 921, and probably, though not certainly, before he received the title of Gaon in 928; so Assaf in Davidson-Assaf-Joel, *Siddur R. Saadja Gaon*, 22f. Saadia's principles in choosing *piyyuṭim* are summarized by Assaf at 21; for his testimony to the great number from which he selected Yose's Tekiata, see 225.

[60] Kalir's poem is printed with comments by J. Kaufmann (Even-Shemuel), *Midrashe Ge'ullah*, 2nd edn. (Hebrew: Jerusalem-Tel Aviv, 1954), 109–16; for that in Saadia's name see S. Stein, 'Saadya's Piyyut on the Alphabet', in Rosenthal, *Saadya Studies*, 206–26.

(a) The kingdom

Kingdom is the explicit and traditional theme of the first poem of the Tekiata (Mishnah, Rosh ha-Shanah 4.6). Yose's *kingdom* at the end of each line takes up the last word of Obadiah 21 (above, p. 331), the much-quoted *malkhuyyoth*-text, which unites the national and theocentric elements of messianism.[61] The opening description of the conquest has prepared for the allusion to the downfall of Edom, which, after the mournful central section (above, p. 331), opens the concluding passage. The *hairy man* inherited for a while (above, p. 331), but (lines 30ff.):

> the *smooth man* was exalted to be *lord over the brethren* [Gen. 27:29], and
> to Jeshurun again shall there turn back the KINGDOM
> [cf. Lev. R. 13, n. 61 above];

> as it is written in the law, And he shall be [or, 'And there shall be a'] king in Jeshurun, when the heads of the people and the tribes of Israel were gathered together [Deut. 33:5; see p. 17, n. 58, above].

This text is the first of the *malkhuyyoth*, which are now interwoven with couplets from the poet into a series of prayers and predictions concerning redemption. These appear to form two successive sequences dealing largely but not entirely with the same events. First, the lines on the downfall of Edom, just quoted, are followed by prayer for the establishment of the messianic kingdom in Jerusalem (in words close, as Mirsky notes, to the fourteenth Benediction of the Tefillah):[62]

> Stir and awake the *joy of the whole earth*,
> and establish thy throne in the city of the KINGDOM.
> (line 33, introducing Ps. 48:3)

Before Israel, the bride in the 'fair city', the divine glory is to be revealed (lines 35f., introducing Isa. 24:23). The link between bride and city is now grounded

[61] Thus it forms the last words of Lev. R. 13, in which the four unclean beasts of Lev. 11:4–7 are the four kingdoms, Rome the swine (*ḥazir*) 'returning (*maḥzereth*) the crown to its owners' (text and notes in Krauss, *Griechen und Römer*, 20, n. 35); and it is the climax of *Zerubbabel* (A. Jellinek, *Bet ha-Midrasch* (6 parts, reprinted Jerusalem, 1967), 11, 57, line 4 from bottom). Cohen, 'Esau as Symbol', 19f. gives discussion; for the question how far the theocentric climax of 1 Cor. 15:28 is comparable, see e.g., W. D. Davies, *Paul and Rabbinic Judaism*, 2nd edn. (London, 1962), 292–8; pp. 218–19, above.

[62] Translated and discussed in E. Schürer, G. Vermes, F. Millar and M. Black, *The History of the Jewish People in the Age of Jesus Christ*, rev. edn., vol. ii (Edinburgh, 1979), 458, 461.

by lines 39f., recalling that 'the redeemed from Zoan' in the Exodus foresaw in the Spirit their plantation in the holy place (Exod. 15:17, about to be quoted). One of the scarce Pentateuchal kingdom-texts is thereby incorporated,[63] and a confident recollection of past redemption is introduced. The line on the divine glory is then elucidated, in the same tone of confidence, by a prediction that the Shekhinah will indeed come back to the Temple.

> The gates of the Dwelling were cut down, of the everlasting House
> [1 Kings 8:13]
> for from between them there ceased the KINGDOM.
> The Holy One shall come within them for ever,
> and then shall they *lift up their head*, when thou renewest the
> KINGDOM.
>
> (lines 43f., introducing Ps. 24:7f., 9f.)

Now Yose reverts to the sombre present, hopefully interpreted as a permitted lengthening of the days (in implied answer to arguments like that of Chrysostom) before Edom's appointed end (line 48). Here there accordingly seems to begin a second sequence of references to what is fundamentally the same series of redemptive events. Obadiah 21 is introduced (line 49) by a prayer for victory:

> Contend, O *saviours*, take the glory from Edom:
> and set upon the Lord the majesty of the kingdom.

It is followed by an equally earnest prayer for the national purity appropriate to redemption, quoting and introducing Num. 23:21.

> Vanity God hates, and he upon our tongue
> sought truth, and there was none; and far away went the KINGDOM.
> Shaddai, turn aside iniquity from thy hosts:
> and let them shout unto thee the *shout* of the KINGDOM.
>
> (lines 51f.)

This sharply messianic exegesis, interpreting captivity as punishment and praying for divine cleansing that the kingdom may be hastened, is partly paralleled in Targum Pseudo-Jonathan, where 'the shout of a king' is indeed 'the call to arms of king Messiah'. There is no comparable urgency in the Targum, however, where Israel is seen as already free from iniquity, interpreted as

[63] L. J. Liebreich, 'Aspects of the New Year Liturgy', *HUCA* xxxiv (1963), 125–76 (140) notes the great shortage of kingdom-texts in the Pentateuch.

idolatry—that *he hath not beheld iniquity in Jacob* being similarly emphasized in the midrash.[64] There is an even more marked contrast between Yose and the non-messianic Onkelos on this verse (seeing Israel are not idolaters, the Memra and Shekhinah abide with them), followed later by Rashi (God abides with Israel despite her sins).[65] Here Yose's messianism clearly diverges from what was to become the royal road of interpretation.

The next couplet, introducing Ps. 93:1, takes up its words beforehand and gives them two messianic interpretations; these are analogous with its application especially to the Exodus and Sinai in contemporary homily.[66]

Thou shalt *bind on majesty*, and *gird thyself with strength*—
that no more may there be rule by a stranger in the kingdom;
Thou shalt *establish the world*—for the wicked one shall be *shaken out* [Job 38:13]
but one has set righteousness for his feet [Isa. 41:2], and he shall be crowned with kingdom.

(lines 54f.)

The verbs in the allusions to the Psalm-verse can be construed as either prayers or predictions; the latter sense seems more probable in view of the causal clause in the second line of the Hebrew. The 'stranger', then, will rule no longer, the 'wicked one' will be 'shaken out', and a righteous figure will be crowned (*yuṣnaf*; the royal association of *ṣanif* (Isa. 62:3) is taken up by Yose in respect of the sacerdotal mitre, *miṣnefeth*, at *'azkhir gevuroth*, 161). It is probably the Messiah who is crowned (Mirsky). The 'wicked one' may therefore be the current ruler of the 'kingdom of wickedness', the downfall of which is closely linked in contemporary midrash with Messiah's advent (e.g. PRK 5.9, Mandelbaum, 97).[67] The existing plural 'wicked' of Job 38:13, to which allusion is made would, however, have suited a reference to the 'wicked

[64] The Targums are surveyed by S. H. Levey, *The Messiah: An Aramaic Interpretation* (Cincinnati, 1974), 19. Neofiti's version of 'the shout of a king' is close to Ps.-Jon. (A. Diez Macho, *Neophyti I*, vol. iv (Madrid, 1974), 227). The first words of the verse are cited in Lev. R. 1.12 (Margulies, 27) and PRK S. 1.4 (Mandelbaum, 44).

[65] A. Berliner, *Der Kommentar des Salomo b. Isak über den Pentateuch*, 2nd edn. (1905, reprinted Jerusalem, 1962), 329.

[66] PRK 22.5 (Mandelbaum, 330) (the sending of the Flood and the giving of the Law); PRK S. 6.5 (Mandelbaum, 469) (the division of the Sea); Midrash Tehillim *ad loc.*, quoted in *Yalkut Shimeoni* on the Writings (Wilna, 1909), no. 847, 946 (both the Sea and Sinai).

[67] The passage is quoted as typical of many others by S. Schechter, *Some Aspects of Rabbinic Theology* (reprinted New York, 1961), 101; see also p. 331, below.

kingdom' equally well. Thus 'the time has come for the wicked men to be broken', PRK, *loc. cit.* (Mandelbaum, 97). It is striking, therefore, that Yose, without obvious metrical reason, has changed the word into the singular. He very possibly means, although the passage is not clear enough for certainty, to indicate the Gentile ruler conceived as anti-christ, who in *Zerubbabel* is termed 'that wicked one' and is indeed, as in, Targ. Isa. 11:4, 'the wicked' slain by the Messiah 'with the breath of his lips' (Isa. 11:4; p. 368, below).[68]

The last couplet, introducing Deut. 6:4, predicts that God shall 'break the staff of wickedness that rules in the KINGDOM' ('the staff of the wicked' (Isa. 14:5), is mentioned at PRK, *loc. cit.*), shall abolish idols, and for ever shall be called 'the only One to reign in KINGDOM'. If the previous couplet does indeed refer to antichrist, the train of thought will be comparable with that of *Zerubbabel*: 'and at once after him [Armilus] *the kingdom shall be the* LORD'S' (Obadiah 21).[69]

The events of the first sequence are: downfall of Edom, Messiah's throne set up in Jerusalem, return of Shekhinah to Temple. Those of the second sequence are: downfall of Edom, destruction of 'the wicked one' (probably antichrist), God rules alone. The first sequence significantly fails to end with this reference to the final sole rule of God. The omission enhances the likelihood that the second reference to the downfall of Edom (line 48) leads back into the same series of events at a slightly later stage. The servitude envisaged is clearly continuous with that of the present. Line 48 cannot then itself refer to resurgence of 'the wicked kingdom' during the messianic age. Such resurgence would, however, be presupposed by the line on the 'wicked one', if it is rightly taken of antichrist. The midrashim likely to be near Yose's time envisage a threat to the messianic kingdom well after its beginning. Thus Messiah will come and then disappear for a time, during which his faithful followers will have tribulation; or at his advent Gog and Magog will plan their war 'against the LORD and against his anointed' (Ps. 2:2); or 'the days of the Messiah' can be distinguished from, and placed before, 'the days of Gog and Magog'.[70] Yose

[68] Jellinek, *Bet ha-Midrasch*, ii, 56, lines 11f. 14 (*'otho rasha'*); 'Armilus the wicked' (*rasha'*) in the commentary on the Song of Songs under the name of Saadia reprinted by Even-Shemuel, *Midrashe Ge'ullah*, 131, line 7. Job 38:13 is comparably interpreted of the days of antichrist by Gregory the Great, *Moralia* 29.6 (10–11) (*PL* lxxvi, 482).

[69] Jellinek, *Bet ha-Midrasch*, ii, 57, line 4 from the bottom.

[70] PRK 5.8 (Mandelbaum, 92) (on Song of Songs 2:9); PRK 9.11 (Mandelbaum, 159) = Lev. R. 27.11 (Margulies, 646); Lev. R. 30.5 (Margulies, 701).

appears to expect the attack at the end of the messianic age, or of a distinct stage in it. Herein he would be close to the third midrashic passage and to Rev. 20:7f. as well as to *Zerubbabel*.[71] The events envisaged in the poem as a whole would accordingly be: downfall of Edom, messianic reign in Jerusalem, Shekhinah returns to temple, antichrist rises and is destroyed, God rules alone.

The third poem of the Tekiata, *I will flee for help*, has comparable but not identical messianic references. Synagogue, recalling how the three kingdoms have been cast down for her (above p. 333), prays 'from the teeth of iron' of the fourth beast (Dan. 7:7):

> 'The measure of my end he has not made known to me:
> when in my land shall *the turtle-dove* give VOICE?'
>
> (line 25)

'The voice of the turtle' (Song of Songs 2:12) is 'the voice of king Messiah' in an exegesis ascribed to the third-century R. Johanan and found among other places at PRK 5.9 (Mandelbaum, 97). This interpretation fits well here, and is followed by Mirsky, who cites the parallel from Pesikta Rabbati 75.1. God himself, however, is certainly the subject of the further allusion to the Song of Songs: 'when I hear my Beloved knocking at my doors' (5:2), which shortly afterwards introduces the first of the *shofaroth*, Exod. 19:16 (lines 29f.; above, p. 333).

Further *shofaroth* are now introduced by couplets describing the giving of the Law (before Ps. 47:6), praying for the gathering of the exiles (Zech. 10:8; version at p. 333 above), praying that the commandments may be treasured (Exod. 19:19), and noting that the end symbolized by New Year is accompanied by judgment (Ps. 81:4f.). Isa. 18:3 is introduced by lines on the resurrection:

> A sound from the grave, a cry from *the rock* [Isa. 42:11]
> *as the dry-boned* from *the dust* give VOICE.
> See, *an ensign on the mountains*, and the voice of *a trumpet* in the land,
>   to cause a cry of joy to be heard from the silent with no VOICE.
>
> (lines 47f.)

The circumstances are unclear. The resurrection is not expressly separated from the events of the messianic age, such as the ingathering. The 'end' looked for in

[71] Gog and Magog come before the days of the Messiah, by contrast, in the tradition of Hanan bar Tahlifa in Sanh. 97*b* (discussed, without reference to this point, by Schäfer, 'Hoffnungen', 15f.).

line 25 is the beginning of the messianic age, and the same word *qeṣ* is taken up in the couplet on New Year and judgement immediately preceding that on the resurrection. Further, Isa. 18:3, 'earth', is so re-used in line 48 as to make the rendering 'land' adopted above possible. These indications are not conclusive, but they are consistent with the view that Yose is presupposing the widespread rabbinic association of the resurrection with Palestine in the messianic age (Ezek. 37:11–14). Saadia says that most in his time expected the resurrection at the messianic redemption; *Zerubbabel* expresses this expectation, and it is the principal theme of Kalir's messianic poem already mentioned.[72] Yose is perhaps more likely to have envisaged it before the defeat of antichrist, with the two last-named sources, than afterwards, as in the specially-constructed scheme of Saadia.

The next couplet introducing Exod. 20:18, predicts that the 'deceived heart' (Isa. 44:20) shall no more be led astray (cf. *ʾahallelah ʾelohay*, 51; above, p. 343), and prays: 'Bring back to me as of old the law, the inheritance', doubtless reckoning with the complete observance possible in the messianic age (Maimonides (above, p. 340) sums up this well-marked topic).[73] A couplet introducing Psalm 150 tells of the 'understanding' poured forth in David's psalms, which teach praise to the ruler of all. The reference to David in prophetic terms as 'the man understanding in speech' (line 54) may perhaps have messianic overtones; compare 'all the words of the songs and praises of David, son of Jesse, thy servant and anointed' at the end of the Sabbath morning *Nishmath*.[74] The next and last couplet, introducing the final text, Zech. 9:14, recalls first the victory of the sons of Zion over the sons of Greece (Zech. 9:13), and then predicts battle against Teman (Edom) in the words of the text.

In the whole passage three sequences can be discerned, each beginning from present corporate recollection of the past. In the first, the congregation, longing with Synagogue to know 'the measure of my end', look forward to the coming of the messianic age and the ingathering; in the second, they recall

[72] Saadia, *ʾEmunoth we-Deʿoth*, 7. 1, ET by S. Rosenblatt (New Haven, 1948), 264f; *Zerubbabel* in Jellinek, *Bet ha-Midrasch*, ii, 56; Kalir in Even Shemuel, *Midrashe Geʾullah*, 113–16. The dead in Palestine rise first, according (for example) to PRK 22.5*a* (Mandelbaum, 330 (apparatus to line 12)). On the continuity between rabbinic texts and apocalyptic like Zerubbabel on this topic, see A. Marmorstein, *Studies in Jewish Theology* (London, 1950), 160.

[73] So Synagogue says (Song of Songs 5:2): '*I sleep*—in lack of God's commandments; *nevertheless my heart wakeneth*—ready to obey them', PRK 5.6 (Mandelbaum, 87).

[74] T. Kronholm, *Seder R. Amram Gaon*, Part ii (Lund, 1974), 71, and 14 of the Hebrew text.

the giving of the Law (Exod. 19:19), looking to the 'end' (of the year and the present captivity), with its accompanying heavenly judgment, and to the resurrection; in the third, again recalling Sinai (Exod. 20:18), they look once more to the overthrow of Edom and the beginning of the messianic age. The newly-mentioned events are the ingathering and the resurrection.

The messianic events encountered in the two poems accordingly are: downfall of Edom, messianic reign in Jerusalem, Shekhinah returns to Temple, ingathering of exiles, resurrection of the dead, antichrist rises and is destroyed, God rules alone. The events have been linked with texts from the *malkhuyyoth* and *shofaroth*, but there is likely to have been a degree of free choice among these texts in Yose's time.[75] Yose nevertheless draws on a fund of messianic ideas according to need rather than versifying them systematically.

His strong messianism has so far evinced two characteristics generally seen as typically rabbinic. It is theocentric, clear allusion to the messiah being rare; and it is concerned with Law, as emerged especially in the prayer 'Bring back the law'. A fuller characterization must, however, also take into account the messianism of the Avodah poems, with their special concentration on sanctuary and sacrifice.

(b) The temple service

A description of the Day of Atonement service, quoting and paraphrasing Mishnah, Yoma, is the kernel of the Avodah poems. It begins from a citation of Lev. 8:34, well compared and contrasted by L. Ligier with the Gospel-citation opening the narrative of institution in the eucharistic anaphora.[76] Elbogen argued, on the basis of Geniza texts, that this description originally constituted the Avodah in its entirety.[77] Since before Yose,[78] however, it had been prefaced with a recital of God's works from Creation to the institution of the Tabernacle-

[75] Heinemann in Heinemann-Petuchowski, *Literature of the Synagogue*, 60; Liebreich, 'New Year Liturgy', 139–41, argues that the prophetic verses had to be eschatological passages from the Latter Prophets.

[76] L. Ligier, SJ, 'Autour du sacrifice eucharistique: anaphores orientales et anamnèse juive de Kippur', *Nouvelle revue théologique*, lxxxii (1960), 40–55 (52, 54).

[77] I. Elbogen, *Studien zur Geschichte des jüdischen Gottesdienstes* (Berlin, 1907), 56f; Mirsky, *Yosse ben Yosse*, 25, also refers to J. M. Grintz's suggestion that a Qumran 'Prayer for the Day of Atonement' (1Q34 2+1) was an Avodah.

[78] The Avodah *'attah bara'tha'eth ha-'olam kullo* (discussed below at p. 355) published by Elbogen, *Studien*, 116f., is set earlier than Yose by Mirsky, *Yosse ben Yosse*, 26.

service: in Elbogen's view, a poetic device of one early writer, who was then imitated by most others.[79] In view of the many parallels with Ecclesiasticus, Roth suggested that the form grew from an original that combined the relevant parts of the Praise of the Fathers with Mishnah, Yoma.[80] Mirsky reinforces this view by pointing to the Creation-poem, Ecclus. 42:15–43:33, which precedes the Praise of the Fathers; and he compares the belief, evinced for example at Gen. R. 1.4, that both the Temple and repentance (the business of the Day of Atonement) existed before Creation. The recital in the Avodah shows that the Temple service completes the tale of the works of Creation, and that the world is founded upon it.[81]

The literary form of the Avodah thus reflects the conviction that the Temple service is bound up with the work of Creation. The deep roots of this conviction, in such biblical passages as Ps. 78:69, are also probably to be traced beneath other liturgical institutions of Yose's time. Mishnah, Taanith 4.2–3 obliges the lay members of a *maamad* to read the story of Creation while the priests of the course concerned are ministering in the Temple. The Babylonian Gemara, *27b*, gives the reason as 'were it not for the *maamadoth*, heaven and earth could not stand'. The priestly courses appear to have continued after 70 to fast and to read daily the relevant portion of Genesis 1 as 'part of the trend commemorating the ancient Temple ritual'.[82] Among midrashic echoes of the same conviction a special kinship with the Avodah form appears in the interpretation of Num. 7:1 at PRK 1.4 and 5 (Mandelbaum, 9 and 11): 'After the Tabernacle was set up, the earth became stable.'

The *anamnesis* of the Temple service in these poems is, despite the bitter sense of loss already noted, in some degree an actualization. 'Whenever they read the order of sacrifices I will deem it as if they had offered them before me, and I will grant them pardon' (Taanith 27*b*). Hence the recital, made in lively awareness of the service as the crown of Creation, in a measure anticipates the restoration expected in redemption.

[79] Elbogen, *Studien*, 58f.

[80] Roth, 'Ecclesiasticus', 177.

[81] Mirsky, *Yosse ben Yosse*, 26–9.

[82] E. E. Urbach, ''Mishmarot and Ma'amadot', *Tarbiz* xlii (1973), 304–27; the quotation is from the English summary, p. v. Cf. Urbach, 'Additional Note', *Tarbiz* xliii (1974), 224; Z. Ilan, 'A Broken Slab Containing the Names of the Twenty-Four Priestly Courses Discovered in the Vicinity of Kissufim', ibid., 225f.; Stein in Rosenthal, *Saadya Studies*, 221; Baron, *History*, vii, 90; Schürer-Vermes-Millar, *History of the Jewish People*, ii, 245–50.

S. Stein has observed that the Gemara of Taanith in the Babylonian Talmud, which in a section already quoted (27*a*–28*a*) deals with the duties of the priestly courses, significantly ends by describing a dance of the redeemed (31*a*).[83] His observation is confirmed by the arrangement of Lev. R. 11, in which the first ministrations of Aaron and his sons (Lev. 9:1) are interpreted by Prov. 9:1–4 (Wisdom's 'house' being expounded successively of the world, the Temple and the days of Gog and Magog, the Torah, and the Tabernacle), and the chapter is ended (11:9) by the same tradition, with different attestation and proof-texts, on the dance of the righteous round the Holy One in the Time to Come. Discoveries of poems and synagogal inscriptions concerning the priestly courses have confirmed that throughout the Talmudic period Palestinian priests were ready, in S. W. Baron's words, 'to spring into immediate action upon the advent of Messiah, and without delay to restore the ancient ritual to full operation'.[84]

The whole Avodah-form accordingly possesses messianic overtones. The restoration of the Service, which it looks to and in some degree realizes, will be the fulfilment of God's purpose from before the world and the sure token of his redemption. Some more specific allusions to redemption in Yose's interpretation can now be noted.

(i) The rebuilding of the Temple. The throne of glory, to which the Temple corresponds, is mentioned, as Mirsky notes, immediately after the Law as created before the world.[85]

> Then before a thousand generations it [the Law] came into mind,
> and from it is the preparation of all the works of the pattern [1 Chron 28:19].
> In the height he set the throne of his majesty,
> spread his cloud and stretched it out as a curtain for a tent.
> It shall not be taken down, and none of its stakes shall be removed,
> until its end come and it is renewed with a word.
>
> (*ʾazkhir gevuroth*, 10–12)[86]

Here the Law, as in Gen.R. 1.1, is the plan of Creation, but line 10*b* uses the words of 1 Chron. 28:19, which refer to the building of the *Temple* after the

83 Stein in Rosenthal, *Saadya Studies*, 221.

84 Baron, *History*, vii, 90; CIIP 1145.

85 Mirsky, *Yosse ben Yosse*, 27, also quoting *ʾattah konanta ʿolam be-rov ḥesed*, 3 and 5, and *ʾasapper gedoloth*, 2.

86 This poem is translated (apart from a passage at the end) with comments by A. Murtonen, *Materials for a Non-Masoretic Hebrew Grammar*, vol. i (Helsinki, 1958), 107–13.

heavenly pattern. Murtonen brings this out by rendering *mal'akhoth*, 'works', as 'services', and noting *tavnith*, 'pattern', as an allusive name for 'sanctuary'. In the next line 'height' is linked by Mirsky with Jer. 17:12: 'a glorious high throne from the beginning is the place of our sanctuary'; and *'ohel*, tent or tabernacle, taken here from the description of the heavens in Isa. 40:22, has an obvious sacred application, to occur shortly in line 26 where Joshua is *meshareth 'ohel*, the minister of the tabernacle. The double meaning is sustained, in line 12, which alludes to Isa. 33:20, where the 'tabernacle that shall not be taken down' is Jerusalem. Thus line 12*b*, on the appointed end and renewal of the heavens, speaks also of the end and renewal of the earthly Temple.

(ii) The Messianic Banquet. Gen. 1:21, on the creation of sea monsters, fish and fowl, is linked with the Banquet, as in Targum and midrash, in both the longer Avodah-poems. In *Thou hast established the world in the multitude of mercy*, lines 18–22, the Banquet is connected with the dietary laws, as in Targ. Ps.-Jon. *ad loc.*; Leviticus Rabbah at 13.3; 22.10 (Margulies, 278f., 522f.) indeed presents it as the future compensation for eating *kosher*. In I *will recount the mighty works*, however, the Banquet receives a sacrificial interpretation also. From 'the fleeing ones of the deeps' (Isa. 27:1; Ps. 148:7) created on the Fifth Day

> He stored up some for the everlasting banquet …
> Tall fowl sprouted from the pool of waters
> for them that *eat at the king's table*, and the army of his hosts …
> There multiplied from the earth horned beasts for sacrifice,
> creatures to eat, cattle and creeping things.
> He fattened Behemoth with the produce of *a thousand hills* [Ps. 50:10],
> for on the day of his sacrifice *he will bring near his sword* [Job 40:19].
> (*'azkhir gevuroth*, 28*a*, 29, 31f.)

Although the question of uncleanness is expressly mentioned in the omitted line 30, the emphasis here falls, by contrast with the sources already noted, less on diet than on sacrifice. Creation provides both for the priests who 'eat at the king's table' (Ezek. 41:22) and for the lay Israelite. The messianic banquet will be just such a sacrificial meal. With the due slaughter implied in line 32 we may contrast Lev. R. 13.3, where the monsters kill one another, although this too is interpreted as ritual slaughter. A similarly 'sacrificial' view of the Banquet may also be found at 1QS*a* 2.11–22, where however the model appears to be not the whole-offerings but the priestly participation in the Shewbread from the altar-table of Ezek. 41:22, associated with the meal of the messianic Prince in the Temple described at Ezek. 44:3ff.[87] Likewise, in Targ. Cant. 8:2, Israel conducts Messiah into the Temple for 'the feast of Leviathan'.[88]

(iii) The Akedah. The binding of Isaac is interpreted as the equivalent of 'a lamb for a burnt offering' (Gen. 22:8) and the pledge of future redemption. Isaac is 'the basket of first-fruits' (Deut. 26:2) and 'the lamb' (*'azkhir gevuroth*, 92f.; cf. *'anusah le-ezrah*, 8; above, p. 299). Zunz drew attention to the emphasis in the Avodah poems on readiness for sacrifice.[89] This emphasis may well come to Yose by inheritance. In an Aramaic poem dated earlier than Yose by J. Heinemann 'the father did not spare his son, and the son did not delay' (language almost identical with that of *'azkhir gevuroth*, 92*b*, quoted below); and Isaac declares, in heavily Graecized diction: 'Happy am I that *Kyrios* has chosen me from the whole *kosmos*.'[90] The link between freely-accepted trials, sacrifice and atonement is very close (above, p. 299).

He bore like a giant the weight of temptations,
and by command to slaughter his only son thou didst try him, and he stood.
The father rejoiced to bind, and the son to be bound;
for by this will be justified (God's) carried ones in the chastisement.
Thou didst appoint his atonement (*kofer*) a ram, and it was
reckoned to him righteousness;
on this day will *we* hear: I have found atonement.
(*'atta konanta 'olam be-rov ḥesed*, 58–60)

Zunz brings out the emphasis of the last line by rendering 'we also', and for *kofer* has *Lösung*, 'setting free' or 'absolution'.[91] *'aqad*, 'bind', is the term for tying the lamb of the *Tamid* before slaughter.[92]

Similarly in *'azkhir gevuroth*, 92–4, 'the father did not spare, the son did not delay' and 'the Good and Merciful One' said 'We will accept your [plural]

[87] M. Black, *The Scrolls and Christian Origins* (London, 1961), 108–11, 146f.

[88] Levey, *The Messiah*, 130–2; on the monsters' deaths in Kalir, other poets including Yose, and the midrash, see J. Schirmann, 'The Battle between Behemoth and Leviathan According to an Ancient Hebrew Piyyut', *Proceedings of the Israel Academy of Sciences and Humanities* iv (1969–70), 327–69 (338–40, 362).

[89] Zunz, *Die synagogale Poesie*, 136f.

[90] J. Heinemann, 'Remnants of Ancient Piyyutim in the Palestinian Targum Tradition', *Hasifrut* iv (1973), 362–75 (366f.).

[91] Zunz, *Die synagogale Poesie*, 137.

[92] Mishnah, Tamid 4.1; the point is emphasized by P. R. Davies and B. D. Chilton, 'The Aqedah: A Revised Tradition-History', *CBQ* xl (1978), 535.

deed as that of priest and victim' (*zoveaḥ we-nizbaḥ*, 'sacrificer and sacrificed'). Again, in *'asapper gedoloth* Abraham's ten trials (above, p. 335) culminated in the command

to make his son an offering,[93] and he did not hesitate.
The lamb was delivered to the sword, and the burning of fire:
JAH will look upon him as ashes when we are in distress.

(*'asapper gedoloth*, 16f.)

Throughout, the efficacy of the Akedah is expressed as that of a burnt offering. The terms are mainly those known from Amoraic texts, the last quotation being close to those, like Ber. 62*b*, which speak as if Isaac had in truth been offered.[94] In the context of the Avodah, however, emphasis falls rather on the importance of the sacrificial rites prefigured on Mount Moriah (the Temple-mount, *'eyn lanu kohen gadol*, 25; above, p. 332) than on the value of the binding of Isaac as their substitute. The recital of the Day of Atonement offerings will soon follow. Ligier has noted the striking resemblance between Yose and contemporary eastern and western Church teaching on Christ as both priest and victim.[95] There is probably an element of conscious or unconscious reaction to such teaching in Yose's presentation of the binding of Isaac; but in the setting of the Avodah his interpretation remains true to the early understanding of the passage as a prefiguration of the Temple service, and of the atonement and future redemption that the service betokens.[96]

(iv) The redemption from Egypt. The Exodus, foreshadowing redemption to come, is described with markedly sacerdotal emphasis. The similarly coloured Ecclus. 45 only hints at the story, but Yose tells it to the glory of the house of Levi. Jacob became father of the twelve tribes, and

The third was set aside to behold the King's face,
to sing and to minister, to enter his chambers.

(*'azkhir gevuroth*, 105)

[93] *shay*, often used for *qorban* in Yose; see Mirsky, *Yosse ben Yosse*, 69.

[94] S. Spiegel, *The Last Trial* (New York, 1967), 41–4; cf. 102f. (willingness of father and son), 114f. (atonement, Cant. R. on 1.14).

[95] Ligier, 'Autour du sacrifice eucharistique', 55, citing among other texts the Liturgies of S. Basil and S. Chrysostom in F. E. Brightman, *Liturgies Eastern and Western*, vol. i (Oxford, 1896), 318, lines 34–5, and 378, lines 5–6 (σὺ γὰρ εἶ ὁ προσφέρων καὶ προσφερόμενος).

[96] See P. R. Davies, 'Passover and the Dating of the Aqedah', *JJS* xxx (1979), 59–67, on the early interpretation of the passage, and apologetic elements in its development.

This line on Levi is echoed in the account of the service at line 186 of the same poem; the high priest, seeming like an angel in his vesture (line 157), will be 'seeing the King's face and entering his holy chamber'. This stress on the angelic privilege shared by the priesthood recalls the view expressed in contemporary Day-of-Atonement homily that Nadab and Abihu abused it by 'eating and drinking' the vision of God (Exod. 24:11 in PRK 26.9 (Mandelbaum, 396) and Lev. R. 20.10 (Margulies, 466f.)); the High Priest could indeed be described as an angel, Lev. R. 21.12 (Margulies, 493). These passages, like Yose here, continue the tendency to compare priests with angels seen at Jub. 31:14; 1QS*b* 4.24–6 (from 'Recueil des Bénédictions').

Meanwhile, however, the poem describes the blossoming of Levi's rod or tribe in his three sons (Exod. 6:16) until like 'a goodly vine' (Ezek. 17:8) Amram his grandson sprouts into 'a priest, a shepherd, and a woman that is a prophetess'—Aaron, Moses and Miriam (line 110). The order of reference, following Exod. 6:20 (Aaron and Moses, only) rather than Mic. 6:4 (the three, with Moses first), is significant of what follows (line 111):

> When the *time of love* drew near [Ezek. 16:8] his blossom was established
> to break the bonds of Zoan, and to breach the hedge of the handful
>   [the sea, Isa. 40:12].

It is, then, through the blossoming of the levitical vine that redemption was accomplished, when Israel was brought near to the Bridegroom. After three lines on Moses' sanctification in the cloud, and his miracles, and a line on Miriam and her merits, Yose ascribes the pillar of cloud and fire to Aaron's merit (lines 116f., each beginning with Levi's *lamed*):

> The escort of clouds of majesty was granted to the beloved ones
> at the hands of a priest ministering *in peace and equity* [Mal 2:6];
> With him and with his seed a covenant of salt was made
> that there might never fail the covenant of the salt of offerings of
>   sweet savour [Num. 18:19; Lev. 2:12f.].

An entirely priestly passage on the company of Korah (in the spirit of Ecclus. 45:18–20) and the duties of the priests as laid down by Moses in Lev. 8 now leads to the quotation of Lev. 8:34: 'As he hath done this day, so the LORD hath commanded to do, to make an atonement for you.' This text, as noted above, opens the narrative of the rites and ceremonies of the Day of Atonement.

The redemption from Egypt has been presented as part of the annals of Levi. The same pattern is followed more briefly in *ʾattah konanta ʾolam be-rov ḥesed*, 66–72, on the blossoming of the 'stem of Levi' (line 67; cf. Isa. 11:1). The much briefer *ʾasapper gedoloth* encompasses the matter in lines 20–3, without mentioning the Exodus. The three offspring of Amram were 'for a king, and for a seeress, and to minister and do priestly service' (line 20), Aaron receiving the last but the fullest and most honorific reference. Lines 21f. immediately begin the description of priestly duties, Lev. 8:34 being quoted after line 22.

That this presentation was traditional in Yose's time is suggested by the bare bones of it visible in what is considered an earlier Avodah, *ʾattah baraʾthaʾeth ha-ʿolam kullo*, lines 12–16[97] Here Levi 'the third' (cf. *ʾazkhir gevuroth*, 105, above, p. 353) is separated; God's eyes are set on one of his descendants, 'Aaron the chief of thy saints' (Ps. 106:16); to him it has been explained how he shall enter the holy place. Yose has adorned this structure with the momentous narrative of redemption, which now appears as wrought through the fruitful vine of the Levitical priesthood; the effect is to underline the redemptive significance of the recital of the order of priestly service that follows.

(v) The Day of Atonement. The high priest's glory is described first when he vests himself and secondly when he comes forth from the holy of holies. The atoning value of each garment that he puts on is described (*ʾazkhir gevuroth*, 152–86; *ʾattah konanta ʾolam be-rov ḥesed*, 93–119; no treatment in *ʾasapper gedoloth*). Among the collective sins of Israel thus absolved are the selling of the 'righteous one', Joseph (the vestment, *ʾazkhir gevuroth*, 160; *ʾattah konanta ʿolam be-rov ḥesed*, 98) and the making of the golden calf (the jewel of the breastplate, *ʾazkhir gevuroth*, 174; *ʾattah konanta ʿolam be-rov ḥesed*, 110). Strong consciousness of the first of these sins emerges also in the midrash *ʾElleh ʾezkerah*, where the Hadrianic martyrs suffer for this fault of their forefathers; for the second, compare *I fear amid my doings*, line 51. The messianic significance of this acute awareness of corporate sin has been noted above at p. 330. Atonement for these sins may be presumed to hasten the messianic age.

Two items in the vesture in fact recall kingdom rather than atonement. It is at once noted that the 'anointed for war' divines by these garments, and that

[97] Text in Elbogen, *Studien*, 117.

the Urim forecast defeat or victory (Num. 27:21). Hence 'Praise God, sons of a *great nation* (Deut. 4:7); the herald of salvation is near at all times' (*'azkhir gevuroth*, 156). The phrase is taken up at the end of the poem, where the high priest is the herald of salvation (line 269, quoted below). The priest 'anointed for war' (Deut. 20:2–9, Mishnah, Soṭah 8) is a messianic figure at PRK 5.9 (Mandelbaum, 97) where together with Elijah, king Messiah and Melchizedek he is one of the 'four carpenters' of Zech. 2:3 (1:20) who are 'the flowers' to 'appear on the earth' at the messianic age (Song of Songs 2:12). A similarly messianic note is struck in the description of the mitre (above, p. 344).

> The crown of his head was in royal majesty (*be-hod ha-melukhah*),
> mitred in fair linen *for glory and for beauty*.
>
> (*'azkhir gevuroth*, 161)

In the parallel, *'attah konanta 'olam be-rov ḥesed*, 161, it is 'a royal diadem', *nezer ha-melukhah*. The description recalls the Hasmonaean priest-kings, *mekhahane melukhah* (*'ahallelah 'elohay*, 28; above, p. 328), (whose victory over the third kingdom Yose can mention in a messianic context, as at the end of *'anusah le-'ezrah* (above, p. 347).

At the end of the Avodah the High Priest emerges from the holy of holies.

> His appearance shines out as when the sun comes forth *in his might*
> [Judg. 5:31; Rev. 1:16];
> he is sending to those that sent him *righteousness* and *healing* [Mal. 3:20].
> The hope of the congregation is for the coming forth of a skilled man,
> a herald of salvation and proclaimer of forgiveness.
>
> (*'azkhir gevuroth*, 268f.)

The high priest speaks of God's forgiveness, and the attendant of the scapegoat 'gives good tidings of forgiveness' (*ibid.*, 273) by attesting that the scarlet thread is whitened (Yoma 6.8); then

> *Perfect and upright* they lead him to his dwelling,
> and they make rejoicing as he comes forth without harm.
> *Happy are the people that are in such a case* … [Ps. 144:15]
>
> (*ibid.*, lines 275f.)

The high priest coming forth as the sun represents all Israel as 'the messenger of the congregation' (line 268); cf. 'faithful messenger' (*'asapper gedoloth*, line 59). The righteousness and healing that he brings make them perfect and upright.

The sacerdotal vesture in Yose is both priestly and kingly, the token at once of divine forgiveness and reunion with Israel, and of royalty to be restored. The emphasis laid on the proclamation of forgiveness by 'the herald of salvation' so vested corresponds not only to acute consciousness of sin, but also to a longing for the kingdom that sin delays.

The messianic events expected by Yose can now be listed as: downfall of Edom, messianic reign in Jerusalem, Shekhinah returns to Temple, ingathering of exiles, messianic banquet, resurrection of dead, antichrist rises and is destroyed, God rules alone. As has been noted, they are not described by the poet in this sequence, and the place given here to so important an event as the resurrection can be no more than probable (above, pp. 346–7). It is nevertheless significant that a relatively compact body of liturgical poetry for the 'Days of Awe' can yield so full a picture of messianic expectation. To note the importance of the subject in Yose is the first step towards the fuller characterization of his messianism that can now be attempted.

Its thematic importance corresponds, first of all, to Yose's striking *urgency* of tone. This is especially audible in the Tekiata, where each poem builds up to a final section on redemption. The *malkhuyyoth* pray (above, pp. 342–3):

> Stir and awake the *joy of the whole earth* …
> Contend, O *saviours*, take the glory from Edom …
> let them shout unto thee the *shout* of the KINGDOM.

(where Yose's messianism diverges from the line to be taken by classical exegesis of Num. 23:21). The *zikhronoth* move from the petition: 'Look, O God, upon the dwellers in the gardens' (above, p. 336) to: '*Purchase us the second time* [Isa. 11:11], for we are forgotten out of REMEMBRANCE [line 57, introducing Ps. 74:2: 'Remember thy congregation whom thou didst purchase of old'). In the third poem, 'When in my land shall *the turtle-dove* give VOICE?' (p. 346), is soon followed by the petitions of the *shofaroth* (pp. 333, 347): 'Visit the house-sparrow … bring back to me as of old the law, the inheritance', and the final militant prediction (Zech. 9:14; p. 347): 'Thou shalt blow *the trumpet; with the whirlwinds to Teman* then *shall go forth* the VOICE.' In the Avodah-poems 'the hope of the congregation' (*'azkhir gevuroth*, 269; above,

p. 356) is directed primarily towards the Day-of-Atonement declaration of divine pardon. 'The end of days' (Dan. 12:13; *ʾattah konanta ʿolam be-rov ḥesed*, line 1) is also in mind, however; the Temple will be renewed, and the day of sacrifice for the everlasting banquet will come (above, p. 351); the remembrance of the work of creation culminating in the service of the Tabernacle, and the recital of the order of sacrifice for atonement, are themselves implicitly messianic (pp. 350–1). Similarly, the systematic account of Temple rites and ceremonies that can no longer be performed, in *We have no high priest*, intensifies hope for the restoration of God's presence (p. 332). The specially clear note of urgency in the Tekiata recalls that it was intended not as hymnody simply, but as liturgy (above p. 327); it is formally comparable with messianic prayers of the *Tekiata de-vey Rav* (p. 327, n. 16). Earnest petition is therefore appropriate to its purpose. An estimate of Yose's messianism must still reckon with the fact that its expression has the 'fervent piety' (S. W. Baron)[98] suited to this traditional form, and that it won for itself a place in the mainstream of Jewish liturgy.

A second obvious characteristic is Yose's nationalism. The synagogue of Israel, rather than mankind or the individual, is at the heart of his thought (p. 329). This might seem too commonplace for comment, did it not contrast, as seen already (above, pp. 330–1), with the messianism of the hymn-like prayers—among the most important antecedents of Yose's poetry—that introduce *malkhuyyoth, zikhronoth* and *shofaroth* in the *Tekiata de-vey Rav*. These exhibit, not entirely without particularist passages, a universalism marked by such expressions as 'all sons of flesh shall call upon thee'.[99] From the same *malkhuyyoth* (including Obadiah 21) quoted after this passage Yose, so bitterly lamenting the oppression of the fourth kingdom, characteristically emphasizes not only the kingdom of the LORD, but his vengeance on the heathen (above, p. 343).

Obadiah 21, promising that when the saviours judge the mount of Esau the kingdom shall be the LORD's, links nationalism with a characteristic picked out above as typically rabbinic, Yose's *theocentricity*. This was especially noticeable in the third poem of the *Tekiata*, where an allusion to the messiah in the language of the Song of Songs (above, p. 346) occurs in the midst of

[98] Baron, *History*, vii, 93.

[99] Translation from text in Goldschmidt, *Maḥzor la-yamim ha-norʾaim*, i, 243; cf. 327 n. 16 above.

a sustained application of the imagery of bridegroom and bride not to the Messiah, but to God himself and his people. Similarly, suffering, closely bound up with messianism as we have seen it to be, marks the Synagogue and her representative patriarchs, martyrs and wise men, but not the Messiah himself. There is little trace of that meditation on the messianic figure, in which he can appear as a sufferer, that is evident in rabbinic tradition before Yose's time. The theme of the Deity himself as Israel's bridegroom and earth's sovereign by far preponderates over that of the Messiah, to whom only three reasonably clear allusions have been noticed. As quotation has made plain, this theocentricity combines intense reverence with extreme boldness, in the manner of the haggadah. Hence the bridegroom imagery that in Church tradition, from 2 Cor. 11:2 onwards, is characteristically christological (although the christology is itself theocentric; 1 Cor. 3:23), in Yose is directly theological.

Concern with Torah, the other characteristic already noted as rabbinic, is present but not pre-eminent. Torah is the pattern of the universe, and the dietary laws are envisaged in Creation (above, pp. 350–1); the Wise and their converse are dear to God (pp. 336–7), and Israel longs to keep the Law, given at 'the time of love' in the first redemption, wholly and wholeheartedly in the messianic age (p. 347). Yet Yose does not strongly emphasize the place in the divine economy of the Oral Law and its rabbinic elucidation. Herein he differs from such a rabbinic presentation of Israel's relation with God as the Targum to the Song of Songs (below, pp. 361–2); and his position seems to correspond to the fact that he is only moderately influenced by rabbinic material (above, p. 326).

More obvious, especially in the Avodah poems, is the *levitical flavour* of Yose's messianism. The rebuilding of the Temple is central to his hopes; the messianic banquet is sacrificial, and the Akedah prefigures the sacrifices to be restored, the promise of pardon going with them; the first redemption was wrought through the levitical priesthood, whose ministry is the appointed means of reconciliation between Israel and her Beloved (above, pp. 350–7). Outside the Day-of-Atonement compositions, the return of the Shekhinah to the Temple is a prominent theme of the *malkhuyyoth* (p. 343). Like the midrashic passages compared above, Yose's poems attest the lively continuance of the concern with priesthood and sacrifice manifest in the Qumran writings (cited above pp. 351, 354) or the Epistle to the Hebrews.

With his concern for the Temple-service we may link a last important note of his messianism, *consciousness of sin* and desire for reconciliation with God. When Israel sinned, 'far away went the KINGDOM'; God is asked to purify her for the messianic age (above, p. 343), when the heart will no more be led astray (the evil *yeṣer*, in rabbinic terms that Yose does not use, will lose its power) (p. 347); then, as the first redemption promised, forever will she be the seal upon his heart (p. 333).

Conclusions

(a) The relations of suffering with messianism in Yose

The corporate sufferings underscored by Yose, servitude and the loss of the Temple service, answer (as we saw) to the twin hopes of his messianism, with its series of redemptive events in realm and sanctuary culminating in the sole rule of God. The foregoing summary has shown, however, that suffering is not related to messianism simply as deprivation to the hope of restoration, in precise correspondence. Such a correspondence is indeed envisaged, as appears in the characteristics of urgency, nationalism and levitical concern identified above. There is also, however, a more integral relation between suffering and hope. Yose indeed, as noted above, has no suffering Messiah among the representatives of suffering Israel; Isa. 53:7 is characteristically applied to Synagogue herself (*'anusah le-'ezrah*, line 3; above, p. 332). Yet, as seen in the first part of this study, Yose gives the Synagogue's present suffering a double interpretation as at once punitive and meritorious; and this theological interpretation is related to the theocentricity of his messianism, his levitical concern as concern with the means of atonement, his consciousness of sin and love of God's Law. An approach to his consolation from its biblical links with tribulation, the messianic significance of which Scholem has emphasized, thus leads to the miraculous as well as the this-worldly elements in his view of redemption. In present, historical suffering he hopes indeed for the overthrow of Edom and the restoration of Israel; but present suffering itself, viewed as punishment and merit, implies a larger hope of reconciliation and reward with God—who returns to the bride of youth in the beloved dwelling, who receives acceptable sacrifice and service, and who raises the dead.

(b) Yose and rabbinic messianism

Yose's messianism hopes above all for the establishment of God's kingdom and the return of the divine Bridegroom to his sanctuary and people. This hope embraces a series of expectations, from the downfall of Edom and the return of the Shekhinah to the resurrection of the dead, the defeat of antichrist and God's sole rule. His presentation of them is urgent, nationalist but theocentric; concerned with God's Law, and concerned still more obviously with sanctuary, sacrifice, sin and atonement.

These expectations are known from rabbinic sources, and their presentation has typically rabbinic features in its restrained treatment of the Messiah and its concern with Torah (although the latter is less strongly marked, as already noted, than we might expect). On the other hand, the reflection of so unified a series of expectations within a relatively confined space itself contrasts with the more fragmentary and unschematized presentations of messianic traditions in Talmud and midrash; and the unqualified urgency of Yose's petitions for the kingdom, like the fervency with which he affirms the value of sanctuary and sacrifice, is at variance with the more cautious tenor of the midrash. Thus Leviticus Rabbah, as Joseph Heinemann observes,[100] depicts messianic joys (e.g. 13.3; above, p. 351), but bridles expectation by reserve on the manner and time of their coming; and when it affirms sacrificial atonement (e.g. 11; above, p. 350), also inculcates the atoning value of good works.

A similar difference of emphasis emerges in comparison with the Targum of the Song of Songs, wherein, as in Yose, the Song is the story of Israel's relation with God. The redaction of the Targum is ascribed to rabbinic circles in seventh- or eighth-century Palestine; R. Loewe also takes note of its contact with interpretations in the name of the third-century Palestinian R. Johanan (above, p. 346) and his contemporaries.[101] Four features of the Targum are specially noted by Loewe: the prominence that it accords to Oral Torah as the central theme in Israel's story of salvation; emphasis on Israel's sin (which can receive apparently gratuitous notice, as in Yose; above, p. 333); affirmation of atonement through Tabernacle, Temple and sacrifice; and restriction of Messiah's role in redemption, with concentration on that of the Deity

[100] Heinemann, 'Art of Composition', 821, 825f., and 'Profile of a Midrash', 146–8.
[101] Loewe, 'Apologetic Motifs', 161, 168; P. S. Alexander, *The Targum of Canticles* (London, 2003), 1–9.

himself. These points add up, Loewe suggests, to a mute repudiation of the Christian understanding of atonement. The striking fact that Yose shares the last three of the Targum's notable features may further suggest, in line with Loewe's indication of possible sources, that both draw on a common exegetical tradition, perhaps already marked by the apologetic concern that has also seemed possible in Yose (above, pp. 336, 353). However that may be, Yose, who has so much in common with the Targumist, fails to share (as noted above) his characteristically rabbinic emphasis on Oral Torah. Further, Yose's urgency is opposed to a lesser feature of the Targum, its dissuasion from premature messianism.

These contrasts may in part correspond, as in the case of the treatments of suffering discussed above, to the formal contrast between congregational self-expression in Yose and the address *to* the congregation that in different modes lies beneath the literary traditions of midrash and Targum. Yose's characteristic concerns are shared, however, by the other two sources, which simply balance them with other emphases. These answer not merely to the pastoral demands of homily and biblical paraphrase, but also to the conviction that Israel's present life according to *halakhah* is an acceptable offering. Had this fundamental rabbinic conviction been close to Yose's heart, he would probably have expressed it in connection with his unmistakable love of the commandments. Instead, more strongly conscious of the tendency to sin in suffering Israel's present life, he characteristically prays: 'Bind on the commandments, lest they fly from me as an eagle' (*ʾanusah le-ʿezrah*, 39, introducing Exod. 19:19; above, p. 346).

Yose's failure to magnify the Oral Torah and to neutralize his messianic urgency thus corresponds to a lack of emphasis in these poems on the validity of Israel's present observance. Without this emphasis, but with a lively awareness of present suffering, concern for sin and the appointed means of atonement is thrown into bolder relief, and the hope for redemption is correspondingly intensified. This muting of a characteristically rabbinic note in the sphere of thought recalls Yose's limited use of rabbinic terms in the sphere of language. Yose's messianism constantly draws, as we have seen, on the material of rabbinic midrash; but distinctiveness over against the *ethos* of the midrash is epitomized in his introduction to Num. 23:21 (above, pp. 343, 360). Here he avoids expressing the midrashic confidence, echoed in Rashi's comment, that

God 'hath not beheld iniquity in Jacob'; but prays instead for the removal of iniquity and the hastening of the kingdom.

(c) Yose and the New Testament

Yose's poems, largely scriptural in language, draw on biblical writings and interpretations known in New Testament times, together with exegesis of later date. This material subserves an integration of experienced suffering with messianic hope. The corporate afflictions of the Synagogue are interpreted not only as deserving compensation, but as constituting tokens of coming reconciliation and reward with God. The voice of the congregation cries directly to the divine Bridegroom.

Among the few New Testament passages formally comparable with Yose's poems are the hymns in Revelation to God—and the Lamb. Other literary forms attest this same new Church-consciousness of relation to God through Christ. The Bridegroom now is the crucified Messiah (above, p. 359). Yose's bold biblical images of the Almighty's longing for the bride of youth are not far from the spirit of contemporary midrash, wherein God's 'undefiled' in the Song of Songs is his 'twin' whose pain he shares.[102] Nevertheless these poems are, in Rachel Rosenzweig's phrase, projecting on to God himself Israel's own human solidarity in woe.[103] For the New Testament writers, by contrast, the historical Passion of Christ means that the Bridegroom's sufferings are primary and determinative in a way for which there is no parallel in Yose. The corporate sufferings of the New Testament Church are accordingly related to those of the Lord. The contrast is heightened by Yose's combination of theocentric fervour with reserve on the Messiah's role. A comparable difference is discerned by P. Prigent between the christocentric visions of Revelation and their Jewish apocalyptic counterparts, wherein specifically messianic concern is often subsumed in the longing for intervention by God himself.[104] Yet Yose's poems also highlight the debt that he shares with the New Testament writers to their common source, the

[102] PRK 5.6 (Mandelbaum, 87f.); the parallel Cant. R. on S.2 is discussed with other passages on God's identification with Israel's suffering in Rosenzweig, *Solidarität*, 93–9.

[103] Ibid., 203.

[104] P. Prigent, 'Apocalypse et apocalyptique', in J.-E. Ménard (ed.), *Exegèse biblique et judaïsme* (= *Recherches de science religieuse* xlvii (1973), 157–407) (Strasbourg, 1973), 126–45 (133).

application of bridal imagery to redemption in such passages of Hebrew scripture as Jeremiah 2.[105]

The importance of suffering and messianism in Yose's poems evinces their thematic closeness to the New Testament. The Mishnah and Tosefta, by contrast, are concerned with the community's continual observance in daily life. This concern is by no means absent from the New Testament, but the Mishnah characteristically evokes a constant and ordered world, whereas the New Testament atmosphere is formed especially by hopes akin to those met in Yose.[106] Such hopes also appear in post-Mishnaic rabbinic writings like the midrashim quoted above; but in emphasis, as just noted, the midrash can differ from Yose just where Yose seems to recall the urgent tone of the New Testament. It can perhaps be said that the restraint and confidence noted above at these points in the midrash come nearer to the serenity of the Mishnah. By the same token, the contrast in atmosphere between the Mishnah and the New Testament to some extent recurs in a contrast between the overall tranquillity of the Mishnah and the urgency of Yose.

The hopes manifest in different ways both in the midrash and in Yose are expressed at a time when Christianity has become prominent. Under one aspect their expression is inevitably an implied response to Christianity, but it also owes much to the impetus of inner-Jewish messianic hopes. The currency of these hopes in the community at the time of the Mishnah has appeared earlier in this book especially in the ancient Jewish biblical versions and interpretations, from the Septuagint to the Targums (see for example chapter 9, above).

A small body of poems has been studied here, but Yose speaks for the congregation and was subsequently felt to have done so worthily. Hence it is not insignificant that in Yose tranquil daily observance is galvanized, as we saw in comparison with rabbinic messianism, by consciousness of sin and urgent hope for redemption. Herein, as already noted from time to time, Yose takes up themes of other Jewish sources as well as the New Testament. Concern with sin and redemption is comparably prominent in the Qumran

[105] The general New Testament debt to such passages is vividly expounded by J. P. M. Sweet, *Revelation* (London, 1979), 279, 301f. (on Rev. 19:7; 21:9); a post-biblical instance is Od. Sol. 42, discussed by B. McNeil, 'Suffering and Martyrdom in the Odes of Solomon', in Horbury and McNeil (ed.), *Suffering and Martyrdom in the New Testament*, 136–42.

[106] J. Neusner, *A History of the Mishnaic Law of Purities*, vol. xxi (Leiden, 1977), esp. 322f., and *Judaism: The Evidence of the Mishnah* (Chicago and London, 1981), 235–6, 268–9.

hymns and the Eighteen Benedictions. Atonement through the ministrations of the priesthood in sanctuary and sacrifice is important not only in Yose, but at Qumran, in the background of such New Testament books as Hebrews and Revelation, in midrashic and Targumic passages noted above, in patristic references to Judaism like that of Chrysostom,[107] and perhaps also in the explanation of archaeological evidence such as the course-inscriptions.

Yose's poems thus illustrate some concerns associated with messianic redemption which had earlier been prominent in the New Testament, whereas the Mishnah has a strikingly different atmosphere. On the other hand, the Targums and some rabbinic midrash, spanning the period between the New Testament and Yose, once again reflect these concerns. The New Testament can then be judged to embody some themes which, despite their absence from the Mishnah, continued to influence Judaism. They found their voice in sources close to the congregation: in Targumic interpretation, in midrashic homily, and above all in the prayer and poetry rendered by the synagogue precentor.

[107] With Chrysostom, C. *Iud.* 6.5 (above. p. 301); cf. Origen, *In Num. hom.* 10.2 (Jewish lament that without sacrifice sin remains unforgiven, *PG* xii, 638) and *Princ.* iv.1.3 (loss of priestly ministrations, *PG* xi, 347f.; J. A. Robinson, *The Philocalia of Origen* (Cambridge, 1893), 10, discussed by N. R. M. de Lange, *Origen and the Jews* (Cambridge, 1976), 45, 97; further comments in *JTS* N.S. xxx (1979), 326.

11

Antichrist among Jews and Gentiles

Antichrist seems as native to Christianity as the devil with horns and a tail. This impression receives learned support in much recent scholarship. Thus G. C. Jenks, C. E. Hill and L. J. Lietaert Peerbolte all contend that the figure of Antichrist is a Christian development. In earlier years, by contrast, it had been considered originally Jewish by Wilhelm Bousset, Moritz Friedländer, Louis Ginzberg and Israel Lévi. Then, however, Paul Billerbeck (1926), concisely summarizing a wealth of material, urged that, despite appearances, there was virtually no contact in substance between ancient Jewish literature and the New Testament on Antichrist; in Jewish sources the messiah had political opponents, but the Christian Antichrist was a religious figure.[1] More recently Stefan Heid, in a book finished in 1990, accepted that Bousset was fundamentally right. A contrast between Christian and Jewish sources, in some ways recalling that drawn by Billerbeck, has nevertheless returned to prominence. For Jenks (1991), Hill (1995) and Lietaert Peerbolte (1996), the expectation of an enemy specifically opposed to the messiah first occurs among the earliest Christians, rather than among the non-Christian or pre-Christian Jews. Pre-Christian traditions, it is urged, refer to an eschatological tyrant, a final attack by evil powers, or the accompanying false prophecy, rather than a messianic opponent who can properly be termed Antichrist.

Yet, just as Belial with horns now looms up hauntingly in Qumran texts (see 11Q Apocryphal Psalms[a], col. iv, lines 6–7), so it may be asked again, a hundred years after Bousset, whether Antichrist is not pre-Christian and Jewish as well as Christian. With regard to the Jews in the Roman empire this question frames itself more precisely. In the early empire, was Antichrist a Jewish counterpart of Greek and Roman notions concerning the great enemy

[1] Billerbeck in Strack and Billerbeck, *Kommentar*, iii, 637–40, on 2 Thess. 2:3.

of a saviour king? If so, Jews and gentiles would have shared, in this as in many other respects, a broadly similar pattern of hopes and fears for the future.[2]

I. The wicked one

First, was an Antichrist already envisaged by Jews in the early Roman empire? They might be expected to have imagined such a figure, because biblical texts which were important in messianic hope naturally emphasize victory over enemies; see for example three passages which were all later connected with an arch-enemy of the messiah, Num. 24:17 (the star from Jacob smites the corners of Moab), Isa. 11:4 (with the breath of his lips he shall slay the wicked), and Ps. 2:2 (the kings of the earth rise up, and the rulers take counsel together, against the Lord and against his anointed). Moreover, from the Persian period onwards it was expected that a tyrannical king would oppress Israel and the nations just before the decisive divine victory. This thought is already suggested by the placing of the prophecy of Gog of Magog in Ezek. 38–9, after the prophecies of a David to come and the revival of the dry bones, and before the description of new Jerusalem; and the expectation is developed or alluded to in Dan. 7:8, 24–7, 8:9–11, 23–6, on the little horn which signifies a king of fierce countenance; Ass. Mos. 8:1 ('regem regum terrae', cf. Ps. 2:2 'kings of the earth'); and 2 Esd. 5:6 ('et regnabit quem non sperant qui inhabitant super terram'). The time-honoured representation of oppressive rulers or kingdoms as monstrous beasts often marks this line of thought, as in Daniel and later on in Revelation. An influence of the expectation of an evil king on the texts associated with messianic victory is suggested by Ecclus. 36:12 in the Hebrew textual tradition ('destroy the *head* of the corners of Moab'; cf. Num. 24:17; Jer. 48:45; and Ass. Mos. 8:1 '*king* of the kings of the earth'); but it cannot simply be assumed that oracles which speak of many enemies of the messiah, like the psalms cited above, had at the time of the Roman principate been generally interpreted as also indicating one great anti-messianic overlord.

[2] A similar observation is made on different grounds by F. G. Downing, 'Common Strands in Pagan, Jewish and Christian Eschatologies in the First Century', *Theologische Zeitschrift* li (1995), 196–211.

Of course such a messianic opponent was envisaged by Jews later on. In the Byzantine period he is the subject of the legend of Armilus the wicked, attested in the early seventh-century book *Zerubbabel* and elsewhere. Here Armilus slays messiah son of Joseph, and is himself slain by messiah son of David, as prophesied in Isa. 11:4 ('with the breath of his lips he shall slay the wicked').[3] Elements of this story, without the name Armilus, can be identified in midrash and piyyut. So the possibly fifth-century poet Yose ben Yose, in his New-Year composition *ahallelah elohay* which incorporates the series of *malkhuyyoth* texts, writes (line 55)

> ... the wicked one shall be *shaken out* [Job 38:13],
> but one has set righteousness for his feet [Isa. 41:2], and he shall be crowned with KINGDOM.[4]

Here Yose seems to reflect the notion of Antichrist—'the wicked one', in line with Isa. 11:4—being removed by the messiah of righteousness; note that the plural 'wicked ones' of Job 38:13 have become singular. Compare a probably earlier midrash found in Lev. R. 27.11 = PRK 9.11, in Midrash Tehillim 2.4 (on Ps. 2:2), and elsewhere, in the name of the third-century haggadist R. Levi, on Gog and Magog (speaking as a single figure) planning war 'against the Lord and against his messiah', as envisaged in Ps. 2:2. This messianic psalm could indeed be called 'the chapter of Gog and Magog', followed by 'the chapter of Absalom' (Ps. 3, ascribed in its title to the time of Absalom's revolt), as can be seen from a comment on the juxtaposition of the two psalms repeated by Abbahu of Caesarea in the name of his mid-third-century teacher Johanan, who settled in Tiberias (Babylonian Talmud, Ber. 10a); this designation of Ps. 2 presupposes that the messiah's enemy is Gog and Magog. The messianic antagonist is similarly assumed in a famous explanation of the closed Mem in the prophecy 'of the increase of government' in Isa. 9:6 (7), cited as given by Bar Kappara (early third century) in Sepphoris; the Holy One sought to make Hezekiah the messiah, and Sennacherib Gog and Magog (Babylonian

[3] Text in Ad. Jellinek, *Bet ha-Midrasch*, ii (Leipzig, 1853, reprinted Jerusalem, 1967), 54–7; the related midrash *Signs of the Messiah*, as reprinted by Jellinek, *ibid.*, 58–63 from *Abqat Rokhel* (Amsterdam, 1696), includes a note that Armilus is 'he whom the nations call *anticristo*' (Jellinek, *ibid.*, xxii, 60). For the dating of the Armilus legend in the time of Heraclius see A. Sharf, *Byzantine Jewry* (London, 1971), 54.

[4] Text in A. Mirsky, *Yosse ben Yosse: Poems* (Jerusalem, 1977), 94, discussed by Horbury, 'Suffering and Messianism', 162–5 (pp. 344–5, above).

Talmud, Sanh. 94a). At the time of this explanation, the conception of Gog and Magog as the messiah's opponent needed no special justification. These three midrashim citing third-century teachers together suggest that war between Gog and Magog and the messiah will have been a familiar and uncontroversial expectation in Caesarea and Galilee under the Jewish patriarchs, by the end of the age of the Severi.

Nevertheless, even as early as this, the possibility of Christian influence on Jewish messianic hopes cannot be ruled out. Jewish notions of an opponent of the messiah are commonly thought to be less well attested, or not attested at all, at the beginning of the Roman imperial period. The earliest full descriptions of Antichrist, identified by that name, are Christian, and they come from sources of the second and third centuries—Irenaeus, Tertullian, Origen, and the exegetical works attributed to Hippolytus. Moreover, the first attestations of the Greek word *antichristos* are Christian, being found—here without fuller explanation or description—in two of the three Johannine epistles of the New Testament, probably written towards the end of the first century (1 John 2:18, 22; 4:3; 2 John 7). The 'antichrists' are those who deny that Jesus is the messiah (1 John 2:18–23); their emergence fulfils the familiar teaching that 'Antichrist is coming'. Probably they led their followers into or back to the majority Jewish community; but even if they are to be understood simply as the founders of a separate party within the Christian body, their leadership will still have had a political significance for the Christian community which suits the traditional depiction of the messianic opponent as a ruler. Accordingly, the emphasis on false teaching in these Johannine passages on Antichrist should not be sharply contrasted with the emphasis on oppressive rule in the traditions on the messianic opponent—which themselves include the motif of false teaching, in the conception of the beast with the mouth speaking great things (Dan. 7:8).[5]

Antichrist, then, was certainly an important early *Christian* conception. Nevertheless, the Christian references to him include much to suggest that, like the figure of the Christ or messiah, he derived from pre-Christian Judaism in its Greek and Roman setting. This view is consonant with the lack of explanation of the Antichrist figure in the New Testament, and it is supported by Jewish sources from the end of the Second Temple period which describe

[5] Such a contrast is drawn, for example, by Billerbeck in Strack and Billerbeck, *Kommentar*, iii, 637–8; Hill, 'Antichrist', 100; Lietaert Peerbolte, *Antecedents*, 338.

an Antichrist-like figure without using this term, naming him rather as the wicked one, Gog, or Beliar.[6] These sources can be said to bridge the gap between the biblical passages already noted, which attest the expectations of messianic victory and of a final arch-enemy of Israel without explicit interconnection between them, and the rabbinic passages also noted above, which suggest that the notion of a great messianic opponent was familiar under the Jewish patriarchate in the third century.

Against this background it can be seen that the technical Greek term *antichristos*, although it is known only from Christian sources, need not necessarily be Christian in origin. It is true that the distribution of the word can readily suggest that it is a Christian coinage. *Antichristos* first occurs in the Johannine epistles, and it is not used by other Greek Jewish or early Christian writings which speak of an identical or similar figure, notably the Sibylline Oracles (but *antichristos* is somewhat inconvenient for their metre), 2 Thess. 2:1–13; Rev. 11–20, the Didache and Justin Martyr; it next occurs in Polycarp and Irenaeus—second-century authors who knew the Johannine writings. Hence a specifically Johannine origin for the word has been regarded as a strong possibility.[7]

Yet, in the Johannine epistles *antichristos* is not treated as a new word, but as belonging to a teaching which is already current—'Antichrist is coming' (1 John 2:18, cf. 4:3); and the gospel of John, which is very close to the epistles in style and vocabulary, attests for the first time one or two other words which were probably non-Christian Jewish technical terms, notably the Hellenized Aramaic *messias* and the Greek *aposynagogos*, 'excluded from assembly' (John 1:41, 4:25, 9:22, 12:42, 16:2). *Christos*, used both in John and elsewhere in the New Testament, was likewise taken over from the contemporary Jewish vocabulary. The same may well have been true of *antichristos*. Comparable Jewish uses of compounds with *anti-* are exemplified by ἀντίδικος, in Ben Sira's grandson's rendering of the prayer for the crushing of the arrogant enemy in Ecclus. 36:7, or the verb ἀντιβασίλευω in Josephus' depiction of John of Gischala as a rival sovereign over against the remainder of the Zealot party (*B.J.* iv 395), or ἀντίθεος, in Philo's warning against the season of good

6 The Coptic Apocalypse of Elijah on the 'lawless one' does the same, but despite Jewish elements in its source-material (Frankfurter, *Elijah*, 104) it is not cited in the present argument as a Jewish document.

7 Hengel, *The Johannine Question*, 171–2, n. 69, citing R. E. Brown.

fortune which is 'against God' and put in the place of God (Num. 14:9 LXX, as interpreted in *Post. C.* 122–3). (Is Philo here thinking in part of current associations of Fortune with the supreme deity, as seen in Horace, *Od.* i 34–5 and elsewhere?)

Even the technical term 'Antichrist', therefore, is by no means clearly of Christian origin. However that may be, the figure which the term describes—the great enemy to be slain by the messiah—is probably pre-Christian. In his argument for this view, Bousset pointed especially to the passage in the twelfth chapter of the book of Revelation describing how the great red dragon seeks to devour the man-child borne by the woman clothed with the sun; building on H. Gunkel's interpretation of Rev. 11–12 as a fragment of a myth of the messiah, and noting also that much developed exegesis is presupposed in the second-century and later Christian texts on Antichrist, Bousset urged that an 'antichrist myth' was also known at the time of the New Testament writers.[8] Criticism has fastened on his inferences from Christian evidence, including relatively late material, to a connected myth envisaged as in circulation at the time of Christian origins; but perhaps too little credit has been given to the support for his view found in Jewish sources of the Second Temple period, notably the Septuagint, the Sibylline Oracles, 2 Esdras and 2 Baruch, and the Qumran texts.

First, messianic expectations of this period included a judgment scene in which the messiah condemned and executed his great adversary. This scene was associated with an exegesis of Isa. 11:4 'but with righteousness shall he judge the poor, and reprove with equity for the meek of the earth: and he shall smite the earth with the rod of his mouth, and with the breath of his lips he shall slay the wicked'. In the LXX the Hebrew of the second part of the verse is rendered 'he shall smite the earth with the word of his mouth, and with a breath through the lips shall he remove the impious'. In the context of chapter 10 the wicked one in question can readily be understood as a threatening king, Sennacherib in Isaiah's time or the great foe of the messiah yet to come. The application of Isa. 11:4 to the destruction of a special future enemy is of course found in the New Testament. Thus a judgment scene is presupposed with allusion to this verse in 2 Thess. 2:8 'then shall be revealed the lawless

[8] Bousset, *Legend*, especially 15, 152–90, 214–17, 247–9.

one, whom the Lord Jesus shall remove by the breath of his mouth, and shall destroy by the epiphany of his advent'; and Isa. 11:4 is also vividly pictorialized in Revelation, where the enemies of the two witnesses are destroyed by fire from the Lord's mouth (Rev. 11:5), and the conquering messiah has a sword coming out of his mouth (Rev. 1:16, 2:13, 16, 19:15, 21). In the vision of Rev. 19:11–21 the messiah judges in righteousness (verse 11; cf. Isa. 11:4), and with the sword of his mouth he is to smite the nations (verse 15; cf. Isa. 11:4); the beast who leads the kings of the earth (cf. Ps. 2:2; Ass. Mos. 8:1) and his false prophet would be slain by it, as their followers are, if the two leaders were not preserved to be cast into the lake of fire (verses 19–21; cf. Isa. 11:4 'he shall slay the wicked').

These Christian texts of the first century in 2 Thessalonians and Revelation evidently presuppose a scene built on Isa. 11:4. This point gives the passages a unity which would not be recognized if they were simply classified according to their descriptions of the opponents. Their shared dependence on Isa. 11:4 suggests the existence of a prophetically-based myth of the messiah and his adversary, on the lines suggested by Gunkel and Bousset, and their early date underlines the likelihood that it is originally Jewish; but on the basis of this evidence alone the possibility that an Antichrist myth first emerged in the intense messianism of the rise of Christianity would still remain.

Yet the judgment scene associated with this passage of Isaiah is also attested in non-Christian Jewish sources of the same period. Thus in the apocalypses of Ezra and Baruch, to be dated not long after the destruction of Jerusalem by Titus, the messiah, taking his stand on mount Zion, first rebukes, and then destroys, the fourth kingdom—here the Roman empire. The sequence of reproof and execution found in both apocalypses once again follows Isa. 11:4 ('judge … and reprove …: smite the earth … and … slay the wicked'). In the Ezra-apocalypse the kingdom is personified individually in the eagle-vision of chapter 11, but emphasis later falls on the nations and the multitude who support its oppressive rule (see 2 Esd. 11:36–46, 12:30–3, 13:4–11, 27–8, 35–8). The influence of Isa. 11:4 'with the rod of his mouth, and with the breath of his lips', and of the understanding of it attested in the LXX 'with the *word* of his mouth', is seen in the motif of destruction by the messiah's voice, which is also the law (2 Esd. 12:1–3, 13:4, 10–11, 38). (This emphasis on the godlike power of his voice also approximates the description to contemporary praise of rulers.)[9] In the Syriac apocalypse of Baruch, on the other hand, the destruction of all the hosts of the fourth kingdom is reported first; the stream and the vine of Baruch's dream-vision destroy the forest first of all, and finally the great cedar which is its last survivor (2 (Syriac) Baruch 37–9). This vision is inspired by passages including Ps. 80:15–18, but also, notably in the present context, Isa. 10:34 (a verse followed immediately by Isa. 11:1–4) 'he shall cut down the thickets of the forest, and Lebanon shall fall by a mighty one'—Lebanon, on the exegetical convention followed here, standing for a gentile king.[10] In the interpretation of Baruch's dream, correspondingly, the last leader of the fourth kingdom is finally singled out and brought to mount Zion for the reproof and execution suggested by Isa. 11:4; 'my messiah will charge him with all his iniquities …, and afterwards he shall put him to death' (2 (Syriac) Baruch 40:1–2). Here there is close resemblance to the execution of the beast and the false prophet by the judgment of the messiah in Rev. 19. Thus—to view the apocalypses of Ezra and Baruch together—the conception of a single messianic opponent is not absent from 2 Esdras, where it is adumbrated by the contest between the lion and the eagle; but it takes particularly clear and concrete form in 2 Baruch, which seems to envisage the messiah as putting the Roman emperor to death. Both apocalypses are shaped by Isa. 11:4, considered—as is evident especially from 2 Baruch—in its larger context.

A brief depiction of this messianic judgment scene is given in a third source close in date to the two apocalypses, Sib. 5:101–10. Here the conqueror of Persia who attacks Egypt from the west grows formidably great and threatens 'the city of the blessed', like the he goat from the west in Dan. 8:5–12; but 'a king sent from God against him | shall destroy all great kings and mighty men; | and so shall there be judgment upon men from the Immortal' (lines 108–10). As in 2 Esdras, the end of 'him' is less emphasized than the general destruction of his kings and warriors, but it is clear that the messiah has one great adversary. The description based on Daniel leads to a judgment scene at Jerusalem like that associated with Isa. 11:4, a verse which is recalled,

[9] Compare Acts 12:22 'the voice of a god, and not of a man' (Agrippa I), with Tacitus, *Ann.* xvi 22, on Nero (Thrasea Paetus never sacrificed 'pro salute principis aut caelesti voce') and other passages discussed by S. Loesch, *Deitas Jesu und antike Apotheose* (Rottenburg a. N., 1933), 18–24.

[10] The influence of Isa. 10:34 here is brought out by G. Vermes in Vermes *et al.*, 'Seminar on the Rule of War from Cave 4 (4Q 285)', 90; on the conventions followed in the interpretation of 'Lebanon' see Gordon, *ibid.*, 93–4 (urging that in 4Q 285, discussed below, it is simultaneously equated with 'king' and 'nations').

without any detailed correspondence, by the emphasis in lines 108–10 on judgment and destruction of foes after the victory of the God-sent king over his enemy at Jerusalem. The Sibylline passage is also broadly compatible with the myth of Nero's return, which is utilized below in lines 137–54. This point indicates the similarity, noted further below, between the Jewish conception of a messianic adversary and non-Jewish expectations in the Roman empire.

Further attestations of this messianic judgment scene are found in the Dead Sea Scrolls. First, in a fragment which has been attributed to the Rule of War (4Q285, fragment 5), in the course of a continuous exegesis of Isa. 10:34–11:5, it is said that 'there shall slay him the Prince of the Congregation, the Branch of David'. The foe to be slain by the Davidic messiah is unnamed because of lacunae, but will be connected with the Kittim mentioned in a surviving phrase; probably he is 'the king of the Kittim' who leads the enemy army in the War Scroll (15:2).[11] The scene imagined then corresponds exactly with that described in 2 (Syriac) Baruch. Comparably, the Blessing of the Prince of the Congregation prays, once again taking up Isa. 11:4, that with the breath of his lips he may slay the wicked (1QSb col. v, lines 24–5). This slaying is mentioned yet again in the fragmentary commentary on Isa. 10:33–11:5 in 4Q161.[12] Here the 'high ones of stature' (10:33) are 'the mighty men of the Kittim' (line 5), and 'Lebanon' in 10:34 seems likely again to be their chief or king, although the relevant text is lacking (beginning of line 8); later in this fragment (lines 16–18) 'he shall slay the wicked' is interpreted of the branch of David who will slay 'his [en] emy' (singular).[13] The description of his rule and judgment includes a mention of Magog (line 20), which recalls the rôle of Gog and Magog as the foe of the messiah, already noted in connection with rabbinic interpretation of Ps. 2.

Still other biblical passages were probably drawn into this scene in contemporary exegesis, for example Ps. 68:30–31 on the gifts brought by kings and the rebuke administered to 'the beast of the reeds', who seems to be linked with the Kittim in a fragmentary commentary on Ps. 68 (1Q16).[14] In midrash

[11] For text and discussion see P. S. Alexander and G. Vermes, '4QSefer ha-Milhamah'.
[12] J. M. Allegro, *Qumrân Cave 4*, i (DJD v, Oxford, 1968), 13–15, and Plate v; translation also in F. García Martínez, *The Dead Sea Scrolls Translated* (ET by W. G. E. Watson, Leiden, 1994), 186.
[13] *'w]ybw* (line 18) is taken by Allegro and García Martínez as a defectively written plural and rendered 'his enemies', but the more straightforward rendering 'his enemy', in the singular, seems preferable against the background sketched above. Vermes and Gordon do not discuss this question in their comments on 4Q 161 in Vermes, 'Seminar on the Rule of War from Cave 4 (4Q 285)'.
[14] So J. T. Milik in D. Barthélemy and J. T. Milik, *Qumrân Cave 1* (DJD i, Oxford, 1955), 82.

and piyyut this beast is Rome; so, in a poetic account of the succession of the four Danielic kingdoms, 'to the beast of the reeds then he sold the land' (Yose ben Yose, *ʾanusah leʿezrah*, line 23).[15] Now in an exegesis of Ps. 68:30–1 attributed to the early-third-century Ishmael b. Jose b. Halafta (who himself is said to have repeated it as something that 'my father said') Rome is rebuked by or in the presence of the messiah—who has accepted gifts from the other gentile monarchies (Exod. R. 35.5, on Exod. 26:15; Babylonian Talmud, Pes. 118b). In this interpretation the judgment scene considered above seems to have been linked with the old and widely-attested scene in which the messiah receives gifts from the nations; for the latter scene see Ps. Sol. 17:31; 2 Esd. 13:13; cf. Ps. 72:10–11, Isa. 66:20; Ber. R. 78.12, on Gen. 33:11 (quoting Ps. 72:10); Midrash Tehillim 88.6, on verse 4 (quoting Isa. 66:20). In the dream-vision of 2 Esd. 13:1–13 the two scenes are already connected, through a messianic interpretation of Isa. 66:5–24; and with the Qumran material in view it may be suggested that they were also linked in the Second Temple period on the basis of Ps. 68:30–1.

These passages do not comprise all the Qumran material relevant to discussion of Antichrist.[16] Thus the present writer thinks that the figure called 'son of God' in the Aramaic prophecy in 4Q246 is probably once again the expected evil king.[17] Similarly, the conflict between Melchizedech and Melchiresha (see 11Q Melchizedek, 4Q Amram (in Aramaic) and 4Q280) can be interpreted with fair probability as one between angelic spirits who take human form as the messiah and his great opponent.[18] These positions cannot be presented here, but the argument does not depend upon them. The view that a messianic opponent was envisaged in the Second Temple period is supported, rather, by the less-discussed scene of messianic judgment of 'the wicked one'

[15] Mirsky, *Yosse*, 108; the context is summarized in Horbury, 'Suffering and Messianism', 151 (p. 333, above).

[16] Lietaert Peerbolte, *Antecedents*, 257–86 gives a valuable survey, including interpretations of the 'son of God' and Melchizedek texts which differ from those mentioned below, but not including discussion of the texts on a messianic judgment scene which have just been considered.

[17] See Vermes, 'Miscellanea', 301–3 (probably the last ruler of the final world empire). Collins, *Scepter*, 154–72 prefers a messianic interpretation.

[18] Collins, *Scepter*, 176 understands Melchizedek as an angelic saviour, not a messiah. The view that Melchizedek is a messianic figure, put forward by J. Carmignac and others, is freshly argued by P. A. Rainbow, 'Melchizedek as a Messiah at Qumran'; see also Chapters 1 and 4, pp. 85–6, 165–6, above. This view of Melchizedek would be consistent with the ancient opinion that, together with Elijah, king messiah, and the Priest anointed for war, Melchizedek is one of the 'four smiths' of Zech. 2:3–4 (1:20–1) who come to cast down the horns of the nations who threaten Judah (PRK v 9, and elsewhere).

which some Hebrew texts discovered at Qumran share with Jewish prophecies known through Christian transmission. In the exegesis represented in the first three Qumran texts, Isa. 11:4 was regularly interpreted of the execution of 'the wicked', probably the ruler of the Kittim, by the branch of David. This interpretation was also connected with other scriptural passages, including the prophecy of Gog and probably also Ps. 68, as suggested by 1Q16 in the light of 2 Esdras and the midrash. This understanding of Isa. 11:4 will therefore have been familiar among Jews at the beginning of the Herodian period. It will have influenced both the Christian and the Jewish texts from the end of this period which have just been considered—2 Thessalonians, Revelation, and the apocalypses of Ezra and Baruch. Moreover, it had already helped to shape an imagined scene of messianic judgment, found again in the fifth Sibylline book, which can properly be called an element in a myth of the messiah and his arch-enemy. This story could also be attached to other biblical texts, as the rabbinic passages on Gog discussed above have shown, and from the Second Temple period onwards it was sometimes linked with the related scene in which the messiah receives tribute from the nations.

As a pendant to what now appears as a regularly envisaged Isaianic scene one may note Jerome's allegation that Bar Kokhba pretended to breathe fire by a trick (*adv. Rufinum* iii 31). Probably this reproduces a Jewish tradition hostile to Bar Kokhba, once again with allusion to Isa. 11:4; compare the talmudic legend that he was slain because the rabbis saw that he did not fulfil Isa. 11:3 'he shall not judge by the sight of his eyes' (Babylonian Talmud, Sanh. 93b).

From among other evidence pointing in the same direction as the judgment-scene of the 'wicked one' of Isa. 11:4, two further old identifications of the messiah's adversary may be briefly outlined. First, as already noted, Gog and Magog constitute his foe in rabbinic interpretation current in the third century; and in the fragmentary 4Q161, representing exegesis known during the Herodian period, Magog is named in the context of the messiah's rule over all the nations.[19] The likelihood that the name is connected here with opposition, in line with rabbinic exegesis and with Targum Ps.-Jonathan on Num. 11:26, cited below, is strengthened by Septuagintal references to Gog. Thus in the third century B.C. Num. 24:7 is rendered in the LXX (presupposing

[19] Material on Gog and Magog is gathered by Billerbeck in Strack and Billerbeck, *Kommentar*, iii, 638 (on 2 Thess. 2:3), 831–40 (on Rev. 20:8–9), and Perez Fernandez, *Tradiciones mesiánicas*, 282–6.

mg(w)g for MT *m'gg*) 'there shall come forth a man … his kingdom shall be higher than Gog'. Here Gog is already the messianic opponent. In the prophets, the end of Amos 7:1 is rendered 'behold, one locust was king Gog' (presupposing *gwg* where MT has *gzy*). This oracle could be understood of Sennacherib's invasion (so Jerome), but in the light of Num. 24:7 LXX it seems likely that the translator took it of a future adversary. Comparably, Amos 4:13 LXX includes the phrase 'announcing to men his messiah' (presupposing *mšḥw*; cf. MT *mhšḥw*). Both these Septuagintal renderings in Amos fit the messianic close of the book (9:11–15).[20] On a distinct but closely related line of interpretation, the third Sibylline book, in a passage reflecting Jewish Egypt perhaps during the second century b.c., locates 'the land of Gog and Magog' in Ethiopia (cf. Ezek. 38:5) and predicts its doom as a 'house of judgment' drenched in blood (Sib. 3:319–21).

The wide early circulation of the understanding of Gog and Magog as the enemy to be destroyed by the messiah is further confirmed by its occurrence in the prophecy of Eldad and Medad according to the Targum: 'Gog-and-Magog and his forces go up to Jerusalem and fall into the hand of king messiah' (Num. 11:26 in Neofiti and the Fragment Targum). 4Q161, if rightly restored, similarly says that the Kittim or their leaders 'will be given into the hand of his great one' (fragments 8–10, line 8). Pseudo-Jonathan at Num. 11:26 on 'the king from the land of Magog' who is overlord of other kings and princes is comparable with and longer than Neofiti and the Fragment Targum, but does not specify the messiah. Its phrasing, however, confirms that 'Magog' in 4Q161 should be understood primarily of the land, as in Ezek. 38:3 and Sib. 3:319. The prophecy of Eldad and Medad mentioned in Pseudo-Philo's Biblical Antiquities (20.5, exactly corresponding to an earlier prophecy on Joshua in the Targums on Num. 11:26) and quoted in Greek in the Shepherd of Hermas (*Vis.* ii 3, 4, roughly corresponding to a phrase in Pseudo-Jonathan on the king from Magog) may well have included a version of this oracle on Gog. The identification of the great messianic adversary as Gog is therefore

[20] According to the Greek of Codex Vaticanus (B), Ecclus. 48:17b, on Hezekiah, runs 'and he led Gog into their midst'. Γώγ is probably an inner-Greek corruption of Γίων 'Gihon' (see J. H. A. Hart, *Ecclesiasticus: The Greek Text of Codex 248* (Cambridge, 1909), 219–20), but it suggests knowledge of the close connection in Jewish thought between Hezekiah and the messiah, illustrated above from Bar Kappara's saying in Babylonian Talmud, Sanh. 94a. As Hezekiah's captive, Gog is the messianic adversary. Expectation of Hezekiah is judged to have been lively at the end of the Second Temple period by Hadas-Lebel, ' "Il n'y a pas de messie pour Israël" '.

continuously attested in Jewish sources from the Septuagint Pentateuch to the Targums and rabbinic literature, and 4Q161 can be understood in connection with this series of interpretations.

A second old identification of the messianic opponent names him Beliar. Belial or Beliar has of course become the name of an archdemon in Qumran texts, the Testaments of the Twelve Patriarchs, and elsewhere, often with the emphasis on deception found in biblical texts using *beliyyaʿal* (e.g. Deut. 13:14); but in Sib. 3:63–74 and in Asc. Isa. 4.1–18 (a Christian insertion following the pattern of the messianic judgment scene) Beliar also takes the form of an earthly leader. Thus the Sibyl predicts that Beliar will come forth from the Sebastenoi to lead many astray by delusive miracles, including raisings of the dead; but when the divine threats come near to fulfilment, he and his followers will be burnt up by a fiery power from the deep (Sib. 3:63–74). J. J. Collins, following the view that the Sebastenoi are the line of the Augusti, takes the passage as alluding to the return of Nero, which is well attested elsewhere in the Sibyllines, as noted above.[21] He rejects the alternative interpretation of Sebastenoi as inhabitants of Sebaste (Samaria), urging that there is no parallel in Jewish writings for the notion of a Samaritan anti-messiah.

Yet the Samaritan interpretation has much to be said for it. It fits the hostility towards Samaritans evident in the later Second Temple period, for example in Ben Sira (50:25–6), Pseudo-Philo (Biblical Antiquities 25.10–11, on idolatrous images of 'the holy nymphs' buried at Shechem) and Josephus; this hostility is linked with Beliar in the Ascension of Isaiah, 2:1–3:12 (a probably Jewish portion of the work), where a Samaritan false prophet accuses Isaiah under Manasseh, who serves Beliar. Moreover, despite the apparent lack of Jewish reference to a Samaritan 'anti-messiah', Josephus (*Ant.* xviii 85–6) describes the leader of a Samaritan uprising under Pontius Pilate as a deceiver who claimed to show the hiding-place of the sacred vessels deposited by Moses, according to a tradition which is satirized in the allegation about hidden idols in Ps.-Philo, as cited above;[22] figures like this Samaritan leader could exemplify the seductive deception attributed to Beliar 'from the Sebastenes'. There is nothing

[21] J. J. Collins in J. H. Charlesworth (ed.), *The Old Testament Pseudepigrapha*, i (London, 1983), 360; his interpretation is followed by Lietaert Peerbolte, *Antecedents*, 332–3.

[22] Other references to this Jewish allegation based on Gen. 35:4, including Ber. R. 81.4 (idols hidden beneath the Samaritan temple), are gathered by C. T. R. Hayward, 'Jacob's Second Visit to Bethel in Targum Pseudo-Jonathan', in P. R. Davies and R. T. White (eds.), *A Tribute to Geza Vermes* (Sheffield, 1990), 175–92 (176–80).

in this Sibylline passage itself to suggest the Nero myth, but on the other hand it agrees with Jewish expectations; the raising of the dead is associated with the days of the messiah in the Qumran 'messianic apocalypse' (4Q521, 3, lines 1 and 12), and Beliar's destruction by fire from the sea recalls the fire sent forth (cf. Isa. 11:4) by the man who comes up from the sea and flies with the clouds in 2 Esd. 13:3–4. The passage need not then be dated after Nero, but could be tentatively ascribed to the Hasmonaean or Herodian period, since it probably assumes the status of Beliar as an archdemon. Like its early Christian counterpart in Asc. Isa. 4, however, it presents a Beliar incorporate who could justly be compared with a messiah, as occurs implicitly when St. Paul asks 'What is the concord of Christ with Beliar?' (2 Cor. 6:15).

It is noteworthy that 2 Thess. 2:8, quoted already, calls the evil opponent to be slain by the messiah not 'wicked' (ἀσεβής, as Isa. 11:4 LXX), but 'lawless' (ἄνομος); this choice of adjective is probably influenced by the contextual use of the noun ἀνομία in the phrases 'man of lawlessness' and 'mystery of lawlessness' (2:3 and 7), but that in turn recalls the noun used to render Belial in the LXX Pentateuch (ἀνόμημα, Deut. 15:9). Probably therefore Beliar lies just beneath the surface here.

In this name the associations of false teaching and seduction to idolatry are uppermost, but they are compatible with the portrait of a king or leader, like Manasseh in the Ascension of Isaiah or the Samaritan leader under Pilate in Josephus.

The great foe to be slain by the messiah was therefore a familiar figure in Jewish biblical interpretation of the Second Temple period. His execution was central in a wisely-attested scene of messianic judgment, which was shaped especially by exegesis of Isa. 11:4. This scene has long been known from the New Testament (2 Thessalonians and Revelation) and from 2 Esdras, 2 Baruch and the Fifth Sibylline, but its Jewish origins and its familiarity in the pre-Christian period have been confirmed by interpretations of Isaiah in Hebrew texts discovered at Qumran. This material further suggests that, as later happened in rabbinic interpretation, the scene of the messiah's victory over his adversary could be linked with the scene in which he receives offerings from the gentile nations. Gunkel and Bousset were right, therefore, in positing a myth of the messiah and his opponent, in the sense of a number of scenes which were regularly depicted and linked.

The opponent was above all the last leader of the fourth kingdom, in some cases clearly the Roman emperor. He could be named as Gog, in an interpretation of Ezek. 38–9 which goes back at least to the Septuagint Pentateuch and independently attests that the messiah's adversary was familiar in exegesis of the Second Temple period. The naming of the adversary as Beliar brings out the motif of seduction which in any case belongs to the portrait of the evil king (Dan. 7:8, etc.); the 'political' and the 'religious' opponent are not so clearly differentiated as Billerbeck suggested, and the Christian Antichrist, as is noted below, retains markedly political traits.[23] The portrait of the messiah, as noted in passing, comparably receives motifs from current political flattery. The 'wicked one' of Second Temple Jewish exegesis is continuous with the opponent later attested in rabbinic interpretation, but he is also continuous with the Christian Antichrist—as is evident from the New Testament examples of the messianic judgment scene, and from Christian adoption and elaboration of the anti-Roman apocalypses of Ezra and Baruch and the Sibylline Oracles. Antichrist therefore came to belong to specifically Christian expectations and conceptions of the Roman empire; but he is an originally Jewish figure, and in the early imperial period he symbolizes Jewish dissent from Roman assumptions of *imperium* granted *sine fine*.

II. Titan

Such Roman assumptions were also, however, touched by fears expressed through myths which closely resemble Jewish prophecies of opposition to the heaven-sent king. This point has already begun to emerge from the Sibylline Oracles, where the messianic opponent fits readily into the general Sibylline theme of *bella, horrida bella*. The same point was already expressly made in the ancient world, where resemblances between biblical tradition and mythology were often noted,[24] by observers who scrutinized the Christian expectation

[23] Hence the church fathers whom Hill, 'Antichrist', 99–101 views as combining separate emphases on false teaching and on political power could be regarded rather as continuing both sides of a single pre-Christian Jewish tradition.

[24] See, for example, Philo, *Gig.* 58, on Gen. 6:4 (Moses did not follow the myth of the giants); on Christian traditions, 2 Pet. 1:16 (again claiming independence of myth); on the other hand, Justin, *I Apol.* xxii (if you accept analogous myths, you can accept Christian teaching), and Tertullian, *Apol.* xxi 14 *recipite interim hanc fabulam, similis est vestris.*

of Antichrist. Thus, from within the Christian tradition, elements in this expectation were compared with the myth of the Titans and the giants which Philo discussed, as just noted, in connection with the giants of Gen. 6:3. 'Titan' is regarded as the most plausible interpretation of the number of the beast in Rev. 13:8 by Irenaeus, writing towards the end of the second century. Not only (he notes) does TEITAN add up to 666, but it is thought to be a divine name, being often applied to the sun; it has a show of vengeance which suits a figure claiming to vindicate the oppressed; and it is a royal, or rather a tyrannical name (Irenaeus, *Haer.* v 30, 3).

Here Irenaeus clearly shares the political interpretation of the myth of the war of the Titans. Pretenders to the throne, *tyranni* or *adfectatores tyrannidis*, were familiar in the Roman empire.[25] In Hesiod's *Theogony* the Titans are Cronus, father of Zeus, and his brothers and sisters. Cronus, aided by the vigilance of the other Titans, swallowed his children, but Zeus and others survived; Clement of Alexandria (*Protr.* ii 15) relates how the Titans tore the child Dionysus in pieces. The Titans struggled with Zeus and the Olympians for power, aided by giants, but were thrown down. The sun is called 'Titan' (often in Roman poetry, e.g. Virgil, *Aen.* iv 119) as son of the Titan Hyperion (Hesiod, *Theogony*, 371). The name Titan also individually belonged (according to a rendering of the myth given by Euhemerus and incorporated into Sib. iii:97–154) to a brother of Cronus, who fought with him for the kingdom when their father died. A Latin version of Euhemerus, made by Ennius, is quoted by Lactantius, who also knew the version in Sib. iii (Lactantius, *D.I.* i 14). Hesiod links the name with *tisis*, vengeance (*Theogony* 209). Rulers were associated with the sun, as Augustus had been,[26] and praised as avengers; so Pliny (*Panegyric* 35–6) stressed that Trajan provided *ultio* against informers. The giants similarly were avenging the wrongs of the Titans and their mother Earth (in Claudian, *Gigantomachia* 27 she addresses the giants as *exercitus ultor*). Antichrist therefore appears to Irenaeus—who has based his description on Daniel, quoted at length, as well as 2 Thessalonians and Revelation—above

[25] For these expressions see HA Avidius Cassius v 1 (Aemilius Parthenianus wrote a history of *adfectatores tyrannidis*, including Avidius Cassius), Pescennius Niger i 1 (those whom other men's victories made *tyranni*).

[26] So Apollo, Augustus' patron, and Sol—linked but not necessarily identical—are both invoked by Horace, *Carmen Saeculare*, lines 1 and 9 (Phoebe … alme Sol). Irenaeus does not quote the Sibyl, but he may perhaps also have had in view the oracle Sib. 3:652 'and then God will send a king from the sun', later quoted as a prophecy of Christ by Lactantius, *D.I.* vii 18, 7.

all as a plausible pretender to power, a figure recalling the Titans who tried to storm Olympus.

The resemblance between the Antichrist myth and the myth of the Titans was also noted at about the same time, perhaps under Marcus Aurelius, by Celsus, the pagan critic of Christianity.[27] He says that the Christian doctrine of the devil and 'Satanas', and the teaching of Jesus that Satan will appear like himself and will manifest great and glorious works, usurping the glory of God, rests on a misunderstanding of the enigmas of the Greek myths of a divine war. He specifies 'the mysteries which affirm that the Titans and Giants fought with the gods, and … the mysteries of the Egyptians which tell of Typhon and Horus and Osiris' (Origen, *c. Celsum* vi 42). These myths of course overlapped in their theme of contention for the throne, and had in common the figure of Typhon or Typhoeus, slain by Zeus in Greek mythology but also identified with the Egyptian Seth (Plutarch, *Isis and Osiris*, 371B). The Greek gigantomachy also had a long history in art, including the altar of Pergamum. In literature, comparably, the *Titanomachia* was a lost member of the epic cycle, and the Titans and the giants occupy surviving Greek poets from Hesiod onwards, and Latin writers from Ennius to Claudian (both cited above). Geographically, the legend was linked especially with volcanic areas of Asia Minor (the district of Catacecaumene near Philadelphia, Strabo, *Geog.* xiii 4, 11), Sicily and Campania; the battle of the giants took place on the Phlegraean Fields in Campania, and Typhon was buried alive beneath Cumae, Procida, Ischia and Etna (Pindar, *Pyth.* i, epode 1; Virgil, *Aen.* ix 715–16).

Celsus in this passage alludes directly or indirectly to Rev. 12:8, on the casting out of the devil or Satanas, and to Christ's prophecy of those who will arise and give signs and wonders to lead astray (Mark 13:21–3). Origen in his reply therefore deals both with Satan, on the basis of Revelation here, and with Antichrist, as suggested by Christ's prophecy. Celsus has urged that all this Christian material is a misunderstanding of what he takes to be the profoundly significant myths of the Titans and of Typhon and Osiris. His point of course has its place in a broader argument among pagans, Jews and Christians over the allegorization of mythology. In the present context, however, it is notable

[27] On the date of Celsus' work see H. Chadwick, *Origen: Contra Celsum* (Cambridge, 1953, corrected reprint 1965), xxvi–xxviii (on balance, probability lies with a date in the period 177–80).

as a pagan identification of mythological counterparts to the Antichrist myth, converging with the contemporary inner-Christian association of Antichrist and Titan found in Irenaeus.

The resemblances between Typhon in particular and the evil king as attested in Daniel are richly documented from both Greek and Egyptian legend by J. W. van Henten; he shows that the Danielic depiction of Antiochus IV has been influenced by the originally Egyptian stereotype of a 'Typhonic king', but in the course of this argument he brings out the significance of Typhon as a symbol of threat to order and sovereignty in the wider Greek world under the Hellenistic monarchies and later.[28] In the present context it is only necessary to note the continuance and development of such symbolism in the early Roman empire.

First, the probable influence of Sibylline oracles on the Augustan poets should be recalled. When Virgil made the Sibyl of Cumae Aeneas' guide to the underworld, he indicated among other things a debt to Sibylline writings. Individual oracles circulated in Rome, and a form of what is now the third Sibylline book was known there by the middle of the first century b.c.[29] Against the dark background of the civil wars at home and the Parthian threat in the east, Virgil in his early work invoked the hopes of 'Cumaean song' in the Fourth Eclogue, possibly but not plainly drawing on the Jewish prophecies of prosperity in Sib. 3 as preserved (lines 18–25, 28–30 in the Eclogue have been compared with Sib. 3:619–24, 743–59, 787–94). At about the same time Horace, in Epode 16.1–14, appears to echo the third Sibylline book in language as well as in his more characteristically Sibylline theme of woe.[30] Rome is falling through her own strength in the civil wars, 'suis et ipsa Roma viribus ruit' (line 2; cf. Sib. 3:364 Ῥώμη ῥύμη 'Rome a mere alley' or 'Rome a ruin'). The ashes of the City will be trampled by a barbarian victor, mounted and no doubt Parthian, who will scatter Roman bones; 'barbarus heu cineres insistet victor … ossa Quirini (nefas videre) dissipabit insolens' (lines 11–14). Mythical imagery is lacking, but the nightmare of the fall of Rome at the hand of an eastern foe corresponds to woes which were to be developed in the later

[28] van Henten, 'Antiochus', especially 228–36.

[29] H. W. Parke, edited by B. C. McGing, *Sibyls and Sibylline Prophecy in Classical Antiquity* (London, 1988), 143–4 (Alexander Polyhistor used Sib. iii).

[30] C. W. Macleod, 'Horace and the Sibyl', reprinted from *Classical Quarterly* N.S. xxix (1979), 220–1 in Colin Macleod, *Collected Essays* (Oxford, 1983), 218–19.

Jewish Sibyllines by integration with the expected return of Nero from the east, as noted above (see Sib. 4:119–22, 137–9; 5:143–8, 361–4, and compare the Antichrist of Asc. Isa. 4:2–4 'a lawless king, the slayer of his mother'). The Sibyl had incorporated Greek mythology, including Euhemerus' version of the war of the Titans, as noted above; these prophetic passages from Virgil and Horace show, on the other hand, how fully the poets who commended the Augustan peace and at once became classical in the empire (Virgil was soon read at the outposts of empire, Masada and Hadrian's Wall) shared the thought-world of the Greek Jewish prophecies heralding the messiah and his adversary.

Secondly, the myth of the Titans and giants was brought into connection with the figure of a saviour-king—Augustus—in the longest of Horace's group of 'Roman odes' (*Od.* iii 4, lines 37–80). A resemblance to the Jewish and Christian Antichrist myth emerges strongly. The Muses aid Caesar with their gentle counsel, Horace writes; and we know that Jupiter, the just ruler of the universe, overthrew the impious Titans with a thunderbolt—'scimus ut impios | Titanas immanemque turbam | fulmine sustulerit caduco' (lines 42–4). Here, according to the convention of court poetry, Jupiter stands for Augustus, who in the following fifth ode of the third book is hailed as the 'present god' come to reign here in earth on Jupiter's behalf (*Od.* iii 5, 1–4). Yet, in one of the most striking statements of the fourth ode, Jupiter had been terror-struck; 'magnum ille terrorem intulerat Jovi | fidens iuventus horrida brachiis' (lines 49–50). The force of the prominently-placed 'great terror' is brought out with spirit in Philip Francis' English version:

> … the fierce Titanian brood
> Whose horrid youth, elate with impious pride,
> Unnumbered, on their sinewy force relied;
> Mountain on mountain piled they raised in air,
> And shook the throne of Jove, and bade the Thunderer fear.

This fear is consistent with the formidable character which Typhon bears in other poets, notably in the Egyptian motif of the flight of the gods before him, a flight which in Ovid includes Jupiter.[31] Nevertheless, Jupiter, the slayer of Typhon, usually stands his ground; in Pindar's first Pythian ode,

[31] Ovid, *Metam.* v 321–31, quoted with other texts by van Henten, 'Antiochus', 228–31.

which is similarly supporting a ruler and influenced this ode of Horace,[32] the punishment of Typhon is central (his body stretches underground from Cumae to Etna), and there is no mention of any fear on the part of Zeus. In Horace here Typhoeus is mentioned (line 53), but the fear is inspired by the collective appearance of the Titans and giants. Their terrifying impact remains startling, therefore, and recalls the formidable aspect of the messianic opponent and his followers, notably the sometimes monstrous form which stands for a king of fierce countenance, as in Dan. 7–8. Moreover, the general symbolism of the myth as used in Horace is comparable with that of the messianic judgment-scene; both involve the omnipotent deity and his vice-gerent, and in both the evil power which would usurp rightful sovereignty is overthrown.

I can then perhaps say with Horace (*Od.* iii 4, 69–70) 'testis mearum centimanus Gyas | sententiarum'. To summarize, a myth of a messianic opponent, in the sense of regularly envisaged and interconnected scenes in which the opponent figures, appeared in the first part of this study to have been current among Jews from before the time of Pompey and throughout the Roman period. Its specifically anti-messianic focus was strong enough to warrant Bousset's term 'antichrist myth'. It could include an emphasis on false teaching as well as usurpation. Despite the contrast between Christian and Jewish views drawn in much study of Antichrist, Christian notions of Antichrist derived from Jewish tradition. Jewish tradition on this subject also, however, had many points of correspondence with non-Jewish expectations current in the Greek and Roman world. The myth of the Titans and the giants was picked out by both Christian and pagan observers as particularly close to the Antichrist myth. In the Greek age the figure of Typhon symbolized a threat to rightful monarchy, and influenced the Danielic depiction of Antiochus IV, as J. W. van Henten showed. With the Roman empire in view, it can be added that in the late Roman republic and the principate the Augustan poets entered into the thought-world of Jewish messianic and anti-messianic prophecy especially through the medium of Sibylline literature. Against this background, finally, the treatment of the Titans in Horace's longest Roman ode has suggested that it may not be out of place to speak of Antichrist among gentiles as well as Jews in the Roman empire.

32 E. Fraenkel, *Horace* (Oxford, 1957), 276–85.

Literature

P. S. Alexander and G. Vermes (eds.), '4QSefer ha-Milhamah', in *Qumran Cave 4. xxvi Cryptic Texts* (ed. S. Pfann); *Miscellanea Part I* (ed. P. Alexander and others) (*DJD* xxxvi, Oxford, 2000), 228–46

W. Bousset, *Der Antichrist in der Überlieferung des Judentums, des Neuen Testaments und der alten Kirche. Ein Beitrag zur Auslegung der Apokalypse* (Göttingen, 1895); ET, with a Prologue on the Babylonian Dragon Myth, by A. H. Keane, *The Antichrist Legend. A Chapter in Christian and Jewish Folklore* (London, 1896)

———, 'Antichrist', *ERE* i (1908), 578–81

J. J. Collins, *The Scepter and the Star* (New York, 1995)

D. Frankfurter, *Elijah in Upper Egypt: The Apocalypse of Elijah and Early Egyptian Christianity* (Minneapolis, 1993)

M. Friedländer, 'L'Anti-Messie', *REJ* xxxviii (1899), 14–37

L. Ginzberg, 'Antichrist', *JE* i (1901), 625–7

M. Hadas-Lebel, ' "Il n'y a pas de messie pour Israël car on l'a déjà consommé au temps d'Ézéchias" (TB Sanhédrin 99a)', *REJ* clix (2000), 357–67

S. Heid, *Chiliasmus und Antichrist-Mythos. Eine frühchristliche Kontroverse um das Heilige Land* (Bonn, 1993)

M. Hengel, *The Johannine Question* (ET by John Bowden, London and Philadelphia, 1989)

J. W. van Henten, 'Antiochus IV as a Typhonic Figure in Daniel 7', in A. S. van der Woude (ed.), *The Book of Daniel* (Leuven, 1993), 223–43

C. E. Hill, 'Antichrist from the Tribe of Dan', *JTS* N.S. xlvi (1995), 99–117

W. Horbury, 'Suffering and Messianism in Yose ben Yose', in W. Horbury and B. McNeil (eds.), *Suffering and Martyrdom in the New Testament* (Cambridge, 1981), 143–82 (chapter 10, above)

G. C. Jenks, *The Origins and Early Development of the Antichrist Myth* (BZNW lix, Berlin and New York, 1991)

I. Lévi, 'Le ravissement du Messie à sa naissance', *REJ* LXXIV (1922), 113–26

L. J. Lietaert Peerbolte, *The Antecedents of Antichrist: a traditio-historical study of the earliest Christian views on eschatological opponents* (Leiden, 1996)

S. Loesch, *Deitas Jesu und antike Apotheose* (Rottenburg a. N., Württemberg, 1933)

M. Pérez Fernández, *Tradiciones mesiánicas en el Targum palestinense* (Valencia and Jerusalem, 1981)

P. A. Rainbow, 'Melchizedek as a Messiah at Qumran', *Bulletin for Biblical Research* vii (1997), 179–94

H. L. Strack and P. Billerbeck, *Kommentar zum Neuen Testament aus Talmud und Midrasch* (Munich, i (1922), ii (1924), iii (1926), iv 1 (1928), iv 2 (1928); index volumes by K. Adolph and J. Jeremias, v (1956), vi (1961))

G. Vermes and others, 'The Oxford Forum for Qumran Research: Seminar on the Rule of War from Cave 4 (4Q285)', *JJS* xliii (1992), 85–94

G. Vermes, 'Qumran Forum Miscellanea i', *JJS* xliii (1992), 299–305

12

The Cult of Christ and the Cult of the Saints

The Christ-cult was the most important but not the only manifestation of its kind in the early church. In the second century it stands beside the cult of angels and the cult of martyrs and saints, as appears from Justin Martyr and the Martyrdom of Polycarp. Already in the Epistle to the Hebrews, correspondingly, those who draw near to Mount Sion encounter the angels, the spirits of the just and Jesus Christ (Heb. 12:22–4). In all three cases the quest for origins leads through the New Testament writings into Greek and Roman as well as Jewish thought and practice.[1]

Angels have long been prominent in inquiry into the origins of the Christ-cult, the martyrs and saints rather less so. This is partly because reverence for angels has obvious antecedents in post-exilic Judaism. The cult of martyrs and saints, however, arguably also has some Jewish roots. These have been explored by a series of students, including A. Schlatter, J. Obermann, E. Bickerman, E. Bammel, J. Jeremias, J. Lightstone, W. Rordorf, J. Wilkinson, J. W. van Henten and A. M. Schwemer. On the other hand, despite this inquiry, the mainly Christian character of the cult of the saints is widely asserted, for example by P. R. L. Brown, D. Satran, J. Taylor and G. W. Bowersock. In this paper, however, it is urged that a case for the importance of a Jewish factor in the development of the cult of saints can be made on lines slightly different from those which have been most generally followed; and that Jewish developments which anticipated and ran concurrently with the Christian cult of the saints also constituted a factor in the rise of the cult of Christ.

The cult of a hero, ruler, deity or saint can embrace private and domestic as well as more broadly corporate observance. Delehaye, 123–5, discussing

[1] Details of works cited by author and short title are listed in conclusion. I gratefully acknowledge questions from hearers of this paper, including J. W. van Henten, A. T. Kraabel and K. W. Niebuhr, and a series of valuable comments from M. N. A. Bockmuehl.

problems of identifying and defining cult in the case of martyrs, picked out corporate commemoration as the essential sign of cult. In the present study, concerned with Christ and Jewish as well as Christian heroic and saintly figures, the word 'cult' is comparably used only when corporate or public, not merely private observance is envisaged. With regard to the Jewish community, the scattered direct evidence for public commemoration and frequentation of tombs is interpreted here against its sometimes neglected background of a widely shared conception of a class of holy persons, and a communal transmission of visions of them and legends about them.

I

Consideration of the cults of Christ and of the saints together is encouraged by the history of debate about them. In ancient and modern times both have recalled Greek and Roman cults of heroes, sovereigns and divinities. A derivation of the Christian from the Greek and Roman customs has been proposed and resisted in both cases.

In antiquity, Christian apologists for the cult of both Christ and the martyrs not only stressed the difference between Christian and pagan usage, but also exploited the resemblance.[2] In the case of the martyr-cult, the charge of pagan origin which apologists rebutted indeed found some acceptance within the Christian sphere. Thus, in a famous inner-Christian attack on the cult of the saints at the beginning of the fifth century Vigilantius said, on the use of lights, 'I see what is almost a rite of the gentiles introduced in the churches under the pretext of religion' (Jerome, *c. Vigilantium* 4); similarly, it was a Manichaean accusation that the church 'turned the idols into martyrs' (Augustine, *c. Faustum* xx 4 and 21). Augustine himself, in his campaign to check eating and drinking at commemorations of the martyrs, could call this custom a concession to gentile Christians deprived of the pagan festivals (*Ep.* xxix 9). These objections endorsed an earlier non-Christian impression, mockingly embodied in the charge that Christians would worship martyrs instead of 'the crucified one'

[2] On the examples given below, and other texts, see J. B. Lightfoot, *The Apostolic Fathers*, Second Part, iii (2nd edn., London: Macmillan, 1889), 395, on *Mart. Polyc.* xvii; Lucius-Anrich, 325–36; Frend, 'North African Cult', 162–4.

(Martyrdom of Polycarp xvii 2–3) or 'as gods' (Eusebius, *H.E.* viii 6, 7), 'adding many corpses newly dead to the corpse of long ago' (Julian, *c. Galilaeos* 335B). Augustine repeatedly distinguished between the cult of God himself and the honour paid to the martyrs. This point is stressed in his preaching, significantly for the inclination of his people, but he also polemically shows that martyrs are stronger than gods and heroes (both points in *C.D.* viii 26–7, and *Serm.* 273, on Fructuosus and his companions, sections 3 and 6–9). In contemporary Syria, comparably but in more strongly Hellenic terms, Theodoret (*Affect.* viii) distinguished the pagan cult of θεοί from the Christian cult of the martyrs as θεῖοι ἄνθρώποι; but he also argued that the martyrs' shrines and festivals had replaced and improved upon those of the old gods, and that Greeks should find the cult of the martyrs as great patrons at their tombs fully justified by its likeness to their own tomb-oriented cult of heroes as guardians who ward off evil—ἐσθλοί, ἀλεξίκακοι, φύλακες θνητῶν ἀνθρώπων (Hesiod, *Op.* 123, on the golden race, in the form quoted by Plato, *Rep.* v 468E–469A and *Crat.* 397E, passages also quoted by Theodoret).

The same two-edged argument served to defend the cult of Christ. Apologists had to distinguish the Christ-cult from pagan usage, as Origen did when answering Celsus' charge that it was no different from the cults of Antinous, Asclepius, Dionysus or Heracles (*c. Celsum* iii 36–8, 42–3). On the other hand, resemblances to pagan custom were exploited from the second century onwards in response to the charge of atheism. It was stressed that Christianity indeed has, in the system of worship which includes the cult of Christ, something corresponding to Greek and Roman reverence for the gods. So Justin says 'We reverence and worship [God], and the Son, and the army of good angels, and the prophetic spirit' (Justin Martyr, *I Apol.* vi).[3] Similarly, still stressing resemblances, apologists could defend the narratives of the wonderful birth and works of Christ as like the Greek myths of beneficent heroes, and could prize the hopeful legends that Tiberius recommended Christ to the senate for apotheosis (*consecratio*) (so Tertullian, *Apol.* v 1–2, xxi 14 and 29–30), or that pagans set up a statue in honour of Christ the healer at Paneas (Eusebius, *H.E.* vii 18, 2–4).

[3] For similar phrases see Athenagoras, *Leg.* x, and Rev. 1:4–5; their use in the apologists is set against the background of contemporary Platonic theologies of a demiurge, a world-soul and assistant divine creators by Stead, 584–5.

In modern times, not dissimilarly, the two Christian cults have been both derived and differentiated from the cult of heroes in a debate which still continues. Criticism of W. Bousset's case for gentile influence on the Christ-cult issued in intensive inquiry into Jewish antecedents, but aspects recalling Greek and Roman custom have also been reconsidered. Thus H.-D. Betz takes it that the gospels, like the later Christian apologetic just reviewed, reflect both the influence of the hero-cult and reaction against it. In study of Judaism in connection with the Christ-cult the importance of Greek influence is stressed by M. Hengel, but this aspect has been somewhat over-shadowed by varied recent explorations of angelic and mediatorial figures and of what may be called the specifically Christian element in origins.

Modern discussion of the saints has run parallel. In the epoch of *Religionsgeschichte* their cult was derived from the hero-cult by E. Lucius (1904), soon followed by F. Pfister on the continuity between pagan and Christian attitudes to relics, and by E. Nourry with a more popular treatise in the rationalist interest, *Les saints successeurs des dieux*. H. Delehaye rejected this conclusion in the course of his own further work on Greek and Roman as well as Christian material. In more recent study, as noted already, inquiry into Jewish roots of the cult has gone side by side with rejection of pagan derivation (as by Brown, 5–6) and reassertion of its primarily Christian character. T. Klauser, however, showed that pagan as well as Jewish and Christian factors should be recognized. In 1960, in the light of Jeremias' work, he characterized the martyr-cult as a largely Christian development with some Jewish antecedents. In 1974, however, he added that this development could not be dissociated from contemporary pagan custom.

In both cases, then, contemporary observers of early Christian custom, inside as well as outside the church, noted its likeness to the hero-cult; and in both cases some modern historians have found significant continuities between the hero-cult and the Christian usage. In what follows an attempt is made, accordingly, to hold together these two Christian cults in exploration of their origins. It is accepted here that there is much truth in the ancient and modern indications of a common Greek and Roman background for them both; but it will be argued in the two following sections that full justice has perhaps still not been done to Jewish development of beliefs and customs recalling both the hero-cult and the Christian cult of the saints. Identification of this trend in ancient Judaism then suggests, as outlined in section IV below, another avenue of approach to study of the Jewish roots of the Christ-cult.

II

How fully did this Jewish development anticipate and resemble the Christian cult of the saints? In this section a case for substantial anticipation and resemblance will be outlined, starting from the New Testament, through a mainly chronological review of some landmarks in the evidence and the history of study; and an approach slightly differing from those most widely followed will be suggested. Then the following section will set some signs of corporate commemoration and veneration in Jewish custom against the background of Jewish conceptions of a saintly class and transmission of visions and legends. It will be argued that continuity in Jewish practice and thought on this matter can be traced from well before to well after the time of Christian origins.

For both sections it is important that, among Christians as well as Jews in antiquity, biblical saints remained primary, although in both communities post-biblical figures were added to them. The abiding pre-eminence of biblical figures among Christians in the later Roman empire emerges not only from liturgical formulae like 'patriarchs, prophets, righteous, apostles, martyrs, confessors' (*Const. Ap.* viii 12), but also from the great preponderance of biblical apocrypha over martyrology in surviving Greek and probably also pre-Islamic Coptic papyri (Clarysse, 392–5). The cult of saints in Christian antiquity was in this respect considerably closer to ancient Jewish life and thought than was the later western Christian cult, with its main orientation towards ecclesiastical figures.

To begin now with the New Testament, Jewish antecedents for the Christian cult of the saints are suggested by a number of passages. One group of these refers to the glory and after-life of the patriarchs and prophets. Thus Abraham, Isaac, and Jacob are alive (Mark 12:26–7 and parallels); they will be in the kingdom of heaven (Matt. 8:11), together with all the prophets (Luke 13:28); 'the fathers' are a glory of Israel (Rom. 9:5); even now Abraham is favourably placed in the after-life, with Lazarus carried by the angels into his bosom (Luke 16:22–31); apparitions of Moses and Elijah are seen by the disciples (Mark

9:4 and parallels); the return of Elijah, Jeremiah, or John the Baptist can be expected (Matt. 16:19 and parallels); many bodies of the saints who sleep in their memorials arise at the death of Christ (Matt. 27:52–3); the patriarchs from Abel to Moses, together with prophets, judges, kings, and righteous ones, form a cloud of witnesses surrounding Christians on earth (Heb. 12:1), and are encountered in the heavenly Jerusalem as or among the spirits of the perfected just (Heb. 12:23, quoted above as linking the spirits of the just and Jesus Christ); similarly, the souls of the (probably Christian) slain are under the altar in heaven (Rev. 6:9–11).

A second group of passages, highlighted especially by Jeremias, deal with tombs of saints. The dead in general are οἱ ἐν τοῖς μνημείοις (John 5:28; cf. Isa. 26:19 LXX ἐγερθήσονται οἱ ἐν τοῖς μνημείοις), and special mention is made of the tombs of prophets and righteous (Matt. 23:27–9; Luke 11:44, 47); memorials holding the bodies of the saints outside Jerusalem (Matt. 27:52–3, already cited); the tomb of David (Acts 2:29); the tomb of the patriarchs in Shechem (Acts 7:16); the bones of Joseph (Heb. 11:22, in the context of the cloud of witnesses, already cited); and, by allusion, the tomb of Rachel near Bethlehem (Matt. 2:18).

A third group, of indirect importance, reflects the dignity ascribed to apostles and martyrs.[4] Apostolic bodily and spiritual presence is a formidable honour (as in Rom. 15:18–19; 1 Cor. 4:21, 5:4; Phil 1:26; Acts 5:1–11, 12–13); power inheres in the apostolic shadow or clothing (Acts 5:15, 19:12; cf. Mark 5:28 and parallels, on the garments of Christ); and the 'victor' will share the messianic throne and judgment (as in Rev. 2:26–7, 3:21; cf. 6:9–11, on the slain, quoted above). The dignity presupposed derives from Christ's pre-eminence, but the specifically Christian reverence reflected here forms a further indirect sign of customary Jewish honour for the righteous.

Earlier Jewish writings illustrate these New Testament texts. Literary forms corresponding to praise and invocation of saints appear respectively in the laudatory πατέρων ὕμνος of Ecclesiasticus and in the Song of the Three Children, calling on the spirits and souls of the righteous in a context of martyr-like sacrificial death. The activity and glory of the righteous departed, the prophets and the patriarchs are pre-supposed in the Wisdom of

4 On apostolic presence, shadow, and garb see Funk; van der Horst, 61–4; Pfister, 620.

Solomon on the coming victory of the righteous souls, and on the holy souls, and the glories of the fathers (3:1, 4:7, 5:1, 7:27, 19:24). Many other works roughly contemporary with these are relevant. Thus literature attested in the Qumran finds includes, from probably non-sectarian sources, hagiography on patriarchs and later worthies (as in Jubilees, Genesis Apocryphon, Testaments of Judah and Levi, Visions of Amram, Psalms of Joshua, Tobit); within sectarian writings, comparable treatment of the Teacher of Righteousness; and in both types of source, expectations of the return of the great (Melchizedek, probably also the Teacher of Righteousness), the prayers of righteous souls (Book of Noah = 1 En. 9:10; 1 En. 22:5–7), and the resurrection and glory of the righteous (Deutero-Ezekiel, 1 En. 10 and 22 (4QEn *c–d*), 1QH xiv (vi) 34).

From these and other writings there emerge, further, some widespread concerns which help to form a setting for reverence for the saints. Thus care for relics and tombs need not imply hope for bodily resurrection, but it readily coheres with it. Similarly, thoughts of the prayers and the glory of righteous souls are encouraged by concern for the soul here (Philo, *Spec. Leg.* i 77, on the health-bringing half-shekel λύτρα for the soul, Exod. 30:12); or hereafter (2 Esd. 7:75; Syriac Apocalypse of Baruch 21:12–18); or in both respects, as when Lev 16:31 'ye shall afflict your souls' (on the Day of Atonement) is interpreted as 'ye shall fast *for* your souls' (Fragment Targum; Ps.-Philo, *Ant. Bibl.* 13.6; cf. Philo, *Spec. Leg.* ii 196 χρηστὰ ἐλπίζοντες).

2 Maccabees, however, has three narratives of special note. The first, on Eleazar and on the seven brethren and their mother (6:18–7:42), deals with what a Christian would call martyrdom, and mentions intercession (7:37–8). The second tells how Judas Maccabaeus sacrificed and prayed on behalf of Jews fallen in battle whose amulets attested a lapse into idolatry (12:38–45). Lastly, Judas' vision of Onias and Jeremiah praying for Jerusalem is described (15:11–16). These passages presuppose intercession by martyrs and righteous souls, awaiting future glory. Not surprisingly, the sixteenth-century Dominican Sixtus Senensis (Sisto da Siena) called Maccabees 1–2 *vehementer utiles* 'for confuting the heresies especially of our own times; for in 2 Maccabees there are very clear testimonies concerning Purgatory, and that prayers should be made for the dead, and concerning the prayers of the saints' (Sixtus Senensis, *Bibliotheca Sancta* (1566), viii 12; Cologne: P. Cholin, 1626, 829).

2 Maccabees, an abridgement of Jason of Cyrene's five-book history, was issued with its two prefatory festal letters before Pompey's time, perhaps as early as 124 B.C. (so M. Goodman in Schürer *et al.*, 532–4; similarly, J. C. H. Lebram and J. W. van Henten in van Henten, *Entstehung*, 248–9). Bowersock, 9–13, suggests that the section on martyr-like deaths (6:18–7:42), which (by contrast with the emphasis of the book elsewhere) lacks any reference to the temple, may have been interpolated at a relatively late date, perhaps after the destruction of Jerusalem by Titus; but any looseness in its attachment to the context is also well accounted for by 'the painful labour of abridgement' (2:26), and its silence on the temple follows naturally from the author's or abridger's remark that even the temple is of less account in God's eyes than the nation (ἔθνος, 5:19)—which is prominent, together with the 'race' (γένος), in the ensuing story of the brethren (7:16, 37–8). The section on martyrdom has other thematic links with the rest of the book. Thus, admiration for the choice of death rather than idolatry, even in appearance (6:21–8), agrees with fear and grief on behalf of the dead who did appear to have lapsed (12:38–45); similarly, the effectual intercession of the faithful brethren (7:37–8) coheres well with the heavenly intercession of the righteous (15:11–16). Finally, it has been shown that in vocabulary this section is close to 9:1–18 and is indistinguishable from the rest of the historical narrative, in the structure of which it is pivotal (van Henten in *Entstehung*, 132–6, 248). Bowersock's redating of 6:18–7:42 therefore seems unlikely. More probably, this section comes from the Hasmonaean period, like the material in 2 Maccabees on the saints and the afterlife with which it is thematically linked.

Thus the New Testament, in the light of the Apocrypha and other pre-Christian Jewish writings, could reasonably be interpreted as attesting a Jewish view of departed patriarchs, prophets and others as living (Mark, Matthew, Luke), interceding (2 Maccabees, Luke), and present, none the less, in their tombs (Matthew). It also attests a corresponding Jewish custom of honouring the tombs of the patriarchs, prophets and righteous (Matthew and Luke-Acts). This is confirmed by Josephus on the patriarchal tomb in Hebron and Abraham's terebinth nearby (*B.J.* iv 532–3, using the word δείκνυται of both), and on the miraculous protection of the tomb of David and Solomon (*Ant.* xvi 179–83), and by Cassius Dio (lxix 14, 2) on the ill-omened collapse of the monument of Solomon. Later evidence includes targumic and rabbinic texts attesting reverence for and hagiographical treatment of patriarchs, prophets, kings, the slain, and the disciples of the Wise. In this material viewed as a whole the recurrent conception of patrons who appear in visions and whose tombs are honoured recalls aspects of the hero-cult, but is particularly close to the Christian cult of saints.

Three further bodies of evidence have formed landmarks in discussion, but some inferences often drawn from them are not presupposed here. First, at the end of a narrative of the Maccabees in the sixth-century Antiochene chronicler John Malalas, Antiochus IV's successor Demetrius is said to have given Judas Maccabaeus their remains, 'and they buried them in Antioch the Great in the place called Kerateon, for there was a synagogue of the Jews there; for Antiochus had punished them a little outside the city of Antioch, on the ever-weeping mountain opposite Zeus Casius'.[5] Their story as transmitted in the midrash appears in one amplified form of the *Book of Comfort* by the eleventh-century Nissim ibn Shahin of Cairouan with the addition that 'king Caesar' had them buried in one grave and built a synagogue over them.[6] It has been concluded (for example, by Bammel, 81–2; Jeremias, *Heiligengräber*, 21–3, 124; Cohen, 158–9) that an ancient Antiochene synagogue stood at the martyrs' reputed tomb. Yet Malalas may reflect a provenance-narrative attached to the Antiochene Christian cult of the Maccabees (as noted by Dupont-Sommer, 71), in a church which had been a synagogue—perhaps an adaptation of Josephus on the restoration of plunder from the Jerusalem temple to the Jews of Antioch by Antiochus IV's successors (*B.J.* vii 44); and the additional note in the textual tradition of the *Book of Comfort* recalls many similar notices of tombs at synagogues in mediaeval Jewish itineraries. These passages indicate ancient Christian and mediaeval Jewish veneration of a Maccabaean tomb at Antioch, but need not imply an earlier Jewish cult (Rajak, 68–9). This should not be ruled out, but it is not presupposed here.

[5] L. Dindorf (ed.), *Joannis Malalis Chronographia*, viii, reprinted in *PG* 97.324 (the context is discussed by Bickerman).

[6] Obermann, 'Sepulchre'; Obermann, *The Arabic Original of Ibn Shâhîn's Book of Comfort, known as the Hiibbûr Yaphê of R. Nissîm b. Ya'aqobh* (New Haven, CT: Yale University Press, 1933), Plate XXVI (f.24b); p. 28; S. Abramson (ed.), *R. Nissim Gaon: Libelli Quinque* (Jerusalem: Mekize Nirdamim, 1965), 367–8 (Nissim's original text probably said only that he had told their tale elsewhere; ET by W. M. Brinner, *An Elegant Composition concerning Relief after Adversity* (New Haven and London: Yale University Press, 1977), xx; 29, n. 7; 32.

Secondly, in the Testaments of the Twelve Patriarchs their lives and prophetic visions are treated hagiographically, their burial at Hebron is stressed, they are to rise from the dead among the first (Test. Judah 25:1, Benj. 10:6–7), and the related Judaean burial sites of Rachel and Zilpah or Asenath are mentioned (Test. Jos. 20:3). It is assumed that Levi and Judah are pre-eminent. This point, viewed together with Qumran attestation of the Testament of Levi, suggests that the work has a pre-Christian Jewish core. The Testaments were accordingly a pillar of Jeremias' *Heiligengräber*, together with the Lives of the Prophets.

In the present writer's view, the hagiographical features of the Testaments should probably be assigned to their pre-Christian core, through comparison with 2 Maccabees and Josephus. Here, however, the Testaments, Christian in their present form (as M. de Jonge especially has underlined), are not used as direct evidence for Jewish thought and custom. Instead, they contribute to the argument as a witness to continuity between Judaism and Christianity, an aspect of them which de Jonge (206–7) has also stressed; comparable continuity between Jewish and Christian usage at the end of the Second Temple period is suggested here.

Thirdly, the Lives of the Prophets have evoked similar debate. They expand on birth and burial places and the miracles performed there. Jeremias followed predecessors, including S. Klein, in viewing the Lives as a Christian version of Jewish material; its Jewish source was compiled at latest not long after Bar Kokhba, and more probably before Titus captured Jerusalem. D. Satran, on the other hand, allows that individual Jewish traditions may have contributed to the Lives, but maintains that the composition as a whole should be regarded as a Byzantine Christian work; he takes a position questioned here, that at the end of the Second Temple period there was no Jewish cult of the saints sufficiently developed to provide a *Sitz im Leben* for a Jewish writing on these lines. A. M. Schwemer, by contrast, argues for a Jewish source earlier than the destruction of the temple, and traces in a detailed commentary the contacts of the Lives with Jewish tradition. In the present writer's view the Lives, suitable as they were to Byzantine Palestine, probably also attest much earlier Jewish veneration of the prophets and their tombs. Here, however, this is not taken for granted.

Lastly, this review of some landmarks should include two archaeological finds published after Jeremias' *Heiligengräber*. First, in the necropolis of Beth

Shearim in south-western Galilee, walled meeting places with stone benches were identified over two of the catacombs. This interpretation of the finds, advanced by N. Avigad in 1971 in the light of rabbinic texts (see below), seemed to strengthen the possibility that in the third and fourth centuries Jews, not unlike Christians, assembled at tombs to honour the dead, despite Pentateuchal warnings of impurity there (Num. 19:16–19, noted in Didascalia xxvi (vi 21–2) as ostensibly discouraging Christian cemetery assemblies); the Mishnah indeed envisages that people dwell among tomb-monuments, and that they may touch the sides of them without uncleanness (Erub. 5.1, Ohol. 7.1). It therefore seems inexact to speak of 'a fundamental difference of ideas' between Jews and Christians on the dead (with Lane Fox, 447–8). Obermann, 'Sepulchre', 263–5 more justly recognized among ancient Jews a tendency to revere relics and tombs alongside the tendency to restrict contact with the dead.

Secondly, Old Testament scenes hitherto unattested in Christian art were found at the fourth-century Via Latina catacomb in Rome, published by A. Ferrua in 1960; their contacts with the haggadah strengthened the view already advanced on the basis of other evidence by E. R. Goodenough and others that early Christian paintings of the Old Testament saints might have had Jewish models (see, for example, G. Stemberger on the depictions of the patriarchs). The impression left by targum and midrash that Jews treated the biblical worthies hagiographically was thereby reinforced.

The literary and archaeological evidence just reviewed suggests that Jews regarded their saints as inspired patrons and honoured their tombs at least from the Hasmonaean period onwards. This can be said without the appeal to an inferred Jewish cult of the Maccabees which has sometimes been made, and without citation of the Testaments of the Twelve Patriarchs and the Lives of the Prophets, which are prominent among the many sources adduced by Jeremias. Although these works probably preserve ancient Jewish tradition, it is desirable to see if a case can be made, as has been attempted here, simply by confronting the rich New Testament material with evidence generally accepted as Jewish.

The argument outlined so far may at this point be further elucidated by an addition to the text as first printed. Some of the objections envisaged above were expressed again in a study of Jewish pilgrimage in Greek and Roman Egypt by A. Kerkeslager, published in the year when this essay first appeared, and not available when the foregoing paragraphs were written. He brings forward further material for discussion with regard to holy places, notably in an extended argument for Jewish interest in Mount Sinai, and for the currency throughout the Greek and Roman periods of the identification of Sinai with a mountain near Madyan in north-western Arabia (Kerkeslager, 146–213). He judges the material specifically from Egypt, however, to be sparse (103), although his treatment of it could have included two Egyptian Jewish institutions which he does not discuss, the festival and place of prayer founded at 'rose-bearing Ptolemais' in lower Egypt (3 Macc. 7:17–21), and the Septuagint-festival of Pharos (section III (i), below). On the question of Jewish concern with the righteous and holy departed, not simply in Egypt but also elsewhere, he correspondingly stresses the limited nature of evidence for pilgrimage to tombs in the Second Temple period, and the possible discontinuities between Jewish and Christian custom.

On evidence for Jewish pilgrimage, he accepts that the Testaments of the Twelve Patriarchs reflect non-Christian Judaism, but follows D. Satran in regarding the Lives of the Prophets as essentially a Christian work; he does not mention A. M. Schwemer's commentary and argument for earlier dating. He emphasizes that, if the evidence of the Lives and of an inferred Jewish cult of the Maccabees is excluded, Jewish pilgrimage to tombs in the Second Temple period may seem far more limited than was suggested by Jeremias (Kerkeslager, 134–8; cf. 143–4, on the Egyptian burial and translation of Jeremiah described in the Lives of the Prophets). In the argument offered above it was urged, however, that even if these debated bodies of evidence are excluded, and the Testaments of the Twelve Patriarchs as well, the New Testament, 2 Maccabees and other sources of the Second Temple period still exhibit departed patriarchs, prophets and others as saint-like figures whose tombs are honoured.

Secondly, Kerkeslager tends to minimize continuity between Jewish and Christian observance by noting conflict of opinion on the righteous dead among Jews at the time of Christian origins, the seemingly greater importance of kinship and national identity in Jewish observance, and the potential influence among Jews later on of fresh developments, especially the tendency to treat rabbis as holy men and the growth of the Christian cult of the saints (Kerkeslager, 132–6, 140–2, 224).

Conflict of opinion on the departed is considered in the reviews of evidence for commemoration and for concepts of a saintly class in sections III (i) and (ii), below; Christian influence is considered at the end of III (i). It is urged here that, despite differences of opinion on after-life, the trend towards regarding the mighty and righteous dead as a company of the holy who are dear to God was strong at the end of the Second Temple period. That appears plainly when, as in the present argument, evidence for pilgrimage and the honouring of tombs is viewed together with literary and other evidence, already substantial by the end of the Second Temple period, for commemoration of the righteous and for the presupposition of a body of righteous departed and the circulation of legends concerning them (sections III (i)–(iii), below).

It is in this context that the veneration of rabbis is illustrated in section III (i) below in connection with Meron, Khirbet Shema and Beth Shearim, in III (ii) from Beth Shearim epitaphs of departed teachers, and in III (iii) from dream-visions of rabbinic teachers and from narratives of Simeon b. Yohai and his son. For the argument offered here, there is no need to deny that such veneration of near-contemporary figures will have given fresh impetus to commemoration of the fathers and righteous of old, as seems to have been the case at an earlier time in 2 Maccabees, in the vision of the recently-dead Onias together with the prophet Jeremiah. What is suggested, rather, is that a long-standing tradition of commemoration will have been continually renewed by the incorporation into it of contemporary righteous or slain, from the Second Temple period onwards (compare Ecclesiasticus and Hebrews, as cited at the beginning of III (ii), below).

Hence the argument outlined here and below does not rule out the possibility of Christian influence, but treats it as converging with inner-Jewish tradition which has also already played a part in the development of Christian custom. Similarly, contrasts between Jewish and Christian observance need not be ruled out, but it is urged that resemblances also be given due weight; thus Kerkeslager (142) justly notes that the encouragement of pilgrimage centres by Herod the Great (see chapter 3, above) and by later Christian bishops is comparable, but he does not allow this point to modify his overall contrast between Jewish and Christian practice. Other modifications to this contrast could be suggested. Thus the importance of kindred and nation which for Kerkeslager (139–40, 142, 146) characterizes Jewish as opposed to Christian pilgrimage finds some correspondence in the quasi-national church-consciousness exemplified in the Christian martyr-cult (Van Henten, 'The Martyrs as Heroes of the Christian People'). A further contrast is drawn by Kerkeslager (140–2) between third-century and later Christian hope for benefits from honoured saints, and earlier Jewish care for the departed without expectation of prayers from them—care envisaged either simply as a duty (notably in Tobit) or as a means of gaining public esteem (as gospel passages on the adornment of sepulchres might suggest). This contrast too can be modified, however, by reference to the early depictions of the prayer of righteous souls noted above from 1 Enoch and 2 Maccabees, and to the even earlier biblical view that God specially remembers the patriarchs, the matriarchs and the meek—a Pentateuchal view which underlies, as noted in section III (i) below, Philo's conviction that the ancestors intercede effectually for their descendants.

Hence, although the developed Christian cult of the saints should not be unthinkingly merged with Jewish practice of the Second Temple period, there are striking indications of continuity between Jewish and Christian custom and belief. Such continuity is further illustrated, as noted above, when discussion of pilgrimage and tombs is enlarged to include other forms of commemoration of the departed and beliefs and legends about them. These further topics are considered in the following section.

III

The material reviewed so far has documented the treatment of the departed righteous as patrons and the honour given to their tombs, before, during, and after the time of Christian origins. Now this mainly chronological review of evidence, beginning from the New Testament, needs supplementation by fuller treatment of forms of commemoration, and the accompanying conceptions of a saintly class and legends of the righteous.

(i) Commemoration

The prime importance of public commemoration as evidence for cult was noted above, with reference to Delehaye on the martyrs. In their case a festal day forms the central commemoration. For the holy and righteous of ancient Judaism the anniversary of death will also in some cases have been marked, with fasting and with eulogy, and sometime with assembly at tombs; but a further range of public commemorative practice comes into view, connected with biblical reading, prayer and festivals.

First, as already noted, the majority of these figures were biblical. Their naming when the law and the prophets were publicly read will have functioned as commemoration, recalling the legends which enhanced their individual vitality, and their place as lively members of the congregation of saints (see below).

Secondly, they were remembered in communal prayer. In the Hebrew Bible the remembrance of individual figures is already important within the broader remembrance of divine deliverance which became characteristic of post-exilic Israel (Childs, 74–80). God remembers the patriarchs and matriarchs (Gen. 8:1, 19:39, 30:22; Lev. 26:45; Ps. 105:42), and the meek (Ps. 9:12, 18); these passages are echoed in Ezekiel Tragicus 106, discussed in chapter 2, above, and in Philo (*Praem.* 165–6) when he says that the founders of the race are remembered by God, and intercede effectually. In other biblical passages, God is asked to remember them again, as in Exod. 32:13; Deut. 9:27 (patriarchs); 2 Chron 6:42; Ps. 132:1 (David). This petition was later continued in prayer for remembrance of the patriarchs and their covenant, as in 2 Macc. 1:2, 1:25, and the Words of the Luminaries, 4Q504 fr.3 ii, 505 fr.124, and later in the request for remembrance of the fathers and the messiah together with all Israel in the prayer *ya'aleh ve-yavo'* in the festal Amidah (Sopherim 19.7, 42b; Elbogen, Heinemann and Scheindlin, 51, 112; Singer and Brodie, 52); on comparable Christian prayer for remembrance of the people and the saints, and on midrashic association of the remembrance-prayer in 2 Chron. 6:42 with David's body, see this section, below. Israel likewise remembers divine deliverance specifically at the hand of the patriarchs and Moses and Aaron (Isa. 63:11; Ps. 77:20, 105:5–27), and the righteous are remembered (Ps. 112:6; Prov 10:7); as noted above, in later hymnody they are praised (Ecclus. 44:1–15), and their souls are called on to bless the Lord (Dan. 3:86 LXX). Many of these texts from the Hebrew Bible were included before the time of the Mishnah among the Remembrance-verses recited at New Year (R.H. 4.5). The biblical prominence of the remembrance of the righteous encouraged its continuation, and formed part of the context in which their stories were read and amplified.

Thirdly, commemoration of the righteous formed an element in many festivals and fasts. The three pilgrim feasts, especially Passover, were of course connected with Moses, their founder or renewer in the exodus (Lev. 23:44, Josephus, *Ant.* iv 203), and with David and Solomon, Hezekiah and Josiah; they came to be linked also with the patriarchs, as in Jub. 6:17–27 (Noah and Weeks), 16.20–31 (Abraham and Tabernacles). In the later Roman empire, the fasts of Ninth Ab and the Day of Atonement were connected not only with destruction and sin but also with the martyrs under Antiochus and Hadrian (Obermann, 'Sepulchre'), and Purim was preceded on 12th Adar by commemoration of martyrs under Trajan (Horbury, 'Pappus', 290); and the network of association between the biblical saints and the feasts and fasts is evident in the *piyyuṭim* for the various days and seasons (instances in Horbury, 'Yose', 152–5, 169–71; pp. 334–8, 352–3, above).

Post-biblical figures like the Maccabees, the Hadrianic martyrs and venerated rabbis were therefore drawn through the feasts and fasts into the company of the biblical saints. This association is somewhat comparable with the commemoration of Old Testament saints together with others in eastern church calendars, and in Christian prayer like that of *Const. Ap.* viii 12, quoted above, asking God to remember Old Testament and later saints, the departed, and the faithful (for similar formulae from Cyril of Jerusalem, Epiphanius and the Liturgy of S. James see Brightman and Hammond, 56–7, 466, 469 n. 13).

Fourthly, in the Second Temple period some individual commemorations resemble pagan and Christian days in honour of heroes, monarchs and martyrs. The pious observed a calendar of fasts and feasts (Zech. 7:3–5, 8:19; Judith 8:6; Megillath Taanith) which will have included commemorations on the lines of the recurrent public mourning envisaged for Josiah (2 Chron. 35:25), Gedaliah (seventh-month fast as interpreted in the name of Simeon b. Yohai, R.H. 18b), and Jephthah's daughter (Ps.-Philo, *Ant. Bibl.* 40.8). In these instances it was probably envisaged that notable figures received a more widespread form of the mourning customary on the anniversary of the death of a father or teacher (Ned. 12a names these anniversaries together with the fast of Gedaliah). Two greater festivals instituted in this period are strongly linked with the righteous: Hanukkah with its founders, Judas and his brethren (1 Macc. 4:59; 2 Macc.

10:1–8), and with the tribal princes through the reading of Num. 7 (Meg. 3.6; chapter 5, p. 192 above); and Purim, with Esther and Mordecai (14th Adar was 'the Mardochaean Day', 2 Macc. 15:36). Similarly, the annual Septuagint-feast on the Pharos island will have included honour to the translators, whom Philo calls spirit-possessed (*Mos.* ii 7) and whose cells were shown to visitors (Meg. 9a; Ps.-Justin, *Coh. Gr.* 13). Interest in individuals appears too when villains are remembered beside heroes; the Mardochaean Day was preceded by the impious Nicanor's Day (2 Macc. 15:36; Meg. Taan. xii 3), and Purim condemns Haman and Zeresh while exalting Mordecai and Esther.

Another public observance, in this case a network of local observances, is formed by frequentation of the tombs of the righteous. New Testament indications of this custom can be confirmed, as noted above in section II, even when the Testaments of the Twelve Patriarchs and the Lives of the Prophets are left aside. A further indirect confirmation is offered by attestations of concern for the bodies and bones of saints, including Ecclus. 46:12, 49:10 (the judges and the twelve prophets); Matt. 27:53 (buried saints), Acts 2:29, 13:34–7 (David) and Heb. 11:22 (Joseph), cited above in section II. This concern coheres with interpretation of Ezek. 37 as a prophecy of resurrection (4Q385.2 (Deutero-Ezekiel); Justin, *I Apol.*, 52; Dura Europus synagogue, north wall). It later reappears dramatically in the view that the dedication of Solomon's temple was accomplished through the bodily presence of the departed David. Since fire descended to consume the sacrifices only after Solomon had prayed 'remember the mercies of David thy servant' (2 Chron. 6:42–7:1), in Palestinian rabbinic exposition it came to be held that this grace—and also the admission of the ark into the Holy of Holies (Ps. 24:7–10)—was obtained not just by the merits of David (so Judah b. Ezekiel in the name of Rab, M.K. 9a, Shabb. 30a), but through his bodily presence and intercession; either he was raised to life again, as David's own psalm 'for the dedication of the temple' might suggest (Ps. 30:1, 4), or Solomon brought his coffin into the temple when he prayed 'Remember'. Midrash Qoheleth (Eccl. R.) iv i (4), Pes. R. ii, 6b, on Ps. 30:1, and Tanhuma (Wilna, 1833, reissued New York and Berlin: Horeb, 1927), Exodus, Wa'era, 7, f. 96a–b, on Exod. 7:1, give both these interpretations; Tanhuma Buber, Exodus, f.11a–b, on Exod. 7:1, has the second interpretation only.[7]

[7] For further sources see L. Ginzberg, *The Legends of the Jews, iv* (Philadelphia: Jewish Publication Society of America, 1968), 296, n. 65; the importance here attached to David's relics was underlined by Smith, *Studies*, i, 131–2, n. 73.

Interpretation of tomb-visits with this concern in view likewise appears in rabbinic texts. Caleb went to the tomb of the patriarchs at Hebron to seek their intercession, praying 'my fathers, seek mercy for me' (Soṭah 34b, in the name of Raba). The development of a relic-oriented pilgrimage centre is reflected in the story of the pious theft of the body of Eleazar, son of Simeon ben Yohai, by the people of Meron in Galilee from nearby Gischala; his sainted father, buried in Meron, had provoked them to this deed by repeated dream-apparitions (PRK xi 23, among other places).

Can assembly at tombs be envisaged among ancient Jews, as these rabbinic stories in conjunction with pre-rabbinic sources suggest, on the lines followed by Christians at martyr-tombs and in associated churches? Vitringa, 219–20, answered Yes, judging that ancient synagogues were often built at notable sepulchres. He compared Matt. 23:29 with the mediaeval Jewish itineraries of Benjamin of Tudela and others, where venerated tombs in the Holy Land and elsewhere are often said to be at or near a synagogue; so the thirteenth-century itinerary of Jehiel of Paris registers tombs just mentioned 'At Meron, in the synagogue: R. Simeon b. Yohai and R. Eleazar his son' (Grünhut and Adler, ii, 141). From the years between the New Testament and these mediaeval texts Vitringa cited Lam. R., Proem, 25, on 2 Chron. 32:33 'they made him [Hezekiah] honour at his death'; Judah b. Simon (fourth century) explained: they built a house of assembly (*beth va'adh*) above the tomb of Hezekiah, and when they went up to it they used to say to him 'Teach us'. Vitringa stressed that the historical accuracy of all these reports mattered less for his argument than their presuppositions.

In later study, however, mediaeval synagogue-tombs were linked with Islamic influence, although Obermann ('Sepulchre', 265) urged that some of the synagogues concerned were probably pre-Islamic. More recently, excavations at Khirbet Shema, the ancient Galilaean Tekoa, near Meron, showed that the monument known as the Mausoleum of Shammai and two other tombs were 'strikingly proximate' to the third—and fourth-century synagogue (Meyers, Kraabel and Strange, 121–2). This is among evidence which led Cohen, 168–9, to judge that in antiquity synagogues were sometimes deliberately built near tombs.

This question is still discussed, but Beth Shearim finds, as noted above in section II, have been among evidence prompting reconsideration of the broader question of assembly at tombs. The tiers of stone seating within an apsed wall above the monumental façades of catacombs 14 and 20 at Beth Shearim were interpreted in the light of Lam. R. on Hezekiah by N. Avigad as houses of assembly, where the mighty dead beneath were eulogized and remembered in prayer and study (Avigad, 44–5, 83). A courtyard with benches at a monumental tomb in Jericho has been judged to attest this custom at the end of the Second Temple period (Hachlili and Killebrew, 112).

Literary and archaeological material therefore strongly suggests that Jews in antiquity did assemble at tombs to honour the dead. Such customs have been ascribed to Christian influence (as by Bickerman, 204; Smith, i, 131–2, n. 73; Taylor, 324–5; Tsafrir, 375); but it is unlikely to be their main source, given the relatively early witness to this practice at Jericho, and the New Testament and other pre-rabbinic evidence noted above.

To summarize, commemoration of various kinds can be traced from the Second Temple period down to the later Roman empire: in public bible-reading and prayer; in the association of the pilgrim-feasts with the patriarchs; in the foundation of festivals like Purim, Hanukkah, and the Septuagint-feast, marking deliverance or blessing accorded at the hand of individuals; and in commemoration on the lines followed for the notable dead, including annual fast-days, and often involving assembly and eulogy at a venerated tomb.

The potential significance of commemoration in its simplest forms is underlined by instances of invocation (Dan 3:86 LXX; Mark 15:35; Lam. R. Proem 25; Soṭah 34b). The correlated expectation of intercession by the saints has appeared in 2 Macc. 7:37–8, 15:14 (cited in the previous section) and in Philo, *Praem.* 165, and Soṭah 34b (this section, above). Warnings that such intercession is excluded, at judgment day (2 Esd. 7:102–5; 2 Baruch 85:12) or altogether (Ps. Philo, *Ant. Bibl.* 33.5), seem to presuppose widespread reliance on it (as expressed in Ps.-Philo, *Ant. Bibl.* 33.4).

(ii) The assembly of saints

This scattered yet continous evidence for commemoration of various kinds corresponds to continuous but perhaps somewhat neglected evidence for the vitality of ancient Jewish conceptions of the company of departed saints. In the Greek and Roman periods Jews (like Christians) lacked general terms corresponding to modern English 'saint', although a step in this direction was taken when *sanctus* was used to render both ἅγιος and ὅσιος in Latin biblical versions. Jews recognized, nevertheless, a glorious company of the holy and righteous—'our fathers', biblical ἔνδοξοι or *'anshe hesedh* (Ecclus. 44:1) to whom might be added others more recent (Ecclus. 50:1; Heb. 11:35), extending to the whole company of the departed 'righteous' (1 En. 25:7). Groups identified among them included 'the fathers' and 'the prophets', encountered above in the biblical Apocrypha, the New Testament, rabbinic and patristic writings, and 'the slain', common to Rev. 6:10 and rabbinic usage, as in the Midrash of the Ten Martyrs, 'the ten slain by the kingdom', *'asarah haruge malkuth* (Reeg, 4*–6*). Old Testament and New Testament adjectives in the fields of 'righteous' and 'holy' are well known as applied to the whole community (a usage stressed by Delehaye, 1–73, and Proksch and Kuhn on ἅγιος), and, in the second case, also to the angels; but departed saints are also described in these terms in biblical and later texts, as emerges in part from Büchler, Mach, Schrenk on δίκαιος, and Hauck on ὅσιος. These descriptions give further witness to the importance of a saintly class for Jews in antiquity.

In general presentations of ancient Judaism the conception of a saintly class has accordingly had some limited notice. Examples include Bousset and Gressmann, 189–90, 198–9, on the martyrs and patriarchs and their merits, against the background of the pious movements of the later Second Temple period; Volz, 353–5, on the heavenly 'Gemeinde der Heiligen' envisaged in views of the hereafter; and Urbach, 487–511, assessing the place of the legends and merits of the righteous in rabbinic thought. Sometimes, however, the conception as a whole has remained implicit, when attention has been concentrated on one aspect of it, such as the merit of the fathers (as in Moore, i, 536–44). Not dissimilarly, E. P. Sanders implies the importance of ideas of a saintly class when he includes Philo (*Praem.* 165) on the founders of the race as remembered by God, and general Jewish hope for a purified community, within his depiction of 'common Judaism'; but he does not specifically discuss the broader circle of practice and belief associated with the tombs of the righteous (Sanders, 272, 290–4). Hence the conception of an assembly of saints is readily associated with the ancient church, but its currency among Jews can easily be overlooked.

From the Second Temple period onwards, however, many held that the holy and righteous rest in the tomb, but their souls form a favoured company; at the time of redemption, they will appear in glory, together with the angels and perhaps fighting on their side. These views were not shared by those who 'say that there is no resurrection, neither angel nor spirit' (Acts 23:8); but they were of long standing when Christianity arose, and continued to be potent in the Jewish community.

In the Greek period, development towards this outlook appears in the LXX Pentateuch. Thus the phrase 'souls (spirits) of the righteous', which became widespread (1 En. 22:9; Dan. 3:86 LXX, Wisd. 3:1; Heb. 12:23, cited above; 2 Esd. 7:99; Sifre Deut. 344, quoted below), seems already to be familiar when Balaam is made to ask that his soul may die ἐν ψυχαῖς δικαίων (Num. 23:10 LXX). Again, in the Blessing of Moses, Hebrew which may be translated 'all his holy ones are in thy hands' is rendered 'all the ἡγιασμένοι are under his hands' (Deut. 33:3 LXX). These 'sanctified' could be taken as all Israel, with Targums Onkelos and Ps.-Jonathan, and probably with Acts 20:32, 26:18, alluding to Deut. 33:3; but a more specialized understanding was also current, for the verse was applied to martyrs in particular (4 Macc. 17:19), just as Jacob and the patriarchs in particular as well as the Lord's whole portion in general were 'sanctified' (so, in prayers, 2 Macc. 1:25, cited above, on 'the fathers'; 3 Macc. 6:3 ἐπὶ ἡγιασμένου τέκνα Ἰακώβ, μερίδος ἡγιασμένης σου λαόν). The familiarity of such special interpretations is suggested by their later recurrence. Sifre on Deut. 33:3 includes two exegeses recalling 4 Macc. 17:19: the 'holy' in God's hands are those who have given up their souls for Israel, like Moses and David; or they are 'the souls of the righteous' (*naphshotheyhem shel tsaddiqim*) in their storehouse, 'bound up in the bundle of life' (Sifre Deut. 344). With this line of interpretation in view, it seems likely that Wisd. 3:1 'the souls of the righteous are in the hand of God' is based on Deut. 33:3 in a form closer to MT than LXX, 'all his holy ones' being understood as the souls of the righteous.

The souls of the righteous were therefore identified as a group from the time of the LXX Pentateuch onwards, and by the end of the Second Temple period their seven orders in their *promptuaria* are elaborately described (2 Esdr 7:88–101); the 'holy' could now be envisaged not just as Israel or the angels, but also as the martyrs or the righteous. The use of adjectives corresponding to 'righteous' and 'holy' confirms the currency of the conception of a company of saints. δίκαιοι, 'righteous ones', already documented, recurs in this sense among early Christians, as in 1 Clem. 30.7 οἱ πατέρες ἡμῶν οἱ δίκαιοι, and by reflection in such phrases as *epistolae Pauli, viri iusti* (*Mart. Scill.* 12), and in quotation of Ps. 115:6 (116:15) on the death of the 'pious' as *honorabilis mors* iustorum (Tert. *Marc.* iv 39, 8; Cypr. *Test.* iii 16, *Fortunat.* xii). The range of terms such as 'holy' or 'pious', also current in this sense, could include honorific reference to the sanctity of rulers, as in second-century application of ὅσιος and *sanctus* to the Roman emperor (Delehaye, 4–5; *IEphes.* 3217 τοῦ ὁσιωτάτου Αὐτοκράτορος).[8]

For *qedoshim*/ἅγιοι, 'holy', see, as well as passages quoted in connection with Deut. 33:3: Isa. 4:3 LXX (ἅγιοι), on the righteous remnant; in Qumran texts, *qedoshey 'ammo* (1QM vi 6, xvi 10; 4Q511 (Songs of Sage) fr. 2 i.6), probably referring to a special group (at 4Q511 fr. 35.1–8, human holy ones seem to be associated with angels; see Puech, 583–4, n. 58); Rev. 15:6, 16 (ἅγιοι); and Rev. 13:10, 14:12 (ὑπομονὴ τῶν ἁγίων), where 'holy' has probably replaced 'meek' in an existing biblical phrase (Ps. 9:19 'hope of the meek'). Established terminology is thus followed when the Matthaean 'saints' asleep in their tombs are ἅγιοι (Matt. 27:52), and is later continued with *qedoshim* when 'the saints who are in the earth' (Ps. 16:2) are the buried saints (Midrash Tehillim xvi 2), or, in Ber. R. (Wilna: Romm, 1887) 97.1, in the name of Azariah (fourth century), the patriarchs are addressed by Jacob in the words of Ps. 34:10 'Ye his holy ones'.

For ὅσιοι/*hasidim*, 'pious', see Dan 3:87 LXX (ὅσιοι καὶ ταπεινοὶ τῇ καρδίᾳ); 2 (Syriac) Baruch 85:1, where intercession has been made by the righteous and prophets and 'pious' (*ḥsy*, probably reflecting ὅσιοι);[9] Ps.-Philo, *Ant. Bibl.* 33.6 (Deborah lamented as *sancta*). Jewish as well as gentile usage could then have been evoked by a Leontopolis epitaph (*c.* 150–50 B.C.) ending ψυχὴ δ' εἰς ὁσίους ἔπετε (*CIJ* 1510 = Horbury and Noy, 33, line 10). The patriarchs as a company of ὅσιοι were likewise in view when Philo (*Praem.* 166) wrote that the souls of the founders of the nation can intercede in virtue of their ὁσιότης.

[8] Quoted by P. G. W. Glare, with A. A. Thomson, *Greek-English Lexicon: Revised Supplement* (Oxford: Clarendon Press, 1996), 232, s. ὅσιος.

[9] The reading wherein 'holy' lacks the copula and can be taken to qualify 'prophets' is preferred by Bogaert, ii, 157, on the ground that righteous and prophets form a pair in 85.3 and 12; but 85.12 in fact has the triad fathers, prophets, and righteous, answering well to a triad in 85.1. On Syriac *hsy'* as regularly rendering ὅσιος see Puech, 23.

All these terms recur correspondingly in later Jewish funerary contexts. Epitaphs at home and abroad quote Prov. 10:7 'the memory of the righteous is for a blessing' (LXX μετ' ἐγκωμίων) (Avigad, 184–5, nos. 25–6; Noy, ii, no. 276); in the Midrash of the Ten Martyrs, God himself utters this text over R. Ishmael (Reeg, 54*–57*). In Rome the deceased are wished sleep with the ὅσιοι or δίκαιοι (Noy, ii, index, 545) (compare *cum sanctis, cum spirita sancta* in Christian epitaphs, Delehaye 30–1). In Palestine, you could be lamented with the cry 'alas, the pious; alas, the meek' (Tos. Soṭah 13.3), and be buried, if qualified, in the 'cave of the pious' (M.K. 17a); at Beth She'arim departed teachers figure as πατέρες ὅσιοι (Schwabe and Lifschitz no. 193) and *qedoshim* (Avigad no. 17).

Lastly, this company of departed saints will be vindicated in glory (1 En. 25:5–6; Dan 12:3; Wisd. 3:4–8, 5:16–17). The pattern followed in Wisdom for the righteous was outlined for ὅσιοι in the LXX Psalter, showing how verses on *hasidim* were understood in the Hasmonaean period. 'The Lord loves judgment and will not forsake his pious; they shall be guarded for ever' (Ps. 36: (37)28); he guards their souls, beasts may eat their flesh and their blood may be shed, but their death is precious (τίμιος) in his sight, they will be gathered to him when he comes manifestly, and vengeance on the heathen is their glory (Pss 96(97):10); 78(79):2–3 (applied to the slain 'Asidaeans', 1 Macc. 7:17); 115:6 (116:15); 49(50):5; 149:9). The ὅσιοι and δίκαιοι are similarly envisaged in the Psalms of Solomon, for example 14:3–10 (Büchler, 128–95). The first phase of their vindication is exemplified by Jephthah's daughter in Ps.-Philo, *Ant. Bibl.* 40.4; her death is precious in God's sight, an allusion to Ps. 116:15 (115:6) implying that she is one of his saints, and she goes straight into the bosom of the matriarchs, *in sinum matrum suarum*. Similarly, in later midrash, the martyred R. Ishmael will be 'in the bosom of the righteous ones', probably the patriarchs (Semahoth 8.8, 47a). Vindication is completed in 'the day of mercy of the righteous' (Ps. Sol. 14:6), envisaged in later prayer when New Year petitions inserted in the Amidah speak of the coming of 'the son of Jesse, thine anointed' and the exultation of the righteous, upright, and pious (Elbogen, Heinemann and Scheindlin, 118–19; modern text in Singer and Brodie, 327–8).

From the Second Temple period onwards, therefore, many Jews envisaged an assembly of departed saints or righteous souls, intercessors who awaited a glorious vindication. This familiar Christian tenet was inherited from and shared with Jews. Commemoration in its various forms took place against this background.

(iii) Legend

One further set of mental furnishings must be indicated in this sketch of the background against which Jews commemorated the righteous. A complex of exegetical legend incorporated the biblical saints into an expanded biblical narrative, already rich in the Greek period, and later manifest in targum, midrash and *piyyuṭ*, as exemplified above. The strongly hagiographical character of this tradition is not always brought to the fore in modern study, but it was underlined by the Qumran literary finds noted above in section II, for instance the portrait of Abraham as intercessor and healer in the Genesis Apocryphon. Other early examples of such portraiture include Habakkuk as Daniel's victualler (Bel and the Dragon 33–9), and (here recalling gentile cult) Moses as Thoth-Hermes in Artapanus (Eus. *P.E.* ix 27, 6), and probably Joseph as Serapis (Tert. *Nat* ii 8; A. Z. 43a, in the name of Judah b. Ilai, discussed by Mussies). The vitality of the biblical saints in communal thought emerges especially when those who are little more than names in scripture receive full depiction, as happens with Kenaz in Ps.-Philo or Serah daughter of Asher in the midrash. Post-biblical figures perhaps acquired their own legends or 'acts', comparable with those of the Christian martyrs, as is suggested by rabbinic references to the death of Akiba (Goldberg) and to the Trajanic martyrs Pappus and Lulianus (Horbury, 'Pappus'); but in any case they were brought into the broader legendary tradition on the biblical saints, in the manner exemplified at the beginning of III (ii) above from Ecclesiasticus and Hebrews, and as their share in festal commemoration and tomb-veneration would suggest. Thus homily for the Paschal season as represented in PRK, cited above, passes from the recovery of Joseph's coffin from the Nile and its escort through the wilderness with the not dissimilar ark of God, by way of an apparition of Serah (who looks down from above during R. Johanan's exposition to describe the divided Red Sea), and stories of the Hadrianic martyrs and Simeon b. Yohai and his son, to a final suggestion that each tribe brought up the bones of its own patriarch from Egypt (PRK xi 12–25). Here narratives of biblical and rabbinic saints are brought together within the context of reverence for the bones of the patriarchs.

In the later Roman empire the biblical saints appear in Jewish representational art, as attested in third-century wall-painting at Dura Europus and mosaic in later Palestinian synagogue remains; when these are viewed together with non-Jewish evidence from the Roman catacombs, including the Via Latina paintings mentioned above, and also from early illustrated biblical manuscripts, it seems likely that Jewish representation of the saints of Israel in art was not restricted to Syria and Palestine. This Jewish phenomenon, in its early phases at the end of the second century, would have been contemporary with the earliest evidence for Christian representation of saints, for example in the Acts of John 27–9 and in Irenaeus on the Carpocratians (*Haer.* i 25, 6).

Lastly, just as the potential significance of commemoration was underlined by instances of invocation (at the end of part i in this section, above), so the vitality of the figures portrayed in legend or art is confirmed by accounts of their appearance in dream or vision. Examples have been met above in 2 Macc. 15:11–16 (Onias and Jeremiah); Mark 9:4–5 (Moses and Elijah); and PRK xi 13 (Serah), 23 (Simeon b. Yohai). The cultivation of such visions is attested when Ecclesiastes Rabbah (ix 10, 1–2) names some who fasted to obtain dream-visions of the dead (Horbury, 'Pappus', 289).

In section II it was shown from selected literary and archaeological evidence, including rich New Testament material but without appeal to a Jewish cult of the Maccabees or to the Testaments of the Twelve Patriarchs and the Lives of the Prophets, that from the Hasmonaean period onwards many Jews regarded the righteous and holy departed as patrons and honoured their tombs. Now in section III various kinds of commemoration have been identified (part i), including but not restricted to assembly at tombs, and accompanied by invocation; and a sketch has been offered of background conceptions which encouraged commemoration and endued it with significance. The souls of the righteous formed an assembly of intercessors, expecting a glorious vindication (this section, part ii); they included the honoured names of scripture and recent history, actualized in detailed legend, ultimately represented in synagogue art, and sometimes seen throughout the period in dream or vision (part iii).

Public commemoration against this background can appropriately be called cult. These righteous and holy, often honoured at tombs, resembled Greek and Roman heroes as strongly as the Christian martyrs did in Theodoret's argument (section I, above); but ancient Jewish practice and belief in this area had a still closer resemblance to the Christian cult of saints. This emerges especially, as noted already, when it is remembered that in antiquity the two communities were to a great extent oriented towards the same set of biblical and early post-biblical righteous and holy. Moreover, commemoration against the background sketched here was already prevalent in the Second Temple period; it was inherited as well as shared by Christians.

IV

These considerations open a further avenue towards the origins of the cult of Christ. It arose in a setting in which the departed righteous could be honoured as patron-intercessors. Of course the Christ-cult is not simply one further instance of this honour. Those who invoke Christ call themselves his own, and name him together with God (1 Cor. 1:2–3, 3:23, 8:6). These characteristics indeed recall attitudes to Moses (John 9:28; Exod. 14:31; Num. 21:5; Acts 6:11), but thereby point also to other aspects of the setting, above all, in the writer's view, to reverence for Christ as messianic king (Horbury, *Jewish Messianism and the Cult of Christ*).

Yet, as this example shows, there were also continuities between approaches to the saints in Judaism and to Christ in Christianity. Two were indicated by Jeremias and endorsed by Wilkinson, 464–5. First, Christ's rôle as patron-intercessor (Rom. 8:34; Heb. 7:25) was characteristic of the righteous (cf. 1 John 2:1 on Christ 'the righteous' as παράκλητος); it may be added that at John 16:26, where the disciples loved by the Father do not need Christ's intercession, they themselves implicitly acquire this rôle. Further, 'the messiah of righteousness' (4QpBless on Gen. 49:10) is one of the righteous, even though he is not thereby fully classified.

Secondly, concern for the tombs of the righteous would have made Christian concern for the tomb of Christ inevitable from the first. This view traverses some interpretation of Mark 16:6 οὐκ ἔστιν ὧδε· ἠγέρθη, now including H. D. Betz's suggestion (138–9) that the saying is meant to rule out treatment of Christ as a hero, a chthonian demigod whose power is bound up with his tomb in the earth; the cult of heroes would have been familiar to Christians, as Betz emphasizes, but the gospel material noted in section II, above, including Matt. 27:52–3, Mark 9:5, suggests that they also inherited Jewish concern for saints and their tombs. Against this background, the saying would be meant to affirm that the reason for the known emptiness of this tomb was the resurrection. The following words ἴδε ὁ τόπος ὅπου ἔθηκαν αὐτόν are indeed consistent with encouragement of pilgrimage.

Links between the cult of Christ and the cult of the saints of Israel have been identified, therefore, but arguably the relationship between the two extends further than these observations alone would suggest. First, the messianic king is associated with the circle of the Fathers, the Holy, the Righteous and the Slain; they include figures closely connected with messianic expectation, notably Moses, Elijah, David and Hezekiah, and the messiah himself can be classified as righteous, as just noted. Correspondingly, the exegetical narratives of the advent and deeds of the messiah, based especially on Gen. 49, Num. 24 and Isa. 11 and already attested in the Greek Pentateuch and Qumran exegesis, belong to the larger network of legends of the biblical and later righteous discussed above. These interconnections are reflected in the synoptic tradition when Jesus is identified within a range of possibilities afforded by past and recent Israelite saints, together with the messiah (Mark 6:14–15, 8:28–9). The apparition of Moses and Elijah to the disciples at the Transfiguration (Mark 9:4) underlines the point that Christ is pictured in connection with the company of the prophets and the righteous.

Then, correspondingly, the circle of ideas on the status and work of Christ overlaps with that surrounding the saints of Israel, as instanced already in the treatment of Christ as intercessor. Other common elements include the expectation of the return or replication of notable figures, such as Moses, David, Elijah, Jeremiah and John the Baptist, and the consideration of such figures as spiritual or angelic, for example Moses, *sanctus et sacer spiritus* (Ass. Mos. 11:16). Again, there is a strong case for connection between conceptions of 'effective death' as attested in Jewish accounts of the righteous slain and in New Testament Christology (van Henten, 'Martyrs as Heroes', 311–12).

The development of the cult of Christ will then have been associated from the beginning in various ways with the ascription of honour to the saints of Israel. The Christ-cult had distinctive features, as noted already, but the Jewish reverence for the glorious company of departed saints with which it was linked will have helped to form a favourable environment for its growth. For the Jewish and Christian cult of saints, as for the cult of Christ, there were Greek and Roman counterparts; but the immediate origins of both Christian cults lay rather in Jewish tradition and custom which itself belonged to the Greek and Roman as well as the Jewish world.

Literature

N. Avigad, *Beth She'arim, Volume Three, The Archaeological Excavations during 1953–1958: The Catacombs 12–23* (Jerusalem, 1971)

E. Bammel, 'Zum jüdischen Märtyrerkult', *TLZ* LXXVIII (1953), cols. 119–26, reprinted with addendum in E. Bammel, *Judaica* (Tübingen, 1986), 79–85

H. D. Betz, 'Heroenverehrung und Christusglaube. Religionsgeschichtliche Beobachtungen zu Philostrats Heroicus', in H. Cancik, H. Lichtenberger and P. Schäfer (eds.), *Geschichte-Tradition-Reflexion: Festschrift für Martin Hengel zum 70. Geburtstag* (3 vols., Tübingen, 1996), ii, 119–39

E. Bickerman, 'Les Maccabées de Malalas', reprinted from *Byzantion* xxi (1951) in idem, *Studies in Jewish and Christian History*, ii (Leiden, 1980), 192–209

P. M. Bogaert, *L'apocalypse syriaque de Baruch* (2 vols., Paris, 1969)

W. Bousset and H. Gressmann, *Die Religion des Judentums im späthellenistischen Zeitalter* (3rd edn., Tübingen, 1926)

G. W. Bowersock, *Martyrdom and Rome* (Cambridge, 1995)

F. E. Brightman and C. E. Hammond, *Liturgies Eastern and Western*, i (Oxford, 1896, reprinted 1967)

P. Brown, *The Cult of the Saints, Its Rise and Function in Latin Christianity* (London, 1981)

A. Büchler, *Types of Jewish-Palestinian Piety from 70 B.C.E. to 70 C.E.: the Ancient Pious Men* (London, 1922)

B. S. Childs, *Memory and Tradition in Israel* (London, 1962)

W. Clarysse, 'The Coptic Martyr Cult', in Lamberigts and van Deun (eds.), *Martyrium*, 377–95

S. J. D. Cohen, 'Pagan and Christian Evidence on the Ancient Synagogue', in L. I. Levine (ed.), *The Synagogue in Late Antiquity* (Philadelphia, 1987), 159–81

E. Dassmann, K. Thraede and J. Engemann (eds.), *Akten des XII. Internationalen Kongresses für Christliche Archäologie* (2 vols., JAC Ergänzungsband xx, 1–2, Münster, 1995)

H. Delehaye, *Sanctus* (Brussels, 1927)

A. Dupont-Sommer, *Le Quatrieme Livre des Machabées* (Paris, 1939)
I. Elbogen, supplemented by J. Heinemann and others, ET by R. P. Scheindlin, *Jewish Liturgy: A Comprehensive History* (Philadelphia, New York and Jerusalem, 1993)
W. H. C. Frend, *Martyrdom and Persecution in the Early Church* (Oxford, 1965)
———, 'The North African Cult of Martyrs', in T. Klauser, E. Dassmann and K. Thraede (eds.), *Jenseitsvorstellungen in Antike und Christentum: Gedenkschrift für Alfred Stuiber* (JAC Ergänzungsband ix, Münster, 1982), 154–67
R. W. Funk, 'The Apostolic Parousia: Form and Significance', in W. R. Farmer, C. F. D. Moule and R. R. Niebuhr (eds.), *Christian History and Interpretation: Studies Presented to John Knox* (Cambridge, 1967), 249–68
A. Goldberg, 'Das Martyrium des Rabbi Aqiva. Zur Komposition einer Märtyrererzählung (bBer 61b)', *FJB* xii (1984), 1–82
L. Grünhut and M. N. Adler (eds.), *Die Reisebeschreibungen des R. Benjamin von Tudela* (2 vols, Jerusalem, 1903)
R. Hachlili and A. Killebrew, 'Jewish Funerary Customs during the Second Temple Period, in the Light of Excavations at the Jericho Necropolis', *PEQ* cxv (1983), 109–32
F. Hauck s. ὅsioi, *TWNT* v (1954), 88–92
J. W. van Henten (ed.), *Die Entstehung der jüdischen Martyrologie* (Leiden, 1989)
———, 'The Martyrs as Heroes of the Christian People: some Remarks on the Continuity between Jewish and Christian Martyrology, with Pagan Analogies', in Lamberigts and van Deun (eds.), *Martyrium*, 303–22
———, *Maccabean Martyrs as Saviours of the Jewish People* (Leiden, 1997)
W. Horbury, 'Suffering and Messianism in Yose ben Yose', in W. Horbury and B. McNeil (eds.), *Suffering and Martyrdom in the New Testament* (Cambridge, 1981), 143–82
———, *Jewish Messianism and the Cult of Christ* (London, 1998)
———, 'Pappus and Lulianus in Jewish Resistance to Rome', in J. Targarona Borrás and A. Sáenz Badillos (eds.), *Jewish Studies at the Turn of the Twentieth Century: Proceedings of the Sixth EAJS Congress, Toledo, July 1998* (2 vols., Leiden, Köln and Boston, 1999), 289–95
——— and D. Noy, *Jewish Inscriptions of Graeco-Roman Egypt* (Cambridge, 1992)
P. W. van der Horst, *Hellenism-Judaism-Christianity* (Kampen, 1994)
J. Jeremias, *Heiligengräber in Jesu Umwelt* (Göttingen, 1958)
———, 'Drei weitere jüdische Heiligengräber', *ZNW* lii (1961), 95–101
M. de Jonge, 'Test. Benjamin 3:8 and the Picture of Joseph as "a Good and Holy Man" ', in van Henten, *Entstehung*, 204–14
A. Kerkeslager, 'Jewish Pilgrimage and Jewish Identity in Hellenistic and Early Roman Egypt', in D. Frankfurter (ed.), *Pilgrimage and Holy Space in Late Antique*

Egypt (Religions in the Graeco-Roman World cxxxiv; Leiden, Boston and Köln, 1998), 99–225

T. Klauser, 'Christlicher Märtyrerkult, heidnischer Heroenkult und spätjüdische Heiligenverehrung. Neue Einsichten und neue Probleme', *Arbeitsgemeinschaft für Forschung des Landes Nordrhein-Westfalen, Geisteswissenschaften, Heft 91* (Cologne and Opladen, 1960), reprinted with addendum in T. Klauser, ed. E. Dassmann, *Gesammelte Arbeiten zur Liturgiegeschichte, Kirchengeschichte, und christlichen Archäologie* (JAC Ergänzungsband III, Münster: Aschendorff, 1974), 221–9

M. Lamberigts and P. van Deun (eds.), *Martyrium in Multidisciplinary Perspective. Memorial Louis Reekmans* (BETL cxvii, Leuven, 1995)

R. Lane Fox, *Pagans and Christians* (London, 1986)

J. N. Lightstone, *The Commerce of the Sacred: Mediation of the Divine among Jews in the Graeco-Roman Diaspora* (Chico, 1984)

E. Lucius, ed. G. Anrich, *Die Anfänge des Heiligenkults in der christlichen Kirche* (Tübingen, 1904)

R. Mach, *Der Zaddik in Talmud und Midrasch* (Leiden, 1957)

E. M. Meyers, A. T. Kraabel and J. F. Strange, 'Ancient Synagogue Excavations at Khirbet Shema', *Upper Galilee, Israel 1970–1972* (AASOR xlii, Durham, NC, 1976)

G. F. Moore, *Judaism in the First Centuries of the Christian Era: the Age of the Tannaim* (2 vols., Cambridge, MA, 1927)

G. Mussies, 'The Interpretatio Judaica of Sarapis', in M. J. Vermaseren (ed.), *Studies in Hellenistic Religions* (Leiden, 1979), 189–214

E. Nourry, under the nom de plume P. Saintyves, *Les saints successeurs des dieux* (Paris, 1907)

D. Noy, *Jewish Inscriptions of Western Europe* (2 vols., Cambridge, 1993, 1995)

J. Obermann, 'The Sepulchre of the Maccabean Martyrs', *JBL* 1 (1931), 250–65

F. Pfister, *Der Reliquienkult im Altertum* (two continuously paginated parts, Giessen, 1909, 1912, reprinted in one volume, Berlin, 1974)

O. Proksch and K. G. Kuhn s. ἅγιος, *TWNT* i (1933), 88–114

E. Puech, *La croyance des Esséniens en la vie future: immortalité, résurrection, vie éternelle? Histoire d'une croyance dans le judaïsme ancien* (two continuously paginated parts, Paris, 1993)

T. Rajak, 'The Maccabaean Martyrs in Jewish Memory: Jerusalem and Antioch', in R. S. Boustan, K. Herrmann, R. Leicht, A, Yoshiko Reed and G. Veltri (ed.), *Envisioning Judaism: Studies in Honor of Peter Schäfer* (2 vols., Tübingen, 2013), 63–79

G. Reeg (ed.), *Die Geschichte von den Zehn Märtyrern* (Tübingen, 1985)

W. Rordorf, 'Wie steht es um den jüdischen Einfluss auf den christlichen Märtyrerkult?', in J. van Amersfoort and J. van Oort (eds.), *Juden und Christen in der Antike* (Kampen, 1990), 61–71

E. P. Sanders, *Judaism: Practice and Belief, 63 BCE–66 CE* (London, 1992)

D. Satran, *Biblical Prophets in Byzantine Palestine: Reassessing the Lives of the Prophets* (Leiden, New York and Cologne: Brill, 1995)

A. Schlatter, *Der Märtyrer in den Anfängen der Kirche* (BFCT xix. 3, Gütersloh, 1915), reprinted in A. Schlatter, *Synagoge und Kirche bis zum Barkochba-Aufstand* (Stuttgart, 1966), 237–304

G. Schrenk s. đikaioV, *TWNT* ii (1935), 184–93

E. Schürer, ET revised by G. Vermes, F. Millar, M. Goodman, M. Black and P. Vermes, *The History of the Jewish People in the Age of Jesus Christ, iii.1* (Edinburgh, 1986)

M. Schwabe and B. Lifschitz, *Beth She'arim, Volume Two, The Greek Inscriptions* (Jerusalem, 1967)

A. M. Schwemer, *Studien zu den frühjüdischen Prophetenlegenden Vitae Prophetarum* (2 vols. and Synopsis of text, Tübingen, 1995, 1996)

S. Singer and I. Brodie, *The Authorised Daily Prayer Book* (London, 5722–1962)

M. Smith, ed. S. J. D. Cohen, *Studies in the Cult of Yahweh* (2 vols., Leiden, New York, and Cologne, 1996)

G. C. Stead, 'The Origins of the Doctrine of the Trinity', *Theology* LXXVII (1974), 508–17, 583–8

G. Stemberger, 'Die Patriarchenbilder der Katakombe in der Via Latina im Lichte der jüdischen Tradition', *Kairos* N.F. xvi (1974), 19–78

J. E. Taylor, *Christians and the Holy Places* (Oxford, 1993)

Y. Tsafrir, 'Jewish Pilgrimage in the Roman and Byzantine Periods', in Dassmann, Thraede and Engemann (eds.), *Akten des XII. Internationalen Kongresses für Christliche Archäologie*, i, 369–76

E. E. Urbach, *The Sages* (ET, 2nd edn., Cambridge, MA, and London, 1979)

C. Vitringa, *De synagoga vetere* (Franeker, 1696)

P. Volz, *Die Eschatologie der jüdischen Gemeinde* (2nd edn., Tübingen, 1934, reprinted Hildesheim, 1966)

J. Wilkinson, 'Visits to Jewish Tombs by Early Christians', in Dassmann, Thraede and Engemann, *Akten des XII. Internationalen Kongresses für Christliche Archäologie*, i, 452–65

Index of Subjects

Index of Authors

Index of References

Old Testament

Pseudepigrapha

Inscriptions

Classical authors

Legal writers

Christian

Qumran